R. Gupta's®

General Knowledge DIGEST

With Objective Type Questions

A Unique Collection of Pointwise Facts on **Indian History, Geography, Economy, Polity, General Science, Computer, Miscellaneous Facts and Figures related to India and World, Abbreviations, Books & Authors, Awards & Honours and Sports for Various Competitive Examinations**

by

RPH Editorial Board

RAMESH PUBLISHING HOUSE, NEW DELHI

Published by
O.P. Gupta *for* Ramesh Publishing House

Admin. Office
12-H, New Daryaganj Road, Opp. Officers' Mess,
New Delhi-110002 ✆ 23275224, 23245124

E-mail: info@rameshpublishinghouse.com
For Online Shopping: www.rameshpublishinghouse.com

Showroom
• Balaji Market, Nai Sarak, Delhi-6 ✆ 23282525 📱 9354373464
• 4457, Nai Sarak, Delhi-6, ✆ 23918938

Book Code: R-1739

ISBN: 978-93-89480-03-0

Price: ₹ 395

Printed at: Kamal Enterprises, Delhi

CONTENTS

General Knowledge DIGEST

- Indian History
- World : Miscellaneous
- Geography
- India : Miscellaneous
- Indian Economy
- Abbreviations
- Indian Polity
- Books & Authors
- General Science
- Awards & Honours
- Computer
- Sports

ANCIENT MEDIEVAL MODERN

Indian History

ANCIENT INDIA

SOURCES OF ANCIENT INDIAN HISTORY

- Literary and Archaeological records are the two main categories that give evidences of Ancient Indian History.
- The literary source includes literature of Vedic, Sanskrit, Pali, Prakrit, and other literature along with other foreign accounts.
- The archaeological source includes epigraphic, numismatic, and other architectural remains.
- The Vedas give reliable information about the culture and civilization of the Vedic period, but do not reveal the political history.
- Ashtadhyayi (eight chapters), written by Panini, is a book on grammar that gives excellent information on the art of writing in sutra (precepts).
- The Buddhist books are called as Jataka stories. They have been given some historical importance because they are related with the previous births of the Buddha. There are more than 550 such stories.
- The *Dharmasutras* and the *Smritis* were the rules and regulations for the general public and the rulers. It can be equated with the constitution and the law books of the modern concept of polity and society. For example, *Manusmriti.*
- *Arthashastra* is a book on statecraft written by Kautilya during the Maurya period. The book is divided into 15 parts dealing with different subject matters related to polity, economy, and society.
- *Mudrarakshasha* is a play written by Visakha datta. It describes the society and culture of that period.
- *Malavikagnimitram* written by Kalidasa gives information of the reign of Pusyamitra Sunga dynasty.
- *Harshacharita*, written by Banabhatta, throws light on many historical facts about which we could not have known otherwise.
- Vakpati wrote *Gaudavaho,* based on the exploits of Yasovarman of Kanauj.
- *Vikramankadevacharita*, written by Bilhana, describes the victories of the later Chalukya king Vikramaditya.
- *Rajatarangini*, written by Kalhana, is the best form of history writing

valued by modern historians. His critical method of historical research and impartial treatment of the historical facts have earned him a great respect among the modern historians.

- The Sangam literature is in the form of short and long poems consisting 30,000 lines of poetry, which arranged in two main groups *i.e., Patinenkilkanakku* and the *Pattupattu*. It describes many kings and dynasties of South India.
- Herodotus in his book Histories (written in many volumes) describes about the Indo-Persian relations.
- A detailed account of the invasion of India by Alexander was written by Arrian.
- Megasthenes came in the court of Chandragupta Maurya. He had written about the Indian society and culture in his book called as 'Indica'. Though the original work has been lost, but it had been frequently quoted in the works of later writers.
- A book 'Periplus of the Erythrean Sea' written by an anonymous Greek author who settled in Egypt on the basis of his personal voyage of Indian coast in about A.D. 80 gives valuable information about the Indian coasts.
- In the second century A.D., Ptolemy had written a geographical treatise on India.
- Hiuen-Tsang had given valuable account about Harshavardhana and some other contemporary kings of Northern India.
- Fa-Hien and Hiuen-Tsang traveled many parts of the country and they have given an exaggerated account of Buddhism during the period of their visit.
- Hiuen-Tsang mentioned Harsha as a follower of Buddhism while in his epigraphic records, Harsha mentions himself as a devotee of Siva. Such contradictions may be considered due to the fact of multi-religious nature of Indian rulers, which might confuse a foreigner.
- Al-Biruni gave important information about India. He was Arab scholar and contemporary of Mahmud of Ghazni.

THE HARAPPAN CIVILISATION (2500-1750 BC)

- The earliest excavations in the Indus valley were done at Harappa in the West Punjab and Mohenjodaro in Sindh. Both places are now in Pakistan.
- The findings in these two cities brought to light a civilisation. It was first called the 'The Indus Valley Civilisation'. But now it is called the Harappan Civilisation because it was first discovered in 1921 at the modern site of Harappa.

Major Cities and their Special Features

Mohen-Jo-Daro

- It is situated on the right bank of the Indus.
- It is the largest of all the Indus cities.
- The most important building found here is the Great Bath 11.89 m long, 7.01 m broad and 2.44 m deep.
- Its floor is made of burnt bricks set in gypsum and mortar.
- It must have served as a ritual bathing site.

- The Great Granary found here is the largest building, measuring 150 feet length × 50 feet breadth.
- It is located within the citadel and its presence implies the existence of a centralised tax collecting agency.

Harappa

- It was the first Indus site to be discovered and excavated in 1921 and is located on the left bank of the Ravi.
- This site has two large and imposing ruined mounds. The western mound represented the citadel, outside which were important structures identified with workmen's quarters, working floors and granaries.
- The granaries located outside the citadel are a series of brick platforms forming the basis of two rows of six rows of granaries.

Kalibangan

- It is situated on the southern bank of the Ghaggar river in Ganganagar district, Rajasthan.
- It has witnessed both the pre-Harappan and Harappan-cultural phase.
- The most important discoveries of pre-Harappan phase is the plan of a parallelogram citadel with well-laid-out houses.
- The excavations have revealed the evidence of the ploughed field, knowledge of copper technology and rich remains of the earthen-vessels, a few of which continued even in subsequent Harappan cultural phase.

Lothal

- Is a coastal site located in Gujarat at the head of the Gulf of Cambay.
- The most important structure discovered here is the dockyard built with brick.
- The dockyard suggests that Lothal was an important port of entry into the area covered by the Harappa civilization.
- The Harappans maintained maritime relations with Mesopotamia and other places through Lothal.
- This is the only site where horse remains have been found.

Banawali

- It is in Hissar district in Haryana.
- It witnessed both Pre-Harappa and Harappa-cultural phase similar to those of Kalibangan.
- The remains of streets and drains have been found at Banawali.
- A good quantity of barley and a good amount of pottery has been discovered at Banawali.

Chanhu-Daro

- It is a very small hamlet on the eastern bank of the Indus river, south-east of Mohen-Jo-Daro.
- It is only site which had yielded curved-bricks used for building bins, bath-tubs, water tanks, wells etc.
- It appears to have been a manufacturing centre of toys like terracotta rattles, decorated carts with humped oxen, toy-fish etc.

Surkotada

- Bead making was a popular industry here.
- It must have been a toy manufacturing centre.
- There was a shopping complex at the site.

Dholavira

- It is the latest city to be excavated in the Great Rann of Kutch in Gujarat.
- It is one of the largest site after Mohan-Jo-Daro and Harappa.
- The city was enclosed by massive walls with fortifications, bastions and an intricate system of conduits for water with small dams, drains and tanks.

Salient Features of the Harappan Culture

Town Planning

- The Harappan Civilization was primarily Urban.
- Mohenjodaro and Harappa were the planned cities.
- The large-scale use of burnt bricks in almost all kinds of constructions are the important characteristics of the Harappan culture.
- Another remarkable feature was the underground drainage system connecting all houses to the street drains which were covered by stone slabs or bricks.
- The most important public place of Mohanjodaro is the Great Bath measuring 39 feet length, 23 feet breadth and 8 feet depth.

Economic Life

- Agriculture was the most important occupation. In the fertile soils, farmers cultivated two crops a year.
- Wheat and barley were the main crops grown besides sesame, mustard and cotton.
- Animals like sheep, goats and buffalo were domesticated. The use of horse is not yet firmly established.
- Bronze and copper vessels are the outstanding examples of the Harappan metal craft.
- Foreign trade was mainly barter type and conducted with Mesopotamia, Afghanistan and Iran.
-

Imports	From
• Gold	Kolar (Karnataka), Afghanistan, Persia (Iran)
• Silver	Afghanistan, Persia (Iran), South India
• Copper	Khetri (Rajasthan), Baluchistan, Arabia
• Tin	Afghanistan, Bihar
• Lapis Lazuli & Sapphire	Badak-shan (Afghanistan)
• Jade	Central Asia
• Steatite	Shaher-i-Sokhta, Kirthar Hills
• Amethyst	Maharashtra
• Agate, Chalcedonies & Carnelians	Saurashtra & West India

- The Sumerian text refer to trade relations with 'Meluha' which was the name given to the Indus region.
- *Shatughai* & *Mundigaq* were the Indus sites found in Afghanistan.
- The Sumerian texts also refer to two intermediate stations—Dilmun (Bahrain) & Makan (Makran coast). Susa & Ur are Mesopotamian places where Harappan seals have been found.
- Remains of dockyard have been discovered at **Lothal** in Gujarat.

Social Life

- Jewelleries such as bangles, bracelets, fillets, girdles, anklets, ear-rings and finger rings were worn by women. These ornaments were made of gold, silver, copper, bronze and semi precious stones.

- Fishing was a regular occupation while hunting and bull fighting were other pastimes.

Script

- Most of the inscriptions were engraved on seals. It is interesting to note that the Indus script has not yet been deciphere.

Religious Life

- The Pipal tree was used as a religious symbol.
- The origin of the *'Swastika'* symbol can be traced to the Harrapan Civilization.
- The chief male deity was Pasupati, (proto-Siva) represented in seals as sitting in a yogic posture with three faces and two horns. He is surrounded by four animals (elephant, tiger, rhino, and buffalo each facing a different direction). Two deer appear on his feet.
- The chief female deity was the Mother Goddess represented in terracotta figurines. Mother Goddess represented fertility.
- The Indus people believed in life after death. They buried their dead in huge earthen pots along with food and ornaments. The articles used by them in their daily life were also kept in those pots.

THE VEDIC PERIOD

Rig Vedic Age or Early Vedic Period (1500-1000 B.C.)

- The Early Vedic period is known from the **Rig Veda**.
- The Rig Veda refers to Saptasindhu or the land of seven rivers. This includes the five rivers of the Punjab, namely, Jhelum, Chenab, Ravi, Beas and Sutlej along with the Indus and Saraswati.
- Historians view that the Aryans came from Central Asia. They entered India through the Khyber Pass between 2000 B.C. and 1500 B.C. They first settled in seven places in the Punjab region which they called Sapta Sindhu. Slowly, they moved towards the Gangetic Valley.
- The Aryan civilisation was a Rural civilisation.

Political Organisation

- According to the Rig Veda, the most mentioned river—Sindhu, the most pious river—Saraswati.
- According to Rig Veda, the Famous Dasrajan war was mutual struggle of Aryans.
- The Dasrajan war gives names of ten kings who participated in a war against *Sudas* who was *Bharata* king of *Tritsus* family.
- The ten kings were of the states of Purus, Yadus, Turvasas, Anus and Druhyus along with five others viz. Alinas, Pakhtas, Bhalanas, Sibis & Vishanins.
- The battle was fought on the bank of *Parushani* (Ravi) and *Sudas* emerged victorious.
- During this period, the kingdom was tribal in character. Each tribe formed a separate kingdom.
- The basic unit of political organisation was *kula* or family.
- Several families joined together on the basis of their kinship to form a village or grama. The leader of grama was known as *gramani*.

- A group of villages constituted a larger unit called visu. It was headed by *vishayapati*.
- The highest political unit was called *jana* or tribe.
- There were several tribal kingdoms during the Rig Vedic period such as Bharatas, Matsyas, Yadus and Purus. The head of the kingdom was called as *rajan* or king.
- There were two popular bodies called the *Sabha* and *Samiti*. The former seems to have been a council of elders and the latter, a general assembly of the entire people.

Social Life

- Family was the basis of the society.
- The head of the family was known as *grihapathi*.
- Women were given equal opportunities as men for their spiritual and intellectual development.
- There were women poets like Apala, Viswavara, Ghosa and Lopamudra during the Rig Vedic period.
- Wheat and barley, milk and its products like curd and ghee, vegetables and fruits were the chief articles of food.
- The eating of cow's meat was prohibited since it was a sacred animal.
- Chariot racing, horse racing, dicing, music and dance were the favourite pastimes.

Economic Condition

- The Rig Vedic Aryans were pastoral people and their main occupation was cattle rearing. Their wealth was estimated in terms of their cattle. When they permanently settled in North India, they began to practise agriculture.
- Carpentry was another important profession and the availability of wood from the forests cleared made the profession profitable. Carpenters produced chariots and ploughs.

Religion

- The early Vedic religion was naturalistic.
- The mode of prayer was recitation of *mantras*.
- Sacrifice was offered for *Praja* (children), *Pasu* (cattle) and *Dhana* (wealth) and not for spirtual upliftment of misery.
- Believed in one Supreme God.
- Did not believe in idol worship.
- Worshipeed the forces of nature as the manifestations of one Supreme God.
- Indra, Agni, Varuna, Surya, Rudra, Yama, Soma, Marut, Dyaus, Vayu and Prajanaya. Prithvi, Saraswati, Usha, Aditi were female deities. They were not given the same position as male gods.

Later Vedic Period (1000-600 B.C,)

- This age is also called as the Epic Age because the two great epics the Ramayana and Mahabharata were written during this period.
- The Sama, Yajur, Atharva Vedas, Brahmanas, Aranyakas, Upanishads and the two epics are the sources of information for this period.

Political Organisation

- Larger kingdoms were formed during the later Vedic period. Kingdoms like Kosala, Videha, Kuru, Magadha, Kasi, Avanti and Panchala came into existence.

- Many jana or tribes were amalgamated to form *janapadas* or rashtras in the later Vedic period.
- The king performed various rituals and sacrifices to strengthen his position. They include Rajasuya (consecration ceremony), Asvamedha (horse sacrifice) and Vajpeya (chariot race).
- Kingship became hereditary.
- Kings assumed titles like Ekrat, Samrat and Sarvabauma.
- In later Vedic times, the *vidhatha* completely disappeared.
- The *sabha* and *samiti* continued to hold the ground, but their character changed.
- Women were no longer permitted to sit in the sabha, and it was now dominated by nobles and Brahmanas.
- During this period collection of taxes and tributes seems to have become common. They were probably deposited with an officer called *sangrihitri.*
- In the discharge of this duties, the king was assisted by the priest, the commander, the chief queen and a few other high functionaries.

Economic Condition

- Iron was used extensively in this period and this enabled the people to clear forests and to bring more land under cultivation. Agriculture became the chief occupation.
- Taxes like Pali, Sulk and Bhaga were collected from the people.
- The Later Vedic people were familiar with the sea and they traded with countries like Babylon.
- A class of hereditary merchants *(vaniya)* came into existence. Vaisyas also carried on trade and commerce.
- Besides *nishka* of the Rig Vedic period, gold and silver coins like *satamana* and *krishnala* were used as media of exchange.
- Cattle still constituted the principal form of movable property. Elephants were tamed.
- However, the idea of private possession of land gradually began to crystallize.
- Wheat was also cultivated during this period along with barley. Rice is mentioned in sources but was not an important crop at this time.
- The later Vedic Aryans used four types of pottery—Black and Red Ware, Black Slipped Ware, Painted Grey Ware (PGW), and Red Ware.
- The black and red earthen pots were used around 600 BC by the people of Koshala.

Social Life

- The four divisions of society (Brahmins, Kshatriyas, Vaisyas and Sudras) or the Varna system was thoroughly established during the Later Vedic period.
- Child marriages had become common.
- According to the religious texts, the life of an individual was divided into four stages or Ashramas. They were Brahmacharya or student life, Graihasta or life of a father and husband. Vanaprasta or life as a hermit and finally Sanyasa or total renunciation of the world.
- The Ashrama system was formed to attain 4 purusharthas. They were *Dharma, Artha, Kama* and *Moksha.*
- Women were not sent to the Gurukula. However, women like Gargi and Maitreyi were educated.
- The institution of *Gotra, i.e.,* the clan appeared in Later Vedic Period.

Religion

- Gods of the Early Vedic period like Indra and Agni lost their importance. Prajapathi (the creator), Vishnu (the protector) and Rudra (the destroyer) became prominent during the Later Vedic period.
- Pushan, who was supposed to look after cattle, came to be regarded as the god to the *sudras*.
- Important female deities during the Later Vedic Age were : Usha (Goddess of Dawn), Aditi (Mother of Gods), Prithvi (Earth Goddess), Aryani (Forest Goddess) and Saraswati (River deity).
- The mode of worship changed considerably. Prayers continued to be recited, but they ceased to be the dominant mode of placating the gods.
- Sacrifices became far more important, and they assumed both public and domestic character. The Chief priests who were engaged in performing the sacrifices were—Hotri (invoker), Adhvaryu (executor) and Udgatri (singer).

EVOLUTION OF JAINISM

- Rishabhanath and Aristhanemi are the two Tirthankaras of Jainism mentioned in Rig Veda that proves the antiquity of Jainism.
- Rishabhanath had been mentioned an incarnation of Narayana in Vayu Purana and Bhagwat Purana.
- Rishabhnath was the first Tirthankara of Jainism. The traditions of Jainism say that he was a king and renounced the kingdom in favour of his son, Bharata, and became an ascetic.
- The name *Bharatavarsha* is after Bharata, the son of Rishabhanath as per the Puranic traditions.
- Parsvanath was the twenty-third Tirthankara, he renounced the world at the age of thirty and attained the enlightenment (perfect knowledge) after nearly three months of intense meditation and spent the remain-ing life as a religious teacher. He had lived 250 years before Mahavira.

Mahavira

- Vardhamana Mahavira was the twenty-fourth and the last Tirthankara of Jainism.
- Mahavira was born about 540 B.C. in the village Kunda-grama near Vaisali. He was the only son of Siddhartha and Trisala. Siddhartha was the head of famous Kshatriya Jnatrika clan and Trisala was the sister of Chetaka, an eminent Lichchhavi noble of Vaisali. Chetaka's daughter was married to the king of Magadha, Bimbisara.
- Mahavira was married to Yasoda and lived a life of a householder. After the death of his parents, Mahavira left his home at the age of thirty, and became an ascetic.
- Mahavira had practiced most rigorous asceticism for the next twelve years and attained *kaivalya* at the age of 42 years.
- In 468 B.C., Mahavira passed away at Pawapuri at the age of 72 years. He spent 30 years of his life in preaching his teachings.
- Four doctrines of Parsvanath are:
  - Non-injury to living beings,
  - Speaking the truth,
  - Non-possession of property, and
  - Not stealing.
- Vardhaman Mahavira accepted four doctrines of Parsvanath and added Celibacy as a fifth one to them.

➡ Celibacy is the complete renunciation and free from any possessions. Mahavira asked his followers to discard even their clothes.

Jain's Mythology

➡ The universe is eternal.

➡ The world is not created, maintained, or destroyed by a God, but it functions through a universal or eternal law.

➡ Jains did not deny the existence of God, but they simply ignored.

➡ The existence of the universe is divided into cycles of progress (Utsarpini) and declines (Avasarpim). It functions through the interaction of living souls (Jiva) and everything in the universe has a soul.

➡ The souls are found not only in the living beings like animals and plants, but also in stones, rocks, water, etc.

➡ The purification of the soul is the purpose of living.

➡ Only the pure soul after being released from the body resides in heaven.

➡ The soul, which has finally set itself free, rises at once to the top of the universe, above the highest heaven where it remains in an inactive omniscient bliss through eternity. It is known as 'Nirvana' in the Jainism.

➡ According to Jainism, salvation is possible only by:
- Deserting all belongings,
- A long course of fasting,
- Self-mortification,
- Study, and
- Meditation.

➡ Jainism, therefore, says that the monastic life is essential for salvation.

➡ According to the Jaina tradition, the king Chandragupta Maurya has supported Jainism. He had accepted Jaina religion and abdicated the throne and died as a Jaina Bhikshu in the southern part of India.

➡ Two hundred years after the death of Mahavira (during the reign of Chandragupta Maurya), a terrible famine broke out in Magadha. Bhadrabahu was the chief of the Jaina community at that time.

➡ Bhadrabahu went to Karnataka with his followers and Sthulabhadra remained in Magadha as the in-charge of Jainism.

➡ Bhadrabahu convoked a council at Patliputra, in which the Jaina canon was arranged.

➡ Later in the 5th century A.D., the Jaina canon was further rearranged when the Jainas returned from south India. From where Jainism divided into two sects.

➡ Those who returned from southern India held that complete nudity is an essential part of the teachings of Mahavira while the monks in Magadha began to put on white clothes.

➡ Those who put on white robes known as 'Svetambaras' and those who were star naked were called as 'Digambaras.'

Jain Council	Year	Venue	Chairman	Patron	Result
1st Jain Council	300 BC	Patliputra	Sthulabhadra	Chandragupta Maurya	Compilation of 12 Angas
2nd Jain Council	512 AD	Vallabhi	Devardhi Kshmasramana	—	Final compilation of 12 Angas & 12 Upangas

EVOLUTION OF BUDDHISM

➡ Gautama Budhha was born in 563 B.C. He was the son of Suddhodhan and Mayadevi. His father Suddhodhan was the eminent king of Sakya republic.

➡ Gautama was married to Yasodhara at an early age. Gautama was shocked at the sight of an old man, a diseased person, a dead body. Thereafter, he was attracted by the saintly appearance of an ascetic. One night he renounced the worldly life and left his home, wife, and son.

➡ After leaving home, Gautama studied for some time in the philoso-phical schools of two renowned teachers. Thereafter, six years of profound meditation led to the discovery of truths. Gautama became the 'Buddha' *i.e.*, the enlightened one.

➡ The main principle of Buddha's teachings is represented by the 'Four Noble Truths (Arya-Satyas)' as:

- Dukkha (the world is full of sorrow)
- Dukkha Samuddaya (that causes the sorrow)
- Dukkha Nirodha (sorrow can be stopped)

Teachings of Buddha

➡ Desire is the root of all human sadness and the assured way of ending unhappiness was the elimination of desire.

➡ Death is certain and there is no escape from it which lead to rebirth and caused further suffering. One could get out of this chain of suffering by attaining Nirvana (salvation).

➡ To achieve the final salvation (Nirvana) Buddha suggest 'Ashtangika marga' (the eight-fold path). These eight fold paths are:

- Right speech
- Right action
- Right means of livelihood
- Right exertion
- Right mindfulness
- Right meditation
- Right resolution, and
- Right view.

➡ The ultimate aim of life is to attain Nirvana, which means freedom, from further birth and death.

➡ Nirvana is the eternal state of peace and bliss or liberation from the cycle of birth and death.

➡ Buddha had summarized the whole process in three words viz.

- Seela (Right conduct),
- Samadhi (Right concentration), and
- Prajna (Right knowledge).

➡ According to Buddha, Seela and Samadhi lead to Prajna, which is the direct cause of nirvana.

➡ Buddha advocated "The Middle Path" in which extremes are avoided.

➡ Buddha visited to the Deer Park (modern Sarnath), Kasi after his enlightenment and gave his first Sermon (lecture).

➡ His first sermon was known as "Set in Motion, the Wheel of Law".

➡ The followers of the Buddha fell into two categories:

- ***Upasakas*** *i.e.*, the lay followers who lived with family; and
- ***Bhikshus*** *i.e.*, monks who renounced the world and led the life of an ascetic.

➡ Bhikshus lived as a commune called 'Sangha' founded by Buddha himself. In Buddhism, all the followers enjoyed equal rights irrespective of their Varna and Jati.

Buddhist Council	Year	Venue	Chairman	Patron	Result
1st Buddhist Council	483 BC	Saptaparni Cave, Rajagriha	Mahakassapa	Ajatashatru (Harayanka Dynasty)	Compilation of Sutta-Pitaka & Vinaya Pitaka by Ananda & Upali respectively
2nd Buddhist Council	383 BC	Chullavanga Vaishali	Sabbakami	Kalashoka (Shisunaga Dynasty)	(i) The monks of Vaishali wanted some change in rites. (ii) Schism into Sthaviravadins rites.
3rd Buddhist Council	250 BC	Ashokarama Vihar, Patliputra	Mogaliputta Tissa	Ashoka (Maurya Dynasty)	(i) Compilation of Abhidhamma Pitaka (ii) Decision to send missionaries to various parts of the world
4th Buddhist Council	98 AD	Kundala Vana, Kashmir	Chairman-Vasumitra Vice chairman	Kanishka (Kushana Dynasty)	(i) Compilation of Mahavibhasha shastra (Sanskrti comment on Tripitaka) (ii) the division of Buddhists into Hinayanists & Mahayanists.

- Women were also allowed to join the Sangha and were known as 'Bhikshunis.'
- Buddha debated in the language of the common people.
- Buddha and his followers used to travel from place to place, and preach for eight months in a year; and, four months, during the rainy season, they stayed at one place.
- Buddha died in the year 483 B.C. at Kushinagar at the age of 80.
- The ashes of Buddha after cremation were distributed among his followers.
- The followers kept these ashes in caskets and built 'Stupas' over them. One example of such Stupa is *Sanchi* Stupa.

MAHAJANAPADAS

- The term Maha Janapada was used to mean a large territorial unit capable of bearing taxes and various impositions. It comprised several Janapadas.
- A Janapada consisted of several thousand villages. The Kautilyan Janapada comprised 3200 villages.
- Though the process of large-scale settlements had started much earlier in the Punjab and the upper Gangetic Plains it was only in the middle Gangetic plains that large states emerged in the 6th century B.C.

List of Maha Janapadas

1. Kashi	2. Kosala
3. Anga	4. Magadha
5. Vajji	6. Malla
7. Chedi	8. Vansa (Vatsa)
9. Kuru	10. Panchal
11. Matsya	12. Surasena
13. Asvaka	14. Avanti
15. Gandhara	16. Kamboja

- Certain material conditions favoured the rise of large-scale state in the middle Gangetic plains.
- The alluvial soil helped the rise of large-scale settlements.
- Iron was available in large quantities.
- The people developed the art of transplanting paddy.
- The farmers were, therefore, in a position to support their households and dependants and able to pay taxes.
- Anguttara Nikaya speaks about sixteen Maha Janapadas.

- The existence of these states in the middle Gangetic zone and its periphery is supported by the finds of the Northern Black Polished Ware (NBPW), punch-marked coins and craft-activities.

RISE OF MAGADHA

- Magadha was one of the sixteen great states which flourished during Buddha age. It comprised the modern district of Patna and part of Gaya.
- It was the first state to make a successful bid for supremacy and establish its suzerainty.

Haryanka Dynasty

- The first important king of Magadha was Bimbisara who was a scion of Haryanka-Kula.
- He was helped in his political career by his matrimonial alliances.
- His first wife was a sister of Prasenjit, the king of Kosala who gave him the dowry of a village in Kasi. His second wife was Chellana, daughter of the Lichchhavi chief, Chetaka. His third wife was Khema, daughter of the king of Madra.
- His capital was Girivraja (Rajagriha) which was planned by Maha-govinda. It was enclosed by five hills and also girded with stone walls.
- After securing his western and northern frontiers, Bimbisara opened his first campaign against Anga to the south-east which controlled the trade and the routes to the sea-ports in the Gangetic delta which, in turn, had commercial contacts with Burma and the east coast of India and was thus economically a valuable support to the Magadha. Anga was conquered and annexed to Magadha.
- With the conquest of Anga and the peaceful acquisition of Kasi began the expansion of Magadha.
- Bimbisara maintained friendly relations with both the neighbouring and distant powers.
- His diplomatic and matrimonial relations must have helped him considerably in the aggressive policy initiated by him.

Ajatashatru

- Ajatashatru continued his father's policy of expansion and turned his attention to the north and the west.
- He started a war with Prasenajit, the Kosala king who could not forgive him for death of the widowed Kosala princess who died, unable to stand the death of her husband, Bimbisara. He, therefore, revoked his gift of the Kasi village.
- This led to a war between the two. At first, Ajatashatru won. But soon the tables were turned. In the end, peace was concluded.
- Prasenajit restored to Ajatashatru; the disputed village of Kasi and also gave his daughter in marriage to him.
- According to Jaina texts Ajatashatru was the conqueror of the powerful political confederacy which dominated eastern India and comprised 36 republican states — 9 Mallaki, 9 Lichchhavi and 18 Ganarajas of Kasi and Kosalas.
- Ajatashatru realised that the Lichchhavis were the nerve-centre of the confederacy and that if they were beaten, the whole confederacy would crumble.
- They also came to know that the chief strength of the Lichchhavis lay in their inner unity.

- Ajatasatru decided to sow seeds of discord among the Lichchhavis. His work bore fruit after three years.
- The Lichchhavis came to be divided hopelessly. Torn by disunion, the Lichchhavis fell an easy prey to Ajatasatru. The war ended in a complete victory for Ajatasatru.
- The success over the Lichchhavis brought him into conflict with King Pradyota of Avanti.
- To meet the danger from Avanti, he strengthened the fortifications of Rajagriha.

Sisunaga Dynasty

- **Sisunaga:** Sisunaga destroyed the power of the Pradyotas of Avanti and added it to the Magadha. He also annexed the kingdoms of Vatsa and Kosala.
- Thus, Magadha absorbed all the important states in north India that flourished in the age of Buddha.

The Nandas

- The Nandas who usurped the throne of the Sisunaga dynasty were of low origin. They were the first non-Kshatriya dynasties that ruled in India. The Nandas are sometimes described as the first empire builders of India.
- They inherited the large kingdom of Magadha and desired to extend it further. For this purpose, they built up a vast army of 20,000 cavalry, 200,000 infantry, 3000 elephants etc.
- **Mahapadma Nanda:** The name of the founder and the first king of the Nanda dynasty is differently given in different texts. The Puranas call him Mahapadma while the Buddhist call him Ugrasena (who possessed of a terrible army).
- The Puranas describe him as a second Parsurama, the exterminator of the entire Kshatriya race and as one who made himself the sole sovereign in the country and brought it under the umbrella of one authority which was not challenged.
- The Kshatriya dynasties thus overthrown were the Aikshvakus, Panchalas, Kasis, Kalingas, Kurus, Asmakas, Mithilas, Surasenas and Vitihotras.
- The early inscriptions of Mysore speak of the Nanda rule over Kuntala (Southern part of Bombay and north-western parts of Mysore).
- All these show that Mahapadma had built up a great empire which was not a loose federation but was built on a solid foundation.

MAURYAN DYNASTY

Chandragupta Maurya

- Chandragupta Maurya had ruled during the period of 322-298 B.C.
- Chandragupta Maurya has been described as a descendant of the Kshatriya clan of the Moriyas branch of Sakyas. They lived in Pipphalivana, in eastern Uttar Pradesh.
- With the help of Kautilya, Chandra gupta raised a large army and launched campaigns. He first overthrew the Greek kshatrapas ruling in the region of north-western India.
- The Sandrocottas mentioned in the Greek literature has been identified with Chandragupta Maurya.
- The Junagarh rock inscription describes that a dam for irrigation was constructed on the Sudarshana Lake by Pushyagupta, a provincial governor of Chandragupta Maurya.

- The Jain tradition confirms that in his old age, Chandragupta abdicated the throne and retired to Shravanabelagola in Karnataka with his teacher Bhadrabahu (a Jain ascetic).
- In about 305 B.C. Chandragupta defeated the army of the Greek Kshatrapa Seleucus who had succeeded Alexander in the eastern part of his empire.
- The Greek writers stated that a treaty was concluded between Seleucus and Chandragupta in which Seleucus accepted the territories of Kandahar, Kabul, Herat, and Baluchistan and Chandragupta presented him 500 elephants.
- The treaty was followed by a matrimonial alliance between the two in which Seleucus married his daughter to Chandragupta Maurya.
- Seleucus sent Megasthenese as his ambassador to the court of Chandragupta.
- Plutarch writes, "Sandrocottas who had by that time mounted the throne overran and subdued the whole of India with an army of 600,000".

Bindusara (298-273 B.C.)

- Bindusara, the son of Chandragupta Maurya, ascend to throne after his father.
- According to the Tibetan historian, Taranath, Chanakya continued as a minister of Bindusara after Chandragupta Maurya Hemachandra, Jain scholar, also confirms this fact.
- Divyavadana mentions that Bindusara appointed his eldest son Sumana (or Susima) as his viceroy at Taxila and Ashoka at Ujjain. It also mentions that when a revolt broke out at Taxila, Ashoka was sent to restore peace as Susima fails to suppress it.
- Bindusara continued his policy of friendly relations with Hellenic world.
- Dionysius was the Egypt ambassador came to the court of Bindusara.
- Pliny mentions that Ptolemy Philadelphus, king of Egypt sent him as an ambassador.
- Bindusara had been given the credit of south Indian conquest, but most of the scholars believe that this was done by his father Chandragupta Maurya.

Ashoka (273-232 B.C.)

- Ashoka succeeded to the throne after the death of his father Bindusara in 273 B.C.
- Janapada Kalyani or Subhadrangi was his mother.
- Ashoka was very cruel in his early life and captured the throne after killing his 99 brothers. But it appears an exaggerated figure.
- Ashoka was the first king in the Indian history who has left his records engraved on stones.
- The Ashokan inscriptions are found at 47 places in different regions of India, Nepal, Pakistan, and Afghanistan.
- Ashoka's name occurs only in copies of Minor Rock Edict-I found at three places in Karnataka and one in Madhya Pradesh. Whereas in all other inscriptions, he mentioned himself as 'Devanampiya' and 'Piyadasi' meaning beloved of the gods.
- Ashoka's inscriptions were written in four different scripts, namely:
  - Greek languages and scripts used in Afghanistan area;

- Aramaic languages and scripts used in west Asia;
- Prakrit language and Kharosthi script used in Pakistan area; and
- Prakrit language and Brahmi script used in rest of the inscriptions.

Decline of Mauryan Empire

➥ Ashoka ruled for almost 40 years and died in 232 B.C.

➥ oon after Ashoka's death, the empire broke up and the decline of the Mauryan Empire set in.

➥ In a period of about 50 years after Ashoka's death, seven kings followed him in succession.

➥ The empire was divided into an eastern and western part. The western part was governed by Kunala, Samprati and others.

➥ The eastern part with southern India was governed by six successors of Mauryan kings from Dasarath to Brihadratha. They were having their capital at Pataliputra.

➥ The power and prestige of the Mauryan Empire were challenged by Andhras (in the south India) and continuous attacks of Greek king in the west.

➥ The king Brihadratha was killed by Pushyamitra who was the commander-in-chief of the army.

Mauryan Governance

Polity and Administration

➥ The king was the head of the state. The king used to issue ordinances known as 'Sasana'. He possessed the judicial, the legislative, and the executive powers.

➥ Sasanas are available in the form of 'Edicts of Ashoka'.

➥ The Mauryas king had to follow the law of the country given by law givers and had to govern according to the customs of the land. He could not do whatever he liked.

➥ The king was assisted in administration by 'Mantriparishad', which was a Council of Ministers.

➥ Adhyakshas (superintendent) were officers who performed a special task.

➥ The Mauryan Empire was divided into provinces. *Pradeshikas* was another officer of the Mauryan administration. He was the provincial governor.

➥ Bindusara appointed his son Ashoka as Governor of the Avanti region and posted him at Ujjain.

➥ Asoka's elder brother Susima was posted at Taxila as the Governor of the northwestern provinces.

➥ The important provinces were directly under Kumaras (princes); however, the total number of provinces is not known.

➥ The Mauryan kingdom was divided into different provinces, which were subdivided into the districts and each district was further divided into groups of five to ten villages.

➥ The village was the smallest unit of an administration.

➥ The *Pradeshika* was the head of district administration. He used to tour the entire district every five years to inspect the administration of areas under his control. A group of officials worked in each district under him.

➥ *Gramika* was the head of the village. He was assisted in village administration by the "village elders".

- The villages, during this time, enjoyed substantial autonomy. Most of the disputes of the village were settled by Gramika with the help of village assembly.
- The Arthashastra mentions the highest salary being 48,000 Panas and the lowest 60 Panas. There was a wide range of scales in salary.

Society & Economy during Mauryas

Society

- Megasthenese mentioned that during this period, the society was comprising seven castes, namely:
  - Philosophers
  - Farmers
  - Soldiers
  - Herdsmen
  - Artisans
  - Magistrates and
  - Councilors.
- Megasthenese, however, failed to comprehend the Indian society properly and confused among the terms Jati, Varna, and the occupation.
- Chaturvarna system continued to govern the society.
- The urban way of life developed and the craftsmen enjoyed a high place in the society.
- Teaching continued to be the main job of the Brahmans.
- Buddhist monasteries were developed as important educational institutions. Taxila, Ujjayini, and Varanasi were famous educational centers.
- Technical education was generally provided through guilds, where pupils learnt the crafts from the early age.
- The joint family system was the norm in the domestic life.
- The widows had been given respect in the society. All stree-dhana (bride-gift and jewelry) belongs to her. Offences against women were severely dealt with.
- Megasthenese mentioned that slavery did not exist in India.

Economy

- Largely, the population was agriculturists and lived in villages. The state helped people to bring new areas under cultivation by cleaning the forest. But certain types of forests were protected by law.
- A number of crops like rice, coarse grains (kodrava), sesame, pepper, and saffron, pulses, wheat, linseed, mustard, vegetable and fruits of various kinds and sugarcane were grown.
- The state also owned agricultural farms, cattle farms, dairy farms, etc.
- Water reservoirs and dams were built by the state for irrigation. Steps were taken to distribute and measure this water for irrigation.
- Megasthenese mentioned about the extraordinary skill of craftsmen.
- Junagarh inscription of Rudradaman mentions that Pushyagupta (Chandragupta's governors) was responsible for building a dam on Sudarshana Lake near Girnar in Kathiawad.
- They had foreign trade with the western countries. The main items of trade were indigo, various medicinal substances, cotton, and silk. The foreign trade was carried on by the land as well as by the sea.
- Special arrangements were made for facilitation of the trade like security of trade-routes, provisions of warehouses, godowns, and other means of transport.

- The trade was regulated by the state and the trader had to get a license to trade.
- The state also had the machinery to control and regulate the weights and measures.
- The land tax was one-fourth to one-sixth of the produce. The tax was also levied on all the manufactured goods.
- The toll tax was levied on all items, which were brought for sale in the market.
- The income from the king's own land or estate was known as 'sita'.
- Brahmans, children, and handicapped people were exempted from paying the taxes.
- The main industries during this period were textile, mining and metallurgy, ship-building, jewelry making, metal working, etc.
- The guilds settled the disputes of their members. A few guilds issued their own coins.
- Important ports : Bharukachch/ Bharoch & Supara (Western Coast), Tamralipti in Bengal (Eastern coast).
- During Mauryan period, the punch-marked coins (mostly of silver) were the common units of transactions.

Mauryan Art & Architecture

- Art and architecture had developed substantially during the Mauryan period.
- The main examples of the Mauryan art and architecture are:
  - Remains of the royal palace and the city of Pataliputra;
  - Ashokan pillars and capitals;
  - Rock cut Chaitya caves in the Barabar and Nagarjuni hills;
  - Individual Mauryan sculptures and terracotta figurines; etc.
- Megasthenese had described in detail about the famous city of Pataliputra (modern Patna). He describes it as it was stretched along the river Ganga in the form of a parallelogram. It was enclosed by a wooden wall and had 64 gates.
- Seven rock-cut caves in the Barabar and Nagarjuni hills were built during this period.
- The pillars represent the masterpiece of Mauryan sculpture. Each pillar is made of single piece of sandstone, only their capitals, which are beautiful pieces of sculpture in form of lion or bulls, are joined with pillar on the top.
- Four lion capital at Sarnath & Sanchi. Lioned capital of Sarnath was adopted as 'National Emblem' of India on 26 Jan., 1950.
- The Mauryan artisans who started the practice of hewing out caves from rocks for monks to live in. The earliest example are Barabar caves (Sudama, World Hut, Chaupada of Karna, Rishi Lomesh) in Gaya (Ashokan). The other examples are Nagarjuni caves in Gaya (Dasharath).
- Stupas were built throughout the empire to enshrine the relics of Buddha. Of these, the most famous are at Sanchi & Bharhuta.

POST-MAURYAN INDIA

- There are multiple causes for the decline of the Mauryan empire such as weak successors, partition of empire and administrative abuses after Ashoka's reign.
- After the death of Ashoka, his successors were not able to keep the vast Mauryan Empire intact.

- Kalinga declared its independence and in the farther south, the Satavahanas established their independent rule.
- The Mauryan rule was confined to the Gangetic valley and it was soon replaced by the Sunga dynasty.

Sungas and Kanvas

- The founder of the Sunga dynasty was **Pushyamitra Sunga**, who was the commander-in-chief under the Mauryas.
- He ascended the throne of Magadha in 185 B.C.
- Pushyamitra was a staunch follower of Brahmanism. He performed two asvamedha sacrifices.
- After the death of Pushyamitra, his son Agnimitra became the ruler.
- Agnimitra was a great conqueror. He was also the hero of the play *Malavikagnimitram* written by Kalidasa.
- During their rule there was a revival of Brahminical influence. The Bhagavata religion became important.
- 'Patanjali, author of the 'Mahabhasya', was born at Gonarda in Central India. Patanjali was the priest of 2 Asvamedha Yajnas, performed by Pushymitra.
- In arts, the Bharhut Stupa is the most famous monument of the Sunga period.
- The fine gateway railing which surrounds the Sanchi stupa, built by Ashoka, constructed during the Sunga period.
- The last Sunga ruler was Devabhuti, who was murdered by his minister Vasudeva Kanva, the founder of the **Kanva dynasty**.
- The Kanva dynasty ruled for 45 years. After the fall of the Kanvas, the history of Magadha was a blank until the establishment of the Gupta dynasty.

Satavahanas

- The most important of the native successors of the Mauryas in the Deccan and in central India were the Satavahanas.
- The Satavahanas are considered to be identical with the Andhras who are mentioned in the Puranas.
- According to some Puranas altogether the Andhras ruled for 300 years and this period is assigned to the rule of the Satavahana dynasty.
- The earliest inscriptions of the Satavahanas belong to the first century B.C., when they defeated the Kanvas and established their power in parts of central India.
- The early Satavahana kings appeared not in Andhra, but in Maharashtra where most of their early inscriptions have been found.
- They set up their power in the upper Godavari valley, which at present produces rich and diverse crops in Maharashtra.
- The fortunes of the family were restored by Gautamiputra Satakarni (A.D. 106-130).
- He called himself the only brahmana, defeated the Sakas and destroyed many kshatriya rulers. He claims to have destroyed the Kshaharata lineage to which his adversary Nahapana belonged.
- He also occupied Malwa and Kathiawar which lay under the control of the Sakas.
- The successors of Gautamiputra ruled till A.D 220.

- The coins and inscriptions of his immediate successor Vasisthiputra Pulumayi (A.D 130-154) are found in Andhra, and show that by the middle of the second century this area had become a part of the Satavahana kingdom.
- He set up his capital at Paithan or Pratisthan on the Godavari in Aurangabad district.
- The Sakas resumed their conflict with the Satavahanas for the possession of the Konkan coast and Malwa.
- Yajna Sri Satakarni (A.D. 165-194), one of the later kings, recovered north Konkan and Malwa from the Saka rulers.
- He was a lover of trade and navigation.
- His coins have been found not only in Andhra but also in Maharashtra, Madhya Pradesh, and Gujarat.

Chedi

- The information derived from Hathigumpha inscription of **Kharavela** the greatest ruler of Kalinga of this dynasty.
- He constructed caves on the Udaygiri hill near Bhuvaneshwar.

CENTRAL ASIAN CONTACTS AND THEIR RESULTS

The Indo-Greeks

- A series of invasions took place from about 200 B.C.
- The first to cross the Hindukush were the Greeks, who ruled Bactria, lying south of the Oxus river in the area covered by north Afghanistan.
- Two Greek dynasties ruled north-western India on parallel lines at one and the same time.
- The most famous Indo-Greek ruler was Menander (165-145 B.C.). He is also known by the name Milinda.
- He had his capital at Sakala (modern Sialkot) in Punjab, and he invaded the Ganga-Yamuna doab.
- He was converted to Buddhism by Nagasena, who is also known as Nagarjuna.
- The Indo-Bactrian rule is important in the history of India because of the large number of coins which the Greeks issued. The Indo-Greeks were the first rulers in India to issue coins which can be definitely attributed to the kings.
- The Indo-Greeks were the first to issue gold coins in India, which increased in number under the Kushans.
- The Greek rule is also memorable on account of the introduction of Hellonistic art features in the north-west frontier of India, giving rise to the Gandhara art.

The Sakas

- The Greeks were followed by the Sakas, who controlled a much larger part of India than the Greeks did.
- There were five branches of the Sakas with their seats of power in different parts of India and Afghanistan.
- Although the Sakas established their rule in different parts of the country, only those who ruled in western India held power for any considerable length of time, for about four centuries or so.
- The most famous Saka ruler in India was Rudradaman-I (A D 130-150).
- He ruled not only over Sindh, Kutch and Gujarat, but had also recovered from the Satavahanas Konkan, the Narmada valley, Malwa and Kathiawar.

- He is famous in history because of the repairs he undertook to improve the Sudarsana lake in the semi-arid zone of Kathiawar.
- Rudradaman was a great lover of Sanskrit. Although a foreigner settled in India, he issued the first-ever long inscription in chaste Sanskrit.

The Parthians

- The Saka domination in north-western India was followed by that of the Parthians, and in 'many ancient' Indian Sanskrit texts the two peoples are together mentioned as Saka-Pahlavas.
- In fact they ruled over this country on parallel lines for some time.
- Originally the Parthians lived in Iran, from where they moved to India.
- In comparison with the Greeks and the Sakas they occupied only a small portion of north-western India in the first century.
- The most famous Parthian king was Gondophernes, in whose reign St. Thomas is said to have come to India for the propagation of Christianity.

The Kushans

- The Parthians were followed by the Kushans, who are also called Yuechis or Tocharians.
- The Kushans were one of the five clans into which the Yuechi tribe was divided.
- A nomadic people from the steppes of north, Central Asia living in the neighbourhood of China, the Kushans first occupied Bactria or north Afghanistan where they displaced the Sakas.
- Gradually they moved to the Kabul valley and seized Gandhara by crossing the Hindukush, replacing the rule of the Greeks and Parthians in these areas.
- Finally they set up their authority over the lower Indus basin and the greater part of the Gangetic basin.
- The first dynasty was founded by a house of chiefs who were called Kadphises and who ruled for 28 years from about A.D. 50.
- It had two kings. The first was Kadphises I, who issued coins south of the Hindukush. He minted coppers in imitation of Roman coins.
- The second king was Kadphises II, who issued a large number of gold money and spread his kingdom east of the Indus.
- The house of Kadphises was succeeded by that of Kanishka.
- Its kings extended the Kushan power over upper India and the lower Indus basin.
- The early Kushan kings issued numerous gold coins with higher gold content than is found in the Gupta coins.
- Although the gold coins of the Kushans are found mainly west of the Indus, their inscriptions are distributed not only in north-western India and Sindh but also in Mathura, Sravasti, Kausambi and Varanasi.
- Kushan coins, inscriptions, sculptures and structures found in Mathura show that it was their second capital in India, the first being Purushapura or Peshawar.
- The most famous Kushan ruler was Kanishka.
- He started an era in A.D. 78, which is now known as the Saka era and is used by the Government of India.

- Kanishka extended his whole-hearted patronage to Buddhism. He held a Buddhist council in Kashmir, where the doctrines of the Mahayana form of Buddhism were finalized.
- Kanishka was also a great patron of art and Sanskrit literature.
- The successors of Kanishka continued to rule in north-western India till about A.D. 230, and some of them bore typical Indian names such as Vasudeva.

GUPTA EMPIRE

Chandragupta I (320-334 A.D.)

- The first important king of the Gupta dynasty was Chandragupta I.
- He married a Lichchhavi princess from Nepal, which strengthened his position.
- The Guptas were possibly vaisyas, and hence marriage in a "kshatriya family gave them prestige.
- Chandragupta I seems to have been a ruler of considerable importance because he started the Gupta era in A.D. 319-20, which marked the date of his accession.

Samudragupta (335-380 A.D.)

- The Gupta kingdom was enlarged enormously by Chandragupta I's son and successor Samudragupta (335-380 A.D.).
- He was the opposite of Ashoka. Ashoka believed in a policy of peace and non-aggression, but Samudragupta delighted in violence and conquest.
- His court poet Harishena wrote a glowing account of the military exploits of his patron.
- In a long inscription the poet enumerates the peoples and countries that were conquered by Samudragupta.
- The inscription is engraved at Allahabad on the same pillar as carries an inscription of the peace-loving Ashoka.
- Meghavarman, the ruler of Sri Lanka, sent a missionary to Samudragupta for permission to build a Buddhist temple at Gaya.
- Samudragupta never knew any defeat, and in this sense he is called the Napoleon of India.

Chandragupta II (380-414 A.D.)

- The reign of Chandragupta II saw the high watermark of the Gupta empire.
- He extended the limits of the empire by marriage alliance and conquests. Chandragupta married his daughter Prabhavati with a Vakataka prince who belonged to the brahmana caste and ruled in central India.
- Chandragupta II conquered western Malwa and Gujarat, which had been under the rule of the Sakas for about four centuries by that time. The conquest gave Chandragupta the western sea coast, famous for trade and commerce.
- This contributed to the prosperity of Malwa, and its chief city Ujjain. Ujjain seems to have been made the second capital by Chandragupta II.
- The exploits of a king called Chandra are glorified in an iron pillar inscription fixed near Qutb Minar in Delhi.
- He established Gupta authority in north-western India and in a good portion of Bengal.

- Chandragupta II adopted the title of Vikramaditya.
- The court of Chandragupta II at Ujjain was adorned by numerous scholars including Kalidasa and Amarasimha.
- It was in Chandragupta's time that the Chinese pilgrim Fa-hsien (399-414) visited India and wrote an elaborate account of the life of its people.

Successors of Chandragupta II

- **Kumaragupta** (415-455) was the son and successor of Chandra-gupta II. His reign was marked by general peace and prosperity.
- Kumaragupta was the founder of the Nalanda University.
- Kumaragupta was followed by **Skandagupta** who ruled from A.D. 456 to A.D. 468.
- After Skandagupta's death, many of his successors like Purugupta, Narasimhagupta, Buddhagupta and Baladitya could not save the Gupta empire from the Huns. Ultimately, the Gupta power totally disappeared due to the Hun invasions and later by the rise of Yasodharman in Malwa.

Life in the Gupta Age

System of Administration

- In contrast to the Mauryas the Gupta kings adopted pompous' titles such as *parmeshvara, maharajadhiraja* and *paramabhattaraka*.
- This signifies that they ruled over lesser kings in their empire.
- Kingship was hereditary, but royal power was limited by the absence of a firm practice of primogeniture.
- The throne did not always go to the eldest son.
- The Guptas made munificent gifts to the brahmanas, who expressed their gratitude by comparing the king to different gods.
- The king maintained a standing army, which was supplemented by the forces occasionally supplied by the feudatories.
- Chariots receded into the background, and cavalry came to the forefront.
- Horse archery became prominent in military tactics.
- In the Gupta period land taxes increased in number, and those on trade and commerce decreased.
- Probably the king collected taxes varying from one-fourth to one-sixth of the produce.
- In addition to this, whenever the royal army passed through the countryside the local people had to feed it.
- The peasants had to supply animals, foodgrains, furniture, etc., for the maintenance of royal officers on duty in the rural areas.
- In central and western India the villagers were also subjected to forced labour called *vishti* for serving the royal army and officials.
- The judicial system was far more developed under the Guptas than in earlier times. Several law-books were compiled in this period.
- For the first time civil and criminal law were clearly defined and demarcated.
- In bureaucracy, kumaramatyas were the most important officers appointed by the king in the home province and possibly paid in cash.
- The Guptas organized a system of provincial and local administration.

- The empire was divided into divisions (*bhuktis*), and each, *bhukti* was placed under the charge of an *uparika*.
- The *bhuktis* were divided into districts (*vishayas*), which were placed under the charge of *vishayapati*.
- In eastern India the *vishayas* were divided into *vithis*. which again were divided into villages.
- The village headman became more important in Gupta times. He managed the village affairs with the assistance of elders.

Economy

- Till A.D. 550 India carried on some trade with the Eastern Roman empire, to which it exported silk.
- Around A.D. 550 the people of the Eastern Roman empire learnt from the Chinese the art of growing silk. This adversely affected the export trade of India.
- In the middle of the fifth century a guild of silk weavers left their original home in western India in the country of Lata and migrated to Mandasor, where they gave up their original occupation and took to other professions.
- The striking development of the Gupta period was the emergence of priestly landlords at the cost of local peasants.
- Land grants made to the priests certainly brought many virgin areas under cultivation.
- From the economic stand point, we may classify land under the Gupta period into 5 groups : 1. *Kshetra Boomi:* Cultivable land, 2. *Khila:* Waste land, 3. *Vastu Bhoomi:* Habitable land, 4. *Charagah Bhoomi:* Pasture land, 5. *Aprahata Bhoomi:* Forest land.
- *Bhaga*, *Bhoga*, *Bali* and *Uparikara* were a form of taxes.
- The Guptas issued the largest number of gold coins in ancient India, but in gold content, Gupta coins are not as pure as Kushanas.
- The ports of the East coast: Tamralipti, Ghantashala and Kandura—handled the North-Indian trade with South-East Asia; and those of the West coast—Bharoach, Chaul, Kalyan and Cambay—traded with the Mediterranean and West Asia.

Social Developments

- Land grants to the brahmanas on a large scale suggest that the brahmana supremacy continued in Gupta times.
- The Guptas who were originally vaisyas came to be looked upon as kshatriyas by the brahmanas.
- The castes proliferated into numerous subcastes as a result of two factors. On the one hand a large number of foreigners had been assimilated into the Indian society, and each group of foreigners was considered a kind of Hindu caste.
- Since the foreigners mainly came as conquerors they were given the status of the kshatriya in society.
- The Hunas, who appeared in India towards the close of the fifth century, ultimately came to be recognized as one of the thirty-six clans of the Rajputs.
- The other reason for the increase in the number of castes was the absorption of many tribal peoples into brahmanical society by way of land grants.
- The position of sudras and women improved in this period. They were now permitted to listen to the epics and the Puranas.

- From the seventh century onwards the sudras were mainly represented as agriculturists.
- During this period the untouchables increased in number, especially the chandalas. The chandalas appeared in society as early as the fifth century B.C.
- Chandalas lived outside the village and dealt in meat and fish.
- Early marriages were advocated and often pre-puberty marriages took place.
- The first example of Sati appears in Gupta time in 510 AD in Eran in Madhya Pradesh. (Bhanugupta's Eran Inscription-510 AD).
- Women were denied any right to property except for *Stridhana* in the form of jewellery and garments.

Art and Culture

- The Gutpa period is called the **Golden Age** of ancient India.
- Both Samudragupta and Chandragupta II were patrons of art and literature.
- Samudragupta is represented on his coins playing the lute (vina), and Chandragupta II is credited with maintaining in his court nine luminaries or great scholars.
- In the Gupta period we find an over two metre high bronze image of the Buddha, which was recovered from Sultanganj near Bhagalpur.
- Fa-hsien saw an over 25 metre high image of the Buddha made of copper, but it is not traceable now.
- In the Gupta period beautiful images of the Buddha were made at Sarnath and Mathura.
- The greatest specimen of Buddhist art in Gupta times is provided by the Ajanta paintings.
- For the first time we get in the Gupta period images of Vishnu, Siva and some other Hindu gods.
- The Gupta period was poor in architecture.
- All we get is a few temples made of brick in Uttar Pradesh and a stone temple. We may mention the, brick temples of Bhitargaon in Kanpur, Bhitari in Ghazipur and Deogarh in Jhansi.
- The Buddhist university at Nalanda was set up in the fifth century, and its earliest structure, made of brick, belongs to this period.

Literature

- Kalidasa wrote a number of books including *Ritusanhar*, *Raghuvansam*, *Meghadutam*, *Kumarasambhavam* etc.
- *Vayu Purana*, *Vishnu Purana*, *Ramayana*, *Mahabharata* and *Manu Smriti* were re-written.
- *Madrarakshasa* (Visakhadatta), *Kiratarjuniya* (Bharavi), *Panchatantra* (Vishnu Sharma), *Kamasutra* (Vatsyayan) etc. were written in this period.

HARSHAVARDHANA (606-647 A.D.)

- Prabhakara Vardhana was the founder of the Vardhana dynasty. He had two sons, Rajya Vardhana and Harsha Vardhana and a daughter Rajyasree.
- Prabhakara Vardhana was a mighty warrior. After his death, his son Rajya Vardhana succeeded him. But, soon his enemies murdered him. So Harsha became the ruler of Thaneswar in A.D. 606. He ruled upto A.D. 647.

- The most important military campaign of Harsha was against the Western Chalukya ruler Pulakesin II. But Pulakesin II, the Chalukya king, defeated him.
- The Aihole inscription of Pulakesin II mentions the defeat of Harsha by Pulakesin, who after this achievement assumed the title *Paramesvara.*
- Harsha's last military campaign was against the kingdom of Kalinga in Orissa and it was a success.
- Initially, Harsha was the follower of Hindu religion. Later, he became a Buddhist and followed Mahayana Buddhism.
- Harsha shifted his capital from Thaneswar to Kannauj.
- During Harsha's reign, Hiuen Tsang, the Chinese pilgrim, visited India. He stayed for about fourteen years in India.
- In A.D. 644, Harsha called for a Buddhist Council at Kannauj in the honour of Hiuen Tsang's visit to India. It lasted for 23 days.
- Harsha was a great patron of learning. His biographer Banabhatta adorned his royal court. Besides *Harshacharita,* he wrote *Kadambari.* Other literary figures in Harsha's court were Matanga Divakara and the famous Barthrihari, who was the poet, philosopher and grammarian.
- Haridatta and Jayasena were patronised by Harsha.
- Harsha himself authored three plays—*Ratnavali, Priyadarsika* and *Nagananda.*
- Nalanda University became the principal seat of learning during Harsha's time.
- Harsha died in A.D. 647.

PALLAVAS EMPIRE

- The Pallavas established their kingdom in Tondaimandalam by Simhavishnu with its capital at Kanchipuram.
- Other great Pallava rulers were Mahendravarman I, Narasimhavarman I, and Narasimhavarman II.

Mahendravarman-I (600-630 A.D.)

- Mahendravarman I was a follower of Jainism in the early part of his career. He was converted to Saivism by the influence of the Saiva saint, Thirunavukkarasar alias Appar.
- The long-drawn Pallava – Chalukya conflict began during his period.
- He also wrote a Sanskrit drama called *Mattavilasaprahasana*. He was also a composer of music.

Narasimhavarman-I (630-668 A.D.)

- Narasimhavarman I was also known as Mamalla, which means 'great wrestler'.
- His victory over Pulakesin II in the Battle of Manimangalam near Kanchi is mentioned in Kuram copper plates. The Pallava army under General Paranjothi pursued the retreating Chalukya army, entered Chalukya territory, captured and destroyed the capital city of Vatapi. Narasimhavarman I assumed the title 'Vatapikonda'.
- During his reign, Hiuen Tsang visited the Pallava capital Kanchipuram.
- Narasimhavarman I was the founder of Mamallapuram and the monolithic rathas were erected during his reign.

Narasimhavarman-II or Rajasimha

- The Shore temple at Mamallapuram and the Kailasanatha temple at

Kanchipuram were built in this period.

- The Pallava rule lasted till the end of the ninth century A.D. The Chola king Aditya I defeated the last Pallava ruler Aparajita and seized the Kanchi region. With this, the rule of Pallava dynasty came to an end.

Pallavas Art and Architecture

- The Pallavas introduced the art of excavating temples from the rock. In fact, the Dravidian style of temple architecture began with the Pallava rule.
- Mahendravarman I introduced the rock-cut temples.
- Pallava architecture is represented by the monolithic *rathas* and Mandapas found at Mamallapuram. The five *rathas*, popularly called as the *Panchapanadava rathas*, signifies five different styles of temple architecture.
- Rajasimha introduced the structural temples. These temples were built by using the soft sand rocks.
- The Kailasanatha temple at Kanchipuram is the greatest architectural masterpiece of the Pallava art.

CHALUKYAS

- Pulakesin I was the founder of the Chalukya dynasty. He established a small kingdom with Vatapi or Badami as its capital.

Pulakesin-II

- **Pulakesin II** was the contemporary of Harsha Vardhana.
- There was a battle between Harsha and Pulakesin II on the banks of the river **Narmada**. Pulakesin II defeated Harsha.
- In his first expedition against the Pallavas, Pulakesin II emerged victorious. But he suffered a humiliating defeat at the hands of Narasimhavarman I near Kanchi. Subsequently, the Chalukya capital Vatapi was captured and destroyed by the Pallavas.
- Kirtivarman II was the last of the rulers of the Chalukyas. He was defeated by Dantidurga, the founder of the Rashtrakuta dynasty.

Art and Architecture

- The Chalukyas were great patrons of art. They developed the Vesara style in the building of structural temples.
- The structural temples of the Chalukyas exist at Aihole, Badami and Pattadakal (Virupaksha temple). Cave temple architecture was also famous under the Chalukyas. Their cave temples are found in Ajanta, Ellora and Nasik.
- The best specimens of Chalukya paintings can be seen in the Badami cave temple and in the Ajanta caves.

RASHTRAKUTAS

- **Dantidurga** was the founder of the Rashtrakuta dynasty. He defeated the Gurjaras and captured Malwa from them. Then, he annexed the Chalukya kingdom by defeating Kirtivarman 2II. Thus, the Rashtrakutas became a paramount power in the Deccan.
- Dantidurga was succeeded by Krishna I.
- Krishna I built the magnificent rock-cut monolithic Kailasa temple at Ellora.
- Probably the greatest Rashtrakuta rulers were Govinda III (793-814), and Amoghavarsha (814-878).

- After a successful expedition against Nagabhatta of Kanauj and the annexation of Malwa, Govind III turned to the south.
- The king of Lanka and his minister who had been negligent of their own interests, were captured and brought over as prisoners to Halapur.
- Two statues of the lord of Lanka were carried to Manyakhet, and installed like pillars of victory in front of a Shiva temple.
- Amoghavarsha ruled for 68 years but by temperament he preferred the pursuit of religion and literature to war.
- He was himself an author and its credited with writing the first Kannada book on poetics.
- He was a great builder, and is said to have built the capital city Manyakhet so as to excel the city of Indra.
- There were many rebellions in the far fung Rashtrakuta empire under Amoghavarsha.
- These could be barely contained, and began afresh after his death.
- His grandson Indra III (915-927) re-established the empire.
- After the defeat of Mahipala and the sack of Kanauj in 915, Indra III was the most powerful ruler of his times.
- According to al-Masudi who visited India at that time, the Rashtrakuta king Balhara or Vallabharaja, was the greatest king of India and most of the Indian rulers accepted his suzerainty and respected his evvoys.
- He possessed large armies and innumerable elephants.
- Krishna III (934-963) was the last in a line of brilliant rulers.
- He was engaged in a struggle against the Paramaras of malwa and the eastern Chalukyas of Vengi.
- He also alunched a campaign against the Chola ruler of Tanjore, who had supplanted the Pallavas of Kanchi.
- Krishna III defeated the Chola king, Parantaka 1 (949), and annexed the northern part of the Chola empire.
- He then pressed down to Rameshwaram and set up a pillar of victory there and built a temple.
- After his death, all his oppents united against his successor. The Rashtrakuta capital, Malkhed was sacked and burned in 972. This marked the end of the Rashtrakuta empire.
- The Rashtrakuta rule in the Deccan lasted for almost two hundred years till the end of the tenth century.

CHOLA EMPIRE

- Cholas became prominent in the ninth century and established an empire comprising the major portion of South India. Their capital was Tanjore.
- The founder of the Chola kingdom was Vijayalaya.

Rajaraja-I (985-1014 A.D.)

- The most powerful Chola kings were Rajaraja I and his son Rajendra I. Rajaraja ruled from A.D. 985 to A.D 1012. He had conquered the neighbouring Pandya kingdoms and extended his conquest upto the Northern part of Ceylon.
- The extent of the Chola empire under Rajaraja I included the Pandya, Chera and the Tondaimandalam regions

of Tamil Nadu and the Gangavadi, Nolambapadi and the Telugu Chola territories in the Deccan and the northern part of Ceylon and the Maldive Islands beyond India.

- Rajaraja I completed the construction of the famous Rajarajeswara temple or Brihadeeswara temple at Tanjore in 1010 A.D.

Rajendra-I (1014-1044 A.D.)

- During the reign of Rajendra I the whole of Sri Lanka was made part of the Chola Empire.
- He reasserted the Chola authority over the Chera and Pandya countries.
- He defeated Jayasimha II, the Western Chalukya king and the river Tungabhadra was recognised as the boundary between the Cholas and Chalukyas.
- He also defeated the Shailendra or Srivijaya King Vijayatunga-varman.

Chola Government

- The king was the most important person in the Chola administration. All authority rested in his hands, but he had a council of ministers to advise him.
- The kings often went on tours in order to keep better touch with the administration.
- The Cholas maintained a large army consisting of infantry, cavalry and elephants which were called the three limbs of the army.
- The Chola empire was divided into *mandalams* or provinces and these, in turn, were divided into *valanadu* and *nadu*.
- Sometimes, princes of the royal family were appointed governors of provinces.
- Officials were generally paid by giving them assignments of revenue-bearing lands.
- We know more about village government in the Chola empire from a number of inscriptions.
- We hear of two assemblies, called the Ur and the sabha or mahasabha. The Ur was a general assembly of the village.
- This was a gathering of the adult men in the brahmana villages which were called *Agraharas*.

RAJPUT KINGDOMS IN NORTH INDIA

Prathiharas

- Nagabhatta I founded this dynasty. Kannuaj was their capital.
- The most famous king of the Prathiharas was king Mihira Bhoja. He ruled from 836 A.D. to 885 A.D.
- Mihira Bhoja's son Mahendrapal was also equally great and powerful. Under his rule, the Prathihara empire reached its zenith.
- Mahendrapala extended his power over Magadha and Bengal. His court was adorned by Rajshekhar who wrote *Kapurmanjari, Kavya Mimansa, Bal Ramayana, Bal Bharat, Vidhsaal, Bhrinjika, Prapanch Pandav,* and *Bhuvan Kosh-Harvilas* etc.
- During Mahmud Ghazni's raid on Kannauj, Rajyapala fled from the battlefield and was murdered by *Vidyadhara* Chandella.
- Yashpal was the last ruler of this dynasty. By A.D. 1090 the Garhwalas conquered Kannauj.

Chauhans

- Another branch of the Rajputs was the Chauhans of Ajmer.
- This kingdom was founded at the end of the 8th century A.D. The famous king of this dynasty was Visaldeva. He captured Delhi from the Tomaras.
- The last and the most powerful king of this dynasty was Prithviraj Chauhan. He defeated Muhammad of Ghor in the First Battle of Tarain in 1191 A.D. But in the next year Prithviraj was defeated and killed by Muhammed of Ghor in the Second Battle of Tarain.

Chandellas

- The Chandellas had ruled the region called Bundelkhand.
- The important rulers of this dynasty were Dhanga and Kirtivarman.
- The famous Vishnu Temple was built by Yashovarman at Khajuraho in 955 A.D. He made Mahoba his capital. Two other temples of this period are the Parshwanath Jain temple and the Kandariya Mahadeva temple at Khajuraho.
- The last ruler of this dynasty was defeated by Qutb-ud-din Aibak. And thus came the end of the Chandella rule in Bundelkhand.

Paramaras

- Upendra was the founder of this dynasty.
- The most important king of this dynasty was Bhoja (1010 A.D.-1055 A.D.). He dug a very big lake (more than 250 square miles). It is situated to the South East of Bhopal.

Palas of Bengal

- The Pala empire was founded by Gopala, probably in 750 when he was elected king by the notable men of the area to end the anarchy prevailing there.
- He was succeeded in 770 by his son Dharmapala who ruled till 810.
- Dharmapala was defeated by the Rashtrakuta ruler, Dhruva. He revived the Nalanda university and also founded the Vikramashila University near Bhagalpur.
- Devapala, the son of Dharmapala, who succeeded to the throne in AD 810 and ruled for 40 years, extended his control over Pragjyotishpur (Assam) and parts of Orissa.
- Pala rulers were great patrons of Buddhist learning and religion.
- The Pala rulers also had close cultural relations with Tibet. The noted Buddhist scholars, Santarakshita and Dipankara (called Atisa), were invited to Tibet, and they introduced a new form of Buddhism there.
- The Palas had close trade contacts and cultural links with South Asia.
- The trade with South-east Asia was very profitable and added greatly to the prosperity of the Pala empire.
- The powerful Sailendra dynasty, which was Buddhist in faith and which ruled over Malaya, Java, Sumartra and the neighbouring islands, sent many embassies to the Pala court and sought permission to build a monastery at Nalanda, and also requested the Pala ruler, Devapala, to endow five villages for its upkeep.

MEDIEVAL INDIA

ARAB CONQUEST OF SIND

- In 712 A.D., Muhammad bin Quasim invaded Sind. Quasim defeated Dahir, the ruler of Sind and killed him in a well-contested battle. His capital Aror was captured.

Mahmud of Ghazni

- Mahmud is said to have made seventeen raids into India.
- The initial raids were against the Hindu Shahi kingdom in which its king Jayapala was defeated in 1001.
- Anandapala fought against Mahmud but he was also defeated in the Battle of Waihind, the Hind Shahi capital near Peshawar in 1008.
- In 1024, Mahmud marched from Multan across Rajaputana, defeated the Solanki King Bhimadeva I, plundered Anhilwad and sacked the famous temple of Somanatha. This was his last campaign in India. Mahmud died in 1030 A.D.
- Mahmud patronized art and literature. Firdausi was the poet-laureate in the court of Mahmud. He was the author of Shah Namah. Alberuni stayed in Mahmud's court and wrote the famous *Kitab-i-Hind*, an account on India.

Muhammad Ghori

- Taking advantage of the decline of the Ghaznavid empire, Muizzuddin Muhammad popularly known as Muhammad Ghori brought Ghazni under their control.
- In 1175, Muhammad Ghori captured Multan and occupied whole of Sind in his subsequent expeditions. In 1186 he attacked Punjab, captured it from Khusru Malik and annexed it to his dominions.
- Prithviraj Chauhan defeated Ghori in the battle of Tarain near Delhi in 1191 A.D.
- In the Second Battle of Tarain in 1192, Muhammad Ghori thoroughly routed the army of Prithiviraj, who was captured and killed.
- After his brilliant victory over Prithviraj at Tarain, Muhammad Ghori returned to Ghazni leaving behind his favourite general Qutb-ud-din Aibak to make further conquests in India.
- Aibak consolidated his position in India by occupying places like Delhi and Meerut.
- In 1193, Aibak prepared the ground for another invasion by Muhammad Ghori. This invasion was directed against the Gahadavala ruler Jayachandra. Muhammad routed Jayachandra's forces. Kannauj was occupied by the *Muslims* after the battle of Chandawar.
- The Battles of Tarain and Chandawar contributed to the establishment of Turkish rule in India.

DELHI SULTANATE

- The Muslim invasions into India had ultimately resulted in the establishment of Delhi Sultanate which existed from A.D. 1206 to 1526.
- The five dynasties which ruled Delhi were:
  - The Slave dynasty 1206-1290
  - The Khilji dynasty 1290-1320

- The Tughlaq dynasty 1320-1414
- The Sayyid dynasty 1414-1451
- The Lodi dynasty 1451-1526

Slave Dynasty

➥ The Slave dynasty was also called Mamluk dynasty. Mamluk was the Quranic term for slave.

Qutb-ud-din Aibak (1206-10)

➥ Qutb-ud-din Aibak was the first Sultan of Delhi.

➥ Qutb-ud-din Aibak0 was a slave of Muhammad Ghori, who made him the Governor of his Indian possessions.

➥ After the death of Ghori in 1206, Aibak declared his independence. He assumed the title Sultan and made Lahore his capital.

➥ Muslim writers call Aibak *Lakh Baksh* or giver of lakhs because he gave liberal donations to them.

➥ He built the famous Quwat-Ul-Islam mosque at Delhi. He began the construction of the famous Qutb Minar at Delhi but did not live long to complete it. It was later completed by Iltutmish.

➥ Aibak died of injuries received in a fall from his horse while playing chaugan (Polo) in 1210.

➥ Aibak was succeeded by his son Aram Baksh, who was replaced by Iltutmish after eight months.

Iltutmish (1211-36)

➥ Iltutmish belonged to the Ilbari tribe and hence his dynasty was named as Ilbari dynasty.

➥ He shifted his capital from Lahore to Delhi.

➥ He received the mansur, the letter of recognition, from the Abbasid Caliph in 1229 by which he became the legal sovereign ruler of India.

➥ He organised the *Iqta system* and introduced reforms in civil administration and army.

➥ Apart from completing the construction of Qutub Minar at Delhi, the tallest stone tower in India (238 ft.), he built a magnificent mosque at Ajmer.

➥ Iltutmish introduced the Arabic coinage into India and the silver *tanka* weighing 175 grams became a standard coin in medieval India.

➥ Iltutmish had also created a new class of ruling elite of forty powerful military leaders, known as *chahalgani/ chalisa*.

➥ Iltutmish died in A.D. 1236. Before his death Iltutmish nominated his daughter Razia as his successor.

Raziya (1236-40)

➥ She was the first and last Muslim lady who sat on the throne of Delhi.

➥ She appointed an Abyssinian slave Yakuth as Master of the Royal Horses.

➥ In 1240, Altunia, the governor of Bhatinda revolted against her. She went in personally to suppress the revolt but Altunia killed Yakuth and took Raziya prisoner.

Ghiyas-ud-din Balban (1266-87)

➥ Ghiyas-ud-din Balban, who was also known as Ulugh Khan, served as Naib or regent to Sultan Nasiruddin Mahmud.

➥ Balban introduced rigorous court discipline and new customs such as prostration and kissing the Sultan's feet to prove his superiority over the nobles.

- He also introduced the Persian festival of *Nauroz* to impress the nobles and people with his wealth and power. He established a separate military department—*diwan-i-arz* and reorganized the army.
- Balban was determined to break the power of the Forty, the Turkish nobles. He spared only the most obedient nobles and eliminated all others by fair or foul means.
- Balban died in 1287.
- When Balban died, one of his grandsons Kaiqubad was made the Sultan of Delhi. After four years of incompetent rule, Jalaluddin Khilji captured the throne of Delhi in 1290.

Khilji Dynasty

Jalaluddin Khilji (1290-96)

- The founder of the Khilji dynasty was Jalaluddin Khilji.
- The important event of Jalaluddin's reign was the attack on Devagiri in the Deccan. His nephew and son-in-law Ala-ud-din Khilji plundered Devagiri and defeated its ruler Ramachandra Deva and returned to Kara. During the reception there, Ala-ud-din Khilji treacherously murdered his father-in-law Jalaluddin Khilji and usurped the throne of Delhi.

Ala-ud-din Khilji (1296-1316)

- Ala-ud-din Khilji was the greatest ruler of the Khilji Dynasty.
- He was the first Muslim ruler to extend his empire right upto Rameshwaram in the South and adopted the title of *'Sikandar-i-Azam'*.
- Ala-ud-din Khilji sent Nusrat Khan and Ulugh Khan to capture Gujarat in 1299. The king and his daughter escaped while the queen was caught and sent to Delhi. Kafur, an eunuch, was also taken to Delhi and later he was made the Malik Naib – military commander.
- In 1303, Ala-ud-din stormed the Chittor fort. Raja Ratan Singh and his soldiers fought valiantly but submitted. The Rajput women including Rani Padmini performed *jauhar*. This Padmini episode was graphically mentioned in the book *Padmavath* written by Jayasi.
- Ala-ud-din sent his favourite General Malik Kafur to attack Devagiri, Warangal, Mysore and Madurai. Malik Kafur advanced as far as Rameshwaram. He had returned to Delhi with enormous booty.
- The Sultan had built a new city called Siri near Delhi.
- Amir Khusrau the great Persian poet, patronised by Balban, continued to live in Ala-ud-din Khilji's court also and was given the title *'Tuti-i-Hind'*.
- He imposed two other taxes—grazing tax (*charai*) and house tax (*ghari*), both of which were traditional.
- In order to avoid the problems created by the nobles, Alauddin issued four important ordinances. The first ordinance aimed at confiscation of the religious endowments and free grants of lands. By the second ordinance Ala-ud-din reorganised the spy system. An army of informers was created and their duty was to spy on all that happened in the Empire and submit reports to the Sultan. The third ordinance prohibited the use of wine. The fourth ordinance issued by Alauddin laid down that nobles should not have social gatherings and they should not inter-marry without his permission.
- He introduced the system of *Dagh* or the branding of house and *Chehra* or preparation of the descriptive role.

- Alauddin ordered that all land was to be measured and then the share of state was to be fixed. The post of special officer called *Mustakhraj* was created for the purpose of collection of revenue.
- The peasants had to pay half the produce as land revenue.
- Alauddin sought to fix cost of all commodities. For the purpose, he set up three markets at Delhi. One market for food grains, the second for costly cloth and third for horses, slaves and cattles. Each market was under the control of a high officer called *Shahna* who maintained a register of the merchants and strictly controlled the shopkeepers and the prices. The check on market was kept by two officers—*Diwan-i-Riyasat* and *Shahana-i-Mandi*.
- All goods for sale were brought to an open market called the *Sarai-i-Adl*.
- Many forts were built by him and most important of them was Alai Fort. He also constructed the *Alai Darwaja*, the entrance gate to Qutub Minar. He also built the palace of thousand pillars called *Hazar Situn*.

Mubarak Khilji (1316-1320)

- After Alauddin's death, his son Mubarak Khilji ascended the throne.
- He was the first Sultan who declared himself the Khalifa and took the title 'Al-wasiq-Billah'.
- He was killed and succeded by Nasiruddin Khusrau Shah who became the only Hindu convert to sit on the throne of Delhi.

Tughlaq Dynasty

Ghiyasuddin Tughlaq (1320-1325 A.D.)

- He was the founder of the Tughlaq Dynasty.
- From an ordinary person, he rose to the position of provincial governor of Dinapur under Alauddin Khilji.
- He repelled the Mongol invaders several times.
- He killed Khusro Khan, the usurper and became the sultan.
- He was a wise and generous ruler.
- Taking advantage of the confusion that prevailed after the death of Alauddin Khilji, many governors and rulers of the distant provinces declared their independence.
- In 1323, he defeated the ruler of Warrangal and annexed his territory.
- A war of succession was going on in Bengal. Ghiyasuddin took an advantage of such a situation and invaded Bengal. He suppressed the rebels and in this way Bengal also become a part of his empire.
- On his way back to Delhi, he defeated the ruler of Tirhut which he also annexed.

Muhammad bin Tughlaq (1325-1351)

- He is best remembered as a ruler who undertook a number of bold experiments, and showed a keen interest in agriculture.
- He was deeply read in religion and philosophy and had a critical and open mind.
- He conversed not only with the Muslim mystics, but also with the Hindu yogis and Jain saints such as Junaprabha Suri.
- He was also prepared to give high offices to people on the basis of merit, irrespective of whether they belong to noble families or not.
- He transferred the capital from Delhi to Deogiri (which he renamed

Daulatabad) which has been the base for the expansion of the Muslim rule in South India.

- He introduced the token currency. There was a shortage of silver in the world in the 14th century. Muhammad Tughlaq decided to introduce a bronze coin which was to have the same value as the silver tanka. The government was not able to prevent people from forging the new coins, and soon the new coins began to be greatly devalued in the markets.
- He made an ill-advised financial experiment in the Doab between the Ganga and Yamuna. He not only increased the rate of taxation but also revived and created some additional *Abwabs* or *cessess*.
- The Sultan created a new department of Agriculture called *Diwan-i-Kohi*. The main objects of this Department was to bring more land under cultivation by giving direct help to peasants.
- The Sultan had a vision of universal conquest. He decided to conquest Khurasan and Iraq and mobilized a huge army for the purpose.
- He led Quarachil expedition. The expedition was launched in Kumaon hills in Himalayas allegedly to counter Chinese incursions. It also appears that the expedition was directed against some refractory tribes in Kumaon Garhwal region with the objects of bringing them under Delhi Sultanate. The first attack was a success but when the rainy season set in, the invaders suffered terribly.

Firoz Shah Tughlaq (1351-1388 A.D.)

- The nobles and theologians at the court selected Muhammad's cousin Firoz Shah as the next Sultan. He gave a number of important concessions to the theologians.
- He tried to ban practices with the orthodox theologians considered un-Islamic. Thus, he prohibited the practice of Muslim women going out to worship at the graves of saints.
- He persecuted a number of Muslim seats which were considered heretical by the theologians.
- He refused to exempt the Brahmanas from the payment of Jaziya since this was not provided for in the Shariat.
- He decreed that whenever a noble died, his son should be allowed to succeed his position including his Iqta and if he had no sons, his son-in-law and in his absence his slave.
- Firoz extended the principle of heredity to the army. Soldiers were allowed to rest in peace and to send in their place their sons. The soldiers were not paid in cash but by assignment on land revenue of villages. This novel technique of payment led to many abuses.
- The new system of taxation was based on Quran. Four kinds of taxes sanctioned by the Quran were imposed and those were Kharaj, Zakat, Jaziya and Khams. Kharaj was the land tax, which was equal to 1/10 of the produce of the land, Zakat was 2½% tax on property, Jaziya was levied on non-Muslims Khams was 1/6 of the booty captured during war.
- *Jaziya* was introduced for the first time by Firoz Shah.
- A new department of Diwan-i-Khairat was set up to make provision for marriage of poor girls.
- He was a great builder, to his credit are cities of Fatehabad, Hissar,

Jaunpur and Firozabad. During his Bengal campaign he renamed Ikdala as Azadpur and Pandua as Firozabad. The two pillars of Ashoka, one from Topra and another from Meerut were brought to Delhi.

Timur's Invasion (1398-99)

- Amir Timur or Timurlane was a mighty conqueror of Central Asia. His capital was at Samarqand.
- He invaded India in 1398 during the reign of Nasiruddin Mahmud Shah.
- He occupied Delhi on December 18, 1398 and remained there for 15 days. Delhi was sacked and plundered.
- The Tughlaq empire could never recover from such a terrible blow and came to an end in 1412.
- There was disorder and confusion in the country. Delhi was ruined and depopulated.
- India's wealth was drained off to foreign countries.

The Sayyid Dynasty (1414-1451 A.D.)

- Khizr Khan, a lieutenant of Timur captured Delhi. He was a Sayyid and so his dynasty is called the Sayyid Dynasty.
- Khizr Khan ruled till 1421, but his whole reign was marked by utter chaos and disorder.
- He was succeeded, after his death, by his son Mubarak Shah (1421-34).
- During his reign the Subedars of Punjab, Bhatinda and Doab broke out in revolt and the whole of his period was spent in trying to suppress them.
- He died in 1434 and was succeeded by his son Mohammad Shah (1434-45).
- During his reign, the ruler of Malwa invaded Delhi, which was however, saved by the valiant Subedar of Lahore, Bahlol Lodhi.
- After Mohammad Shah's death, his son Alauddin Alam Shah (1445-51) proved incompetent.
- He himself handed over the reigns of his kingdom to Bahlol Lodhi and himself retired to Badaun.

The Lodhi Dynasty (1451-1526 A.D.)

- The Lodhi dynasty was the first Afghan or Pathan dynasty in India. Sher Shah Suri founded the next.

Bahlol Lodhi (1451-1488)

- He was the founder of the Lodhi dynasty.
- He founded the rule of the Lodhi dynasty by usurping the throne from the last of the Sayyid rulers, Alauddin Alam Shah.
- He was a strong and brave ruler. He tried to restore the glory of Delhi by conquering territories around Delhi and after continuous wars for 26 years, he succeeded in extending his authority over Jaunpur, Itawa, Mewar, Sambhal, Gwalior etc.
- He was a kind and generous ruler.
- He was always prepared to help his subjects.
- Though he was himself illiteratre he extended his patronage to art and learning. He died in 1488.

Sikandar Lodhi (1488-1517 A.D.)

- On Bahlol's death, his second son, Nizam Khan, ascended the throne under the title of Sikandar Shah Lodhi.
- He conquered Bihar and Tirhut.

- He transferred the capital from Delhi to Agra, a city he founded.
- Sikandar was the most capable monarch of the Lodhi dynasty.
- His administration was strict and impartial.
- He organised an efficient system of espionage.
- In religious matters, however, he was a bigot and an uncompromising enemy of Hiduism.
- He charged 'jaziya' and 'pilgrim's tax' from the Hindus with severity.
- He is also considered a patron of scholars and philosophers and he got many sanskrit works translated into Persian.

Ibrahim Lodhi (1517-1526 A.D.)

- On Sikandar's death his eldest son, Ibrahim, became the Sultan.
- He asserted the absolute power of the sultan and often insulted the Afghan nobles.
- At last Daulatkhan Lodhi, the governor of Punjab, invited Babar, the king of Kabul, to overthrow Ibrahim.
- Babur seized the opportunity and inflicted a crushing defeat on Ibrahim Lodhi in the First Battle of Panipat in 1526.
- Ibrahim was killed in the battle and with him the Delhi Sultanate came to an end.

Administration Under the Delhi Sultanate

- The Delhi Sultanate was an Islamic state with its religion Islam.
- The office of the Sultan was the most important in the administrative system. He was the ultimate authority for the military, legal and political activities.
- The post of *Naib* was the most powerful one. The *Naib* practically enjoyed all the powers of the Sultan and exercised general control over all the departments.
- The military department was called *Diwan-i-Ariz*. It was headed by *Ariz-i-mumalik*.
- *Diwan-i-Rasalat* was the department of religious affairs. It was headed by chief *Sadr*.
- The head of the judicial department was the chief *Qazi*.
- The department of correspondence was called *Diwan-i-Insha*.
- The provinces under the Delhi Sultanate were called *Iqtas*.
- The governors of the provinces were called the *muqtis* or *walis*.
- The provinces were divided into *shiqs* and the next division was *pargana*. The *shiq* was under the control of *shiqdar*. The *pargana* comprising a number of villages was headed by *amil*.
- The village remained the basic unit of the administration. The village headman was known as *muqaddam* or *chaudhri*. The village accountant was called *patwari*.
- **Officers during Sultanate**
  - **Mustaufi-i-Mamalik:** The Auditor General to check expenditure.
  - **Mushrif-i-Mamalik:** The Accountant General
  - **Sadr-us-Sadr:** Head of Diwan-i-Risalat
  - **Muftis:** Expounded Quranic Law
  - **Muhatsib:** Censor of public morals
  - **Khazain:** The Treasurer

- **Barids:** Intelligence agents
- **Waqia Navis:** News reporters
- **Wakil:** Controlled royal household
- **Kotwal:** Police officer

➥ The lands were classified into three categories:

- **Iqta land** – lands assigned to officials as iqtas instead of payment for their services.
- **Khalisa land** – land under the direct control of the Sultan and the revenues collected were spent for the maintenance of royal court and royal household.
- **Inam land** – land assigned or granted to religious leaders or religious institutions.

Cultural Development During Sultanate Period

Art and Architecture

➥ The Turks introduced arches, domes, lofty towers or *minarets* and decorations using the Arabic script.

➥ The most magnificent building of the 13th century was the *Qutub Minar* which was founded by Aibek and completed by Iltutmish. This seventy one metre tower was dedicated to the *Sufi* saint Qutb-ud-din Bakthiyar Kaki.

➥ Ala-ud-din Khilji added an entrance to the *Qutub Minar* called *Alai Darwaza*.

➥ The buildings of the Tughlaq period were constructed by combining arch and dome.

➥ Muhammad-bin-Tughlaq built the tomb of Ghyas-ud-din Tughlaq on a high platform. The Kotla Fort at Delhi was the creation of Firoz Tughlaq. The Lodhi garden in Delhi was the example for the architecture of the Lodhis.

Music

➥ New musical instruments such as *sarangi* and *rabab* were introduced during this period.

➥ Amir Khusrau introduced many new *ragas* such as *ghora* and *sanam*. He evolved a new style of light music known as *qwalis* by blending the Hindu and Iranian systems. The invention of *sitar* was also attributed to him.

➥ The Indian classical work *Ragadarpan* was translated into Persian during the reign of Firoz Tughlaq.

Literature

➥ The most famous historians of this period were Hasan Nizami, Minhaj-us-Siraj, Ziauddin Barani, and Shams-Siraj Afif.

➥ Barani's *Tarikh-i-Firoz Shahi* contains the history of Tughlaq dynasty.

➥ Minhaj-us-Siraj wrote *Tabaqat-i-Nasari,* a general history of Muslim dynasties up to 1260.

➥ Amir Khusrau's *Khazain-ul-Futuh* speaks about Ala-ud-din's conquests. His famous work *Tughlaq Nama* deals with the rise of Ghyias-ud-din Tughlaq.

Literature of Delhi Sultanate

Book	Author	Historical Importance
Tahqiq-i-Hind	Alberuni	Alberuni was an Arabian scholar who wrote about the Slave dynasty
Tabaqat-i-Nasiri	Minhaj-us-Siraj	Gives an account of Iltutmish's reign
Laila-Majnu	Amir Khusrau	Court poet of Ala-ud-din Khilji
Khazain-ul-Futuh	Amir Khusrau	Describes conquests of Ala-ud-din Khilji

Book	Author	Historical Importance
Tughlaq-Nama	Amir Khusrau	Gives account of Ghiyas-ud-din's reign
Nuh-Siphir	Amir Khusrau	Poetic description of Ala-ud-din Khilji
Fatawah-i-Jahandari	Ziauddin Barani	Gives an account of the Tughlaq dynasty
Tarikh-i-Firoz Shahi	Ziauddin Barani	Gives an account of Firoz Shah's Reign
Fatwah-i-Firoz Shahi	Firoz Shah	Gives an account of his Reign
Kitab-fi-Tahqiq	Alberuni	About Indian Sciences
Qanun-e-Masudi	Alberuni	About astronomy
Jawahar-fil-Jawahir	Alberuni	About mineralogy
Qamas	Firozabadi	Arabic words dictionary
Taj-ul-Maathir	Hasan Nizami	History of Ilbaris, the slave dynasty
Chach Namah	Abu Baker	History of Sindh region
Lubab-ul-Alab	Bhukhari	Persian anthology
Khamsah	Amir Khusrau	Literature and Poems
Shah Namah	Firdausi	About Mohmud Ghazni's reign
Kitab-ul-Rehla	Ibn Batutah	A travelogue with Stories
Miftah-ul-Futuh	Amir Khusrau	Jalaluddin's Conquest and Life
Multa-ul-Anwar	Amir Khusrau	Literary Masterpieces
Ayina-i-Sikandari	Amir Khusrau	Literary Masterpieces
Hasht Bihisht	Amir Khusrau	Literary Masterpieces
Shirin Khusrau	Amir Khusrau	Literary Masterpieces
Tarik-i-Firoz Shahi	Shams-i-Shiraj Afif	History of Tughlaqs

BHAKTI MOVEMENT IN MEDIEVAL INDIA

- The medieval Bhakti movement was the direct result of the influence of the spread of Islam in India.

Sufi Movement

- The Sufis were Muslim saints who came originally from Persian and Arabian countries.
- The two separate groups among the Sufis were the Chisti and the Suhrawardi.
- The most famous of the Sufi saints of India was Khwaja Moin-ud-din Chisti, who settled in Ajmer which became the centre of his activities.
- Baba Farid and Nizamuddin Auliya were other great Sufi saints.
- Another well known Sufi saint was Bahauddin Zakariya who came under the influence of another famous mystic Shihabuddin Suhrawardi. His branch of Sufi saints was known as the Sufis of the Suhrawardi Order.

Sufi/Saints Orders

Order	Saints
Chisti Silsilah	Khwaja Moinuddin Chisti Shaikh Haminuddin Nagauri 'Sultan Tapikin' Khwaja Qutbuddin Bakhtiyar Kaki Khwaja Fariduddin Masud 'Ganj-i-Shakar' Shaikh Nizamuddin Auliya 'Mehboob-i-Shakar' Amir Khusrav 'Turkullah' Shaikh Nasiruddin Mahmud 'Chirag-i-Delhi'

Order	Saints
Suhrawardhi Silsilah	Shaikh Bahauddin Zakariya 'Shaikh-ul-Islam' Shaikh Jalaluddin Tabrizi
Firdausi Silsilah	Shaikh Badruddin Smarkandi Shaikh Sharfuddin Yaha Maneri
Shattari Silsilah	Shaikh Abdullah Shattari Muhammad Ghaush
Qadirya Silsilah	Shaikh Nayamatullah Qadiri Shaikh Nizamatullah Sayyid Muhammad Gilani Abdul Quadir Gilani Shaikh Pir Mahammad 'Main Pir'
Qalandari Silsilah	Abu Ali Qalandar Sayyid Murtaza
Naqsbandi Silsilah	Khwaja Bahauddin Naqsbandi Khwaja Baqi Billah Shaikh Ahmd Sirhnidi 'Mujeddid Alif-i-Saani' Khwaja Mir Dard 'Ilm-Ilahi Muhammad'
Raushaniya sect	Bayazid Ansari
Mahadewi Movement	Mahammad Madhi of Jaunpur

Bhakti Movement

Shankaracharya

- In the 9th century **Sankara** started a Hindu revivalist movement giving a new orientation to Hinduism.
- He was born in Kaladi in Kerala. His doctrine of *Advaita* or Monism was too abstract to appeal to the common man.

Ramanuja

- In the 12th century, Ramanuja, who was born at Sriperumbudur near modern Chennai, preached *Visishtadvaita*.
- According to Ramanuja, God is *Sagunabrahma*. He also advocated *prabattimarga* or path of self-surrender to God.

Ramananda

- Ramananda was born at Allahabad. He was originally a follower of Ramanuja. Later, he founded his own sect and preached his principles in Hindi at Banaras (Varanasi) and Agra.
- His disciples were:
  - Kabir, a Muslim weaver;
  - Raidasa, a cobbler;
  - Sena, a barber;
  - Sadhana, a butcher;
  - Dhanna, a Jat farmer;
  - Narahari, a goldsmith and
  - Pipa, a Rajput prince.

Kabir

- Among the disciples of Ramananda the most famous was Kabir.
- He was born near Banaras (Varanasi) to a brahmin widow. But he was brought up by a Muslim couple who were weavers by profession.
- He preached that both the Hindus and the Muslims are the children of a single God. He had no faith in idol worship, religious rituals and ceremonies. He taught that Allah and Eswar, Ram and Rahim are one and the same.
- The devotees of Kabir were known as Kabir Panthis.

Guru Nanak

- Guru Nanak was the founder of the Sikh religion. He started free community kitchens called 'Guru ka Langar'.
- He was born in Talwandi near Lahore.
- Nanak's teachings were in the form of verses. They were collected in a book called the *Adi Granth*. Later *Adi Grantham* was written in a script called *Gurmukhi*.
- In the seventeenth century, the Khalsa had become a strong military group. It was the time when the Sikhs distinguished themselves from other people by the means of five characteristics (popular as '5Ks'), namely:
  - Kesha (hair),
  - Kangha (comb),
  - Kara (iron bracelet),
  - Kripan (dagger), and
  - Kachchha (under-wear).
- The holy book of the Sikhs is popularly known as 'Guru Granth Sahib'. It contains verses from Kabir, Namdeva and other Bhakti and Sufi saints.

Chaitanya

- Chaitanya, a great devotee of Lord Krishna, was a saint from Bengal.
- He popularised 'Sankritan' or public singing of God's name. His songs are still very popular in Bengal. He was addressed 'Mahaprabhu' by his followers.

Tulsidas

- Goswamy Tulsidas was a devotee of Rama.
- Tulsidas composed the famous *Ram-charitmanas*, the Hindi version of Ramayana.

Vallabhacharya

- A great saint of the Krishna Bhakti cult of vaishnavism, who propounded the philosophy of *Pushti Marg*.

Meerabai

- Meerabai was a Rajput princess.
- Mirabai was a great devotee of Krishna and she became popular in Rajasthan for her bhajans.

Jnanadeva

- Jnanadeva was the founder of the Bhakti Movement in Maharashtra in the thirteenth century. It was called Maharashtra dharma.
- He wrote a commentary of *Bhagavat Gita* called *Jnaneswari*.

Namdeva

- Namdeva was a waterman by birth. He hailed from Maharashtra. He composed beautiful hymns in Marathi.
- He worshipped Vishnu in the form of Lord Vithoba. Some of his verses are included in the Guru Granth Sahib, the holy book of the Sikhs.

Eknath

- He was a family man who started that in order to lead a religious life, staying in institution or monasteries.

Shankara Deva

- He was the founder of Vaishnava devotional movement in Assam.

Tukaram

- Tukaram was a saint who lived in Maharashtra.
- He composed a large number of verses in Marathi called Abhangas or devotional songs in praise of Panduranga or Krishna.

BAHMANI AND VIJAYANAGAR KINGDOMS

- The break up of the Delhi Sultanate provided an opportunity for the rise of a number of kingdoms in the Deccan.
- After the decline of the Tughlaqs, there arose two important kingdoms in the Deccan. They were the Bahmani and Vijayanagar kingdoms.

Vijayanagar Empire

- It was founded by Harihar and Bukka in A.D. 1336. They had earlier served under the Kakatiya ruler of Warangal Prataprudra-II.
- Harihara I annexed Hoysala and Kadamba kingdoms. His wife Ganga Devi wrote Madura Vijayam.
- During the period of Bukka-I the tussle with Bahamanid Sultans started. He fought with the Bahamanid Sultan Muhammad Shah I.
- 10,000 Muslims were inducted by him in his army, and he became the first king of Vijayanagar to do so. Feroz Shah began an invasion during his time.
- Devaraya II had various names like Gajabetekara, Proudha, Devraya, etc. He authored a commentary on the Braham sutra.
- Abdur Razzaq visited his court.

The Saluva Dynasty (1486-1505 A.D.)

- Saluva Narsimha (1486-91) founded the Saluva Dynasty.
- Tirumal and Immadi Narasimha : Both were minors during the regency of Narsa Nayaka. Vasco Da Gama landed in Calicut during his region in 1498.

Krishna Deva Raya (1509-1530)

- The Tuluva dynasty was founded by Vira Narasimha.
- The greatest of the Vijayanagar rulers, Krishna Deva Raya belonged to the Tuluva dynasty.
- Albuquerque sent his ambassadors to Krishna Deva Raya.
- He was a great patron of literature and art and he was known as Andhra Bhoja.
- Eight eminent scholars known as Ashtadiggajas were at his royal court. Pingali Suranna and Tenali Ramakrishna were other important scholars.
- Krishna Deva Raya himself authored a Telugu work, *Amukthama-lyadha* and Sanskrit works, *Jambavati Kalyanam* and *Ushaparinayam*.
- He built the famous Vittalaswamy and Hazara Ramaswamy temples at Vijayanagar.
- Many temples of this period consist of several mandapams or halls meant for ritual, dance and music performances. Gopurams and Kalyana mandapas constructed by the Vijayanagar kings are found in the Kanchipuram, Chidambaram, Vellore, Virinchipuram and Tiruchi temples.
- Krishna Deva Raya renovated Virupaksha temple in A.D. 1510.
- Krishna Deva was also a great builder. He built a new town near Vijayanagara and dug an enormous tank which was also used for irrigation purposes.
- After the death of Krishna Deva (1530), there was a struggle for succession among his relations since his sons were all minors.

- Ultimately, in 1543, Sadashiva Raya ascended the throne and reigned till 1567. But the real power lay in the hands of a triumvirate in which the leading person was Rama Raja.
- Rama Raja was able to play off the various Muslim powers against one another.
- He entered into a commercial treaty with the Portuguese whereby the supply of horses to the Bijapur ruler was stopped.
- In a series of wars he completely defeated the Bijapur ruler, and also inflicted humiliating defeats on Golconda and Ahmadnagar.
- It seems that Rama Raja had no larger purpose than to maintain a balance of power favourable to Vijayanagara between these three powers.
- At length, they combined to inflict a crushing defeat on'Vijayanagara at Bannihatti, near Talikota, in 1565. This is also called the battle of Talikota or the battle of Rakshasa-Tangadi.
- Rama Raja was surrounded, taken prisonerand immediately executed. It is said that 1,00,000 Hindus were slain during the battle. Vijayanagara was thoroughly looted and left in ruins.

The Bahmani Kingdom (1347-1526)

- The Bahmani kingdom was founded in 1347 by Hasan Gangu who revolted and proclaimed his independence, from the Sultanate.
- He assumed the title of *Alauddin Bahmani* (Also Bahman Shah). Gulbarga was his capital.
- He divided his kingdom into four *Tarafs* (provinces) and placed each one under a *Tarafdar* (Governor).
- He was succeeded by Muhammad Shah I (1358-73) whose reign was chiefly occupied in waging savage wars against Vijayanagar and Warangal.
- Some of the other notable rulers of the dynasty were Firoz Shah (1397-1422) who twice defeated Vijayanagar but was ultimately defeated at Pangul.
- Ahmad Shah (1422-33) who conquered Warangal and shifted the capital to Bidar was also known as Wali on account of his association with a sufi, Gesu Daraz.
- Humayun (1451-61) famous for his minister, Khwaja Mahmud Gawan.
- Muhammad Shah III (1463-82) whose reign saw Mahmud Gawan expand the Kingdom as never before.
- In his campaign against Vijaynagar in 1481 he even reached and plundered Kanchi. He over-ran Dabhol and Goa on the western coast.
- However, Gawan was a Persian by birth and hence disliked by the 'Deccani' chiefs who were native. The Deccani party conspired against him and got him executed in 1481.
- Gradually, the Bahmani Kingdom declined in power till in 1526, Amir Barid usurped the throne. Thus the dynasty came to end.

Deccan Sultanate

- Five independent kingdoms rose on the ruins of the Bahmani kingdom, namely Berar, Bidar, Ahmadnagar, Golconda and Bijapur.
- **Berar:** It was the first province to break loose from the Bahmani Kingdom when in 1484, Fathulla, the governor of Gowilgarh, revolted against Mahmud Bahmani.
- The dynasty he founded was called the Imad Shahi dynasty because he

borne the title of Imadoul-Mulk. His capital was at Elichpur.

- The dynasty lasted for about 90 years until 1574 when it was annexed by Ahmadnagar.
- **Bidar:** The kingdom comprised the territory around the Bahmani capital.
- Qasim Barid, a former minister of Mahmud Gawan, had become its de facto ruler as early as 1492. But he and his successor hesitated from assuming formal ranks until 1527.
- The dynasty lasted till 1619 when, it was annexed by Bijapur.
- **Ahmadnagar:** In 1490, Malik Ahmad, the governor of Junmar, successfully revolted and established himself as an independent sovereign.
- He founded the city of Ahmadnagar and along with, the Nizam Shahi dynasty.
- Frequently embroiled in wars with Bijapur and Golkonda, it formed a Subha of Akbar's Empire and was finally annexed to the Mughal in 1637 under Shahjahan.
- **Golkonda:** Founded the last of all (1518), the Golkonda kingdom comprised the ruins of the Kakatiya principality of Warangal and was extensive, fertile and rich in territory.
- It was founded in 1518 by a Turkish officer, Sultan Quli Qutub Shah, who was appointed the Governor of Golkonda by Mahmud Gawan. He moved the capital from Warangal to Golkonda.
- Like Bijapur, Golkonda too became a famous centre of art and architecture and is famous for its tombs which were made of granite.
- Golkonda fort and Charminar are its famous examples of architecture.
- The state was finally annexed to the Mughal Empire by Aurangzeb in 1687.
- **Bijapur:** Out of the five kingdoms of the Deccan Sultanate, Bijapur was the most important.
- It was founded by Yusuf Adil Shah, who waged wars against Vijayanagar and his neighbours but his great achievement was the recovery of Goa from the Portuguese commander, Albuquerque, though the Portuguese retook it in 1510.
- He was succeeded by his minor son, Ismail Shah, who recovered Raichur Doab from Vijayanagar.
- During the reign of Ibrahim Adil Shah, the kingdoms of Golkonda, Bidar and Ahmadnagar attacked Bijapur but it was well defended by its able minister Asad Khan.
- Ibrahim died in 1557 and was succeeded by his son, Ali Adil Shah.
- Ibrahim Adil Shah II (1579-1626) was perhaps the greatest of the Adil Shah kings. He was a good administrator and introduced a very efficient system of revenue settlement.
- He was tolerant of all creeds and faiths. He kept friendly relations with the Portugese and allowed them to preach Christianity in his dominions.

MUGHAL EMPIRE

Babur

- Babar was the founder of the Mughal Empire in India. His original name was Zahir-ud-din Muhammad. He was related to Timur from his father's side and to Chengez Khan through his mother.
- On 21st April, 1526 the first Battle of Panipat took place between Babar

and Ibrahim Lodhi. Lodhi was killed in the battle. Babar's success was due his cavalry and artillery.

- Babar was the first one to use guns or artillery in a battle on the Indian soil.
- Babar defeated Rana Sanga of Mewar in the battle of Kanwah in A.D. 1527. Babur assumed the title Ghazi.
- Babar occupied Malwa after defeating its ruler Medini Rai in A.D. 1528. He defeated the Afghan noble of Bihar, Mahmud Lodi, in the battle of Ghagra in A.D. 1529.
- Babar died at Agra in 1530 at the age of forty seven.
- Babar was a soldier-scholar and wrote his own autobiography called Babar Nama in Turkish language.

Humayun

- Humayun succeeded to the throne of Delhi in A.D. 1530.
- Sher Shah defeated Humayun at Chausa in A.D. 1539 and again at Kannauj in A.D. 1540.
- After losing his kingdom, Humayun became an exile for the next fifteen years.
- He married Hamida Banu Begam who gave birth to Akbar at Amarkot in A.D. 1542.
- In 1555, Humayun defeated the Afghans and recovered the Mughal throne. After six months, he died in 1556 due to his fall from the staircase of his library.

Sher Shah Suri

- The founder of the Sur dynasty was Sher Shah, whose original name was Farid.
- Sher Shah became the ruler of Delhi in 1540.
- Sher Shah organized a brilliant administrative system. The central government consisted of several departments. The king was assisted by four important ministers:
  - Diwan-i-Wizarat—also called as Wazir—incharge of Revenue and Finance.
  - Diwan-i-Ariz—incharge of Army.
  - Diwan-i-Rasalat—Foreign Minister.
  - Diwan-i-Insha—Minister for Communications.
- Sher Shah's empire was divided into forty seven sarkars.
- Chief Shiqdar (law and order) and Chief Munsif (judge) were the two officers incharge of the administration in each sarkar.
- Each sarkar was divided into several parganas. Shiqdar (military officer), Amin (land revenue), Fotedar (treasurer) Karkuns (accountants) were incharge of the administration of each pargana.
- He issued the coin called *Rupia* and fixed standard weight and measures all over the empire.
- He also improved communications by building several highways. He built the *Grand Trunk Road* (G.T. Road), that runs from Calcutta to Peshawar.
- He set up cantonment in various parts of his empire and strong garrison was posted in each cantonments.
- He introduced the principle of local responsibility for local crimes. Muqaddams were punished for failure to find culprits.
- Land was measured and 1/3rd of the average was fixed as land tax. The peasant was given a *patta* (title deed) and a *qabuliyat* (deed of agreement) which fixed the peasant's rights and

taxes. Zamindar were removed and the taxes were directly collected.

- Sher Shah introduced new silver coins called "Dam" and they were in circulation till 1835. He built a new city on the banks of the river Yamuna near Delhi. Now the old fort called Purana Quila and its mosque is alone surviving. He built a Mausoleum at Sasaram, which is considered as one of the master pieces of Indian architecture.
- After Sher Shah's death in 1545 his successors ruled till 1555 when Humayun reconquered India.

Akbar

- When Akbar ascended the throne in A.D. 1556 he was only 14 years old. His guardian Bairam Khan served him as a faithful minister and tutor.
- Bairam Khan, along with Akbar met Hemu in the second Battle of Panipat in 1556. Hemu was initially successful, but lost his consciousness after an arrow hit him. Akbar killed him.
- Battle of Haldighati, was fought between Rana Pratap of Mewar and Mughal army led by Man Singh and Asif Khan. Some historian say that this battle was indecisive but some say that Rana Pratap was defeated.
- Birbal died in a campaign against the Yusuf-Zahis.
- The Ibadat Khana was built in 1575, so that religious discussions could take place here. Purshottam Das (Hindu), Maharaji Rana (Parsi), Harvijaya Suri (Jain), Monserate and Aquaviva (Christian) partook in the discussions that were held here.
- In 1579, the 'Khutba', which was composed by Faizi in his own name, was read by Akbar.
- The proclamation of 'Mazhar' took place in 1579, and Akbar was given the title 'Imam-i-Adil', The discussions that took place in Ibabat Khana were brought to a stop in 1582.
- 'Din-i-Ilahi' was enunciated in 1582.
- As put forward by Badauni, Akbar wished to establish a new religion. Birbal, Abdul Fazl and Faizi became a part of the Din-i-Ilahi.
- The land revenue system of Akbar was called Zabti or Bandobast system. It was further improved by Raja Todar Mal. It was known as Dahsala System.
- By Dahsala System, Todar Mal introduced a uniform system of land measurement. The revenue was fixed on the average yield of land assessed on the basis of past ten years.
- The land was also divided into four categories – Polaj (cultivated every year), Parauti (once in two years), Chachar (once in three or four years) and Banjar (once in five or more years).
- Akbar died in A.D. 1605 after a glorious reign of 50 years. Before his death, Akbar nominated his son Salim to the throne.

Jahangir

- When Akbar died, Prince Salim succeeded with the title Jahangir (Conqueror of World) in 1605.
- Jahangir's eldest son, Khusrau, rebelled against him. He was arrested and put into prison. Guru Arjun Dev, the fifth Sikh Guru, who assisted him was killed for refusal to pay a fine.
- In 1611, Jahangir married Mehrunnisa who was known as Nurjahan (Light of World).

- During Jahangir's reign Captain William Hawkins and Sir Thomas Roe visited his court.
- Sir Thomas Roe secured permission from Jahangir in A.D. 1615 to trade at Surat.
- Nurjahan's elder brother Asaf Khan was appointed as Khan-i-Saman, a post reserved for the nobles.
- In 1612, Asaf Khan's daughter, Arjumand Banu Begum (later known as Mumtaj), married Jahangir's third son, prince Khurram (later Shahjahan).
- Amar Singh of Mewar submitted in 1615. Malik Ambar was successful in capturing Ahmadnagar from the Mughals. In 1620, Jahangir annexed Kangra.
- A chain of justice was hung outside his palace.
- Qandhar was occupied from Shah Abbas of Persia in 1622.
- Jahangir died in A.D. 1627.

Shahjahan

- A war of succession between Khurram and Shahryar ensued after Jahangir's death. Shahryar was killed. Khurram assumed the title Shahjahan or "King of the World" and ruled for 30 years.
- Mother's name: Jagat Gosai/Jodha Bai (daughter of Raja Jagat Singh).
- In 1631-32, he defeated the Portuguese.
- In addition to Jahangir's empire, Nizam Shahi's dynasty of Ahmadnagar was brought under Mughal control (1633) by Shahjahan. The Deccan Sultanate of Bijapur and Golconda accepted his suzreighnty in 1636.
- He sent his army to Balkh in order to secure the defence of North-Western India (1647). Shajahan who had recovered Kandhar (Afghanistan) in 1638 from the Iranians lost it again in 1647 despite three campaigns under prince Murad, Aurangzeb and Dara.
- The reign of Shahjahan is generally considered as the Golden Age of the Mughal period.
- Shahjahan is called as the Prince of Builders. He had built the Jama Masjid and Red Fort in Delhi and Taj Mahal in Agra.
- Fine arts like painting, music and literature reached high level of development during Shahjahan's time.
- Shah Jahan fell ill in A.D. 1657. A war of succession started among his four sons for the throne. Aurangazeb imprisoned Shah Jahan in A.D. 1658. The Emperor remained in prison during his last days. He died in A.D. 1666.

Aurangazeb

- Aurangzeb ruled for almost 50 years. During his long reign period, the Mughal Empire reached its territorial climax.
- Aurangzeb stretched his territory from Kashmir (in the north) to Jinji (in the south), and from the Hindukush (in the west) to Chittagong (in the east).
- In 1686, Aurangzeb imprisoned prince Muazzam on a charge of intriguing with the ruler of Golconda, and kept him in prison for 12 long years. His other sons also had to face his wrath on various occasions.
- Aurangzeb's personal life was marked by simplicity. He had the reputation of being orthodox, God fearing Muslim. In a course of time, he began to be regarded as a *zinda pir*, or "a living saint."

- While taking his stand on the Hanafi school of Muslim law, which had been traditionally followed in India, Aurangzeb did not hesitate in issuing secular decrees, called 'zawabit'.
- At the beginning of his reign, Aurangzeb prohibited the *kalma* being inscribed on coins, as it trampled underfoot or be defiled while passing from one hand to another.
- Aurangzeb banned the festival of Nauroz, as it was considered as Zoroastrian practice favored by the Safavid rulers of Iran.
- Aurangzeb appointed *Muhtasibs* in all the provinces. Their major work was to see that people lived their lives in accordance with the sharia.
- In 1669, Aurangzeb took a number of measures, which have been called puritanical, but many of them were of an economic and social character, and against superstitious beliefs. Likewise, he prohibited singing in the court and the official musicians were pensioned off. The instrumental music and naubat (the royal band) were, however, continued.
- Aurangzeb withdrawn the practice of *jharoka darshan* or showing himself to the public from the balcony (initiated by Akbar). He considered it a superstitious practice and against Islam.
- Aurangzeb banned the ceremony of weighing the emperor against gold and silver and other articles on his birthdays. However, because of majority of social demand, Aurangzeb had to permit this ceremony for his sons when they recovered from illness.
- Aurangzeb prohibited astrologers from preparing almanacs. But the order was disobeyed by everybody including members of the royal family.
- To promote trade among the Muslims who depended (almost) exclusively on state support, Aurangzeb exempted Muslim traders from the payment of cess. However, Aurangzeb found that the Muslim traders were taking undue advantages of this and cheating the state; therefore, he reinstated it, but kept it at half of what was charged from others.
- Aurangzeb again introduced the jizyah (or the poll tax) (it was abolished by Akbar). According to the sharia, in a Muslim state, the payment of jizyah was obligatory, for the non-Muslims.

Mughal Administration

- The Mughals established an imperial state in the true sense free from even shadowy allegiance to an external authority like the Caliphate, and exercised unrivalled power over vast territories.
- The Mughal empire was a centralised disposition based on military power.
- It rested on two pillars: the absolute authority of the emperor and the strength of the army.
- The emperor was the supreme commander of the armed forces, and all other commanders were appointed and if necessary-removed by him.
- He determined the rank of every *mansabdar* and allotted *Jagirs* for the maintenance of the *mansabdar*. He was the fountain of justice as also the supreme judge.
- He made laws and issued adminis-trative ordinances which had the forces of laws, although the principles of *shariat* (Islamic law) were generally adhered to.

- In the days of Babur and Humayun there was a prime minister, known as *vakil*, who was entrusted with large powers in civil and military affairs.
- During the early years of Akbar's reign, Bairam Khan, as *vakil*, virtually served as regent for the minor sovereign. After Bairam Khan's fall, the all-important department of finance, taken away from the *vakil*, was placed in charge of the *wazir* (or *diwan*).
- After the virtual disappearance of the *vakil*, the *wazir* became the emperor's 'minister *par excellence*' *i.e.* prime minister.
- The emperor was the commander-in-chief of the entire army. The minister who looked after the administration of the army was called *Mir Bakshi*. He was in charge of recruitment, equipment and discipline of the troops. The salary bill of all mansabdars had to be calculated and passed by his office.
- Towards the end of Aurangzeb's reign the expansion of the empire necessitated the appointment of four *Bakshis:* the chief or first *bakshi*, and the second, third and fourth *bakshis*.
- The *khan-i-saman* held independent charge of the household department and the *karkhanas*.
- The *sadr-us-sudur* had three important functions. He acted as the emperor's chief adviser in ecclesiastical matters. He was in charge of the disbursement of imperial grant for religious, educational and charitable purposes. He was the chief justice of the empire.

High Officials

- The *muhatasib* (censor of public morals) was primarily an ecclesiastical officer whose duty was to regulate the lives of the people. He also performed certain secular duties, such as the examination of weights and measures, enforcement of fair prices in the market, recovery of debts and restoration of fugitive slaves to their owners.
- There was *diwan* of the *khalisa* in-charge of the crown lands. The *diwan-i-tan* looked after matters relating to the jagirs.
- *Daroga-i-dak* chauki who was in charge of the imperial post.
- The *mir-i-arz* who was in charge of petitions.
- The *Mir-i-mal*, or the officer in charge of the privy purse and the *Mir tuzuk* or the master of ceremonies.

Important Books of Medieval India

Books	Writer
Kitab-ul-Hindi	Al Beruni
Kanun-al-Masudi	Al Beruni
Tarikha-i-Yamini	Utbi
Taaj-ul-Masir	Hasan Nizami
Tabaqat-i-Nasiri	Minhaz-ul-Siraj
Khallq Bari	Amir Khusrau
Tughlaq Nama	Amir Khusrau
Tarikh-i-Alai	Amir Khusrau
Mitah-ul-Futuh	Amir Khusrau
Tarikh-i-Firuz Shahi	Barani
Fatwah-i-Jahandari	Barani
Fautuhat-i-Firozshahi	Firoz Shah Tughlaq
Tarikh-i-Firuz Shahi	Shams-i-Siraj-Afif
Zafarnama	Yazdi
Siyasatnama	Nizami Tusi
Tarikh-i-Mubarakshahi	Ahmad Sirihindi
Futuh-us-Salatin	Isami
Rehala	Ibn Batuta
Baburnama	Babur
Humayunnama	Gulbadan Begum
Tarikh-i-Rashidi	Mirza Haider
Tarikh-i-Humayuni	Jauhar Aftabchi
Tarikh-i-Shershai	Abbas Khan Serwani

Books	Writer
Akbarnama	Abul Fazl
Mantakhab-ul-Tawarikh	Babauni
Tabakat-i-Akbari	Nizamuddin Ahmad
Badshahnama	Abdul Hamid Lahori
Alamgirnama	Mirza Mohd. Qasim
Muntakhab-ul-Lubab	Khafi Khan
Masir-i-Lamgiri	Mustaid Khan
Nuskha-i-Dilkhush	Bhimsena
Fauthuhat-i-Alamgiri	Ishwar Das
Khulassat-i-Tawarikh	Sujan Rain Khatri

THE MARATHAS

Chhatrapathi Shivaji Maharaj (1627-1680)

- Chhatrapathi Shivaji Maharaj was born at Shivner in 1627. His father was Shahji Bhonsle and mother Jija Bai.
- Shivaji's military conquests made him a legendary figure in the Maratha region.
- Shahji gave him the Jagir of Poona. He first captured Torna in 1646.
- In the next two years he conquered Chakan, Kondana and Purandhar.
- In 1656, he captured Javli from Chandra Rao More. He also acquired the port towns of Kalyana and Bhivandi. He raided the Portuguese settlement at Daman and received tribute from them.
- In 1659, Afzal Khan was sent by Ali Adil Shah of Bijapur in order to teach Shivaji a lesson. Shivaji used his tiger claws to kill Afzal Khan.
- Aurangzeb, in 1660, sent the Viceroy of Mughal Deccan, Shaista Khan, to attack the Maratha territories. The war raged on till 1663.
- In 1664, Shivaji attacked Surat, the chief port of the Mughals and plundered it.
- Aurangazeb sent Raja Jai Singh of Amber to fight against Shivaji. He made elaborate preparations and succeeded in besieging the Purander fort where Shivaji lodged his family and treasure. Shivaji opened negotiations with Jai Singh and the Treaty of Purander was signed in 1665.
- In 1674, Shivaji crowned himself at Raigarh and assumed the title Chhatrapathi. Shivaji died in 1680.

Shivaji's Administration

- Shivaji was also a great administrator. He laid the foundations of a sound system of administration. He was assisted by a council of ministers called Ashtapradhan.
  - Peshwa–Finance and general administration. Later he became the prime minister.
  - Sar-i-Naubat or Senapati–Military commander, a honorary post.
  - Amatya–Accountant General.
  - Waqenavis–Intelligence, posts and household affairs.
  - Sachiv–Correspondence.
  - Sumanta–Master of ceremonies and Foreign Minister
  - Nyayadish–Justice.
  - Panditarao–Charities and religious administration.
- The revenue system of Shivaji was based on that of Malik Amber of Ahamadnagar. Lands were measured by using the measuring rod called kathi.
- Shivaji reduced the powers of the existing deshmuks and kulkarnis. He appointed his own revenue officials called karkuns.
- Chauth and Sardeshmukhi were the taxes collected not in the Maratha

kingdom but in the neighbouring territories of the Mughal empire or Deccan Sultanates.

- Chauth was one-fourth of the land revenue paid to the Marathas in order to avoid the Maratha raids. Sardeshmukhi was an additional levy of ten per cent on those lands which the Marathas claimed hereditary rights.

Shambhaji (1680-1689)

- Shambhaji, the eldest son of Shivaji, found a faithful adviser in a Kanauji Brahmin on whom he conferred the title of *Kavi Kalash*.
- Aurangzeb was determined to crush Shambhaji.
- In 1689, Shambhaji and Kavi Kalash were captured by a Mughal general and put to death.
- Rajaram was crowned by the Maratha ministers at Raigarh as Shambhaji's son, Shahu, was too young.
- Then Raigarh was captured by the Mughals.

Peshwas

Balaji Viswanath (1713-1720)

- He began his career as a small revenue official and was given the title of 'Sena Karte' (maker of the army) by Shahu in 1708.
- He became Peshwa in 1713 and made the post the most important and powerful as well as hereditary.
- He played a crucial role in the final victory of Shahu over the Mughals by winning over almost all the Maratha sardars to the side of Shahu.
- He concluded an agreement with the Sayyid brothers (1719) by which the Mughal emperor (Farukhsiyar) recognised Shahu as the king of the Swarajya.

Baji Rao-I (1720-1740)

- Baji Rao, eldest son of Balaji Viswanath, became Peshwa at the young age of 20.
- He was considered the greatest exponent of guerrilla tactics after Shivaji and Maratha power reached its zenith under him.
- Baji Rao I conquered Bassein and Salsette from the Portuguese (1733).
- He also defeated the Nizam-ul-Mulk near Bhopal and concluded the Treaty of Durai Sarai, by which he got Malwa and Bundelkhand from the latter (1737).
- He led innumerable successful expeditions into north India to weaken the Mughal empire and to make the Marathas the supreme power in India.

Balaji Baji Rao (1740-1761)

- Popularly known as *Nana Saheb*, he succeeded his father at the age of 20.
- After the death of Shahu (1749), the management of all state affairs was left in his hands.
- In an agreement with the Mughal emperor (Ahmad Shah), the Peshwa (1752) was to protect the Mughal empire from internal and external (Ahmad Shah Abdali) enemies in return from the Chauth.

THE SIKHS

- Guru Nanak Dev was the founder of Sikhism, the religion that draws its elements from both Hinduism and Islam.

- Name of the ten Sikh Gurus and their works are given below:
  - **Guru Nanak Dev (1469-1539AD):** The founder of Sikhism.
  - **Guru Angad Dev (1504-1552AD):** Developed Gurmukhi, the script used for the Punjabi language and composed 62 hymns that were later included in the **Guru Granth Sahib**.
  - **Guru Amar Das (1479-1574AD):** Became Guru at the age of 73. His most famous hymn, Anand Sahib, is part of Sikh daily ritual.
  - **Guru Ram Das (1534-1581AD):** Founded Amritsar, the holy city of Sikhism. His followers dug the pool that became the holy lake surrounding the Golden Temple.
  - **Guru Arjun Dev (1563-1606AD):** Collected the hymns of previous Gurus and added 2616 of his own to form the Guru Granth Sahib, the holy book of Sikhism. He also built the Golden Temple.
  - **Guru Hargobind (1595-1644AD):** The son of Guru Arjun. Proclaimed that the Guru is a military leader as well as spiritual leader, leading to conflict with the Mughal emperor Shah Jahan.
  - **Guru Har Rai (1630-1661AD):** Grandson of Guru Hargobind.
  - **Guru Har Krishan (1656-1664AD):** Younger son of Guru Har Rai. Became guru at the age of 5 and died of smallpox at the age of 8.
  - **Guru Tegh Bahadur (1621-1675AD):** Great-uncle of Guru Har Krishan. Was barred from Amritsar by Sikh rivals, so founded the Sikh center of Anandpur. Executed by Aurangzeb.
  - **Guru Gobind Singh (1666-1708AD):** Son of Guru Tegh Bahadur. Second only to Guru Nanak in importance. Exemplifying the Sikh ideal of the heroic saint-soldier. Founded the Khalsa and Sikh baptism, composed many poems, and nominated the Sikh sacred text as the final and enduring Guru.

Ranjit Singh

- Maharaja Ranjit Singh was born in 1780 AD in Gujranwala, which is now located in modern day Pakistan, into the Sandhawalia family.
- Ranjit Singh's father Maha Singh was the commander of the Sukerchakia misl and controlled a territory in west Punjab based around his headquarters at Gujranwala.
- Ranjit Singh was a great Indian ruler of his time and founder of Sikh rule in the Punjab.
- Maharaja Ranjit Singh died in 1839 AD at the age of 59.
- The Sikh Power was broken by the British after the death of Ranjit Singh.

AUTONOMOUS STATES

Mysore

- **Haidar Ali** began his career as soldier became the faujdar of Dindigul.
- He defeated the British in 1st Anglo-Mysore war but died during the second Anglo-Mysore war.
- Haidar ali was succeeded by his son **Tipu Sultan** in 1782.
- Haidar Ali conquered several territories and led to the rise of Mysore as one of the leading Indian Powers.

- In the third Anglo-Mysore war Maratha and Nizam aided the British, Cornwallis captured the territory and by Treaty of Seringapatnam Tipu ceded half of his territory.
- Tipu Sultan died on May, 1799 while fighting the British forces in the Fourth Anglo-Mysore War.
- Tipu was commonly known as the 'Tiger of Mysore'.
- Dr. APJ Abdul Kalam, the former President of India, called Tipu Sultan the innovator of the world's first war rocket.

Bengal

- In 1717, **Murshid Quli Kahn** was appointed as Subedar, *i.e.*, governor by Mughal emperor. He transferred the capital from Dacca to Murshidabad.
- In 1740-56 **Alivardi Khan** prevented the English and the French from fortifying their factories.
- He was succeeded by his grandson **Sirajuddaula**.
- Battle of Plassey was fought on 23 June, 1757. Owing to the conspiracy the Nawab was defeated.
- **Mir Jafar (1757-60)** granted undisputed right to free trade in Bengal, Bihar and Orissa to Britishers. He was forced to abdicate in favour of his son-in-law Mir Qasim.
- **Mir Qasim** shifted the capital from Murshidabad to Munger.
- Battle of Buxar (1764) between the British and the three allies Mir Qasim, Shuja-ud-daula of Awadh and Shah Alam II. The allies were defeated.
- **Mir Jafar** was again placed on the throne.
- The victory made the British the defacto rulers of Bengal, Bihar and Orissa.

Carnatic

- It was founded with Arcot as its capital in 1725 by Saadutullah Khan.
- Lord Wellesley pensioned off the last Nawab and annexed the state (1801).

Hyderabad

- Chinquilich Khan was appointed as Wazir of the Mughal empire but disgusted with the Mughal court politics. He conferred the title of 'Nizam-ul-Mulk'.
- Nizam founded the state of Hyderabad.
- Nizam's death was followed by a war of succession (1748-60), after which a series of weak successors ruled as allies of the British.

Awadh

- **Saddat Khan** appointed as the Governor of Awadh in 1722, founded an autonomous state.
- **Safdar Jung (1739-54)** appointed as the Wazir of the Mughal empire was also granted the province of Allahabad.
- **Shuja-ud-daula (1754-75)** defeated in the battle of Buxar against the British, lost Allahabad and Kara.
- **Asaf-ud-daula (1775-97)** concluded the treaty of Faizabad and transferred the capital to Lucknow in 1775.
- Last ruler was **Wazid Ali Shah** when Lord Dalhousie annexed the Awadh.

MODERN INDIA

THE ADVENT OF THE EUROPEANS

The Portuguese

- Vasco-da-Gama, a Portuguese explorer, sailed through the route of cape of Good Hope and reached near Calicut on 20th May, 1498 A.D. He was cordially received by King Zamorin, the local ruler.
- Vasco-da-Gama founded a factory at Cannanore on his second visit to India in 1501. In due course, Calicut, Cochin and Cannanore became the Portuguese trading centres.
- Francisco Almeida came to India in 1505. He was the first Governor of Portuguese possessions in India.
- The real founder of Portuguese power in India was Alfonso de Albuquerque. He captured Goa from the rulers of Bijapur in 1510. It was made their headquarters.

The Dutch

- The United East India Company of the Netherlands founded a factory at Masulipatnam in 1605. They built their first fort on the main land of India at Pulicut in 1609, near Madras (Chennai). They captured Nagapattinam from the Portuguese.
- They made Agra, Surat, Masulipatnam and Chinsura in Bengal as their trading centres.

The Danes

- The Danish East India Company was established in 1616 in Denmark.
- They came to South India and founded a factory at Tranquebar (Tharangambadi) in 1620. They also made settlements at Serampore near Calcutta (Kolkata).

The French

- The French East India Company was established in 1664 under the inspiring and energetic leadership of Colbert, the economic adviser of the French King Louis XIV.
- In 1667, the first French factory was established at Surat by Francis Caron who was nominated as Director-General. In December 1669, another French factory was established at Masulipatnam.
- Francis Caron was replaced by Francis Martin. He founded the settlement of Pondicherry (Puducherry) in 1674 under a grant from Sher Khan Lodi, the Sultan of Bijapur. He made Pondicherry (Puducherry) as the French headquarters.
- The French had gained settlements in Chandranagore, Balasore and Quasim Bazar. On the Malabar coast the French got Mahe in 1725, Karaikal on the coromandal coast, became a French settlement in 1739.

The English

- The East India Company sent Sir William Hawkins to the court of the Mughal Emperor Jahangir in 1609 to obtain permission to erect a factory at Surat.
- In 1615, Sir Thomas Roe, another British merchant, came to Jahangir's court. He stayed for three years and succeeded in getting permission to set up their trading centres at Agra, Surat, Ahmedabad and Broach.

- In 1639, Francis Day, an English merchant bought the site of Madras from a local Nayak, who was the subordinate of the ruler of Chandragiri. He built a fortified factory called Fort St. George.
- Charles II leased out Bombay (Mumbai) to the East India Company. King Charles got Bombay as dowry after his marriage with Portuguese Princess.
- In 1690, the British got permission from Aurangazeb to build a factory on the site of Calcutta. In 1696 a fort was built at that place. It was called Fort William.

CONQUESTS

Conquest of Bengal

- Under the royal firman of 1717, granted by the Mughal Emperor Farrukhsiyar, the English East India Company acquired privileges which allowed them the freedom to export and import their goods without being levied any taxes, in Bengal. Through the firman of 1717, the British were granted the right to utilise passes, called 'dastaks', in order to move their goods freely.
- The Company servants were also permitted to trade but were not covered by the firman. They were required to pay the same taxes as Indian Merchants.
- When Sirajuddaulah ascended the throne of Bengal, conflict arose between him and the British. He was faced with grave challenges from his rivals Ghasiti Begum of Dacca and Shaukat Jung of Purnia. Apart from this, he was also wary of the British.
- He was strictly against the misuse of dastaks.
- Sirajuddaulah asked both the English and the French to pull down their fortifications. The French complied but the English refused to obey.
- The seizing of the English Factory at Qasim Bazaar, was Siraju-ddaulah's response, and he subsequently took over Fort William in 1756. The so called Black Hole episode of Holwell took place during this occupation of Calcutta.
- A strong military and naval force under Colonel Clive and Admiral Watson arrived from Madras. They took over Calcutta once again, and plundered Hoogli in early 1757. The Treaty of Alinagar was forced upon the Nawab in February 1757, through which each and every demand of the British was conceded.
- By this time the English had decided to remove Siraj and place a putppet in his place. They conspired with the leading men of the Nawab's court such as Manikchand, Amirchand, Jagat Seth, Mir Jaffar and Rai Durlabh.
- The rival met each other in the battle field of Plassey. The fateful battle was a battle only in name. The major part of Nawab's army was led by traitors. Sirajuddaulah was put to death by Mir Jaffar's son Miran.
- Mir Jaffar was installed as the Nawab by the English. In doing so, the Company allowed itself to be granted undisputed right to free trade in Bihar, Bengal and Orissa. The English was also granted the zamindari of 24 Parganas.
- Besides Jaffar also paid huge sums of bribe to officials of the company.
- The Company's demands soon drained Mir Jaffar's treasury. When the English saw that their demands were not being met by Mir Jafar, they

removed him and installed his son-in-law, Mir Qasim, in his place.

- Mir Qasim granted the zamindari of the districts of Burdwan, Midnapore and Chittagong, to the English as a reward for instating him as the Nawab.
- In order to evade internal custom duties, he also checked the Company's misuse of the firman of 1717.
- In 1763, war broke out between the English and Mir Qasim, and the Nawab was defeated in a series of encounters.
- Mir Qasim escaped to Awadh. It is over there that he forged an alliance with Shujauddaulah, the Nawab of Awadh, and the exiled Mughal emperor Shah Alam II in an attempt to oust the English from Bengal.
- They fought against the British in the Battle of Buxar on 22 October 1764 and were utterly defeated. The turned out to be the most decisive battle in India's history. It resulted in the firm settling of the British in Bengal, Bihar and Orissa and positioned Awadh at their mercy. Mir Jaffar was reinstated as the Nawab of Bengal and Nizamuddaulah ascended the throne after his death.
- Nizam-ud-daulah signed the Treaty of Allahbad in 1765 by which most of Nawab's army was disbanded and the administration of Bengal was placed in the hands of a deputy Subahdar who was to be nominated by the Company.
- The Company got the Diwani of Bihar, Bengal and Orissa from the Mughal emperor. This system is known, in history, as the 'dual government'.
- The dual government in Bengal was brought out by Robert Clive. Through the dual government, the real power was bestowed upon the English, while the administration was taken care of by the Nawab of Bengal.
- Warren Hastings ended the dual government.

Annexation of Sind

- There were three important causes to annex Sind to the British Empire (*i*) commercial possibilities of the Indus; (*ii*) British fear to expansion of Russian empire to the east and; (*iii*) British desire to increase its influence in Persia and Afghanistan.
- Lord Auckland forced the Amirs to sign the subsidiary treaty in 1839. Lord unnecessarily provoked the Amirs of Sind into a war.
- After defeating the Baluchis and expulsion of Shr Mohammad (Amir of Mirpur) by Napier, Sind was annexed to the British Empire in 1843.

Annexation of Awadh

- The enmity between Awadh and British started in 1764 from the Battle of Buxar. In this battle, the English defeated the combined forces of Shuja-ud-daulah (Awadh); Mughal emperor Shah Alam II; and the Nawab of Bengal, Mir Qasim.
- The accusation of misgoverning his state and of refusing to being about reforms was put on Nawab Wajid Ali Shah. This was the reason, using which the British annexed his state in 1856.
- The annexation was justified by Lord Dalhousie, when he stated that 'the British government would be guilty in the sight of God and man, if it were any longer to aid in sustaining by its continuance an administration fraught with suffering of millions'.
- It is one of the causes for the Revolt of 1857.

Wars of Indian States with the British

	War	Year	Place	Peace Treaty	Year
1.	First Carnatic War	1744-48	Fort St. David St. Thome	Treaty of Aux-La Chappell	1748
2.	Second Carnatic War	1749-54			
3.	Battle of Plassey	1757			
4.	Third Carnatic War	1756-63	Wandiwash	Treaty of Paris	1763
5.	Third Battle of Panipat	1761			
6.	Battle of Buxar	1764			
7.	First Anglo-Mysore War	1767-69	Arcot	Treaty of Madras	1769
8.	First Anglo-Maratha War	1775-82			
9.	Second Anglo-Mysore War	1780-84	Arcot; Porlo Novo	Treaty of Mangalore	1784
10.	Third Anglo-Mysore War	1790-92	Travancore; Seringapatnam	Treaty of Seringapatnam	1792
11.	Fourth Anglo-Mysore War	1799	Seringapatnam	Tipu Sultan was killed	
12.	Second Anglo-Maratha War	1803-05			
13.	Anglo-Gorkha War	1814-16		Treaty of Sugauli	1816
14.	Third Anglo-Maratha War	1817-19			
15.	First Anglo-Burmese War	1826		Treaty of Yandaboo	1826
16.	First Anglo-Sikh War	1845-46	Mudki; Ferozshah Buddiwal; Aliwal and Sabraon	Treaty of Lahore	1846
17.	Second Anglo-Sikh War	1848-49	Ramnagar; Chillianwal and Gujarat (in Punjab)	Punjab was annexed	
18.	Second Anglo-Afghan War	1878-80			

THE GREAT REVOLT OF 1857

Causes of the Revolt

Political Causes

- The British policy of annexations had disturbed the political equilibrium in the country.
- The indiscriminate application of the "Doctrine of Lapse" by Lord Dalhousie had caused widespread discontent.
- The overthrow of Nawab Wajid Ali Shah of Awadh, annexation of several Hindu principalities and forfeiture on the ex-Peshwa's pension had alarmed the Princely States.
- The annexation of Princely States was not a blow to the princely families alone, but to their dependent subjects as well.

Administrative and Economic Causes

- The annexation of Indian states produced startling economic and social consequences under the British rule. Not only was the Indian aristocracy deprived of power and position, but all high posts, civil and military, were reserved for the Europeans. Racial discrimination was evident everywhere.

- The administrative machinery of the East India Company was inefficient and inadequate.
- The land revenue policy was most unpopular.
- Many districts in the newly annexed states were in permanent revolt. Many taluqdars (hereditary landlords) were deprived of their position and resources.
- Large estates were confiscated and auctioned off.
- Thus the new land revenue settlements made by the East India Company in the newly annexed states, made the aristocracy poor without benefiting the peasantry, who fell into the clutches of unprincipled money-lenders and groaned under the weight of heavy assessments and excessive duties.
- The judicial system that the Company introduced in India became an instrument of oppression.

Social and Religious Causes

- The Traditional Indian social system and culture appeared to be in danger under the reformist zeal of the British administrators.
- The sway of leaders of orthodoxy both maulvis and pandits regarding common law in matters of succession, inheritance, etc. was challenged.
- The Religious Disabilities Act of 1856 modified Hindu customs; a change in religion did not debar a son from inheriting the property of his heathen father.
- The Indian mind was getting increasingly convinced that the English were conspiring to convert them into Christianity.

Military Causes

- There was widespread discontent amongst the Indian soldiers serving in the British army, in which the majority of the soldiers and junior officers were Indians. The Indian soldiers resented their low pay and poor prospects of promotion.
- Indian soldiers serving overseas were either not given overseas allowances (bhatta) at all or paid much lower than the European soldiers serving in the British army, which was one of the major causes of discontent among Indian soldiers.
- Another cause of military discontent was the General Service Enlistment Act, which made it compulsory for all recruits to cross the seas whenever ordered to do so.
- The details of the "greased cartridge" issue, which, however, was not the main cause of discontent, are as follows: Shortly before the Revolt of 1857 the new Royal Enfield rifle had been introduced.
- The new type of cartridge used with it had caps allegedly greased with the fat of cow or pig. Before loading the cartridge, the cap had to be removed with the teeth. This issue is said to have agitated both Hindu and Muslim soldiers.

Beginning and Spread of the Revolt

- The Revolt was sparked off on March 29, 1857 when a section of Indian soldiers of the 19th and 34th Native Infantry posted at Barrackpur near

Kolkata mutinied and a Brahmin soldier, Mangal Pandey, killed two British army officers. The mutiny was suppressed, Mangal Pandey tried and executed and the 19th and 34th Native Infantry disbanded.

- About two months later, on May 10, 1857 the soldiers of the 3rd Cavalry Regiment at Meerut refused to touch the greased cartridges and broke out in open rebellion.
- Next day the rebellious soldiers of Meerut marched to Delhi and proclaimed the old Mughal emperor Bahadur Shah II as the King Emperor of Hindustan.
- The success of the rebellion in Delhi created a sensation in various parts of North and Central India and rebellions broke out in Awadh, Ruhelkhand, West Bihar and many other towns and cities of the North-Western Provinces.
- On June 4, the soldiers of the 2nd Cavalry and 1st Native Infantry mutinied at Kanpur and killed several British men, women and children. The leader of the revolt at Kanpur was Dhondu Pant alias Nana Saheb, the adopted son of Peshwa Baji Rao II who was living in exile at Bithur near Kanpur.
- Nana Saheb, assisted by his devoted follower Tantiya Tope, assumed the role of a conquering hero and was proclaimed the Peshwa.
- At Jhansi Rani Lakshmibai, the widowed queen of Raja Gangadhar Rao, the last Maratha ruler of Jhansi, led the rebellion.
- At Lucknow Begum Hazrat Mahal, the queen of Nawab Wajid Ali Shah of Awadh declared her 11 year old son Birjis Qadar as Nawab and the whole of Awadh rallied round her authority.
- In Bihar a local Rajput Zamindar Kunwar Singh, an old man of eighty, who held extensive estates in Arrah, raised the banner of rebellion, which soon spread to many parts of Bihar, including Danapur near Patna, Chotanagpur, Ranchi, Palamu etc.
- Several towns of North-Western and Central Provinces, such as Aligarh, Etawah, Farrukhabad, Bareilly, Banda, Hamirpur etc. also rose in rebellion and independent governments were setup there under the former local chiefs.

Causes of Failure of the Revolt

Some of the important factors for its failure are described as under :

- The Revolt was not inspired by any positive and creative idea. It had no vision of a higher social order or higher political system.
- It lacked plan, programme and funds. The only thing which united the rebels was their desire to eliminate the British rule.
- The Revolt remained confined to a small part of North India, primarily Ruhelkhand, Awadh, Delhi and parts of Central India and Bihar.
- The rebel leaders lacked political leadership, military experience and strategic perception.
- There was no single great leader who could fuse the scattered elements into a consolidated force of great momentum, with a definite policy and action.

SOCIAL AND CULTURAL AWAKENING

Rammohan Roy and Brahmo Samaj

- He is regarded as the first great leader of modern India.

- Rammohan Roy possessed great love and respect for the traditional philosophic systems of the East; but, at the same time, he believed that Western culture alone would help regenerate Indian society.
- He vigorously opposed worship of idols, rigidity of caste, and prevalence of meaningless religious rituals. He condemned the priestly class for encouraging and inculcating these practices.
- In 1820, he published his *Precepts of Jesus* in which he tried to separate the moral and philosophic message of the New Testament, which he praised, from its miracle stories.
- In 1829 he founded a new religious society, the Brahma Sabha, later known as the Brahmo Samaj, whose purpose was to purify Hinduism and to preach theism or the worship of one God.
- The new society was to be based on the twin pillars of reason and the Vedas and Upanishads. It was also to incorporate the teachings of other religions.
- The Brahmo Samaj laid emphasis on human dignity, opposed idolatry, and criticised such social evils as the practice of Sati.
- The best example of his life-long crusade against social evils was the historic agitation he organised against the inhuman custom of women becoming *Sati*.
- He was a stout champion of women's rights. He condemned the subjugation of women and opposed the prevailing idea that women were inferior to men in intellect or in a moral sense.
- He attacked polygamy and the degraded state to which widows were reduced.
- Rammohan Roy was one of the earliest propagators of modern education which he looked upon as a major instrument for the spread of modern ideas in the country.
- In 1817, David Hare, who had come out to India in 1800 as a watchmaker but who spent his entire life in the promotion of modern eduation in the country, founded the famous Hindu College. Rammohun Roy gave most enthusiastic assistance to Hare in this and his other educational projects.
- In addition, he maintained at his own cost an English school in Calcutta from 1817 in which, among other subjects, mechanics and the philosophy of Voltaire were taught.
- In 1825 he established a Vedanta College in which courses both in Indian learning and in Western social and physical sciences were offered.
- He celebrated the success of the Revolution in Spanish America in 1823 by giving a public dinner.
- He condemned the miserable condition of Ireland under the oppressive regime of absentee English landlordism.

Young Bengal Movement

- Its leader and inspirer was the young Anglo-Indian Henry Vivian Derozio, who was bom in 1809 and who taught at Hindu College from 1826 to 1831.
- Derozio possessed a dazzling intellect and followed the most radical views of the time drawing his inspiration from the great French Revolution.
- He was a brilliant teacher who, in spite of his youth, attached to himself a host of bright and adoring students.
- He inspired these students to think rationally and freely, to question all

authority, to love liberty, equality and freedom, and to worship truth.

- Derozio and his famous followers, known as the Derozians and Young Bengal, were fiery patriots.
- Derozio was perhaps the first nationalist poet of modern India.
- Derozio was removed from the Hindu College in 1831 because of his radicalism and died of cholera soon after at the young age of 22.
- The Derozians attacked old and decadent customs, rites and traditions. They were passionate advocates of women's rights and demanded education for them.
- They carried on public agitation on public questions such as the revision of the.Company's Charter, the freedom of the Press, better treatment for Indian labour in British colonies abroad, trial by jury, protection of the ryots from oppressive zamindars, and employment of Indians in the higher grades of government services.
- Surendranath Banerjea, the famous leader of the nationalist movement, described the Derozians as "the pioneers of the modern civilization of Bengal".

Ramakrishna and Vivekananda

- Ramakrishna Paramhansa (1834-1886) was a saintly person who sought religious salvation in the traditional ways of renunciation, meditation, and devotion (*bhakti*).
- In his search for religious truth or the realisation of God he lived with mystics of other faiths, Muslims and Christians.
- He again and again emphasised that there were many roads to God and salvation and that service of man was service of God, for man was the embodiment of God.
- It was his great disciple, Swami Vivekananda (1863-1902), who popularised his religious message and who tried to put it in a form that would suit the needs of contemporary Indian society.
- Vivekananda proclaimed the essential oneness of all religions and condemned any narrowness in religious matters.
- He was convinced of the superior approach of the Indian philosophical tradition.
- He himself subscribed to Vedanta which he declared to be a fully rational system.
- Vivekananda criticised Indians for having lost touch with the rest of the world and become stagnant and mummified.
- Vivekananada condemned the caste system and the current Hindu emphasis on rituals, ceremonies, and superstitions, and urged the people to imbibe the spirit of liberty, equality, and free thinking.
- In 1896, Vivekananda founded the Ramakrishana Mission to carry on humanitarian relief and social work.

Swami Dayananda and Arya Samaj

- The Arya Samaj undertook the task of reforming Hindu religion in North India. It was founded in 1875 by Swami Dayananada Saraswati (1824-1883).
- Swami Dayananda believed that selfish and ignorant priests had perverted Hindu religion with the aid of the Puranas which he said were full of false teachings.

- For his own inspiration, Swami Dayananda went to the Vedas which he regarded as infallible, being the inspired word of God, and as the fount of all knowledge.
- He rejected all later religious thought if it conflicted with the Vedas.
- He believed that every person had the right of direct access to God.
- Moreover, instead of supporting Hindu orthodoxy, he attacked it and led a revolt against it.
- He was opposed to idolatry, ritual and priesthood,. and particularly to the prevalent caste practices and popular Hinduism as preached by *brahmins*.
- He also directed attention towards the problems of men as they lived in this real world and away from the traditional belief in the other world.
- He also favoured the study of western sciences.
- Interestingly enough, Swami Dayanand had met and had discussions with Keshub Chandra Sen, Vidyasagar, Justice Ranade, Gopal Hari Deshmukh and other modern religious and social reformers.
- In fact, the ideas of the Arya Samaj with its Sunday meeting resembled the practices of the Brahmo Samaj and the Prarthana Samaj in this respect.
- Some of Swami Dayanand's followers later started a network of schools and colleges in the country to impart education on western lines. Lala Hansraj played a leading part in this effort.
- On the other hand, in 1902, Swami Shradhananda started the Gurukul near Hardwar to propagate the more traditional ideals of education.
- The Arya Samajists were vigorous advocates of social reform and worked actively to improve the condition of women, and to spread education among them.
- They fought untouchability and the rigidities of the hereditary caste system.
- They were thus advocates of social equality and promoted social solidarity and consolidation.
- At the same time, one of the Arya Samaj's objectives was to prevent the conversion of Hindus to other religions. This led it to start a crusade against other religions.

Theosophical Society

- The Theosophical Society was founded in the United States by Madam H.P. Blavatsky and Colonel H.S. Olcott, who later came to India and founded the headquarters of the Society at Adyar near Madras in 1886.
- The Theosophist movement soon grew in India as a result of the leadership given to it by Mrs. Annie Besant who had come to India in 1893.
- The Theosophists advocated the revival and strengthening of the ancient religions of Hinduism, Zoroastrianism, and Buddhism.
- They recognised the doctrine of the transmigration of the soul.
- They also preached the universal brotherhood of man.
- It was a movement led by westerners who glorified Indian religions and philosophical tradition. This helped Indians recover their self-confidence, even though it tended to give them a sense of false pride in their past greatness.

- One of Mrs. Besant's many achievements in India was the establish-ment of the Central Hindu School at Benars which was later developed by Madan Mohan Malaviya into the Benaras Hindu University.

Sayyed Ahmad Khan and the Aligarh School

- Movements for religious reform were late in emerging among the Muslims. The Muslim upper classes had tended to avoid contact with western education and culture, and it was mainly after the Revolt of 1857 that modern ideas of religious reform began to appear.
- A beginning in this direction was made when the Muhammedan Literary Society was founded at Calcutta in 1863.
- This Society promoted discussion of religious, social, and political questions, in the light of modern ideas and encouraged upper and middle class Muslims to take to western education.
- The most important reformer among the Muslims was Sayyid Ahmad Khan (1817-1898).
- He was tremendously impressed by modern scientific thought and worked all his life to reconcile it with Islam.
- This he did, first of all, by declaring that the Quran alone was the authoritative work for Islam and all other Islamic writings were secondary.
- Even the Quran he interpreted in the light of contemporary rationalism and science.
- All his life he struggled against blind obedience to tradition, dependence on custom, ignornce and irrationalism.
- He urged the people to develop a critical approach and freedom of thought.
- He also warned against fanaticism, narrow-mindedness, and exclusiveness, and urged students and others to be broadminded and tolerant.
- Sayyid Ahmad Khan believed that the religious and social life of the Muslims could be improved only by imbibing modern western scientific knowledge and culture.
- As an official he founded schools in many towns and had many western books translated into Urdu.
- In 1875 he founded at Aligarh the Muhammedan Anglo-Oriental College as a centre for spreading western sciences and culture. Later, this College grew into the Aligarh Muslim University.
- Sayyid Ahmad Khan was a great believer in religious toleration.
- Believing that a person's religion was his or her private affair, he roundly condemned any sign of religious bigotry in personal relations.
- In particular he wrote in favour of raising the women's status in society and advocated removal of purdah and spread of education among women.
- He also condemned the customs of polygamy and easy divorce.

Religious Reform among the Parsis

- Religious reform was begun among the Parsis in Bombay in the middle of the 19th century. In 1851, the Rehnumai Mazdayasan Sabha or Religious Reform Association was started by Naoroji Furdonji, Dadabhai

Naoroji, S.S. Bengalee, and others. It campaigned against the entrenched orthodoxy in the religious field and initiated the modernisation of Parsi social customs regarding the edcation of women, marriage and the social position of women in general.

Religious Reform among the Sikhs

- Religious reform among the Sikhs was begun at the end of the 19th century when the Khalsa College was started at Amritsar.
- But the reform effort gained momentum after 1920 when the Akali Movement rose in the Punjab.
- The main aim of the Akalis was to purify the management of the gurudwaras or Sikh shrines.
- The Sikh masses led by the Akalis started in 1921 a powerful Satyagraha against the mahants and the Government which came to their aid.
- The Akalis soon forced the Government to pass a new Sikh Gurudwaras Act in 1922 which was later amended in 1925.

NATIONAL MOVEMENT (1885-1947)

Early Political Associations

- The British Indian Association — 1851, Bengal
- The Bombay Association — 1852
- East India Association — 1856, London
- Madras Native Association — 1852
- Poona Sarvojanik Sabha — 1870
- The Madras Mahajana Sabha — 1884

Indian National Congress (1885)

- Allan Octavian Hume, a retired civil servant in the British Government took the initiative to form an all-India organization. Thus, the Indian National Congress was founded and its first session was held at Bombay in 1885. W.C. Banerjee was its first president. It was attended by 72 delegates from all over India.
- The second session was held in Calcutta in 1886 and the third in Madras in 1887.
- Surendranath Banerjee was called the Indian Burke. He founded the Indian Association (1876) to agitate for political reforms. He had convened the Indian National Conference (1883) which merged with the Indian National Congress in 1886.
- In the beginning, the British Government welcomed the birth of the Indian National Congress. In 1886, Governor-General Lord Dufferin gave a tea garden party for the Congress members in Calcutta. The government officials had also attended Congress sessions. With the increase in Congress demands, the government became unfriendly.
- Between 1885 and 1905, the Congress leaders were moderates. The Moderates had faith in the British justice and goodwill. They were called moderates because they adopted peaceful and constitutional means to achieve their demands.
- The only demand of the Congress granted by the British was the expansion of the legislative councils by the Indian Councils Act of 1892.
- In 1905, Gopal Krishna Gokhale founded the Servants of India Society to train Indians to dedicate their lives to the cause of the country.

Indian National Movement

- The period from 1905 was known as the era of extremism in the Indian National Movement.
- The important extremist leaders were Lala Lajpat Rai, Bal Gangadhar Tilak, Bipin Chandra Pal and Aurobindo Ghosh.

Causes for the Rise of Extremism

1. The failure of the Moderates to win any notable success other than the expansion of the legislative councils by the Indian Councils Act (1892).
2. The famine and plague of 1896-97 which affected the whole country and the suffering of the masses.
3. The economic conditions of the people became worse.
4. The ill-treatment of Indians in South Africa on the basis of colour of skin.
5. The immediate cause for the rise of extremism was the reactionary rule of Lord Curzon:
   - He passed the Calcutta Corporation Act, (1899) reducing the Indian control of this local body.
   - The Universities Act (1904) reduced the elected members in the University bodies. It also reduced the autonomy of the universities and made them government departments.
   - His worst measure was the Partition of Bengal (1905).

The Partition of Bengal and Swadeshi Movement

- The partition of Bengal officially came into effect on October 16, 1905.
- Its announcement set off a mighty upsurge which brought people and political leaders of all shades of opinion together.
- **Vande Mataram** overnight became the national song for the whole country.
- The day the partition came into effect (October 16, 1905) was observed in Bengal as a day of mourning.
- On the suggestion of Rabindranath Tagore the day of partition was further observed as Rakhi Bandhan Day.
- To offer more active resistance, it was decided to boycott goods.
- People vowed not to purchase British cloth, salt, sugar or anything else manufactured in England.
- This was the beginning of the *Swadeshi movement*, which within a few years transformed the Indian political scene.
- The *Swadeshi* movement quickly gathered force. Bonfires of British cloth demonstrated the people's determination not to rely on foreign products. The sale of English goods fell dramatically as Bombay mills worked overtime to meet the demand for *swadeshi* textiles.
- It became a matter of pride to wear coarse ***dhotis*** made on local handlooms rather than the fashionable Manchester textiles.
- The ***Swadeshi*** movement gave a tremendous impetus to Indian industry.

The Foundation of All-India Muslim League

- The partition of Bengal had created a communal divide.
- Shortly after the partition scheme was announced, a Muslim deputation, most of its members belonging to

the aristocracy, led by the Agha Khan, the spiritual head of the Khoja Muslim community, met Lord Minto at Simla on October 1, 1906.

- The address presented by the deputation claimed a privileged position for Indian Muslims on the grounds of political importance, military service (i.e. enlistment in the Army) and the historical memories of their lost political glory.
- The Simla Deputation was followed in Eastern Bengal by Muslim meetings in support of the partition of Bengal.
- Demonstrations in support of official policies were encouraged by the Government as a counter-stroke to the Swadeshi movement.
- Nawab Habibulla (or Salimullah) of Dacca, favoured by Lord Curzon, took the leadership of the pro-partition movement.
- In the wake of these developments, a meeting was held at Dacca on December 30, 1906, where it was decided to form a political association, called the All-India Muslim League, with three objectives:
    - to promote among Muslims loyalty to the British Government;
    - to protect and advance the political rights of the Muslims and
    - to prevent the rise among the Muslims of any feeling of hostility towards other communities without prejudice to other objects of the League.
- During the years 1907-9, the main programme of the Muslim League was to fight for consolidation and extension of separate electorates.
- The Amritsar session of the League, held in 1908, demanded a separate electorate for the Muslims, which was conceded to them by the Morley-Minto reforms in 1909.

The Surat Split

- The Swadeshi movement also cast its shadow on the growing differences between the Moderate and Extremist groups in the Congress.
- The Varanasi session of the Congress, presided over by G.K. Gokhale in 1905, recorded its protest against the partition of Bengal.
- But the Moderates were not ready to extend open support to boycott which was in conflict with their policy of "petition and persuasion".
- The growing differences between the Moderates and the Extremists came to the fore at the Surat session of the INC in 1907, when against the wishes of the Extremists, who preferred Lala Lajpat Rai, Ras Behari Ghosh was chosen as President.
- The issues on which the split came were the resolutions on self-government, boycott and National Education.
- The Surat session ended in pandemonium and the Moderates, who constituted the majority of the delegates, gained complete control over the Congress organisation.
- The Moderates eventually decided to have no truck with the Extremists, who seceded from the INC.

The Morley-Minto Reforms or The Indian Councils Act, 1909

- In view of the seething unrest and troubles in India, both of them decided to work out a scheme for the reform of the Legislative Councils.
- Passed by the British Parliament in 1911, the new statute, officially called the Indian Councils Act (1909), was popularly known as Minto-Morley Reforms.

➥ The main features of this Act were :

- It increased the membership of non-officials in the Imperial and Provincial Legislative Councils.
- The effective principle introduced by the Indian Councils Act, 1892, was further extended, so that in 1910 more than a hundred indirectly elected Indians took their seats in the Councils.
- In the Provincial Legislature, the non-official members had the majority, but an official majority was retained at the Centre.
- The Act provided for the appointment of an Indian to the Viceroy's Executive Council, as well as the Provincial Executive Councils.
- The powers of the Legislature were also improved. The members could ask questions and even debate the budget, but could not vote on it. They could introduce legislative proposals, but could not enact laws.
- The greatest evil of the Act of 1909 was the grant of separate electorate to the Muslims. The Muslim representatives to the Councils were elected not from the general electorate, but from a separate electorate consisting of Muslims alone. This meant in effect that the Muslim community was recognised as a completely separate section of the Indian nation.

➥ The Minto-Morley Reforms satisfied neither the Moderates nor the Extremists.

➥ The Lahore session of the INC in 1909 expressed its strong disapproval of separate electorate formed on the basis of religion.

Revolutionary Movement in India and Abroad

The First Phase of Revolutionary Movement

➥ One of the earliest terrorist deeds was done in Poona in 1897 by two young Chapekar brothers, Damodar and Balkrishna, when they murdered two notorious British officials, Rand and Amherst.

➥ They were later arrested and sentenced to death.

➥ The Chapekar brothers were associated with the revolutionary society Hindu Dharma Sangha. The Arya Bandhav Samaj was another society formed under the inspiration of Tilak.

➥ Foremost among the revolutionary associations in Maharashtra was the Abhinava Bharat Society founded by Vinayak Damodar Savarkar in 1904.

➥ The educational institutions provided a fertile breeding ground for the revolutionary ideas and activities of the society, which established branches in various towns of Maharashtra and Central Provinces.

➥ Anant Lakshman Karkare, a leading member of this Society, murdered Jackson, the District Magistrate of Nasik.

➥ This led to the arrest and trial of the revolutionaries of this Society in the Nasik Conspiracy case and 27 of them were found guilty and punished.

➥ V.D. Savarkar's brother Ganesh was transported for life for seditious writings and inciting war against the British Government.

➥ In the Madras Province, Nilkantha Brahmachari and Vanchi Aiyar founded a secret Bharatha Matha Association.

- Aiyar killed Ashe, the District Magistrate of Tiruneveli in 1911 and later on committed suicide.
- In the Punjab, revolutionary terrorism had some links with recurring famines and increase in the land revenue and irrigation taxes.
- As early as in 1904, one J.M. Chaterji, whose family had settled in Saharanpur, founded the Bharat Mata Society.
- Later he was joined by Lala Hardayal, Ajit Singh and Sufi Amba Prasad.
- The deportation of Lala Lajpat Rai and Sardar Ajit Singh provided further stimulus to the revolutionary feelings in the Punjab.
- Bengal was in the forefront of revolutionary terrorist activities.
- The revolutionary movement in Bengal derived its inspiration from the works of Bankim Chandra Chatterji and exhortations of Swami Vivekananda and Aurobindo Ghosh.
- One of the earliest and best known revolutionary societies in Bengal was the Anushilan Samiti.
- Satish Chandra Bose and Pramathanath Mitra played a leading role in founding this society; Aurobindo Ghosh and Sister Nivedita, the Irish discipline of Swami Vivekananda, greatly encouraged and supported it.
- Another Anushilan Samiti was founded in Dacca (now Dhaka).
- The Dacca Anushilan Samiti was led by Pulin Behari Das and had about 500 branches in East Bengal.
- *Atmonnati Samiti*, founded by Bipin Behari Ganguly, was another revolutionary society of Bengal.
- Sakharam Ganesh Deuskar, a Marathi scholar who was proficient in Bengali, provided a link between the revolutionaries of Bengal and Maharashtra.

Revolutionary Movements Outside India

- During this period, revolutionary activities and propaganda were conducted by Indians settled abroad, especially in the United Kingdom, the USA, France, Afghanistan and Germany.
- The India Home Rule Society, one of the earliest revolutionary societies outside India, was founded by Shyamji Krishna Varma who had settled in London in 1897.
- He gathered a group of Indian revolutionaries around him, the most prominent among whom were V.D. Savarkar, Hardayal and Madan Lal Dhingra.
- Shyamji Krishna Varma founded the Indian Home Rule Society with the object of securing Home Rule for India.
- For this purpose he started a paper, ***Indian Sociologist*** and founded the Indian House in London.
- The growing revolutionary approach of Shyamji and his associates drew the attention of the British Government and ***The Times*** and other newspapers in London criticised Shyamji and his associates. Shyamji thereupon left London and settled Paris and the political leadership of India House came to be vested on V.D. Savarkar.
- Savarkar's colleague Madan Lal Dhingra shot dead Curzon Wyllie on July 1, 1909 in London. Madan Lal Dhingra was arrested then hanged.
- Later on, Savarkar was arrested and sent to India to undergo trial in the Nasik Conspiracy case and other charges.

Bhikaiji Cama's Movement

- Madam Bhikaiji Rustam K.R. Cama, an associate of Shyamji Krishna Varma, left India in 1902 and was engaged in making revolutionary propaganda against the British rule, both in Europe and America.
- She and Sardar Singh Rana lived in Paris and attended the International Socialist Congress at Stuttgart (Germany) in August 1907, as representatives of India.
- Madam Cama made a fiery speech exposing the disastrous results of the British rule in India and at the conclusion of the conference unfurled the National Flag of India—a tricolour in green, yellow and red.

The Ghadar Party Movement

- At the turn of the century, a large number of Indians had settled down in the USA and Canada.
- About 1906, these Indians started nationalistic activities in the USA and began to publish material against the British rule in India.
- Taraknath Das, one of the leading Indians in the USA, formed the Indian Independence League in California in 1907 and the next year he began to publish the paper ***Free Hindustan***. Its object was to spread revolutionary ideas among Indians living in the USA.
- In November 1913 the ***Hind Association of America*** was founded by Sohan Singh Bhakana. It decided to publish a weekly paper ***Ghadar*** or ***Hindustan Ghadar,*** in commemoration of the Revolt of 1857, in English, Urdu, Marathi and Gurumukhi, which gave the association its hallowed name the ***Ghadar Party***.
- Lala Hardayal was the guiding spirit of the Ghadar Party movement.
- Among other notable revolutionaries outside India were Raja Mahendra Pratap and Barkatullah who, with the support of Germany and Russia, set up the Provisional Government of India in Kabul.

The Home Rule Movement

- The outbreak of the First World War and release of Tilak in 1914 after the completion of his prison term, accelerated the launching of the Home Rule Movement by Tilak and Mrs. Annie Besant, both of whom decided to work in close cooperation to launch the movement.
- The idea of starting a Home Rule League originated with Mrs. Besant.
- Realising that no real progress could be achieved without securing self-government, she plunged herself into political struggle.
- She was equally convinced that the Moderates, who at that time controlled the Congress, were too weak to work for Self-Government.
- The definite campaign for Home Rule began with the publication of a weekly review, ***The Commonwealth***, on January 2, 1914.
- The paper adopted as its cardinal programme, "religious liberty, national education, social reform and political reform" aiming at self-government for India within the British Commonwealth.
- Two Home Rule Leagues were founded to pursue this programme, both Leagues being supportive of each other.
- Tilak founded the ***Indian Home Rule League*** in April 1916 and five months later in September 1916 Mr. Annie Besant started the ***Home Rule League***.

- There was an informal understanding between the two Leagues that Mrs. Besant's field of work would cover the whole of India, except Maharashtra and Central Provinces, where Tilak's League would carry on the work.
- Both launched a propaganda in favour of Home Rule through their respective papers—Mrs. Besant's ***Commonwealth*** and ***New India*** and Tilak's ***Mahratta*** and ***Kesari***.
- Both of them undertook an extensive lecture tour to instruct the masses on Home Rule.
- To suppress this movement which was growing in popularity, the British Government in July 1916, instituted a case against Tilak for certain speeches he had delivered at the Home Rule meetings; Mrs. Besant too was interned in 1917.
- These repressive measures, however, did not weaken the Home Rule movement.
- After Montagu's Declaration (August 1917) Mrs. Besant dropped her League, but Tilak continued his movement.

The Lucknow Pact (1916)

- The Lucknow session of the I.N.C. in 1916 was a memorable event on account of two important developments.
- The first was the readmission of the Extremists, who had been expelled from the I.N.C. nine years earlier. Thus the Lucknow session was the first meeting of the united Congress.
- The second development was the bond of alliance between the Congress and the Muslim League.
- During the simultaneous annual sessions of the League and the Congress held at Lucknow in December 1916, both passed resolutions separately for a joint scheme of constitutional reforms and reached an agreement to cooperate in the political field on the basis of a common programme.
- This agreement is generally known as the ***Lucknow Pact*** or the ***Congress-League Scheme***.
- The Lucknow Pact opened the way to future resurgence of communalism in Indian politics.

The Government of India Act, 1919

Features of Act

The principal features of the Act of 1919 were:

- A provision was made for classification of central and provincial subjects.
- The provincial subjects were divided into two groups: Reserved and Transferred. The Reserved subjects were with the Governor and Transferred subjects with the Indian Ministers. This division of subjects, known as 'Dyarchy' or dual government in the provinces, was the most important feature of the Act.
- The Reserved subjects included essential areas of law enforcement such as justice, police and revenue.
- The Transferred subjects included education, public health, public works, etc. The ministers in charge of them were to be responsible to provincial Legislative Councils.
- No Bill of the Legislature could be deemed to have been passed unless assented to by the Governor-General. The latter could, however, enact a Bill without the assent of the Legislature.
- The Governor-General's control over the Indian finances was also kept intact.

- The Act provided for the establishment, for the first time, in India of a Public Service Commission.

Anti-Rowlatt Satyagraha (1919)

- In view of the growing revolutionary terrorism and the on-going First World War, the Governor-General Chelmsford had appointed a Committee (the Sedition or Rowlatt Committee) under the Presidentship of Sydney Rowlatt, a Judge of the King's bench in London, to investigate the nature and extent of revolutionary activities and to suggest legislation, if necessary, to deal effectively with them.
- The Rowlatt Committee, which submitted its Report in April 1918, made a comprehensive review of the activities of militant nationalists and recommended special legislation, both punitive and preventive in character.
- Two Bills based on the Rowlatt Committee's recommendations were placed before the Imperial Legislative Council.
- One was dropped; the other—the Anarchical and Revolutionary Crimes Act—was passed in March 1919.
- It provided for speedy trial of offences by a Special Court consisting of three High Court Judges.
- There was no appeal from this Court and it could accept evidence not admissible under the Indian Evidence Act.
- Besides, this Provincial Governments were given wide powers to search a place and arrest a suspected person without warrant.
- As soon as the Government introduced the two Bills (February 6, 1919), Gandhiji decided to organise a *Satyagraha* campaign.
- He criticised the so-called Rowlatt Acts as "unjust, subversive of the principles of liberty and destructive of elementary rights of the individual".
- A *Satyagraha Sabha* was established, with Gandhiji as its president, to organise the campaign.
- In the first stage of the anti-Rowlatt *Satyagraha,* volunteers courted arrest through formal defiance of the law.
- The second stage was to launch a country-wide ***hartal*** or strike on April 6, 1919. This was followed by mass protest and mob violence in Bombay, Ahmedabad and several other towns.
- The anti-Rowlatt Act ***Satyagraha*** transformed the Congress into a national body, with a new ideology and a new strategy under a new leader.

The Jallianwala Bagh Massacre

- The anti-Rowlatt Act agitation was particularly severe in the Punjab which was suffering from the aftereffects of wartime repression, forcible recruitment and the influence of the revolutionaries.
- The movement provoked a ***hartal*** in many parts of the Punjab and violent disturbances took place.
- Within a week of the ***hartal*** of April 6, a considerable part of the Punjab was aflame and the authorities put down the rebellion through such measures as "no civilised Government in modern times has ever been known to take against its own subjects."
- The Lieutenant Governor, Gen. Michal O'Dwyer, had already earned notoriety as an oppressive administrator.

- On April 9, 1919, he ordered the arrest of two local Congress leaders, Dr. Satyapal and Dr. Kitchlew, who were associated with the Reception Committee for the annual session of the I.N.C. to be held in December 1919.
- To protest against their arrest and the British repression, a public meeting was held at Jallianwala Bagh in Amritsar on April 13, 1919, where O'Dwyer arrived with armoured cars and troops and fired on an unarmed peaceful crowd without warning, killing nearly 1,000 people and scores of others.
- The massacre of Jallianwala Bagh was followed by martial law and a veritable reign of terror prevailed in the Punjab.
- To protest against the Jallianwala Bagh tragedy Rabindranath Tagore surrendered the knighthood conferred on him by the British Government and Sir Sankaran Nair, a former president of the I.N.C., resigned his membership of the Viceroy's Executive Council.

The Khilafat Movement (1920-22)

- The Jallianwala Bagh massacre took place at a time when the Indian Muslims were extremely agitated over the pan-Islamic Khilafat issue, which originated as a result of Turkey's entry into the First World War as an ally of Germany against Britain.
- The Sultan of Turkey, ruler of the vast Ottoman empire, was the Caliph (or Khalifa) of the Islamic world.
- In the First World War Turkey was defeated, the Ottoman Empire was dismembered and the Sultan of Turkey was deprived of all real authority even in the remaining dominions, as he was placed completely under the control of a High Commission appointed by the Allied powers.
- The Muslims of India regarded the treatment of Turkey as a great betrayal on the part of Britain and other Allies and early in 1920 the Indian Muslims started a vigorous agitation to bring pressure on Britain to change its policy towards Turkey.
- This Khilafat Movement grew in strength on account of the sympathy and support which the Muslims received from Mahatma Gandhi, who was elected President of the All India Khilafat Conference in November 1919.
- The Amritsar session of the INC, held in December 1919, gave a great fillip to the Khilafat agitation.

The Non-Cooperation Movement (1920-22)

- The Non-Cooperation movement, which was the first mass movement launched under the leadership of Mahatma Gandhi, was launched to press three main demands: (*i*) the Khilafat issue; (*ii*) the redressal of the Punjab wrongs and (*iii*) the attainment of ***Swaraj***.
- The programme of the movement had two main aspects: Destructive and Constructive.
- Under the first category came:
  - surrender of titles and honorary offices and resignation from nominated seats in local bodies;
  - refusal to attend official and non-official functions;
  - gradual withdrawal of children from officially controlled schools and colleges;

- boycott of British courts by lawyers and litigants;
- refusal on the part of the military, clerical and labour classes to offer themselves as recruits for service in Mesopotamia;
- boycott of elections to the Legislative Councils by candidates and voters and
- boycott of foreign goods.

➥ The constructive programme of the Non-Cooperation movement comprised:

- setting up of arbitration boards to take the place of courts;
- founding of national schools and colleges, where students leaving government schools and colleges might continue their education;
- promotion of ***Swadeshi***;
- popularisation of ***Charkha,*** and ***Khadi***;
- raising a Volunteer Corps.

➥ The AICC meeting at Vijayawada on March 31, 1921, outlined two more programmes; (*vi*) to collect one crore rupees for the Tilak Memorial Swarajya Fund; and (*vii*) to introduce 20 lakh charkhas into Indian households.

The Swarajya Party

➥ After the suspension of the Non-Cooperation movement the Congress was left without any political programme.

➥ Some congress leaders, such as C. Rajagopalachari and Dr. Rajendra Prasad, busied themselves with the constructive programme: hand-spinning on ***charkha,*** uplift of the ***Harijans,*** popularisation of temperance, etc.

➥ But a group of Congressmen, led by Motilal Nehru and Chitta Ranjan Das, wished to contest the elections in 1923 organised under the Government of India Act, 1919 and thus gain entry into the legislatures.

➥ Opinion within the Congress was thus divided between two schools of thought: the 'no-changers', who were opposed to Council entry and the 'pro-changers', who wanted to contest the elections.

➥ At the Gaya session of the Congress, held in December 1922, the 'no-changers', led by C. Rajagopalachari, defeated the 'pro-changers'.

➥ Thereupon, Chitta Ranjan Das, himself a pro-changer who had presided over the Gaya session, resigned from the Presidentship of the Congress.

➥ With Motilal Nehru and other 'pro-changers' he formed the Congress-Khilafat-Swarajaya Party, commonly known as the ***Swarajya Party***.

➥ Through successful propaganda, the new party rapidly gained in strength.

➥ The ***Swarajya Party*** set up a separate organisation with C.R. Das as its president and Motilal Nehru as secretary.

➥ The party pledged itself to a policy of "uniform, continuous and consistent obstruction with a view to make government through the (central) Assembly and (Provincial) Councils impossible."

➥ It had the active support of Congressmen like Vittalbhai Patel, Madan Mohan Malviya and M.R. Jayakar.

➥ The elections to the legislatures were held in November 1923.

➥ They won 42 out of the 101 elective seats in the Central Legislature Assembly.

- In the 1926 elections, though the Swarajya Party won 40 seats in the Central Legislature and half of the seats in Madras, in other Provinces it suffered badly.
- The *Swarajists* finally walked out of the Legislature in 1930.
- By early 1930 the Swarajist sun had set.

Simon Commission

- According to a provision of the Government of India Act, 1919, a Statutory Commission was to be appointed ten years after the passage of the Act, that is in 1929, to inquire into the working of the Act and to propose further reforms, if needed.
- But the then Conservative Government in London pre-empted its appointment by two years, for fear that a Labour Government, which was seen to be likely to come to power in the forthcoming General Election, might appoint a Statutory Commission composed of members with liberal and pro-India views.
- The Commission was composed of seven British members of Parliament, with Sir John Simon as its Chairman. It had no Indian member.
- Such composition of a Commission, intended to decide on the political future of India, was not acceptable to enlightened Indian political opinion.
- The INC, at its session held in Madras in December 1927, resolved to boycott the Commission "at every stage, everywhere and in every form".
- A complete *hartal* was observed in Bombay and other cities on February 3, 1928, the day the Simon Commission landed in Bombay.
- Wherever the Commission visited, complete *hartal* was observed and processions were taken out with the slogan, "Simon Go Back".
- The Simon Commission paid two visits to India in 1928 and 1929.
- It submitted its Report in May 1930, which was later discussed at the Round Table Conference held in London.

Nehru Report—1928

- The Nehru Committee submitted its Report on August 28, 1928, which was accepted by the All-Parties conference at Lucknow and passed with the only dissenting vote of M.A. Jinnah.
- Some important features of the Nehru Report were:
  - India must be given Dominion status, which meant independence within the British Commonwealth.
  - India would be a Federation, having a bicameral Legislature at the Centre to which the Ministry would be responsible.
  - The Governor-General would be only the constitutional head with the same powers as the British Crown.
  - There was to be no separate electorate.
  - Citizenship was also defined and fundamental rights enunciated.
- Since the British Government did not accept or spurn the Nehru Report, the Congress passed the Poorna Swarajya Resolution at its Lahore session (1929).
- With that, the Nehru Report itself became infructuous.

Fourteen Points of Jinnah

- M.A. Jinnah, the leader of the Muslim League, did not accept the Nehru Report on the ground that it discarded separate electorates for the minorities.

- The League wanted more safeguards for muslims.
- Jinnah thereafter drew up a list of demands, the so-called Fourteen Points, which represented the minimum demands of the Muslims.
- These included:
  - separate electorate for Muslims to be retained and supplemented by other concessions, such as one-third Muslim representation in the Central Cabinet and in all provincial Cabinets (although the Muslims constituted only one-fourth of the total population);
  - creation of Muslim majority provinces and
  - reservation of posts for Muslims in all services of the State, etc.
- The essence of Jinnah's Fourteen Points was to strike a profitable bargain with the Congress or to reject the Nehru Report.

The Civil Disobedience Movement

- The Congress Working Committee had authorised Mahatma Gandhi to determine the time, place and the issue on which the Civil Disobedience movement was to be launched.
- Gandhiji decided to inaugurate the movement by violating the Salt Laws on the sea-coast at Dandi.
- Mahatma Gandhi launched the Salt Satyagraha on March 12, 1930, when he marched from his Sabarmati Ashram (Ahmedabad) with some eighty hand-picked followers.
- After a 24-day long march he symbolically broke the Salt laws at Dandi on April 5, 1930.
- The breaking of the Salt Laws formally inaugurated the Civil Disobedience movement.

Programme of the Civil Disobedience Movement

Among the programmes outlined for the Civil Disobedience movement were the following:

- The violation of the Salt Law and other laws;
- Non-payment of land-revenue, rent or other taxes;
- Boycott of law courts, legislatures, elections, Government functions, Government schools and colleges;
- Boycott of foreign goods and cloth and burning of foreign cloth;
- Peaceful picketing of shops selling liquor and other intoxicants;
- Organising mass strikes and demonstrations;
- Resigning Government jobs and not joining the civil, military or police services.

Gandhi-Irwin Pact (March 5, 1931)

- During the course of the Civil Disobedience movement the Simon Commission Report had been published and to consider its recommendations the First Round Table Conference was summoned in London, in November 1930.
- The Congress boycotted the Conference, but other parties such as the Liberals, the Muslim League, the Hindu Mahasabha and the Princely States attended it.
- The absence of the Congress, however, rendered the conference pointless.
- Some of the Liberal leaders like Tej Bahadur Sapru, V.S. Sastri and M.R. Jayakar, on their return from the Conference appealed to Mahatma Gandhi to seek an interview with the Viceroy.

- To create appropriate conditions for talks between the Viceroy and the Congress leaders, other Congress leaders were released and Viceroy Lord Irwin invited the Congress for talks.
- The Congress authorised Gandhiji to negotiate a settlement with the Viceroy.
- After prolonged Gandhi-Irwin talks an agreement, known as the Gandhi-Irwin Pact, was signed between the two on March 5, 1931.

Communal Award

- The Second Round Table Conference having failed to resolve the questions of electoral representation to different religious communities and the depressed classes, authorised the British Prime Minister to resolve it.
- Accordingly, Prime Minister Ramsay Macdonald announced his 'Communal Award' on August 16, 1932.
- According to this Award the Muslim, European and Sikh voters would elect their candidates by voting in separate communal electorates.
- There was also provision for separate electorate for the Depressed Classes, officially described as Scheduled Castes, as a separate community.
- Macdonald, however, promised to accept any alternative scheme mutually agreed upon by the Hindus and the Depressed Classes.

Poona Pact

- Gandhiji's fast caused great alarm and anxiety all over the country and Pandit Madan Mohan Malaviya summoned a conference of various castes and political parties, including Dr. B.R. Ambedkar, the leader of the Depressed Classes League.
- The conference finally arrived at an agreement in Poona on September 25, 1932, the sixth day of Gandhiji's fast.
- A common electorate of all the Hindus was agreed upon, subject to two conditions.
- First, 148 seats in different Provincial Legislatures were reserved for the Depressed Classes in place of 71 as provided in the Communal Award.
- Secondly, 18 per cent of the seats in the Central Legislature were reserved for the Depressed Classes.

The Government of India Act, 1935

- The Government of India Act, 1935, was unique in many respects. It was the longest piece of legislation ever passed by the British Parliament.
- It was the last constitutional measure introduced by the British in India and it survived for the longest period.
- It provided the groundwork for the negotiations that led to the final transfer of power into Indian hands.
- Some of its main features were:
  - It provided for the establishment of a 'Federation of India' consisting of Governor's Provinces and Princely States.
  - Dyarchy was withdrawn from the Provinces and implanted at the Centre.
  - The proposed Federal Legislature was to be bicameral, with a Council of States with 250 members and a Federal Assembly of 375 members.
  - A threefold division of subjects was made—Federal, Provincial and concurrent.

- Provision was made for the establishment of a Federal Court, with original, appellate and advisory jurisdiction. Appeals from its decisions lay to the Privy Council in London.
- The most important feature of the Act was Provincial Autonomy.

August Offer

➡ On 8 August, 1940, Viceroy issued from Simla a statement that was intended to break the constitutional deadlock.

➡ The statement is famous as August Offer. It made the following three points:

- An immediate expansion of the Viceroy's Executive Council by inducting into that body a number of representative Indians.
- The establishment of a War Advisory Council comprising represent-atives of British India and the Indian States, the Council to meet at regular intervals.
- The promotion of practical steps to arrive at an agreement among Indians on the form which the post-War representative body would take, the method by which it should arrive at its conclusions and a definition of the principles and outlines of the constitution itself.

The Individual Satyagraha (1940-41)

➡ Disillusioned with the August offer, the Congress decided to launch Individual Satyagraha, which was intended to preach openly against the War.

➡ It was launched on October 17, 1940 and as soon as an individual (or a small group was arrested), another took his place.

➡ One of the first Satyagrahis was Vinobha Bhave. But the movement created little enthusiasm and Mahatma Gandhi suspended it on December 17, 1940.

➡ On January 5, 1941, the campaign was started again. During the second phase of the movement, more than 20,000 Satyagrahis were arrested.

The Indian National Army

➡ Ras Behari Bose, an Indian revolutionary who had taken political refuge in Japan in 1915, organised the *Indian Independence League* with the support of Indian living in South-east Asia.

➡ In March 1942, Ras Behari convened a Conference in Tokyo at which it was decided to form the Indian National Army (INA) or Azad Hind Fauj.

➡ The nucleus of the INA was composed of the Indian soldiers who had surrendered to the Japanese troops after the fall of Singapore.

➡ The INA was initially organised by Captain Singh, an Indian officer of the British army in Malaya who had surrendered to the Japanese.

➡ In June 1942, Ras Behari Bose convened another Conference of the Indian Independence League in Bangkok, which decided that INA would fight for India's independence.

➡ The Bangkok Conference also invited Subhas Bose to come to Japan.

➡ He reached Tokyo in June 1943. Shortly afterwards, Ras Behari Bose resigned the Chairmanship of the Indian Independence League and Subhas Bose, was named as the Supreme Commander of the INA.

The Cripps Proposals

➡ Sir Stafford Cripps spent three weeks in India (March-April 1942) and after discussions with the Indian leaders, announced his proposals in the form of a Draft Declaration, which may be summarised as under :

- The British Government's object was the creation of a new Indian Union, which would have Dominion status.
- A Constitution-making body, consisting of the elected representatives from the British Provinces and the Princely States was to be set up immediately after the war.
- The Constitution framed by this body would be accepted and implemented subject to two conditions: (*a*) any Province of British India not prepared to accept this Constitution would retain its present constitutional position. With such non-acceding Provinces, the British Government might agree upon a new Constitution, giving them the same status as the Indian Union. (*b*) Every Princely State would be free to adhere to the Constitution or decline to do so.
- During the War an Executive Council would be set up, composed of leaders of the principal sections of the Indian people. But the British Government would retain control of the defence of India as a part of their War effort. In exchange for these concessions, Britain asked for India's support in its war efforts.

The Quit India Movement (August 1942)

- The Congress Working Committee, which met at Wardha on July 14, 1942, passed a long resolution, generally called the 'Quit India' resolution.
- The All-India Congress Committee, which met in Bombay on August 7, 1942, ratified the Wardha Resolution with overwhelming majority.
- It sanctioned the non-violent mass struggle under the leadership of Gandhiji, but provided also for the contingency of his arrest.
- Mahatma Gandhi, in his speech after the passage of the Quit India resolution, said: "Every one of you should from this moment onwards consider yourself a free man or woman and act as if you are free... I am not going to be satisfied with anything short of freedom. We shall do or die. We shall either free India or die in the attempt."
- The place where the AICC met and ratified the Quit India Resolution is now known as the August Kranti Maidan.
- The AICC meeting ended at around midnight on August 8, 1942. During that very night the police arrested Mahatma Gandhi, Maulana Abul Kalam Azad and all eminent Congress leaders. Within a week almost everyone who mattered in the Congress organisation was arrested.

Wavell Plan and Simla Conference (June 25, 1945)

- On June 14, Wavell broadcast a plan, popularly known as the Wavell Plan.
- The essence of the plan was the formation of a new Executive Council at the Centre, in which all but the Viceroy and the Commander-in-Chief would be Indians.
- All portfolios except defence would also be held by the Indian members.
- The Executive Council was an interim arrangement, which was to govern the country until such time that "a new permanent constitution could be agreed upon and come to force".
- To consider these proposals and to progress towards the formation of the proposed Executive Council, a

Conference of 21 Indian political leaders was invited to the summer capital of Simla in June 1945.

- The leaders included Maulana Abul Kalam Azad, the then President of the Congress, M.A. Jinnah, the leader of the Muslim League, the leaders of the Nationalist Party, Scheduled Castes, Sikhs, etc.
- Jinnah, however, sabotaged the Simla Conference. He objected to the inclusion of any non-League Muslims in the Executive Council, with the claim that the Muslim League was the sole representative of Indian Muslims; the Congress therefore had no right to nominate Muslim members to the Executive Council.
- Abul Kalam Azad, who represented the Congress at the Simla Conference, is of the view that the failure of Simla Conference marked a watershed in India's political history.

General Elections in India (December 1945)

- The Second World War came to an end with the surrender of Japan on August 15, 1945.
- A month before, in the general elections held in Britain, the Conservative Party of Winston Churchill was defeated and the Labour Party headed by Clement Attlee came to power with a resounding victory.
- Sir Pethick Lawrence was appointed the new Secretary of State for India in the new Labour Government.
- The first step taken by the Attlee Government was to hold general elections in India, which had been held last in 1945.
- In the election results announced in December 1945, the Congress made its presence felt in the Central Legislative Assembly as also the Provincial Legislatures.
- In the Central Assembly, the Congress secured 91.3 per cent votes in the General Constituencies; the Muslim League won every Muslim seat.
- In the Provincial Legislature, the Congress won absolute majority in Bombay, Madras, United Provinces, Bihar, Orissa and Central Provinces. In the NWFP the Congress won 30 seats (including 19 Muslim) while the Muslim League got only 17.
- In the Punjab a Coalition Government of the Congress, Akalis and the Unionists was formed. The Muslim League could secure majority only in Bengal and Sind.

Ratings Mutiny (February 1946)

- On February 18, 1946, a section of Indians serving in the Royal Indian Navy, known as ratings (non-commissioned officers and sailors) mutinied in Bombay.
- They went on a hunger strike in protest against untold hardships regarding pay and food and the most outrageous racial discrimination, in particular derogatory references to their national character.

The Cabinet Mission

- The Cabinet Mission, composed of three British Cabinet Ministers—Sir Pethick Lawrence, the Secretary of State for India, Sir Stafford Cripps, President of the Board of Trade and A.V. Alexander, First Lord of the Admiralty—arrived in New Delhi on March 24, 1946.

- The Cabinet Mission announced its own recommendations on May 16, 1946. Its main recommendations were as under :
  - The unity of India had to be retained.
  - The demand for Pakistan, as demanded by the Muslim League, was rejected on the ground that it would not solve the communal minority problem. In addition, partition would create many serious problems in defence, communications and other areas.
  - There was to be a Union of India, consisting of the British Provinces and the Princely States. The Union Government and its Legislature were to have limited powers, dealing with only defence, foreign affairs and communications. The Union would have the powers necessary to raise the finances to manage these subjects.
  - All subjects other than the Union subjects and all residuary powers would vest in the Provinces.
  - The Princely States would retain all subjects and all residuary powers other than those ceded to the Union.
  - The Provinces were grouped into three categories—A, B and C. Group A was to consist of Madras, United Provinces, Bihar, Central Provinces and Orissa; Group B was to comprise (the Muslim-majority areas) of the Punjab, Sind, NWFP and Baluchistan; Group C was to include Bengal and Assam (where the Muslims had small majority over the rest).
- The Congress agreed to the proposals relating to the Constituent Assembly, but rejected the proposal regarding the formation of an Interim Government, because the Muslim League had been given disproportionate representation.
- The Muslim League at first accepted the Cabinet Mission plan on June 6, 1946, but on July 29 withdrew its acceptance and called upon Muslims "to resort to Direct Action to achieve Pakistan".

Direct Action Day (August 16, 1946)

- The Muslim League now took a course of action which had no parallel in the recorded history of India.
- The Direct Action Day, fixed for August 16, was an invitation to the worst communal holocaust.
- On August 16 and the days following it bands of Muslim rowdies went on rampage of in-discriminate killings, arson, rape and looting.
- This communal madness soon spread to other parts of North India, particularly East Bengal and Bihar.
- What followed Direct Action Day was a virtual civil war between the Hindus and Muslims.
- Amidst this insanity and unreason, the lone symbol of sanity, courage and dignity was the seventy-seven year old Mahatma Gandhi, who went to Noakhali to restore peace.

The Interim Government (September 2, 1946)

- The Viceroy Lord Wavell invited Jawaharlal Nehru, the leader of the largest party in India, to form an Interim Government, which was sworn in on September 2, 1946.
- It was composed of 12 members (including 3 Muslims) nominated by the Congress with Jawaharlal Nehru as its Vice-President.

- It was the first time since the coming of the British that the Government of Indian was in Indian hands.
- The Muslim League at first refused to join the Interim Government, but was persuaded to change its stand.
- On October 13 five Congress appointees resigned to make way for the League's nominees.
- It became clear, however, that the Muslim League joined the Interim Government not to work sincerely and cooperate with the Congress, but to paralyse the functioning of the new Government.
- Liaqat Ali, who was given the Finance portfolio, used his position to bring this about. The tactics of the League effectively brought the business of the Government to a virtual standstill.

The Constituent Assembly (December 9, 1946)

- In the meantime elections to the Constituent Assembly were held between July and December 1946 and the Constituent Assembly met for the first time on December 9, 1946 with Dr. Rajendra Prasad as its President.
- The Muslim League, adhering to its resolution rejecting the Cabinet Mission Plan, refused to join the Constituent Assembly and began to press its demand for Pakistan.

Attlee's Declaration (February 20, 1947)

- British Prime Minister Attlee announced on February 20, 1947, in the House of Commons, that the British would quit India after transfering power "into responsible hands not later than June 1948".
- Attlee apparently believed the announcement of the terminal date for the British withdrawal from India would bring pressure on the Indian people to settle their differences before then.
- Attlee also announced the appointment of Lord Mountbatten as Viceroy in place of Lord Wavell.

The June Third Plan

- The June third Plan laid down the following procedure:
  - The Provincial Legislative Assemblies of Bengal and the Punjab would meet in two parts separately, one representing the Muslim-majority districts and the other representing the remaining districts, to decide by vote for the partition of the provinces.
  - In case of Sind and Baluchistan a straight forward decision was to be taken by their respective Provincial Legislatures.
  - In the case of the North-West Frontier Province, the choice was to be made by the people through a referendum. A similar referendum was to be held in the Muslim-majority district of Sylhet in Assam.
  - Paramountcy in the Princely States would not be transferred to either of the successor States. In theory this meant that the Princely States would not become sovereign entities when the British left India.

The Implementation of June Third Plan

- The Congress Working Committee, which met on June 3, 1947, approved of the partition plan; the All India Congress Committee, which met in New Delhi on June 14-15, ratified the approval.

The Indian Independence Act (July 1947)

- Soon after partition was decided upon, the Indian Independence Bill was drafted, which was passed by the British Parliament in July 1947.
- Its main provisions were as follows :
  - The Act provided for setting up two independent Dominions, to be known as India and Pakistan, from August 15, 1947.
  - The Legislature of each Dominion would have full power to make laws for that Dominion. No Act of the British Parliament passed after August 15, 1947, would have validity in either Dominion. In short, the jurisdiction of the British Parliament over India would cease from that date.
  - With effect from August 15, 1947, the British Government would cease to have any responsibility for the Government of British India and all Treaties and Agreements between His Majesty's Government and the rulers of Indian (Princely) States or any authority in tribal areas would lapse.
  - The two Dominions, as also the Provinces would be governed 'as nearly as may be' in accordance with the Act of 1935 unless and until the Constituent Assembly concerned made other provision.
  - Provision was made for the division of the Armed Forces and the Civil Services between the new Dominions. Each Dominion would exercise authority over its armed forces and civil services.

The Integration of Princely States

- Under the Indian Independence Act, British paramountcy over the Princely States was to lapse on August 15, 1947.
- In theory this meant that the States would become sovereign entities when the British left India. It was to the credit of Vallabhbhai Patel and V.P. Menon who successfully brought about the integration of Princely States.
- Sardar Patel, who was both stern and statesman like, persuaded the Princes that it was in their own interest to join the Indian Union.
- After protracted negotiations a settlement was arrived at, and rulers of all States geographically contiguous to India, with the exception of Hyderabad, Junagarh and Kashmir, signed the Instrument of Accession and Stand-still Agreement with India before August 15, 1947.
- The Nawab of Junagarh wanted to accede to Pakistan, but a popular uprising against him forced him to flee to Pakistan.
- The Maharaja of Kashmir acceded to India in October 1947 when irregular Pakistani troops invaded his state.
- The Nizam of Hyderabad was forced to accede to the Indian Union under the pressure of internal anarchy and military action against him.

MULTIPLE CHOICE QUESTIONS

1. The important public place discovered at Mohenjo-daro was:
A. the great bath
B. the great granary
C. the great cemetery
D. the acropolis

2. Indus script is:
A. bonstrophedon
B. indeographic
C. cuneiform
D. logographic

3. Indus seals:
A. were purely secular in character
B. were used as means of exchange by Harappans
C. reveal their religions character
D. were exported in big numbers

4. Who among the following was the first to suggest the similarity between Sanskrit language of Aryans, Greeks and Latin?
A. Sir Williams Jones
B. Monier Williams
C. Max Muller
D. None of the above

5. Which was not the cause of Aryans Victory over the Dasas or Dasyus?
A. Use of chariots in war
B. Use of horses in war
C. Use of metal armours and helmets
D. Use of elephant in war

6. The important characteristics of the vedic religion were:
1. Goddes like 'prithvi', 'Aditi' and 'Usha'
2. Goddes are co-equal to their male-partners
3. Predominance of male dieties.
4. Worship of nature.

Codes:
A. only 3 and 4
B. only 2 and 4
C. only 1 and 4
D. only 1 and 3

7. Which of the following statement is not correct regarding Indra?
A. He was the god exclusively associated with sacrifices.
B. He was known as 'Purandara' or breaker of forts
C. He killed the evil dragon 'Virata'
D. He was the god of Thunder.

8. Which of the following region was called "Aryavarta"?
A. From Yamuna upto West Bengal
B. Punjab and Delhi Region
C. The whole of northern India
D. The region beyond Vindhya mountain

9. In India Varna law enjoyed:
A. Legal Sanction only
B. Religious Sanction only
C. Economic Sanction only
D. The Sanction of both the state and religion.

10. Which statement on asceticism is correct?
A. The Atharva Veda after refers to ascetics as Vratyas
B. By the time of the Upanishads, asceticism was widespread
C. Vratya was a priest of non-vedic fertility cult which involved ritual dancing and flagellation
D. All of the above.

11. Mahayana Buddhism originated in:
A. Andhra Pradesh, 1st Century B.C.
B. Bihar, 1st Century A.D.
C. Kashmir, 3rd Century B.C.
D. Bengal, 2nd Century A.D.

12. Where has the Rummindei Pillar been erected?

A. The birth place of the Budha
B. The place where he preached his sermon first
C. The place where the Budha died
D. The place where he attained enlightenment

13. Early Schism in Buddhism divided the Buddhist order into:

A. Sthavirvadins and Mahasanghikas
B. Mahasanghikas Sunyavadins
C. Sunyavadins and Sarvastivadins
D. Sthavirvadins and Sarvastivadins

14. The Bhabru Edict records Ashoka's faith in:

A. Tisaranam
B. Toleration
C. Dharmavijya
D. Solicitude for the Welfare of the people

15. Which one of the following statement on the social life in the Sangam era is **not** correct?

A. The widows had to cut off their hair, discard all ornaments and eat only the plainest food.
B. Civil and military offices were held by the rich peasants called velalas.
C. Caste distinction existed.
D. Tolkappiar calls the commercial community as vaisigas.

16. Which was the most important city under Chandragupta Maurya?

A. Pataliputra B. Kausambi
C. Ujjain D. Taxila

17. The administrative system of Chandragupta consisted of:

A. Autonomous king
B. Decentralisation
C. Centralised bureaucracy
D. Mantri Parishad that had the right to over rule King's decision.

18. Which one of the following was not a feature of the industrial life of the Gupta period?

A. The artisans were held in high esteem.
B. There were also royal foundries.
C. Liquor was produced throughout the country.
D. Bonded labourers were also employed in the industries.

19. Who were Sarthavaha?

A. They were caravan traders
B. They were grain merchants
C. They were money lenders
D. They were brokers.

20. Decentralisation of administrative authority in the Gupta period was caused by:

A. increased in grants of land and villages with fiscal and administrative immunities to priests and temples.
B. preponderant authority of provincial governors.
C. weak authority of general government.
D. the belief of the Guptas in provincial autonomy.

21. Rashtrakutas continual struggle with the Pratiharas and the Palas was fostered by the fact that:

A. the possession of Kannauj would enhance their prestige
B. they attached great importance to the control of Malwa and Gujarat
C. they wanted to guard the trade routes
D. they wanted to safeguard their outer flank

22. Which fact relating to the Rashtrakutas is of significance?

A. Patronage extended to Jainism
B. Acquiescence of Muslim rule in Sind and the preaching of Islam

C. Patronage of Sanskrit Scholars such as Rajashekhara
D. Earliest work on poetics in Kannada by Amoghavarsha

23. Where was ginger of the best quality produced during the period of the Sultanate?
A. Malabar B. Konkan
C. Carnatic D. Gujarat

24. What is a farman?
A. Paper document by which lands made over to the grantees.
B. Sultan's judicial pronouncement.
C. Descriptive roll
D. An important gift

25. Match the following dynasties with their founders:

(*a*)	Bijapur	1.	Qutb Shah
(*b*)	Ahmadnagar	2.	Amir Ali Bario
(*c*)	Golkunda	3.	Yusuf Adil Shah
(*d*)	Bidar	4.	Malik Ahmad
(*e*)	Berar	5.	Fateh Ullah Imad Shah

Codes:

	(*a*)	(*b*)	(*c*)	(*d*)	(*e*)
A.	3	4	1	2	5
B.	3	1	4	5	2
C.	2	5	1	3	4
D.	5	3	2	1	4

26. Who was the founder of the Bahamani kingdom?
A. Ala-ud-din Hasan
B. Gangoo
C. Ismail Mukh
D. Muhammad Shah II

27. Which among the following is not applicable to Vijaynagar period.
A. Sati was prevalent
B. Polygamy was known
C. Dowry system was prevalent
D. Child marriage was unknown

28. Pick out the wrong match
A. Mirat-i-Sikandar-Lodis
B. Burhan-i-Ma'qsir-Bahman
C. Riyaz-us-Salatin-Bengal
D. Rajatarangini-Kashmir

29. In South India the architecture of the Bahmanis was a composite mixture of several elements. Which of the following was not one of them?
A. Turkish B. Indian
C. Mongoloid D. Egyptian

30. The Ist Sultan of Delhi who initiated the policy of associating Indian Muslims with administration was
A. Balban
B. Feroz Tughlaq
C. Iltutmish
D. Alauddin Khilji

31. Ranjit Singh did
1. organise his army on western lines with the help of Europeans
2. cooperate with Zaman Shah of Afghanistan when the latter invaded Punjab in 1799
3. recruit only Sikhs as soldiers
4. establish modern foundaries to manufacture Canon

Codes:
A. 1, 2 and 3 B. 1, 2 and 4
C. 2 and 4 D. 3, 4

32. Arrange the following successors of Ranjit Singh in the chronological order
1. Sher Singh
2. Kharak Singh
3. Dalip Singh
4. Nao Nihal Singh

Codes:
A. 2, 4, 1 and 3
B. 2, 1, 4 and 3
C. 1, 3, 2 and 4
D. 1, 4, 3 and 2

33. After the recovery of Calcutta in January 1757 by the English under Clive, Siraj-ud-Daula signed a treaty with the English conceding almost all their demands. What is the name of this treaty?

A. Treaty of Alinagar
B. Treaty of Calcutta
C. Treaty of Fulta
D. Treaty of Kasimbazar

34. All the information concerning the so-called, "Black Hole episode" is found in a single-sided account of it by an Englishman. What is the name of this Englishman?

A. William Hamilton
B. John Surman
C. Holwell
D. Stephenson

35. Murshid Quli Khan did not

1. stop paying tribute and homage to the Mughal emperor, though he was practically independent.
2. transfer parts of Jagir lands into Khalsa lands.
3. introduce the system of revenue farming in place of direct revenue collection by Govt. officials.
4. discriminate between Hindus and Muslims in providing employment opportunities?

Codes:

A. 1 and 2 B. 2 and 4
C. 1 and 3 D. 1 and 4

36. Which of the following was not alive at time of Shivaji's coronation in 1674?

A. Gaga Bhatt
B. Tukaram
C. Dadaji Kondadeo
D. Ram Das

37. Shivaji was assisted by a council of 8 ministers called the 'Astha Pradhan'. Match the following 4 ministers with their respective functions.

(*a*) Peshwa 1. General administration
(*b*) Amatya 2. Foreign affairs
(*c*) Nyayadhisha 3. Justice
(*d*) Samant 4. Finance

Codes:

	(*a*)	(*b*)	(*c*)	(*d*)
A.	1	2	3	4
B.	1	4	3	2
C.	1	3	2	4
D.	1	4	2	3

38. The annexation of some Indian states by Dalhousie was cancelled by the court of Directors. Who were they?

1. Sambalpur 2. Baghat
3. Nagpur 4. Udaipur
5. Jhansi

Codes:

A. 2, 3 and 4 B. 2, 3 and 5
C. 1 and 2 D. 2 and 4

39. What is the chronological sequence in which following places witnessed sepoy revolts?

1. Naushera 2. Delhi
3. Meerut 4. Hoti Mardan

Codes:

A. 2, 3, 1 and 4
B. 3, 2, 1 and 4
C. 4, 3, 2 and 1
D. 1, 3, 4 and 2

40. Which of the following Acts were passed by the British Government in 1856?

1. Hindu Widow Remarriage Act
2. Abolition of Sati
3. Religious Disabilities Act
4. General Service Enlistment Act

Codes:

A. 1 and 2 B. 2 and 4
C. 1, 3 and 4 D. 1, 2 and 3

41. The Quit India Movement was launched in:

A. 1939 B. 1941
C. 1942 D. 1945

42. Muslim League for the first time gave a call for a separate state in:

A. 1916 B. 1929
C. 1937 D. 1940

43. Gandhiji launched his first mass movement in India in:

A. Champaran B. Wardha
C. Sabarmati D. Bardoli

44. Kuka Movement was started by:

A. the Congress
B. the Muslim League
C. the Army
D. the Sikhs

45. The Home Rule Movement was started by:

A. Mrs Annie Besant
B. Mahatma Gandhi
C. G.K. Gokhale
D. M.A. Jinnah

46. Civil Disobedience Movement was launched in:

A. 1920 B. 1928
C. 1930 D. 1932

47. Dandi March marked the beginning of:

A. Non-Cooperation Movement
B. Civil Disobedience Movement
C. Quit India Movement
D. Split in the Congress

48. In the 1937 provincial elections, the Congress party got majority in:

A. only one assembly
B. no assembly
C. all assemblies
D. most of the assemblies

49. The British government reacted to the Poona Pact by:

A. accepting the agreement
B. rejecting the agreement
C. accepting the modifications
D. none of the above

50. The main demand of the Congress resolution in Wardha in 1942 was:

A. release of all political leaders
B. universal franchise
C. unconditional withdrawal by the British
D. elections to the provincial legislatures

ANSWERS

1	2	3	4	5	6	7	8	9	10
A	D	B	A	D	A	A	B	D	D
11	**12**	**13**	**14**	**15**	**16**	**17**	**18**	**19**	**20**
A	A	A	A	D	A	C	A	A	A
21	**22**	**23**	**24**	**25**	**26**	**27**	**28**	**29**	**30**
B	B	A	A	A	A	D	A	C	B
31	**32**	**33**	**34**	**35**	**36**	**37**	**38**	**39**	**40**
B	A	A	C	D	C	B	D	B	C
41	**42**	**43**	**44**	**45**	**46**	**47**	**48**	**49**	**50**
C	D	A	D	A	C	B	D	A	C

Geography

GENERAL GEOGRAPHY

- ❑ Geography is the description of the earth.
- ❑ The term *geography* was first coined by Eratosthenese, a Greek scholar (276-194 BC.).
- ❑ The word has been derived from two roots from Greek language *geo* (earth) and *graphos* (description).

THE UNIVERSE

- ➥ Existing matter and energy are together known as Universe.

Galaxy

- ➥ A galaxy is a huge system of billions of stars, clouds of dust and gases.
- ➥ Our solar system is a part of *Milky Way* galaxy.
- ➥ There are millions of galaxies that make the Universe.

Solar System

- ➥ The Sun, eight planets, satellites and some other celestial bodies known as asteroids and meteoroids form the solar system.
- ➥ Mercury, Venus, Mars, Jupiter and Saturn can be seen from Earth with the naked eyes.
- ➥ Uranus and Neptune were discovered after the invention of telescope.

Sun

- ➥ The Sun is in the centre of the solar system.
- ➥ The Sun is a mixture of gases. It consists of 92% hydrogen, 7.8% helium and 0.2% other gases.
- ➥ It provides the pulling force that binds the solar system.
- ➥ The Sun is about 150 million km away from the earth.
- ➥ The Sun shines as a consequence of the fusion of hydrogen into helium, which is constantly taking place in its core.
- ➥ A persistent stream of protons and electrons is blowing out of the corona and sweeping over the whole solar system. This stream is called Solar Wind.

- The sun is an ultimate source of energy for life on Earth.
- The energy of sun comes from the fusion of hydrogen into helium.
- Sunlight takes 8 min, 16.6 sec to reach earth.
- Ecliptic is an imaginary annual path of Sun across the sky.

Planets

- There are eight planets in our solar system. In order of their distance from the sun, they are: Mercury, Venus, Earth, Mars, Jupiter, Saturn, Uranus, and Neptune.
- All the planets of the solar system move around the sun in fixed paths. These paths are elongated. They are called orbits.

Mercury

- Mercury is nearest to the sun. It takes only about 88 days to complete one round along its orbit.
- Maximum diurnal range of temperature.
- It has no atmosphere and no satellite.

Venus

- Venus is considered as 'Earth's-twin' because its size and shape are very much similar to that of the earth.
- Popularly known as Evening star and Morning star. It is seen in the east in the morning and in the west in the evening. It is not possible to see it all over the night.
- Brightest object after sun and moon (because of 70% albedo, the reflecting power).
- *Closest* planet to earth.
- It is the hottest planet in Solar System.
- Rotates backward (clockwise) unlike others.
- It has no satellite.

Mars

- Also called Red Planet.
- It has a thin atmosphere comprising of nitrogen and argon.
- It is marked with dormant volcanoes and deep chasms where once water flowed. Recent explorations have thrown light on the possibilities of existence of life here.
- The highest mountain here is named 'Nix Olympia', which is three times higher than Mount Everest.
- It has 2 satellites—Phobos and Deimos.

Jupiter

- Largest of all planets. Called Lord of the Heavens.
- It gives off more energy than it receives from the sun, because of the heat inside.
- Its atmosphere contains hydrogen, helium, methane and ammonia.
- A great red spot is detected on it. It represents a huge storm—a super hurricane, existing for hundreds of years, without abating. This storm is probably powered by Jupiter's internal heat.
- It has the fastest rotation time (9.8 hr) in the Solar System.
- Revolution: 12 years.
- Its prominent satellites are Europa, Gannymede and Callisto. Gannymede is the largest satellite of Solar System.

Saturn

- Second in size after Jupiter.
- Least density of all (30 times less dense than earth).
- Unique feature is its system of rings (3 well defined). These are separate particles that move independently in circular orbits.
- Its prominent satellite is Titan.

Uranus

- Identified as a planet in 1781 by *William Hershel.*
- Seems to rotate from north to south as it is inclined at an angle of 98° to its orbit.
- Surrounded by a system of 9 faint rings.
- Its prominent satellites are Miranda, Ariel, etc.

Neptune

- Appears as 'Greenish Star'.
- Has 5 faint rings.
- Discovered by *J.G. Galle* of Berlin in 1846.
- Its prominent satellites are Triton and Nereid.

Pluto

- Pluto is now the second largest known dwarf planet in the Solar System.
- Since its discovery by Clyde Tombaugh in 1930, Pluto was considered the ninth planet from the Sun. In August, 2006, the International Astronomical Union (IAU) Redefined the term 'planet', and classified Pluto, Ceres and Eris as dwarf planets.
- Now, Pluto has been given the number 134340.

Planets : In Figures

Planet	Distance from Sun (in million km)	Diametre (in km)	Rotation Period	Revolution Period
Mercury	5.79	4878	58.65 days	88 days
Venus	10.82	12102	257 days	225 days
Earth	14.96	12755	23 hrs, 56 min, 4.091 sec	365 days, 5 hrs, 48 min, 45.51 sec
Mars	22.79	6787	Almost 24 hrs	687 days
Jupiter	77.83	142800	9.8 hrs	12 years
Saturn	142.70	120500	10.3 hrs	29 years
Uranus	287.96	51400	10.8 days	84 years
Neptune	497.06	48600	15.7 days	165 years

Asteroids

- Apart from the stars, planets and satellites, there are numerous tiny bodies which also move around the sun. These bodies are called asteroids.
- They are found between the orbits of Mars and Jupiter.
- The largest asteroid is the **Ceres**.

Meteoroids

- The small pieces of rocks which move around the sun are called meteoroids. Sometimes these meteoroids come near the earth and tend to drop upon it. During this process due to friction with the air they get heated up and burn. It causes a flash of light.

- Sometimes, a meteor without being completely burnt, falls on the earth and creates a hollow.

Comets

- It has a head and a tail. Its tail originates only when it gets closer to the sun. The tail can be 20-30 million km long. It always point away from the sun because of the force exerted by solar wind and radiation on the cometory material.
- Hailey's comet: Reappears after 76 years. Last seen in 1986.
- Comet Smith-Tuttle: Can collide with earth on Aug. 17, 2116. Will create an impact of about 1.6 million times that of Hiroshima bomb.
- Comet Shoemaker Levy-9: Collided with Jupiter between July 16 and 21, 1994.

The Earth

- The earth is the third nearest planet to the Sun.
- The Earth is 23½° tilted on its axis and thus makes 26½° angles.
- From the outer space, the earth appears blue because its two-thirds surface is covered by water. It is, therefore, called a blue planet.
- It is the densest of all planets.
- Circumference: 40,232 km. Area: 510 million sq. km. Average distance from sun: 149 million-km.
- *Perihelion*: Nearest position of earth to sun. The earth reaches its perihelion on January 3 every year at a distance of about 147 million-km.
- *Aphelion*: Farthest position of earth from sun. The earth reaches its aphelion on July 4, when the earth is at a distance of 152 million km.
- The shape of the earth is oblate spheroid or oblate ellipsoid (*i.e.*, almost spherical, flattened a little at the poles with a slight bulge at the centre).

Earth : Rotation & Revolution System

Rotation

- Rotation is the movement of the earth on its axis. Due to this rotation, day and night occur.
- The earth takes about 23 hours 56 minutes and 4 seconds to complete one rotation around its axis.
- The period of rotation is known as the earthday. This is the daily motion of the earth.

Revolution

- The Earth also on its inclined axis revolves around the Sun and thus produce seasons.
- The movement of the earth around the sun in a fixed path or orbit is called Revolution.
- Earth takes 365¼ days (one year) to revolve around the sun.

The Moon

- Earth has only one satellite, that is, the moon.
- Its diameter is only one-quarter that of the earth. It is about 3,84,400 km away from us.
- The moon moves around the earth in about 27 days. It takes exactly the same time to complete one spin. As a result, only one side of the moon (only 59% of its surface) is visible to us on the earth.
- Moonlight takes 1.3 sec. to reach earth.

Equinoxes

- These are dates when days and nights are equal. During these days the sun shines directly over the equator.
- March 21: Vernal Equinox
- Sept. 23: Autumnal Equinox

Solstice

- The time of the year when the difference between the length of days and the length of nights is the largest.
- During these days the sun shines directly over the tropics.
- June 21: Summer Solstice
- Dec 22: Winter Solstice

Midnight Sun

- It is a phenomenon, observable in the latitudes 66½° North and South (or the Arctic and Antarctic Circles) where the sun does not sink below the horizon during summer. This results due to the tilt of the earth's axis, each hemisphere being inclined towards the sun during its summer.
- North Pole experiences day from 21st March to 23rd September.
- South Pole experiences day from 23rd September to 21st March.

Latitude

- Imaginary lines drawn parallel to the equator. Measured as an angle whose apex is at the centre of the earth.
- The equator represents 0° latitude, while the North Pole is 90°N and the South Pole 90°S.
- 23½°N represents Tropic of Cancer while 23½°S represents Tropic of Capricorn.
- 66½°N represents Arctic Circle while 66½°S represents Antarctic Circle.
- There are total 181 latitudes including the equator. Each parallel of latitude is a circle, but they are not equal. The circle becomes smaller towards the poles. Equator is the 'Greatest Circle' that can be drawn on the earth's surface.

Longitude

- It is the angular distance measured from the centre of the earth. On the globe the lines of longitude are drawn as a series of semicircles that extend from the North Pole to the South Pole through the equator. They are also called meridians.
- The distance between any two meridians is not equal. At the equator, 1 degree = 111 km. At 30°N or S, it is 96.5 km. It goes on decreasing this way until it is zero at the poles.
- There are 360 meridians of longitude. The prime meridian is a longitude of 0°, passing through the Royal Observatory at Greenwich near London.
- Each meridian of longitude is a semi-circle. 180° meridian (International Date Line) lies exactly opposite to 0° meridian. Such points are called ANTIPODAL POINTS.
- The earth is divided into 24 longitudinal zones, each being 15° or 1 hour apart in time (4 minutes/degree).

Longitude and Time

- Places that are on the same meridian have the same local (sun) time. Since the earth makes one complete revolution of 360° in 24 hours, it passes through 15° in one hour or 1° in 4 minutes.
- The earth rotates from west to east, hence places east of Greenwich see

the sun earlier and gain time where places west of Greenwich see the sun later and lose time.

➥ India, whose longitudinal extent is approx. 30°, has adopted only one time zone, selecting the 82.5°E for the standard time which is 5 hours and 30 minutes ahead of GMT (Greenwich Mean Time).

International Date Line

➥ It is the 180° meridian running over the Pacific Ocean, deviating at Aleutian Islands, Fiji, Samoa and Gilbert Islands.

➥ Travellers crossing the Date Line from west to east repeat a day and travellers crossing it from east to west lose a day.

ECLIPSES

➥ Sun is the only source of light for both the Earth and Moon. Eclipses occur when the light thus received is either blocked by the earth or by the Moon.

➥ Eclipses occur when either the Earth moves behind the Moon's shadow or the Moon moves behind the Earth's shadow.

Lunar Eclipse

➥ Lunar eclipses occur only when the following conditions are met.
- The Sun, Earth and Moon must be aligned in a straight line.
- The Earth must be positioned between the Sun and the Moon.
- The Moon must be in its full phase (Full Moon).

Solar Eclipse

➥ Solar eclipses occur only when the following conditions are met.
- The Sun, Earth and Moon must be aligned in a straight line.
- The Moon must be positioned between the Sun and the Earth.
- Must be a New Moon day.

➥ A total solar eclipse thus lasts for less than eight minutes at any one place on Earth. The earth is in total darkness for those eight minutes.

THE STRUCTURE OF THE EARTH

The Crust

➥ It is the outermost solid part of the earth. It is brittle in nature.

➥ The thickness of the crust varies under the oceanic and continental areas.

➥ Oceanic crust is thinner as compared to the continental crust.

➥ The mean thickness of oceanic crust is 5 km whereas that of the continental is around 30 km.

➥ It is made up of heavier rocks having density of 3 g/cm^3.

The Mantle

➥ The portion of the interior beyond the crust is called the mantle.

➥ The mantle extends from Moho's discontinuity to a depth of 2,900 km.

➥ The upper portion of the mantle is called asthenosphere.

➥ It is the main source of magma that finds its way to the surface during volcanic eruptions.

➥ It has a density higher than the crust's (3.4 g/cm^3).

➥ The crust and the uppermost part of the mantle are called lithosphere. Its thickness ranges from 10-200 km.

- The lower mantle extends beyond the asthenosphere. It is in solid state.

The Core

- The core-mantle boundary is located at the depth of 2,900 km.
- The outer core is in liquid state while the inner core is in solid state.
- The density of material at the mantle core boundary is around 5 g/cm^3 and at the centre of the earth at 6,300 km.
- The core is made up of very heavy material mostly constituted by nickel and iron.
- It is sometimes referred to as the nife layer.

ROCKS

- The earth's crust is composed of rocks.
- A rock is an aggregate of one or more minerals.
- Rock may be hard or soft and in varied colours. For example, granite is hard, soapstone is soft. Gabbro is black and quartzite can be milky white.
- Rocks do not have definite composition of mineral constituents.
- Feldspar and quartz are the most common minerals found in rocks.
- Petrology is science of rocks.
- There are different kinds of rocks which are grouped under three families on the basis of their mode of formation.
- They are:
  - Igneous Rocks — solidified from magma and lava.
  - Sedimentary Rocks — the result of deposition of fragments of rocks by exogenous processes.
  - Metamorphic Rocks — formed out of existing rocks undergoing recrystallisation.

Igneous Rocks

- As igneous rocks form out of magma and lava from the interior of the earth, they are known as primary rocks.
- The igneous rocks (Ignis – in Latin means 'Fire') are formed when magma cools and solidifies.
- When magma in its upward movement cools and turns into solid form it is called igneous rock.
- The process of cooling and solidification can happen in the earth's crustor on the surface of the earth.
- Granite, gabbro, pegmatite, basalt, volcanic breccia and tuff are some of the examples of igneous rocks.

Sedimentary Rocks

- The word 'sedimentary' is derived from the Latin word sedimentum, which means settling.
- Rocks (igneous, sedimentary and metamorphic) of the earth's surface are exposed to denudational agents, and are broken up into various sizes of fragments. Such fragments are transported by different exogenous agencies and deposited.
- These deposits through compaction turn into rocks. This process is called lithification.
- In many sedimentary rocks, the layers of deposits retain their characteristics even after lithification.
- Depending upon the mode of formation, sedimentary rocks are classified into three major groups:

- **Mechanically formed:** sandstone, conglomerate, limestone, shale, loess etc. are examples.
- **Organically formed:** geyserite, chalk, limestone, coal etc. are some examples.
- **Chemically formed:** chert, limestone, halite, potash etc. are some examples.

Metamorphic Rocks

- The word metamorphic means 'change of form'.
- These rocks form under the action of pressure, volume and temperature (PVT) changes.
- Metamorphism occurs when rocks are forced down to lower levels by tectonic processes or when molten magma rising through the crust comes in contact with the crustal rocks or the underlying rocks are subjected to great amounts of pressure by overlying rocks.
- Metamorphism is a process by which already consolidated rocks undergo recrystallisation and reorganisation of materials within original rocks.
- In the process of metamorphism in some rocks grains or minerals get arranged in layers or lines. Such an arrangement of minerals or grains in metamorphic rocks is called foliation or lineation.
- Sometimes minerals or materials of different groups are arranged into alternating thin to thick layers appearing in light and dark shades. Such a structure in metamorphic rocks is called banding and rocks displaying banding are called banded rocks.
- Metamorphic rocks are classified into two major groups — foliated rocks and non-foliated rocks.
- Gneissoid, granite, syenite, slate, schist, marble, quartzite etc. are some examples of metamorphic rocks.

ATMOSPHERE

- Atmosphere is a mixture of different gases and it envelopes the earth all round. It contains life-giving gases like oxygen for humans and animals and carbon dioxide for plants.
- The atmosphere provides a natural "warming effect", maintaining the temperatures and climates in which life forms on the Earth have evolved to survive.
- The air is an integral part of the earth's mass and 99 per cent of the total mass is confined to the height of 32 km from the earth's surface.

Composition of the Atmosphere

- The atmosphere is composed of gases, water vapour and dust particles.
- The proportion of gases changes in the higher layers of the atmosphere in such a way that oxygen will be almost in negligible quantity at the height of 120 km.

Permanent Gases of the Atmosphere

Constituent	Formula	Percentage by Volume
Nitrogen	N_2	78.08
Oxygen	O_2	20.95
Argon	Ar	0.93
Carbon dioxide	CO_2	0.036
Neon	Ne	0.002
Helium	He	0.0005
Krypton	Kr	0.001
Xenon	Xe	0.00009
Hydrogen	H_2	0.00005

- Carbon dioxide is meteorologically a very important gas as it is transparent to the incoming solar radiation but opaque to the outgoing terrestrial radiation. It absorbs a part of terrestrial radiation and reflects back some part of it towards the earth's surface. It is largely responsible for the *green house effect*.
- Ozone is another important component of the atmosphere found between 10 and 50 km above the earth's surface and acts as a filter and absorbs the *ultra-violet rays* radiating from the sun and prevents them from reaching the surface of the earth.

Layers of the Atmosphere

- The atmosphere consists of different layers with varying density and temperature.
- Density is highest near the surface of the earth and decreases with increasing altitude.
- The column of atmosphere is divided into five different layers depending upon the temperature condition. They are: troposphere, stratosphere, mesosphere, ionosphere and exosphere.

Troposphere

- The troposphere is the lowermost layer of the atmosphere.
- Its average height is 13 km and extends roughly to a height of 8 km near the poles and about 18 km at the equator.
- All changes in climate and weather take place in this layer. Weather phenomena such as clouds, lightning, thunder, storms and rain take place in this layer.
- The zone separating the tropsophere from stratosphere is known as the tropopause.

Stratosphere

- The stratosphere is found above the tropopause and extends up to a height of 50 km.
- One important feature of the stratosphere is that it contains the ozone layer.
- This layer absorbs ultra-violet radiation and shields life on the earth from intense, harmful form of energy.
- In contrast to the troposphere, water vapour is not found in this layer. Therefore, weather changes do not take place in this layer. Moreover, the wind blows horizontally and therefore the conditions are conducive for aeroplanes to fly with great speed and a long distance.

Mesosphere

- The mesosphere lies above the stratosphere, which extends up to a height of 80 km.
- The upper limit of mesosphere is known as the mesopause.
- This layer protects the Earth from the falling meteors, otherwise these meteors will damage the surface of the Earth.

Ionosphere

- The ionosphere is located between 80 and 400 km above the mesopause.
- It contains electrically charged particles known as ions, and hence, it is known as ionosphere.
- Radio waves transmitted from the earth are reflected back to the earth by this layer.
- Temperature here starts increasing with height.

Exosphere

- The uppermost layer of the atmosphere above the ionosphere is known as the exosphere.
- This is the highest layer but very little is known about it.

Ozone-Depleting Substances

- A family of compounds known as chlorofluorocarbons (CFCs) have the most significant effect on the ozone layer.
- CFCs contain different proportions of three elements: carbon (C), fluorine (F) and chlorine (Cl).
- CFCs were produced and used extensively as refrigerants starting in the early 1930's after a scientist named Medgley discovered this gas.

Atmospheric Pressure

Pressure and Winds

- The atmosphere is made up of various gases, water vapours and dust particles. All of these components carry a specific weight, which exerts pressure on the earth's surface. This pressure is popularly known as the atmospheric pressure.
- Air has weight and therefore it exerts air pressure or atmospheric pressure. Pressure is felt maximum at the surface and it decreases with height.

RELATION BETWEEN PRESSURE AND WIND

Ferrel's Law : In the northern hemisphere, wind deflects towards right and in the southern hemisphere it is vice-versa. This means that in the northern hemisphere, the wind deflects clockwise and in the southern anti-clockwise. This is called deflection of wind and because of high and low pressure the wind tends to be deflected instead of being straightened.

- It is about 2.7 kg per sq. cm *i.e.* 1013.2 millibar, water vapour decreases the pressure, the movement of the earth also affects pressure.
- The atmospheric pressure is measured by an instrument, called the barometer.
- It is shown on the map by Isobars. Isobars are the lines that join the places having equal atmosphere pressure.
- Atmospheric pressure is inversely proportionate to temperature, *i.e.*
  high temperature ⇒ low pressure
  low temperature ⇒ high pressure
- Like temperature, the atmospheric pressure decreases with height. It decreases at an average rate of about 34 mb per 300 mts of height.
- These variations in pressure (high and low) cause a horizontal movement of air called winds.

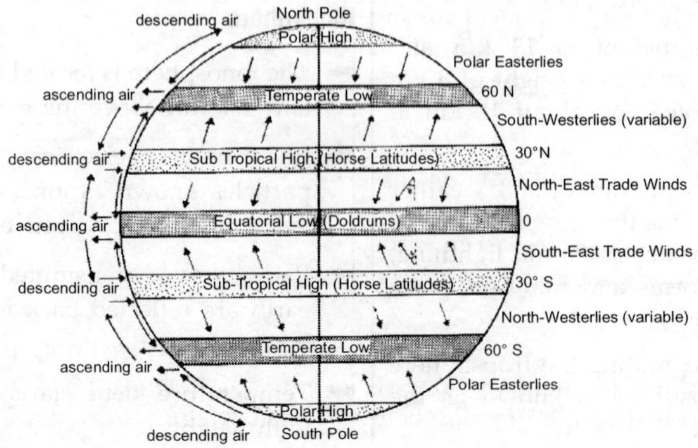

Doldrum

- A belt of low pressure, popularly known as equatorial trough of low pressure, extends along the equator within a zone of 5 degree N and 5 degree S latitudes. This is the belt of calm or doldrums because of light and variable winds.
- This belt is subjected to seasonal and spatial variations due to northward and southward movement of the overhead sun (summer and winter solstices).

Horse Latitude

- The dynamically induced subtropical high pressure belt extends between 30°-35° latitudes in both the hemispheres.
- This belt separates two wind systems, viz. trade winds and westerlies.
- This zone 30°-35° is characterized by weak and variable winds and calm.
- It is known as horse latitude because of the fact that in ancient times horse be sailed through the calm conditions of these latitudes.

Trade Winds

- They blow with great force and in constant direction.
- Therefore, helpful to traders to sail. Trade winds bring heavy rainfall.
- They sometimes contain intense depressions.
- They blow from north-east towards the equator, in the northern hemisphere and from south-east towards the equator, in the southern hemisphere.

Polar Belt

- Temperature is permanently low, so this region is the high pressure belt.
- In the northern hemisphere, they blow north east and in southern hemisphere, south east.
- The polar easterlies blows towards the temperate low pressure belt. They are extremely cold as they come from Tundra and Icecap region. They are more regular in the south than the north.

Westerlies

- From the Subtropical High Pressure Belts, winds blow towards the Low Pressure Belts.
- Under the effect of Coriolis Force, they become the South-Westerlies in the northern hemisphere and North-Westerlies in the southern hemisphere.
- This warming effect and other local pressure differences have resulted in a very variable climate in the temperature zones, dominated by the movement of cyclones and anticyclones.

Easterlies

- It is extremely cold winds as it comes from Tundra and Ice-Cap regions. It is more regular in the south than in the north.
- It blows from the Polar Easterlies towards the Temperate Low Pressure Belts.
- It is deflected to the right to become the N.E. Polar Winds in the Northern Hemisphere and to the left to become the S.E. Polar Winds in the Southern Hemisphere.
- These polar cold winds converge with warm westerlies near 60-65° latitudes and form polar front or mid-latitude front which becomes the centre for the origin of temperate cyclones.

Monsoon Winds

- Derived from the Arabic word 'mausim', meaning season, 'monsoon' is applied to winds whose direction is reversed completely from one season to the next.
- Land masses of Asia and North America powerfully control the temperature and pressure conditions in the northern hemisphere.
- As pressure conditions control winds, these areas also develop wind systems, quite independent of the belted wind system in the southern hemisphere.

Summer Monsoon

- During summer, a 'thermal' or 'heat' low is developed over southern Asia in the lower levels of the atmosphere. It is a cyclone with a considerable air flow.
- From the Indian Ocean and the south-western Pacific warm, humid air moves northward and northwestward into Asia passing over India, Indo-China and China.
- This air flow accompanied by heavy rainfall constitutes the summer monsoon in southeast Asia.

Winter Monsoon

- Reverse air flow from that of summer takes place in winter in Asia. The land area is dominated by a strong centre of high pressure from which there is an outward flow of air.
- Blowing southward and south-eastward towards the equatorial oceans, the winter monsoon brings dry, clear weather for several months.
- In North America, there is an alternation of temperature and pressure conditions between winter and summer, but the differences are not as remarkable as in southeast Asia.
- Australia also shows a monsoon effect but it reverses the conditions of Asia, being in the southern hemisphere.

Jet Stream

- The term was introduced in 1947 by Swedish-born US meteorologist Carl-Gustaf Rossby, and it is used to describe a very strong steady westerly wind blowing at high altitudes (6,000 to about 1400 metres above the earth's surface) just below the tropopause.
- It is usually confined to a narrow band and its speed reaches up to 350-450 kmph. The highest streams occur during winter.
- There are two main jet streams: (*a*) polar front jet stream, irregular in its location and commonly discontinuous; (*b*) subtropical jet stream (between 20° and 30° latitudes, north and south)—it is fairly consistent for a given season.
- In the northern hemisphere, the strongest jets flow across Japan and the United States.
- The jets have an important role in the weather changes.

Local Winds

- These winds affect only a limited area and blow for short periods of time, and are generated by immediate influences of the surrounding area.
- Most local winds are developed by depression: these are of considerable environmental importance as they may affect the plants and animals when dry and extremely hot or cold.

Table of Local Wind

Name	Place	Name	Place
Chinook	Andes and Rockies	Friagem/Surazo	Brazil
Yamo	Japan	Mistral	Rhone valley of France
Tramontane	Central Europe (North-easterly from the Alps and the Mediterranean)	Bora	Adriatic coast
Samun	Iran	Karaburan	Tarim basin, Central Asia
Norwester	New Zealand	Haboob	Sudan
Berg	South Africa	Harmattan	Central Africa
Santa Ana	California	Zonda	Argentina
Sirocco	North Africa to Southern Europe	Leveche	Spain
Khamsin	North Africa to Eastern Mediterranean	Gibli	Libia
Brickfielders	Victoria Province of Australia	Pampero	South America
Tropical Cyclone	**Nomenclature**	**Tropical Cyclone**	**Nomenclature**
Hurricane	Caribbean sea	Typhoons	South China sea
Willy-Wilies	Australia	Baguio	Philippines
Taifu	Japan	Cyclone	Indian Ocean

Land and Sea Breeze

- During the day the land gets warmer than the sea producing low pressure over the land into which cooler air moves from over the sea. Thus the local wind that blows from sea to land during the day is called sea breeze.
- It reaches the maximum strength during the mid-afternoon when temperature difference between the land and the sea is greater, and dies out by the evening as the sun's heat diminishes.
- It is best developed in tropics when conditions are calm and the sky is clear, but can also be observed in temperate areas under similar conditions.
- During the night the land cools more quickly than the sea and a reverse process sets in. Land breeze is a cool wind that blows from the land to the sea (or a large lake, etc.) during the night.
- It occurs when night time radiation cools the land and the air in contact with the ground surface.
- The atmospheric pressure over the land is raised relative to that over the sea resulting in a difference of pressure and the flow of air towards the sea from land.
- Land breeze is most common in tropical areas but may also occur in high latitudes particularly when the weather is calm.
- Land breeze is not as strong as sea breeze.

Mountain and Valley Winds

- These are local winds responding to local pressure gradients set up by heating or cooling of the lower air.

➥ During the day when the slopes are intensely heated by the sun, the air in contact with the slopes is also heated by conduction from the ground. This warmed-up air rises and is replaced by the air moving up from the valley, thus creating an upslope wind during the day.

➥ It is particularly well developed when one side of the valley is heated much more than the other, for example, the valleys which have an east-west trend in mid and high latitudes.

➥ When the same slopes have been cooled at night by radiation of heat from ground to air, the wind moves valleywards.

➥ The wind is at its strongest just before sunrise when radiational cooling is greatest. Valley winds are a kind of anabatic winds.

Anabatic Winds

- This wind is caused by thermal (heat) processes. Anabatic winds occur over slopes which are heated by the sun.
- Air which is in contact with slopes that are warmed expands upward and cool and sinks over neighbouring valleys.

Katabatic Winds

- Katabatic winds occur over slopes which are cooled. Katabatic winds occur where air in contact with sloping ground is colder than air at the same level away from the hillside over the valley.
- Katabatic winds may lead to the formation of frost, mist and fog in valleys.

HYDROSPHERE

Divisions of the Ocean Floors

➥ The ocean floors can be divided into four major divisions:

- the Continental Shelf;
- the Continental Slope;
- the Deep Sea Plain;
- the Oceanic Deeps.

➥ Besides, these divisions there are also major and minor relief features in the ocean floors like ridges, hills, seamounts, guyots, trenches, canyons, etc.

Continental Shelf

➥ The continental shelf is the extended margin of each continent occupied by relatively shallow seas and gulfs. It is the shallowest part of the ocean showing an average gradient of 1° or even less. The shelf typically ends at a very steep slope, called the shelf break.

➥ The width of the continental shelves vary from one ocean to another. The average width of continental shelves is about 80 km.

➥ The shelves are almost absent or very narrow along some of the margins like the coasts of Chile, the west coast of Sumatra, etc.

➥ On the contrary, the Siberian shelf in the Arctic Ocean, the largest in the world, stretches to 1,500 km in width.

➥ The depth of the shelves also varies. It may be as shallow as 30 m in some areas while in some areas it is as deep as 600 m.

➥ The continental shelves are covered with variable thicknesses of sediments brought down by rivers, glaciers, wind, from the land and distributed by waves and currents. Massive sedimentary deposits received over a long time by the continental shelves, become the source of fossil fuels.

Continental Slope

➥ The continental slope connects the continental shelf and the ocean basins.

- It begins where the bottom of the continental shelf sharply drops off into a steep slope.
- The gradient of the slope region varies between 2-5°.
- The depth of the slope region varies between 200 and 3,000 m.
- The slope boundary indicates the end of the continents. Canyons and trenches are observed in this region.

Deep Sea Plain

- Deep sea plains are gently sloping areas of the ocean basins.
- These are the flattest and smoothest regions of the world. The depths vary between 3,000 and 6,000m.
- These plains are covered with fine-grained sediments like clay and silt.

Oceanic Deeps or Trenches

- These areas are the deepest parts of the oceans. The trenches are relatively steep sided, narrow basins. They are some 3-5 km deeper than the surrounding ocean floor.
- They occur at the bases of continental slopes and along island arcs and are associated with active volcanoes and strong earth-quakes.
- As many as 57 deeps have been explored so far; of which 32 are in the Pacific Ocean; 19 in the Atlantic Ocean and 6 in the Indian Ocean.

Tides

- The periodical rise and fall of the sea level, once or twice a day, mainly due to the attraction of the sun and the moon, is called a *tide*.
- The moon's gravitational pull to a great extent and to a lesser extent the sun's gravitational pull, are the major causes for the occurrence of tides.
- Another factor is centrifugal force, which is the force that acts to counter balance the gravity.
- Together, the gravitational pull and the centrifugal force are responsible for creating the two major tidal bulges on the earth.

Types of Tides

- **Semi-diurnal tide:** The most common tidal pattern, featuring two high tides and two low tides each day. The successive high or low tides are approximately of the same height.
- **Diurnal tide:** There is only one high tide and one low tide during each day. The successive high and low tides are approximately of the same height.
- **Mixed tide:** Tides having variations in height are known as mixed tides. These tides generally occur along the west coast of North America and on many islands of the Pacific Ocean.
- Tides based on the Sun, Moon and the Earth Positions.
- The height of rising water (high tide) varies appreciably depending upon the position of sun and moon with respect to the earth. Spring tides and neap tides come under this category.
- **Spring tides:** The position of both the sun and the moon in relation to the earth has direct bearing on tide height. When the sun, the moon and the earth are in a straight line, the height of the tide will be higher. These are called spring tides and they occur twice a month, one on full moon period and another during new moon period.
- **Neap tides:** Normally, there is a seven day interval between the spring tides and neap tides. At this time the sun and moon are at right angles to each

other and the forces of the sun and moon tend to counteract one another. The Moon's attraction, though more than twice as strong as the sun's, is diminished by the counteracting force of the sun's gravitational pull.

- Once in a month, when the moon's orbit is closest to the earth (perigee), unusually high and low tides occur. During this time the tidal range is greater than normal.
- Two weeks later, when the moon is farthest from earth (apogee), the moon's gravitational force is limited and the tidal ranges are less than their average heights.
- When the earth is closest to the sun (perihelion), around 3rd January each year, tidal ranges are also much greater, with unusually high and unusually low tides.
- When the earth is farthest from the sun (aphelion), around 4th July each year, tidal ranges are much less than average.
- The time between the high tide and low tide, when the water level is falling, is called the ebb.
- The time between the low tide and high tide, when the tide is rising, is called the flow or flood.

Important Oceans

Pacific Ocean

- It is one third of the globe; has a triangular shape.
- Average depth is 4572 m (14,040 ft.).
- It has highest number of islands (more than 2,000), grouped in three categories:
  - **Continental Islands:** Aleutian islands, Chilean islands, British Columbia (islands of Canada).
  - **Island Arcs and Festoons:** Kurile islands, Japanese Archi.
  - **Scattered and Smaller Islands:** Hawaiian islands, Fiji islands, Micronesian islands (Marshal island).
- Continental Canyons are less deeper. It's course is dendritic. It's less steeper. The width is lesser.
- Important seas in the Pacific Ocean are Bearing Sea, Okhotsk Sea, Japan Sea, Coral Sea, Yellow Sea, Java Sea, China Sea, Tasman Sea, Arafura Sea.

Atlantic Ocean

- 1/6 of the geographical area (29,637,962 sq. mi) and half the area of Pacific ocean.
- It is 'S' shaped.
- It is located between North and South America in the west and between Europe and Africa in the east.
- Important Continental Shelf are found at Hudson Bay, Baltic sea, North sea, Davis Strait, Denmark Strait, British Isles, Iceland, St. Helena, West Indies, Trinidad, Falkland, S. Orkneys.
- Important Atlantic Ridges are:
  - Dolphin Rise and Challenger Rise north of Equator
  - New Foundland, Azores Rise, Sierra Leon, Para Rise, Unea Ridge.

Indian Ocean

- It is smaller than the Atlantic and Pacific Ocean;
- Formed by the blocked mountains of Gondwana land;
- Average depth is 4,000 m. (12,800 ft);
- Important seas are: Mozambique Channel, Red Sea, Persian Gulf, Andaman Sea, Arabian Sea, Bay of Bengal.
- Important islands are : Madagascar, Sri Lanka, Zanzibar Island, Comoros

Island, Mauritius, Caragos Island, Diego Garcia Island, Seychelles Island, Victoria, Mahe, Price Edward Island, St. Paul, Maldives, Lakshdweep, Andaman and Nicobar.

Ocean Currents

- The ocean currents are the most important of the movements in the oceanic water. The ocean current is the general movement of a mass of water in a fairly defined direction over great distances.
- Ocean currents can broadly be divided into two types: (*i*) warm current, and (*ii*) cool or cold currents.
- Those that flow from equatorial regions polewards have a higher surface temperature and are warm currents.
- Those that flow from polar regions equatorwards have a lower surface temperature and are cold currents.
- The origin and nature of the movement of the currents are related to four sets of factors :
  - factors related to earth's rotation (gravitational force and force of deflection).
  - factors originating outside the sea (atmospheric pressure, winds, etc.).
  - factors originating within the sea (pressure, salinity, etc.), and
  - factors modifying the ocean currents (direction and shape of the coast, seasonal variations, etc.).
- In the Northern Hemisphere, the currents move to their right and in the Southern Hemisphere to their left.
- However, as an exception, in the northern part of the Indian Ocean, the direction of currents changes in response to the reversal of the monsoon winds. Warm currents move towards the cold seas and cold currents towards the warm oceans.
- The direction of currents in the Northern and Southern Hemispheres is determined by Coriolis force or Ferrel's law.

Major Ocean Currents

Pacific Ocean

- **North Equatorial Current:** A warm current, it flows westwards in the north of the equator. This current is produced by the north-east trades.
- **South Equatorial Current:** A warm current, it flows westwards in the south of the equator. This current is produced by the south-east trades.
- **Kuro Siwo Current:** The north-east trade winds blow the north equatorial current off the coasts of the Philippines and Formosa into the East China Sea as the Kuro Siwo or Kuroshio or Japan current. It is a warm current.
- **North Pacific Current:** From the south-east coast of Japan, the current flows right across the ocean from west to east as the North Pacific current. North Pacific current is a warm current.
- **Alaska Current:** A cold current, Alaska current flows anti-clockwise along the coast of British Columbia and Alaska. This current is a branch of the North Pacific current.
- **Californian Current:** A cold current, the Californian current flows southwards along the Pacific coastline of the USA. This current is caused by the upwelling of colder water from greater depths due to the southward deflection of the North Pacific Current. The Californian current eventually joins the North Equatorial Current, thus completing the cycle.

➡ **Peru or Humboldt Current:** Reaching the south western coast of South America, the South Pacific Current turns northward as Peru current. It is a cold current.

➡ **Counter Equatorial Current:** Between the North and the South Equatorial Currents, a current flows from west to east which is known as the Counter Equatorial Current, a warm current.

➡ **Oya Siwo or Oyashio Current:** The Cold Alaskan current or Bering current creeps southwards from the narrow Bering strait and is joined by the Okhotsk current (a cold current) to meet the warm Japan current as the Oya Siwo or Oyashio (a cold current).

Atlantic Ocean

In the Atlantic Ocean, the steady trade winds in north and south of the equator drive two streams of surface water westward. They are known as North and South Equatorial Currents. They are warm currents. Other important currents of the Atlantic Ocean are as follows:

➡ **Guinea Current:** A current called the Equatorial Counter Current flows from west to east between the two main equatorial currents. It is known as the Guinea current off the West African coast.

➡ **Brazil Current:** The South Equatorial Current is split into two branches near Cape de Sao Roque (Brazil). One branch turns south as the warm Brazilian current.

➡ **Gulf Stream:** It is a warm current of sea water. It originates in the eastern Gulf of Mexico before flowing past Florida and the eastern seaboard of the USA. The warm Gulf stream combines with the prevailing south-westerly winds to produce the temperate climate of north-west Europe and keeps the Norwegian coast ice-free during the winter months.

➡ **Canary Current:** It is a cold current which flows southwards past Madeira and the Canaries off the Atlantic coast of North Africa. It is caused by the upwelling of colder water from greater depths owing to the southward deflection of the west wind drift in the North Atlantic and the transference of surface water back across the Atlantic by the North Equatorial Current.

➡ **Labrador Current:** The Labrador current (warm) flows southwards along part of the east coast of Canada and meets the warm Gulf Stream. The confluence of these two currents, one hot and the other cold, produces the famous fogs around Newfoundland.

➡ **Benguela Current:** It is a cold ocean current flowing northwards off the coast of South West Africa. It is characterised by the upwelling of relatively cold water and has an associated effect on the coastal climate of the region.

➡ **Florida Current:** It is one of the important ocean currents of the North Atlantic. It commences as a branch of the North Equatorial Current, which enters the Caribbean and then returns to the Atlantic Ocean through the Florida Straits as the Florida current.

Indian Ocean

The current circulation in the Indian Ocean is different from those of the Atlantic and the Pacific Oceans. Important Indian Ocean currents are:

➡ **South-West Monsoon Drift:** In summer, when the dominant wind is the south-west monsoon, the currents are blown from a south-westerly direction as the South-West Monsoon Drift.

- **North-East Monsoon Drift:** In winter, the dominant northeast monsoon blows the currents from the north-east as the North-East Monsoon Drift.
- **West Wind Drift:** A cold current, the West Wind Drift moves across the ocean in the higher latitudes from west to east. One of the branches of this cold current turns northwards along the west coast of Australia. This current, known as West Australian Current, flows northward to feed the South Equatorial Current.
- Regional Currents in the Indian Ocean include the Agulhas current and Mozambique current.

Principal River Systems of the World

- **Nile (Africa):** The longest river, 6650 km; White Nile originates from Lake Albert in Uganda and Blue Nile from Ethiopia; the two join together at Khartoum in Sudan to form River Nile. After flowing through Egypt (the river's longest course), it falls into the Medi-terranean Sea near Alexandria.
- **Amazon (South America):** Originates from the Andes Mountain in Peru; tributaries come from Bolivia, Ecuador and Venezuela; the river flows mainly through Brazil and falls into the Atlantic Ocean.
- **Yangtze Kiang (Asia):** Rises in north-east Tibet; and flows mainly through China, draining into the East China Sea.
- **Mississippi-Missouri (North America):** Mississippi rises in Lake Itasca in Minnesota state of USA; Missouri joins it at Saint Louis, together, they flow into the Gulf of Mexico at New Orleans.
- **Mackenzie (North America):** Rising in Great Slave Lake, it flows through Canada to Mackenzie Bay in the Arctic Ocean.

Longest Rivers of the World

Name	Country/ Continent	Length (in km)	Name	Country/ Continent	Length (in km)
Nile	Mediterranean Sea	6650	Murray-Darling	Australia	3780
Amazon	S. America	6437	Volga	Russia	3690
Mississippi-Missouri	USA	6020	Zambezi	Africa	3540
Yangtze Kiang	China	5494	Mederia	S. Ameica	3218
Ob-Irtysh	Russia	5410	Purus	S. America	3200
Zaire	Africa	4700	Yukon-Teslin	Alaska-Canada	3185
Lena	Russia	4400	Rio-Grande	USA-Mexico	3040
Hwang Ho	China	4344	Indus	Asia	2900
Mackenzie	Canada	4241	Brahmaputra (India)	Aisa	2900
Mekong	Asia	4180	Ganga	India	2510
Niger	Africa	4180	Godawari	India	1450
St. Lawrence	Canada-USA	4023	Narmada	India	1290
Parana	S. America	4000	Krishna	India	1290
Yenisey	Russia	3804			

➡ **Mekong (Asia):** Rises in Tibet, enters China through which it flows and later forms, for some distance, the borders between Thailand and Laos and falls into the South China Sea.

➡ **Niger (Africa):** Rising near Sierra Leone, it crosses Niger and flows mainly through Nigeria and enters the Atlantic Ocean at the Gulf of Guinea.

➡ **Murray-Darling (Australia):** Murray rises in the Australian Alps; Darling, its biggest tributary, joins it in the state of New South Wales. Both empty into the Indian Ocean at Encounter Bay.

➡ **Volga (Europe):** Rises in Valdai Plateau north-west of Moscow, Russia, and enters the Caspian Sea at Astrakhan.

➡ **Danube (Europe):** Rises near Baden in Germany, flows through Austria, Hungary, Czech Republic, Slovak Republic and Serbia, crosses Romania and enters the Black Sea.

Important Cities on River Banks (World)

Sr.No.	City	Country	River
1.	Adelaide	Australia	Torrens
2.	Amsterdam	Netherlands	Amsel
3.	Alexandria	Egypt	Nile
4.	Ankara	Turkiye	Kazil
5.	Bangkok	Thailand	Chao Praya
6.	Basra	Iraq	Eupharates and Tigris
7.	Baghdad	Iraq	Tigris
8.	Berlin	Germany	Spree
9.	Bonn	Germany	Rhine
10.	Budapest	Hungary	Danube
11.	Bristol	UK	Avon
12.	Buenos Aires	Argentina	Laplata
13.	Chittagong	Bangladesh	Majyani
14.	Canton	China	Si-Kiang
15.	Cairo	Egypt	Nile
16.	Chung King	China	Yang-tse-kiang
17.	Cologne	Germany	Rhine
18.	Dandzing	Germany	Vistula
19.	Dresden	Germany	Elbe
20.	Dublin	Ireland	Liffy
21.	Hamburg	Germany	Elbe
22.	Kabul	Afghanistan	Kabul
23.	Karachi	Pakistan	Indus
24.	Khortoum	Sudan	Confluence of Blue & White Nile
25.	Lahore	Pakistan	Ravi
26.	Leningrad	Russia	Neva

Sr.No.	City	Country	River
27.	Lisbon	Portugal	Tagus
28.	Liverpool	England	Messey
29.	London	England	Thames
30.	Moscow	Russia	Moskva
31.	Montreal	Canada	St. Lawrence
32.	Nanking	China	Yang-tse-kiang
33.	New Orleans	U.S.A	Mississipi
34.	New York	U.S.A	Hudson
35.	Ottawa	Canada	Ottawa
36.	Paris	France	Seine
37.	Philadelphia	U.S.A	Delaware
38.	Perth	Australia	Swan
39.	Prague	Czech Republic	Vitava
40.	Quebec	Canada	Sl. Lawrence
41.	Rome	Italy	Tiber
42.	Rotterdam	The Netherlands	New Moss
43.	Stalingrad	Russia	Volga
44.	Shanghai	China	Yang-tse-kiang
45.	Sidney	Australia	Darling
46.	Saint Louis	U.S.A	Mississippi
47.	Tokyo	Japan	Arakava
48.	Vienna	Austria	Danube
49.	Warsaw	Poland	Vistula
50.	Washington D.C.	U.S.A.	Potomac
51.	Yangoon	Myanmar	Irawaddy

AGRICULTURE

Main Crops

Rice

- Grown under humid conditions in tropical areas receiving good rainfall.
- Requires (20°C–30°C) of temperature. Rainfall (100-250 cm).
- Intensive cultivation is practised in monsoonal Asia where it is grown for subsistence purpose.
- Compared to wheat, Rice has not much commercialised in the world trade.
- China, India and Indonesia are top rice producers.

Wheat

- Originated in Asia Minor and Middle East.
- Grown mechanically on extensive farms.
- Temp. 16°C–27°C.
- Best wheat comes from Chernozem soils (Ukranian Black Earth), brown prairies and grey brown podzolic soils of the deciduous forest regions.
- The Polder Lands (reclaimed from sea) Belgium and the Netherlands

with their fertile marine clay or riverine silt gives high wheat yields.

- An open, rolling topography with adequate drainage is needed. Terraced wheat farming is unusual, except in Japan and China.
- Spring wheat is grown in colder north of the Canadian Prairies and in parts of the Continental steppes and Siberia.
- China, India and Russia are the three top producers.

Maize

- 18-27°C of temperature
- 60-115cm of rainfall
- Grown on wide range of soils.
- In mountainous areas where soils may be thin and slopes are steep, maize can survive when other cereals fails to take root. 75-90% of worlds' production is consumed for feeding animals.
- USA, China, Brazil are major producers.

Barley

- Grown in a wide range of climate, topographical and soil environment, where wheat fails to survive grown in:
  - Subarctic regions
  - Semiarid regions
  - High Altitudes
  - Light Loamy Soils
- Used as human food, animal and malting (beer and whisky)
- Europe accounts for half of the world's total production.
- Russia, Australia and France are major producers.

Rubber

- Needs 21-27°C of temperature
- 50-250 cm of rainfall, evenly distributed throughout the year.
- Deep, friable well drained soils are ideal. Acidic soils are also suitable.
- Land should be flat or gently undulating
- Rubber trees sheds its leaves annually despite its equatorial habitat. This is known as Wintering.

Cotton

- Originates in Eurasia.
- Varieties:
  - Long staple (Egypt, Sudan, Peru and USA).
  - Medium staple (Bulk of world cotton output mainly in USA and CIS).
  - Short staple (Mainly in Asia. But many regions have now shifted to medium and long staple cotton).
- Requires warm climate (25°C or more), (50-110 cm) of rainfall.
- It does badly in wet conditions.
- Medium loamy soils with good drainage.

Jute

- Grown in hot tropical condition with plently of moisture.
- Heavy rainfall and rich alluvial soil are favourable.

Tea

- Native to hill slopes of Monsoon Asia.
- One of the hardiest tropical shrubs.
- Cultivation in the tiny tea gardens of China and the large tea estates of India is basically similar.
- Requirements : Temperature 15-25°C, rainfall 100 cm (evenly distributed), well drained acidic soils.

  Types
  - Black Tea (from India and Sri Lanka) used in Europe and America.

- China Tea or Green Tea (or Sencha): Consumed in Far East.

Coffee

- ➡ Native of Southern Ethiopian highlands. Dutch introduced coffee in East Indies (highly flavoured Java Coffee)
- ➡ Mocha (from Arabian Peninsula)
- ➡ Blue Mountain coffee (Jamaica and other West Indies)

  Types

  - Arabica most important in world trade, Grown in Brazil and East Africa.
  - Robusta West African variety. It is hard and poorer in quality.
  - Liberica High yielding, moderate quality.

Cocoa

- ➡ Indigenous to tropical America
- ➡ The consumption of cocoa is greatest where the standard of living is highest
- ➡ Varieties : Cacao Carioua (Tropical America) and Cacao Forastero (West Africa)
- ➡ Unlike tea or coffee, it thrives in a tropical lowland environment. Often grown with banana.

MINERALS

- ➡ Minerals are naturally occurring substances having a definite chemical composition.
- ➡ They are grouped into classes, generally as rocks, non-metallic, mineral fuels and metals.

Important Minerals

- ➡ **Asbestos:** It is fibrous mineral produced largely in Russia, China and Brazil.
- ➡ **Bauxite:**
  - A light weight durable metal, aluminium is obtained from bauxite which is its principle ore (the raw material of any mineral).
  - Chief producers of bauxite are Australia, Gini, China, Brazil, USA and Russia.
- ➡ **Copper:**
  - Though found in pure state also, most of the copper is obtained from copper oxides and sulphides which are the chief ores of this metal.
  - Chile, Peru, China, USA, Canada and Armenia are the leading producers.
  - China has recently increased production of copper joining the club of the top ten producers.
- ➡ **Chromium:** It is a metal used for making high quality alloy steel. South Africa, Kazakhstan, Turkiye, India are its leading producers.
- ➡ **Diamonds:** It is a non-metallic precious stone. It is also the hardest substance. The leading producers are Russia, Botswana, Canada.
- ➡ **Gold:**
  - Gold occurs either in alluvial or placer deposits or as reefs or lobes underground. Due to its non-reactive character it is considered a noble metal.
  - China, Australia, Russia, USA and Canada are the leading producers.
  - Witwaters rand is the most important gold mining region of South Africa.
- ➡ **Iron Ore:**
  - Iron is the most widely used metallic substance and it forms the foundation of modern industrial civilisation. It is also one of the most widely occuring minerals.
  - Commercial ores of iron are magnetite (more than 60% iron), haematite (50% to 65% iron), limonite (less than 50% iron) and siderite.
  - The leading producers of iron ore are Australia, China, Brazil, India, and Russia.

➡ **Lead:**

- Lead sulphide or galena is the chief ore of lead. This metal occurs in association with zinc.
- Chief producers of lead are China, Australia, USA, Peru and Canada.

➡ **Manganese:**

- Manganese is used for making steel. Its main ores are pyrolusite and psilomelane.
- Leading producers of manganese are South Africa, Australia, China, Brazil and India.

➡ **Mercury:** It is a metal which normally occurs in a liquid state. Chief producers are China, Kazakhstan, Chile and Australia.

➡ **Mica:**

- It is a non-metallic mineral. It is a bad conductor of heat and electricity and finds application in electrical appliancesandahostofotherindustries.
- Brazil, China, South Africa, India and USA are the leading producers.

➡ **Nickel:**

- The chief ore of nickel is pentlaudite. Nickel finds application in a host of areas including electroplating.
- The leading producers of nickel are Indonesia, Philippines, Canada and Russia.

➡ **Platinum:**

- Like gold, platinum is also a noble metal. It is one of the rarest metals also.
- South Africa, Russia, Zimbabwe, Canada and Columbia are the chief producers.

➡ **Silver:**

- It is another precious metal. The most important ore of silver is argentite. It occurs mostly in association with lead and zinc.
- Chief producers of silver are Mexico, Peru, China, Chile and Poland.

➡ **Tin:**

- Tin is found mostly in the form of alluvial or placer deposits. Cassiterite or tinstone is its cheif ore.
- China, Indonesia, Peru, Brazil, Malaysia and Bolivia are the chief producers.

➡ **Tungsten:**

- It is a very heavy metal and has a high melting point. It is used for making alloy steel.
- China, USA, Russia, Canada and Bolivia are the leading producers.

➡ **Uranium:**

- Being a radio-active mineral, uranium is the basic raw material for atomic energy. Its chief ores are uranite and pitchblende.
- Chief producers are Kazakhstan, Canada, Australia, Russia, Niger and Namibia.

➡ **Zinc:**

- It is another metallic mineral finding application in a variety of areas. One of its chief uses is for galvanizing. Zinkblende and calamine are the main ores of zinc and it occurs in association with lead.
- The chief producers of zinc are China, Australia, Peru, Canada, and India.

INDUSTRY

Major Industries of the World

Iron and Steel Industry

➡ The iron and steel industry forms the base of all other industries and, therefore, it is called a basic industry. It is basic because it provides raw material for other industries such as machine tools used for further production.

➡ It may also be called a heavy industry because it uses large quantities of bulky raw materials and its products are also heavy.

- The industry is one of the most complex and capital-intensive industries and is concentrated in the advanced countries of North America, Europe and Asia.
- In Asia, the important centres include Nagasaki and Tokyo-Yokohama in Japan; Shanghai, Tientsin and Wuhan in China; and Jamshedpur, Kulti-Burnpur, Durgapur, Rourkela, Bhilai, Bokaro, Salem, Visakhapatnam and Bhadravati in India.
- In U.S.A, most of the production comes from the north Appalachian region (Pittsburgh), Great Lake region (Chicago-Gary, Erie, Cleveland, Lorain, Buffalo and Duluth) and the Atlantic Coast (Sparrows Point and Morisville). The industry has also moved towards the southern state of Alabama. Pittsburg area is now losing ground. It has now become the "rust bowl" of U.S.A.
- In Europe, U.K., Germany, France, Belgium, Luxembourgh, the Netherlands and Russia are the leading producers.
- The important steel centres are Birmingham and Sheffield in the U.K.; Duisburg, Dortmund, Dusseldorf and Essen in Germany; Le Creusot and St. Ettienne in France; and Moscow, St. Petersburgh, Lipetsk, Tula, in Russia and Krivoi Rog, and Donetsk in Ukraine.

Cotton Textile Industry

- Cotton textile industry has three sub-sectors i.e. handloom, powerloom and mill sectors.
- Handloom sector is labour-intensive and provides employment to semi-skilled workers. It requires small capital investment.
- China, India, U.S.A, Pakistan, Uzbekistan, Egypt produce more than half of the world's raw cotton.
- The U.K, NW European countries and Japan also produce cotton textile made from imported yarn.
- Europe alone accounts for nearly half of the world's cotton imports.
- The industry has to face very stiff competition with synthetic fibres hence it has now shown a declining trend in many countries.

Woollen Textile Industry

- Europe accounts for nearly two-thirds of the world's woollen mill capacity and production.
- Australia is the leading producer of woollen textiles in the world. China and USA are other important producers.
- It may be noted here that some of the largest wool producing countries—Australia, New Zealand, South Africa and Argentina—hardly have a strong industrial base.
- Important centres of woollen production in the world are as follow:
  - **Russia:** Central industrial district around Moscow; Leningrad.
  - **Japan:** Osaka-Kobe region and Tokyo-Yokohama region.
  - **USA:** Lawrence and Providence in New England, Philadelphia, and the Piedmont area in the south.
  - **UK:** Bradford, Huddersfield and Leeds in the West Riding of Yorkshire region.; Tweed Valley of Scotland; Lancashire and south-west England.
  - **France:** Lille, Roubaix and Tourcoing.
  - **Germany:** Ruhr coalfields at Barmen and Elberfield; and Aachen coalfields region.

Silk Textile Industry

- China, India, Uzbekistan, Japan, USA, France, Taiwan, Germany and UK are the most important producers of silk textiles in the world.
- The East Asian region, which includes China and Japan, account for about 85 per cent of the production of raw silk.

- China is the largest producer of silk textiles as well as of raw silk. The region however, produces only about 35 per cent of natural silk fabrics. Japan and China are the major suppliers of the raw silk to various countries, including the USA, which produce silk fabrics using imported raw materials. The USA is the largest silk importer and consumer in the world.
- Important silk producing centres in the world are as follows:
  - **China:** Central and southern China and the Shandong (Shantung) peninsula.
  - **Japan:** Central and southern Honshu, especially in upland areas.
  - **USA:** New Jersey, Pennsylvania and New York.
  - **France:** Lyons and Grenoble
  - **Italy:** Milan

Jute Textile Industry

- The first jute mill was started in Dundee (Scotland) in 1838.
- Today, jute industry is spread in many countries of the world, such as India, Bangladesh, China, Germany, UK, France and Italy.
- Almost all the world production comes from India and Bangladesh. Chittagong, Narayanganj, Khulna, Ghorashal and Narsindhi are some of the famous locations of jute mills in Bangladesh.
- Bangladesh is the leading exporter of raw jute, whereas India exports more jute goods.
- USA, Russia, Australia, Canada, Argentina are the most important buyers of jute goods in the world.

Synthetic Textiles Industry

- Man-made or synthetic fibres were produced commercially at the end of the 20th century but only came into prominence during the 1920s and 1930s.
- The true synthetics derived from petroleum rather than from natural cellulose have only been developed on a larger scale since the World War II.
- The main producers of synthetic fibres are the industrialised countries, such as the USA, Japan, Germany, former USSR and UK.
- In Britain, the first rayon plants were set up in Lancashire and the Midlands.
- In the USA, synthetic fibre plants are concentrated in the south and New England.
- Japan began to make synthetic textiles in the 1920s. Japanese synthetic textile industries are concentrated around the Inland Sea with ready access to imported petroleum.

Sugar Industry

- Sugar production has been carried on since ancient times, but modern sugar industry developed in the first decade of the twentieth century.
- The basic raw material is sugarcane.
- There are over 100 countries in the world producing sugar. The leading sugarcane producing countries are also the leading producers of sugar.
- Brazil, India, China, Mexico, Thailand, Cuba and Australia are the leading producers of cane sugar in the world, while the European countries and the USA are the leading producers of beet sugar.

Paper Industries

- The pulp and paper industry comprises companies that use wood as raw material and produce pulp, paper, board and other cellulose-based products.

- The industry is dominated by North American (United States and Canada), northern European (Finland, Sweden, and North-West Russia) and East Asian countries (such as East Siberian Russia, China, Japan, and South Korea).
- Australasia and Brazil also have significant pulp and paper enterprises.
- The United States had been the world's leading producer of paper until it was overtaken by China in 2009. China is the largest producer of paper in the world.

Petrochemical Industry

- The development of petrochemical industries took place in North America and Europe after the World War II.
- In the USA, Chicago, Toledo, Philadelphia, Delaware and Los Angeles have large petrochemical complexes.
- The major European petrochemical complexes are located on the coasts of Southern North Sea and the English Channel (Antwerp, Rotterdam and Southampton), Ruhr region in Germany, and Le Havre-Roven-Marselles region in France.
- There are also a number of petro-chemical complexes in the Central Asian Republics, Russia, West Asia and India.

Towns and Industries

Sr.No.	Town	Country	Industry
1.	Aberdeen	Scotland (UK)	Granite mining
2.	Abadan	Iran	Oil refineries
3.	Baku	Azerbaijan	Petroleum
4.	Bangkok	Thailand	Shipping
5.	Belfast	N. Ireland (Ulster)	Ship-building, linen
6.	Buenos Aires	Argentina	Dairy products
7.	Cadiz	Spain	Cork
8.	Chicago	USA	Gramophone, agricultural implements, meat products
9.	Dhaka	Bangladesh	Jute
10.	Detroit	USA	Automobiles
11.	Dresden	Germany	Optical and photo-graphic instruments
12.	Dundee	Scotland (UK)	Jute, linen
13.	Essex	England (UK)	Engineering works
14.	Geneva	Switzerland	Watches
15.	Glassgow	Scotland (UK)	Engineering works
16.	Glassgow	Scotland (UK)	Machinery, Textiles
17.	Havana	Cuba	Cigars, Sugar
18.	Hollywood	USA	Films
19.	Johannesbourg	South Africa	Gold mines
20.	Kansas	USA	Meat packing
21.	Leeds	England(UK)	Woollen garments
22.	Los Angeles	USA	Films, Oil mining
23.	Lyons	France	Silk
24.	Melbourne	Australia	Chocolate
25.	Milan	Italy	Silk

Sr.No.	Town	Country	Industry
26.	New Orleans	USA	Cotton
27.	Northampton	UK	Leather goods
28.	Oporto	Portugal	Wine
29.	Oslo	Norway	Paper
30.	Ottawa	Canada	Paper
31.	Pittsburgh	USA	Iron and Steel
32.	Plymouth	England (UK)	Ship-building
33.	Port Louis	Mauritius	Sugar
34.	Sheffield	England (UK)	Cutlery
35.	Rotterdam	Netherlands	Ship-building
36.	Teheran	Iran	Carpets
37.	Tokyo	Japan	Rayon and Textiles
38.	Venice	Italy	Glass
39.	Vienna	Austria	Glass
40.	Wellington	New Zealand	Dairy products
41.	Yenang Yaung	Myanmar	Oil fields

POPULATION

- Broadly, 90 per cent of the world population lives in about 10 per cent of its land area. The 10 most populous countries of the world contribute about 60 per cent of the world's population. Of these 10 countries, 6 are located in Asia.
- Those regions having density greater than hundred persons per square kilometres. It includes the areas of East Asia (China, Japan, S. Korea and Taiwan), South Asia (India, Pakistan, Bangladesh, Sri Lanka and Nepal), North Western Europe (France, UK, Germany, Netherlands, Poland, Belgium, Luxembourg, Ireland, Denmark, Spain, Portugal and Italy).
- Desert, arid and semiarid areas. Exceptions occur where towns have emerged in deserts owing to the mining of gold and other precious metals (e.g. Kalgoorlie and Coolgardie in Australia and Crippel Creek in USA etc.).

Largest Population

Rank	Country	Population 2024	Rank	Country	Population 2024
1.	India	1,450,935,791	11.	Mexico	130,861,007
2.	China	1,419,321,278	12.	Japan	123,753,041
3.	United States	345,426,571	13.	Egypt	116,538,258
4.	Indonesia	283,487,931	14.	Philippines	115,843,670
5.	Pakistan	251,269,164	15.	Congo, Dem. Rep.	109,276,265
6.	Nigeria	232,679,478	16.	Vietnam	100,987,686
7.	Brazil	211,998,573	17.	Iran	91,567,738
8.	Bangladesh	173,562,364	18.	Turkiye	87,473,805
9.	Russia	144,820,423	19.	Germany	84,552,242
10.	Ethiopia	132,059,767	20.	Thailand	71,668,011

➡ Mountainous Regions, Exceptions occur where minerals are found, like some pockets in Peru and Bolivia. In Kishtwar (J&K), mining of precious stones have led to the emergence of settlements.

Smallest Population

Rank	Country	Population 2024	Rank	Country	Population 2024
1.	Vatican City (Holy See)	1,000	11.	Andorra	85,708
2.	Nauru	9,692	12.	Seychelles	94,633
3.	Tuvalu	11,147	13.	Antigua & Barbuda	95,882
4.	Palau	21,516	14.	Saint Vincent & the Grenadines	101,844
5.	San Marino	33,779	15.	Tonga	106,398
6.	Monaco	30,727	16.	Micronesia	103,643
7.	Liechtenstein	38,547	17.	Kiribati	109,367
8.	Saint Kitts & Nevis	53,094	18.	Grenada	112,207
9.	Marshall Islands	75,684	19.	Saint Lucia	165,510
10.	Dominica	74,027	20.	Samoa	201,316

Source: Population 2024, StatisticsTimes.com

Tribes of the World

➡ **Bora** : W. Amazon Basin.

➡ **Bantu** : Negroes of central and Southern Africa

➡ **Sakai** : Malaya Island.

➡ **Semang** : Malaya hilly area.

➡ **Papuan** : Pacific ocean.

➡ **Bushman** : S. Africa's Kalahari Desert.

➡ **Pygmies** : Extremely short-statured people of the Congo (Zaire) Basin.

➡ **Bedouins** : Arab (Hamad and Nefad desert)

➡ **Berbers** : Tribals of Morocco, Algeria and Tunisia.

➡ **Bindibu** : Natives of Western Australia.

➡ **Gaucho** : Nomads of Pampas in Uruguay and Argentina.

➡ **Hamites** : Dark-skinned Muslims in N.W. Africa

➡ **Masai** : Tanganika, Kenya, East Uganda.

➡ **Khirghiz** : People of the steppe type region (Central Asia, Russia).

➡ **Kikuyu** : A tribe in Kenya.

➡ **Lapps** : People of European tundra.

➡ **Eskimo** : Greenland, Alaska and Tundra.

➡ **Samoyed** : People of the Asiatic tundra Western Siberia (North USSR).

➡ **Semites** : Jews and Ethiopeans.

➡ **Yakagir** : Siberia.

➡ **Punan** : Central Boroneao.

➡ **Kazak** : Russia.

➡ **Masai** : A Negro tribe of east Africa.

➡ **Maya** : Mexico, Guatemala and Honduras.

➡ **Maori** : New Zealand

➡ **Magyar** : Hungary.

➡ **Papuans** : Tribal's of New Guinea.

➡ **Tartars** : A mixed group of people in Siberia

➡ **Veddas** : The racial stock of Srilanka

➡ **Yakuts** : People in the tundra region in the USSR

➡ **Boer** : S.Africa.

➡ **Afridi** : Pakistan.

➡ **Zulu** : S.Africa (Natal).

INDIAN GEOGRAPHY

PHYSICAL FEATURES

- India is the seventh largest country in the world covering an area of 32,87,263 sq. km.
- The mainland stretches from latitude 8°4′ to 37°6′ north and from longitude 68°7′ to 97°25′ east of Greenwich.
- Due to vast longitudinal extent, the time difference between the two extreme points in the east and west is of two hours.
- As such, time along the standard meridian of India (82°30′E) passing through Prayagraj is taken as the Indian Standard Time for country.
- The tropic of Cancer (23°30′N) passes through middle of India is situated on the northern frings of the Indian Ocean.
- Its land frontier is 15,200 kilometres long. Its northern borderland is mountainous.
- India has a coastline of 6,100 kilometres in the mainland.
- The total length of the coastline of the mainland and Lakshdweep Islands and Andaman and Nicobar Island is 7,516.6 km.
- The Gulf of Mannar and the Palk Strait separate India from Sri Lanka.
- The Andaman and Nicobar Islands in the Bay of Bengal and Lakshadweep in the Arabian Sea are parts of the Indian territory.
- Indira Point (earlier called **Pygmalion Point)** in Great Nicobar in the Andaman and Nicobar Islands is the southernmost Point of India.

Physiographic Divisions of India

- The Indian sub-continent is characterised by a great diversity in its physical features. It may be divided in the following physiographic units:

The Northern Mountain

- The region extends all along the northern border of the country, from the eastern border of West Pakistan to the frontiers of Myanmar of about 2500 km. with an average width of about 240 km; occupied by the Himalayan ranges. This covers an area of about 5,00,000 km^2.
- It consists of the *Hindukush, Karakoram* and the *Himalayas* proper.
- Almost all the highest peaks of the world are in Karakoram and the Himalayas.
- There are three major fold axes represent the *Himadri* (Greater Himalaya), *Himachal* (Lesser Himalaya) and the *Shivaliks* (Outer Himalaya) extending almost uninterrupted throughout its length.
- The Himadri, the asymmetrical and the northern most range of the Himalaya owes its scenic beauty to glacier and lofty snowy peaks. Its average elevation is 6000 m.
- The Gangotri and Jamnotri are found in Himdari. This range has a granitic core, flanked by metamorphosed sediments.
- It has the credit of having the world's 14 highest peaks ranging between the Everest (8848m), Kanchenjunga (8,598 m), Dhaulagiri (8,172 m), Nanga Parbat (8,126 m) and Nanda Devi (7,817 m) are the famous peak.

- The Himachal or the Lesser Himalayas forms the central chain composed mainly of highly compressed and altered rocks varying from Algonkian or pre-Cambrian to Eocene in age.
- In general, the alternating ranges and valleys acquire an elevation of about 3700 m and 4500 m respectively. Its asymmetrical structures at places provide it a more or less hogback look.
- The Shivaliks in the south, which extend from the Potwar Plateau on the west to the Brahmaputra valley on the east and have an average height of over 1,000m represent the outermost range of the system with roughly a hogback appearance, a steeply sloping southern and a gently sloping northern face.
- These newer and river-borne deposits derived from the rising Himalaya represent the most recent phase of the Himalayan orogeny i.e., from Middle Miocene to the Lower Pleistocene.
- The range, bordered on the north by flat-floored structural-longitudinal or erosional valleys called the Doons is characterised by fault scarps, anticlinal valleys and synclinal ranges.

IMPORTANT FACTS

Total Area	:	32,87,263 sq. km
Land Frontier	:	15,200 sq. km
Coast Line	:	7516.6 km
North to South	:	3214 km (between the extreme latitudes)
East to West	:	2933 km (between the extreme longitudes)
Exclusive Economic Zone	:	200 nm from its shores
Longest River	:	Ganga
Largest Lake	:	Chilka Lake
Largest Lake (Fresh Water)	:	Wular Lake
Highest Point	:	Mt. K2 (8611 m.)
Highers Point of Himalaya	:	Kanchenjunga (8,598 m)
Lowest Point	:	Kuttanad (–2.2 m)
Northernmost Point	:	Siachen Glacier near Karakoram Pass
Southernmost Point	:	Indira Point, Great Nicobar, Andaman & Nicobar Islands.
Southernmost Point of India (Mainland)	:	Cape Comorin (Kanya Kumari)
Westernmost Point	:	West of Ghuar Mota, Gujarat
Easternmost Point	:	Kibithy, Arunachal Pradesh

Regional Divisions of Himalayas

Apart from these longitudinal sub-divisions, the Himalaya exhibit regional characteristics and as such, the following regions have been identified:

(*a*) Kashmir or Northwestern Himalayas:

- It comprise a series of ranges such as the Karakoram, Ladakh, Zaskar and Pir Panjal.
- The northeastern part of the Kashmir Himalayas is a cold desert, which lies between the Greater Himalayas and the Karakoram ranges.
- The famous Dal Lake of Kashmir lies between the Greater Himalayas and the Pir Panjal range.

- **Important Glaciers:** Baltoro and Siachen.
- **Important Passes:** Zoji La on the Great Himalayas, Banihal on the Pir Panjal, Jojila-Zaskar on the Zaskar and Khardung La on the Ladakh range.
- **Important Lakes:** Fresh water lake are: Dal Lake and Wular lake and salt water lakes such as Pangong Tso and Tso Moriri.
- **Important Rivers:** The river Indus, and its tributaries such as the Jhelum and the Chenab.
- **Duns:** The southernmost part of the region consists of longitudinal valleys known as 'duns'. Jammu dun and Pathankot dun are important examples.
- **Famous Places of Pilgrimage:** Vaishno Devi, Amarnath Cave, Charar-e-Sharif.

Passes through the Mountain Wall

(*i*) The Khybar Pass (1,000 m) is the most famous of all. It leads from Peshawar to Kabul. Most of the invaders in the past came through this opening in the Northern Mountain Wall.

(*ii*) The Gomal Pass: (1,525 m) South of the khybar pass there is the Gomal Pass. This pass served as a trade route passing through the districts of Waziristan (now in Pakistan).

(*iii*) The Bolan Pass: (1,800 m) lies between the Sulaiman and the Kirthar Ranges. It leads from Kandahar to Quetta.

(*iv*) The Shipki Pass leads from the Himachal Pradesh to Tibet.

(*b*) The Himachal and Uttarakhand Himalayas:

- This part lies approximately between the Sutluj in the west and the Kali (a tributary of Ghaghara) in the east.
- **Two Major River Systems,** the Indus and the Ganga. Tributaries of the Indus include the Ravi, the Beas and the Sutluj, and the tributaries of Ganga flowing through this region include the Yamuna, the Gomti and the Ghaghara.
- **Three Ranges of Himalayas** are prominent in this region, (*i*) Great Himalayan range, (*ii*) the Lesser Himalayas (which is locally known as Dhauladhar in Himachal Pradesh and Nagtibba in Uttarakhand) and (*iii*) the Shivalik range from the North to the South.
- **Tourism:** In this region the Lesser Himalayas, has altitude between 1,000-2,000 m. Some of the important hill stations are Dharamshala, Mussoorie, Shimla, Kaosani and the cantonment towns and health resorts such as Shimla, Mussoorie, Kasauli, Almora, Lansdowne and Ranikhet, etc., were developed in this region.
- **Dun formations:** Some important duns located in this region are the Chandigarh-Kalka dun, Nalagarh dun, Dehradun, Harike dun and the Kota dun, etc. *Dehradun* is the largest of all the duns with an approximate length of 35-45 km and a width of 22-25 km.
- **Places of Pilgrimage** such as the Gangotri, Yamunotri, Kedarnath, Badrinath and Hemkund Sahib are also situated in this part. The region is also known to have five famous Prayags (river confluences).

(*c*) The Darjeeling and Sikkim Himalayas

- They are flanked by Nepal Himalayas in the west and Bhutan Himalayas in the east. It is relatively small but is a most significant part of the Himalayas.
- **Rivers:** It is known for its fast-flowing rivers such as Tista.
- **Mountain Peaks like** Kanchenjunga (Kanchengiri), and deep valleys.

- **Duar Formation:** In place of the Shivalik here, the 'duar formation' are important, which have also been used for the development of tea gardens. Duars like Dun's are also deposit filled Lacustrine valleys.

(*d*) The Arunachal Himalayas

- These extend from the east of the Bhutan Himalayas up to the Diphu pass in the east. The general direction of the mountain range is from southwest to northeast.
- **Important Mountain Peaks:** Kangtu and Namcha Barwa. These ranges are dissected by fast-flowing rivers from the north to the south, forming deep gorges. Brahmaputra flows through a deep gorge after crossing Namcha Barwa.
- **Important Rivers:** The Kameng, the Subansiri, the Dihang, the Dibang and the Lohit. These are perennial with the high rate of fall, thus, having the highest hydro-electric power potential in the country.

(*e*) The Eastern Hills and Mountains

- These are part of the Himalayan mountain system having their general alignment from the north to the south direction. They are known by different local names. In the north, they are known as Patkai Bum, Naga hills, the Manipur hills and in the south as Mizo or Lushai hills. These are low hills, inhabited by numerous tribal groups practising Jhum cultivation.
- **Rivers & Lakes:** The Barak is an important river in Manipur and Mizoram. 'Loktak' Lake in Manipur at the centre.

The Indus-Ganga-Brahmaputra Plain

The Great Plain of India is formed by the Indus, Ganga and the Brahmaputra rivers. This is the largest alluvial tract of the world extending for 3,200 kilometres between the mouths of the Ganga and the Indus, all along the foot of the mountain rim with a width varying from 150 to 300 kilometres. It is subdivided into:

➡ **The Punjab Plain:** The western part of Punjab Plain lies between the western part of Pakistan and the eastern part of India. Its tributaries are divided into many doabs. ***Bist-Jalandhar Doab*** between Beas and Sutlej rivers, ***Bari Doab*** between Beas and Ravi Rivers, ***Rachna Doab*** between Ravi and Chenab, ***Chaj Doab*** between Chenab and Jhelum, ***Sind Sagar Doab*** among Jhelum, Chenab and Indus. It has low flood plains called **Bet** and its border is called ***Dhaya.***

➡ **The Ganga Plain:** It lies in Uttar Pradesh, Bihar and Bengal. It covers 3.57 lakh sq. km. of area. The tributaries of Ganga on its north are the **Gomti, Ghaghra, Gandak, Kosi, Mahanadi, Kali,** and in the South are **Chambal, Son, Betwa** and **Ken**. It comprises of **Bhabar, Terai, Khadar** and **Bhangar Belts.**

➡ **Bhabar:** It lies along the foot of the Shivaliks from the Indus to the Tista. It is 8 to 16 kms parallel to Shivalik foot hills at the break up of the slope. It comprises of pebble-studded rocks, which are highly permeable. Due to permeability of the rocks, the steams disappear. This region is not much suitable for agriculture.

➡ **Terai:** It lies to the south of the Bhabar and run parallel to it. It is 20 to 30 kms wide. The underground streams of the bhabar re-emerge on the surface and give birth to marshy area. Most parts of the Terai area are reclaimed for agriculture.

➡ **Bhangar:** This is the older alluvium in river beds in the form of terraces found above the flood plain level. These terraces are often impregnated with calcareous concretions or 'kankars'. 'Barind plains' in the deltaic region of Bengal and 'bhur formations' in the middle Ganga-Yamuna doab are two regional variations of bhangar. Barind plains are actually the older delta of Ganga, formed during the pleistocene, later lifted and eroded into low uplands with extensive laterite formations.

➥ **Khadar Belt:** It lies in low land areas after the Bhangar Belt. It is made up of fresh newer alluvium which is deposited by the rivers flowing down the plains. It is distributed over eastern U.P., Bihar and West Bengal. It is known as 'Bet' in Punjab.

➥ **The Deltaic Plain of Bengal:** It is situated in West Bengal. It is far more extensive. The doab between Ganga and Brahmaputra rivers in the north is also included in it which is called Para-delta.

➥ **The Assam Plain or Brahmaputra Plain:** This plain extends for a distance of about 640 km. from Dhubri to Sadiya. This plain is formed by the sediment brought by the Brahmaputra, and its tributaries.

Peninsular Plateau

➥ This plateau is situated in a triangular form in Southern India. Its southern apex is rising from the height of 150 m above the river plains upto an elevation of 600-900 m in Kanyakumari. On its eastern side Bay of Bengal and on the Western side the Arabian Sea is present.

➥ It is the oldest landmass of India whose general elevation is 600-800 metres. Its eastern and western sides are represented by Eastern Ghats and Western Ghats. This vast plateau is 1600 kms. long in north-south direction and 1400 kms. wide in east-west direction. The Narmada-Tapi trough divides this great plateau into the Malwa Plateau and the Deccan Plateau.

The Coastal Plains

➥ The Great Plateau is flanked by narrow coastal strips on both west and east sides along the Arabian Sea and the Bay of Bengal respectively. These are commonly known as the West Coastal plain and the East Coastal plain.

The Western Coastal Plain

➥ The Western Coastal Plain spreads from Gujarat to the Kanyakumari. It is uneven and has been dissected by numerous fast-flowing rivers—the Narmada and the Tapti are among them. The plain is divided into two parts—the northern and the southern. The northern part from Gujarat to Goa is called Konkan coast while the southern Malabar coast from Goa to the Kanyakumari. Konkan is 50-80 kms. wide and characterized by estuaries while Malabar is characterised by lagoons, estuaries and back waters (Kayals). Lagoons are salt water lakes, separate from the main sea by sands bars and spits.

The Eastern Coastal Plain

➥ It is the coast along the Bay of Bengal from Odisha to Kanyakumari known as the East Coastal Plain. It also has two part—the northern and southern. The northern part is North circar plain and the southern is Coromandel plain. The Mahanadi, the Godavari, the Krishna and the Cauvery are major rivers which originate from the great plateau and form deltas at their mouth. A chain of bars is found along the coast that has given birth to numerous lagoons. The Chilka and the Pulicat present good example of lagoons.

WESTERN GHATS

- It extends from the Tapi river in the north and Kanyakumari in the south and forms the western boundary of the Deccan Plateau. Its length is about 1600 km.
- The block mountains were formed due to the down warping of a part of the land into the Arabian Sea. Harishchandra, Mahabaleshwar, Kalsubai and Salher are important peaks in this region. Thalghat and Bhorghat are the important passes for roads and railways.
- It has average elevation of 1220 m. Few peaks are above 1500 m e.g. Kudremukh (1892) and Pushpagiri (1714).
- The Nilgiris (Eastern Ghats) join the Sahyadris (Western Ghats) to form a mountain knot where highest point is Doddabetta (2637m).
- In the south of Nilgiri lies the Palghat Gap which connects Tamil Nadu with Kerala. In the South of Palghat, Anaimudi (2695m) is a knot which is joined by three hills, viz. the Anaimalai hills (1800-2000m) in the north, the Palni hills (960-1200m) in the N.E. and the Cardamom or Elamalai hills in the south.
- The Anaimalai constitutes a series of plateau with rolling topography. Here hill slopes support tea, coffee, cinchona. Kodaikanal hill station (2195m) is located on the southern edge of the Palni hills, Tambraparni has it source near Agastya Malai forming a series of waterfalls (Bajiatirtham and Papanasam). The highest peak in the Western Ghats is Anaimudi with a height of 2,695 m. They rise steeply from the West Coast. The hills are continuous. All the rivers of the Deccan plateau rise in the Western Ghats.

EASTERN GHATS

- It depict true Mountain characteristic between Mahanadi and Godavari (peaks are Nimalgiri at Koraput, Mahendragiri at Ganjam).
- In between the Krishna River and Chennai they continue as the Kondavidu hills mainly composed of Quartzites and Slates.
- The Nallamalai (900-1100m) and Palkonda hills are composed of Cuddapah and Kurnool formations.
- Nilgiris (blue mountains) provide the converging site for three mountain ranges: the Sahyadri joining opposite of the Makurti peak; the Southern Ghats across the Palghat in the south and the Eastern Ghats in the north eastern corner.
- The highest peak in the Eastern Ghats is Mahendragiri at Vishakhapatnam with a height of 1,500 m. They rise gently from the east coast. The hills are discontinuous. Rivers cut the valleys through the Eastern Ghats. Two notable inlets in the western coastal plains are the Gulf of Kachchh and Gulf of Khambhat. The lake Vembanad, about 63 km in length is the largest lake.

The Islands

- The Islands of India are usually divided into two parts (*a*) Islands close to the coast (*b*) Islands distant from the coast.
- The Andamans and Nicobars are a cluster of Islands stretched almost in a line. There are as many as 200 islands in the Andaman groups which extending upto 350 kilometres. There are 19 islands in the Nicobar group. Some of the island extend from 60 to 100 km, forming a cluster south of the Andaman group.
- Lakshadweep islands are formed of coral deposits are called atolls. The word is originally derived from the Malayalam word 'Atolu'.

DRAINAGE SYSTEM

- The area drained by a single river system is called a drainage basin or river basin. The rivers in India have been more of less adjusted to its physical conditions.

- It is largely influenced by the evolution of three fold physiographic divisions. The origin of rivers can be categorised into two groups (*i*) the Himalayan rivers and (*ii*) the peninsular rivers.

The Himalayan Rivers

- The Himalayan Rivers have very large basins. These rivers aided by the bold features of Himalayan relief, continue to perform intensive erosional activity.
- Another striking feature of the Himalayan rivers is seen in their flow pattern which is perennial and is derived from rainfall as well as the snow-melt.
- The rivers originating in the Himalayan mountain complex consists of 3 systems: (*i*) the Indus system (*ii*) the Ganga system and (*iii*) the Brahmaputra system.

The Indus System

- This system comprises river Indus and its five tributaries—Chenab, Jhelum, Ravi, Beas and Sutluj.
- **The Indus** rises from a glacier near Bokhar Chan in Tibet at an altitude of 5,180 metre near the Mansarovar lake and enters Indian territory in Jammu and Kashmir. It is known as Singi Kham ban or Lion's mouth.
- The Indus flows south-westwards across Pakistan to reach the Arabian Sea east of Karachi.
- The Indus is considered as one of the largest rivers of the world, with the catchment area of 1,165,000 sq. km of which as much as 321,289 sq. km lies in India and with a total length of 2,880 km (in India 709 km).
- **The Jhelum:** The Jhelum is an important tributary of the Indus. It rises from a spring at Verinag, situated in the south-eastern part of the valley of Kashmir. Its Sanskrit name is Vitasta and is called Veth in Kashmir. Its total length is 725 km and drainage area is 28,490 km^2 in India and it flows in India and Pakistan. It joins the Chenab near Jhang in Pakistan.
- **The Chenab:** It is called Asikini in Sanskrit and is formed by the confluence of Chandra and Bhaga in H.P., so is called Chandra Bhaga in H.P. It flows north-westwards and runs parallel to Pir Panjal for some distance. Its length is 1180 km in India and its catchment area is 26,755 sq. km in India. The main tributary is Tavi.
- **The Ravi:** It rises west to the Rohtang Pass in the Kullu hills of H.P. and flows between Pir Panjal and Dhauladhar ranges. Its Sanskrit name is Iravati. It meets Chenab and enters Panchnad. Its length is 725 km and has a catchment area of about 5,957 sq. km.
- **The Beas:** Its Sanskrit name is Vipasha and it rises from the southern end of Rohtang Pass at the height of 4,000 m. It makes the famous Kullu Valley. It is 460 km long. Its catchment area is about 26,000 sq. km. It meets the Sutlej near Harike.
- **The Sutlej:** Its Sanskrit name is Shatdru. It originates from Rakas lake at an altitude of 4,630 m in Tibet. It flows for about 1,050 km and drains 24,087 km^2 of area in India. It is very important tributary as it feeds the canal system of Bhakra Nangal Project, Harike and Sirhind.

The Ganga System

- **The Ganga** originates as Bhagirathi from Gangotri glacier. The river acquires its name after its head-streams—Alaknanda and Bhagirathi uniting at Devaprayag. The main southern tributary is the Son while, Yamuna is its left bank tributary besides the minor streams of the Tons and the Punpun.

- On its left bank, the Ganga, however, receives a larger number of tributaries, including the Ramganga, Gomati, Ghaghra, Gandak, Kosi and the Mahananda.
- **The Yamuna:** It is the longest tributary of the Ganga. It has its source in the Yamunotri glacier on Banderpunch range. Its basin area is 359,000 km^2. It joins river on its right bank at Prayag. The confluence of the Ganga and Yamuna is called Sangam. Agra is an important city situated on the banks of Yamuna. Chambal and Betwa are tributaries of Yamuna.
- **The Sharda or Saryu:** It is known as Kali in the Himalayas, the Sharda in Pilibhit and Kheri districts and Chauka before it joins the right bank of Ghaghara. It rises in the Milan glacier in the Nepal Himalayas. It runs along the Indo-Nepal boundary and leaves Himalayas at Baramdeo.
- **The Ramganga:** The river is the left bank tributary of the Ganga. It rises near Nainital and has a length of 690 km meets Ganga near Farrukhabad.
- **The Gomti:** It is the tributary of the Ganga which rises in the plains and not in the hills. It meets the Ganga down Varanasi.
- **The Ghaghra:** It originates in the glaciers of Map chachungo. This river rises parallel to the Ganga in U.P. and its source is east of the Ganga. The river Sharda (Kali or Kali Ganga) joins it in the plains before it joins the Ganga near Chapra. It is 1,080 km long and its catchment area is 127,500 sq. km.
- **The Gandak:** It rises near Sino-Nepal boundary and drains the central part of Nepal. It is called the Narayani in Nepal. It is 425 km long in India and drains 9540 km^2 is India. It comprises streams namely Kali Gandak and Trishul Ganga. It meets the Ganga near Bankipur in Bihar.
- **The Kosi:** The Kosi has its source to the North of Mt. Everest in Tibet where its main stream Arun rises. After crossing the Central Himalayas in Nepal it is joined by Son Kosi from the West and the Tamil Kosi from the east. It forms Sapt Kosi after the uniting with River Arun. It drains eastern Nepal and enters Saharsa district of Bihar in numerous channels. The river is notorious for shifting its course, depositing silt and causing floods. It joins the Ganga at Kursela.
- **The Damodar:** It occupies the eastern margins of the Chhotanagpur plateau where it flows through a rift valley. The Barakar is its main tributary. The Damodar finally joins the Hugli. River Damodar is known as the Sorrow of Bengal.
- **The Mahananda:** It is another tributary of the Ganga rising in the Darjeeling hills. It joins the Ganga as its last left bank tributary in West Bengal.
- **The Son:** It is a large south bank tributary of the Ganga, originating in the Amarkantak plateau. After forming a series of waterfalls at the edge of the plateau, it reaches Arrah, west of Patna to join Ganga.

The Brahmaputra River System

- It is formed by the Brahmaputra river which is about 2900 km in length. It has its origin in the Chemayundung glacier of the Kailash range near the Mansarovar Lake. From here it traverses eastward longitudinally for a distance of nearly 1200 km in a dry and flat region of Southern Tibet and is known as ***Tsang-Po*** which means the Purifier.

- It emerges as a turbulent and dynamic river after carving out a deep gorge in the Central Himalayas near Namcha Barwa (7,755 m).
- The river emerges from the foothill under the name of ***Siang*** or ***Dihang***. It is also known as Brahmaputra as it turns southwards in Arunachal Pradesh and enters Assam.
- The Brahmaputra's tributaries are Tista, Subansiri, Barali, Manas, Dhansiri, Buri and Dihing.
- The world's largest river island, named ***Majauli*** is situated in river Brahmaputra (Assam).

Peninsular Rivers

- **The Krishna** is the second largest east-flowing Peninsular river which rises in the Mahabaleshwar Hills and flows eastwards towards the south and into the Bay of Bengal. Bhima is its largest tributary. The other large tributaries are Koyna, Tungabhadra, Varna, Panchagana and Dudhaganga.
- **The Kaveri** is known as the "**Ganga of the South**". It rises in the Coorg district of Karnataka. Its important tributaries are Kabini, Bhavani and Amravati. It has several rapids and waterfalls in its course. At Sivasamundram it plunges from a height of 100 m forming the famous Siva Samundram Falls. It forms a large delta in Tamil Nadu before flowing into the Bay of Bengal.
- **The Godavari** is the largest-river of the Deccan Plateau. Its basin covers about 10% of the total area of India. It is called **Vridha Ganga** or **Dakhsin Ganga** because of its huge size. It rises in the Western Ghats in the Nasik district of Maharashtra. It flows for several kilometres through a gorge before reaching the city of Nasik. After flowing through Maharashtra, the Godavari flows through the Telangana. It forms a large delta at its mouth before draining into the Bay of Bengal. The Darna, Pravara, Manjra, Pranhita and Indravati are its important tributaries.
- **The Narmada** rises on the Amarkantak Plateau in the Maikala Range from a spring at a height of 1060 m. It flows west and south-west through a valley between the Vindhya and the Satpura ranges. At Bheraghat, it drops through a height of 15 m forming the famous Marble Falls. It then flows through a gorge and forms a large estuary before flowing into the Gulf of Khambhat.
- **The Tapi** also known as Tapti rises from Multai in the Betul district in the Satpura Hills. It flows westwards, north of Surat and into the Gulf of Khambhat. The Purna, Girna and Panjhara are its large tributaries.
- **The Mahanadi** has its source in the Maikala Hills in Madhya Pradesh and flows through the state of Orissa. It forms a very large delta before flowing into the Bay of Bengal.
- **The Sharavati** in Karnataka is well known for its Gersoppa (Jog) Falls. During the Monsoon season these falls can be considered as one of the world's greatest waterfalls. But like all rivers of the Deccan Plateau, the Sharavati has very little water in the dry season.
- **The Sabarmati and the Brahmani:** These two rivers interposed between the Ganga and the Mahanadi deltas

and drain an area of 21,674 sq. kms and 36,300 sq. kms. respectively. Jharkhand, Orissa, West Bengal and Madhya Pradesh share the drainage basin of these two rivers. The Brahmani is known as south Koel in its upper reaches in Jharkhand.

➡ **The Sabarmati and the Mahi:** Sabarmati and Mahi drain from the north-west part of Peninsular India. The Sabarmati originates in the Aravalli hills and flows for a distance of 300 kms. to fall in Arabian Sea. The Mahi originates in the east of Udaipur and drains an area of 34,842 sq. kms. and Sabarmati drains an area of 21,674 sq. kms. Mahi falls into the Gulf of Khambhat.

➡ **The Chambal:** It originates in the Vindhya range and flows towards the north generally in a gorge upto Kota. From Kota it turns to the north-east direction and reaches Pinahat then it turns to the east and runs nearly parallel to the Yamuna before joining it at Etawah in Uttar Pradesh. It is 1050 kms in length.

CLIMATE

Seasons in India

➡ The climate of India is described as tropical monsoon. Even northern India, lying beyond the tropical zone, acquires a tropical touch marked by the relatively high temperatures.

➡ The large size of the country and its varied relief play a crucial role in determining the climatic variations in different parts of India. But the seasonal rhythm of the monsoon is apparent throughout India.

➡ The most characteristic feature of the monsoons is the complete reversal of winds. It eventually leads to the alternation of seasons.

➡ India is known as the 'land of the endless growing season'. The year is divided into four seasons:

1. Cold Weather Season

- The Southern branch of the jet stream occupies its position south of the Himalayas, which is accompanied with the restoration of light northeast trade winds (monsoons) to the surface.
- Withdrawal of the inter tropical convergence zone and formation of anti cyclonic cell over north western India results in dry weather, over most of the areas in the country.
- There is general increase of temperature from North to South. Isotherms run almost parallel to the latitudes (in January 21°C isotherm runs through the middle of the country connecting Tapti estuary to the Mahanadi delta).
- In the western India Punjab, Haryana, West U.P and Northern Rajasthan experience Less than 15°C.
- In South India the isotherm, tend to bend southward and run parallel to the coast. The western coast is warmer than the eastern coast.
- This season is characterized by the inflow of depression from the west to north-west.
- Fine weather, clear sky, low humidity, absence of rainfalls, low temperature and large diurnal variation are usual feature of the winter season.
- North east parts of India also get some rainfall during this season.

2. The Hot and Dry Weather

- A low pressure area occupies the northern part of the Bay of Bengal during October, which moves southward and get deflecting towards, the coromandal coast thereby producing rains on this coast.

- The presence of inter-tropical convergence and the easterly depression are responsible for these rains.
- Hot and Dry Weather is characterized by low pressure system, high temperature, unstable pressure and wind circulation.
- The dust storms of Punjab and Haryana, the Loo of UP, the Norwesters (Kalbaisakhis) of W. Bengal and cyclonic depressions of the eastern coast produce a stormy and turbulent weather.
- The rains caused by thunderstorm in Karnataka are called '**Cherry Blossoms**'. These are beneficial for coffee plantation. Elsewhere in South India they are known as '**Mango Showers**'.
- Hot, dry and dusty westerly winds blow in the northern western parts of the country is known as Loo.
- **Norwester/Kalbaisakhi** (Dark Clouds in the month of Baisakh) occurs in Assam and West Bengal. These are thunderstorms, accompanied with strong winds and heavy rainfall. This is good for the tea crop in Assam and the jute and rice in West Bengal. In Assam these storms are called **Bardoli Chherha**.

3. The Wet Season

- The southern branch of the western jet is withdrawn from south of the Himalaya therby leading to the formation of dynamic depression over the surface.
- The ITC shifts northwards allowing equatorial westerlies to shift in the subcontinent. Indian subcontinent receives bulk of its rainfall (around 80%) from the southwest.
- The Arabian Sea current causes rainfall all along the Western Coast, Western Ghats, Gujarat, Maharashtra, parts of M.P and Rajasthan.
- While crossing the Sahyadris (Western Ghats), the monsoon current produce heavy rainfall on the windward and scanty rainfall on the leeward side therby producing a rain shadow area.
- The rainfall is also erratic on the leeward side, which results in frequent drought in Maharashtra and Karnatka. The Tamil Nadu coast goes dry in this season.
- The Arabian Sea branch meets the Bay of Bengal branch over Chhotanagpur Plateau producing copious rainfall.
- Absence of moutain barrier in Kutch, parallel position of the Aravalli, effect of the hot and dry air results in failure of Arabian Sea branch to produce adequate rainfall.
- The Bay of Bengal branch, obstructed by the eastern hill is deflected westward towards the Ganga Plain.
- The Entrapped current in the valleys of Meghalaya produces very heavy rainfall [Chera-punji (1087 cm) and Mawsynram (1141 cm)].
- The weather is also affected by a number of cyclonic depressions entering the country through the Bay of Bengal and the Arabian Sea. About 20 to 25 such depressions develop during monsoon period.
- With the exception of J & K and parts of Tamil Nadu, most of the country receives heavy rainfall.

4. Season of Retreating Monsoon

- South-West Monsoon begins to retreat from the second or third week of September. Unlike the Sudden burst, the retreat is highly gradual.
- The southerly branch of the jet stream returns to its winter position by October and this is accompanied by the restoration of light North East trade winds to the surface.
- Cloudiness and moisture are low except in the southern parts of the Peninsula. It is this retreating monsoon which brings rain to the Tamil Nadu coast as North East Monsoon.

MECHANISM OF MONSOONS

High temperatures in the months of May and June result in the formation of a low pressure zone along the Indo-Gangetic plains. The axis of this 'monsoon trough', oriented from the north-west to the south-east, shows periodic movements that play an important role in predictions of the monsoons.

The explanations given by Dr P. Koteshwaram and Prof F. Flohn identify an area of rising air motion formed by the atmosphere over the Tibet plateau. Due to the rotation of the earth, the ascending air is deflected to the India west coast as a return current from a south-westerly direction. The air gets laden with moisture as a result of the evaporation process when it moves across the Indian Ocean.

EL NINO AND THE INDIAN MONSOON

El Nino is a warm oceanic current that flows along the western coast of South America, as a temporary replacement of the cold Peru current. The system involves oceanic and atmospheric phenomena with the appearance of warm currents off the coast of Peru in the Eastern Pacific and affects weather in many places including India. It is merely an extension of the warm equatorial current. This results in : (i) the distortion of equatorial atmosphere circulation; (ii) irregularities in the evaporation of sea water; (iii) reduction in the amount of planktons which further reduces the number of fish in the Sea. It is also called the Peru of Humboldt. It is a complex weather system that appears once every three to seven years, bringing drought, floods and other weather extremes to different parts of the world.

SIGNIFICANCE OF MONSOON RAINS

The monsoons are the single largest factor affecting the Indian economy as agriculture is directly dependent upon the monsoon rains. About 53% of the country's cropped area depend upon these rains. The remaining area is also irrigated with rain water stored in tanks and reservoirs. The cropping pattern is also determined by the quantity of rainfall. And so, the erratic nature of the monsoon greatly affects the agricultural output. Rainfall is important for generation of hydro-electricity which makes up for two-fifths of the total power generation.

NATURAL VEGETATION AND WILDLIFE

➡ Natural vegetation in India is influenced by altitude (in the Himalayan region) and rainfall.

➡ On the basis of altitude, the Himalayan region has vegetations of tropical to tundra regions, namely tropical wet-evergreen and semi-evergreen forests, the tropical deciduous, and the thorn forests.

➡ India is the 10th in the world and 4th in Asia in plant diversity. It is one of the 17 'mega-diversity' countries of the world.

➡ India has the two richest bio-diversity spot, one in the Eastern Himalyas and other in the Western Ghats.

➡ India's biological diversity which is estimated to be over 47,000 plant species represents about 7% of the world flora and 6.5% of the world fauna respectively.

➥ The distribution of vegetation in the Himalayas is mostly along the vertical plane. The Shivaliks or the outer Himalayas are covered with tropical moist deciduous flora of which the sal is an important species of economic significance.

➥ The vegetation followed, at higher elevation are evergreen oak, chestnut and some ash and beech. This is a typical subtropical wet hill vegetation.

➥ At higher altitude the vegetation is replaced by chir and chil trees, representative of subtropical moist hill flora.

➥ Pine, cedar, silver fir, and spruce are the most important species found between the altitudes 1,600 metres to 3,300 metres. These conifer trees typical of the dry temperate region found in the inner Himalayan ranges.

Classification of Natural Vegetation

➥ The natural vegetation of India is diverse owing to varied biotic conditions as well as unequal rainfall.

➥ A noteworthy classification of Indian vegetation is given by Champion and Seth who base it on three factors—temperature, altitude and rainfall. They have evolved eight broad types.

1. Tropical Evergreen or Rain Forests

- These are dense forests of luxuriant growth which look evergreen as their trees shed leaves at different times of the year.
- They are prevalent in areas where the annual rainfall is over 200 cm and the average annual humidity exceeds 77 per cent. The annual temperature is 25°C to 27°C on an average.
- Mahogany, Bamboo, Ivory Wood, Ebony, Rubber trees are the economically significant trees of these forests.
- Such forests are found in the north-east, eastern regions of subtropical Himalaya (Tarai), western portions of the Western Ghats and Andaman and Nicobar Islands. The forests are sub-divided as follows:

(a) *Tropical Wet Evergreen Forests:* They are found in areas where the annual rainfall is above 250 cm. The many storeyed forests have an undergrowth of bamboos, ferns, canes and climbers. They contain economically valuable species such as Ebony, Rosewood, Iron wood, Champa, Toon, etc. Such forest is found in the north-eastern states, the Andaman and Nicobar Islands and western parts of the Western Ghats.

(b) *Tropical Semi-Evergreen Forests:* Found in regions where the annual rainfall is below 200 cm, these forests have evergreen trees mixed with deciduous ones. The mean annual temperature in these forests ranges from 24°C to 27°C and humidity is about 80 per cent. Important trees include Champa, Canes, Ferns, Orchids, Rosewood, Benteak, Kadam, Semul, Laurel, etc. These forests occur in regions of upper Assam, lower eastern Himalaya, Odisha, and the Andaman and Nicobars.

(c) *Tropical Moist Deciduous Forests:* Also called the Monsoon forests, they occur where annual rainfall is 150 to 200 cm and the mean annual temperature is about 26-27°C. The forests are characterised by few species and the undergrowth is of canes and bamboos. Humidity varies from

60 to 80 per cent. They are found in the interior of the Indian Plateau and the Sivalik east of the Yamuna river. Sal, Teak, Tendu, Sissoo, Mahua, Sandal, Shisham are the important trees. The trees shed their leaves during spring and early summer.

(d) ***Littoral or Swamp Forests:*** Also called tidal forests, these occur in and around the tidal creeks and along the deltas of the rivers Ganga, Mahanadi, Krishna and Godavari. The trees, mainly evergreen, have profuse growth and stilt-like roots. The densest trees are found in the great Sunderban delta which has the sundari trees in abundance. Rhizophora and Nipa fruiticans (a type of palm) also grow in these forests. On the tropical tide-washed coasts where mud and silt have accumulated, dense mangrove forests flourish.

2. Dry Tropical Forests

- Such forests are mostly prevalent in regions with an annual rainfall of 90 to 130 cm, a mean annual temperature of 23 to 27°C and humidity ranging between 50 and 60 per cent.
- They are subdivided into following types.

(a) ***Tropical Dry Deciduous Forests:*** They run from the Himalayan foothills to Kanyakumari and comprise important trees like Bijasal, Teak, Tendu, Amaltas, Khair, Palas, Rosewood and Axlewood. The tracts of these forests have a low canopy of grasses and shrubs in some places which has been cleared for agriculture or casuarina plantations.

(b) ***Tropical Thorn Forests:*** These are mostly prevalent in those areas where rainfall is very low, i.e., 50 cm to 70 cm, the mean annual temperature is 25°C to 27°C and humidity is rather low, i.e., less than 47 per cent. Kutch, Saurashtra, Punjab, Haryana, Rajasthan, the Upper Ganga plains and the Deccan Plateau consist of such forests. Small trees such as Khair, Babul, Thor, Khejra, Kanju, Ak and Neem are found in these forests.

(c) ***Tropical Dry Evergreen Forests:*** From Tamil Nadu to Nellore, such type of forests cover areas where the mean rainfall is about 100 cm, the annual temperature is 28°C and the mean annual humidity is 74 per cent. Trees are 12 m high with canopies. Bamboos are rare and the grass is not conspicuous. The important species of trees are Khirni, Jamun, Kokko, Toddy Palm, Casuarina, Neem, Cane, etc.

3. Riparian Forests

- They are common in wet places particularly along river banks and other wetlands where rainfall is less than 50 cm.
- Short trees and grasses such as Munj and Kans are abundant. Neem, Shisham, Pipal, Babul, Tamarind are common in such regions.

4. Subtropical Broad Leaved Hill Forests

- Such forests are common in the highlands of Bastar, Pachmari, Palani Hills, Khasi Hills on the lower slopes of the Himalaya in Assam and West Bengal.

- The mean annual temperature is about 18°C to 21°C, the mean annual rainfall is about 75 to 125 cm and the humidity is 80 per cent.
- With an abundance of evergreen trees, these forests are called Shola forests in southern India.

5. Montane Wet Temperate Forests

- Generally at a height of 1800-3000 m above sea level especially in the hills of Kerala, Tamil Nadu and the eastern Himalaya, the forests occur in regions with a mean annual temperature of about 11°C to 14°C and a mean annual rainfall of 150 to 300 cm.
- The important trees are Oaks, Magnolia, Chilauni, Birch, Plum, Michilus, Deodar and Hemlock.

6. Montane Moist Temperate Forests

- Such type of forests occur in the temperate eastern and western Himalaya, i.e., in Jammu and Kashmir, Himachal Pradesh, Punjab, Uttarakhand, Sikkim and Darjeeling.
- They are mainly composed of coniferous species generally 30 to 50 m high Mosses and ferns that grow on trees.
- The important trees are Pine, Deodar, Silver Fir, Oak, Beach, Rhododendrons, Maple, etc.

7. Alpine Forests

- As the name suggests, these forests cover the Alpine areas in the Himalayas, i.e., at a height of 2880 m to 3700 m.
- They constitute dwarf shrubs of Juniper, Fir, Pine, Birch and Rhododendrons. On the southern Himalayan slopes, the Alpine forests degenerate into a low evergreen scrub.
- On the northern slopes of the Himalaya, they represent a dry, xerophytic vegetation.

8. Grasslands

- Though the Indian grasslands are not comparable to the savanna or steppe, they do occur on wet soil ground and in the sal belt and some hilly areas.
- They are sub-divided as follows.

  (a) ***Low-land Grasses :*** Occurring in regions receiving 31 to 200 cm of rainfall where the temperature is high during summers, they are found in the plains of upper India—Punjab, Uttar Pradesh, Haryana, Bihar and north-west Assam. These grasses grow on different soil type and are suitable for cattle-breeding.

  (b) ***Upland or Hilly Grasses :*** They are found at a height of over 1,000 m in the Himalaya and in the cleared forest areas of the Western Ghats in the Karnataka region. They are found among small tracts of Shola forests in South India.

  (c) ***Riverine Grasses :*** Found in the northern part of India, they form the Bhabar pastures which are important grazing grounds for buffaloes and cattle.

Wildlife Reserves and National Parks

➡ The wildlife reserves in India may broadly be classified in two types: National Parks and Wildlife sanctuaries.

➡ Wildlife Sanctuaries have the special purpose of preserving animals and birds. National Parks protect the entire ecosystem.

Famous National Parks in India

State/UT	National Parks
Andaman and Nicobar Islands	Campbell Bay, Galathea Bay, Mahatma Gandhi Marine Wandoor, Middle Button Island, Mount Harriett, North Button Island, Rani Jhansi Marine, Saddle Peak, South Button Island
Andhra Pradesh	Papikonda, Rajiv Gandhi (Rameswaram), Sri Venkateswara
Arunachal Pradesh	Mouling, Namdapha
Assam	Dibru-Saikhowa, Kaziranga, Manas, Nameri, Rajiv Gandhi Orang
Bihar	Valmiki
Chhattisgarh	Guru Ghasidas (Sanjay), Indravati (Kutru), Kanger Valley
Goa	Mollem
Gujarat	Vansda, Blackbuck (Velavadar), Gir, Marine (Gulf of Kachchh)
Haryana	Kalesar, Sultanpur
Himachal Pradesh	Great Himalayan, Inderkillam, Khirganga, Pin Valley, Simbalbara
Jammu & Kashmir	City Forest (Salim Ali), Dachigam, Hemis, Kishtwar
Jharkhand	Betla
Karnataka	Anshi, Bandipur, Bannerghatta, Kudremukh, Nagarahole (Rajiv Gandhi)
Kerala	Anamudi Shola, Eravikulam, Mathikettan Shola, Pambadum Shola, Periyar, Silent Valley
Madhya Pradesh	Bandhavgarh, Fossil, Kanha, Madhav, Panna, Indira Priyadarshini Pench, Sanjay, Satpura, Van Vihar
Maharashtra	Chandoli, Gugamal, Nawegaon, Pench (Jawaharlal Nehru), Sanjay Gandhi (Borivilli), Tadoba.
Manipur	Keibul-Lamjao
Meghalaya	Balphakram, Nokrek Ridge
Mizoram	Murlen, Phawngpui Blue Mountain
Nagaland	Intanki
Odisha	Bhitarkanika, Simlipal
Rajasthan	Mukundra Hills, Desert, Keoladeo Ghana, Ranthambhore, Sariska
Sikkim	Khangchendzonga
Tamil Nadu	Guindy, Gulf of Mannar Marine, Indira Gandhi (Annamalai), Mudumalai, Mukurthi
Telangana	Kasu Brahmananda Reddy, Mahaveer Harina Vanasthali, Mrugavani.
Tripura	Clouded Leopard, Bison (Rajbari)
Uttar Pradesh	Dudhwa
Uttarakhand	Corbett, Gangotri, Govind, Nanda Devi, Rajaji, Valley of Flowers
West Bengal	Buxa, Gorumara, Jaldapara, Neora Valley, Singalila, Sunderban

Famous Wildlife Sanctuaries in India

State/UT	Wildlife Sanctuaries
Andhra Pradesh	Kolleru Lake, Nagarjuna Sagar, Sri Venkateswara, Pulicat
Arunachal Pradesh	Mehao
Assam	Sonai, Rupai, Pabha

State/UT	Wildlife Sanctuaries
Bihar	Kaimur, Bhimbandha
Chhattisgarh	Sitanadi
Gujarat	Narayan Sarovar, (Wild Ass) Nal Sarovar
Haryana	Sultanpur
Himachal Pradesh	Kugti, Rupi Bhawa, Govind Sagar
Jammu and Kashmir	Karakoram, Ramnagar
Jharkhand	Hazaribagh, Dalma
Karnataka	Ghatprabha, Dandili, Sharavathi, Ranganathittu, Ranebennur
Kerala	Waynad, Mudimalai, Idukki
Madhya Pradesh	Panchmarhi, Gandhi Sagar
Maharashtra	Koyna, Chandoli, Radhanagari, Karnala, Gautalu, Yaval, Melghat
Mizoram	Murien
Nagaland	Fakim
Odisha	Ushakothi, Karlapat, Chilka Lake, Bhittarkanika
Punjab	Govind Sagar, Abohar, Harike
Rajasthan	Mount Abu
Tamil Nadu	Mundanthurai, Kodikkarai, Indira Gandhi, Vedantangal
Telangana	Kawal, Eturnagram, Papikonda.
Tripura	Trishna
Uttarakhand	Kedarnath
Uttar Pradesh	Katernighat, Sohagbarwa, Ranipur, Chandraprabha
West Bengal	Jaldapara

SOILS

- India has varied relief features, landforms, climatic realms and vegetation types. These have contributed in the development of various types of soils in India.
- On the basis of genesis, colour, composition and location, the soils of India have been classified into:
  - Alluvial soils
  - Black soils
  - Red and Yellow soils
  - Laterite soils
  - Arid soils
  - Saline soils
  - Peaty soils
  - Forest soils.

Alluvial Soils

- Alluvial soils are widespread in the northern plains and the river valleys. These soils cover about 45 per cent of the total area of the country.
- They are depositional soils, transported and deposited by rivers and streams. Through a narrow corridor in Rajasthan, they extend into the plains of Gujarat.
- In the Peninsular region, they are found in deltas of the east coast and in the river valleys.
- The alluvial soils vary in nature from sandy loam to clay. They are generally rich in potash but poor in phosphorous.

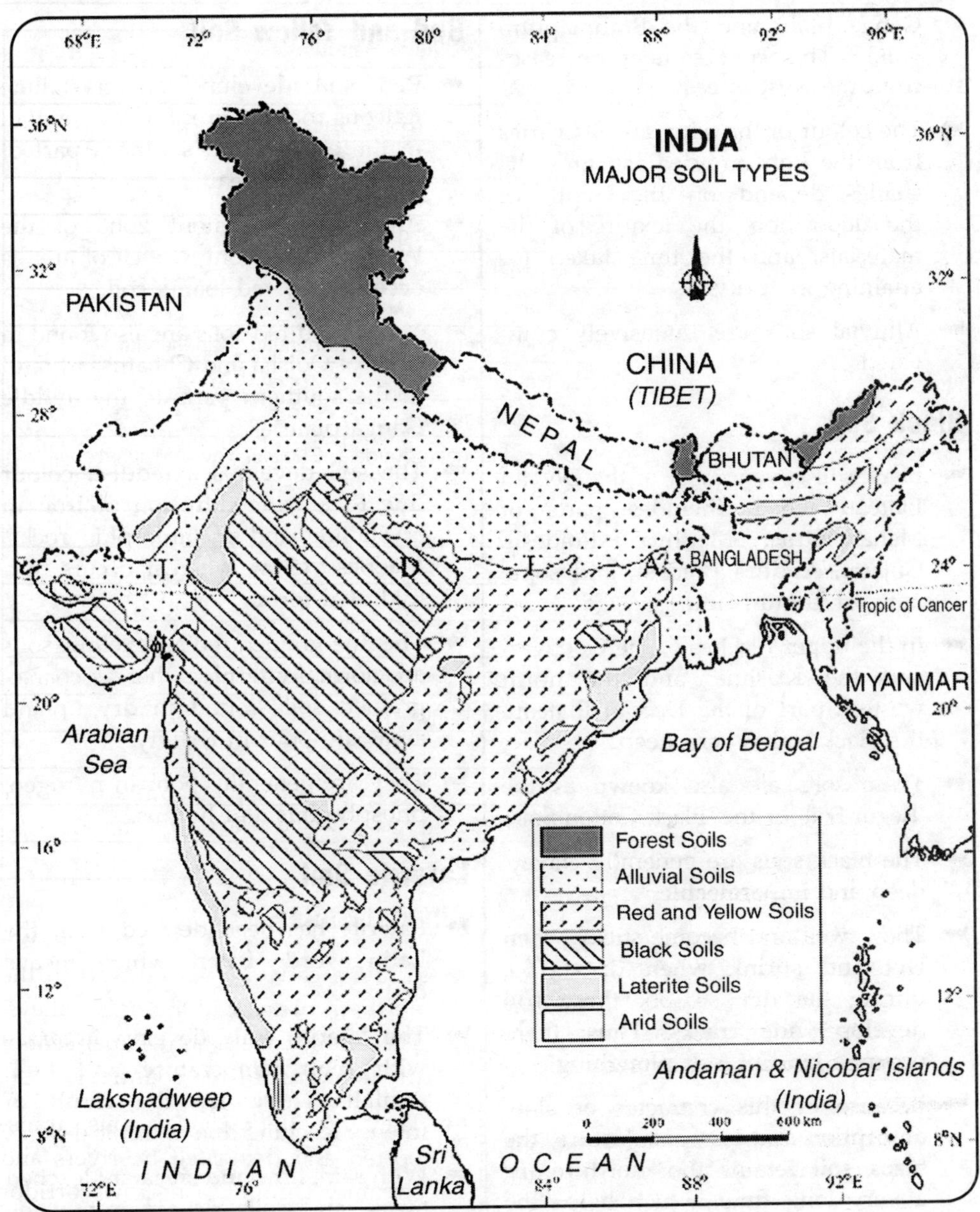

- In the Upper and Middle Ganga plain, two different types of alluvial soils have developed, viz. ***Khadar*** and ***Bhangar***.
- ***Khadar*** is the new alluvium and is deposited by floods annually, which enriches the soil by depositing fine silts.
- ***Bhangar*** represents a system of older alluvium, deposited away from the flood plains.
- Both the Khadar and Bhangar soils contain calcareous concretions (Kankars).
- These soils are more loamy and clayey in the lower and middle

Ganga plain and the Brahmaputra valley. The sand content decreases from the west to east.

- The colour of the alluvial soils varies from the light grey to ash grey. Its shades depend on the depth of the deposition, the texture of the materials, and the time taken for attaining maturity.
- Alluvial soils are intensively cultivated.

Black Soil

- Black soil covers most of the Deccan Plateau which includes parts of Maharashtra, Madhya Pradesh, Gujarat, Andhra Pradesh and some parts of Tamil Nadu.
- In the upper reaches of the Godavari and the Krishna, and the north western part of the Deccan Plateau, the black soil is very deep.
- These soils are also known as the 'Regur Soil' or the 'Black Cotton Soil'.
- The black soils are generally clayey, deep and impermeable.
- They swell and become sticky when wet and shrink when dried. So, during the dry season, these soil develop wide cracks. Thus, there occurs a kind of 'self ploughing'.
- Because of this character of slow absorption and loss of moisture, the black soil retains the moisture for a very long time, which helps the crops, especially, the rain fed ones, to sustain even during the dry season.
- Chemically, the black soils are rich in lime, iron, magnesia and alumina. They also contain potash. But they lack in phosphorous, nitrogen and organic matter.
- The colour of the soil ranges from deep black to grey.

Red and Yellow Soil

- Red soil develops on crystalline igneous rocks in areas of low rainfall in the eastern and southern part of the Deccan Plateau.
- Along the piedmont zone of the Western Ghat, long stretch of area is occupied by red loamy soil.
- Yellow and red soils are also found in parts of Odisha and Chhattisgarh and in the southern parts of the middle Ganga plain.
- The soil develops a reddish colour due to a wide diffusion of iron in crystalline and metamorphic rocks. It looks yellow when it occurs in a hydrated form.
- The fine-grained red and yellow soils are normally fertile, whereas coarse-grained soils found in dry upland areas are poor in fertility.
- They are generally poor in nitrogen, phosphorous and humus.

Laterite Soil

- Laterite has been derived from the Latin word 'Later' which means brick.
- The laterite soils develop in areas with high temperature and high rainfall. These are the result of intense leaching due to tropical rains.
- With rain, lime and silica are leached away, and soils rich in iron oxide and aluminium compound are left behind.
- Humus content of the soil is removed fast by bacteria that thrives well in high temperature.
- These soils are poor in organic matter, nitrogen, phosphate and calcium, while iron oxide and potash are in excess.

- Hence, laterites are not suitable for cultivation; however, application of manures and fertilisers are required for making the soils fertile for cultivation.
- Red laterite soils in Tamil Nadu, Andhra Pradesh and Kerala are more suitable for tree crops like cashewnut.
- The laterite soils are commonly found in Karnataka, Kerala, Tamil Nadu, Madhya Pradesh and the hilly areas of Odisha and Assam.

Arid Soils

- Arid soils range from red to brown in colour. They are generally sandy in structure and saline in nature. In some areas, the salt content is so high that common salt is obtained by evaporating the saline water.
- Due to the dry climate, high temperature and accelerated evaporation, they lack moisture and humus.
- Nitrogen is insufficient and the phosphate content is normal.
- Arid soils are characteristically developed in western Rajasthan, which exhibit characteristic arid topography.
- These soils are poor and contain little humus and organic matter.

Saline Soils

- They are also known as Usara soils.
- Saline soils contain a larger proportion of sodium, potassium and magnesium, and thus, they are infertile, and do not support any vegetative growth. They have more salts, largely because of dry climate and poor drainage.
- They occur in arid and semi-arid regions, and in waterlogged and swampy areas. Their structure ranges from sandy to loamy.
- They lack in nitrogen and calcium.
- Saline soils are more widespread in western Gujarat, deltas of the eastern coast and in Sunderban areas of West Bengal.
- In the Rann of Kuchchh, the Southwest Monsoon brings salt particles and deposits there as a crust.
- Seawater intrusions in the deltas promote the occurrence of saline soils.
- In the areas of intensive cultivation with excessive use of irrigation, especially in areas of green revolution, the fertile alluvial soils are becoming saline.
- Excessive irrigation with dry climatic conditions promotes capillary action, which results in the deposition of salt on the top layer of the soil.
- In such areas, especially in Punjab and Haryana, farmers are advised to add gypsum to solve the problem of salinity in the soil.

Peaty Soils

- They are found in the areas of heavy rainfall and high humidity, where there is a good growth of vegetation. Thus, large quantity of dead organic matter accumulates in these areas, and this gives a rich humus and organic content to the soil. Organic matter in these soils may go even up to 40-50 per cent.
- These soils are normally heavy and black in colour. At many places, they are alkaline also.
- It occurs widely in the northern part of Bihar, southern part of Uttarakhand and the coastal areas of West Bengal, Odisha and Tamil Nadu.

Forest Soils

- As the name suggests, forest soils are formed in the forest areas where sufficient rainfall is available.
- The soils vary in structure and texture depending on the mountain environment where they are formed.
- They are loamy and silty on valley sides and coarse-grained in the upper slopes.
- In the snow-bound areas of the Himalayas, they experience denudation, and are acidic with low humus content. The soils found in the lower valleys are fertile.

AGRICULTURE

Agricultural Seasons

India has three cropping seasons.

- **Kharif Crops:** These are the crops which are sown at the beginning of the South West monsoon season (June to July) and are harvested at the end of the same season (September and October). Major crops grown in this season include rice, jowar, barja, groundnut, jute, cotton, sesamum, some pulses such as moong, urad etc.
- **Rabi Crops:** These are the crops sown at the beginning of the cold season (October to December) and harvested at the beginning of the warm season (March to April). They include wheat, gram, barley, potatoes, jowar, oil seeds such as linseed, rape, and mustard.
- **Zaid:** It is categorised into two groups:
  - **Zaid Kharif Crops:** These are sown in August and September and are harvested in December and January. Most of the oil seeds like mustard are grown in this season.
  - **Zaid Rabi Crops:** These crops are sown at the beginning of the hot season in February and March and are harvested in the months of April and May. Summer vegetables and fodder crops like jowar, maize, water melons, cucumbers etc. are important among these crops.

Major Crops

1. Rice

- **Temperature:** Early growing stage 16°C-20°C. Ripening stage 18°C-32°C
- **Rainfall:** 150-300 cm (heavy).
- **Soil:** Alluvial soil with clayey sub-soil
- **Area and State:** Telangana, W. Bengal, Uttar Pradesh, Punjab, Andhra Pradesh, Bihar, Odisha, Karnataka, Assam, Maharashtra
- **Highest yield:** West Bengal

2. Wheat

- **Temperature:** Early growing stage 10°C-15°C. Ripening stage 25°C-28°C
- **Rainfall:** 50 cm-100 cm
- **Soil:** Well drained, heavy textured soil with lime. Grows well on alluvial and black soil.
- **Area and State:** Uttar Pradesh, Madhya Pradesh, Punjab.

3. Maize

- **Temperature:** 21°C-27°C cannot stands frost at any stage.
- **Rainfall:** 50 cm-100 cm, Sunshine promotes growth. Cool, dry conditions necessary at ripening stage.
- **Soil:** Nitrogen-rich loamy soil
- **Area and State:** Karnataka, Bihar, Maharashtra, Telangana, Madhya Pradesh.

4. Millets

- **Temperature:** 27°C-32°C Survives high temperatures and drought conditions.
- **Rainfall:** 50 cm-120 cm, knowns as "drop crop" does not require much rain
- **Soil:** Can be grown in less fertile soil where rice cannot be grown.
- **Area and State:** Jowar and Bajra grown in Maharashtra, Karnataka, A.P., M.P., T.N., U.P., Gujarat, Rajasthan.

5. Pulses

- **Temperature:** 20°C-30°C
- **Rainfall:** 50-75 cm
- **Soil:** Dry, light soil
- **Area and State:** Madhya Pradesh, Maharashtra, Rajasthan, Uttar Pradesh.

6. Sugarcane

- **Temperature:** Grows best in areas with temperature between 20°C to 28°C.
- **Rainfall:** A long rainy season is required. Dry winter season during rpening and harvesting is ideal.
- **Soil:** Needs deep fertile soils, which are water retentive, usually grown on flat or undulating lowlands.
- **Area and State:** Uttar Pradesh, Maharashtra, Karnataka, Tamil Nadu, Andhra Pradesh and Gujarat.

7. Cotton

- **Temperature:** Temperature about 25°C or more is ideal, plenty of sunshine during the growing period is essential.
- **Rainfall:** Between 510 mm and 1115 mm. is required, better crop can be grown in semi-arid conditions.
- **Soil:** Medium Loams with good drainage are ideal. Soil especially suited for cotton growing is black cotton soils of the north west Deccan in India.
- **Area and State:** Gujarat produces most of the cotton in India, followed by Maharashtra, Telangana, Tamil Nadu, Madhya Pradesh, Karnataka and Chhattisgarh.

8. Jute

- **Temperature:** Temperature between 27°-30°C, growing period is three to four months, grows well in hot tropical conditions.
- **Rainfall:** Between 1150 mm and 2400 mm is needed.
- **Soil:** Requires rich river alluvial soil, especially where annual floods renew the fertility of the soil.
- **Area and State:** India ranks top in both the production and area. Most of its production comes from West Bengal, other producers are Bihar, Assam, Odisha, Uttar Pradesh and Tripura.

9. Tea

- **Temperature:** Temperature of over 21°C during the growing season.
- **Rainfall:** Between 1270 mm and 6350 mm. with no prolonged dry season.
- **Soil:** Well-drained, loamy or forest soil rich in organic matter, slightly acidic and without calcium.
- **Area and State:** India is the second leading producer of tea after China. Main tea growing areas are Darjeeling in West Bengal, the Brahmaputra valley in Assam and the Nilgiris in the south.

10. Coffee

- **Temperature:** Between 14°C to 26°C, mean monthly temperature should not drop below 11°C.
- **Rainfall:** Requires 1,016 mm to 2,030 mm rain fall, but willl not tolerate stagnant water.
- **Soil:** Well-drained volcanic soils are the best.
- **Area and State:** It is grown in Karnataka, Kerala and Tamil Nadu on the hill of Nilgiris, Cardamom, Palni and Annamalai. It is also grown on a limited scale in some non-traditional areas in Odisha, West Bengal, Assam and Madhya Pradesh.

11. Rubber

- **Temperature:** Requires constant high temperature of around 27°C, which should not fall below 21°C.
- **Rainfall:** Rainfall should be 1525 mm. to 2540 mm, it should be evenly distributed through the year.
- **Soil:** Deep, friable, well drained soils are ideal as they promote root development.
- **Area and State:** Thailand is the largest single producer. In India, Kerala is a leading producer. Kerala is followed by Tamil Nadu, Karnataka, Andman Nicobar and Assam.

12. Vegetables

- Vegetables constitute the most important food next only to cereals and milk. Important vegetable crops grown in the country are potato, tomato, onion, brinjal, cabbage, cauliflower, okra peas.
- India occupies second position in the production of cauliflower, onion, brinjal, cabbage, potato and tomato production in the world and contributes about 13% of the world's vegetable production.

13. Flowers

- Flower cultivation has been practised in India to generate income and employment opportunities, promote enhancement of exports.
- It has been identified as an Extreme Focus Area for exports such as jasmine, marigold, chrysanthemum, tuberose, crossandra and aster.
- Commerical cultivation of cut floweres such as rose, orchids, galdiolus, carnation, anthurium, gerbera and lilies has also become popular.

IRRIGATION

- Irrigation in India is very important in view of the overwhelming significance of agriculture in the national economy and the unpredictability of the monsoon.
- The country has good resources for irrigation in the form of groundwater and surface sources such as rivers. Both types of sources are used extensively.
- The country has an irrigation potential of about 140 million hectares.

Means of Irrigation

Wells & Tubewells

- Wells form the most widely distributed source of irrigation in India and account for more than 46 per cent of the net irrigated area.
- Well irrigation is more important in the Great Plains, the delta regions of the Mahanadi, the Godavari, the Krishna and the Kaveri, and the

weathered areas of the peninsular region in the Narmada and Tapti valleys. Gujarat, Maharashtra, Uttar Pradesh, Punjab and Haryana are important states where tubewell irrigation is practiced.

- In Madhya Pradesh, Karnataka and Tamil Nadu too land is irrigated by wells.

Tanks

- The tanks are a common source of irrigation in the peninsular region.
- West Bengal, Bihar and Odisha also have several irrigation tanks of the excavated type, in contrast to the more or less natural depressions of the peninsular region.
- This means of irrigation accounts for only about eight per cent of the net irrigated area in India.
- This means of irrigation can be most successfully employed only in areas having natural depressions where rainwater can be accumulated.
- Tank irrigation is more common in the Karnataka plateau, eastern Madhya Pradesh, Chhattisgarh, interior Odisha, interior Andhra Pradesh and Tamil Nadu.

Canals

- Although canal irrigation was introduced only in the last century, this means of irrigation has already become the most important among all means of irrigation.
- Ideal conditions for development of this means of irrigation include level land and presence of perennial rivers from which the canals can be taken out.
- Canals account for more than 24 per cent of net irrigated area in India.
- About half the net canal-irrigated area lies in Uttar Pradesh, Punjab, Haryana and Andhra Pradesh, and the rest mostly in West Bengal, Tamil Nadu, Bihar, Rajasthan, Karnataka and Maharashtra.

Major Power and Irrigation Projects

S.No.	Name of the Project	Location	State	Purpose
1.	Nagarjuna Sagar multipurpose project	River Krishna	AP, Telangana	Irrigation, Hydro-electricity
2.	Pochampad project	River Godavari	AP, Telangana	Irrigation
3.	Lower Sileru project	River Sileru (Godavari)	AP, Telangana	Hydro-electricity
4.	Kakarpara project	River Tapi,	Gujarat	Irrigation
5.	Kothagudam project	Singareni coalfields	AP, Telangana	Thermal power
6.	Kosi project	River Kosi	Bihar, Nepal	Flood control, Irrigation, Hydro-electricity
7.	Gandak project	River Gandak	UP, Bihar	Irrigation, Hydro-electricity
8.	Dhuvaran power Station	Kheda district	Gujarat	Thermal power
9.	Sabarigiri (Pamba Kakki) project	River Pamba-Kakki	Kerala	Hydro-electricity
10.	Idukki project	Rivers Periyar Cheutheni, Idukki	Kerala	Hydro-electricity

S.No.	Name of the Project	Location	State	Purpose
11.	Chambal project	River Chambal	Rajasthan, MP	Irrigation, Hydro-electricity
12.	Tawa project	River Tawa (Narmada)	MP	Irrigation
13.	Korba project	near Korba coalfields	Chhattisgarh	Thermal power
14.	Satpura power station	Patharkada coalfields	MP	Thermal power
15.	Koyna project	River Koyna	Maharashtra	Hydro-electricity
16.	Nagpur power station	Koradi, near Nagpur city	Maharashtra	Thermal power
17.	Tungabhadra multipurpose project	River Tungabhadra	Karnataka, AP	Irrigation, Hydro-electricity
18.	Upper Krishna project	River Krishna	Karnataka	Irrigation
19.	Sharavati project	River Sharavati near Jog Falls	Karnataka	Hydro-electricity
20.	Hirakud multipurpose project	River Mahanadi	Odisha	Irrigation, Hydro-electricity
21.	Mahanadi Delta project	River Mahanadi	Odisha	Irrigation
22.	Talcher power station	near Talchar	Odisha	Thermal power
23.	Bhakra-Nangal multipurpose project	River Sutlej	HP, Punjab Haryana	Irrigation, Hydro-electricity
24.	Rajasthan Canal project	River Sutlej in Punjab	Rajasthan Headworks in Punjab	Irrigation
25.	Kundah project	River Kundah	Tamil Nadu	Hydro-electricity
26.	Neyveli power station	Neyveli	Tamil Nadu	Thermal power
27.	Ramganga multi-purpose project	Chuisot stream near Kalagarh	Uttarakhand	Irriigation, Hydro-electricity
28.	Matatilla multi-purpose project	River Betwa	UP, MP	Irrigation, Hydro-electricity
29.	Rihand scheme	River Rihand	UP	Hydro-electricity
30.	Obra power station	Obra	UP	Thermal power
31.	Damodar Valley project	River Damodar	Jharkhand, shared with West Bengal	Flood control, irrigation, Hydro-electricity
32.	Ukai project	River Tapi	Gujarat	Irrigation

S.No.	Name of the Project	Location	State	Purpose
33.	Mahi project	River Mahi	Gujarat	Irrigation
34.	Ghataprabha project	River Ghataprabha	AP and Karnataka	Irrigation
35.	Bhima project	River Bhima	Maharashtra	Irrigation
36.	Sardar Sarowar project	River Narmada	Gujarat and MP	Irrigation and Hydro-electicity
37.	Banasagar project	River Son	MP, Chhattisgarh, UP and Jharkhand	Irrigation
38.	Dul Hasti project	River Chenab	Jammu & Kashmir	Hydro-electricity
39.	Salal project	River Chenab	Jammu & Kashmir	Hydro-electricity
40.	Thein Dam project	River Ravi	Punjab	Irrigation, hydro-electricity
41.	Malaprabha project	River Malaprabha	Karnataka	Irrigation
42.	Jayakwadi project	River Godavari	Maharashtra	Irrigation
43.	Beas project	River Beas	Punjab & Haryana	Hydro-electricity
44.	Sharda Shayak	River Ghaghra	UP	Irrigation
45.	Mayurakshi project	River Mayurakshi	W Bengal	Irrigation, Hydro-electricity
46.	Rana Partap Sagar project	River Chambal	Rajasthan	Hydro-electricity
47.	Suratgarh Super-Thermal Project	Suratgarh	Rajasthan	Thermal Power
48.	Mettur	River Kaveri	Tamil Nadu	Hydro-electricity
49.	Pallivasal	River Mundirapujha	Kerala	Hydro-electricity
50.	Papanasam Project	River Tambiraparani	Tamil Nadu	Hydro-electricity
51.	Loktak Project	Lake Loktak	Manipur	Hydro-electricity
52.	Tehri Project	River Bhilangana (Ganga)	Uttarakhand	Hydro-electricity
53.	Farakka Project	Ganga	West Bengal	Irrigation
54.	Damanganga	River Damanganga	Gujarat	Irrigation and river link
55.	Girna	River Girna	Maharashtra	Irrigation and river link
56.	Pamba	River Pamba	Kerala	River conservation and irrigation
57.	Tapovan-Vishnugarh	River Alaknanda	Uttarakhand	Hydro-electricity
58.	Omkareshwar	River Narmada	Madhya Pradesh	Hydro-power and irrigation

MINERAL RESOURCES

- India is rich in mineral resources. But these are not equally distributed in the country.
- Most of the mineral resources found in the area of Deccan plateau, Chhattisgarh, Jharkhand, Madhya Pradesh, Odisha, Karnataka, Maharashtra and Tamil Nadu.

Important Minerals

Iron Ore

- China is the largest producer in the world. India ranks fourth in production.
- India produces four types of iron ores, Haematite, Magnetite, Limonite and Siderite.
- Karnataka has the Largest reserve of Magnetite ore followed by Odisha, Jharkhand, Chhattisgarh and Andhra Pradesh.
- Odisha has the largest reserve of haematite followed by Jharkhand, Chhattisgarh and Karnataka.
  - **Odisha:** In Odisha main producing areas are Mayurbhanj, Keonjhar and Sundargarh.
  - **Chhattisgarh:** Dantewada, Bastar, Durg, Rajnadgaon, Raigarh, and Bilaspur districts are main producers.
  - **Karnataka:** Important areas are—Bellary, Chitradurga (Bababudan Hills) Chikmaglur, Bijapur, Dharwad, Tumkur and Shimoga districts.
  - **Jharkhand:** Major producers are Noamundi and Gua in Singhbhum, Daltonganj in Palamau.
  - **Andhra Pradesh and Telangana:** Anantpur, Khammam, Krishna, Kurnool, Cuddapha and Nellore.
  - **Goa:** Pirna adol, Tolsia, Borgadogar, and Rivora are important regions, minings are open and mechanised, mainly exported to Japan.

Manganese

- Occur mainly in the Dharwar system of rocks.
- Odisha has the highest reserve followed by Karnataka, Madhya Pradesh, Maharashtra, and Goa.
- Odisha is the leading producer followed by Maharashtra, Madhya Pradesh and Karnataka.
  - **Odisha:** Keonjhar, Sundargarh, Koraput, Kalahandi and Bolangir.
  - **Maharashtra:** Main regions are—Nagpur-Bhandara Belt, and Ratnagiri.
  - **Madhya Pradesh:** Balaghat, Chhindwara, Jabalpur and Jhabua.
  - **Karnataka:** Bellary, Uttar kannad, Shimoga, Tumkur and Belgaum.
  - **Jharkhand:** Birmitrapur in Chaibasa, Singhbhum, Hazaribagh and Dhanbad districts.

Copper

- Important non-ferrous metal, earliest metal used by man.
- Highest reserve in Rajasthan followed by Madhya Pradesh, Jharkhand, Andhra Pradesh and Gujarat.
- Madhya Pradesh is largest producer followed by Rajasthan.
  - **Madhya Pradesh:** Malajkhand in Balaghat district, Sidhi and Jabalpur.
  - **Rajasthan:** Khetri Belt in Aravalli range, Kho Dariba near Alwar, Delwara and Debari in Udaipur districts are important mining centres.
  - **Jharkhand:** Mosabani, Rakha and Ghatshila.

- **Andhra Pradesh & Telangana:** Agnigumdala belt near Guntur.

Bauxite

➡ Mainly spread over the eastern ghats.

➡ Scattered in Laterite rocks.

➡ Odisha ranks first in reserve followed by Andhra Pradesh, Gujarat, Chhattisgarh and Maharashtra.

➡ Odisha is the largest producer followed by Gujarat, Jharkhand and Maharashtra.

- **Odisha:** More than half of country's production comes from this state alone. Kalahandi-Koraput belt is famous for its production.
- **Gujarat:** Another important producer in the country. Bhavnagar-Junagarh–Amreli Belt is the main region.
- **Jharkhand:** Ranchi, Palamau, Lohardaga and Muri.
- **Maharashtra:** production comes mainly from-Kolhapur, Ratnagiri, Thane, Satara and Kolaba.

Lead

➡ It occurs in the cambrian rocks and the vindhayan sediments.

- **Rajasthan:** Reserves 88.61 per cent of the country's total mainly from the Zawar region of Udaipur. Other areas in Rajasthan include Rajpura-Dariba area of Bhilwara, Ajmer, Alwar, Banswara and Sawai Madhopur.
- **Andhra Pradesh and Telangana:** Cuddapah, Guntur and Kurnool.
- **Odisha:** Sambalpur, Kalahandi and Sundargarh.

Zinc

➡ Sphalerite is the chief ore.

➡ Largely used for galvanising or coating iron and steel.

- **Rajasthan** has a monopoly in zinc production. Main areas are–Zawar in Udaipur district. This area has two main zones of mineralisation.
  (*i*) Pipli mine to Barla mine
  (*ii*) Mochia Magra, Balaria.
- Other producing areas are Bhilwara, Ajmer, Alwar and Sawai Madhopur.

➡ Bhotang of Sikkim, Riasi of Jammu and Kashmir, Almora and Tehri Garhwal of Uttarakhand are other producing areas of the country.

Gold

➡ Karnataka is the largest producer of gold in the country. It has a monopoly in production of gold. Kolar, Hutti in Rachur and Gulbarga are main gold fields.

➡ Ramagiri in Andhra Pradesh

➡ Nilgiri and Coimbatore in Tamil Nadu

➡ Singhbhum in Jharkhand

➡ Kozhikode in Kerala

➡ Largest resources of gold ore (primamy) are located in Bihar, followed by Karnataka, Rajasthan, West Bengal, Andhra Pradesh and Madhya Pradesh.

Silver

➡ Silver is found in the galena ores that may have up to one per cent of the metalic mineral.

➡ Zawar mines in Udaipur, **Rajasthan**

➡ **Andhra Pradesh including Telangana** is one of the main producers of silver in the country. Guntur, Cuddapah, and Kurnool districts are important producers.

➡ **Jharkhand** including Bihar is the other important producer of silver.

Singhbhum, Dhanbad and Dumka Districts are important producers.

- Vadodara in **Gujarat**, and
- Baramula in **Jammu and Kashmir**.

Mica

- India is the most important mica producing country in the world and it supplies 80 per cent of the world requirements of black mica.
- **Andhra Pradesh (including Telangana)** is the largest producer of mica in the country. Mica is extracted from Nellore in Gudur district. Kalichedu, Kalyanarama, Sitaram, Pallimita and Basayar are important mines. In less quantity it is found in Krishna, Visha, Khapatanam, and Anantpur districts.
- **Rajasthan** is the second largest producer in the country. Jaipur, Udaipur, Bhilwana, and Ajmer are important producers.
- In **Jharkhand** Mica is extracted from the Hazaribagh belt with Koderma. High quality mica is produced in Koderma district.
  - Gaya, Mungyr and Bhagalpur in **Bihar**
  - Hasan and Mysore in **Karnataka**.
  - Bastar and Bilaspur in **Chhattisgarh**
  - Balaghat and Chhindwara in **M.P.**
  - Ratnagiri in **Maharashtra**
  - Koraput, Mayurbhanj and Ganjam in **Odisha**.

Diamond

- Found in scattered crystals in an igneous rock called Kimberlite, also come from alluvial sources.
- Panna Belt of Madhya Pradesh, Raipur of Chhattisgarh and Kurnool in Anantpur district of Andhra Pradesh, are important producers.

Graphite

- Also called black lead, graphite occurs along with metamorphic rock.
- Odisha, Arunachal Pradesh, Jammu & Kashmir, Jharkhand and Tamil Nadu possesses more reserve.

Gypsum

- A hydrated calcium sulphate found in the sedimentary rocks.
- Jodhpur region of Rajasthan, Coimbatore in Tamil Nadu, Gujarat and Uttarakhand are important producing regions.

Magnesite

- A refractory mineral, one of the important minerals of magnesium.
- A substantial quantities of resources are established in Uttarakhand, Rajasthan, Tamil Nadu, Andhra Pradesh, Himachal Pradesh and Jammu & Kashmir.

Lime stone

- Found in rocks constituting calcium carbonate.
- Karnataka is the leading state followed by Andhra Pradesh, Gujarat, Rajasthan, Meghalaya, Chhattisgarh, Madhya Pradesh and Odisha.

Dolomite

- Mainly produced in Chhattisgarh (Durg), Madhya Pradesh, Andhra Pradesh and Odisha (Birmitrapur, Bildih and Khatepur).

INDUSTRY

Iron and Steel Industry

- The location of iron and steel industry in India has been primarily influenced by considerations of transportational costs in procuring raw materials such as iron ore, coal and limestone.

➥ The country's richest iron ore deposits lie in the iron belt extending from Gurumahisani Hills in the Mayurbhanj region in Odisha to Singhbhum district of Jharkhand.

➥ Coal is another important raw material for the iron and steel industry. Raniganj (West Bengal) and Jharia (Jharkhand) have abundance of good quality coal.

Steel Plants in India

Name	Location	Owner
Tata Iron and Steel Corporation (TISCO)	Jamshedpur (Jharkhand)	Tata Steel
Visvesvaraya Iron and Steel Plant	Bhadravati (Karnataka)	SAIL
Bhilai Steel Plant	Chhattisgarh	SAIL
Durgapur Steel Plant	Durgapur (West Bengal)	SAIL
Bokaro Steel Plant	Jharkhand	SAIL
Chandrapur Ferro Alloy Plant	Chandrapur (Maharashtra)	SAIL
IISCO Steel Plant	Asansol (West Bengal)	SAIL
Salem Steel Plant	Tamil Nadu	SAIL
Rourkela Steel Plant	Odisha	SAIL
Vijaynagar Steel Plant (Karnataka) and Power	Hospet, Bellary	Jindal Steel
Vishakhpatnam Steel Plant	Vishakhpatnam (A.P)	Rashtriya Ispat Nigam

Aluminium Industry

➥ The location of the aluminium industry is governed mainly by the availability of bauxite.

➥ Hence, the aluminium industry is mostly located in areas producing bauxite and having cheaper availability of hydro-electricity as in West Bengal, Uttar Pradesh, Maharashtra, and Tamil Nadu.

➥ It was in the year 1938 that India for the first time Produce aluminium at Alupuram Reduction Works of the Indian Aluminium Company. This company was later on converted into a public company in 1944.

Indian Aluminium Company Limited (INDAL)

➥ The Indian Aluminium Company Limited is an integrated plant having three units at different places for the production of aluminium ingots into sheets.

➥ The reduction plant of alumina is located at Alupuram in Kerala and the fabrication plant at Belur manufactures aluminium sheets, rods, aluminium paste, electric conductors, domestic utensils, etc.

➥ In order to achieve the economics of scale, a second smelter was set up at Hirakud.

Hindustan Aluminium Corporation Limited (HINDALCO)

➥ The Hindustan Aluminium Corporation Limited is located at Renukoot near Mirzapur in Uttar Pradesh.

Bharat Aluminium Company (BALCO)

➥ The Bharat Aluminium Company has set up two units at Korba and Ratnagiri to utilise bauxite ores of Amarkantak in Madhya Pradesh and of Udaigiri-Dhargarvadi region in Maharashtra, respectively.

➥ Other important industrial units engaged in the smelting of aluminium include: Bharat Aluminium Company (MALCO) of Mettur, and the Aluminium Corporation of India at Jayakaynagar (near Asansol, West Bengal).

Paper Industry

- Paper industry comes under the category of forest-based industry. Paper is made from cellulose or fibre.
- The first paper mill in the country was set up at Serampore (Bengal) in 1832, which failed.
- In 1870, a fresh venture was started at Ballygunj near Kolkata.
- The planned development of paper and paperboard industry began after independence.
- In 1950, there were 17 paper mills with installed capacity of 1.6 lakh tonnes. At present, there are nearly 850 mills in the country.
- The statewise distribution of paper industry is as follows.
    - **West Bengal:** The state had the advantage of an early start. Bamboo as the raw material was available from Assam, Bihar and Odisha in the vicinity and sabai grass from Madhya Pradesh. Major paper manufacturing centres in the state are Titanagar, Kakinara, Naihatti, Kolkata and Baranagore.
    - **Maharashtra:** Mumbai, Pune, Ballarpur and Kamptee produce paper and Vikhroli, Kalyan and Goregaon produce paper-boards here.
    - **Andhra Pradesh (including Telangana):** Rajamundry and Sirpur produce paper here.
    - **Madhya Pradesh:** Indore, Bhopal, Sehore and Shahdol are the major paper-producing centres.
    - **Karnataka:** Belagola (using bagasse) and Shimoga are the main paper-producing centres.
    - The other states known for paper production are Uttar Pradesh, Bihar, Odisha, Haryana, Tamil Nadu, Gujarat and Kerala.

Cement Industry

- Cement is made mainly from limestone and clay. Other raw materials include shale, coal and gypsum. Thus, cement factories are located near limestone deposits.
- The cement plants at **Bhadravati** (Karnataka) and **Chaibasa** (Jharkhand) use slag and the plant at **Sindri** uses sludge.
- At **Dalmia Dadri** in Haryana, there is a cement plant based on *kanker* (limestone nodules).
- The major cement producing Centres are as follow:
    - **Andhra Pradesh (including Telangana):** Karimnagar, Kurnool, Vijaywada, Krishna, Sullupet and Anantpur.
    - **Rajasthan:** Bundi, Sawai Madhopur, Chittorgarh, Udaipur.
    - **Tamil Nadu:** Tirunelveli, Ramanathpuram, Tiruchirappalli, Salem and Coimbatore.
    - **Madhya Pradesh:** Jabalpur and Gwalior.
    - **Chhattisgarh:** Durg and Raipur.
    - **Gujarat:** Ahmedabad, Sikka, Sewree, Dwarka, Porbandar, Sewalia and Ankaleshwar.
    - **Jharkhand:** Sindri, Ranchi, Palamau, Chaibasa and Japla.
    - **Karnataka:** Shahbad, Wadi, Kurkunta, Bagalkot, Bhadravati and Tumkur.
- At present, there are nearly 200 large cement plants.

Sugar Industry

- After Brazil, India is the largest sugar producer in the world and it leads in sugarcane production.
- The major centres of sugar industries are as follows :
  - **Uttar Pradesh:** There are two belts—one in western Uttar Pradesh and the other in eastern Uttar Pradesh. The western belt includes Meerut, Saharanpur, Muzaffarnagar, Bijnor and Moradabad, and the eastern belt includes Gorakhpur, Deoria, Basti and Gonda.
  - **Bihar:** It is an extension of the eastern Uttar Pradesh belt, which includes Darbhanga, Saran, Champaran and Muzaffarpur.
  - **Maharashtra:** Nasik, Pune, Satara, Sangli, Kolhapur, Sholapur are the centres well integrated in the cooperative sector in terms of cultivation and suagar factories.
  - **Tamil Nadu:** In this state Nalikupuram, Pugulur, Coimbatore and Pandyarajpuram are famous for producing sugar.
  - **Karnataka:** Munirabad, Shimoga and Mandya are the main centres.
  - **Punjab:** Mainly in the eastern side, in Phagwara and Dhuri.

Cotton Textile Industry

- The first successful cotton textile mill was set up at Mumbai by Parsi entrepreneurs.
- The major centres of cotton textiles production are as follows :
  - **Maharashtra:** Mumbai is the focal point, the industry is spread in Sholapur, Kolhapur, Pune, Jalgaon, Akola, Sangli and Nagpur.
  - **Gujarat:** Besides Ahmedabad, other cotton textiles centres are Surat, Vadodara, Bharuch, Bhavanagar, Nadiad, Porbandar, Rajkot and Navsari.
  - **Tamil Nadu:** Coimbatore, Chennai, Tirunelvelli, Madurai, Tuticorin, Salem, Virudhnagar and Pollachi are the major cotton textile industry centres.
  - **Karnataka:** Bangalore and its hinterland have attracted cotton textiles industry.
  - **Uttar Pradesh:** The major cotton textiles producing centres are Kanpur, Etawah, Modinagar, Moradabad, Bareilly, Hathras, Agra, Meerut and Varanasi.
  - **Madhya Pradesh:** Indore, Gwalior, Mandsaur, Dewas, Ujjain, Nagda, Bhopal and Jabalpur.
  - **Chhattisgarh:** Rajnandgaon
  - **Rajasthan:** Kota, Jaipur, Sriganga-nagar, Bhilwada, Bhavanimandi, Udaipur and Kishengarh.
  - **West Bengal:** Kolkata, Howrah, Serampore, Shyamnagar, Murshida-bad and Saikia.

Woollen Textile Industry

- The first woollen textiles mill was set up in 1876 at Kanpur.
- Most of the woollen textile mills are situated in **Punjab** along the Amritsar-Gurdaspur-Ludhiana belt, and at Patiala and Dhariwal.
- State–wise producers in the country are given below:
  - **Rajasthan:** Jaipur, Jodhpur, Bikaner
  - **Uttar Pradesh:** Kanpur, Agra, Mirzapur
  - **Madhya Pradesh:** Gwalior
  - **Gujarat:** Jamnagar, Ahmedabad, Vadodara
  - **Maharashtra:** Mumbai
  - **Karnataka:** Bangalore
  - **Jammu and Kashmir:** The state is a large producer of handloom woollen goods and manufacturing is centred around Srinagar.

Silk Textile Industry

- India's silk industry is world's second largest after China.
- **Karnataka** is the largest producer of silk in the country. Major silk-producing centres in the state are Tumkur, Dodballapur, Bangalore and Mysore.
- Other silk-producing states are:
  - **Tamil Nadu:** Dharmapuram, Salem, Coimbatore, Tirunelveli.
  - **Andhra Pradesh (including Telangana):** Karimnagar, Warangal, Mahbubnagar, Kurnool, Ongole, Adilabad.
  - **Jammu and Kashmir:** Srinagar.
  - **Punjab:** Amritsar.
  - **Maharashtra:** Chandrapur.
  - **Madhya Pradesh:** Raigarh.
  - **Uttar Pradesh:** Varanasi, Mirzapur.
  - **Bihar:** Katihar, Bhagalpur.
  - **Jharkhand:** Ranchi.
  - **West Bengal:** Malda, Murshidabad, Bankura.

Jute Industry

- The first modern jute mill in India was set up at Rishra near Kolkata in 1854.
- India tops in production of raw jute and finshed jute goods and second in export of jute goods.
- Nearly 85 per cent of the manufacturing capacity is located in a narrow belt about 100 km long and 3 km wide along River Hooghly.
  - Soil and agronomic conditions suit jute cultivation.
  - The East India Company's initial efforts in and around Kolkata were of great advantage for the industry.
  - This belt is well connected through waterways and rail with the jute-growing areas.
- Other states are Bihar, UP and Odisha.

Synthetic Industry

- Weaving of synthetic fibres began around 1920, when the first rayon plant was set up at Rayonpuram in Kerala.
- Mumbai, Ahmedabad, Delhi, Surat, Kolkata, Amritsar and Gwalior are the centres of this industry.

Other Industries in India

S.No.	Name	Location
1.	Petro-chemical Industry	Trombay, Koyali, Badodara, Chennai, Thane, Bongaigaon
2.	Fertilizer Industry	Nangal, Kanpur, Sindari, Talchar, Barauni, Korba, Alwai, Kalol.
3.	Aircraft Manufacturing	Lucknow, Kanpur, Koraput, Hyderabad, Nasik and Bengaluru.
4.	Shipyard	Kolkata, Vishakhapattnam, Kochi, Mumbai, Goa.
5.	Electronic Goods	Hyderabad, Bhopal, Haridwar, Sonipat, Patiala, Pune.
6.	Shoftware Industry	Bengalure, Vishakhapattanam, Gurugram, Noida, Gandhinagar, Bhubaneshwar.

ENERGY RESOURCES

Coal

- India is third largest producer of coal in the world after China and USA.

- In India, coal is the most abundantly available fossil fuel.
- India is highly dependent on coal for meeting its commercial energy requirements.
- In India coal occurs in rock series of two main geological ages, namely Gondwana, a little over 200 million years in age and in tertiary deposits which are only about 55 million years old.
- The major resources of Gondwana coal, which are metallurgical coal, are located in Damodar valley (West Bengal-Jharkhand). Jharia, Raniganj, Bokaro are important coalfields.
- The Godavari, Mahanadi, Son and Wardha valleys also contain coal deposits.
- Tertiary coals occur in the north eastern states of Meghalaya, Assam, Arunachal Pradesh and Nagaland.
  - It amounts to 60% of total electricity generated.
  - 67% of the commercial needs of energy.
  - Raniganj coal field is the oldest in India (1814).
- Important Coalfields
  - **Jharkhand:** Jharia, Bokaro, Giridih, Karanpura, Ramgarh.
  - **W. Bengal:** Raniganj.
  - **M.P., Chhattisgarh:** Singrauli, Korba.
  - **Andhra Pradesh (including Telangana):** Godavari valley (Singareni) Kantapalli.
  - **Maharashtra:** Chanda, Kamte, Umrer and Bander.
  - **Odisha:** Talcher, Himgir.

Lignites

- Lignite deposits in India is confined to states of Tamil Nadu, Gujarat, Rajasthan, Puducherry, Jammu & Kashmir and Kerala where coal is almost absent.

Petroleum

- The mineral oil resources of India are distributed in three important basins.
- ***Upper Assam or the Naharkatia-Moran, Region***: Major oil wells in this region are Digboi, Naharkatia, Moran, Lakwa, Sibsagar and Rudrasagar.
- ***Bombay High***: This is an offshore source, lying 167 km to the north-west of Mumbai.
- ***Cambay Basin:*** This basin lies in the state of Gujarat and major oil-wells are Ankaleshwar, Kosamba, Kalol, Dhaka, Mahesana, Nawagam and Sobhasan.
- Some recently discovered oil-fields, include:
  - South Heera, Neelam, Gandhar Phase II, Panna and Mukta in the Bombay High basin
  - Ravva oil field in the offshore of Krishna- Godavari basin.
  - Kaveri basin
  - Arunachal Pradesh
  - Andamans.

Natural Gas

- Most of the natural gas is found in association with crude oil. It is obtained as a by-product from petroleum refineries.
- The gasfield at Camaby (Gujarat) is the only non-associated source of natural gas.
- The Ankaleswar gasfield, Bombay High—a comparatively new source, and Morah and Naharkatiya gasfields in Assam are among the main sources.

- It is available as seepages in Nom-Chick, Miao Punga and Laptang Punga in Arunachal Pradesh, areas of the Baramura range in Tripura, and Jwalamukhi and Kangra in Himachal Pradesh.
- Natural gas has also been discoverd in Punjab (Ferozepur district), Jammu and Kashmir (in parts of Mausar-Maradpur) and Tamil Nadu (Thanjavur and Chinglepet districts).

Tidal Energy

- Tides are caused through a combination of forces created by the gravitational pull of the sun and the moon and the rotation of the earth.
- In India, the Gulf of Kutch and the Gulf of Cambay in Gujarat and the delta of the Ganaga in Sunderbans area of West Bengal have so far been known as potential sites for generating tidal power.

Wind Energy

- India has the fifth largest wind power installed capacity in the world.
- The coastal states of Tamil Nadu, Maharashtra, Gujarat and Rajasthan are better placed in regard to wind energy, as constant wind speeds above 10 km per hour are prevalent over coastal regions of these states.
- Tamil Nadu leads the wind power development accounting for about 35 per cent of the total capacity.

Solar Energy

- Solar Energy represents the earth's most abundant energy resource.
- In India, the average global radiation is around 4-7 kWh per sq m per day with about 2,300-3,200 sunshine hours per year, which can be judiciously exploited to meet our ever increasing energy requirements.
- On 16 May 2011, India's first 5 MW of installed capacity solar power project was registered under the Clean Development Mechanism. The project is in Sivagangai Village, Sivaganga district, Tamil Nadu.
- With regard to solar energy production, Rajasthan is one of India's most solar-developed states.
- The French group AREVA solar is currently engaged in constructing a 250 MW concentrated solar power (CSP) installation, which will become the largest CSP installation in Asia.
- A 4,000 MW Ultra Mega Green Solar Power Project (UMPP) is being built near Sambhar Lake in Rajasthan. Upon Completion, it would be world's largest Solar Power Plant.

Nuclear Energy

- Nuclear power is the fourth-largest source of electricity in India after thermal, hydroelectric and renewable sources of electricity.
- India has been making advances in the field of thorium-based fuels, working to design and develop a prototype for an atomic reactor using thorium and low-enriched uranium, a key part of India's three stage nuclear power programme.

Atomic Power Centres

S.No.	Name	Location
1.	Tarapur (India's first, 1969)	Maharashtra
2.	Kota	Rajasthan
3.	Naroura	Uttar Pradesh
4.	Kalpakkam	Tamil Nadu
5.	Kakrapar	Gujarat
6.	Kaiga	Karnataka
7.	Kundankulam	Tamil Nadu

TRANSPORTATION

Railways

- From a modest beginning in April 1853, when the first railway train steamed off from Mumbai to Thana, a distance of 34 km, the Indian Railways, till 31st March 2024 have grown over a route length of 69,181 km.
- Indian Railways' network is the second railways in Asia and fourth biggest railways in the world. It is also the biggest public undertaking in the country.
- **Oldest running locomotive in the world:** Fairy Queen
- **World's longest railway platform:** Shree Siddharoodha Swamiji Railway Station Hubballi (Karnataka), 1507 m.
- The longest train route in India began in July 2013. Vivek Express covers 4278 km (2658 miles), linking Dibrugarh (Assam) with Kanyakumari (Tamil Nadu), taking 82 hours, 40 minutes (3 days, 10 hours, 40 minutes) one way.
- **Longest continuous run-on Indian Railways:** Trivandrum Rajdhani between Vadodara and Kota (328 miles in about 6.5 hrs.)
- **Fastest train in India:** Vande Bharat.
- The metre gauge is found mainly in northern U.P., Bihar, Assam and in parts of Western Rajasthan, Maharashtra, Karnataka & Tamil Nadu.
- The narrow gauge is mainly in mountainous regions and broad gauge is in the rest of the country.

Gauges of Indian Railways

	Gauge	Route (km)
1.	Broad Gauge (1.676 mm)	66,820
2.	Metre Gauge (1.000 mm)	1,159
3.	Narrow Gauge (762 mm & 610 mm)	1,202
	Total	69,181

Konkan Railway Project

- The Konkan Railway project consisting of the 760 km long broad gauge line from Roha (150 km south of Mumbai) to Mangaluru (Karnataka) has been completed.

First Double-decker Train

- India's first double-decker fully air-conditioned train has been put on the wheels. Then Railway Minister Mr. Dinesh Trivedi started it with green flag between Howrah and Dhanbad on Oct. 1, 2011.
- This train, having 9 coaches, consists seven double decker coaches.
- These coaches has been made in Kapurthala Coach Factory. The maximum speed of this train between Howarah and Dhanbad has been fixed at 110 km per hour.

Semi-High Speed Trains

- Nine corridors have been identified for the introduction of semi-high speed trains at 160/200 kilometers per hour (kmph), viz.
  - Delhi-Agra,
  - Delhi-Chandigarh,
  - Delhi-Kanpur,
  - Nagpur-Bilaspur,
  - Mysore-Bengaluru-Chennai,
  - Mumbai-Goa,
  - Mumbai-Ahmedabad,
  - Chennai-Hyderabad; and
  - Nagpur-Secunderabad.

Railway Zones

- The network of railways is divided into 17 zones. One new zone in Vishakhapatnam is in process.

- These zones are headed by a General Manager, who is responsible to the Railway Board for operation, maintenance and financial matters.
- The zones with their headquarters are as follows:

	Name of the Zones	Headquarters
1.	Northern Railway	New Delhi
2.	Western Railway	Church gate Mumbai
3.	South Central Railway	Secunderabad
4.	South Eastern Railway	Kolkata
5.	Central Railway	Mumbai CST
6.	Southern Railway	Chennai
7.	North-Eastern Railway	Gorakhpur
8.	Eastern Railway	Kolkata
9.	North-East Frontier Railway	Maligaon (Guwahati)
10.	East-Central Railway	Hajipur
11.	North Western Railway	Jaipur
12.	East-Coast Railway	Bhubaneshwar
13.	North-Central Railway	Prayagraj
14.	South-Western Railway	Hubballi (Hubli)
15.	Western-Central Railway	Jabalpur
16.	South-East Central Railway	Bilaspur
17.	Kolkata Metro Railway	Kolkata
18.	South Coast Railway	Vishakhapatnam (In Process)

Roads

- India has one of the largest road networks in the world aggregating to about 66.7 lakh km till March 2024.

Golden Quadrilateral Super Highways

- The government has launched a major road development project linking Delhi-Kolkata-Chennai-Mumbai and Delhi by six-lane Super Highways.
- The North-South corridors linking Srinagar (Jammu & Kashmir) and Kanyakumari (Tamil Nadu), and East-West Corridor connecting Silcher (Assam) and Porbander (Gujarat) are part of this project.
- The major objective of these Super Highways is to reduce the time and distance between the mega cities of India.
- These highway projects are being implemented by the National Highway Authority of India (NHAI).

National Highways

- National Highways link extreme parts of the country. These are the primary road systems and are laid and maintained by the Central Public Works Department (CPWD). A number of major National Highways run in North-South and East-West directions. The National Highways Authority of India (NHAI) became operational in February, 1995.

Rural Roads

- Rural roads, which link rural areas and villages with towns, are classified under this category. These roads received special impetus under the *Pradhan Mantri Grameen Sadak Yojana.* Under this scheme special provisions are made so that every village in the country is linked to a major town in the country by an all season motorable road.

Bharat Mala

- The road ministry is planning to construct a road network along the land border to make it easy access to border areas for military and para military forces and to give a boost to cross border trade.
- The scheme, called Bharat Mala, envisages 5,000 km of roads—both construction and upgrades—for ₹ 12,000 crore.
- The road network will stretch from Gujarat in the west to Mizoram in the east and cover 10 other states.

Air Transport

- The scheduled civil air transport in India commenced during 1929-30 when the British, French and the Dutch extended their services to and beyond India.
- The first internal air service was established between Karachi and Chennai via Mumbai in 1922.
- The Civil Aviation centre in Fursatganj near Prayagraj provides, among other things, ground training to the pilots. India has bilateral air services agreements with 88 countries.
- In 1953, the Air India Corporation and the Indian Airlines (now Indian) Corporation were established to operate international air services and domestic air services respectively.
- Air India Limited, a major international carrier, operates services to USA, Europe, Russian Confederation, Gulf/Middle East, East/Far East Asia and Africa.
- **Privatization of Air India:** On January 27, 2022 the Government of India successfully handed over Air India to the Tata Group, nearly 69 years after it was taken from TATAs. The Tata Group, as part of the deal are also handed over the Air India express and a 50% stake in the ground handling arm of Air India SATS. Air India will be the third airline brand in Tata's stable as the conglomerate holds a majority interest in Air Asia India and Vistara. Tata Group chairman N. Chandrashekhar witnessed the formal transfer of the Air India to Tata Group. The Government of India on October 8, 2021 had announced the sale of the national carrier to its original developer–the salt-to-software conglomerate Tata Group at an enterprise value of ₹ 18,000 crore. This is the first major privatisation step in about two decades.
- **Pawan Hans Limited** basically provides helicopter support services to oil sector, hill station and remote areas. It also provides air support services to several customers which include ONGC, Punjab, M.P., Lakshadweep Administration, GAIL, BSF & also caters to private sector.

Major International Airports of India

Name of the Airports	City	States
Rajiv Gandhi International Airport	Hyderabad	Telangana
Sri Guru Ram Dass Jee International Airport	Amristar	Punjab
Lokpriya Gopinath Bordoloi International Airport	Guwahati	Assam
Biju Patnaik International Airport	Bhubaneshwar	Odisha
Gaya Airport	Gaya	Bihar
Indira Gandhi International Airport	New Delhi	Delhi

Name of the Airports	City	States
Veer Savarkar International Airport	Shri Vijaya Puram	Andaman & Nicobar Islands
Sardar Vallabhbhai Patel International Airport	Ahmedabad	Gujarat
Kempegowda International Airport	Bengaluru	Karnataka
Mangalore Airport	Mangalore	Karnataka
Cochin International Airport	Kochi	Kerala
Calicut International Airport	Kozhikode	Kerala
Trivandrum International Airport	Thiruvananthapuram	Kerala
Raja Bhoj Airport	Bhopal	Madhya Pradesh
Devi Ahilyabai Holkar Airport	Indore	Madhya Pradesh
Chhatrapati Shivaji International Airport	Mumbai	Maharashtra
Dr. Babasaheb Ambedkar International Airport	Nagpur	Maharashtra
Pune Airport	Pune	Maharashtra
Zaruki International Airport	Shillong	Meghalaya
Jaipur International Airport	Jaipur	Rajasthan
Chennai International Airport	Chennai	Tamil Nadu
Civil Aerodrome	Coimbatore	Tamil Nadu
Tiruchirapalli International Airport	Tiruchirappalli	Tamil Nadu
Chaudhary Charan Singh Airport	Lucknow	Uttar Pradesh
Lal Bahadur Shastri International Airport	Varanasi	Uttar Pradesh
Netaji Subhash Chandra Bose International Airport	Kolkata	West Bengal

Water Transport

- India has the largest merchant shipping fleet among the developing countries, and ranks 16th amongst the countries with the largest cargo carrying fleet.
- Approximately 90% of the country's trade volume (70% in terms of value) is moved by sea.
- India has a vast coastline of about 7,515 km and over two million sq. km of Exclusive Economic Zone (EEZ).
- The entire coastline is studded with 12 major ports handle about 15,000 Cargo vessels per annum.
- In terms of cargo handling, Mumbai is the biggest port in India.
- India has over 14,500 km. of navigable waterways.
- Inland Waterways Authority of India (IWAI) was set up in 1986 for regulation and development of inland waterways for the purpose of shipping and navigation.
- The Mogul Line Ltd. is operating international tramp trade, Haj services from Mumbai to Jeddah and back, and Konkan passenger service.
- Some of the major private sector shipping companies are the Great Eastern Shipping Co., Essar Shipping Co. Ltd., Chowgule Steam Ship Ltd., Varun Shipping Co. Ltd, Scindia Steam Navigation Company Ltd.
- India has four major ship-building yards; Kochi Shipyard at Kochi, Hindustan Shipyard at Vishakhaptnam, Garden Reach Ship Builders and Engineers at Kolkata

and Mazagaon Dock at Mumbai. All these shipyards are in the public sector.

- There are 12 major ports and 200 minor working ports in the country.
- Major ports are the direct responsibility of the Central Government while minor ports including intermediate ports fall in the concurrent list of the Constitution and are managed and administered by the respective maritime state government.
- Mormugao, Deendayal (Kandla), Mumbai, New Manglore and Cochin are the major ports on the west coast. A new major port J.L. Nehru port at Nhava Sheva off Mumbai is highly developed.
- On the east coast, V.O. Chidambaranar (Tuticorin), Chennai, Vishakhapatnam, Paradip, Kamarajar (Ennore), and Shyama Prasad Mukherjee (Kolkata-Haldia) are the major ports.

Inland Waterways

- Rivers, canals, lakes and coastal areas have important inland waterways from time immemorial. India has about 14,500 km of navigble waterways.
- At present only 3700 km of major rivers are navigable by mechanised flat bottom crafts.

Major National Waterways

- Following are the major National Waterways:
  - The Ganga river, between Prayagraj and Haldia (1620 km).
  - The Brahmaputra river, between Sadiya and Dhubri (891 km).
  - Kottapuram-Kollam stretch of West Coast Canal along with Champakara Canal and Udyogmandal Canal (205 km) (NW-3) in 1993.
  - Kakinada-Puducherry stretch of Canal and Kalurelly Tank, stretches of river Godavari and Krishna (1095 km) in 2008.
  - Talcher-Dhamra stretch of river Brahmani, Geonkhali Charbatia stretch of East Coast Canal, Charbatia-Dhamra stretch of Matai river along with Mahanadi delta river system (620 km.) in 2008.
  - Barak River from Lakhipur to Bhanga (121 km) as sixth National Waterway in 2013.

Pipelines

- Pipelines transport network is a new arrival on the transportation map of India.
- In the past, these were used to transport water to cities and industries.
- Now, these are used for transporting crude oil, petroleum products and natural gas from oil and natural gas fields to refineries, fertilizer factories and big thermal power plants.
- Solids can also be transported through a pipeline when converted into slurry.
- There are five important network of pipeline transportation in the country.
  - From oil field in upper Assam to Kanpur (Uttar Pradesh), via Guwahati, Barauni and Prayagraj. It has branches from Barauni to Haldia, via Rajbandh to Maurigram and Guwahati to Siliguri.
  - From Salaya in Gujarat to Jalandhar in Punjab, via Viramgam, Mathura, Delhi and Sonipat. It has branches to connect Koyali (near Vododara in Gujarat) Chakshu and other places.
  - **Gas pipeline** from Hazira in Gujarat connects Jagdishpur in Uttar Pradesh, via Vijaipur in Madhya Pradesh. It has branch to Kota in Rajasthan, Shahjahanpur, Babrala and other places in Uttar Pradesh.

- **Mumbai High-Mumbai-Ankleshwar-Kayoli Pipeline:** This pipeline connects oilfields of Mumbai High and Gujarat with oil refinery at Koyali. A 210 km long double pipeline connects Mumbai with Mumbai High. It provides facilities for transporting crude oil and natural gas.
- **Jamnagar-Loni LPG Pipeline:** This 1,269 km long pipeline has been constructed by Gas Authority of India Limited (GAIL) at the cost of ₹ 1,250 crore. It connects Jamnagar in Gujarat to Loni near Delhi in U.P. and passes through the states of Gujarat, Rajasthan, Haryana and U.P. This is the longest LPG pipeline of the world.

POPULATION

➥ The first all-India census, though not synchronously taken, was completed in 1872. Since 1881, census in India has been taken regularly every ten years.

➥ Till 1921, India had a chequered rate of growth of population. Therefore, the year 1921 is called the **year of great divide.**

➥ The year 1951 marks the beginning of the three decades of acce-lerated population growth as population almost doubled between 1951 to 1981.

Size and Growth Rate of Population

➥ Total population of India (as on March 1st 2011) 1,210 million. Males 623.2 million, and females 587.5 million.

➥ India supports 17.5% of the total world's population.

➥ India's 'Decadal Growth' of population (2001-2011) is 17.7% (Inter census period 1961-1971 marked the maximum decadal growth of population at 24.8%).

➥ Statewise lowest decadal growth rate (2001–2011) of population is shown by Nagaland (–0.6%) and highest has been registered that of Meghalaya (27.9%).

Population Density

➥ The density of population was increased in all states and union territories between 2001-2011.

Population Density

State/UT	Density	State/UT	Density	State/UT	Density
Delhi	11,320	Dadra & Nagar Haveli	700	Rajasthan	200
Chandigarh	9,258	Goa	394	Uttarakhand	189
Puducherry	2,547	Assam	398	Chhattisgarh	189
Lakshadweep	2,149	Jharkhand	414	Nagaland	119
Daman & Diu	2,191	Maharashtra	365	Himachal Pradesh	123
West Bengal	1,028	Tripura	350	Manipur	115
Bihar	1,106	Andhra Pradesh	308	Meghalaya	132
Kerala	860	Telangana	307	Jammu & Kashmir	124
Uttar Pradesh	829	Karnataka	319	Sikkim	86
Punjab	551	Gujarat	308	Andaman & Nicobar Islands	46
Tamil Nadu	555	Odisha	270	Mizoram	52
Haryana	573	Madhya Pradesh	236	Arunachal Pradesh	17

- Among major states Bihar is the most densely populated state with a population density of 1106 in 2011.
- West Bengal is now the second highest density populated state pushing Kerala to the third place.

Sex Ratio

- Sex ratio is defined as the number of females per thousand males. It is 943 as per census 2011.
- There has been slight improvement in this ratio during the last decade where it increased from 926 in 1991 to 933 in 2001.
- Kerala (1084) and Puducherry (1037) are the two states where sex ratio is in favour of females while, Haryana has the lowest sex ratio (879) in India.

Sex Ratio in India

State/UT	S. Ratio	State/UT	S. Ratio	State/UT	S. Ratio
Andhra Pradesh	996	Kerala	1,084	Telangana	998
Arunachal Pradesh	938	Madhya Pradesh	931	Tripura	960
Assam	958	Maharashtra	929	Uttarakhand	963
Bihar	918	Manipur	992	Uttar Pradesh	912
Chhattisgarh	991	Meghalaya	989	West Bengal	950
Goa	973	Mizoram	976	Andaman & Nicobar Islands	876
Gujarat	919	Nagaland	931	Chandigarh	818
Haryana	879	Odisha	979	Dadra and Nagar Haveli	774
Himachal Pradesh	972	Punjab	895	Daman and Diu	618
Jammu & Kashmir	889	Rajasthan	928	Delhi	868
Jharkhand	949	Sikkim	890	Lakshadweep	947
Karnataka	973	Tamil Nadu	996	Puducherry	1,037

Rural-Urban Composition

- Of the total 1,210 million persons of the country (2011), 833 millions live in rural areas. It is slightly less than three-fourth (68.8 per cent) of the total population.
- **Urban Population:** About 377 million people live in urban areas (2011). They constitute 31.2 per cent of the total population of the country.

Census Year	Rural Population (in %)	Urban Population (in %)	Census Year	Rural Population (in %)	Urban Population (in %)
1901	89.2	10.8	1961	82.0	18.0
1911	89.7	10.3	1971	80.1	19.9
1921	88.8	11.2	1981	76.7	23.3
1931	88.0	12.0	1991	74.3	25.7
1941	86.1	13.9	2001	72.2	27.8
1951	82.7	17.3	2011	68.8	31.2

Literacy

➡ As per the 2011 census, Literacy rate in the country is 73.0 per cent, 80.9 for males and 64.6 for females.

➡ Kerala retained its position by being on top with a 94 per cent literacy rate, closely followed by Mizoram (91.3 per cent).

Literacy of States and Union Territories 2011

States	*Persons*	*Males*	*Females*
Jammu and Kashmir	67.2	76.8	56.4
Himachal Pradesh	82.8	89.5	75.9
Punjab	75.8	80.4	70.7
Chandigarh	86.0	90.0	81.2
Uttarakhand	78.8	87.4	70.0
Haryana	75.6	84.1	65.9
Delhi	86.2	90.9	80.8
Rajasthan	66.1	79.2	52.1
Uttar Pradesh	67.7	77.3	57.2
Bihar	61.8	71.2	51.5
Sikkim	81.4	86.6	75.6
Arunachal Pradesh	65.4	72.6	57.7
Nagaland	79.6	82.8	76.1
Manipur	79.2	86.1	72.4
Mizoram	91.3	93.3	89.3
Tripura	87.2	91.5	82.7
Meghalaya	74.4	76.0	72.9
Assam	72.2	77.8	66.3
W. Bengal	76.3	81.7	70.5
Jharkhand	66.4	76.8	55.4
Odisha	72.9	81.6	64.0
Chhattisgarh	70.3	80.3	60.2
Madhya Pradesh	69.3	78.7	59.2
Gujarat	78.0	85.8	69.7
Daman and Diu	87.1	91.5	79.5
Dadra and Nagar Haveli	76.2	85.2	64.3
Maharashtra	82.3	88.4	75.9
Andhra Pradesh	67.0	74.9	59.1
Telangana	66.5	74.9	57.9
Karnataka	75.4	82.5	68.1
Goa	88.7	92.6	84.7
Lakshadweep	91.8	95.6	87.9
Kerala	94.0	96.1	92.1
Tamil Nadu	80.1	86.8	73.4
Puducherry	85.8	91.3	80.7
Andaman & Nicobar Island	86.6	90.3	82.4

Tribal Population

- Among the ethnic groups of India the Scheduled Tribes hold a significant position. They belong to different ethnic, linguistic and religious groups and have some unique social and economic characteristics.
- The States of Madhya Pradesh, Chhattisgarh Odisha, Bihar, Gujarat, Rajasthan, Maharashtra and West Bengal together account for about 80 per cent of the entire tribal population of the country.

MAJOR TRIBES IN INDIA

- Abors .... Assam
- Apatanis .... Arunachal Pradesh
- Baiga .... Madhya Pradesh, Chhattisgarh, Odisha
- Bhils .... Mostly in Madhya Pradesh and Rajasthan. Also in Gujarat
- Bhotias .... Garhwal and Kumaon regions in Uttarakhand
- Chenchus .... Andhra Pradesh, Odisha
- Gaddis .... Himachal Pradesh
- Garos .... Mehalaya
- Gonds .... Madhya Pradesh and Chhattisgarh. Also in Bihar, Odisha and Andhra Pradesh
- Jarawas .... Little Andamans
- Khasis .... Assam, Meghalaya
- Khonds .... Odisha
- Kol .... Madhya Pradesh, Chhattisgarh, Maharashtra
- Kota .... Nilgiri (Tamil nadu)
- Kuki .... Manipur, Mizoram, Meghalaya
- Lepcha .... Sikkim
- Lushai .... Tripura
- Murias .... Bastar region in Chhattisgarh
- Mikirs .... Assam
- Mundas .... Jharkhand
- Nagas .... Nagaland; some in Assam and NEFA region.
- Oarons (also called Kurukh) .... Jharkhand, Odisha
- Onges .... Andaman and Nicobar Islands
- Santhals .... Birbhum region in Bengal, Hazaribagh, Ranchi and Palamau in Jharkhand
- Sentinelese .... Sentinel Island, Andaman and Nicobar
- Shompens .... Andaman and Nicobar
- Todas .... Nilgiri (Tamil Nadu)
- Varliz .... Maharashtra

MULTIPLE CHOICE QUESTIONS

1. Where is Dibru Saikhowa Biosphere Reserve located?

A. Arunachal Pradesh
B. Assam
C. Manipur
D. Sikkim

2. Which of the following statements are true?

I. The Tropic of Cancer divides India into two halves.
II. The Tropic of Cancer divides Indian International boundary into two halves.
III. Maximum East-West expansion of India lies along the Tropic of Cancer.
IV. Line joining the eastermost and westermost points of India lies to the north of the Tropic of Cancer.

Select the correct answer from the options given below:

A. I and II
B. III and IV
C. II and III
D. I and IV

3. Which of the following Indian States shares its boundary with Bangladesh and Myanmar?

A. Nagaland
B. Tripura
C. Mizoram
D. Manipur

4. From north to south, Western Ghats and locally known as:

A. Sahyadri-Nilgiri-Anaimalai-Cardamom Hills
B. Sahyadri-Anaimalai-Nilgiri-Cardamom Hills
C. Nilgiri-Sahyadri-Cardamom Hills-Anaimalai
D. Sahyadri-Nilgiri-Cardamom Hills-Anaimalai

5. Which of the following rivers does not drain into Arabian sea?

A. Krishna B. Sabarmati
C. Tapi D. Narmada

6. Mango showers are common phenomena in which States of India?

A. Uttar Pradesh and Madhya Pradesh
B. Madhya Pradesh and Karnataka
C. Uttar Pradesh and Tamil Nadu
D. Kerala and Karnataka

7. The dryland farming in India is largely confined to the regions having annual rainfall of:

A. less than 25 cm
B. less than 50 cm
C. less than 75 cm
D. less than 100 cm

8. India is the largest producer as well as the largest consumer and importer of which of the following crops?

A. Wheat B. Cotton
C. Pulses D. Sugarcane

9. Angora wool is extracted from which of the following animals?

A. Sheep B. Goat
C. Rabbit D. Fox

10. Global Gene Bank of rice is situated at:

A. Philippines
B. Pusa, New Delhi
C. Cuttack
D. Hyderabad

11. Sugarcane is a:

A. short day plant
B. long day plant
C. day neutral plant
D. photo insensitive plant

12. Which of the following pairs of Himalayan Glaciers and their location is/are correctly matched?

1. Siachen—Nubra Valley Region
2. Chungphar—Kumaon-Garhwal Region
3. Zemu-Central Nepal Region
4. Gasherbrun—Pir Panjal Range

Select the answer using the code given below:

A. Only 1
B. Only 1 and 2
C. Only 2 and 3
D. Only 3 and 4

13. Consider the following statements regarding the rivers of India:

1. The Barak River, the head stream of the Meghna, rises in the hills of Meghalaya.
2. The Ghaggar River does not drain out to the sea and gets lost in the Rajasthan desert.
3. Puthimari and Manas are important tributaries of the Brahmaputra.

Which of the statements given above is/are correct?

A. Only 1
B. Only 2
C. Only 1 and 2
D. Only 2 and 3

14. Consider the following statements regarding transportation functions associated with important ports:

1. Singapore functions both as a port of call and an entreport.
2. Karwar in India is an example of a naval port.
3. Dover in England is an example of an outport.

Which of the statements given above is/are correct?

A. Only 1
B. Only 3
C. Only 1 and 3
D. Only 1 and 2

15. Cumulonimbus clouds develop from which among the following clouds?

A. Cumulus congestus clouds
B. Cumulus and Nimbostratus clouds
C. Cumulus and Altostratus clouds
D. Cirrocumulus clouds

16. Which of the following Ramsar Wetland sites is not situated in any of the Union Territories of India?

A. Hokera Wetland
B. Point Calimere Wildlife and Bird Sanctuary
C. Tsomoriri Lake
D. Wular Lake

17. How is strong pressure gradient represented on a weather map?

A. Closely spaced isobars
B. Widely spaced isobars
C. Closely spaced isobars at the periphery
D. A set of two widely spaced isobars followed by two closely spaced isobars

18. Which one of the following is not an example of chemical weathering?

A. Acid action
B. Hydrolysis
C. Salt Crystal Growth
D. Oxidation

19. Which of the following statements regarding Arc Volcanoes is/are correct?

1. Arc volcanoes are found near divergent plate boundaries.
2. Some of the world's classical examples of coneshaped stratovolcanoes, such as Mount Fuji in Japan, Mayon in the Philippines are Arc volcanoes.
3. Some of the highest volcanoes on Earth are of the Arc type, notably Nevado Ojos del Salado in the Chilean Andes.

Select the answer using the code given below:

A. Only 2
B. Only 2 and 3
C. Only 1 and 3
D. 1, 2 and 3

20. Which one of the following statements regarding S-waves is not correct?

A. S-waves are slower than P-waves
B. During an earthquake S-waves are less destructive to structures like buildings and highway overpasses
C. S-waves can travel only through solids and cannot travel through the Earth's outer core
D. Seismologists have concluded that the Earth's outer core must be liquid or fluid

21. Which of the following states is/are part of the Ganga Basin?

1. Chhattisgarh
2. Himachal Pradesh
3. Rajasthan

Select the answer using the code given below:

A. Only 1
B. Only 1 and 2
C. Only 2 and 3
D. 1, 2 and 3

22. Which peninsular river has a tributary named 'Kabini'?

A. Godavari
B. Krishna
C. Mahanadi
D. Kaveri

23. Which of the following peaks are situated in India?

1. Dhaulagiri
2. Namcha Barwa
3. Kamet
4. Makalu

Select the answer using the code given below:

A. 1, 2 and 3
B. Only 1 and 3
C. Only 2 and 3
D. Only 2 and 4

24. Which of the following statements regarding River Rhine is/are correct?

1. Rhine River is an important pathway for industrial activity in northern Germany.
2. Port of Rotterdam is located at the mouth of the Rhine River.

Select the answer using the code given below:

A. Only 1
B. Only 2
C. Both 1 and 2
D. Neither 1 nor 2

25. With reference to the continent of 'Antarctica' which of the following statements are correct?

1. It is larger than Europe in terms of area.
2. It has the highest average elevation as compared to all other continent.
3. Mt. Ross is the highest peak of this continent.
4. Waters of the Southern Ocean (West Wind Drift) move in an anticlockwise direction around it.

Select the answer using the code given below:

A. Only 1 and 2
B. Only 1 and 3
C. 1, 2 and 3
D. 2, 3 and 4

26. Name the countries which lie on either side of MacMohan Line?

A. South Vietnam and North Vietnam

B. India and China
C. India and Ceylon
D. France and Germany

27. Which is the largest Gulf in the world?

A. Gulf of Aqaba
B. Gulf of Bengal
C. Gulf of Mexico
D. Gulf of Aden

28. Which of the following are Tropical Grasslands?

1. Savanna
2. Campos
3. Prairie
4. Llanos
5. Steppe

How many of the above options are correct?

A. Only two
B. Only four
C. All five
D. Only three

29. India is the largest producer of which agricultural products?

A. Milk, Pulses and Spicies
B. Rice, Wheat and Cotton
C. Tea, Coffee and Jute
D. Sugarcane, Maize and Oilseeds

30. What does the 38th Parallel Line separate?

A. India from Bangladesh
B. India from China
C. North Korea from South Korea
D. India from Pakistan

31. The Panama Canal Connects:

A. The Pacific and Atlantic Oceans
B. The Pacific and Arctic Oceans
C. The Atlantic and Arctic Oceans
D. The Atlantic and Indian Oceans

32. What is the habitable portion of the world land area?

A. Less than 35%
B. Less than half of it
C. 50%
D. About 75%

33. The largest of all the peninsulas in the world is the:

A. Arabian peninsula
B. Iberian peninsula
C. Indian peninsula
D. Kamehaika peninsula

34. Which of the following is the longest river?

A. Narmada B. Godavari
C. Kaveri D. Krishna

35. Laplands is a group of countries located in:

A. Europe B. Australia
C. Asia D. America

36. The Himalayas constitute the natural boundary between :

A. China and India
B. China and Afghanistan
C. India and Nepal
D. India and Myanmar

37. The city of Khartoum is situated on the banks of:

A. Hudson B. Nile
C. Tiber D. Seine

38. In which continent some of its parts are over 1500 miles from the sea and in which the hottest as well as the coldest climates of the world are to be found:

A. America B. Asia
C. Europe D. Australia

39. Name the place where Blue and White Nile Rivers effect a confluence:

A. Cairo
B. Constantinpole (except Greenland)
C. Khartoum
D. Teheran

40. Which place in the world is known for the least amount of rainfall?

A. Cairo (Egypt)
B. Yarkand (China)
C. Atacama (Chile)
D. Thar (Rajasthan)

41. Australia is the:

A. only continent in the Southern Hemisphere
B. island continent
C. smallest continent
D. all the above points are true

42. Which of the following pairs of Himalayan Passes and the Ranges in which they are located is/are correctly matched?

1. Zoji La—Great Himalayas
2. Banihal Pass—Pir Panjal Range
3. Photu La—Ladakh Range
4. Khardung La—Karakoram Range

Select the answer using the code given below:

A. Only 2
B. Only 4
C. Only 1 and 2
D. 1, 2 and 3

43. Moscow is situated on the river bank of:

A. Moskva
B. Spree
C. Volga
D. Tagus

44. The country Congo is in the ..... continent:

A. European
B. Australian
C. Asian
D. African

45. Which is considered as the most ancient part of the world by historians?

A. Gangestic Valley
B. North Western Indian Valley
C. Southern part of Vindhya Mountain
D. North Eastern part of India

46. The highest peak in Europe is:

A. Mont Blanc
B. Andes
C. Monte Rosa
D. Elburz

47. Where was electricity supply first introduced in India?

A. Darjeeling
B. Kolkata
C. Mumbai
D. Delhi

48. Name the largest island in the world:

A. New Guinea
B. Greenland
C. Madagascar
D. Great Britain

49. Suez Canal joins:

A. London to Paris
B. Tokyo to Osaka
C. Mediterranean to the Red Sea
D. Rangoon to Philippines

50. The Radcliffe Line was drawn on 15th August, 1947 between:

A. India and Myanmar (Burma)
B. Pakistan and China
C. Pakistan and India
D. Pakistan and Nepal

51. Kiel is a:

A. renowned explorer
B. American antelope
C. big American sea bird
D. shipping canal between London and Baltic Sea

52. The Turan Type of Regions have the climate of extremes because:

A. These lie in the interior ports of the continent

B. These have either too much or too less rain
C. These are either on hills or near the deserts
D. None of the above

53. Which country tops in the mining of gold:
A. U.S.A. B. Canada
C. China D. India

54. The largest Fresh water lake is:
A. Lake Superior
B. Caspian Sea
C. Lake Baikal
D. Hind Sea

55. ..... is the most important occupation of the people in the Monsoon Lands:
A. Forestry B. Agriculture
C. Industry D. Mining

ANSWERS

1	2	3	4	5	6	7	8	9	10
B	D	C	A	A	D	C	C	C	A
11	12	13	14	15	16	17	18	19	20
A	A	D	D	A	B	A	C	B	B
21	22	23	24	25	26	27	28	29	30
D	D	C	C	A	B	C	D	A	C
31	32	33	34	35	36	37	38	39	40
A	B	A	B	A	A	B	B	B	C
41	42	43	44	45	46	47	48	49	50
D	A	A	D	C	D	A	B	C	C
51	52	53	54	55					
D	A	C	A	B					

Indian Economy

NATURE AND CHARACTERISTICS

- An underdeveloped economy is characterised, by the existence, in greater or less degree, of unutilised or underutilised manpower on the one hand and of unexploited natural resources on the other.
- This state of affairs may be due to stagnancy of techniques or to certain inhibiting socio-economic factors which prevent the more dynamic forces in economy from asserting themselves.
- The World Bank Report 2017 has classified the world economies into four groups.

  The groups are:
  - low income countries \$1,005 or less;
  - low middle income countries \$1,006-\$3,955;
  - upper middle income countries \$3,956-\$12235;
  - high income countries \$12,235 or more.
- Underdeveloped countries generally had a colonial past and their growth pattern is mainly of dualistic types.
- Dualistic growth refer to the co-existence of developed and under-developed sectors in a country's economy side by side, where one sector or sub-sector experiences perceptible growth and the rest of the economy does not.

Basic Characteristics of Indian Economy

- Indian economy shows a mix of backward and progressive features. It has shed off some of its underdevelopment as it has made forward strides in some of the important areas.
- As a result, it is no longer a stagnating economy as it was during the colonial rule. It is, infact a developing economy.

Predominance of Agriculture

- The secular decline in the share of agriculture sector in GVA continued with a decline from 20.2 per cent in 2020-21 to 19.9 per cent in 2022-23. This is indeed much less than the share of agriculture in Gross Value Added (GVA) in 1950-51 (when it contributed more than 50 per cent).
- The reliance on agriculture in India is far greater than even in some other under-developed countries such as Indonesia, China, Mexico, Brazil etc.

In developed countries like USA and UK, agriculture contributes merely 2 to 4 per cent to the GDP.

Unemployment and Under-employment

- In developed countries, unemployment is of a cyclical nature and occurs due to lack of effective demand.
- In India unemployment is structural and is the result of a deficiency of capital.
- The Indian economy does not find sufficient capital to expand its industries to such an extent that the entire labour force is absorbed.
- Moreover, in the agricultural sector of the Indian economy, a much larger number of labourers are engaged in production than are really needed.
- Accordingly, the marginal product of labour in agriculture is often negligible; it may be zero or may even be negative. Thus there exists 'disguised' or 'concealed' unemployment in agriculture.

Low Capital Formation

- Another basic characteristic of the Indian economy is the existence of capital deficiency which is reflected in two ways—firstly, the amount of capital per head available is low; and secondly, the current rate of capital formation is also low.
- Low capital formation means low rates of growth of national product, unless capital-output ratio declines.

Heavy Population Pressure

- During the decade (2001-2011) population grew from 1,028 million to 1210 million an increase of 172 million. The annual growth rate registered a decline to 1.70 per cent.
- The fast rate of growth of population necessitates a higher rate of economic growth in order to maintain the same standard of living of the population. To maintain a rapidly growing population, the requirements of food, clothing, shelter, medicine, schooling, etc. all rise.
- Thus, a rising population imposes greater economic burdens and consequently, society has to make a much greater effort to initiate the process of growth. Moreover, a rising population leads to an increase in the labour force.

Maldistribution of Wealth

- Inequality in asset distribution is the principal cause of unequal distribution of income in the rural areas.
- This finding by the Reserve Bank is also supported by the National Sample Survey which reveals that in rural areas 27% of households owning less than ₹ 20,000 worth of assets accounted for 2.4% of the total assets.
- Similarly about 24% of the households in the asset range of ₹ 20,000-50,000 owned barely 7.5% of the total assets.
- This implies that nearly 51% of the bottom households owned just 10% of the total assets.
- As against it, 9.6% of the rich households owning assets worth ₹ 2.5 lakhs & above accounted for nearly 49% of total assets.

Low Standard of Living

- In India, the average calorie intake of food is only 2,496 as compared to over 3,400 calories per day in most of the developed countries. This is slightly above the minimum intake for sustaining life-estimated at 2,100 calories.

- Since nearly 29.5 per cent of the population in India lives below the poverty line, it is very doubtful whether the poor get a minimum intake of even 2,100 calories.
- Another factor that has an important bearing on the health of the people is that in India cereals predominate, but in contrast the diet in the advanced countries is rich in content because it includes fruits, fish, meat, butter and sugar. The protein intake is nearly less than half of the level in advance countries.

Prevalence of Low Level of Technology

- Since new techniques are expensive and require a considerable degree of skill for their application in production, the twin requirements for the absorption of new technology are the availability of capital and training of an adequate number of personnel. It is necessary to have a basic minimum level of education among the actual producers in order that the economy can absorb new technology.
- Deficiency of capital hinders the process of scrapping off the old techniques and the installation of the up-to-date and modern techniques. Illiteracy and the absence of a skilled labour force are the other major hurdles in the spread of technology in the economy.

Market Imperfections

- Indian economy faces a number of market imperfections like lack of mobility among production factors from one place to other and lack of specialisations which hinder the optimum utilisation of available resources. All these market imperfections and their results are important reasons for undeveloped state of Indian economy.

NATIONAL INCOME

- National income is defined as the value of all final goods and services produced by the residents of a country, whether operating within the domestic territory of the country or outside, in a year. National income is thus, a monetary expression of the current achievements of the people of a country expressed through their production activities.

National Income Estimates in India

- Dadabhai Naoroji was the first to produce the statistical estimate of average per capita income. In 1873, he calculated that for the year 1867-68, the total national income of British India was Rs. 3,400 million for a population of 170 million or Rs. 20 per head.
- Other individual efforts also were made to estimate the national income, notable among them are William Digby (1899); Findlay Shirras (1911, 1922 and 1931); Shah and Khambatta (1921); V.K.R.V. Rao (1925-29 and 1931-32) and R.C. Desai (1931-40). However, the credit for the first scientific estimate of national income during 1931-32 goes to Prof. V.K.R.V. Rao.
- After Independence, in view of the country's choice of planned development, the importance of the estimates of national income and its various components was recognised.
- Accordingly, the National Income Committee was appointed in 1949, with P.C. Mahalanobis as the Chairman, and D.R. Gadgil and V.K.R.V. Rao as members.
- The Committee was entrusted with the task of preparing a report on the national income and related estimates,

suggesting measures for improving the quality of the available data, and for the collection of further essential statistics and recommending ways and means for promoting research in the field of national income.

Per Capita Income

Author of the Estimate	Year	Per Capita Income At 1948-49 Prices (Rs.)	Per Capita Income At Current Prices (Rs)
Naoroji	1867-68	142	20
Atkinson	1875	172	24.4
Major Baring	1881	184	27
Horne	1891	158	28
Atkinson	1895	178	31.5
Curzon	1902	148	30
Giffen	1903	167	30

Methods of Calculating National Income

Three methods are usually adopted to calculate national income.

1. **Product Method:** S. Kuznets gave a new name to this method, *i.e.,* product service method. In this method net value of final goods and services produced in a country during a year is obtained and the total obtained value is called total final product. This represents Gross Domestic Product (GDP). Net income earned in foreign boundaries by nationals is added and depreciation is subtracted from GDP.
2. **Income Method:** In this method, a total of net incomes earned by working people in different sectors and commercial enterprises is obtained. According to Dr. Bowley and Robertson, incomes of both categories of people-paying taxes and not paying taxes are added to obtain national income. For adopting this method, sometimes a group of people from various income groups is selected and on the basis of their income national income of the country is estimated. In a broad sense, by income method national income is obtained by adding receipts as total rent, total wages, total interest and total profit.

   Symbolically:

   National Income = Total Rent + Total Wages + Total Interest + Total Profit.
3. **Consumption Method:** It is also called expenditure method. Income is either spent on consumption or saved. Hence national income is the addition of total consumption and total savings. For using this method, we need data related to income and savings of the consumers.

   Generally reliable data of saving and consumption are not easily available. There-fore, expenditure method is generally not used for estimating national income.

   In India a combination of production method and income method is used for estimating national income.

Different Concepts of National Income

➡ **Gross Domestic Product (GDP):** It is the monetary value of all final goods and services produced in a country in a year. In GDP, income generated by foreigners in a country is included but income generated by nationals of a country outside the country is not included.

➥ **Net Domestic Product (NDP):** It is the net value of GDP after deducting depreciation of plant and machinery from GDP.

NDP = Gross Domestic Product – Depreciation

➥ **Gross National Product (GNP):** It is the monetary value of all final goods and services produced by the residents of a country in a year.

➥ **Difference Between GDP and GNP:** In GDP, goods and services produced in a country is added, whether it is produced by residents of the country or foreigners. In GNP, the production of foreigners in the country is not included while the production of nationals outside the country is included. In other words, international trade is included in the calculation.

➥ **Net National Product (NNP):** It is the value of GNP after deducting depreciation of plant and machinery

NNP = GNP – Depreciation

➥ **NNP at Factor Cost:** It is the value of NNP when the value of goods and services is taken at the production (cost) point.

➥ **NNP at Market Prices:** It is the value of NNP at consumer point.

NNP at market price = NNP at factor cost + Indirect taxes – Subsidies

➥ **National Income:** In India, net national income at factor cost is called national income.

➥ **Real National Income:** It is the value of national income adjusted for inflation or calculated from some reference point (base year).

Real National Income

$$= \frac{\text{NNP at current prices} \times 100}{\text{Price Index}}$$

➥ **Per Capita Income:** It is the average income (per person) of a country.

Per Capita Income

$$= \frac{\text{National Income}}{\text{Population of the Year}}$$

➥ **Personal Income:** It is the income of the residents (individuals) of a country. To calculate personal income, transfer payments to individuals are added to national income while social security contributions, corporate tax and undistributed profits are subtracted.

Personal Income

= National Income + Transfer Payments – Social Security Contributions – Corporate Tax – Undistributed Profits.

➥ **Disposable Income:** It is the income of individuals at their disposal after paying direct tax liabilities.

Disposable Income

= Personal Income – Direct taxes (e.g., Income Tax)

➥ **Measurement of National Income:** There are three methods of national income estimation to be used in any country. These are:

- Census of Production Method
- Census of Income Method
- Census of Expenditure Method or Census of Consumption—Saving Method

➥ In India, due to non-availability of data, it is not possible to use only one of the above methods. So, in our country a mix of the three methods is used for national income estimation.

PLANNING

➥ Economic Planning means the allocation of limited resources among different uses in such a way as to bring about the maximum welfare of the people.

Objectives of Planning

➥ Planning in India derives its objectives and premises from the Preamble and the Directive Principles of State Policy enshrined in the Constitution.

➥ Based on this, the Planning Commission set out the following four objectives of planning.

- to increase production to the maxi-mum possible extent so as to achieve higher level of national and per capita income;
- to achieve full employment;
- to reduce inequalities of income and wealth;
- to set up a socialist society based on equality and justice and absence of exploitation.

➥ Besides, self-reliance too has been an objective in the long term. Growth with social justice and alleviation of poverty have thus been the primary objectives of Indian planning.

➥ Within this framework, each Five-Year Plan evolves its own short-term objectives taking into account fresh possibilities and existing constraints.

- **Growth:** Economic growth, reflected in a rapid and continuous increase in real national income and per capita income, is an important goal of planning.
- **Social Justice:** One aspect of social dimension is to improve the living standard of the poorest groups in society. The other aspect is the reduction in inequalities in asset distribution.
- Employment: The plans have recog-nized that generation of employment is a crucial factor in the removal of inequalities and raising growth rate.
- Self-Reliance: Self-reliances is not to be confused with self-sufficiency, but means, in Jawaharlal Nehru's words, avoiding "economic imperi-alism" in international trade. Inter-dependence among countries but not subordination to any is the essence of self-reliance. Self-reliance came to be an objective of planning from the Third Plan onwards, but at that time it was adopted to do away with the need for external aid. The goal was concretised in the Fourth Plan. The onwards, it has been a part of the aims of planning.

Types of Planning

➥ **Centralised Planning** presumes complete central control over a major part of the economy.

➥ **Decentralised Planning** is the kind of planning where decision making process is dispersed and the implementation of plans is carried through prices and incentives.

➥ **Structural Planning** involves changes in socio-economic institutions.

➥ **Functional Planning** involves no such changes in the socio-economic structure of the society but planning is done within the framework of existing institutions.

➥ **Fixed-term Plans:** Ordinarily a short-term Plan, say of five years, is divided into annual plans, each annual plan beginning from where the preceding plan left. This way it may be called fixed-term planning.

➥ **Rolling Plans:** A variant of short-term plans is what has come to be known as 'rolling plans'. Two major aspects of rolling plans are:

- In a rolling plan, the central outlay allotment for major sectors within the overall five-year plan targets will be fixed on a yearly basis.
- The five year horizon will be extended each year by changing the select central targets for an additional year.

➡ **Indicative Planning** provides direction for the growth of the economy by spelling out clear goals and providing help in reaching them.

➡ **Imperative Planning** is essentially planning wherein the implementation is provided for, along with its formulation. It not only plan what is desirable but ensures that the economy shapes itself as per plan requirements.

INITIATION OF PLANNING IN INDIA

- **1930:** When our national leaders came under the influence of socialist philosophy, M. Visvesvarayya who was a civil engineer and Dewan of Mysore published his book "Planned Economy in India".
- **1938:** Was the year that witnessed the first attempt to develop a national plan for India when national planning Committee was set up. This committee was set up by Subhash Chandra Bose and chaired by Jawaharlal Nehru.
- **1944:** Eight Industrialists of Bombay including Mr. JRD Tata, GD Birla, Purshottamdas Thakurdas, Lala Shriram, Kasturbhai Lalbhai, AD Shroff, Ardeshir Dalal, & John Mathai working together prepared "A Brief Memorandum Outlining a Plan of Economic Development for India" which was popularly known as Bombay Plan. This plan envisaged doubling the per capita income in 15 years and tripling the national income during this period.
- **August 1944:** The British India government set up "Planning and Development Department" under the charge of Ardeshir Dalal. But this department was abolished in 1946.
- **October 1946:** A Planning Advisory Board was set up by Interim Government to review the plans and future projects and make recommendations upon them.
- **A 10 year People's Plan:** Also came out during that era which was based upon Marxist socialism and drafted by M N Roy on behalf of the Indian federation of Lahore.
- **Another plan called as Gandhian Plan** was put forward by Shriman Narayan Aggarwal in 1944 who was principal of Wardha Commercial College. It was a modest kind of plan.
- **In 1950 Sarvodaya Plan** came out which was drafted by Jaiprakash Narayan inspired by Gandhian plan as well as Sarvodaya idea of Vinoba Bhave. Along with agriculture it emphasized on small and cottage industries as well. It also suggested the freedom from foreign technology and stressed upon land reforms and decentralized participatory planning.

Niti Aayog

➡ 65-year-old Planning Commission has been dissolved and a new institution named NITI Aayog has been constituted by the National Democratic Alliance (NDA) government.

➡ Like Planning Commission the newly established NITI Aayog is also chaired by the Prime Minister.

➡ NITI Aayog or National Institution for Transforming India serves as a government think tank and is meant to reflect changes required in India's governance structures and provide a more active role for the state governments in achieving national objectives.

➡ The newly constituted institution provides governments at the central and state levels with strategic and technical advice across the spectrum of policy making.

➡ The NITI Aayog workes towards the following main objectives:

- To evolve a shared vision of national development priorities, sectors and strategies with the active involvement of States in the light of national objectives.
- To foster cooperative federalism through structured support initiatives and mechanisms with the States on a continuous basis, recognizing that strong States make a strong nation.
- To develop mechanisms to formulate credible plans at the village level and aggregate these progressively at higher levels of government.
- To ensure, on areas that are specifically referred to it, that the interests of national security are incorporated in economic strategy and policy.
- To offer a platform for resolution of inter-sectoral and inter-departmental issues in order to accelerate the implementation of the development agenda.
- To focus on technology upgradation and capacity building for implementation of programmes and initiatives.

Growth Performance in the Five-Year Plans

Sr. No.	Plan	Target	Actual
1.	First Plan (1951-56)	2.1	3.60
2.	Second Plan (1956-61)	4.5	4.21
3.	Third Plan (1961-66)	5.6	2.72
4.	Fourth Plan (1969-74)	5.7	2.05
5.	Fifth Plan (1974-79)	4.4	4.83
6.	Sixth Plan (1980-85)	5.2	5.54
7.	Seventh Plan (1985-90)	5.0	6.02
8.	Eighth Plan (1992-97)	5.6	6.68
9.	Ninth Plan (1997-2002)	6.5	5.50
10.	Tenth Plan (2002-2007)	8.0	7.7
11.	Eleventh Plan (2007-2012)	8.1	7.9
12.	Twelfth Plan (2012-2017)	8	----

12th Five Year Plan (2012-17)

➡ National Development Council has finally approved Draft 12th Five Year Plan in its meeting on December 27, 2012.

➡ As per approved Draft 12th Five Year Plan twenty-five core indicators that are listed below reflect the vision of rapid, sustainable and more inclusive growth.

- Real GDP Growth Rate of 8.0 per cent.
- Agriculture Growth Rate of 4.0 per cent.
- Manufacturing Growth Rate of 7.1 per cent.
- Industrial Sector Growth Rate of 7.6 per cent.
- Service Sector Growth Rate of 9.0 per cent.
- Generate 50 million new work opportunities in the non-farm sector and provide skill certification to equivalent numbers during the Twelfth Five Year Plan.

- Reduce IMR to 25 and MMR to 1 per 1000 live births, and improve Child Sex Ratio (0–6 years) to 950 by the end of the Twelfth Five Year Plan.
- Increase investment in infrastructure as a percentage of GDP to 9 per cent by the end of Twelfth Five Year Plan.
- Increase the Gross Irrigated Area from 90 million hectare to 103 million hectare by the end of Twelfth Five Year Plan.
- Connect all villages with all-weather roads by the end of Twelfth Five Year Plan.
- Complete Eastern and Western Dedicated Freight Corridors by the end of Twelfth Five Year Plan.
- Increase rural teledensity to 70 per cent by the end of 12th Five Year Plan.
- Increase green cover (as measured by satellite imagery) by 1 million hectare every year during the Twelfth Five Year Plan.
- Add 30000 MW of renewable energy capacity in the Twelfth Plan.
- Provide access to banking services to 90 per cent Indian house-holds by the end of Twelfth Five Year Plan.

India's Ambitious 15-Year Vision Plan

NITI Aayog has come forward with a draft 15-year vision plan to catapult the country's economy to more than three times as compared to the present day. The new plan is set to replace the centralised five-year plans the country has been following for decades.

The new plan is accompanied by shorter sub-plans—a seven-year strategy for 2017-24, and a three-year 'Action Agenda' from 2017-18 to 2019-20. No less than 300 specific action points covering a wide range of sectors have been drawn up as part of the 15 year vision.

The salient features of 15-year vision plan are:

- India aims to more than triple the size of its economy in 15 years with Gross Domestic Product (GDP) expected to rise to ₹ 469 lakh crore from ₹ 137 lakh crore in 2015-16. Per capita GDP is expected to rise by three times to ₹ 3,14,667 in 2015-2016.
- NITI Aayog plans to work closely with states to boost infrastructure and services, including regions that require special attention. The government made a big push for Goods and Services Tax (GST), urging the state governments to speed up the legislation of state GST bills.

UNEMPLOYMENT

➥ A person is considered unemployed, if he/she was not working but was either seeking or was available for a work for a relatively longer time throughout the year.

Types of Unemployment

➥ **Cyclical Unemployment:** The main cause of cyclical unemployment is the periodic slackness in business activities. This type of unemployment is generally witnessed in the developed countries.

➥ **Frictional Unemployment:** The temporary unemployment which exists during the period of the transfer of labour from one occupation to another is called frictional unemployment.

➥ **Structural Unemployment:** Basically, India's unemployment is structural in nature, related to the inadequacy of productive capacity to create enough jobs for all those able and willing to work. Not only is the productive capacity much below the needed capacity, it is also found increasing at a low rate.

- This type of unemployment is not a temporary phenomenon in the sense that it will pass of on its own after a lapse of time. It is chronic and is the result of backwardness and low rate of economic development.

➥ **Disguised Unemployment:** When more people are engaged in a job than actually required, they are called disguisedly unemployed. If a part of labour is withdrawn and the total production remains unchanged this withdrawn labour is called as disguised unemployed labour.

➥ **Seasonal Unemployment:**

- Generally, seasonal unemployment is confined to the agricultural sector because nature predominates in agriculture.
- The demand for agricultural labour increases at the time of sowing and harvesting which provides employment for six to eight months and for the remaining period most of the agricultural workers remain unemployed.

Reasons of Unemployment

➥ The reasons for unemployment in India can be categorised under three main heads: (*i*) Underdeveloped nature of economy; (*ii*) Inadequate employment planning; (iii) Rapid growth of population.

➥ In the pre-independence period, the British exploited our resources and destroyed indigenous small-scale and cottage industries. The net burden of surplus workers fell on the already overburdened agricultural sector.

➥ Even in post-independence phase, due to slow rate of capital formation, the economy was not able to generate sufficient infrastructural facilities which could absorb the people searching for jobs. Employment in agriculture is declining.

➥ Also, there has been migration of labour from rural to urban areas.

➥ Employment till recently did not form an integral part of planning strategy. Suitable labour-intensive techniques have not yet been developed. Poor manpower planning is yet another important cause.

➥ There is a mismatch between skills and employment opportunities.

➥ The rapid growth of population further adds to the severity of the problem of unemployment.

➥ The demand for consumption goods increases and the resources meant for capital formation diminish.

➥ Other associated factors are inappropriate technology being used and stunted plan for broadening the resource base.

Various Employment Generation Schemes

Sr. No.	Programme	Year of Beginning	Objective
1.	Community Development Programme (CDP)	1952	Overall development of rural areas with people's participation.
2.	Training Rural Youth for Self-Employment (TRYSEM)	Aug. 15, 1979	Programme of training rural youth for self-employment.
3.	Integrated Rural Development Programme (NREP)	Oct. 2, 1980	All-round development of the rural poor through a programme of asset endowment for self-employment.
4.	National Rural Employment Programme (NREP)	1980	To provide profitable employment opportunities to the rural poor.

Sr. No.	Programme	Year of Beginning	Objective
5.	Development of Women and Children in Rural Areas (DWCRA)	Sept., 1982	To provide suitable opportunities of self-employment to the women belonging to the rural families who are living below the poverty line.
6.	Council for Advancement of People's Action and Rural Technology (CAPART)	Sept. 1, 1986	To provide assistance for rural prosperity.
7.	Jawahar Rozgar Yojana	April 1989	For providing employment to rural unemployed.
8.	Nehru Rozgar Yojana	Oct. 1989	For providing employment to urban unemployed.
9.	Supply of Improved Toolkits to Rural Artisans	July 1992	To supply modern toolkits to the rural craftsmen except the weavers, tailors, embroiders and tobacco labourers who are living below the poverty line.
10.	Employment Assurance Scheme (EAS)	Oct. 2, 1993	To provide employment of at least 100 days in a year in villages.
11.	District Rural Development Agency (DRDA)	1993	To provide financial assistance for rural development.
12.	Swarna Jayanti Shahari Rozgar Yojana (SJSRY)	Dec. 1997	To provide gainful employment to urban unemployed and under-employed poor through self-employment or wage-employment.
13.	Swarna Jayanti Gram Swarozgar Yojana (SJGSY)	April 1999	For eliminating Rural poverty and unemployment and promoting self-employment.
14.	Mahatma Gandhi National Rural Employment Guarantee Act (MNREGA)	Feb. 2, 2006	To provide at least 100 days wage-employment in rural areas.
15.	Pradhan Mantri Kaushal Vikas Yojana	March 2015	To provide skill training to youth.
16.	Deen Dayal Upadhyay Grameen Kaushlya Yojana	Sep. 24, 2015	Skill development of rural youth.
17.	Atal Innovation Mission	2015-16	Atal Innovation Mission and Self Employment and Talent Utilisation
18.	Pt. Deen Dayal Upadhyay Shramev Jayate Scheme	Oct. 16, 2014	To improve employability, skill development and other conveniences for labour.
19.	Twenty Point Programme (TPP)	1975	Poverty eradication and raising the standard of living.
20.	Antyodaya Yojana	1977-78	To make the poorest families of the village economically independent (only in Rajasthan State).
21.	Pradhan Mantri Gram Sadak Yojana (PMGSY)	Dec. 25, 2000	To line all villages with Pacca Road.
22.	Atmanirbhar Bharat Rojgar Yojana	Dec. 9, 2020	To boost employment in formal sector.
23.	PM Vishwakarma Kaushal Samman	2023	For providing assistance to traditional artisans and crafts people.
24.	Dharti Aaba Janjatiya Gram Utkarsh Abhiyan	Sep. 18, 2024	For development of tribal areas and communities.
25.	Prime Minister Dhan Dhaanya Krishi Yojana	2025	It aims to enhance agricultural productivity.

POVERTY

- Poverty can be defined as a social phenomenon in which a section of the society is unable to fulfil even its basic necessities of life.
- When a substantial segment of a society is deprived of the minimum level of living and continues at a bare subsistence level, that society is said to be plagued with mass poverty.
- The countries of the third world exhibit invariably the existence of mass poverty, although pockets of poverty exist even in the developed countries of Europe and America.
- The Planning Commission has adopted an alternative definition of poverty provided by the "Task force on projections of minimum needs and effective consumption demand".

TENDULKAR REPORT ON POVERTY

- The Government of India had set up the Tendulkar Committee after facing criticism about under-reporting its official estimates of rural poverty.
- According to the committee's estimates, the overall poverty rate come to be 37.2 per cent and not 27.5 per cent as was estimated in 2004-05. Similarly, poverty in rural India stood at 41.8 per cent and not 28.3 per cent. Urban poverty rate in 2004-05 came to be 25.7% according to the new estimates.
- States like Odisha, Bihar, Madhya Pradesh, Chhattisgarh and Jharkhand are found to be living under abject poverty.

New Poverty Line

- Those spending over ₹ 32 a day in rural areas and ₹ 47 in towns and cities should not be considered poor, an expert panel headed by former RBI governor C. Rangarajan said in a report submitted to the government. Based on the Suresh Tendulkar Panel's recommendations in 2011-12, the poverty line had been fixed at ₹ 27 in rural areas and ₹ 33 in urban areas, levels at which getting two meals may be difficult.
- The panel's recommendation, however, results in an increase in the below poverty line population, which is estimated at 363 million in 2011-12, compared to the 270 million estimate based on the Tendulkar formula—an increase of almost 35%.
- This means 29.5% of the India population lives below the poverty line as defined by the Rangarajan committee, as against 21.9% according to Tendulkar.

Poverty Line

Committee	Year	Per capita Expenditure per day (₹)		Per capita Average Monthly Expenditure (₹)		All India Poverty Line (Average Monthly Expenditure per Family of 5)	
		Rural	Urban	Rural	Urban	Rural	Urban
Rangarajan	2011-12	32.4	46.9	972	1407	4760	7035
	2009-10	26.7	39.9	801	1198	4005	5990
Tendulkar	2011-12	27.2	33.3	816	1000	4080	5000
	2009-10	22.4	28.7	673	860	3365	4300

Poverty Alleviation & Employment Programmes

Mahatma Gandhi National Rural Employment Guarantee Act

- Evolving the design of the wage employment programmes to more effectively fight poverty, the Centre formulated the Mahatma Gandhi National Rural Employment Guarantee Act (MGNREGA) in 2005.
- Notified on September 7, 2005, MGNREGA aims at enhancing livelihood security by providing at least one hundred days of guaranteed wage employment in a financial year to every rural household whose adult members volunteer to do unskilled manual work.

Swarnajayanti Gram Swarozgar Yojana

- The Swarnajayanti Gram Swarozgar Yojana (SGSY) was launched with effect from April 1, 1999 to bring the assisted poor families above the poverty line by ensuring appreciable sustained level of income over a period of time.
- The programme was a revamp of the erstwhile Integrated Rural Development Programme (IRDP), Development of Women and Children in Rural Areas (DWCRA), Training of Rural Youth for Self-Employment (TRYSEM), Supply of Improved Toolkits to Rural Artisans (SITRA), Ganga Kalyan Yojana (GKY) and Million Wells Scheme (MWS).

National Rural Livelihood Mission — Aajeevika

- Union government has launched **'National Rural Livelihood Mission'** with the aim to eliminate poverty in rural areas. Mrs. Sonia Gandhi on June 3, 2011 launched this Mission from Banswada District of Rajasthan.
- Under this mission, Self-help Groups (SHGs) at the village level is constituted in the form of federation and these SHGs provide beneficial self-employment opportunities to the rural people for ensuring better and stable livelihood.
- The new mission gives focus on women, scheduled caste/scheduled tribes, minorities and disabled people. The mission proposes to include atleast one woman member of the identified poor family in Self-help Group.

Pradhan Mantri Gram Sadak Yojana

- PMGSY was launched on December 25, 2000 as a 100 per cent Centrally-sponsored scheme with the primary objective to provide all-weather connectivity to all the eligible unconnected habitations in the rural areas.
- The programme is funded mainly from the accruals of diesel cess in the Central Road Fund.

Indira Awaas Yojana

- The objective of IAY is to provide financial assistance for construction/ upgradation of houses to BPL rural households belonging to the Scheduled Castes and Scheduled Tribes, freed bonded labourers, non-SC/ST rural households, widows and physically handicapped persons living in the rural areas.
- The scheme is funded on a cost-sharing basis of 75 : 25 between the Centre and the States. However, in the case of NE States, the funding pattern has recently been revised to 90 : 10.

Jawahar Rozgar Yojana

- Prime Minister Rajiv Gandhi announced on 28th April, 1989 the launching of the Jawahar Rozgar Yojana (JRY).
- All the existing rural wage employment programmes were merged into JRY. This implies that National Rural Employment Programme (NREP) and Rural Landless Employment Guarantee Programme (RLEGP) have been merged so as to be brought under this umbrella programme referred to as Jawahar Rozgar Yojana.

Objectives of JRY

- **Primary Objective** — Generation of gainful employment for the unemployed and under-employed, men and women in rural areas.
- **Secondary Objectives** — JRY had several secondary objectives :
  - creation of sustained employment by strengthening the rural infra-structure;
  - creating community and social assets;
  - creating assets in favour of the poor for their direct and continuing benefits;
  - to produce positive impact on wage levels; and
  - to bring about over-all improvement in quality of life in rural areas.

Swarna Jayanti Shahri Rozgar Yojana (SJSRY)

- The SJSRY came into operation in December 1997 through a restructuring and streamlining of the earlier urban poverty alleviation programmes, the Nehru Rozgar Yojana (NRY), the Urban Basic Services for the Poor (UBSP) and the Prime Minister's Integrated Urban Poverty Alleviation Programme (PMIUPEP).
- It seeks to provide employment to the urban unemployed or underemployed living below poverty line and educated up to ninth standard through encouraging the setting up of self-employment ventures or provision of wage employment.

Annapurna Scheme

- Launched as a Centrally-sponsored scheme, "Annapurna" scheme aims at providing food security to indigent senior citizens who have no income of their own and none to take care of them in the villages.
- The scheme envisages provision of 10 kg of foodgrains per month, free of cost, to senior citizens who are eligible for old age pension but are at present not receiving it.

Antyodaya Anna Yojana

- On December 25, 2000, the prime minister announced the implementation of the Antyodaya Anna Yojana (AAY).
- The scheme was to provide an estimated one crore 'poorest of the poor' families in the country 25 kg of wheat or rice per month at the highly subsidised rates of ₹ 2 and ₹ 3 per kg respectively. The quantity was enhanced to 35 kg from April 1, 2002.

Janashree Bima Yojana

- It provides life insurance protection to the rural and urban poor persons below poverty line and marginally above the poverty line.
- The premium under the scheme was ₹ 200 per annum per member. 50 per cent of the premium,

i.e., ₹ 100 was contributed by the member and/or nodal agency/ state government and the balance 50 per cent was met by the Social Security Fund.

- In the event of death (other than by accident) of the member, an amount of ₹ 30,000 is payable. In case of death/total permanent disability due to accident, an amount of ₹ 75,000 is payable. In case of permanent partial disability, due to accident, an amount of ₹ 37,500 is payable.

Aam Admi Bima Yojana (AABY)

- Launched on October 2, 2007, insurance to the head of the family of rural landless households in the country will be provided against natural death as well as accidental death and partial/permanent disability.
- This cover is ₹ 75,000 on death due to accident and permanent disability due to accident, ₹ 37,500 in case of partial permanent disability due to accident and ₹ 30,000 in case of death of a member, prior to terminal date.
- The premium to be charged under the scheme is ₹ 200 per annum per member, 50 per cent of which is to be contributed by the Central government and remaining by state governments.

Rashtriya Swasthya Bima Yojana

- The Rashtriya Swasthya Bima Yojana was formally launched on October 1, 2007.
- All workers in the unorganised sector who come in the category of Below Poverty Line (BPL) and their families will be covered under the scheme.
- The scheme also has a provision of smart card to be issued to the beneficiaries to enable cashless transaction for health care.
- Total sum insured would be ₹ 30,000 per family per annum with Government of India contributing 75 per cent of the annual estimated premium while state governments are expected to contribute 25 per cent of the annual premium as well as any additional premium.

Pradhan Mantri Adarsh Gram Yojana

- Pradhan Mantri Adarsh Gram Yojana (PMAGY) aims for integrated development of selected villages having more than 50% Scheduled Caste (SC) population through implementation of existing scheme of a Central and State Governments in a convergent manner and by utilization of gap filling funds provided as Central Assistance.
- The scheme was launched in 2009-10 on a pilot basis, for the integrated development of 1000 villages in 5 States viz. Himachal Pradesh (Northern Region), Bihar (Eastern Region), Rajasthan (Western Region), Tamil Nadu (Southern Region) and Assam (North-Eastern Region) and further extended in 2015 to another 1500 villages.

National Food Security Scheme-2013

- The National Food Security Scheme has finally launched in August 2013, the birth anniversary of late Prime Minister Rajiv Gandhi, in NCR Delhi, Haryana and Uttarakhand.
- The scheme has been launched through the National Food Security Ordinance, 2013 promulgated by the President of India on July 3, 2013.
- This is a step towards the goal of 'Food for All'.

Sansad Adarsh Gram Yojana

- Launched on October 11, 2014.
- **Main Objective:** Social, cultural, economic, infrastructure deve-lopments in the villages, i.e., development of model villages called 'Adarsh Gram.'
- Each MP should adopt a village of his choice, which should not be his own or his in-laws. This should be turned into a model village by 2016. Then for the next three years, two more villages should be chosen and developed. after 2019, one village should be taken up every year till 2024.

Deen Dayal Upadhyaya Gram Jyoti Yojana (DDUGJY)

- Launched on July 25, 2015.
- **Main Objective:** Electric supply feeder separation (rural households and agricultural) and strengthening of subtransmission and distri-bution infrastructure including metering at all levels in rural areas.
- DDUGJY will help in providing round the clock power to rural households and adequate power to agricultural consumers. The earlier scheme for rural electrificaiton viz. Rajiv Gandhi Grameen Vidyutikaran Yojana (RGGVY) has been subsumed in the new scheme as its rural electrification component.

Shyama Prasad Mukherjee Rurban Mission

- Launched on February 21, 2016.
- **Main Objective:** To create 300 rural cluster across the country and strengthen financial, job, and lifestyle facilities in rural areas.
- Rurban Mission is a solution for both villages and cities in the country that would promote growth of villages and its residents at the place where they are. Under the mission, the government will identify and develop 300 rural clusters with urban like facilities in the next 3 years.

Pradhan Mantri Awas Yojana (PMAY)

- Launched on June 25, 2015.
- **Main Objective:** Achieve housing for all by the year 2022, 2 crore in Urban and 3 crore homes in Rural areas.
- Under the scheme, the government will provide financial asistance to the poor home buyers, interest subsidy on home loan and direct subsidy on homes bought under the scheme.

Atal Mission for Rejuvenation and Urban Transformation (AMRUT)

- Launched on June 24, 2015.
- **Main Objective:** Providing basic services (e.g., water supply, sewerage, urban transport) to house-holds and build amenities in cities which will improve the quality of life for all, especially the poor and the disadvantaged.
- The purpose of Atal Mission for Rejuvenation and Urban Trans-formation (AMRUT) is to
  - ensure that every household has access to a tap with assured suply of water and a sewerge connection;
  - increase the amenity value of cities by developing greenery and well maintained open spaces (e.g., parks); and
  - reduce pollution by switching to public transport or constructing facilities for non-motorized transport (e.g., walking and cycling).

Skill India

- Launched on July 16, 2015.
- **Main Objective:** Train over 40 crore people in India in different skills by 2022.
- The main goal of Skill India Program is to create opportunities, space and scope for the development of talents of the Indian youth.
- The scheme also targeted to identify new sectors for skill development and develop more of those sectors which have already been put under skill development for the last so many years.

SUMAN Scheme

- Aiming zero preventable maternal and newborn deaths in India, the central government on October 10, 2019 launched the Surakshit Matritiva Aashwasan (SUMAN) scheme, under which pregnant women, mothers up to 6 months after delivery, and all sick newborns will be able to avail free healthcare benefits.

Pradhan Mantri Kaushal Vikas Yojana (PMKVY)

- Prime Minister Narendra Modi on January 8, 2017 announced that the government is planning to launch Pravasi Kaushal Vikas Yojana to train Indian youth for overseas employment.
- The programme seeks to train and certify Indians who are seeking overseas employment.
- The objective of this Skill Certification Scheme is to enable a large number of Indian youth to take up industry-relevant skill training that will help them in securing a better livelihood. Individuals with prior learning experience or skills will also be assessed and certified under Recognition of Prior Learning (RPL).

AGRICULTURE

Importance of Agriculture

- The performance of the agricultural sector influences the growth of the Indian economy.
- The share of agriculture and allied sectors in GVA of the country has declined from 20.2 per cent in 2020-21 to 19.9 per cent in 2022-23.
- It accounts more than 46.1 per cent of the employment in the country.
- Apart from being the provider of food and fodder, its importance also stems from the raw materials that it provides to industry.
- The prosperity of the rural economy is also closely linked to agriculture and allied activities.
- Agricultural and allied sector has a share of 16.1 per cent in the country's GDP for FY 2024 at current prices.
- Economic development without agricultural development creates bottlenecks and generate inflationary pressure. This is what has happened in India. Low rate of agricultural development resulted in shortage of food and essential raw materials leading to inflation. Therefore, agricultural development is essential to avoid inflation and to ensure growth with stability.

Green Revolution

- After the drought of 1965-66 and 1966-67, the government enunciated the new agricultural strategy, and put to use the high yielding variety seeds.
- The Green Revolution came on the scene around the middle of the 1960s, beginning with the Kharif crop of 1966.

- The new agricultural strategy was put into practice for the first time in India in the Kharif season of 1966 and was termed High-Yielding Varities Programme (HYVP).
- The HYVP was intoduced in the form of a package programme since it depended crucially on regular and adequate irrigation, fertilizers, high-yielding varieties of seeds, pesticides and insecticides.

Drawbacks of Green Revolution

- The spread of green revolution has remained limited to only a few regions. Excepting Punjab, Haryana and Western Uttar Pradesh practically the whole country has remained untouched by the green revolution.
- Intra-regional disparity has also increased, as not all, but 'only who could aford' took the advantage of new expensive package technology.
- Environmental degradation took as
  - Chemical fertilizers led to problems of entrochication etc.
  - Pesticides killed many nutrient enriching bacteria of the soil.
  - Bio-diversity decreased as mono-culturisation introduced.
- Groundwater went down in areas where wells and tube wells sucked excess of water.
- Irrigation of fields, without proper drainage led to salinization and alkalization of soils.
- As a consequence of the concentration of the new technology in large farms, the inequalities have increased between the rich and the poor in the rural sector.

Second Green Revolution

- In 2004, a second green revolution policy was announced by the government, and even though the next, government at the Centre did not refer to it, the ingredients have been promoted in practice.
- The effort is to increase agricultural production, going beyond just some foodgrains to all sectors.
- It ranges across cropping patterns, diversification, checking post-harvest losses, sustainable practices, soil and water conservation, *et al*.
- It also includes encouraging use of bio-fertilisers, bio-pesticides, and organic farming.
- There is also the elements of improving infrastructure, storage, and value addition—agroprocessing.
- Indeed, the Eleventh Plan vision and strategy for agriculture was largely based on the holistic approach involving the 'second green revolution'.

Rainbow Revolution

The new agricultural policy promises Green Revolution, White Revolution, and Blue Revolution. The Rainbow Revolution also includes 'Foodchain Revolution' to put a check on destroying food-grains, vegetables and fruits. It has described as a policy of promising Rainbow Revolution.

- A focus on Price protection for farmers to suit their requirements.
- Dismantling of restrictions on movement of agricultural commodities.
- Involvement of private sector through Contract Farming.
- 4% targeted annual growth in the development of agriculture.

Land Reforms

- A land reforms package broadly involves the following components:
  - abolition of intermediaries,
  - tenancy reforms (i.e., providing security of tenure),
  - ceiling and redistribution,
  - consolidation, and
  - updating of land records.

Abolition of Intermediaries

- Even during the struggle for independence, it was widely recognised that the stagnation in the Indian agricultural sector was primarily due to exploitative agrarian relations. Zamindars were the chief instrument of exploitation.
- Hence, abolition of zamindari system, along with other intermediary tenure systems, became the topmost priority of land reforms immediately after independence.
- The abolition of intermediaries started in 1948 with the enactment of legislation in Madras. In some other states, the legislations for abolition of intermediaries were passed before 1951.
- West Bengal, the state worst affected by the ravages of absentee landlordism, adopted the legislation in 1954-55. In this way, most of the states had passed the Acts related to abolition of intermediaries by the end of the First Plan.

Tenancy Reforms

- Tenants can be classified into (*i*) occupancy tenants, (*ii*) tenants-at-will, and (*iii*) sub-tenants.
- The rights of tenancy of the occupancy tenants are permanent and heritable. Hence, the occupancy tenants do not face the fear of eviction so long as they pay rent on time.
- But the position of tenants-at-will and sub-tenants is very precarious, since such tenants depend on the mercy of landlords.
- Hence, special laws have had to be enacted and implemented to protect these people.
- These laws relate to: (*i*) regulation of rent, (*ii*) security of tenure, and (*iii*) conferment of ownership rights on tenants.

(*i*) **Regulation of Rent:** The First and the Second Plans recommended that rents should not exceed one-fourth or one-fifth of the gross produce. Various states have passed necessary legislation in this regard, but there are large variations in the rates of rents fixed in different states.

(*ii*) **Security of Tenure :** Legislations have been passed in most of the states to protect tenants from ejectment and grant them permanent rights in land. The purpose of these legislations is to ensure that (*i*) ejectments are lawful, (*ii*) land assumed by an owner is only for personal cultivation, and (*iii*) the tenant is assured of a prescribed minimum area in case of resumption.

(*iii*) **Conferment of Ownership Rights on Tenants:** Legislative provisions have been made in many states for conferment of ownership rights on tenants. Some of the states have acquired ownership of land from landowners and transferred it to tenants. Sub-tenancies have generally been prohibited except in certain cases such as widows, members of armed forces, minors, unmarried women, persons suffering from disabilities, etc.

Ceilings on Agricultural Holdings

- The basic aim of the ceiling laws is to accomplish the elimination of excessive ownership of land.
- Till 2001, only about 73.66 lakh acres were declared surplus in India, out of which only about 53.79 lakh acres were redistributed. Further, different states had adopted different policies regarding land ceiling.
- To bring uniformity in land ceiling policies, a conference of chief ministers was held in 1972.
- A new land ceiling policy was evolved in this conference. The main features of the new policy were as follows:
  - lowering of ceilings to 18 acres of irrigated land and 54 acres of unirrigated land,
  - making family and not the individual as the unit for determining land holding,
  - lowering ceiling for a family of five,
  - declaring benami transaction null and void, and
  - including the land reform laws in the Ninth Schedule of the Constitution, which places them beyond any challenge in any courts of law on the grounds of infringement of Fundamental Rights.
- In the light of this policy, land ceiling legislations were enacted by all the states, except Goa and north-east states. But ceiling limits vary.

Consolidation of Land Holdings

- The basic purpose of consolidation of land holdings is that the owner of several scattered pieces of land be provided with land at one place and it should be equivalent to all pieces of land.
- All the States, except Kerala, Tamil Nadu and Andhra Pradesh have passed the law for consolidation of holdings.
- Updating and Maintenance of Land Records
- With a view to assisting the States/ Union Territories in the task of updating of land records, a Centrally-sponsored Strengthening of Revenue Administration and Updating of Land Records (SRA&ULR) scheme was started in 1987 with the following objectives:
  - strengthening the existing survey and settlement organisations for early completion and preparation of land records in areas where this work still remains to be done;
  - setting up survey and settlement organisations, especially in north-eastern region, where no land records exist;
  - imparting pre-service and in-service training to revenue survey and settlement staff and strengthening of training infrastructure for this purpose;
  - providing facilities for modernisation of survey and settlement operations, printing of survey maps, documents reports, copying and updating of land and crop records, and storage facilities by adopting the latest science and technology inputs; and
  - strengthening revenue machineries at village and immediate supervisory levels on a selective basis so that workload of these functionaries is made manageable.

Agricultural Finance

- Finance is an essential requirement for every productive activity. However, agriculture is up against serious credit problems.
- Besides the large many of the rural folk are groaning under the burden of indebtedness.
- Three types of loans are provided to Indian farmers to meet their financial requirements–
  (*i*) Short term loans (*ii*) Medium term loans (*iii*) Long term loans
- Short term loans are provided for a period of less than 15 months to meet out expenses of routine farming and domestic consumptions. This type of loans is demanded by farmers for purchasing seeds, fertilizers and for meeting out family requirements.
- Medium term loans are provided for a period of 15 months to 5 years to purchase agricultural equipments, animals and for purchasing seeds, fertilizers and for meeting out family requirements.
- Long term loans are provided for a period of more than 5 years. This type of loan is taken by the farmers to purchase land and expensive agricultural equipments and for repayment of old loans.

Sources of Agricultural Finance

- The sources of agricultural finance can be divided into two parts: (*i*) institutional sources, and (*ii*) non-institutional sources.
- The Non-institutional sources include moneylenders, landlords, traders, relatives and commission agents.
- The institutional sources include cooperative societies, commercial banks, regional rural banks, NABARD and RBI.
- Non-institutional sources continue to be important, although their share in the total credit is on the decline.
- At the time of Independence, the most important source of agricultural credit was the moneylender.
- In 1951 moneylenders accounted for as much as 71.6 per cent of rural credit.
- As a result of the efforts undertaken by the government to expand the institutional sources of finance, the importance of non-institutional sources (especially moneylenders) in rural credit has declined significantly.

Co-operative Credit Societies

- The cooperative movement was initiated in 1904 through the establishment of co-operative credit societies.
- Cooperative Credit Societies are based on three-tier structure, except the states in north-east region.
- At the lowest tier are the village level Primary Agricultural Credit Societies (PACSs). PACSs can be formed by any ten or more than ten persons. PACSs provide loans generally for productive purposes.
- At the second tier are the District Central Co-operative Banks (DCBs). DCBs advance loans to the PACSs in time of so that they can fulfil the requirements of agriculture.
- At uppermost tier are the State Co-operative Banks (SCBs). The SCBs advances loans to the DCBs in order to augment their capacity to provide loans to the PACSs. It also co-ordinates and regulates the working of DCBs. For long-term finance, there are land development banks.

Commercial Banks

- The credit supply by commercial banks has been on the increase particularly since the nationalisation of major banks in 1969.
- The share of commercial banks in rural credit was only 0.9 per cent in 1951 which rose to 72 per cent in 2023-24.

Regional Rural Banks

- On the basis of the recommendations of working group, five regional rural banks (RRBs) were initially set up in 1975.
- Their number later rose to 196. As on May 01, 2025; 28 RRBs with more than 22,000 branches are working in India.
- RRBs are sponsored by the government and the commercial banks. The regions for their operations (normally district) are specified.
- RRBs provide credits mainly to small and marginal farmers, rural artisans etc.

National Bank for Agriculture and Rural Development

- NABARD was set up in July 1982. NABARD is the apex bank for rural credit. Its head office is in Mumbai.
- The main functions of NABARD are as follows:
  - NABARD is responsible for the development, policy planning, operational matters, coodination, monitoring, research, training and consultancy, etc., relating credit.
  - It has authority to oversee the functioning of the co-operative sector through its Agricultural Credit Department.
  - It provides short-term credit (upto 18 months) to SCBs.
  - It provides refinance to DCBs and RRBs for medium term credit requirement.
  - It provides refinance for long-term credit requirement to SCBs, land development banks, RRBs and commercial banks.
  - It provides long-term loans to the state governments for a maximum period of 20 years, for contribution to share capital of co-operative credit societies.

INDUSTRIAL DEVELOPMENT

- Industry refers to the economic activities which are connected with raising, producing or processing of goods and services. It also refers to groups of firms producing similar or related goods and services.
- This sector possesses a relatively higher marginal propensity to save and invest, thereby contributing significantly to the achievement of a self-sustaining economy, for
  - Industrialisation leads to an increase in per capita income and provides goods to meet high income demands;
  - It provides increasing avenues for employment of new and skilled labour force;
  - It enables diversifications of the market required at higher stages of development;
  - It provides infrastructural facilities like railways, power generation, etc., for further economic development; and
  - It helps in earning foreign exchange because the income-elasticity of demand for industrial products is much higher than that for agricultural products.

Types of Industries

- We distinguish the industries in terms of capital investments as large, small and tiny sectors.
- On the basis of ownership, we can define a business undertaking as private, public or joint sector enterprise.
- A **private sector** enterprise is one which is owned, managed and controlled by an individual or a group of individuals.
- A **publc sector** enterprise is one which is owned, managed and controlled by the Central government or local authority.
- A **joint sector** enterprise is one which is owned, managed and controlled jointly by the private entrepreneurs and the government. Some examples: Praga Tools Corporation, Cochin Refineries, Indian Rare Earth Limited, etc.

Industrial Policy

- The industrial policy of any government seeks to formulate a philosophy for the pattern of industrialisation.

The Industrial Policy Resolution, 1948

- This policy divided the industries into four broad categories:
- The first category included the manufacture of arms and amm-unition, the production and control of atomic energy and the ownership of railways. This category would belong to the exclusive monopoly of the Central Government.
- Second category included coal, iron, ship-building, aircrafts and telephones. New plants in these industries would be taken only by the Government.
- The third category included certain basic industries such as automobiles, tractors, heavy machinery, machine tools, cement, sugar, etc. The Government of India would regulate these industries because of the importance of these industries.
- The last category included all the other industries except the above. These industries were open to private sector.

Industrial Licensing Act, 1951

- Following the Industrial Policy Resolution of 1948, the Industrial (Development and Regulation) Act of 1951 was passed.
- This Act provided the framework for the licensing and regulation of industrial investment in India.
- The Industrial (Development and Regulation) Act of 1951 has the following objectives:
  - The development and regulation of industrial investments and production accordiing to plan priorities.
  - The encouragement of 'small' industries;
  - The prevention of concentration of ownership of industries in India; and
  - Balanced regional development so as to reduce the inequalities.

The Industrial Policy (1956)

- The first five-year plan started in April 1951 came to an end in 1956. The "Directive Principles" enunciated by the congress laid stress on a new policy for the country and that was a 'socialistic pattern of society'.
- All these changes add developments necessitated for a new policy that came in to operation from 30th April, 1956.

- The main objectives of the policy are as below:
  - To accelerate the rate of economic growth.
  - To expand public sector developing heavy industries.
  - To create more employment opportunity.

New Industrial Policy, 1991

- Making a sharp departure from the Industrial Policy Resolution, 1956, the Government announced a new industrial policy on July 24, 1991.
- The basic philosophy of the new policy has been summed up as: 'continuity with change'.
- The new industrial policy seeks to achieve the following objectives:
  - To maintain a sustained growth in the productivity and gainful employment.
  - To attain international competitiveness.
  - To correct the distortions or weaknesses that may have crept in the industrial structure as it has developed over the last four decadess.
  - To consolidate the strength build up during the last four decades of economic planning and to build on the gain already made.
- The pursuit of these objectives will be tempered by:
  - The need to preserve the environment, and
  - the need to ensure the efficient use of available resources.
- In pursuit of the above objectives, Government has decided to take a series of initiatives in respect of the policies relating to the following areas:
  - Industrial licensing has been abolished for all projects except for a short list of industries related to security and strategic concerns, social reasons, hazardous chemicals and overriding environmental reasons, and items of luxurious consumption.
  - Only six industries groups where security and strategic concerns predominate are under the purview of industrial licensing.

    These are: alcohol, cigarettes, hazardous chemicals, electronics, aerospace and defence-equipment, drugs and pharmaceuticals and industrial explosive. (Drugs and Pharmaceuticals are now exempt from the list)
  - Approval will be given for direct foreign investment up to 51 per cent equity in high priority industries (34 such group of industries have been identified). Such clearance will be available if foreign equity covers the foreign exchange requirement for imported capital goods.

MAHARATANA STATUS

- The Government introduced the Maharatna scheme in February 2010 with the objective to delegate enhanced powers to the Boards of identified large size Navratna CPSEs to facilitate further expansion of their operations, both in domestic as well as global markets.
- Criteria for grant of Maharatna status:
  - Having Navratna status.
  - Listed on Indian stock exchange with minimum prescribed public shareholding under SEBI regulations.

- Average annual turnover of more than ₹ 25,000 crore, during the last 3 years.
- Average annual net worth of more than ₹ 15,000 crore, during the last 3 years.
- Average annual net profit after tax of more than ₹ 5,000 crore during the last 3 years.
- Should have significant global presence/international operations.

➥ The Government has currently (June 2025) conferred Maharatna status to 14 CPSEs namely, (*i*) Indian Oil Corporation Limited, (*ii*) NTPC Limited, (*iii*) Oil and Natural Gas Corporation Limited, (*iv*) Steel Authority of India Limited, (*v*) Coal India Ltd., (*vi*) BHEL, (*vii*) GAIL (*viii*) BPCL, (*ix*) HPCL, (*x*) PGCIL, (*xi*) PFC, (*xii*) RECL and (*xiii*) Oil India Ltd. (*xiv*) Hindustan Aeronautical Ltd. (HAL).

Navratna Status

➥ Criteria for grant of Navratna status: (*i*) Net profit to net worth, (*ii*) manpower cost to total cost of production/services, (*iii*) profit before depreciation, interest and taxes to capital employed, (*iv*) profit before interest and taxes to turnover, (*v*) earning per share and (*vi*) inter-sectoral performance.

➥ A Company must first be Mini Ratna and must have four independent directors on its board before it can be made a Navratna.

List of Navratna Companies (June 2025)

➥ Mahanagar Telephone Nigam Ltd. (MTNL)

➥ Bharat Electronics Ltd. (BEL)

➥ Rail Vikas Nigam Limited

➥ National Mineral Development Corporation (NMDC)

➥ ONGC Videsh Ltd.

➥ National Aluminium Company (NALCO)

➥ Shipping Corporation of India (SCI)

➥ Rashtriya Ispat Nigam Ltd. (RINL)

➥ Neyveli Lignite Corporation Ltd.

➥ Engineers India Ltd.

➥ National Building Construction Corporation Ltd.

➥ Container Corporation of India Ltd.

➥ Rashtriya Chemicals and Fertilizers Limited

➥ IRCON International Limited

➥ RITES Limited

➥ National Fertilizers Limited

➥ Central Warehosing Corporation

➥ Housing and Urban Development Corporation Limited

➥ Indian Renewable Energy Development Agency limited

➥ Nazagon Dock Shipbuilders Limited

➥ Railtel Corporation of India Limited

➥ Solar Energy Corporation of India (SECI) Ltd.

➥ NHPC Limited

➥ SJVN Limited

➥ IRCTC

➥ IRFC

Small Scale Industries

➥ The small enterprises constitute an important segment of the Indian economy, contributing around 45 per cent of the country's manu-facturing output and 40 per cent of its exports.

➥ It provides employment to around 31 million people in the rural and urban areas of the country.

Classification

➡ **Revised MSME Classification (April 01, 2025:**

- *Micro*: Investment in plants and machinery less than ₹ 2.5 crore and Turnover less than ₹ 10 crore.
- *Small:* Investment in plants and machinery greater than ₹ 2.5 crore and less than ₹ 25 crore and Turnover greater than ₹ 10 crore and less than ₹ 100 crore.
- *Medium:* Investment in plants and machinery greater than ₹ 25 crore and less than ₹ 125 crore and Turnover greater than ₹ 100 crore and less than ₹ 500 crore.

Role of Small-Scale Industries in India

➡ **Employment Generation:** After agriculture, small enterprises provide employment to the largest number of people in India.

➡ **Equitable Distribution of National Income:** Small enterprises ensure more equitable distribution of the national income and wealth because: (*i*) the ownership of small scale industries is more widespread than that of large-scale industries; and (*ii*) they possess a much larger employment potential as compared to the large-scale industries.

➡ **Mobilisation of Capital and Entrepreneurial Skills:** A number of entrepreneurs are spread over small towns and villages of the country and large-scale industries obviously cannot utilise them as efficiently as the small scale industries can. Similarly, large-scale industries cannot mobilise savings of the people in areas far away from the urban centres. But this task can be effectively accomplished by setting up a network of small scale industries.

➡ **Regional Dispersal of Industries:** Small scale industries are mostly setup to satisfy local demand and they can be dispersed over all the states very easily. They can also effect a qualitative change in the economy of a state.

➡ **Making Growth Inclusive:** Micro and small enterprises do not just generate the highest employment per capita, but are means to reach inclusive growth. For many families, it is the only source of livelihood.

➡ **Checking Rural-Urban Migration:** By providing villagers and people living in remote areas with a sustainable means of employment, small industries help to check rural-urban migration.

➡ **Ancillary Units for Large Scale Industry:** Small industries often act as ancillary industries for LSIs providing them with raw materials, vital components, and backward linkages.

➡ **Export Contribution:** Small scale industries have contributed greatly to the export potential of India; bulk of exports of this sector consists of such non-traditional items like readymade garments, sports goods, finished leather, leather products, woollen garments and a large number of engineering goods.

BANKING

History of Banking in India

➡ History of Indian banking goes back to 19th century. It was known as 'agency houses'. First successful bank in India was 'Bank of Bengal' set up in 1806.

➡ First commercial bank in the country was Awadh Commercial Bank established in 1881.

➡ In 1921, Imperial Bank of India was set up.

- There were two important steps in the banking sector after independence in 1949:
  - Nationalisation of the Reserve Bank of India
  - Banking Regulation Act which empowered the Reserve Bank of India to control and regulate banking sector in the country.

Nationalisation of Banks

- In 1969, 14 banks with having deposits of more than ₹50 crore were nationalised. In 1980, 6 more banks were nationalized.

List of Banks Nationalised in 1969

- Central Bank of India
- Bank of India
- Punjab National Bank
- Canara Bank
- United Commercial Bank
- Syndicate Bank
- Bank of Baroda
- United Bank of India
- Union Bank of India
- Dena Bank
- Allahabad Bank
- Indian Bank
- Indian Overseas Bank
- Bank of Maharashtra

List of Banks Nationalised in 1980

- Andhra Bank
- Punjab and Sind Bank
- New Bank of India
- Vijaya Bank
- Corporation Bank
- Oriental Bank of Commerce

The structure of banking in India consists of following components:

1. **Central Bank** – Reserve Bank of India (RBI)
2. **Commercial Banks**
   (*a*) Public sector Banks
   (*b*) Private Banks
   (*c*) Foreign Banks
3. **Co-operative Banks**
   (*a*) Primary Credit Societies
   (*b*) Central Co-operative Banks
   (*c*) State Co-operative Banks
4. **Regional Rural Banks**
5. **Development Banks**
6. **Specialized Banks**
   (*a*) Export Import Bank of India
   (*b*) Small Industries Development Bank of India
   (*c*) National Bank for Agricultural and Rural Development
7. **Microfinance institutions**
8. **Development financial institutions**

The Reserve Bank of India

- The Reserve Bank of India (RBI) is the central bank of the country and, as such, the apex institution of our country's monetary system.
- RBI was established on April 1, 1935 under the Reserve Bank of India Act, 1934.
- Initially constituted as a private shareholders' bank with a fully paid-up share capital of ₹ 5 crore, and was given the functions of regulating other banks and being the government's banker.
- The bank was nationalised on January 1, 1949 and became the central banking body of the country.

➡ The executive head of the RBI is called the governor; deputy governors and other executive officers assist in the administration of the bank.

Functions

The functions of the RBI are discussed below:

(*i*) **As a Currency Authority:** The RBI is the sole authority for the issue of currency in India except the one rupee coins (with the signature of the Revenue Secretary) and small coins issued by the Government of India.

(*ii*) **As a Banker to the Government:**

- The RBI acts as a banker to both the Central and the state governments.
- The RBI also manages the public (government) debt. The statutory liquidity ratio (SLR) is the most important instrument for maintaining a 'captive' market for government securities.
- The RBI is authorised to make ways and means advances to the government.
- These short-term loans are repayable within 90 days from the date of advance. (RBI has appointed the State Bank of India as its sole agent for transacting government business.)

(*iii*) **As a Banker's Bank and Supervisor:**

- The RBI has been vested with extensive powers of supervision, regulation and control over commercial and cooperative banks.
- As a bankers' bank, the RBI holds with it a part of the cash reserves of banks, lends them funds, and offers centralised clearing and cheap and quick remittance facilities.

(*iv*) **As a Controller of Money Supply and Credit:** The RBI fulfils this role through its yearly monetary policy. The main control instruments used by the RBI are CRR, SLR, open market operations, lending policy towards banks and control over interest-rate structure of banks through bank rates.

(*v*) **Exchange Management and Control:** The RBI acts as the custodian of the country's foreign exchange reserves, manages exchange control and acts as the agent of the government in respect of India's membership of the International Monetary Fund (IMF).

(*vi*) **Other Functions:**

- The bank performs a number of other developmental works. These works include the function of clearing house arranging credit for agriculture (which has been transferred to NABARD) collecting and publishing the economic data, buying and selling of Government securities and trade bills, giving loans to the Government buying and selling of valuable commodities etc.
- It also acts as the representative of Government in I.M.F. and represents the membership of India.

Instruments of Credit Control

The principal instruments used by the RBI are as follows:

(*i*) **Bank Rate:**

- The RBI uses bank rate as an instrument of credit control.
- Bank rate is the interest rate at which the central bank, (RBI) lends to its clients on long term borrowings.

- The clients are the government (Central/State), banks, financial institutions, NBFCs, etc.
- Now the bank rate serves as a reference rate for other rates in the financial markets.

(ii) Open Market Operations:

- Open market operations refer to the buying and selling of government securities, treasury bills, and other approved securities.
- The RBI also has the power to buy and sell short-term commercial bills.
- RBI has also been taking up 'switch operations', purchasing one loan against the sale of another or vice-versa.

(iii) Cash Reserve Ratio: Banks keep a proportion of their assets in the form of cash—partly as 'cash on hand' and partly as 'balance with RBI'. Such cash is called cash reserves of banks.

(iv) Statutory Liquidity Ratio:

- The statutory liquidity ratio (SLR) is the ratio of the total deposits of a bank that it has to maintain with itself in non-cash form—*i.e.*, of its net demand and time liabilities.
- The Banking Regulation (Amendment) Act, 1962 provides for maintaining a minimum SLR of 25 per cent by the bank against their net demand and time liabilities.

(v) Repo and Reverse Repo Rates:

- **Repo rate** also known as the benchmark interest rate is the rate at which the RBI lends money to the banks for a short term. When the repo rate increases, borrowing from RBI becomes more expensive. If RBI wants to make it more expensive for the banks to borrow money, it increases the repo rate similarly, if it wants to make it cheaper for banks to borrow money it reduces the repo rate.
- **Reverse Repo rate** is the short term borrowing rate at which RBI borrows money from banks. The Reserve Bank uses this tool when it feels there is too much money floating in the banking system. An increase in the reverse repo rate means that the banks will get a higher rate of interest from RBI. As a result, bank prefer to lead their money to RBI which is always safe instead of lending it others which is always risky.

(vi) Selective Credit Controls:

- These controls are directed towards regulating credit for specific purposes or sectors of economic activity.
- The RBI can use these controls to prevent speculative hoarding of essential commodities and check undue rise in prices.
- The techniques of selective credit controls include determination of maximum advances; determination of margin requirements for loans against certain securities (most often relied upon by the RBI in its efforts to check hoarding of essential commodities so as to avert shortages and price rise); and charging discriminatory interest rates on selected advances.
- The RBI may also direct banks about what purpose loans may or may not be given.

Commercial Banks

- Commercial banks have been in existence for many decades.
- They mobilise savings in urban areas and make them available to large and small industrial and trading units mainly for working capital requirements.
- After 1969 commercial banks are broadly classified into nationalized or public sector banks and private sector banks.
- The State Bank of India with another 11 banks are the public sector banks.

The State Bank of India

- The State Bank of India is the largest commercial bank of the country and is among the 100 topmost banks in the world outside the United States of America.
- The State Bank had five subsidiary banks attached to it. These were:
  - State Bank of Bikaner and Jaipur;
  - State Bank of Hyderabad;
  - State Bank of Mysore;
  - State Bank of Patiala; and
  - State Bank of Travancore.
- The all five subsidiary banks of SBI group have been merged with SBI on 1 April, 2017.

10 Public Sector Banks Merged into Four

- The Union Cabinet has approved the merger of 10 public sector banks into four, paving the way for the largest consolidation among the state-owned lenders.
- According to the plan
  - Punjab National Bank has taken over Oriental Bank of Commerce and United Bank.
  - Canara Bank has taken over Syndicate Bank.
  - Union Bank of India has taken over Andhra Bank and Corporation Bank.
  - Indian Bank has been merged with Allahabad Bank.
  - The merger has become effective from April 1, 2020. Consolidation among public sector banks has been on the agenda for the National Democratic Alliance since 2014, when it first came into power. In 2017, State Bank of India was merged with five of its associate banks and Bharatiya Mahila Bank. In 2018, it decided to merge Bank of Baroda with Vijaya Bank and Dena Bank.
  - The government also allowed Life Insurance Corporation of India to take over IDBI bank.
  - After the merger of these banks total number of public sector banks is now 12:
    1. State Bank in India
    2. Punjab National Bank
    3. Bank of Baroda
    4. Canara Bank
    5. Union Bank of India
    6. Indian Bank
    7. Bank of Maharashtra
    8. Punjab and Sindh Bank
    9. Indian Overseas Bank
    10. United Commercial Bank
    11. Central Bank of India
    12. Bank of India

Private Banks

- Private banks are banks that the majority of share capital is held by private individuals.

- To encourage competitive efficiency, the setting up of new private bank is now welcomed.
- Examples of old private sector banks are:
  - Bank of Rajasthan
  - Catholic Syrian Bank
  - Dhanalakshmi Bank
  - Federal Bank
  - ING Vysya Bank
  - Karnataka Bank
  - Karur Vysya Bank
  - Lakshmi Vilas Bank
  - Lord Krishna Bank
  - South Indian Bank
  - Tamilnad Mercantile Bank
- Examples of new generation private sector banks are:
  - Bank of Punjab
  - Centurion Bank
  - HDFC Bank
  - ICICI Bank
  - IndusInd Bank
  - Kotak Mahindra Bank
  - UTI Bank
  - Yes Bank
  - Axis Bank

Foreign Banks

- Foreign banks are registered and have their headquarters in a foreign country but operate their branches in India.
- As on December, 2024, there were 44 foreign banks operating in India. Another 31 foreign banks have their representative offices in India. Among foreign banks, Standard Chartered has the maximum spread of banks branches in India (100 branches) followed by HSBC (26 branches), Citi Bank NA (35 branches) and Deutsche Bank (17).
- Examples of foreign bank functioning in India are:
  - Bank of America
  - Bank of Bahrain & Kuwait
  - Bank of Ceylon
  - Barclays Bank
  - BNP Paribas
  - Ceylon Bank
  - Citibank
  - JP Morgan Chase Bank
  - Sonali Bank
  - Standard Chartered Bank
  - Hongkong & Shanghai Banking Corporation (HSBC)

Regional Rural Banks (RRBs)

- The M. Narisaman committee in 1975 after studying the impact of the Lead Bank Scheme recommended the establishment of rural banks in each district that may be dedicated to rural development.
- The first Gramin Bank started functioning on 2nd October 1975 under an ordinance and subsquently the Regional Rural Banks Act was passed in 1976.
- Regional rural banks perform the following two types of functions:
  - Granting of loans and advances to small and marginal farmers, agricultural workers, cooperative societies including agricultural marketing societies and primary agricultural credit societies for agricultural purposes or agricultural operations or related purposes.
  - Granting of loans and advances to artisans small entrepreneurs engaged in trade, commerce or industry or other productive activities.

Co-operative Banks

- Co-operative banks are banks incorporated in the legal form of co-operatives. Any co-operative society has to obtain a license from the Reserve Bank of India before starting banking business and has to follow the guidelines set and issued by the Reserve Bank of India.
- There are three types of co-operatives banks with different functions:
  - **Primary Credit Societies:** Primary Credit Societies are formed at the village or town level with borrower and non-borrower members residing in one locality. The operations of each society are restricted to a small area so that the members know each other and are able to watch over the activities of all members to prevent frauds.
  - **Central Co-operative Banks:** Central co-operative banks operate at the district level having some of the primary credit societies belonging to the same district as their members. These banks provide loans to their members (*i.e.,* primary credit societies) and function as a link between the primary credit societies and state co-operative banks.
  - **State Co-operative Banks:** These are the highest level of co-operative banks in all the states of the country. They mobilize funds and help in its proper channelization among various sectors. The money reaches the individual borrowers from the state co-operative banks through the central cooperative banks and the primary credit societies.

Development Banks

- Development Banks are banks that provide financial assistance to business that requires medium and long-term capital for purchase of machinery and equipment, for using latest technology, or for expansion and modernization.
- A development bank is a multi-purpose institution which shares entrepreneurial risk, changes its approach in tune with industrial climate and encourages new industrial projects to bring about speedier economic growth.
- These banks also undertake other development measures like subscribing to the shares and debentures issued by companies, in case of under subscription of the issue by the public.

There are two important national level development banks. They are:

1. **Industrial Finance Corporation of India (IFCI)**
   - The IFCI is the first Development Financial Institution in India. It is a pioneer in development banking in India. It was established in 1948 under an Act of Parliament.
   - The main objective of IFCI is to render financial assistance to large scale industrial units, particularly at a time when the ordinary banks are not forth coming to assist these concerns.
   - Its activities include project financing, financial services, merchant banking and investment.
   - Till 1993, IFCI continued to be Developmental Financial Institution. After 1993, it was changed from a statutory corporation to a company under the Indian Companies Act, 1956 and was named as IFCI Ltd with effect from October 1999.

2. **Industrial Credit and Investment Corporation of India (ICICI)**
   - ICICI was set up in 1955 as a public limited company. It was to be a private sector development bank in so far as there was no participation by the Government in its share capital.
   - It is a diversified long-term financial institution and provides a comprehensive range of financial products and services including project and equipment financing, underwriting and direct subscription to capital issues, leasing, deferred credit, trusteeship and custodial services, advisory services and business consultancy.
   - The main objective of the ICICI was to meet the needs of the industry for long-term funds in the private sector.

Specialized Banks

➥ In India, there are some specialized banks, which cater to the requirements and provide overall support for setting up business in specific areas of activity. They engage themselves in some specific area or activity and thus, are called specialized banks.

➥ There are three important types of specialized banks with different functions:

Export Import Bank of India (EXIM Bank)

➥ The Export-Import (EXIM) Bank of India is the principal financial institution in India for coordinating the working of institutions engaged in financing export and import trade. It is a statutory corporation wholly owned by the Government of India.

➥ It was established on January 1, 1982 for the purpose of financing, facilitating and promoting foreign trade of India.

➥ This specialized bank grants loans to exporters and importers and also provides information about the international market.

➥ It also gives guidance about the opportunities for export or import, the risks involved in it and the competition to be faced, etc.

Small Industries Development Bank of India

➥ This specialized bank grant loan to those who want to establish a small-scale business unit or industry.

➥ Small Industries Development Bank of India (SIDBI) was established in October 1989 and commenced its operation from April 1990 with its Head Office at Lucknow as a development bank, exclusively for the small scale industries. It is a central government undertaking.

➥ The prime aim of SIDBI is to promote and develop small industries by providing them the valuable factor of production finance.

➥ Functions of Small Industries Development Bank of India (SIDBI):

(*i*) Initiates steps for technology adoption, technology exchange, transfer and upgradation, and modernisation of existing units.

(*ii*) SIDBI participates in the equity type of loans on soft terms, term loan, working capital both in rupee and foreign currencies, venture capital support, and different forms of resource support to banks and other institutions.

(*iii*) SIDBI facilitates timely flow of credit for both term loans and working capital to SSI in collaboration with commercial banks.

(*iv*) SIDBI enlarges marketing capabilities of the products of SSIs in both domestic and international markets.

(*v*) SIDBI directly discounts and rediscounts bills with a view to encourage bills culture and helping the SSI units to realise their sale proceeds of capital goods/equipment and components etc.

(*vi*) SIDBI promotes employment oriented industries especially in semi-urban areas to create more employment opportunities so that rural-urban migration of people can be checked.

National Bank for Agricultural and Rural Development

➥ It was established on 12 July 1982 by a special Act by the parliament. This specialized bank is a central or apex institution for financing agricultural and rural sectors.

➥ It can provide credit, both short-term and long-term, through regional rural banks.

➥ It provides financial assistance, especially, to co-operative credit, in the field of agriculture, small-scale industries, cottage and village industries handicrafts and allied economic activities in rural areas.

➥ Its important functions are:

(*a*) Takes measures towards institution building for improving absorptive capacity of the credit delivery system, including monitoring, formulation of rehabilitation schemes, restructuring of credit institutions, training of personnel, etc.

(*b*) Co-ordinates the rural financing activities of all institutions engaged in developmental work at the field level and maintains liaison with Government of India, State Governments, Reserve Bank of India (RBI) and other national level institutions concerned with policy formulation.

(*c*) Undertakes monitoring and evaluation of projects refinanced by it.

(*d*) NABARD refinances the financial institutions which finances the rural sector.

(*e*) The institutions which help the rural economy, NABARD helps to develop.

(*f*) NABARD also keeps a check on its client institutes.

(*g*) It regulates the institution which provides financial help to the rural economy.

(*h*) It provides training facilities to the institutions working the field of rural upliftment.

(*i*) It regulates the cooperative banks and the RRB.

Financial Institutions

Microfinance Institutions

➥ Microfinance Institutions are bank-like financial institutions that providing financial services, such as microcredit, microsavings or micro insurance to poor people.

➥ In addition, they also perform the following important functions:

- Provide financing facilities, with or without collateral security, in cash or in kind, for such terms and subject to such conditions as may be prescribed, to poor persons for all types of economic activities including housing, but excluding business in foreign exchange transactions.

- To buy, sell and supply on credit to poor persons industrial and agricultural inputs, livestock, machinery and industrial raw materials.
- To provide professional advice to poor persons regarding investments in small business and such cottage industries as may be prescribed;

Development Financial Institutions (DFIs)

➡ DFIs are specialized financial institutions the Government established to promote investments in the manufacturing and agricultural sectors.

➡ Their functions include:

- Extending financial assistance in the form of medium- and long-term loans, participating in equity capital, underwriting and wherever relevant, acting as issuing house for public shares issues and providing guarantees for loans.
- Specialize in medium- and long-term financing in addition to supplying financial services not normally provided by commercial banks and finance companies.
- In addition, they help in identifying new projects, participate in their promotion, and where appropriate, provide ancillary financial, technical and managerial advice.

Capital Market

➡ Capital market is the market for long-term more than 365 days funds. It includes all facilities and institutional arrangements available for borrowing and lending of term funds (including medium-term).

➡ The capital market may be divided into : (*i*) the securities market; and (*ii*) the financial institutions.

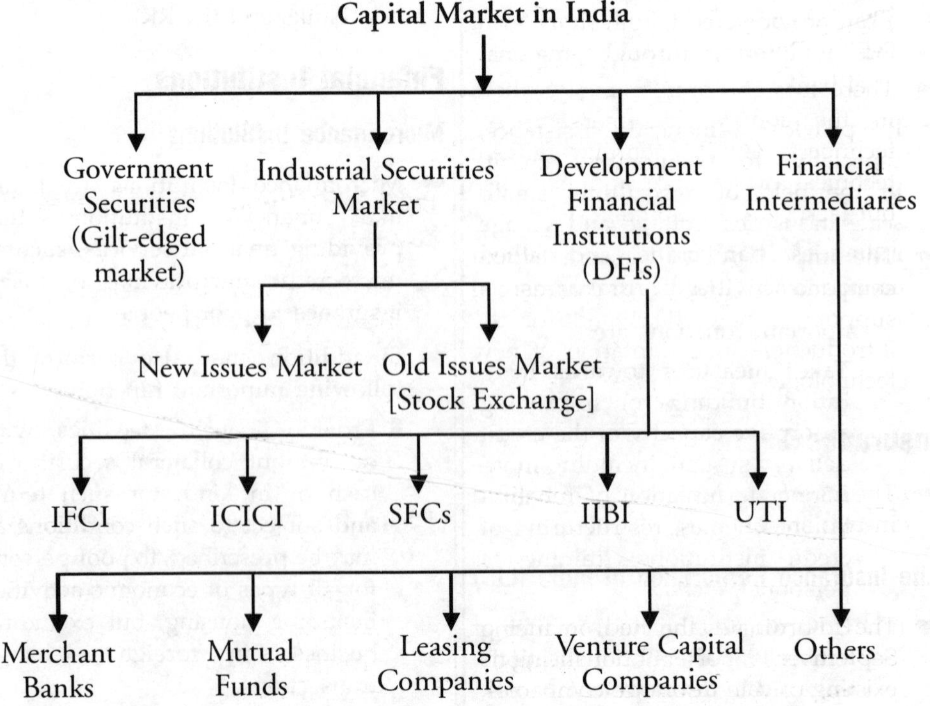

Non-Banking Finance Companies (NBFCs)

Mutual Funds

- In recent years, mutual funds are the most important among the newer capital market institutions.
- Several public sector banks and financial institutions have set up mutual funds on a tax-exempt basis, virtually on the same footing as Unit Trust of India (UTI).
- Their main function is to mobilise the saving of the general public and invest them in stock market securities. Accordingly, they attracted strong investor support and showed significant progress.
- The Government threw the field open to the private sector and joint sector mutual funds.

Venture Capital Funds

- Venture capital financing is one of the more recent entrants into the capital market.
- There is significant scope for them in the context of emergence of technocrat entrepreneurs who have technical competence and expertise but lack ventrue capital.
- The importance of venture capital companies is to give commercial support to new ideas and for the introduction and adaptation of new technologies.

Insurance Sector

- The insurance sector was nationalised in two stages.

Life Insurance Corporation of India (LIC)

- The LIC was established on first of September 1956 after nationalising the existing private insurance companies.
- LIC has a strong social security scheme which is funded by the Social Security Fund (SSF) set up and administered by it since 1989-90.
- The LIC runs three schemes supported by SSF—Janashree Bima Yojana, Krishi Shramik Samajik Suraksha Yojana and Shiksha Sahayog Yojana. These schemes benefit persons and families below the poverty line.

General Insurance Corporation of India (GIC)

- The GIC was formed in November 1972 consequent upon the nationalisation of general insurance business.
- The 107 private companies operating in the field were grouped together into four—National Insurance Company, United India Insurance Company, Oriental Insurance Company and New India Assurance Company, with GIC as the holding company.
- These companies can compete among themselves for all types of general insurance except aviation insurance and crop insurance which are the monopoly of GIC.

Pradhan Mantri Jeevan Jyoti Bima Yojana (PMJJBY)

- The Pradhan Mantri Jeevan Jyoti Bima Yojana (PMJJBY) is a one year life insurance scheme, renewable from year to year, offering coverage for death due to any reason and is available to people in the age group of 18 to 50 years (life cover upto age 55) having a savings bank account who give their consent to join and enable auto-debit.
- The risk cover on the lives of the enrolled persons has commenced from June 1, 2015.

- Under PMJJBY scheme, life cover of ₹ two lakh is available for a one year period stretching from June 1 to May 31 (has been extended upto August 31, 2015) at a premium of ₹ 436 per annum per member and is renewable every year.
- It is offered/administered through LIC and other Indian private Life Insurance companies for enrolment banks have tied up with insurance companies.

Pradhan Mantri Suraksha Bima Yojana (PMSBY)

- The Pradhan Mantri Suraksha Bima Yojana (PMSBY) is aimed at covering the uncovered population at an highly affordable premium of just ₹ 20 per year.
- The scheme will be available to people in the age group 18 to 70 years with a savings bank account who give their consent to join and enable auto-debit on or before May 31 for the coverage period June 1 to May 31 on an annual renewal basis.
- Under the scheme, risk coverage available will be ₹ two lakh for accidental death and permanent total disability and ₹ one lakh for permanent partial disability, for a one year period stretching from June 1 to May 31.
- It is offered by Public Sector General Insurance Companies or any other General Insurance Company who are willing to offer the product on similar terms with necessary approvals and tie up with banks for this purpose.

Credit Rating Agencies

Credit rating was introduced in India in 1988, Indian credit rating institutions are as follows:

- **CRISIL:** Credit Rating Information of India Ltd., the first Indian rating agency, was jointly promoted by ICICI and UTI to rate debenture. Its share capital is held broadly by a large number of banks and financial institutions. Standard and Poor acquired 51 per cent equity in the agency in 2005.
- **ICRA:** Investment Information and Credit Rating Agency of India Ltd. was set up in 1991 by IFCI, LIC, SBI and other financial institutions to rate debt instruments.
- **CARE:** Credit Analysis and Research Ltd., set up in 1993 by IDBI and other financial institutions, public sector banks and private finance companies, rates all types of debt instruments.
- **ONICRA:** Onida Individual Credit Rating Agency of India Ltd., set up in 1995 by private sector finance company, Onida Finance, rates non-corporate, consumers' creditworthiness and debt instruments such as credit cards, housing finance, rental agreements, etc.
- **SMERA:** Small and Medium Enterprises Rating Agency, set up in 2005, is a joint venture of SIDBI, SBI, ICICI Bank, Dun and Bradstreet (an international credit information company), five public sector banks, and CIBIL. Not really a credit rating agency, its data on the overall strength of SMEs are used for rating.
- **CIBIL:** It is the Credit Information Bureau of India Ltd. which was set up in 2004 to maintain a database on individuals' credit records. The credit information is available to banks/financial institutions to assess prospective loan seekers.

PUBLIC FINANCE

- Annual Financial Statement (AFS), the core budget document, shows estimated receipts and disbursements by the Government in a particular year.
- The receipts and disbursements are shown under the three parts, in which Government Accounts are kept viz. (*i*) Consolidated Fund (*ii*) Contingency Fund and (*iii*) Public Account.
- Under the Constitution, Annual Financial Statement distinguishes expenditure on revenue account from other expenditure. Government Budget, therefore, comprises Revenue Budget and Capital Budget.

Revenue Budget

- Revenue Budget consists of the revenue receipts of Government (tax revenues and other revenues) and the expenditure met from these revenues.
- Tax revenues comprise proceeds of taxes and other duties levied by the Union.
- The estimates of revenue receipts shown in the Annual Financial Statement take into account the effect of various taxation proposals made in the Finance Bill.

Sources of Revenue for Central Government

- **Tax Revenue:** It includes taxes on the certain items mentioned in the union list of the seventh schedule and others.
- **Non Tax Revenue:** It includes
  - Borrowings;
  - Income of government undertakings;
  - Income from government properties;
  - Interest earning on loans and advances;
  - Gifts, donation, grants, and aid, etc; and
  - Fees (does not include court fees other than the Supreme Court).

Sources of Revenue for State Government

- **Tax Revenue:** Taxes on the items contained in the state list on the 'seventh schedule' of Constitition which includes land revenue taxes on agriculture, income, sales tax, etc.
- **Non Tax Revenue:** It includes
  - Fee taken in all courts except Supreme Court;
  - Income of government undertakings;
  - Income from the owned property;
  - Borrowings;
  - Royalty from mines, forests, treasure-troves, etc; and
  - Grants in aid.

Taxes

- Article 256 of the Constitution of India says that no tax shall be levied or collected except by the authority of law. In India, the Parliament is the only authority to enact that law in the country.
- **Direct Tax:** In this tax, the impact and incidences is on the same person and shifting of tax burden is not possible. It means that the one who pays the direct tax also bears the burden of the tax. Examples of direct taxes are personal tax, corporate tax, income tax, etc.
- **Indirect Tax:** Indirect taxes are those taxes which are paid by someone who shifts the burden of the tax on some

other person. Therefore, tax impact and tax incidence is on two different people Examples are: excise tax, Goods and Services Tax (GST), etc.

- **Ad Valorem Tax:** It is a kind of indirect tax in which the goods or commodities are taxed as per its value. VAT is an example of Ad Valorem tax.
- **Specific Tax:** It is the tax that is imposed on the basis of special attributes of the commodity. For example, the length, the breadth, the weight is used in the international trade or in case of import-exports.
- **Minimum Alternative Tax (MAT):** It is the minimum tax which a company has to pay even if it does not have any income or has zero income.

Value Added Tax (VAT)

- VAT is the tax levied on the value added at various stages of the output of commodity.
- The value added is measured as the difference between the gross value of output and that of the intermediate goods purchased for the purpose of final disposal.
- For the computation of VAT, the tax credit method is used under which a firm is allowed to deduct the VAT paid by it on its purchase from other units from the VAT which the firm has to pay. This sale invoice has to be shown.
- VAT came into effect on 1 April, 2005, except in the BJP ruled states and Uttar Pradesh. All in all, twenty-five states or union territories implemented VAT in 2005-06.
- Chhattisgarh, Madhya Pradesh, Jharkhand, and Rajasthan implemented VAT with effect from 1 April, 2006.

Service Tax

- It was introduced for the first time in 1984-85 budget at a 5 per cent union service tax on three specific services namely telephone, general insurance and stock brokerage.

Goods and Services Tax

- The Goods and Services Tax (GST) is a comprehensive value-added tax (VAT) levy on manufacture, sale and consumption of goods and services at a national level. This makes India a single, unified market and expected to create a stronger economy.
- After 17 arduous years of negotiations by successive governments at the Centre and in the States, the Narendra Modi government has finally introduced a uniform Goods and Services Tax (GST) regime that converts the country into a single market. The biggest tax reform in Independent India, the Goods and Services Tax (GST), finally rolled out at the midnight hour on June 30, 2017.
- The GST replaces 17 central and state taxes, including services tax, value-added tax, octroi, duties and other charges, except Customs levy, across the country. The tax will create a common market in the $ 2-trillion economy with 1.3 billion people. It is expected to curb "tax terrorism and inspector raj".
- All goods and services have been slotted under six tax slabs: 0 per cent, 3 per cent (for bullion), 5 per cent, 12 per cent, 18 per cent and 28 per cent. There is also a cess, over and above the highest rate, for demerit goods.

List of Taxes Included in GST

Indirect Taxes Included Under GST—

(A) State taxes subsumed in SGST: • VAT/Sales tax/Trade Tax • Entertainment tax (unless it is levied by local bodies) • Luxury tax • Taxes on lottery, betting and gambling • State cess and surcharges to the extent related to supply of goods and services • Entry tax not on in lieu of octroi • Electricity Duty.

(B) Central taxes subsumed in CGST: • Central Excise duty • Special Additional Duty of Custom (SAD) • Additional Custom Duty (CVD) • Additional excise duty • The excise duty levied under The Medical and Toiletries Preparation Act • Service Tax • Additional customs duty, commonly known as countervailing duty (CVD) • Special additional duty of customs (SAD) • Education cess • Surcharges • Tax on advertisement other than in Press/TV/Radio • Taxes on lottery, betting and gambling.

Benefits of GST

➥ GST has been envisaged as a more efficient tax system, neutral in its application and attractive in distribution. The advantages of GST are: • Wider tax base, necessary for lowering the tax rates and eliminating classification disputes. • Elimination of multiplicity of taxes and their cascading effects. • Rationalization of tax structure and simplification of compliance procedures. • Harmonization of center and State tax administrations, which would reduce duplication and compliance costs. • Automation of compliance procedures to reduce errors and increase efficiency. • Reduces transaction costs and unnecessary wastages. • Eliminates the multiplicity of taxation. • One point single tax • Reduces average tax burdens • Reduces the corruption.

Tax Reforms Committees

Year	Committees	Recommendations
1953	**John Mathai Committee**	Groundwork on India's fiscal structure.
1956	**Nicholas Kaldor Committee**	Fiscal structure.
1959	**Mahavir Tyagi Committee**	Fiscal structure.
1961	**Law Commission**	Framed Income-Tax Act.
1971	**K.N. Wanchoo Committee**	Family should be unit of assessment; 1% levy on share capital; reveal donations to political parties; voluntary declarations be abolished.
1978	**C.C. Choksey Committee**	Suggested a central tax code.
1981	**L.K. Jha Committee**	Specialisation by tax departments; selective prosecution; PANs be allotted.
1985	**NIPF&P Report**	Dismantle licence system; regulate political donations.
1991	**R. Chelliah Committee**	Technical offences be compounded; fund computerisation by FIs; corporate tax of 40 per cent.
1995	**Four Departmental Committees**	Assessment, procedures, reliefs and deductions, appeals and institutions.
2001	**Parthasarathy Shome Committee**	Tax Reforms for the Tenth Plan.
2002	**Vijay Kelkar Committee**	To make recommendations on reform of direct and indirect taxes.

Capital Budget

- The capital receipts are loans raised by Government from public, called market loans, borrowings by Government from Reserve Bank and other parties through sale of Treasury Bills, loans received from foreign Governments and bodies, and recoveries of loans from State and Union Territory Governments and other parties.
- Capital payments consist of capital expenditure on acquisition of assets like land, buildings, machinery, equipment, as also investments in shares, etc., and loans and advances granted by Central Government to State and Union Territory Governments, Government companies, Corporations and other parties. Capital Budget also incorporates transactions in the Public Account.

Expenditure

The various sources of government expenditure are as follows:

Non Plan Expenditure:

- **Revenue Expenditure:** Revenue expenditure is the expenditure incurred for the normal running of government departments and provision of various services, interest charges on debt incurred by the government, subsidies etc. In general, any expenditure that does not result in the creation of assets is treated as revenue expenditure.
  - (*a*) Interest payment
  - (*b*) Defence expenditure
  - (*c*) Subsidies
  - (*d*) Economic and social service
- **Capital Expenditure:** Capital expenditure consists mainly of expenditure on acquisition of assets like land, machinery, equipment, investments in shares etc. and loans and advances granted by the central government to state and union territory governments, government companies, corporations and other parties.

Plan Expenditure

- ***Revenue Expenditure:*** It consists
  - (*a*) Central plan
  - (*b*) Central assistance to state
- ***Capital Expenditure:*** It consists
  - (*a*) Loans to States and Union Territories for financing Plan Project.
  - (*b*) Capital expenditure on economic and social development.
  - (*c*) Capital expenditure on defence.

Deficit Financing

- Deficit financing is used to describe the financing of a deliberately created gap between public revenue and public expenditure.
- Deficit financing implies that the total revenue both on the revenue and capital account will not match the total expenditure, both on the revenue and the capital accounts.

Objectives of Deficit Financing

- The use of deficit financing has been considered essential for financing the plans for economic development.
- Deficit financing is advocated for the mobilisation of surplus, idle and unutilised resources in the economy.
- It is an instrument for economic policy for removing the conditions of depression and to raise the level of output and employment.

➥ The deficit financing has been used as a method of meeting the financial needs of the government in the times of war or when it has been considered difficult to mobilise resources.

Relative Sizes of Estimates	Types of Budget
Revenue < Expenditure	Deficit
Revenue = Expenditure	Balanced
Revenue > Expenditure	Surplus

Types of Deficit

There are four different concepts of deficit. They are budget deficit, revenue deficit, primary deficit and the fiscal deficit.

➥ Budget Deficit

- The budget deficit is the difference between the total expenditure and total receipts (current revenue and net internal and external capital receipts) of the government. Thus,

  Budget Deficit = Total Expenditure – Total Receipts

- In this case, total expenditure includes aggregate of both revenue expenditure and capital expenditure. Likewise, total receipts are the addition of revenue receipts and capital receipts. It is this budgetary deficit which is called deficit financing in India.
- **The central government meets its overall budget deficit by:**

  (*i*) net sales of treasury bills to the RBI, (*ii*) reduction of its cash balances.

➥ Revenue Deficit

- The revenue deficit is the excess of government's revenue expenditures over revenue receipts. It gives information on what the government is borrowing for. The revenue deficit implies a repayment burden in the future, not matched by any benefits via investment.

  Revenue Deficit = Revenue Expenditure – Revenue Receipts

➥ Fiscal Deficit

- The fiscal deficit is the difference between the total expenditure of the government and the revenue receipts plus those capital receipts which are not in the nature of borrowing but which finally accrue to the government.

  Thus, Fiscal Deficit = Revenue Receipts + Capital Receipts – Total Expenditure

- In simple terms, fiscal deficit is budgetary deficit plus borrowing and other liabilities.

  Fiscal Deficit = Budget Deficit + borrowing and other liabilities.

➥ Primary Deficit

- It was introduced for the first time in the budget of 1993-94. The primary deficit is the fiscal deficit minus interest payments.

  Thus, Primary Deficit = Fiscal Deficit – Interest Payments.

- Primary deficit indicates, how much government borrowing is going to meet expenses other than interest payments. It reflects the extent to which current government policy is adding to future burdens stemming from past policy.

Zero Based Budgeting

➥ The chief idea in this concept is that for drawing up a budget, the existing level of expenditure should not be taken for granted but should be critically examined.

➥ In other words, while evaluating every programme the government must not think, in terms of increases or decreases in spending but start from a zero base so that it must be justified firstly.

- Zero base budgeting (ZBB) requires the evaluation and judgement on each item of expenditure on its merit and desirability.

Basic Features

- Examination of programmes at various levels of resource allocation and performance.
- Objectives to be formulated by each agency.
- Activities of each agency to be converted into decision packages showing performance at various resource levels.

FOREIGN TRADE AND INVESTMENT

- Foreign trade has played a crucial role in India's economy growing at almost three times the growth of GDP during the last four years.
- India's exports cover a wide range of items including engineering goods, ores and minerals, chemicals and related products, gems and jewellery and of late, petroleum products.
- Imports have increased substantially, bulk of which comprise items like petroleum and crude products fertilizers, precious and semi-precious stones for export production, and capital goods, raw materials, consumables and intermediates for industrial production and techno-logical upgradation.

Export Promotion Schemes

Export Processing Zones

- Before getting converted into Special Economic Zones (SEZs), these Export Processing Zones (EPZs) were playing important role in promoting exports of the country.
- These zones were created to develop such an environment in the economy which may provide capability of facing international competition.
- The Export Processing Zones (EPZs) set up as enclaves, separated from the Domestic Tariff Area by fiscal barriers, were intended to provide a competitive duty free environment for export production.
- All the 8 EPZs located at Kandla & Surat (Gujarat), Santa Cruz (Maharashtra), Kochi (Kerala), Chennai (Tamil Nadu), Vishakha-patnam (Andhra Pradesh), Faeta (West Bengal) and Noida (U. P.) have been converted into Special Economic Zones.

Export-Oriented Units

- Since 1981, the Government intro-duced a complementary plan of EPZ (Now converted into SEZ) scheme for promoting export units (making export of their cent per cent production).
- Under this scheme the Government provides various incentives to increase the production capacity of these units so as to increase exports of the country.
- This scheme offers a wider source of raw materials, hinterland facilities, availability of technological skills, existence of an industrial base and the need for a larger area of land for the project.

Export Houses, Trading Houses and Star Trading Houses

- To increase the marketable efficiency of exporters, the Government intro-duced the concept of export houses, trading houses and star trading houses.

- Those registered exporters who have shown good export perfor-mances over past few years have been given the status of export houses, and trading houses.
- These units are provided some special facilities and benefits by the Government.
- Since April 1, 1994 a new category named **Golden Super Star Trading** Houses was added by the Government which has the highest average annual foreign exchange earning.

Export Promotion Industrial Parks (EPIP)

- A Centrally-sponsored 'Export Promotion Industrial Park (EPIP)' scheme has been introduced in August 1994 with a view to involving the state governments in the creation of infrastructural facilities for export oriented production.
- It provides for 75% (limited to ₹ 10 crore) grant to state government towards creation of such facilities.

Export Development Centres

- The Government has made a plan to invest about ₹ 50,000 crore for developing infrastructure in 23 Export Development Centres identified by Union Commerce Ministry in 1995-96. The major portion of this investment will be made by the Private Sector.

Export Development Centres

1. Tirupur—Hosiery and Weaving Industry.
2. Moradabad—Brass Ware Handicraft.
3. Ludhiana—Heavy Machinery and Hosiery.
4. Surat—Gem and Jewellery.
5. Panipat—Handloom textiles.
6. Alleppi—Coconut and coir.
7. Jalandhar—Sport goods.
8. Ranipat (Amboor)—Leather.
9. Nagpur—Hand-made equipments.
10. Vishakhapatnam—Fish and Fish products.
11. Meerut—Sport goods.
12. Aligarh—Brass locks.
13. Agra—Leather shoes.
14. Khurja—Clay pots.
15. Kanchipuram—Silk.
16. Selam—Hand-made items.
17. Sivakashi—Match boxes.
18. Ambala—Scientific equipments.
19. Rajkot—Engine pump.
20. Wapi (Ankleshwar)—Chemicals
21. Jamnagar—Brass spare parts.
22. Batala—Machine equipment.
23. Bhagalpur—Weaving.

Agricultural Export Zones

- The EXIM policy 2001 introduced the concept of Agricultural Export Zones to give primacy to promotion of agricultural exports and effect a reorganisation of our export efforts on the basis of specific products and specific geographical areas.

Special Economic Zone

- With a view to creating an environment for achieving rapid growth in exports and to provide an internationally competitive and hassle-free environment for boosting exports, a Special Economic Zone Policy was announced in the EXIM Policy 2000.
- The SEZ Act 2005, supported by SEZ rules, came into effect on February 10, 2006.
- The salient features of SEZ schemes are:

- A designated duty free enclave to be treated as foreign territory only for trade operations and duties and tariffs.
- No license required for import.
- Manufacturing, trading and service activities allowed.
- SEZ units to be positive net foreign exchange earners within three years.
- Full freedom for sub-contracting.
- Domestic sales subject to full customs duty and import policy in force.
- No routine examination by customs authorities of export/import cargo.

SEZ Norms Liberalised (2013-14)

➡ Amid dwindling interest in SEZs, the government announced a 'package of reforms' on 18th April, 2013, including easing of land requirement norms and on exit policy, to rekindle investor interest in Special Economic Zones. SEZ, once a major attraction for investors, lost the sheen following imposition of MAT and DDT, certain provisions in the proposed direct tax regime (DTC) besides the global slowdown. Announcing the supplementary foreign trade policy (FTP), the then Union Minister of Commerce Anand Sharma said the government has taken note 'of the fact' that there are acute difficulties in aggregating large tracts of uncultivable land which is vacant to set up SEZ.

- The Minimum Land Area Requirement for SEZ has been reduced by half for different categories of SEZs.
- For multi-product SEZ, minimum land requirement has been brought down from 1000 hectares to 500 hectares and for Sector-Specific SEZs, it has been brought down to 50 hectares.
- Also, there would be no minimum land requirement for setting up IT/ITES SEZs, besides easing of minimum built up area criteria.
- The Government has decided to allow transfer of ownership of SEZ units including sale.

Foreign Investment

➡ Foreign investment is generally in the form of private foreign participation and government collaborations in certain sectors of the domestic economy.

➡ The main advantage of the form of assistance is that generally the foreign investor also brings with him technical expertise, machines, capital goods etc. which are scarce in under-developed countries.

➡ **Direct Foreign Investment:** Foreign capital can enter India in the form of direct investment. Sometimes companies of advanced countries start their subsidiary offices and affiliates in India. Alternately foreigners may subscribe to stocks and debentures of concerns in India. This is known as portfolio investment.

➡ **Foreign Collaboration:** There are three types of foreign collaborations—joint participation between private parties, between foreign firms and Indian Government and between foreign government and Indian Government.

➡ **Loans from International Institutions:** Since 1946, the World Bank and its affiliates have been important suppliers of capital to India. International Monetary Fund (IMF), Aid India Consortium, Asian Development Bank (ADB) and the World Bank have been the major sources of external assistance to India in recent years.

- **External Commercial Borrowing (ECB):** India has also been tapping export credit agencies like the US Exim Bank, the Japanese Exim Bank, ECGC of the UK etc. to obtain a major portion of the commercial borrowing from the capital market.
- **Inter-Government Loans:** Since the second world war there has been a growing tendencies towards direct inter government loans and grants.

Foreign Exchange Convertibility

- Foreign exchange refers to the currencies of foreign countries that can be bought and sold on foreign exchange markets.
- Foreign exchange reserves are liquid assets held by a country's government or central bank to enable them to intervene in the foreign exchange market to influence the exchange rate.
- The exchange rate is the price of one currency in terms of another.
- For use in the external sector, the rupee is convertible into other currencies of the world. The central bank exchanges one country's currency for another.
- Till 1946, the rupee was linked to the British pound-sterling. However, when the International Monetary Fund (IMF) was set up (and India was a founder-member), as per IMF instructions, the external value of the rupee was fixed and maintained in terms of gold or the US dollar. The link with pound-sterling also continued.
- The IMF system of fixed exchange did not last long and in 1975 the Government of India delinked the rupee from pound-sterling and called upon the RBI to determine the exchange rate of the rupee in terms of the exchange rate movements of a basket of currencies—the pound, the US dollar, the yen and the deutsche mark.

Current Account Convertibility

- Current account convertibility means the freedom to buy or sell foreign exchange for the following international transactions: payments due in connection with foreign trade, current business, including services, and normal short-term banking and credit facilities; payments due as interest on loans, and as net income from other investments; payment of moderate amount of amortisation of loans or for depreciation of direct investments; and moderate remittances for family living expenses.
- However, full convertibility on current account does not mean abolition of all controls.
- The RBI can and does intervene to manage volatility, though it does not fix rate target.
- In order to prevent the rupee from appreciating too fast, RBI purchases dollars from the market and sells rupees in return.
- To control inflationary pressure, RBI sells some of the government securities it holds so as to draw out the rupees it has released in the economy.

Capital Account Convertibility

- Capital Account Convertibility (CAC) means freedom to convert local financial assets into foreign financial assets and vice versa at market determined rates of exchange.

- It is associated with changes of ownership in foreign/domestic financial assets and liabilities and embodies the creation and liquidation of claims on, or by, the rest of the world.
- Broadly, capital account convertibility would mean freedom for firms and residents to freely buy into overseas assets such as equity, bonds, property, and acquire ownership of overseas firms besides free repatriation of proceeds by foreign investors.
- The RBI chose a path of gradual and phased move towards capital account convertibility.

Foreign Exchange Reserves

- India's foreign exchange reserve comprise foreign currency assets (FCA), gold, special drawing rights (SDRs) and reserve tranche position (RTP) in the International Monetary Fund (IMF).

Foreign Exchange Reserves (US$ Billion)

Sl. No.	Year	Foreign exchange reserves
1.	2008-09	252.0
2.	2009-10	279.1
3.	2010-11	304.8
4.	2011-12	294.4
5.	2012-13	294.8
6.	2014-15	341.6
7.	2018	529.3
8.	2021	573.4
9.	2023	623.9
10.	Sep. 2024	711.8

MULTIPLE CHOICE QUESTIONS

1. Which age group of children/ adolescents is included in Rashtriya Kishor Swasthya Karyakram?
   A. 10 to 19 years
   B. 8 to 17 years
   C. 9 to 16 years
   D. 8 to 15 years

2. What is the primary objective of the Monetary policy?
   A. Increase government spending
   B. Reduce fiscal deficit
   C. Maintain price stability while ensuring economic growth
   D. Control foreign exchange reserves

3. The economic agenda for achieving the vision of an empowered and inclusive economy focuses on :
   1. Facilitating ample opportunities for citizens, especially the youth, to fulfil their aspirations.
   2. providing strong impetus to growth and job creation.
   3. Strengthening macro-economic stability

   Correct code is:
   A. Only 1 and 2
   B. Only 2 and 3
   C. Only 1 and 3
   D. All of the above

4. The "Cafeteria approach" for family planning was put forward during:
   A. Third plan
   B. Emergency
   C. Annual plans
   D. Janata party rule

5. Which of the following taxs in India is also known as the 'Google tax'?

A. Import Duty
B. Equalisation Levy
C. Securities Transaction Tax
D. Anti-dumping Duty

6. Inflation is caused by:

A. decrease in general spending
B. decrease in money supply
C. increase in industrial and agriculture output
D. increase in general spending or money supply

7. The Bhoomi Rashi Portal is designed for:

A. Digitization of rural land records
B. Assessing agricultural land fertility
C. Land acquisition for infrastructure projects
D. The process to transfer the property in the legal heirs name

8. The main purpose of UTI is:

A. mobilise and channelise small investors' savings
B. regulate the mutual fund industry
C. act as a stabilising agent in the share market
D. coordinate activities of other financial institution

9. The scheme HIRDAY is associated with:

A. free heart treatment of poor below poverty line
B. developing Wi-Fi facility on platforms
C. developing heritage cities
D. cleaning of Ganga River

10. Consider the following statements in relation to Periodic Labour Force Survey:

1. Periodic Labour Force Survey is conducted by National Sample Survey Office.
2. Urban labour data are released every quarter.
3. Rural labour data are released annually.

Which of the above statements are correct?

A. Only 1
B. Only 2 and 3
C. Only 1 and 3
D. All 1, 2 and 3

11. The major function of the Food Corporation of India is:

A. to distribute high yielding variety seeds
B. to extend credit to farmers
C. to control the demand side of foodgrains
D. to check the fluctuation in foodgrain prices by controlling supply

12. Consider the following facts about the Multidimensional Poverty Index:

1. It was developed by Sabina Alkire and James Foster in the year 2010.
2. It was adopted by the United Nations Development Programme (UNDP) in their Human Development Report.
3. It captures overlapping deprivations in health, education and living standards.

How many of the above statements is/are correct?

A. Only one
B. Only two
C. All three
D. None of these

13. Which of the following is referred as Sunrise industry?

A. Coffee
B. Hi-technology
C. Small scale
D. Heavy

14. Which of the following is not a measure of economic growth?

A. Per capita income
B. Gross National Product
C. Net Domestic Product
D. Money in circulation

15. Income Tax in India was introduced by:

A. William Jones
B. Lord Macaule
C. James Wilson
D. Sir Charles Wood

16. A blue chip company is called so because:

A. it produces computer hardware
B. it produces computer software
C. it gives high rains and has low risk
D. it exports most of its produce

17. What is Bharat SHRI?

A. Bharat Shared Repository of Inscriptions
B. Bharat standardized Restoration of Indigenous water bodies
C. A scheme of informal education
D. A scheme of Ministry of AYUSH

18. Poverty line is defined on the basis of:

A. living conditions of people
B. the number of children per family
C. per capita family income
D. the requirement of calories per person

19. The oldest large scale industry of India is in the field of:

A. iron and steel sector
B. jute sector
C. cotton textile sector
D. sugar sector

20. Seasonal unemployment is maximum in:

A. Industrial sector
B. Agricultural sector
C. Service sector
D. Handloom sector

21. The oldest trade union organisation in India is:

A. Hind Mazdoor Sabha
B. Indian National Trade Union Congress
C. All India Trade Union Congress
D. Central Industrial Trade Union

22. Sindri, Haldia and Paradip have:

A. Sea-ports
B. Steel plants
C. Big Multipurpose dams
D. Fertilizer plants

23. Consumer Price Index-Industrial Worker is used:

1. To regulate and determine Dearness Allowance of Central/ State Government employees.
2. In the fixation and revision of minimum wages in scheduled employments.
3. In measuring the inflation in retail prices.

Correct code is:

A. Only 1
B. Only 1 and 2
C. Only 3
D. All of the above

24. Which of the following is not a regional Block in the Global Economic Order?

A. ASEAN B. SAFTA
C. WTO D. NAFTA

25. Which of the following does not contribute to the development of the Indian economy?

A. Rising industrial output
B. Exports' share decreased; imports' share increased; Modern technology
C. Exports' and imports' share increased; Green Revolution
D. Population growth

26. Which of the following statements is/are correct about a blank cheque company?
1. A blank cheque company is a publicly-traded, developmental stage company.
2. It has no established business plan.
3. It may be used to gather funds as a startup.
4. It has the intent to merge or acquire another business entity.
5. Blank check companies are speculative in nature.

Correct code is:
A. Only 1 and 2
B. Only 1 and 3
C. Only 4
D. All of the above

27. Which of the following has largest share in India's imports?
A. Food and allied products
B. Capital goods
C. Fertilizers
D. Fuel

28. 'KUSUM' scheme launched by Government of India is associated with:
A. Female child protection
B. Flower production
C. Solar power plants
D. Promoting plantation

29. Which of the following statements is/are correct about Aroma Mission?
1. It started in UT Jammu & Kashmir with lavender farming.
2. It is focused on the cultivation of aromatic and medicinal plants.
3. Aroma Mission is attracting Startups and agriculturists from across the country.

Correct code is:
A. Only 1
B. Only 2
C. Only 1 and 2
D. All of the above

30. Rupee was made convertible on current account in:
A. 1991 B. 1994
C. 1995 D. 1997

31. The Reserve Bank of India was established in:
A. 1927 B. 1947
C. 1935 D. 1949

32. The foodgrain production in the country in 2023-24 was
A. 172.64 million tonnes
B. 150.04 million tonnes
C. 160.43 million tonnes
D. 332.3 million tonnes

33. The foodgrain production is more during:
A. Rabi season
B. Kharif season
C. Between Kharif and Rabi season
D. No fixed season

34. Purple Revolution is related to:
A. Saree printing
B. Lavender farming
C. Fine arts
D. Performing arts

35. Pradhan Mantri Krishi Sinchayee Yojana focuses on:
1. Accelerated Irrigation Benefits Programme (AIBP)
2. Har Khet Ko Pani
3. Per Drop More Crop
4. Watershed Development

The correct code is:
A. Only 2
B. Only 2 and 3
C. 1, 2 and 3
D. 1, 2, 3 and 4

36. .... is known as the hardware capital of the world.
A. Tokyo
B. Berlin
C. Shenzhen
D. New York

37. "Green Revolution" began in India during the year—
A. 1972-73
B. 1977-78
C. 1967-68
D. 1980-81

38. National Research Centre for Makhana (NRCM) is located at:
A. Darbhanga (Bihar)
B. Malda (West Bengal)
C. Madhubani (Bihar)
D. Saharsa (Bihar)

39. The currencies has the highest value in terms of rupee is:
A. Pound
B. Dollar
C. Euro
D. Saudi Rial

40. Consider the following statements about the 'Yuva Sahakar':
1. Yuva Sahakar is a Cooperative Enterprise Support and Innovation Scheme.
2. It is being implemented by National Cooperative Development Corporation (NCDC).
3. NCDC is a statutory corporation.

Which of the above statments is/are correct?
A. All 1, 2 and 3
B. Only 1 and 3
C. Only 1 and 2
D. None of the above

41. Index 'Residex' is associated with:
A. Share Prices
B. Mutual Fund Prices
C. Land Prices
D. Price Inflation Index

42. Which among the following is not a credit rating agency?
A. CRISIL B. CARE
C. ICRA D. IFCI

43. Which of the following is not an objective of the National Livestock Mission (NLM) scheme?
A. To increase the per animal productivity
B. Genetic improvement of the domestic animals.
C. To protect and preserve indigenous species of cows
D. To ensure availability of quality feed and fodder

44. Which unit of valuation is known as "Paper gold"?
A. Euro dollar
B. Petro dollar
C. GDK
D. SDR

45. The crops grown after the summer monsoon are called?
A. Rabi
B. Kharif
C. Annual
D. Seasonal

46. During which plan, annual compound growth rates was maximum?
A. Second plan
B. Sixth plan
C. Fourth plan
D. Seventh plan

47. Pradhan Mantri Kaushal Vikas Yojana 4.0 is being implemented in close collaboration with which of the following schemes?
1. PM Vishwakarma
2. PM Surya Ghar : Muft Bijli Yojana
3. National Green Hydrogen Mission
4. NAL JAL Mitra

Correct code is:
A. Only 1, 2, 3 and 4
B. Only 1, 3 and 4
C. Only 2, 3 and 4
D. Only 1, 2 and 3

48. Among the following, maximum disbursement has been by:

A. IRDI
B. IDBI
C. ICICI
D. IFCI

49. When was the National Small Scale Industries Corporation formed?

A. 1951 B. 1961
C. 1965 D. 1955

50. Ayushman Bharat Digital Mission (ABDM) was launched in:

A. 2020
B. 2022
C. 2021
D. 2023

ANSWERS

1	2	3	4	5	6	7	8	9	10
A	C	D	D	B	D	C	A	B	C
11	**12**	**13**	**14**	**15**	**16**	**17**	**18**	**19**	**20**
D	C	B	D	D	C	A	D	C	B
21	**22**	**23**	**24**	**25**	**26**	**27**	**28**	**29**	**30**
C	D	D	C	D	D	D	C	D	B
31	**32**	**33**	**34**	**35**	**36**	**37**	**38**	**39**	**40**
C	D	A	B	D	C	C	B	D	A
41	**42**	**43**	**44**	**45**	**46**	**47**	**48**	**49**	**50**
C	D	C	D	B	B	A	B	D	C

Indian Polity

CONSTITUTIONAL DEVELOPMENT OF INDIA

- The Constitution of India, as adopted by the Constituent Assembly in 1949, was not something absolutely new. It was, to a great extent, influenced by the Government of India Act of 1935 that was passed by the British Parliament.
- In order to understand and appreciate the Constitution, it is necessary to glance at the constitutional development during the British rule in India.

Regulating Act of 1773

- With the expansion of political power of the Company, it was felt in England that the affairs of the Company needed some regulation. As a result, the Regulating Act of 1773 came into being. Some of the salient features of the Act were as follows:
  - Subjected the Company's actions to the supervision of the British Government
  - End of Dual government.
  - Governor of Bengal to be the Governor-General of British territories of India.
  - Establishment of Supreme Court in Calcutta.
  - The servants of the Company were forbidden to engage in private trade, accept presents or bribes, etc.

Charter Act of 1813

- Company deprived of its trade monopoly in India except in tea and trade with China. This made the Company more of an administrative body. All Englishmen could trade in India subject to few restrictions.
- A sum of ₹ 1 lakh earmarked annually for education of Indians.
- Further, Christian missionaries were also permitted to come to India and preach their religion.

Charter Act of 1833

- End of Company's monopoly even in tea and trade with China. Company was asked to close its commercial business at the earliest.
- President of Board of Control became the minister for Indian affairs.
- A law member (without power to vote) was added to the Executive Council of the Governor General. Macaulay was the first Law member. This increased the Council's strength to four, with it began the Indian Legislature.

- A law commission was constituted for codification of laws.
- The Act threw open to all, irrespective of religion, place of birth, descent and colour, services under the Company.

Charter Act of 1853

- The Act renewed the powers of the Company and allowed it to retain the possession of Indian territories in trust for the British Crown but not for any specified period.
- The number of members of the Court of Directors was reduced from 24 to 18 of which 6 were to be nominated by the Crown.
- The Law member was made a full member of the Governor General's Executive Council.
- Legislation was treated for the first time as separate from executive functions.
- Questions could be asked and the policy of the Executive Council could be discussed, though the Executive Council could veto a bill of the Legislative Council.
- Recruitment to Civil Services was based on open annual competition examination (excluding Indians).

Government of India Act 1858

- Rule of Company in India ended and that of the Crown began.
- System of Dual government ended. Court of Directors and Board of Control abolished and substituted them with a post of Secretary of State (a member of the British cabinet). He was assisted by a 15-member council (called Indian Council). He was to exercise the powers of the Crown.
- Secretary of State governed India through Governor General.
- Governor General received the title of Viceroy. He represented Secretary of State and was assisted by an Executive Council, which consisted of high officials of the Government.
- A unitary and highly centralized administrative structure was created.

The Indian Council Act 1861

- A fifth member, who was to be a jurist, was added to the Viceroy's Executive Council.
- 6-12 additional members to be added to the Executive Council for legislation purpose. This implied that Viceroy's Executive Council, which was so long composed of officials, would now include certain additional non - official members. Some of non - official seats were offered to natives of high ranks. Thus, a minute element of 'popular' participation was introduced in the legislative process. The additional members, though, had little powers.
- The Executive Council was now to be called Central Legislative Council.
- Viceroy could issue ordinances in case of emergency.

Indian Council Act 1892

- Two improvements in both the Central and the Provincial Legislative Councils were suggested.
- Though the majority of the official members was retained, the non-official members were to be nominated by the Bengal Chamber of Commerce and Provincial Legislative Councils. [The non-official members of the Provincial Councils were to

be nominated by certain local bodies such as universities, district boards, municipalities]. Indian leaders like G.K. Gokhale, Ashutosh Mukherjee, Ras Bihari Ghosh and S.N. Banerjee found their way in the Legislative Council.

- The Councils were to have the powers to discuss the annual statement of revenue and expenditure (i.e. the budget) and of addressing questions to the Executive). They could also put questions, within certain limits, to the Government on matters of public interest after giving six days notice.

Indian Council Act 1909

- Morley was the Secretary of State, while Minto was the Indian Viceroy.
- Legislative Councils, both at the Centre and in the Provinces, were expanded.
- With regard to Central Government, an Indian member was taken in the Executive Council of the Governor General.
- The size of the Provincial Legislative Councils were enlarged by including elected non - official members so that the official majority was gone. Their functions were also increased. Now, they could move resolutions on Budget and on some matters of public matters.
- An element of election was also introduced in the Central Legislative Council, but the official majority was maintained.
- The most notable and retrograde change introduced was that Muslims were given separate representation. Thus, communal representation was introduced.

Government of India Act 1919

- Dyarchy system introduced in the provinces. It was considered to be a substantial step towards transfer of power to the Indians. The Provincial subjects of administration were to be divided into two categories : Transferred and Reserved.
- The Transferred subjects were to be administered by the Governor with the aid of ministers responsible to the Legislative Council. The Governor and the Executive Council were to administer the reserved subjects without any responsibility to the legislature.
- **Devolution Rules:** Subjects of administration were divided into two categories - Central and Provincial. Subjects of all India importance (like railways and finance) were brought under the category of Central, while matters relating to the administration of the provinces were classified as Provincial.
- The Centre was now to have a Bicameral Legislature for the first time. It actually happened after 1935 Act.

Government of India Act 1935

- Provided for the establishment of All - India Federation consisting of the British provinces and the Princely States. The joining of Princely States was voluntary and as a result the federation did not come into existence.
- Dyarchy was introduced at the Centre (e.g., Department of Foreign Affairs and Defence were reserved for the Governor General).
- The Federal Legislature (Central Legislature) was to have two chambers (bicameral)—the Council

of State and the Federal Assembly. The Council of State was to be a permanent body with one - third of its membership being vacated and renewed triennially. The Federal Assembly's duration was fixed for five years.

- It made a 3-fold division of powers: Federal (Central) Legislative List, Provincial Legislative List and the Concurrent Legislative List. Residuary legislative powers were subject to the discretion of the Governor General. Even if a bill was passed by the Federal Legislature, the Governor General could veto it, while even Acts assented to by the Governor General could be disallowed by the King-in-Council.
- Provincial autonomy replaced Dyarchy in Provinces i.e., the distinction between Reserved and Transferred subjects was abolished and full responsible government was established, subject to certain safeguards. They were granted separate legal identity.

Government of India Act 1947

- The division of British India into the two new and fully sovereign dominions of India and Pakistan, with effect from 15 August 1947;
- The establishment of the office of Governor-General in each of the two new countries, as representative of the Crown;
- The termination of British suzerainty over the princely states, with effect from 15 August 1947 (this was intended to encourage the various rulers to accede to one or other of the two new countries);
- The dropping of the use of the title "Emperor of India" by the British monarch (this was subsequently done by King George VI by royal proclamation on 22 June 1948).
- This marked the end of the British rule in India and the emergence of a free India.

COMPOSITION OF THE CONSTITUENT ASSEMBLY

- The Constituent Assembly was constituted in Nov. 1946 under the scheme formulated by the Cabinet Mission Plan.
- The features of the scheme were:
    - The Total strength of the Constituent Assembly was to be 389. After partition, the Constituent Assembly of India had 299 representatives.
    - Each province and princely state (or group of states in case of small states) were to be allotted seats in proportion to their respective population. Roughly, one seat was to be allotted for every million population.
    - The representatives of princely states were to be nominated by the heads of the princely states.
- The elections to the Constitutent Assembly (for 296 seats allotted to the British Indian Provinces) were held in July-August 1946. The Indian National Congress won 208 seats, the Muslim League 73 seats, and the small groups and independents got the remaining 15 seats.
- However, the 93 seats allotted to the princely states were not filled as they decided to stay away from the Constitutent Assembly.
- The Assembly included all important personalities of India at that time, with the exception of Mahatma Gandhi and M.A. Jinnah.

- The Constituent Assembly held its first meeting on December 9, 1946. The Muslim League boycotted the meeting and insisted on a separate state of Pakistan. The meeting was thus attended by only 211 members.
- Dr. Sachchidanand Sinha, the oldest member, was elected as the temporary President of the Assembly, following the French practice.
- Later, on December 11, 1946, Dr. Rajendra Prasad and H.C. Mukherjee were elected as the President and Vice-President of the Assembly respectively.
- Sir B.N. Rau was appointed as the Constitutional advisor to the Assembly.
- The Constituent Assembly had 11 sessions over two years, 11 months and 18 days.
- The Constitution-makers had gone through the constitutions of about 60 countries, and the Draft Constitution was considered for 114 days. The total expenditure incurred on making the Constitution amounted to Rs. 64 lakh.
- On January 24, 1950, the Constituent Assembly held its final session. It, however, did not end, and continued as the provisional parliament of India from January 26, 1950 till the formation of new Parliament after the first general elections in 1951-52.

Committees of the Constituent Assembly

- The Constituent Assembly appointed a number of committees to deal with different tasks of constitution-making. Out of these, eight were major committees and the others were minor committees. The names of these committees and their chairmen are given below:

Major Committees

1. Drafting Committee—Dr. B.R. Ambedkar.
2. Steering Committee—Dr. Rajendra Prasad.
3. Rules of Procedure Committee—Dr. Rajendra Prasad.
4. Union Powers Committee—Jawaharlal Nehru.
5. Union Constitution Committee—Jawaharlal Nehru.
6. Provincial Constitution Committee—Sardar Patel.
7. Advisory Committee on Fundamental Rights and Minorities—Sardar Patel.

   This committee had two important sub-committes:

   - Fundamental Rights Sub-Committee—J.B. Kripalani
   - Minorities Sub-Committee—H.C. Mukherjee.
8. States Committee (Committee for Negotiating with States)—Jawaharlal Nehru.

Minor Committees

1. House Committee—B. Pattabhi Sitaramayya.
2. Finance and Staff Committee—Dr. Rajendra Prasad.
3. Credentials Committee—Alladi Krishnaswamy Ayyar.
4. Committee on the Functions of the Constituent Assembly—G.V. Mavalankar.
5. Order of Business Committee—Dr. K.M. Munshi.
6. Ad-hoc Committee on the National Flag—Dr. Rajendra Prasad.
7. Special Committee to Examine the Draft Constitution—Jawaharlal Nehru.

PREAMBLE

- The term preamble literally means preface, preliminary statement or introduction.
- The Preamble to the Indian Constitution deals with the aims and objectives, the targets and ideals; and the basis and foundations of the Indian Constitution.
- The Preamble is directly related to the Objective Resolution passed by the Constituent Assembly on January 22, 1947.
- WE, THE PEOPLE OF INDIA, having solemnly resolved to constitute India into a [SOVEREIGN SOCIALIST SECULAR DEMOCRATIC REPUBLIC] and to secure to all its citizens: JUSTICE, social, economic and political; LIBERTY of thought, expression, belief, faith and worship; EQUALITY of status and of opportunity; and to promote among them all FRATERNITY assuring the dignity of the individual and the [unity and integrity of the Nation]; IN OUR CONSTITUENT ASSEMBLY this twenty-sixth day of November, 1949, do HEREBY ADOPT, ENACT AND GIVE TO OURSELVES THIS CONSTITUTION.
- The Preamble, in brief, explains the objectives of the Constitution in two ways: one, about the structure of the governance and the other, about the ideals to be achieved in independent India. It is because of this, the Preamble is considered to be the key of the Constitution.
- The objectives, which are laid down in the Preamble, are:

  (*i*) Description of Indian State as Sovereign, Socialist, Secular, Democratic Republic. (Socialist, Secular added by 42nd Amendment, 1976).

  (*ii*) Provision to all the citizens of India i.e.,

  - (*a*) Justice social, economic and political
  - (*b*) Liberty of thought, expression, belief, faith and worship
  - (*c*) Equality of status and opport-unity
  - (*d*) Fraternity assuring dignity of the individual and unity and integrity of the nation.

SOURCES OF CONSTITUTIONAL PROVISIONS

Great Britain	:	Parliamentary form of Government, process of law making, institution of speaker, writ jurisdiction.
America	:	Federal structure, supremacy of the constitution, independent judiciary, Judicial review, impeachment, process of ratification of Constitutional amendments by state Legislatures, Fundamental Rights.
Ireland	:	Directive Principles, Method of the election of President, nomination of members in the Rajya Sabha.
Canada	:	Definition of Indian Federation as an Union of State and giving residuary power to the Union.
Australia	:	Concurrent List.
Germany	:	Emergency provisions.
Former USSR	:	Fundamental Duties
South Africa	:	Constitutional Amendments

CITIZENSHIP

The Constitution provides for a single citizenship. Following categories of persons became citizens of India at the commencement of the Constitution:

1. Persons born and domiciled in India.
2. Persons domiciled in India and either of whose parents was born in India.
3. Persons domiciled in India and residing in India ordinarily for a period of at least five years.
4. Certain categories of people, who had migrated from Pakistan to India.
5. Indians residing abroad but who make an application to acquire Indian citizenship.

Methods for Acquiring Indian Citizenship

The Parliament passed Citizenship Act in 1955, providing for following methods for acquiring Indian citizenship:

1. Citizenship by birth;
2. Citizenship by descent;
3. Citizenship by registration;
4. Citizenship by naturalisation; and
5. Citizenship by incorporation of territory.

The Central Government has the discretion to waive off any or all the conditions of citizenship if it thinks that the applicant has rendered distinguished service to the cause of science, art, philosophy, literature, world peace or human progress in general.

The Loss of Citizenship

Under the provisions of the Constitution, Indian citizenship can be lost in three ways:

- **By renunciation**–if a person holding Indian citizenship as well as another citizenship refutes Indian citizenship voluntarily.
- **By termination**–by operation of law as soon as an Indian citizen voluntarily acquires the citizenship of another country.
- **By deprivation**–the Parliament can, by law, deprive any person of his citizenship by way of the provision of Article 10 of the Constitution if it is satisfied that citizenship was acquired by fraud, false representation; or concealment of material facts. If a person shows disloyalty towards the Indian Constitution; indulges in trade with enemy countries during war; is sentenced to imprisonment for a period of 2 years or more, within 5 years of registration of naturalization, or has been continuously residing out of India for more than 7 years he is liable to lose his citizenship.

FUNDAMENTAL RIGHTS

- People in democractic countries enjoy certain rights, which are protected by judicial system of the country concerned.
- Their violation, even by the State, is not allowed by the courts.
- India respects the rights of the people, which are listed in our Constitution, under the heading "Fundamental Rights".

Classification of Fundamental Rights

Fundamental Rights are classified as:

1. Right to Equality
2. Right to Freedom
3. Right against Exploitation
4. Right to freedom of Religion

5. Cultural and educational Rights
6. Right to Constitutional Remedies
   - The Original Constitution provided for the Right to property but it has been abolished by the 44th Amendment.
   - Right to primary education has been included in Part three under Article 21A.

Right to Equality

Article 14 to 18 deals with the Right to Equality. Article 14, says that "the state shall not deny to any person equality before the law or the equal protection of the laws within the territory of India.

➡ **Equality Before Law:** It is an expression of English common law and is somewhat negative concept implying absence of special privilege on grounds of birth, caste, creed, colour or sex.

Equality before law is second corrollary from Dicey's concept of the "rule of law." It implies that no one is above the law of land. It is the law no one is supreme. However, exceptions are granted to the office of President and Governor.

➡ **Equal Protection of the Law:** It is of American origin and is a more positive concept implying equality of treatment in equal circumstances.

It provides for protective discrimination.

➡ Article 15(1), says "the State shall not discriminate against any citizen on grounds only of religion, race, caste, sex, place of birth or any of them. Besides these 5 grounds, state can prescribe guidelines say; for job in a particular region.

➡ Article 15(2) says "No citizen can be denied access to public places only on the ground of caste sex, race, religion, place of birth or any of them." This Article is a Corollary to Article 17 (against Untouchability).

➡ Article 15(3) says that "nothing in this article shall prevent the state from making special provisions for women and children."

➡ Article 15(4) says that "Nothing in this or in clause (2) of Article 29 shall prevent the state from making any special provision for the advancement of any socially and educationally backward classes of society or for the SCs and STs." This Article was introduced by Ist Amendment.

➡ Article 16(1) provides for equality of opportunity in public employment.

➡ Article 16(2) prohibits discrimination on grounds only of religion, race, sex, descent place of birth or any of them in matters relating to public employment.

➡ Article 16(3) provides for residential qualification in certain category of public employment.

➡ Article 16(4) provides for reservation of seats for the backward classes of citizens in public employment if they are inadequately represented.

➡ Article 16(4A) provides for reservation in promotion for SCs and STs in Government service.

➡ Article 16(5) provides for reservation of seats to offices connected with a religious or dominated institution for members professing the particular religion or belonging to the particular denomination to which the denomination relates.

➡ Article 17 abolishes 'untouchability' and makes its practice, an offence punishable under the law. In view of this, an act was made by Parliament. Untouchability (offences) Act 1955, which is renamed as Civil Rights Protection Act 1976.

- Article 18 abolishes titles and prevents state from conferring title to any person.

Right to Freedom

- Article 19 to 22 deals with the Right to Freedom.
- Article 19(1) includes six freedoms.
  - Freedom of Speech and Expression.
  - Freedom of Assembly.
  - Freedom of Association.
  - Freedom of Movement.
  - Freedom of Residence and settlement.
  - Freedom of profession, occupation, trade and business.
  - included freedom 'to acquire hold and dispose of property' which has been abolished by the 44th Amendment.
- Freedom of the Press is included under Article 19(1)(a).
- Article 20 provides protection against arbitrary and excessive punishment to any person who commits an offence. It can not be suspended during the period of emergency.
- Article 21 guarantees right to life and personal liberty. It says that "No person shall be deprived of his life or personal liberty except according to the procedure established by law." It is the most important Article which has been hailed as backbone of Part III and Part IV of the Constitution by the Supreme Court. It can never be suspended.
- Article 21 is the bedrock from which many rights have been inferred by the Supreme Court.
- Article 22 provides protection against arbitrary arrest and detention. It includes
  - informing the detainee of the cause of his arrest.
  - allowing him to consult and be defended by a legal practitioner of his choice.
  - producing him before a nearest magistrate within the period of 24 hours.

Right Against Exploitation

There are two Articles : 23 and 24 under it.

- Article 23: it seeks to ban traffic in human beings, begar or any form of forced Labour.
- Article 24 it prohibits employment of children below the age of 14 years in any factory or mine or any hazardous condition.

Right to Freedom of Religion

- It includes four rights under Article 25, 26, 27, 28.
- Article 25 entitles everyone the freedom of conscience and the right to process, practice and propagate a religion of one's choice.
- Article 26 grants right to religious denominations to
  - establish institutions for practice or propagating their religion.
  - manage its own affairs in matters of religion.
  - passes and dispose of their immovable property.
- Article 27 provides for exempting religious institutions from paying taxes to state for religious purposes.
- Article 28 deals with religious instruction to be imparted in educational institutions.
  - No religious instruction can be provided in institutions owned and administered by the state.

- Religious instruction may be imparted but pupil may not be compelled to attend them in institutions recognized by the state and receiving aid out of state funds.
- Religious instructions can be imparted and people can be compelled to attend them in educational institutions administered by state established by a religious endowment or religious trust.

Cultural and Educational Rights

It includes Articles 29 and 30.

- Article 29 provides for criteria for determination of minority.
- Article 30 provides that all minorities shall have the right to establish and administer educational institution of their choice.

Right to Constitutional Remedies

- It has only one Article 32. In the words of Dr. Ambedkar Article 32 is fundamental of all Fundamental Rights. This right makes it constitutionally obligatory on the part of the Supreme Court to enforce the Fundamental Rights.

Various Writs

Habeas Corpus

- Habeas corpus literally means 'you shall produce the body'. A writ of habeas corpus is in the nature of an order calling upon the person who has detained another to produce the latter before the court in order to let the court know on what ground he has been confined and to set him free if there is no legal justification for the imprisonment. By this writ, the court secures the body of a person who has been imprisoned to be brought before itself to obtain knowledge of the reason why he has been imprisoned and to set him free if there is no lawful justification for the imprisonment.
- The writ may be addressed to an official or a private person who has another person in his custody and disobedience to the writ is met with punishment for contempt of court. The writ of habeas corpus is a very powerful safeguard to the subject against arbitrary acts not only of private individuals but also of the executive.

Mandamus

- *Mandamus* literally means a command. It demands some activity on the part of the body or person to whom it is addressed. It commands the person to whom it is addressed to perform some public or quasi-public legal duty which he has refused to perform and the performance of which cannot be enforced by any other adequate legal remedy. It is a discretionary remedy.

Prohibition

- The writ of *prohibition* has been defined as an extraordinary judicial writ, issuing out of a court of superior jurisdiction and directed to an inferior court for the purpose of preventing the inferior tribunal from usurping a jurisdiction with which it is not legally vested.

Injunction

- *Injunction* is a judicial process, operating in persona and requiring the person to whom it is directed to do, or refrain from doing, a particular thing.
- Both *injunction* and *prohibition* restrain legal proceedings. *Injunction* is directed to the litigent parties, while prohibition to the court itself.

Injunction recognizes the jurisdiction of the court in which the proceedings are pending, prohibition strikes at such jurisdiction.

Certiorari

- *Certiorari* means *'to be certified'* or *'to be made certain'*. It is a writ issued by a superior to an inferior court of record or other tribunal or officer, exercising a judicial function, requiring the certification and return to the former of some cause already terminated, in cases where the procedure is not according to the course of common law. It is generally issued only after the judgement of the inferior court or tribunal whose proceedings are to be reviewed.
- The effect of *certiorari* is either to quash or affirm the proceedings of the lower court or tribunal. It lies only against substantial errors.

Quo-Warranto

- *Quo Warranto* is proceeding whereby the court enquires into the legality of the claim which a party asserts to a public office and to oust him from its enjoyment if the claim be not well founded.
- The conditions necessary for the issue of a writ of *quo warranto* are as follows:
  - The office must be public and it must be created by a statute or by the constitution itself.
  - The office must be a substantive one and not merely the function or employment of a servant at the will and during the pleasure of another.
  - There has been a contravention of the constitution or a statute or statutory instrument in appointing such a person to that office.

Fundamental Duties

- In modern times generally there is no provision for Fundamental Duties in the constitutions of the world. There are hardly a few constitutions that have such a provision.
- In ancient times, however, the position was very different. In those days emphasis was laid on duties, rather than rights. It was felt that if everyone performs his duties, then the rights would automatically be safeguarded.
- But in 1976 the Indian Parliament felt that there was a need for inclusion of a list of Fundamental Duties in the Indian Constitution.
- Accordingly, Constitution (Forty-Second Amendment) Act, 1976, was passed which added a new part, viz. Part IV A, and a new Article, 51 A, to the Constitution of India.
- The new Part was entitled as Fundamental Duties and it gives a list of ten Fundamental Duties.
- The ten duties are as follows:
  1. To abide by the Constitution and respect its ideals and institutions, the National Flag and the National Anthem.
  2. To cherish and follow the noble ideals which inspired our national struggle for freedom.
  3. To uphold and protect the sovereignty, unity and integrity of India.
  4. To defend the country and render national service when called upon to do so.
  5. To promote harmony and the spirit of common brotherhood amongst all the people of India transcending religious, linguistic and regional or sectional diversities; to renounce practices derogatory to the dignity of women.

6. To value and preserve the rich heritages of our composite culture.
7. To protect and improve the natural environment including forests, lakes, rivers and wild life and to have compassion for living creatures.
8. To develop the scientific temper, humanism and the spirit of inquiry and reform.
9. To safeguard public property and to abjure violence.
10. To strive towards excellence in all spheres of individual and collective activity so that the nation constantly rises to higher levels of endeavour and achievement.

New Addition

11. Clause (K) Art 51A Amendment Act 86th 2002.

    (K) a parent or guardian to provide opportunities for education of his child or as the case may be ward between the age of six and fourteen years.

DIRECTIVE PRINCIPLES OF STATE POLICY

- One of the most noble features of the Indian Constitution given in Part IV Article 36 to 51 deals with the Directive Principles of State Policy.
- Our constitution makers were inspired to include these provisions in the Constitution by the Constitution of Ireland.

Constitutional Provisions

- The various articles on Directive Principles are as follows.
- **Article 38** instructs the state to promote the welfare of people by securing and protecting a social order in which justice (socio-economic and political) shall inform all the institutions of national life.
- **Article 39(a)** talks about state's role in providing adequate means of livelihood to all its citizens.
- **Article 39(b)** provides for state's direction for equitable distribution of resources.
- **Article 39(c)** provides for prevention of concentration of wealth in fewer hands.
- **Article 39(d)** provides for equal pay for equal work, for both; men and women.
- **Article 39(A)** provides for equal justice and free legal Aid.
- **Article 40** says that the state shall organize village Panchayats as units of self-government.
- **Article 41** provides for right to work, public assistance in case of unemployment, old age, sickness and disablement keeping in view the limitations of economic resources.
- **Article 43** provides for living wages for worker and a decent standard of life, leisure and social and cultural opportunities for people.
- **Article 43(A)** provides for participation of workers in the management of industry and other undertakings. It has been added by 42nd Amendment.
- **Article 44** provides for a Uniform Civil Code applicable to the entire country.
- **Article 45** provides free and compulsory education to children till 14 years of age. It has now been made a fundamental right under Article 21A.
- **Article 46** provides for protection of educational and economic interests of weaker sections of the society and in particular, of the scheduled castes and scheduled tribes.

- **Article 47** provides for prohibition of consumption of intoxicating liquor and to raise the level of nutrition and five improvement of public health.
- **Article 48** provides for preserving and improving the breeds and prohibiting the slaughter of cows, calves and other milks and draught cattles.
- **Article 48A** added by 42nd Amendment, provides for protection and improvement of the environment and to safeguard the forests and wild life of the country.
- **Article 49** provides for protection of monuments of historical and national importance.
- **Article 50** provides for separation of judiciary from executive.
- **Article 51** provides for promotion of inter-national peace and security.

THE UNION EXECUTIVE

President of India

- The President of India is the head of state and first citizen of India and the Supreme Commander of the Indian armed forces.
- The President's role, however, is ceremonial; real executive authority is vested in the Council of Minister, headed by the Prime Minister.
- The powers of the President of India is comparable to those of the monarch regent of the UK, the real authority being vested with the people's government.

Qualifications

- A citizen of India who is of 35 years of age or above can be a candidate for the office of the President.
- The Presidential candidate should not hold any office of profit under the government and should be qualified to become a member of the Lok Sabha.

Election Procedure

- The President is elected by an Electoral College consisting of the elected members of both Houses of Parliament *i.e.* Lok Sabha and Rajya Sabha and of the State Legislative Assemblies (Vidhan Sabhas).
- Nominated members of Parliament and members of State Legislative Councils are not members of the Electoral College.
- The election is held by means of single transferable vote system of proportional representation. The voting is done by secret ballot.

Tenure

- The President is elected for a term of five years and is eligible for re-election, though a convention has developed that no President seeks election for the third term.
- However, the first President Dr. Rajendra Prasad was elected for two full terms.
- He/she may resign before the expiry of his term, or the office of President may fall vacant due to his/her death.
- His term of office commences from the date he takes the oath of office.

Removal of the President

- The President can only be removed from office through a process called impeachment.
- An impeachment is a quasi-judicial procedure leading to the removal of a high public official, say, the President as in India, on the grounds of the violation of the Constitution.

- The resolution to impeach the President can be moved in either House of Parliament.
- Such a resolution can be moved only after a notice has been given by at least one-fourth of the total number of members of the House.
- Such a resolution charging the President for violation of the Constitution must be passed by a majority of not less than two-third of the total membership of that House before it goes to the other House for investigation.
- The charges levelled against the President are investigated by the second House. President has the right to be heard or defended when the charges against him are being investigated. The President may defend himself in person or through his counsel.
- If the charges are accepted by a two-third majority of the total membership of the second House, the impeachment succeeds.
- The President thus stands removed from the office from the date on which the resolution is passed.
- This procedure of impeachment is even more difficult than the one adopted in America where only simple majority is required in the House of Representatives to initiate the proceedings.

Powers of The President

- The Constitution has vested the President with vast powers. Broadly the powers of the President can be classified as Executive, Legislative, Financial and Judicial Powers.

Executive Powers

- The President is head of State and executive powers of the Union have been vested in him. The President is empowered to exercise these powers either directly or through officers subordinate to him which means through the Prime Minister and Council of Ministers also. His executive powers are given below :
- The President appoints the Prime Minister and he appoints other ministers on the advice of the Prime Minister. He allocates portfolios among the ministers on the advice of the Prime Minister. He may remove any Minister on the advice of the Prime Minister.
- The President appoints the Chief Justice and other judges of the Supreme Court and High Courts. However, in all judicial appointments, the Chief Justice of India is consulted. Besides the President may also consult such other judges of the Supreme Court as the President may be deemed necessary. While appointing Chief Justice and justices of High Courts the President has to consult the State Governor also.
- In the appointment of High Court judges, the President also consults the Chief Justice of the State.
- The President appoints the Attorney General, the Comptroller and Auditor General of India, the Chief Election Commissioner and other Election Commissioners, the Chairman and Members of Union Public Service Commission (U.P.S.C.).
- He/she also appoints the Governors of States and Lt. Governors of Union Territories. All such appointments are made on the advice of the Union Cabinet headed by the Prime Minister.
- The President is the Supreme Commander of the armed forces. As such, the President makes

appointments of Chiefs of Army, Navy, and Air Force. The President can declare war and make peace.

- In his/her capacity as head of state, the President conducts the country's foreign affairs. The President appoints India's ambassadors and high commissioners in other countries; and receives foreign ambassadors and high commissioners.
- All diplomatic work is conducted in his/her name (by the foreign office and Indian envoys abroad), and all international treaties are negotiated and concluded in his/her name.

Legislative Powers

The President being an integral part of Parliament enjoys many legislative powers. These powers are given below:

- The President summons, and prorogues the Houses of Parliament. He/she may summon the Parliament at least twice a year, and the gap between two sessions cannot be more than six months.
- The President has the power to dissolve the Lok Sabha even before the expiry of its term on the recommendation of the Prime Minister. In normal course he/she dissolves Lok Sabha after five years.
- The President nominates twelve members to Rajya Sabha from amongst persons having special knowledge in the field of literature, science, art and social service.
- The President can call a joint sitting of the two Houses of Parliament in case of a disagreement between Lok Sabha and Rajya Sabha on ordinary bill. So far thrice such joint sittings have been summoned.
- The President has the right to address and send messages to Parliament. The President addresses both Houses of Parliament jointly at the first session after every general election as well as commencement of the first session every year. These addresses contain policies of the government of the day.
- Every bill passed by Parliament is sent to the President for his/her assent. The President may give his/her assent, or return it once for the reconsideration of the Parliament. If passed again the President has to give her assent. Without his/her assent no bill can become a law.
- The President may promulgate an ordinance when the Parliament is not in session.

Financial Powers

- Every financial year the Finance Minister, on behalf of the President, lays an Annual Financial Statement before both the Houses of Parliament.
- A Money Bill cannot be introduced or moved in Lok Sabha except on the recommendation of the President.
- A Bill involving expenditure from the Consolidated Fund of India cannot be passed by either House of Parliament unless President has recommended for it to that House.
- No demand for a grant can be made except on the recommendation of the President.

Judicial Powers

- The President, as head of state, can pardon a criminal or reduce the punishment or suspend, cummute or remit the sentence of a criminal convicted by the Supreme Court or High Courts for an offence against the federal laws.
- The President can pardon a person convicted by a Court Martial.

- His/her power of pardon includes granting of pardon even to a person awarded death sentence. But, the President performs this function on the advice of Law Ministry.
- The President enjoys certain immunities. He/she is above the law and no criminal proceedings can be initiated against him/her.

Emergency Powers

- President is assigned three kinds of emergency powers under Article 352, 356 and 360.
- The Constitution of India has provided for imposition of emergency caused by war, external aggression or internal rebellion. This is described as the National Emergency under Article 352. This type of emergency can be declared by the President of India if he is satisfied that the situation is very grave and the security of India or any part thereof is threatened or is likely to be threatened.
- Such a proclamation of emergency has to be approved by both the Houses of Parliament by absolute majority of the total membership of the Houses as well as 2/3 majority of members present and voting within one month, otherwise the proclamation ceases to operate.
- In case the Lok Sabha stands dissolved at the time of proclamation of emergency or is not in session, it has to be approved by the Rajya Sabha within one month and later on by the Lok Sabha also within one month of the start of its next session.
- Once approved by the Parliament, the emergency remains in force for a period of six months from the date of proclamation.
- In case it is to be extended beyond six months, another prior resolution has to be passed by the Parliament.
- In this way, such emergency continues indefinitely. But if the situation improves the emergency can be revoked by another proclamation by the President of India.
- Under Article 356, the President may issue a proclamation to impose emergency in a state if he is satisfied on receipt of a report from the Governor of the State, or otherwise, that a situation has arisen under which the Government of the State cannot be carried on smoothly.
- In such a situation, proclamation of emergency by the President is called 'proclamation on account of the failure (or breakdown) of constitutional machinery.' In popular language it is called the President's Rule.
- Like National Emergency, such a proclamation must also be placed before both the Houses of Parliament for approval. In this case approval must be given within two months, otherwise the proclamation ceases to operate.
- If approved by the Parliament, the proclamation remains valid for six months at a time. It can be extended for another six months but not beyond one year.
- However, emergency in a State can be extended beyond one year if
  - a National Emergency is already in operation; or if
  - the Election Commission certifies that the election to the State Assembly cannot be held.
- It was in 1951 that this type of emergency was imposed for the first time in the Punjab State.
- The third type of Emergency is Financial Emergency provided under Article 360. It provides that if the

President is satisfied that the financial stability or credit of India or any of its part is in danger, he may declare a state of Financial Emergency.

- Like the other two types of emergencies, it has also to be approved by the Parliament. It must be approved by both Houses of Parliament within two months.
- Financial Emergency can operate as long as the situation demands and may be revoked by a subsequent proclamation.

Vice-President

- The Constitution states that there shall be a Vice-President of India.
- When the office of the President is vacant by reason of his death, resignation or removal the Vice-President becomes the Acting President.
- But when the President is unable to discharge his functions due to absence or illness, the Vice-President discharges his functions as officiating President.

Election Procedure

- Any person who is a citizen of India, has completed the age of 35 years, is qualified to be elected a member of Rajya Sabha and does not hold any office of profit under the Government of India or any State or local authority, can be elected to the office of Vice-President.
- Before entering upon his office, the Vice-President is required to take an oath before the President or some person appointed by him.
- The Vice-President holds office for a term of five years from the date on which he enters upon his office.
- He may send his resignation addressed to the President.
- He can be removed from his office by a resolution of Rajya Sabha passed by a majority of members of the House and agreed to by Lok Sabha.
- The Vice-President is elected by the members of both the Houses of Parliament assembled at a joint meeting.
- The Vice-President of India is elected indirectly by an electoral college consisting of members of both Houses of Parliament, on the basis of proportional representation by means of single transferable vote system. The voting is held by secret ballot.
- All doubts and disputes related to the election of a Vice-President shall be decided by the Supreme Court.

Function of Vice-President

- The Vice-President is the ex-officio Chairman of Rajya Sabha. He presides over the meetings of Rajya Sabha and conducts all its proceedings except when the resolution for his removal is under consideration. He enforces the rules of conduct.
- Whenever there is a division in the House on any issue, he counts the votes and declares the results.
- He gives his ruling whether a resolution or a question is admissible or not.
- Ordinarily, he does not vote but when the House is divided equally on any issue, he exercises casting vote.
- He decides whether an adjournment motion moved by a member is admissible or not.
- He acts as the Chancellor/Visitor of the Central Universities of India.

The Council of Ministers

- The basic idea underlying Parliamentary system is that the head of the state is the nominal executive, the real executive power lies with the Council of Ministers.
- The Council of Ministers is collectively responsible to the lower house of the Parliament.
- As a consequence of conventions, Indian President is vested with all executive power, but he exercises these power duly on the advice of Council of Ministers. The real Executive is the Council of Ministers headed by the Prime Minister.

Powers and Functions

- The Council of Ministers forms the Government of the Union. It is headed by the Prime Minister, who is the head of the Union Government.
- Its powers and functions may be discussed as below:
  - **Legislative Powers:** The Council of Ministers controls the legislature of the Union Government, i.e., Parliament. It formulates its policy, submits and explains it to Parliament for approval. Since it holds majority in Parliament, it is always sure of the acceptance of its policy. The entire legislation of importance passed by Parliament is initiated by the Ministers.
  - **Financial Powers:** The Cabinet controls the financial policy of the Union. It is the Finance Minister who submits the budget to Parliament. Parliament approves the budget expenditure and revenue items in its original form with support of a subservient majority.
  - **Executive Powers:** The Council of Ministers is the executive of the Union. The Ministers preside over the various departments of the government and give direction to the administration. The Cabinet brings about co-ordination of policy among various departments and settles their conflicts. The Cabinet formulates foreign and defence policies of the country and executes the five year plans.

Prime Minister

- The office of the Prime Minister which remains an integral part of the Parliamentary system is a British contribution to the realm of politics. Indians adopted Parliamentary system with the office of Prime Minister from Britain.

Position

- So important is his significance that Morley described him as *"Primus inter pares"* or first among equals. He has also been hailed as "Inter Stellar Luna Minores" or little moon among stars and "key stone of the Cabinet Arch."

Powers and Functions

- **Head of the Government:** While the President is head of the state, the Prime Ministers is head of the Government. In theory all major executive functions are vested in the hands of the President, but exercises them only with aid and advice of the Council of Ministers headed by the Prime Minister.
- **Leader of the Cabinet:** According to Ivor Jennings, "he is a sun around which other ministers revolve like planets." He selects ministers of his council and distributes portfolio amongst them. He acts as Chairman of the Cabinet. He can ask for resignation of an individual Minister or can get him dismissed by the President.

- **Leader of the Parliament:** In this capacity, the Prime Minister
  - determines the dates of meeting, as also its programmes for the session.
  - chief spokesperson of the government in the Parliament.
  - announces the major policy decision of the government.
  - can participate and intervene in all debates in the Parliament.
- **Leader of the Majority Party in the Lok Sabha:** In Parliamentary democracy, usually the leader of majority party in the Lower House is appointed as the Prime Minister. However, in case no party gets majority, the President may appoint a person whom he may deem fit to garner the support of majority.
- **Chairman of the Niti Aayog:** In this capacity he becomes a chairman of super cabinet wherein all chief ministers of states and administrators of Union Territories are represented. It covers all developmental activities undertaken by the centre as well as states.

THE PARLIAMENT

The Indian Parliament or the Union Legislature in India consists of the President and the two houses viz, the Lok Sabha and the Rajya Sabha.

Composition

1. The President.
2. The Lok Sabha or the Lower House or the House of People.
3. The Rajya Sabha or the upper house or council of state.

Functions

1. To enact laws for the administration of the country.
2. To reflect federal sentiment of the Indian polity.
3. To exercise control over the government and ensure limited government.
4. To provide forum for deliberation on issues concerning affairs of the polity.
5. To integrate the polity by providing membership to the representatives.

The Lok Sabha

- The member of the Lok Sabha is elected directly by the people on the basis of universal adult franchise.
- It is also called the popular House or lower House.
- The maximum permissible membership of Lok Sabha is 550 directly elected from the States and Union Territories.
- The Lok Sabha at present consists of 543 members directly elected from the states and Union Territories. By the 104th amendment of the Constitution the reservation for two members of Anglo-Indian community nominated by President have been abolished.
- Certain number of seats have been reserved for Scheduled Castes and Scheduled Tribes in the Lok Sabha.
- The representation to the Lok Sabha is based on population. Therefore UP which is the most heavily populated State in India sends as many as 80 members while smaller States like Mizoram, Nagaland and Sikkim send just one representative each to the Lok Sabha. Only seven members represent Delhi.
- For the purpose of elections to the Lok Sabha, the States are divided into single member constituencies on the basis of population.

Qualifications

- All the citizens of 18 years of age and above are entitled to vote in the elections to Lok Sabha subject to the laws made by the Parliament. Any Indian citizen can become a member of Lok Sabha provided he/she fulfils the following qualifications:
  - He/she should be an Indian citizen.
  - He/she should be not less than 25 years of age.
  - He/she should declare through an oath or affirmation that he has true faith and allegiance in the Constitution and that he will uphold the sovereignty and integrity of India.
  - He/she must possess such other qualifications as may be laid down by the Parliament by law. He must be registered as a voter in any constituency in India.
  - Person contesting from the reserved seat should belong to the Scheduled Caste or Scheduled Tribe as the case may be.

Tenure

- The normal term of Lok Sabha is five years. But the President, on the advice of Council of Ministers, may dissolve it before the expiry of five years.
- In the case of national emergency, its term can be extended for one year at a time. But it will not exceed six months after the emergency is over.
- On several occasions Lok Sabha was dissolved prior to the end of its term. For example the 12th Lok Sabha elected in 1998 was dissolved in 1999.

Representation of States and Union Territories in the Lok Sabha

State/UT	Number of Representatives	State/UT	Number of Representatives
Andhra Pradesh	25	Rajasthan	25
Arunachal Pradesh	02	Sikkim	01
Assam	14	Tamil Nadu	39
Bihar	40	Tripura	02
Goa	02	Telangana	17
Gujarat	26	Uttar Pradesh	80
Haryana	10	West Bengal	42
Himachal Pradesh	04	Chhattisgarh	11
Karnataka	28	Jharkhand	14
Kerala	20	Uttarakhand	05
Madhya Pradesh	29	Andaman & Nicobar Islands	01
Maharashtra	48	Chandigarh	01
Manipur	02	Dadra & Nagar Haveli and Daman & Diu	02
Meghalaya	02	Delhi	07
Mizoram	01	Lakshadweep	01
Nagaland	01	Puducherry	01
Odisha	21	Jammu and Kashmir	05
Punjab	13	Ladakh	01

Sessions

- The Lok Sabha is to meet at least twice a year and the interval between two consecutive sessions shall be less than 6 months.
- A special session of the Lok Sabha can be called if a notice in writing signed by not less than one-tenth of members of the Lok Sabha is given to the Speaker. When such a notice is given to the President he must summon the session within 14 days.

Speaker of the Lok Sabha

- The Lok Sabha elects two of its members as its speaker and Deputy speaker respectively.
- The Speaker is the presiding officer of the House and his office is of great dignity, prestige and authority.
- In the order of precedence he is placed sixth and is bracketed with the Chief Justice of India.
- The office of the speaker has political importance as well. He is the head of the democratically elected representatives of the people.
- He does not resign when the House is dissolved unless and until the new House is formed and it elects another person to be the Speaker.
- When the President resigns, the fact of his resignation is communicated to the Speaker and the House is informed by him of the President's resignation.

Functions of the Speaker

Some of the powers and functions of the speaker are given below :

- The basic function of the Speaker is to preside over the house and conduct the meetings of the House in orderly manner. No member can speak in the House without his/her permission. He/she may ask a member to finish his speech and in case the member does not obey he/she may order that the speech should not be recorded.
- All the Bills, reports, motions and resolutions are introduced with Speaker's permission. He/she puts the motion or bill to vote. He/she does not participate in the voting but when there is a tie i.e. equal number of votes on both sides, he/she can use his casting vote. But he/she is expected to caste her vote in a manner so that her impartiality and independence is retained.
- His/her decisions in all parliamentary matters are final. He/she also rules on points of order raised by the members and his/her decision is final.
- He/she is the custodian of rights and privileges of the members.
- He/she disqualifies a member of his/her membership in case of defection. He/she also accepts the resignation of members and decides about the genuineness of the resignation.
- In case of joint sitting of Lok Sabha and Rajya Sabha, the Speaker presides over the meeting.

The Rajya Sabha

- Also called Upper House or Council of States.

  Composition: Article 80 of the Constitution outlines that:
- Not more than 238 representatives to be sent from States and Union Territories.

- Twelve members to be nominated by the President having special knowledge or practical experience in the field of science, art, literature and social service.

However, the Parliament by law has fixed the total strength of Rajya Sabha to be not more than 245 (233 elected + 12 nominated).

Term

- The Rajya Sabha is a permanent body, not subject to dissolution.
- The term of the members of the house is six years.
- Nearly one-third of the members of the Rajya Sabha retire after every two years.

Representation of States and Union Territories in Rajya Sabha

State/UT	Number of Seats	State/UT	Number of Seats
Andhra Pradesh	11	Jammu & Kashmir	04
Assam	07	Nagaland	01
Bihar	16	Himachal Pradesh	03
Goa	01	Manipur	01
Gujarat	11	Tripura	01
Haryana	05	Telangana	07
Kerala	09	Meghalaya	01
Madhya Pradesh	11	Sikkim	01
Tamil Nadu	18	Mizoram	01
Maharashtra	19	Arunachal Pradesh	01
Karnataka	12	Delhi	03
Odisha	10	Puducherry	01
Punjab	07	Chhattisgarh	05
Rajasthan	10	Jharkhand	06
Uttar Pradesh	31	Uttarakhand	03
West Bengal	16		

Method of Election

- Except for a few members (twelve) who are nominated by the President, the members are elected indirectly by proportional representation by means of single transferrable vote.
- They are elected by an electoral college consisting of elected members of the state Legislative Assemblies. Union Territories elect through the same method by special electoral college.
- A person seeking membership of Rajya Sabha must be 30 years of age.

Parliamentary Privileges

Certain privileges and immunities are granted to members of the Parliament to enable them to work freely and efficiently.

They are as follows :

- Freedom of speech.
- Freedom from arrest in civil cases for duration of session of Parliament and 40 days before and after.
- To summon any person to produce documents or to answer charges for contempt of the house.

- Right to exclude outsiders from the proceedings of the house.
- Power to punish for breach of privileges committed, mode or outside the Parliament.
- Right to regulate its own internal proceedings without interference from any executive or judicial authority.

Parliamentary Committees

- ➥ appointed or elected by the House or nominated by the Speaker/ Chairman.
- ➥ works under the direction of Presiding officer.
- ➥ presents its report to the house or presiding officer.
- ➥ has a Secretariat provided by the House.
- ➥ holds office generally for a year.
- ➥ expected to contain representative of all parties in the House.
- ➥ enables legislature to work on 'Division of Labour.'
- ➥ have been brought into existence under the rule making power of the Parliament.

Ad hoc and Standing Committee

- ➥ Ad hoc Committees are constituted by the House or the speaker as and when the need arises and cease to exist as soon as they complete the work assigned to them.

Public Accounts Committee

- ➥ Committee of House of people.
- ➥ Consists of not more than 15 members of Lok Sabha and 7 members of Rajya Sabha.
- ➥ Elected on the basis of proportional representation.
- ➥ RS members are treated as associate, can not vote.
- ➥ Chairman is a member of opposition party.
- ➥ Scrutinises appropriation accounts of GOI.
- ➥ Scrutinises the report of CAG.
- ➥ Ensures that money is spent in accordance with the Parliaments decisions.
- ➥ Investigations are in the nature of post mortem.

Estimates Committee

- ➥ Committee of House of People.
- ➥ Consists of 30 members
- ➥ Chairman is appointed by speaker.
- ➥ Constituted after presentation of Budget.
- ➥ reports on what economies, improve-ment in organisational efficiency or administration reform may be effected.
- ➥ Scrutinises the expenditure effected by the Government
- ➥ report is not debated.
- ➥ carries its examination throughout the year.

Committee on Public Undertakings

- ➥ Consists of 15 members.
- ➥ 10 members from LS. and 5 from RS.
- ➥ elected by system of proportional represen-tation.
- ➥ Chairman is appointed by the Speaker.
- ➥ mentioned in 4th schedule.
- ➥ involve both pre and post expenditure phases.

THE STATE EXECUTIVE

Governor

- The State executive consist of a Governor and the Council of Minister with the Chief Minister as its head.
- The Governor is the nominal executive head while the Council of Ministers the real executive authority in the State.

Appointments and Tenure

- The Governor of a State is appointed by the President of India.
- There is no bar on reappointment of a Governor either in the same State or in different States.
- The Governor is appointed for a term of five years but normally holds office during the pleasure of the President.
- He/she may resign before the expiry of the term or may be removed by the President earlier.
- As a matter of fact while appointing or removing the Governor the President goes by the advice of the Prime Minister.
- His/her emoluments, allowances and privileges are specified by the law. However, the emoluments and allowances of the Governor cannot be reduced during his tenure.

Qualification

- To be eligible for appointment as Governor of a State
  - a person should be a Citizen of India and
  - must have completed the age of 35 years.
- The Governor cannot be a member of either House of Parliament or of a State Legislature.
- Nor can he hold any office of Profit under any Government.
- If a person who is a member of a legislature is appointed as Governor, he is deemed to have vacated his seat in the legislature the date on which he enters upon his office as Governor.

Powers and Functions of the Governor

The Constitution confers on the Governors large number of functions which may be grouped under five heads: (1) Executive (2) Legislative (3) Financial (4) Judicial (5) Discretionary

- **Executive Powers:** The executive power of the state is vested in the Governor who is empowered to exercise either directly or through officials subordinate to him.
  - He appoints the Chief Minister of the State and other members of the Council of Ministers who hold office during his pleasure.
  - He allocates the business of the Government among the Minister and makes rules for the convenient transactions of such business.
  - The Governor also appoints the Advocate General, the Chairman and other members of the State Public Service Commission.
  - He is consulted in the appointment of the Judges of the High Court of the State. The Governor of Jharkhand, Chhattisgarh, M.P. and Odisha have a special responsibility to see that the Councils of Ministers in their respective States have a Minister incharge on Tribal welfare.
  - The Governor of Assam has certain special powers with respect to the administration of Tribal areas as provided in the Six Schedule of the Constitution.

➥ **Legislative Powers:** The Governor is an integral, part of the State Legislature and performs number of functions in the legislative sphere. He also enjoys legislative powers.

- He convenes the State Legislature, addresses it in person and send messages to it.
- He can also prorogue and dissolve it.
- During every financial year, he causes the Budget to be laid before the House. It is only on his recommendation that demands for grant can be made in the State Legislature.
- Every Bill passed by the State Legislature has to be present to the Governor for his assent. He may assent to it, or withhold it, may reserve it, for the consideration of the President. He may also return the Bill to the Legislature for reconsideration with a message suggesting alterations or modifications. But if it is again passed with or without amendments, he must give his assent thereto. The Governor has, however, no power to return a Money Bill.
- The Governor has also the special legislative power of promulgating ordinances during the recess of the State Legislature.

➥ **Financial Powers:** Before the commencement of every financial year, the Governor causes to be laid before the State Legislature the annual financial statement showing the estimated revenue and expenditure of the State for that year.

- No demand for grant *i.e.* authority to spend any portion of the State revenue, can be made except on the recommendation of the Governor.
- He has also some powers with regard to Money and Financial Bills,
- The State Contingency Fund is also at the disposal of the Governor who can make advances out of it to meet any unforeseen expenditure. Such expenditure must be subsequently authorised by the Assembly.

➥ **Judicial Powers:** The Governor also enjoys certain judicial powers.

- Like the President of India, He too, in empowered to grant pardons, reprieves, respites or to remit or commute the sentence of any person convicted of any offense against any law relating to matter to which the executive power of the state extends.
- He also determines the appointments, postings and promotions of the District Judges, Session Judges and judicial officials.
- His consultation is also sought in the appointment of the judges of the High Court of the State.

➥ **Discretionary Powers:** It is under special circumstance that the Governor may act without the advice of the Council of Ministers. In other words, such powers of the Governor are exercised in his/her own discretion. They are:

- A situation may arise when in the opinion of the Governor there is the breakdown of the constitutional machinery in the State. In such a case, the Governor may report the situation to the President for imposition of the President's Rule in that State.
- A situation may also arise when the Governor may reserve a bill for the consideration of the President.

The Chief Minister

- The duties of the Chief Minister in a State are similar to those of the Prime Minister of the Union.
- As head of the Council of Ministers in a State, he has to communicate to the Governor all decisions of the Council relating to the administration of the affairs of the state and proposals for legislation.
- He has also to furnish any information which the Governor calls for and which is concerned with the administrative and legislative matters of the state.
- It is also one of his duties to place before the Council, if the Governor so requires, any matter on which a decision has been taken by a Minister without consulting his colleagues in the Council.
- Constitution in its Article 163 provides that there shall be a Council of Ministers with the Chief Minister as its head to aid and advise the Governor in the exercise of his functions except when he is required by the constitution to act in his discretion.
- The Governor may choose the Chief Minister from the Legislative Council. There is also no bar on his selecting a nominated member of the Legislative Council as the Chief Minister.

Functions of the Chief Minister

Chief Minister is the head of the Council of Ministers of his State. The constitutional position of the Chief Minister is more or less similar to that of the Prime Minister. The Chief Minister plays an important role in the administration of the State. We can discuss his functions as follows:

1. Chief Minister is the real head of the State Government. Ministers are appointed by the Governor on the advice of the Chief Minister. The Governor allocates portfolios to the ministers on the advice of the Chief Minister.
2. Chief Minister presides over the Cabinet meetings. He/she coordinates the functioning of different ministries. He/she guides the functioning of the Cabinet.
3. Chief Minister plays a key role in framing the laws and policies of the State Government. Bills are introduced by the ministers in the State legislature with his/her approval. He/she is the chief spokesman of the policies of his government both inside and outside the State Legislature.
4. The Constitution provides that the Chief Minister shall communicate to the Governor all decisions of the Council of Ministers relating to the administration and the affairs of the State and proposals for legislation.
5. The Chief Minister furnishes such information relating to the administration of the affairs of the State and proposals for legislation as the Governor may call for.
6. If the Governor so requires, the Chief Minister submits for consideration of the Council of Ministers any matter on which a decision has been taken by a minister but which has not been considered by the Cabinet.
7. The Chief Minister is the sole link of communication between the Cabinet and the Governor. The Governor has the right to be informed by the Chief Minister about the decisions taken by the Council of Ministers.

THE STATE LEGISLATURE

- In most of the States, the Legislature consists of the Governor and the Legislative Assembly (Vidhan Sabha). This means that these State have unicameral Legislature.
- In a few States, there are two Houses of the Legislature namely, Legislative Assembly (Vidhan Sabha) and Legislative council (Vidhan Parishad) besides the Governor. Where there are two Houses, the Legislature, is known as bicameral.
- Six States have the bicameral legislature-viz. Bihar, Karnataka, Maharashtra, Andhra Pradesh, Telangana and Uttar Pradesh.
- The Legislative Assembly is known as lower House or popular House. The Legislative Council is known as upper House.
- Just as Lok Sabha has been made powerful at the Union level, the Legislative Assembly has been made a powerful body in the States.

Legislative Assembly

- There is a Legislative Assembly (Vidhan Sabha) in every State. It represents the people of State.
- The members of Vidhan Sabha are directly elected by people on the basis of universal adult franchise.
- Every State is divided into as many (single member) constituencies as the number of members to be elected.
- In order to become a Member of Vidhan Sabha a person must:
  - be a citizen of India;
  - have attained the age of 25 years;
  - his/her name must be in voters' list;
  - must not hold any office of profit i.e.;
  - should not be a government servant.

The Strength of Vidhan Sabha in States & UTs

	Name of the State	Strength of Vidhan Sabha
1.	Andhra Pradesh	175
2.	Arunachal Pradesh	60
3.	Assam	126
4.	Bihar	243
5.	Goa	40
6.	Gujarat	182
7.	Haryana	90
8.	Himachal Pradesh	68
9.	Karnataka	224
10.	Kerala	140
11.	Madhya Pradesh	230
12.	Maharashtra	288
13.	Manipur	60
14.	Meghalaya	60
15.	Mizoram	40
16.	Nagaland	60
17.	Odisha	147
18.	Punjab	117
19.	Rajasthan	200
20.	Sikkim	32
21.	Tamil Nadu	234
22.	Telangana	119
23.	Tripura	60
24.	Uttar Pradesh	403
25.	West Bengal	294
26.	Chhattisgarh	90
27.	Jharkhand	81
28.	Uttarakhand	70
29.	Puducherry	30
30.	Delhi	70
31.	Jammu & Kashmir	90

- The number of Vidhan Sabha members cannot be more than 500 and not less than 60. However, very small States have been allowed to have lesser number of members. Thus Goa and Mizoram have only 40 members and Sikkim has only 32 members in its Assembly. Uttar Pradesh has 403 seats in the Assembly.

- The tenure of Vidhan Sabha is five years, but the Governor can dissolve it before the completion of its term on the advice of Chief Minister.
- It may be dissolved by the President in case of constitutional emergency proclaimed under Article 356 of the Constitution.
- In case of proclamation of national emergency (under Article 352) the Parliament can extend the term of the Legislative Assemblies for a period not exceeding one year at a time.
- A person can be disqualified from the membership of Legislative Assembly if he holds an office of profit under the Government of India or of a State or is of unsound mind or is an insolvent.
- The House elects its own presiding officer, called Speaker, who conducts its business. During the absence of Speaker from any sitting of the Assembly, the Deputy Speaker, who is also elected by the House, acts as Speaker.

Legislative Council

- The Parliament may, by law, create or abolish a Legislative Council in a State if the Legislative Assembly of that State passes a resolution to that effect by a majority of the total number of members of the Assembly and by a majority of not less than two-thirds of the members present and voting.
- At present, six States (viz. Bihar, Karnataka, Maharashtra, Andhra Pradesh, Telangana and Uttar Pradesh) have Legislative Councils.
- The Legislative Council is the Upper House of a State Legislature.
- The total number of members in the Legislative Council of a State does not exceed one-third of the total number of members in the Legislative Assembly of that State. However, the total number of members in the Legislative Council of a State should, in no case, be less than forty.
- The Vidhan Parishad is partly elected and partly nominated. Most of the members are indirectly elected in accordance with the principle of proportional representation by means of single transferable vote system.
- Different categories of members represent different interests. The composition of the Legislative Council is as follows:
  - One-third members of the Council are elected by the members of the Vidhan Sabha.
  - One-third of the members of the Vidhan Parishad are elected by the electorates consisting of members of Municipalities, District Boards and other local bodies in the State;
  - One-twelfth members are elected by the electorate consisting of graduates in the State with a standing of three years;
  - One-twelfth members are elected by the electorate consisting of teachers of educational institutions within the State not lower in standard than a secondary school who have teaching experience of at least three years;
  - The remaining, i.e. about one-sixth members are nominated by the Governor from amongst the persons having special knowledge in the sphere of literature, science, arts, co-operative movement and social service.

- In order to be a member of the Legislative Council the person concerned should
  - be a citizen of India;
  - have attained the age of 30 years;
  - be a registered voter in the State;
  - not hold any office of profit
- The tenure of every member of the Council is six years but every second year one-third of its members retire and new members are elected. Ten or one-tenth of the total number of members, whichever is greater, forms the quorum of any meeting of the House.

JUDICIAL SYSTEM

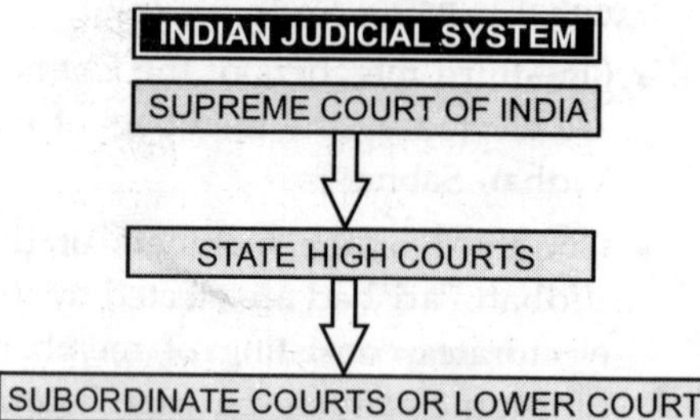

Supreme Court

- The Supreme Court is the highest court of India. It is at the apex of the Indian judicial system.
- It settles the disputes, interprets laws, protects fundamental rights and acts as guardian of the Constitution.
- It consists of a Chief Justice and several other judges.
- At present, the number of other judges is Thirty Three.
- Every judge of the Supreme Court is appointed by the President after consulting such of the judges of the Supreme Court and of the High Courts as President deems necessary. However, while appointing other judges the President has to consult the Chief Justice of India.
- Only such a person can be appointed a judge of the Supreme Court who is a citizen of India and has been a judge of a High Court for at least five years or has been an advocate of a High Court for ten years or is, in the opinion of President, a distinguished jurist.
- The judges of the Supreme Court are paid such salaries as are determined by the Parliament by law. They are also entitled to such privileges and allowances and to such rights in respect of leave of absence and pension as are determined by the Parliament from time to time.
- Every judge of the Supreme Court including the Chief Justice holds office until he attains the age of sixty five years.
- He, however, can resign his post any time by submitting his resignation to the President.
- He can also be removed from his office by the President if each House of Parliament presents an address to him, supported by a majority of the total membership of that House, and by a majority of not less than two-thirds of the members of that House present and voting, for such removal on the grounds of proven misbehaviour or incapacity.
- Every person appointed to be a judge of the Supreme Court is required to take an oath of office before he enters upon his office, before the President or some person appointed by him.
- No person who has held office as a judge of the Supreme Court cannot plead or act in any court or before any authority, within the territory of India.

- If at any time there is no quorum in the Supreme Court for performing its duties, the Chief Justice, with the previous consent of the President and after consultation with the Chief Justice of the High Court concerned, may request one of the judges of a High Court, who otherwise is qualified to be appointed a judge of the Supreme Court, as its ad-hoc judge, for such period as may be necessary.
- The Chief Justice of India may, at any time, with the previous consent of the President, request any retired judge of the Supreme Court or that of a High Court (who otherwise is qualified to be appointed a judge of the Supreme Court) to sit and act as a judge of the Supreme Court. Such a person will be entitled to allowances as the President may determine and shall have all the jurisdiction, powers and privileges that are enjoyed by regular judges.
- The Supreme Court normally sits in New Delhi. But may sit in such other place or places as the Chief Justice of India may from time to time fix with the approval of the President.

Jurisdiction of the Supreme Court

Original Jurisdiction

- The Supreme Court hears directly any dispute,
  - *(i)* between the Government of India and one or more States,
  - *(ii)* between the Government of India and any State or States on one side and one or more States on the other or
  - *(iii)* between two or more States.
- Such a dispute should, however, involve some question of law or fact on which the existence or extent of a legal right depends. The treaties concluded between the Centre and the princely states are excluded from the Court's original jurisdiction.

Appellate Jurisdictions

- The power of a superior/higher court to hear and decide appeals against the judgment of a lower court is called appellate jurisdiction.
- The Supreme Court has vast appellate jurisdiction. It hears appeals against the judgment of the High Courts.
- The appeals can be filled in Civil, Criminal and Constitutional cases.

- **Appeals in Civil Cases:**
  - Disputes relating to property, marriage, money, contract and service etc are called civil cases.
  - If a civil case involves a substantial point of law of public importance needing interpretatation of the Constitution or law, an appeal against the High Court decision can be made to Supreme Court.
  - Earlier the financial limit of such civil cases was ₹ 20,000/- but now according to the 30th Amendment of 1972, there is no minimum amount for taking a civil appeal to the Supreme Court.
  - If substantial question of interpretation of law or Constitution is involved, appeal may be made against the decision of the High Court.
- **Appeals in Criminal Cases:**
  - An appeal may be brought to the Supreme Court against a High Court decision in a criminal case in a number of situations.

- Firstly, if a High Court sets aside an appeal or an order of acquittal passed by a lower court and awards death sentence to the accused, he may bring an appeal to the Supreme Court by right.
- Secondly, appeal can also be made to the Supreme Court if the High Court withdraws a case from a lower court to itself, declares the accused guilty and awards death sentence. In this situation also appeals can be made as a matter of right and without certificate from the High Court.
- The appeal in cases other than these two categories may also be brought to the Supreme Court provided the High Court grants a certificate that the case is fit for appeal to the Supreme Court.
- In case where the High Court refuses to certify a case to be fit for appeal to the Supreme Court, one may seek special leave to appeal from the Supreme Court itself. The Supreme Court may grant such a special leave in its discretion but only in rare cases.

- **Appeals in Constitutional Cases:**
  - A constitutional case is neither a civil dispute, nor concerning a crime. It is a case arising out of different interpretations of Constitution, mainly regarding the fundamental rights.
  - In such Constitutional Cases an appeal can be taken to the Supreme Court only if a High Court certifies that the matter in dispute involves a substantial question of law.
  - If the High Court denies a certificate of fitness to appeal to the Supreme Court, the Supreme Court can use its discretion and grant special leave to appeal to itself in any case it deems fit.

Advisory Jurisdiction

- If at any time it appears to the President that a question of law or fact has arisen or is likely to arise which is of such a nature and of such public importance that it is expedient to obtain the opinion of the Supreme Court upon it he may refer the question to the Court for consideration and the Court may, after such hearing as it thinks fit, report to the President its opinion thereupon.
- However, this advice of the Court is binding neither on the President nor on the parties affected by the opinion.

Review of Judgments

- If the Supreme Court discovers that there are some new facts or evidences or if it is satisfied that some mistake or error took place in its previous decision, it has the power to review the case and alter its previous decisions.
- This is generally done when a review petition is filed. Normally, review is done by a bigger bench than the one that originally decided the case.

High Courts

- Most of the States have a High Court of their own. However, sometimes two or more States share one High Court. A High Court is the highest judicial authority in the State.
- It consists of a Chief Justice and such other judges as the President may from time to time deem it necessary to appoint.
- The Chief Justice is appointed by the President in consultation with the Chief Justice of India and the Governor of that State.

- In appointing other judges the President, besides consulting the Chief Justice of India and the Governor of that State, also consults the Chief Justice of the High Court.
- For the appointment as a judge of a High Court a person should be a citizen of India and should have held a judicial office at least for ten years or has been an advocate of a High Court in any State for at least ten years.
- The judges of a High Court are paid such salaries, as are determined by Parliament by Law. They are also entitled to such privileges and allowances and to such rights in respect of leave of absence and pension as are determined by Parliament from time to time.
- However, Parliament cannot make any change, after their appointment, in the salaries, allowances, privileges, leave of absence and pension etc., adversely affecting them except in case of financial emergency.
- Every Judge of a High Court, including the Chief Justice, holds office until he attains the age of sixty-two years.
- He, however, can resign his post any time by submitting his resignation letter to the President.
- He can also be removed from his office in the same manner as the judges of the Supreme Court.
- No person who has held an office as a permanent judge of a High Court can practice in that High court. However, he can practise in the Supreme Court or in any other High Court.
- The President may increase the number of judges or appoint Additional Judges if so required. A retired High Court judge can also be appointed to act as a judge by the President.
- The President may after consultation with the Chief Justice of India transfer a Judge from one High Court to another High Court.

Appointment of the Judges

- The Additional Judges are appointed in order to meet any temporary increase in the work of court or to dispose of arrears of accumulated work. Their term does not exceed two years.
- An Acting Judge is appointed in place of a permanent judge of the High Court when the latter is away on leave or on some other duty. He acts until the permanent judge has resumed his office.

Jurisdiction of the High Courts

Original Jurisdiction

- Cases of alleged violation of fundamental rights can be started in High Courts, or in the Supreme Court. The High Courts have the power to issue orders to restore the fundamental rights of the people, these orders are called writs.
- A High Court can hear election petition in its original jurisdiction, challenging the election of a Member of Parliament or State Legislative Assembly. It can set aside the election of a member if it finds that he or she used corrupt means in his or her election.

Jurisdiction and Seats of High Courts in India

Sr. No.	Name of High Courts	Year Estd.	Jurisdiction	Seat
1.	Calcutta	1862	West Bengal, Andaman & Nicobar	Kolkata (Benches at Shri Vijaya Puram and Jalpaiguri)
2.	Bombay	1862	Maharashtra, Goa, Dadra & Nagar Haveli and Daman and Diu	Mumbai (Benches at Panji, Nagpur and Sambhaji Nagar)
3.	Madras	1862	Tamil Nadu and Puducherry	Chennai (Bench at Madurai)
4.	Allahabad	1866	Uttar Pradesh	Prayagraj (with Bench at Lucknow)
5.	Karnataka	1884	Karnataka	Bengaluru (Benches at Dharwad and gulbarga)
6.	Patna	1916	Bihar	Patna
7.	Jammu & Kashmir and Ladakh	1928	Jammu and Kashmir, Ladakh	Srinagar and Jammu
8.	Gauhati	1948	Assam, Nagaland, Mizoram and Arunachal Pradesh	Guwahati (Benches at Kohima, Aizawl, Itanagar)
9.	Orissa	1948	Odisha	Cuttack
10.	Rajasthan	1949	Rajasthan	Jodhpur (Bench at Jaipur)
11.	Kerala	1956	Kerala and Lakshadweep	Kochi
12.	Madhya Pradesh	1956	Madhya Pradesh	Jabalpur (Benches at Gwalior & Indore)
13.	Gujarat	1960	Gujarat	Sola (Ahmedabad)
14.	Delhi	1966	New Delhi	NCT of Delhi
15.	Himachal Pradesh	1971	Himachal Pradesh	Shimla
16.	Punjab & Haryana	1975	Punjab, Haryana & Chandigarh	Chandigarh
17.	Sikkim	1975	Sikkim	Gangtok
18.	Jharkhand	2000	Jharkhand	Ranchi
19.	Chhattisgarh	2000	Chhattisgarh	Bilaspur
20.	Uttarakhand	2000	Uttarakhand	Nainital
21.	Manipur	2013	Manipur	Imphal
22.	Meghalaya	2013	Meghalaya	Shillong
23.	Tripura	2013	Tripura	Agartala
24.	Andhra Pradesh	2019	Andhra Pradesh	Amravati
25.	Telangana	2019	Telangana	Hyderabad

Appellate Jurisdiction

- In civil cases, appellate jurisdiction extends to all such cases which involve a higher amount. Any party to a civil dispute, which is dissatisfied with the decision of the District Court may appeal against the decision of the District Court in the High Court.
- It also hears cases relating to patents and designs, succession, land acquisition, insolvency and guardianship.
- The High Courts hear and decide appeals against decisions of the sessions courts in criminal cases. An accused who is found guilty by a sessions court, and awarded a sentence may file an appeal against the verdict of the sessions court. Sometimes even State may appeal against a sessions court judgement for enhancement of punishment.
- The High Court may accept the decision of the sessions court, or alter it and increase or reduce the sentence, or change the nature of sentence, or may acquit an accused.
- However, if an accused is awarded death sentence by the sessions court, the sentence must be confirmed by the High Court before the person is hanged to death. Even if the accused does not file an appeal against death sentence, the State refers it to the High Court for confirmation.

Superintendence of Subordinate Courts

- A High Court has the right of superintendence and control over all the subordinate courts in all the matter of judicial and administrative nature.
- In the exercise of its power of superintendence, the High Court may call for any information from the lower courts; may make and issue general rules and prescribe norms for regulating the practice and proceedings of these courts; and it may issue such directions, from time to time, as it may deem necessary.
- It can also make rules and regulations relating to the appointment, demotion, promotion and leave of absence for the officers of the subordinate courts.

Transfer of Cases to High Court

- If a High Court feels that a case pending in a Subordinate Court, involves a substantial question of law, it may withdraw the case and may either dispose off the case itself or determine the said question of law and return the case to the court from which it was withdrawn for final decision.
- Control over Officers and Servants of the High Court
- Under Article 229, every High Court has been ensured a complete control over the members of the staff.
- The Chief Justice is empowered to appoint officers and servants of its High Court.

Subordinate or Lower Courts in Districts

- In each district of India there are various types of subordinate or lower courts. They are civil courts, criminal courts and revenue courts.
- These Courts hear civil cases, criminal cases and revenue cases, respectively.

Civil Courts

- The Court of the District Judge is the highest civil court in a district to deal with civil cases.

- Very often the same court is called the Court of District and Sessions Judge, when it deals with both civil and criminal cases at the district level. The judge of this court is appointed by the Governor of the State.
- Below the Court of District Judge, there may be one or more courts of sub judges in the district.

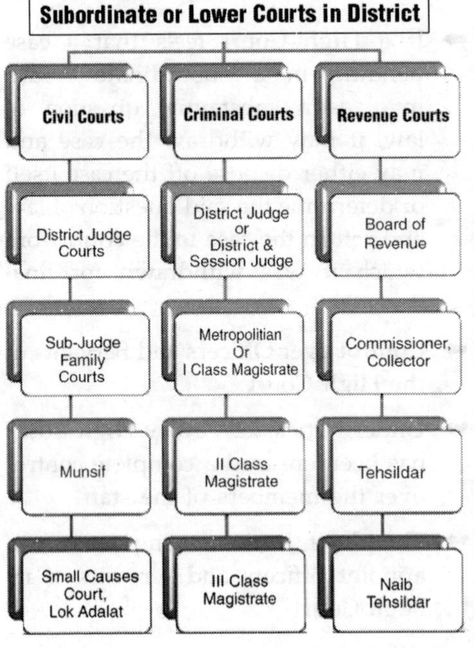

- Separate family courts, which are equal to courts of sub judge, have been established in districts to exclusively hear cases of family disputes, like divorce, custody of children, etc.
- Below them there are courts of munsifs and small causes courts which decide cases involving petty amounts.
- No appeal can be made against the decisions of the small causes courts. All these courts hear and settle civil disputes.
- The Court of the District Judge (called the District Courts) hears not only appeals against the decisions of the courts of sub judges, but also some of the cases begin directly in the Court of District Judge itself.
- Appeals against the decisions of this court may be heard by the High Court of the State.
- Civil Courts deal with cases pertaining to disputes between two or more persons regarding property, divorce, contract, and breach of agreement or landlord-tenant disputes.

Criminal Courts

- The Court of the Sessions Judge (known as Sessions Courts) is the highest court for criminal cases in a district. Below this court, there are courts of magistrates of First, Second and Third class.
- In metropolitan cities like Delhi, Kolkata, Mumbai and Chennai, First Class Magistrates are called Metropolitan Magistrates.
- All these criminal courts are competent to try the accused and to award punishment, as sanctioned by law, to those who are found guilty of violation of law.
- Criminal Courts hear criminal cases which are related to violation of laws. These cases involve theft, dacoity, rape, arson, pick-pocketing, physical assault, murder etc.
- In such cases the guilty person is awarded punishment. It may be fine, imprisonment or even death sentence.

Revenue Courts

- Revenue courts deal with cases of land revenue (It is a sort of tax on agriculture land which the government collects from the farmers) in the State. The highest revenue court in the district is the Board of Revenue. Under it are the Courts of Commissioners, Collectors, Tehsildars and Assistant Tehsildars. The Board of Revenue hears the final appeals against all the lower revenue courts under it.

Family Courts

- The family courts can be set up by the state government under the Family Courts Act 1984. Such courts are usually set up in cities or towns with a population of more than 10 lakh. The main aim of these courts is to promote conciliation and to secure speedy settlement of disputes relating to marriage and family affairs.

Nyaya Panchayats

- The Nyaya Panchayats have been established with the objective of providing speedy and inexpensive justice to the villagers. However, the jurisdiction of the Nyaya Panchayats differs in different states. Usually a Nyaya Panchayat enjoys jurisdiction over one to five Village Panchayats. The Nyaya Panchayats try all petty civil suits relating to property and minor offences within its jurisdiction. The Nyaya Panchayats in most of the states (except Bihar) do not enjoy a power to award imprisonment, and can merely impose fines.

IMPORTANT FUNCTIONARIES

Election Commission

- A three member commission entrusted with the task of supervising and conducting elections. It consists of a Chief Election Commissioner and two Election Commissioners.

Term

- Every Election Commissioner has a term of six years from the date he/she assumes office or till he attains the age of 65 years (whichever is earlier).

Safeguards

- The Chief Election commissioner cannot be removed from his office, except in a like manner and on like grounds as a judge of the Supreme Court. All the three members are entitled to the same salary and other facilities, as are provided to a judge of the Supreme Court.

Functions/Powers

1. Prepare, revise and maintain the voter's list.
2. Delimitation of Constituencies.
3. Advises the President and Governor regarding electoral matters.
4. Determine criteria for recognizing political parties.
5. Settle election disputes.

Union Public Service Commission

- The Union Public Service Commission (UPSC) is the central recruiting agency in India. It is an independent constitutional body in the sense that it is directly created by the constitution of India.

Composition

- The UPSC consists of a chairman and other members appointed by the President of India. The Constitution does not specify the strength of the Commission but has left the matter to the discretion of the President.

- Hence, the composition of the commission is determined by the President. Usually, the Commission consists of 9 to 11 members including the chairman.
- However, the constitution provides that one half of the members of the commission should be such persons who have held office for at least ten years either under the Government of India or the government of a state.
- The constitution also authorises the President to determine the conditions of service of the chairman and members of the commission.
- The chairman and members of the commission shall hold office for a term of six years or until they attain the age of 65 years, whichever is earlier.

Functions

The UPSC performs the following functions:

- It conducts examinations for appointments to the All-India Services, Central Services and public services of the centrally administered territories.
- It advises the President of India on the following.
  - All matters relating to methods of recruitment to civil services and for civil posts.
  - The principles to be followed in making appointments to civil services and posts and in making promotions and transfers from one service to another.
- The additional functions relating to the Services of the Union can be conferred on UPSC by the Parliament. It can also place the personnel system of any local authority, corporate body or public institution within the jurisdiction of the UPSC. Hence the jurisdiction of UPSC can be extended by an act made by the Parliament.
- The UPSC presents, annually, to the President a report on its performance. The President places this report before both the houses of Parliaments, along with a memorandum explaining the cases, if any, where the advice of the commission was not accepted and the reasons for such non-acceptance.

Finance Commission

- Finance Commission is constituted to define financial relations between the centre and the states.
- Under the provision of Artilce 280 of the constitution, the President appoints a Finance Commission for the specific purpose of devolution of non-plan revenue resources.
- The Finance Commission consists of a chairman and four other members.
- According to the qualifications prescribed by parliament, the chairman is selected from amongst persons who have had experience in public affairs, While the members are selected from amongst persons who
  - are, or have been, or are qualified to be appointed judges of the high court; or
  - have special knowledge of the finance and accounts of Governments; or
  - have had wide experience in financial matters and in administration, or
  - have special knowledge of economics.
- The members of the commission hold office for such period as may be specified by the President in his orders and are eligible for re-appointment.

Finance Commissions

Finance Commission	Chairman	Operational Duration
I	K.C. Niyogi	1952-1957
II	K. Santhanam	1957–1962
III	A. K. Chanda	1962–1966
IV	P.V. Rajamannar	1966–1969
V	Mahaveer Tyagi	1969–1974
VI	Brahma Nand Reddy	1974–1979
VII	J.M. Shellet	1979–1984
VIII	Y.B. Chawan	1984–1989
IX	N.K.P. Salve	1989–1995
X	K.C. Pant	1995–2000
XI	A.M. Khusro	2000–2005
XII	Dr. C. Rang Rajan	2005–2010
XIII	Vijay L. Kelkar	2010-2015
XIV	Y.V. Reddy	2015-2020
XV	N.K. Singh	2020-2026
XVI	Dr. Arvind Panagariya	2026-2031

Functions

The main functions of the Finance Commission are:

1. to recommend to the President the basis for distribution of the net proceeds of taxes between the centre and states.
2. to recommend the principles which should govern the grants-in-aid to be given to states out of the Consolidated Fund of India.
3. to tender advice to the President on any other matter referred to the commission in the interest of sound finance.

Central Vigilance Commission (CVC)

- The CVC was established in 1964 on the recommendation of the Santhanam Committee on Prevention of Corruption.
- It was set up by an executive resolution of the Union Government. As such, originally it was neither a constitutional body nor a statutory body.
- In August 1998, the Central Government promulgated an ordinance conferring statutory status on CVC.
- The ordinance provides for the constitution of a multi-member commission headed by a central vigilance commissioner and assisted by not more than two vigilance commissioners.
- They shall be appointed by the President of India on the recommendations of a high powered committee under the chairmanship of the Prime Minister, with the Home Minister and the leader of the opposition in the Lok Sabha as members.

- The CVC shall have a fixed tenure of 4 years as well as the vigilance commissioners shall have a fixed tenure of 4 years subject to the upper age limit of 65 years.
- The Central Vigilance Commissioner can be removed in the same manner as provided for the removal of the Chairman of UPSC.
- After retirement, he is not eligible for any further employment either under the Central Government of State Government.
- The 1998 ordinance has given the CVC wide ranging powers to supervise the functioning of investigating agencies like the CBI and Enforcement Directorate, and recommend appointment of their heads.
- The Central Vigilance Commission is the main agency for preventing corruption in the Central Government.
- It advises the Central Government on all matters relating to the protection and maintenance of integrity in administration. Thus, its role is advisory in the same sense as that of the UPSC.
- The jurisdiction and powers of the commission extends to all those matters which fall within the purview of the executive powers of the Central Government.
- Its jurisdiction covers the following public servants.
    - All the employees of the Central Government (*i.e.* directly employed in the various ministries/departments of the Central Government).
    - All the employees of public undertakings, corporate bodies and other institutions working under the Central Government.
    - All the employees of the Delhi Metropolitan Council and the New Delhi Municipal Committee.
- However, its present jurisdiction is limited to the gazetted officers and officers of equivalent status only. It advises on individual vigilance cases relating to higher civil servants only. It has no power to probe into the cases of political corruption (i.e. against members of Parliament and ministers).

Lokpal

- **Composition:** The Lokpal consists of a chairperson and a maximum of eight members.
- **Applicability:** The Lokpal covers all categories of public servants, including the Prime Minister. But the armed forces do not come under the ambit of Lokpal.

Eligibility

- The person who is to be appointed as the chairperson of the Lokpal should be either of the following: Either the former Chief Justice of India Or the former Judge of Supreme Court Or an eminent person with impeccable integrity and outstanding ability, having special knowledge and expertise of minimum 25 years in the matters relating to anti-corruption policy, public administration, vigilance, finance including insurance and banking, law and management.
- Out of the maximum eight members, half should be judicial members. Minimum fifty per cent of the Members will be from SC/ST/OBC/ Minorities and women.
- The judicial member of the Lokpal should be either a former Judge of the Supreme Court or a former Chief Justice of a High Court.

- The non-judicial member should be an eminent person with impeccable integrity and outstanding ability, having special knowledge and expertise of minimum 25 years in the matters relating to anti-corruption policy, public administration, vigilance, finance including insurance and banking, law and management.

Term of Office

- The term of office for Lokpal Chairman and Members is 5 years or till attaining age of 70 years.
- The salary, allowances and other conditions of service of chairperson are equivalent to Chief Justice of India and members is equivalent to Judge of Supreme Court. If the person is already getting the pension (for being a former judge), the equivalent pension amount will be deducted from the salary.
- The source of salary for Lokpal and Members is Consolidated Fund of India.
- If the chairperson dies in office or has resigned from the post, President can authorise the senior-most Member to act as the Chairperson until new chairperson is appointed. If chairperson is not available for certain functions due to leave, his job will be done by senior most member.

Powers

- The Lokpal has the power of superintendence and direction over any investigation agency including CBI for cases referred to them by the ombudsman.
- As per the Act, The Lokpal can summon or question any public servant if there exists a prima facie case against the person, even before an investigation agency (such as vigilance or CBI) has begun the probe. Any officer of the CBI investigating a case referred to it by the Lokpal, shall not be transferred without the approval of the Lokpal.
- An investigation must be completed within six months. However, the Lokpal or Lokayukta may allow extensions of six months at a time provided the reasons for the need of such extensions are given in writing.
- Special courts will be instituted to conduct trials on cases referred by Lokpal.

Lokayukta

- The institution of Lokayukta was established firsts in Maharashtra in 1971, though Odisha had passed the act in this regard in 1970. The Odisha act came into force in 1983.
- The structure of the Lokayukta is not same in all the states. Some states like Rajasthan, Karnataka, Andhra Pradesh and Maharashtra have created the Lokayukta as well as Uplokayukta, while some other states like Bihar, Uttar Pradesh and Himachal Pradesh have created only the Lokayukta; there being no provision for Uplokayukta.
- There are still other states like the Punjab and Odisha which have designated officials as Lokpal.
- **Appointment:** The Lokayukta and Uplokayukta are appointed by the Governors in most of the states. While appointing, the Governor consults–
  - the Chief Minister
  - Chief Justice of the state High Court
  - the leader of opposition in the state Legislative Assembly.

Lokayukta in States

	States	Created in
1.	Maharashtra	1971
2.	Rajasthan	1973
3.	Bihar	1974
4.	Uttar Pradesh	1975
5.	Madhya Pradesh	1981
6.	Andhra Pradesh	1983
7.	Himachal Pradesh	1983
8.	Odisha	1983
9.	Karnataka	1985
10.	Assam	1985
11.	Gujarat	1986
12.	Punjab	1995
13.	Delhi	1995
14.	Kerala	1999
15.	Jharkhand	2001
16.	Uttarakhand	2002
17.	Chattisgarh	2002
18.	Haryana	2002
19.	Jammu & Kashmir	2002
20.	West Bengal	2003
21.	Tripura	2008
22.	Goa	2011

- **Qualifications:** Judicial qualifications are prescribed for the Lokayukta in the states of Uttar Pradesh, Himachal Pradesh, Andhra Pradesh, Gujarat, Odisha, Karnataka and Assam. But no specific qualifications are prescribed in the states of Bihar, Maharashtra and Rajasthan.
- **Tenure:** In most of the states, the term of office fixed for Lokayukta is of 5 years duration or 65 years of age, whichever is earlier. He is not eligible for reappointment for a second term.
- **Jurisdiction:** There is no uniformity regarding the jurisdiction of Lokayukta in all the states.

(*a*) The Chief Minister is included within the jurisdiction of Lokayukta in the states of Himachal Pradesh, Andhra Pradesh, Gujarat, while he is exculded from the purview of Lokayukta in the states of Maharashtra, Uttar Pradesh, Rajasthan, Bihar and Odisha.

(*b*) Ministers and higher civil servants are included in the purview of Lokayukta in almost all the states. Maharashtra has also included former Ministers and civil servants.

(*c*) Members of states legislatures are included in the purview of Lokayukta in the states of Andhra Pradesh, Himachal Pradesh, Gujarat, Uttar Pradesh and Assam.

(*d*) The authorities of the local bodies, corporations, companies and societies are included in the jurisdiction of the Lokayukta in most of the states.

Comptroller and Auditor General of India

- The Comptroller and Auditor General (CAG) is a guardian of the govt. purse.
- His office has been created by the Constitution. He is appointed by the President.
- Generally, a person with long administrative experience and knowledge of account is appointed to this office.
- He holds office for a term of six years or till he attains the age of 65 years. However, he can relinquish office earlier.

- The President can also remove him from office before the expiry of his term on grounds of proved misbehaviour and incapacity. The President issues orders for removal of CAG only on the recommendation of the two houses of Parliament.

Functions

- The CAG acts as custodian and trustee of the public money. He ensures regularity of expenditure and looks into the wisdom of the expenditure.
- Every year the CAG of India submits a report relating to the accounts of the Union to the President who places the same before the Parliament.

Attorney General of India

- Attorney General is the highest legal officer of the union government and renders legal assistant to it.
- He is appointed by the President and holds office during his pleasure.
- To be eligible for appointment as Attorney General of India, a person must possess the qualifications prescribed for a judge of the Supreme Court.
- He is entitled to such salary and allowances as may be determined by the President.
- The Attorney General is entitled to audience in all courts in the country and can take part in the proceedings of Parliament and its committees. However, he is not given the right to vote.

Functions

- He is the chief legal adviser of the Government of India and gives it advice on all such legal matters which may be referred or assigned to him by the President.
- He also performs such other legal duties as are assigned to him by the President from time to time.

PANCHAYATI RAJ SYSTEM

Rural Local Government

- The term 'Panchayati Raj' in India signifies the system of rural local self-government. It is created in all the states in India by the acts of the state legislatures to establish democracy at the grass roots level.
- It was constitutionalised through the 73rd Constitutional Amendment Act of 1992.
- The scheme was inaugurated by the Prime Minister on 2nd october, 1959, in Rajasthan's Nagaur district. Rajasthan was followed by Andhra Pradesh which also adopted the system in 1959.

73rd Amendment Act of 1992

- This act has added Part-IX to the Constitution of India. It is entitled as 'The Panchayats' and consists of provisions from articles 243 to 243-O.
- In addition, the Act has also added Eleventh schedule to the Constitution. It contains 29 functional items of the Panchayats and deals wih Article 243-G.

The Salient Features of the Act are:

1. **Gram Sabha:** The Act provides for a Gram Sabha as the foundation of the Panchayati Raj system. It is a body consisting of persons

registered in the electoral rolls of a village comprised within the area of Panchayat at the village level. Thus, it is a village assembly consisting of all the registered voters in the area of a Panchayat.

2. **Three-Tier System:** The Act provides for a three-tier system of Panchayati Raj in every state, that is Panchayats at the village, intermediate, and district levels. However a state having a population not exceeding 20 lakhs may not constitute panchayats at the intermediate level.

3. **Reservation of Seats:** The Act provides for the reservation of seats for scheduled castes and scheduled tribes in every Panchayat in proportion of their population to the total population in the Panchayat area. Further, the state legislature shall provide for the reservation of offices of chairpersons in the Panchayat at the village or any other level for the SC and ST.

Urban Local Government

- In the Constitution of India initially there was no provision for the establishment of local self-governing institutions in urban India, though it did make reference, in one of the Directive Principles, about the establishment of Village Panchayats in rural India.
- Lacuna was rectified by the Constitution (Seventy-fourth Amendment) Act, 1992, which provided for the establishment and management of urban local selfgovernment in India.

74th Amendment Act of 1992

- This Act has added Part IX-A to the Constitution of India. It is entitled as "The Municipalities' and consists of provisions from articles 243-P to 243-ZG.
- In addition, the Act has also added Twelfth Schedule to the Constitution.
- It contains 18 functional items of municipalities and deals with Article 243-W.
- The Act gave constitutional status to the municipalities. It has brought them under the purview of justiciable part of the constitution.
- **Composition:**
  - All the members of a municipality shall be elected directly by the people of the municipal area. For this purpose, each municipal area shall be divided into territorial constituencies to be known as wards.
  - The state legislature may provide the manner of election of the chairperson of a municipality.
- **Wards Committees:** There shall be constituted a wards committee, consisting of one or more wards, within the territorial area of a municipality having population of three lakhs or more.
- **Reservation of Seats:**
  - The Act provides for the reservation of seats for the scheduled castes and the scheduled tribes in every muni-cipality in proportion of their population to the total population in the municipal area.
  - Further, it provides for the reservation of not less than one-third of the total number of seats for women (including the number of seats reserved for women belonging to the SCs and the Sts).

MULTIPLE CHOICE QUESTIONS

1. What is the difference between 'vote-on-account' and 'interim budget'?

1. The provision of a 'vote-on-account' is used by a regular Government, while an 'interim budget' is a provision used by a caretaker Government.
2. A 'vote-on-account' only deals with the expenditure in Government's budget, while an 'interim budget' includes both expenditure and receipts.

Which of the statements; given above is/are correct?

A. Only 1
B. Only 2
C. Both 1 and 2
D. Neither 1 nor 2

2. With reference to the Delimitation Commission, consider the following statements:

1. The orders of the Delimitation Commission cannot be challenged in a Court of Law.
2. When the orders of the Delimitation Commission are laid before the Lok Sabha or State Legislative Assembly, they cannot effect any modifications in the orders.

Which of the statements; given above is/are correct?

A. Only 1
B. Only 2
C. Both 1 and 2
D. Neither 1 nor 2

3. According to the Constitution of India, which one of the following statements is not correct?

A. The executive powers of the Union are vested in the President of India
B. The functions President cannot be conferred to any authorities other than the President of India
C. The President of India is elected by an electoral college that consists of all Members of Parliament (both Lok Sabha and Rajya Sabha)
D. A person who has held the office of the President can be eligible for re-election for a second term

4. The powers of the speaker are:

1. To maintain order within the Houses of the Parliament.
2. To interpret the rules of procedure of the Houses of the Parliament.
3. Dissolve the House when there is absence of quorum.

Select the correct answer from the codes given below:

A. 1, 2 and 3
B. Only 1 and 2
C. Only 2 and 3
D. None of these

5. In the Lok Sabha, unless there is a quorum, the Speaker should not conduct the proceedings, to ensure this:

A. The speaker usually counts the heads at the beginning of everyday
B. The Parliamentary Secretariat keeps a watch on the attendance in the house and informs the speaker
C. The attendance register kept at the entrance is monitored
D. The speaker relies only on the members to bring to his notice the lack of quorum

6. Consider the following statements with reference to Attorney General of India:
   1. He holds office during the pleasure of the Prime Minister.
   2. He is not entitled to the privileges of a Member of Parliament.

   Select the correct answer from the codes given below:
   A. Only 1
   B. Only 2
   C. Neither 1 nor 2
   D. Both 1 and 2

7. Which among the following is the correct order mentioned in preamble of the Indian Constitution?
   A. Socialist, Secular, Sovereign, Democratic
   B. Sovereign, Socialist, Secular, Democratic
   C. Secular, Socialist, Sovereign, Democratic
   D. Sovereign, Secular, Socialist, Democratic

8. Which statement is correct about Panchayati Raj?
   A. The Panchayat Samiti and Zila Parishad are constituted with directly elected members
   B. Minimum age is 18 years to contest the election at the Panchayat level
   C. Election of the Panchayati Raj Institutions is conducted under the supervision of the State Election Commission
   D. None of these

9. Which one of the following pairs (Article-Provision) is not correctly matched?
   A. Article 124 — Supreme Court to be a Court of Record
   B. Article 132 — Appellate Jurisdiction of Supreme court
   C. Article 143 — Advisory Jurisdiction of Supreme Court
   D. Article 136 — Special leave to appeal by the Supreme Court

10. Which part of the Indian Constitution deals with the Fundamental Rights?
    A. Part I B. Part II
    C. Part III D. Part IV

11. Who among the following Chief Justices of India ordered the Constitution of a special Bench called 'Social Justice Bench'?
    A. Justice H.L. Dattu
    B. Justice K.G. Balakrishnan
    C. Justice R.M. Lodha
    D. Justice Y.K. Sabharwal

12. Which fundamental right guarantees protection against double jeopardy and self-incrimination?
    A. Right to Freedom of Speech
    B. Right to Life and Personal Liberty
    C. Right to Protection from Arrest and Detention
    D. Right to Protection in Respect of Conviction for Offenses

13. The concept of 'Basic Structure' of the Indian Constitution was first introduced in which landmark Supreme Court case?
    A. Golaknath Vs. State of Punjab
    B. Keshavananda Bharati Vs. State of Kerala
    C. Minerva Mills Vs. Union of India
    D. Indira Nehru Gandhi Vs. Raj Narain

14. In the context of the Panchayati Raj system, which level of Panchayat is directly elected by the people?
    A. District Panchayat
    B. Intermediate Panchayat
    C. Gram Panchayat
    D. All of the above

15. Identify the correct statement regarding the Panchayati Raj system in India.

A. It is a single-tier system with only the Gram Panchayat as the sole level
B. It was constitutionally recognized with the 73rd Amendment Act of 1992
C. The Panchayati Raj Ministry is a Union Ministry directly overseeing the system
D. Zila Parishad forms the lowest tier of the Panchayati Raj system

16. 'The Right to Privacy' is protected as an intrinsic part of which Right under the Indian Constitution?

A. Right to Freedom of Religion
B. Right to Constitutional Remedies
C. Right to Freedom
D. Right against Exploitation

17. The UPSC derives its functions from which of the following sources?

1. The Constitution
2. Parliamentary Laws
3. Executive Rules and Orders
4. Conventions

Select the correct answer from the codes given below:

A. 1 and 3
B. 1 and 2
C. 1, 2, 3 and 4
D. Only 1

18. Which one of the following is correctly matched?

	Constitutional Body	Article
A.	National Commission for Scheduled Castes	— 148
B.	Election Commission	— 165
C.	National Commission for Backward Classes	— 340
D.	Finance Commission	— 263

19. Given below are two statements, one is labelled as Assertion (A) and the other as Reason (R):

Assertion (A): Article 352 of the Indian Constitution deals with the declaration of an emergency.

Reason (R): An emergency may take place at any time.

Select the correct answer from the codes given below:

A. (A) is false, but (R) is true
B. Both (A) and (R) are true, but (R) is not the correct explanation of (A)
C. (A) is true, but (R) is false
D. Both (A) and (R) are true, but (R) is the correct explanation of (A)

20. Match List-I with List-II and choose the correct answer using the codes given below the lists:

List-I	List-II
(a) Consolidated Fund of India	1. Article 266
(b) Finance Commission	2. Article 360
(c) Financial Emergency	3. Article 280
(d) Comptroller and Auditor General of India	4. Article 148

Codes:

	(a)	(b)	(c)	(d)
A.	4	1	3	2
B.	3	1	2	4
C.	1	2	3	4
D.	1	3	2	4

21. Which of the following are envisaged by the Right against Exploitation in the Constitution of India?

1. Abolition of untouchability
2. Prohibition of human trafficking and forced labour

3. Prohibition of employment of children in factories and mines
4. Protection of interests of minorities

Select the correct answer from the codes given below:

A. 3 and 4 B. 2 and 3
C. 1 and 4 D. 1 and 2

22. Consider the following statements:

An Amendment to the Constitution of India can be initiated by the:

1. Lok Sabha
2. Rajya Sabha
3. State Legislatures
4. President of India

Which of the statements is/are correct?

A. 1 and 2
B. 1, 2 and 3
C. 2, 3 and 4
D. Only 1

23. Which of the following are the functions of the Election Commissioner of India?

1. Conduct of elections for the posts of the Speaker and the Deputy Speaker of the Lok Sabha and Deputy Chairman of the Rajya Sabha.
2. Conduct of elections of the Municipal Corporations and Municipalities.
3. Deciding on all doubts and disputes arising out of the above elections.

Select the correct answer from the codes given below:

A. 1 and 3 B. 2 and 3
C. 1 and 2 D. None of these

24. Which one of the following is not a level in the three-tier Panchayati Raj recommended by Balwant Rai Mehta Committee?

A. Gram Panchayat
B. Panchayat Samiti
C. Nyaya Panchayat
D. Zilla Panchayat

25. According to the Lokpal and Lokayuktas Act, 2013 the Lokpal would be appointed by the President after obtaining the recommendations of a Selection Committee, with the Prime Minister as chairperson and consisting, among others, of the following:

1. Chief Justice of India or a Supreme Court Judge nominated by him.
2. Chairman of the Rajya Sabha.
3. Speaker of the Lok Sabha.
4. Leader of Opposition in the Lok Sabha.

Select the correct answer from the codes given below:

A. 2, 3 and 4
B. 1, 2 and 3
C. 1, 3 and 4
D. 1, 2, 3 and 4

26. Which Fundamental Right can be described as the soul and heart of the Constitution:

A. Right to equality
B. Right to prosperity
C. Right to constitutional remedies
D. Right to freedom of speech

27. Ordinances are promulgated by:

A. Prime Minister
B. Lok Sabha Speaker
C. President
D. Rajya Sabha Chairman

28. Indian states have been constituted on the basis of:

A. geographical continuity
B. language
C. administrative convenience
D. economic conditions

29. The Chief Election Commissioner can be removed by:

A. Prime Minister
B. President
C. Supreme Court's Chief Justice
D. Parliament

30. Speaker of the Lok Sabha can only:

A. adjourn the house
B. prorogue the house
C. summon the house
D. dissolve the house

31. Membership of state assembly range from:

A. 30 to 300
B. 40 to 400
C. 50 to 600
D. 60 to 500

32. Salaries of Supreme Court judges are drawn from:

A. Law Ministry Grants
B. Consolidated Fund of India
C. Home Ministry Grants
D. Parliamentary Grants

33. The need of establish Panchayati Raj institutions is prescribed in:

A. Directive Principles
B. Fundamental Rights
C. Preamble
D. Seventh Schedule

34. Which Constitutional amendment curtailed the power of judicial review by the Supreme Court?

A. 24th amendment
B. 42nd amendment
C. 43rd amendment
D. 44th amendment

35. The quorum in Lok Sabha is:

A. 50
B. 55
C. one-fourth of the strength
D. one-tenth of the strength

36. The Prime Minister, who could not face the Parliament even once, was:

A. V.P. Singh
B. Charan Singh
C. Morarji Desai
D. Deve Gowda

37. Among the judicial powers, the President can not:

A. grant pardon
B. grant reprieve
C. grant amnesty
D. grant change of court

38. Provisions of disqualification on ground of defection are listed in:

A. second schedule
B. fourth schedule
C. eighth schedule
D. tenth schedule

39. National emergency can not be imposed in case of:

A. Armed rebellion
B. Political crisis
C. Internal aggression
D. War

40. If Lok Sabha and Rajya Sabha disagree on a constitutional amendment bill:

A. the bill lapses
B. a joint sitting is called
C. Lok Sabha's decision prevails
D. Rajya Sabha's decision prevails

41. The Preamble of the Constitution was amended by:

A. 1st amendment
B. 26th amendment
C. 42nd amendment
D. 44th amendment

42. 18th General Elections were held in:

A. 2021 B. 2024
C. 2022 D. 2023

43. The retirement age for Supreme Court judges is:

A. 58 years B. 60 years
C. 62 years D. 65 years

44. One can be disqualified from voting, only on the grounds of:

A. Age
B. Sex
C. Religion
D. Education

45. Constitutional emergency can be renewed upto:

A. six months
B. two years
C. three years
D. indefinitely

46. First General elections in the country were held in:

A. 1948 B. 1950
C. 1949 D. 1952

47. A total of .... members can be nominated by the President to the Rajya Sabha.

A. 6 B. 12
C. 15 D. 18

48. The Union executive is responsible to:

A. Lok Sabha
B. Rajya Sabha
C. President
D. Supreme Court

49. Attorney-General of India is appointed by:

A. UPSC
B. President
C. Prime Minister
D. Lok Sabha Speaker

50. Time gap between two sessions of Parliament cannot exceed:

A. 3 months B. 6 months
C. 1 year D. no fixed gap

ANSWERS

1	2	3	4	5	6	7	8	9	10
B	C	B	D	B	C	B	C	A	C
11	**12**	**13**	**14**	**15**	**16**	**17**	**18**	**19**	**20**
A	D	B	D	B	C	C	C	B	D
21	**22**	**23**	**24**	**25**	**26**	**27**	**28**	**29**	**30**
B	A	D	C	C	C	C	B	D	A
31	**32**	**33**	**34**	**35**	**36**	**37**	**38**	**39**	**40**
D	B	A	B	D	B	D	D	B	A
41	**42**	**43**	**44**	**45**	**46**	**47**	**48**	**49**	**50**
C	B	D	A	C	D	B	A	B	B

General Science

PHYSICS

Physics is a branch of Science dealing with nature and natural phenomenon. The natural phenomena are expressed in terms of relationship among physical quantities involved.

MEASUREMENTS

- Measurement of any physical quantity involves comparison with a certain basic, arbitrarily chosen, internationally accepted reference standard called unit.
- The result of a measurement of a physical quantity is expressed by a number (or numerical measure) accompanied by a unit.

System of Units

- Several systems of units have been in use to describe measurements.
- The common systems are the CGS system (Centimetre, Gram, Second); the FPS system (Foot, Pound, Second) which is the British system; the MKS system (Metre, Kilogram and Second) and the now internationally accepted which is known as International System of Units (came from French name "Le Systeme International d' Unites"), abbreviated SI.

Quantities and Units

Quantities	Units	Symbols
Length	metre	m
Mass	kilogram	kg
Time	second	s
Electric current	ampere	A
Thermodynamic temperature	kelvin	K
Amount of substance	mole	mol
Luminous intensity	candela	cd

SI Derived Units with Special Names

	QUANTITIES	SI UNITS	
		Names	Symbols
1.	Frequency	hertz	Hz
2.	Force	newton	N
3.	Pressure	Pascal	Pa
4.	Energy, work	joule	J
5.	Power	watt	W
6.	Electric charge	coulomb	C
7.	Capacitance	farad	F
8.	Electric resistance	ohm	W

	QUANTITIES	SI UNITS	
		Names	Symbols
9.	Conductance	siemens	S
10.	Magnetic flux	weber	Wb
11.	Magnetic field	tesla	T
12.	Inductance	henry	H

MOTION AND FORCE

Motion

- **Scalar Quantities:** Physical quantities which have magnitude only and no direction are called scalar quantities.

  Example: Mass, speed, volume, work, time, power, energy, etc.

- **Vector Quantities:** Physical quantities which have magnitude and direction both and obey triangle law are called vector quantities.

  Example: Displacement, velocity, acceleration, force, momentum, torque etc.

- Electric current, though has a direction, is a scalar quantity because it does not obey triangle law.

Distance

- The actual length of path travelled by a body is called the distance (S) travelled or covered by the body. It is a scalar quantity and is measured in metres in SI units.

Displacement

- The shortest distance from the initial to the final position of a body is called displacement of the body.
- Displacement vector is the straight line joining the initial and final position and does not depend on the actual path undertaken by the object between the two positions.

Speed

- Speed is the time rate of change of position. It is measured in metre per second, centimetre per second, kilometre per hour etc. Average speed is the total distance travelled divided by the time taken.

$$\text{Speed} = \frac{\text{distance travelled}}{\text{time taken}} = \frac{s}{t} = \text{m/s}$$

Velocity

- The time rate of displacement (change of position vector) of the particle is called velocity. Thus

$$\text{Velocity} = \vec{v} = \frac{d\vec{S}}{dt},$$

where $\vec{S}$ = displacement

- The velocity is a vector quantity. Its unit is m/s.
- It is of two types: Uniform velocity and Variable velocity.
- Relative Velocity : Relative velocity is the velocity of one body with respect to another body. Suppose two trains A and B are moving parallel to one another with the same velocity and in the same direction. For a passenger in A, B appears to be stationary and vice versa. Thus, the relative velocity of A with respect to B is zero. Also the relative velocity of B with respect to A is zero.
- If A and B are moving in opposite directions. The relative velocity of A with respect to B is twice the velocity of either. Also the relative velocity of B with respect to A is double.
- When two trains cross each other on parallel rails in opposite directions, the velocity of one with respect to the other appears to be higher than its own velocity.

Acceleration

- The time rate of change of velocity is called acceleration.

$$\text{Thus, acceleration} = \vec{a} = \frac{d\vec{v}}{dt}$$

- It is a vector quantity. Its unit is m/s^2.
  - (*a*) **Uniform Acceleration:** If the velocity of a body increases by equal amounts in equal intervals of time, however small, it is said to move with uniform acceleration.
  - (*b*) **Variable Acceleration:** If the velocity of a body increases by unequal amounts in equal intervals of time, however small, it is said to have variable acceleration. The acceleration will be variable if either the magnitude or direction of velocity changes unequally.

Types of Motion

Translatory Motion

- A body has translatory motion, if all the particles move with the same velocity and their paths are parallel. There are two types of translatory motion.

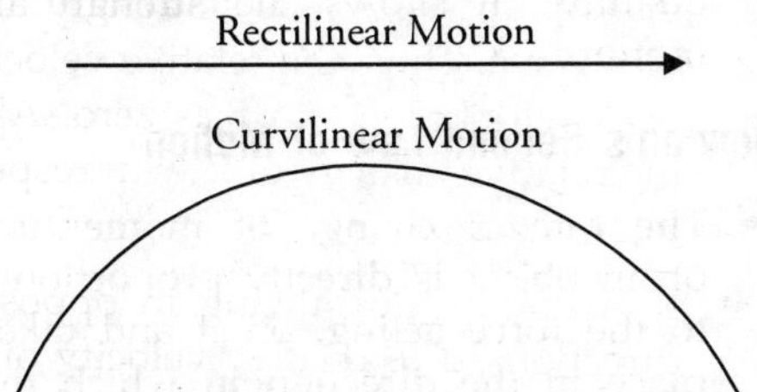

The train moving along a railway track, a body falling freely under the action of gravity, a car moving on the road (except the wheels), are examples of translatory motion. Translatory motion can be along a straight line (rectilinear) or a curved path (curvilinear).

Rotatory Motion

- When a body rotates about a fixed axis, the motion is said to be rotatory. All the particles do not move with the same linear velocity. The particles nearer the axis move with less speed and the particles away from the axis move with more speed.
- Earth rotating about its own axis, spinning top, rotating fly wheel, the motion of the blades of a fan, are examples of rotatory motion.
- A ball rolling on the ground, motion of the cycle wheel, movement of the earth in its orbit around the sun are examples in which these bodies possess translatory and rotatory motions simultaneously.

Circular Motion

- Circular motion is a form of periodic (or cyclic) motion. There are many familiar examples of an object moving in a circle at constant speed, such as the moon around the earth, a satellie in circular oribit around the earth, a cyclist on a circular track at constant speed, and so on.
- **Uniform Circular Motion**
  - An object is undergoing uniform circular motion if it is travelling at a constant speed while moving in a circle. Its main requirement is constant speed and motion in a circle.
  - For uniform circular motion, we have a velocity which is always tangential, and an acceleration which is along the inward radius. Both velocity and acceleration have constant magnitudes but changing directions. Constant speed does not mean that acceleration vanishes.

Projectile Motion

- A body is said to be a projectile when it is projected with some initial velocity, moving in two dimensions and comes down under the influence of gravity. The path of the projectile is called **trajectory.**
- The trajectory of a projectile moving under the influence of a constant acceleration is a **parabola**.
- The projectile motion near the surface of earth consists of two independent motions.
  - *(a)* Horizontal motion at constant speed, it means $a_x = 0$.
  - *(b)* Vertical motion with constant acceleration due to gravity. *e.g.*
    - *(i)* A bullet fired from a pistol.
    - *(ii)* A stone dropped from the window of a moving train.
    - *(iii)* A bomb released from a moving aeroplane.

Oscillatory Motion

- Oscillatory motion is that in which a body moves to and fro about its mean position.

  Example: Motion of a swing, clock pendulum. For example, tie a string around a stone and let it hang freely from a support. Give it a slight push and watch it swing.

Force and Inertia

- It is an observable fact that an isolate object at rest do not start moving of their own accord. Effort is required to move the objects. When we push or pull a table, for instance, we are exerting a force on the table. It is the force exerted by a bat that makes the ball move.
- *Inertia* is the inherent property of objects to remain at rest unless acted upon by a force. Also the property of a body to keep moving with constant velocity in the absence of any force acting on it is its *inertia.* Gelileo discovered the *law of inertia.*
- The property of a body to continue in its state of rest or that of uniform motion in a straight line in the absence of external force is called inertia. ***Newton's first law of motion is the law of inertia.***

Newton's Laws of Motion

Newton's First Law of Motion

- Every body continues in its state of rest or of uniform motion in a straight line unless compelled by some external force to act otherwise.

Momentum

- The product of mass (*M*) of a body and its velocity ($\vec{v}$) is called momentum ($\vec{p}$). Thus $\vec{p} = M\vec{v}$. Its unit is kg m/s. The momentum of an object can be defined as follows:

  momentum = *mass* × *velocity*

  With mass measured in kg and velocity in m/s, momentum is measured in kg m/s. Like force and velocity, momentum is a vector quantity, it shows the strength of motion.

Newton's Second Law of Motion

- The rate of change of momentum of an object is directly proportional to the force acting, on it and takes place in the direction in which the force acts.
- Newton's second law of motion gives *(i)* expression of force, and *(ii)* the direction of force.

Impulse

- When a force acts for a given time, the quantity force × time is called an

Impulse. If force is measured in N and time in *s*, impulse is measured in Ns or kg m/s – both amount to the same thing.

As, Force = $\frac{\text{Gain or change in momentum}}{\text{Time}}$

It follows that:

Force × Time = Gain in momentum in symbols.

$$Ft = mv - mu$$

Application of the Concept of Impulse

1. A cricket player lower his hands while catching a cricket ball. In order to avoid injury he/she increases the time of catch. According to the concept of inpulse, when time of contact increases, the impact of force on hands decreases.
2. Vehicles are provided with shockers.
3. A person receives more injury when falls on a cement floor, than on a sand floor.

Newton's Third Law of Motion

- To every action there is always an equal and opposite reaction.
- Sometimes, we can feel the reacting force. If we fire a rifle, the forward thrust of the projectile is matched by the backward thrust.

Conservation of Momentum

- An important consequence of Newton's third law, in combination with the second, is the law of conservation of momentum which states: *When two or more bodies interact with one another, isolated system their total momentum remains constant, provided no external forces are acting.*

Rocket Propulsion

- One of the spectacular instances in which Newton's third law or the momentum of conservation manifests itself is the flight of a rocket.

Force

- Force is any influence that tends to change the state of rest or the uniform motion in a straight line of a body. The action of an unbalanced or resultant force results in the acceleration of a body in the direction of action of the force or it may, if the body is unable to move freely, result in its deformation.
- Force is a vector quantity, possessing both magnitude and direction; its SI unit is the newton.

Types of Forces

Centripetal Force

- When a body moves along a circular path with uniform speed, the magnitude of the velocity remains the same but its direction changes at every point. It means that there is change in velocity.
- Whenever there is change in velocity, there must be some acceleration.
- As a body has mass also, a force must act upon the body. This force must act along such a direction that the magnitude of the velocity does not change.

Examples:

1. When a bucket containing water is rotated in a vertical circle, water does not fall downward even when the bucket is at the highest point (In Fig.). The centripetal force is provided by the motion. Due to this reason water does not fall.

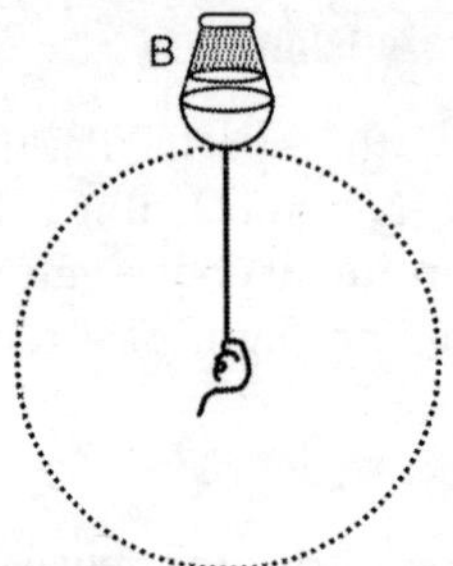

2. In the case of motion of the moon round the earth centripetal force is provided by the gravitational force of attraction of the earth on the moon. Similarly the force of attraction of the sun on the planets provides the necessary centripetal force and the planets revolve round the sun.
3. Electrons revolve round the nucleus in various orbits. The electrons do not collapse into the nucleus. The electrostatic force of attraction of the nucleus on the electron provides the necessary centripetal force and the electron revolves round the nucleus.

- Artificial satellites move round the earth. The force of attraction of the earth on the satellite provides the necessary centripetal force and the satellite revolves round the earth.

Centrifugal Force

- Centrifugal Force is a fictitious or pseudo outward force on a particle rotating about an axis which by Newton's third law is equal and opposite to the centripetal force.
- Like all such action-reaction pairs of forces, they are equal and opposite but do not act on the same body and so do not cancel each other.
- Centrifugal force, representing an inertia reaction, makes itself felt when a car begins to skid. Suppose we make a left turn too sharply or too quickly, the centrifugal inertia force of the turn becomes greater than the friction of the tyres against the road, and the car will start to skid to the right.
- A method commonly used to prevent skidding when rounding a curve is to construct the curved roadway so that the outer part of the road is higher than the inner. This construction is called banking of road.

Friction

- Friction is the force that tries to stop materials sliding over each other.
- There is friction between our hands when we rub them together, and there is friction between our shoes and the ground when we walk along.
- Friction is caused in two ways. First, rougher surfaces have ridges and bumps which catch in each other. Second, all materials are made up of tiny particles called molecules, and these have a tendency to stick to each other when materials are pressed together.
- Friction prevents machinery from moving freely. It also causes any moving parts to heat up.
- To reduce friction, wheels are often mounted on ball or roller bearings and oil is used to make moving surfaces more slippery.
- Friction can also be useful. It gives shoes and tyres 'grip' on the ground, and it is used in most braking systems.

Advantages of Friction

- It would be difficult to sit on a chair without friction.
- It helps in supporting ladders against a wall, or to start cars and trains.

➡ Walking would be impossible if there were no friction between the ground and the soles of our feet or shoes.

GRAVITATION

➡ **Gravity:** The gravitational force of earth is called gravity *i.e.*, gravity is the force by which earch pulls a body towards its centre.

➡ **Variation in *g* (weight = *mg*)**

- value of g decreases with height or depth from earth's surface.
- *g* is maximum at poles.
- *g* is minimum at equator.
- *g* decreases due to rotation of earth.
- *g* decreases if angular speed of earth increases and *g* increases if angular speed of earth decreases.

➡ If angular speed of earth becomes 17 times its present value, a body on the equator becomes weightless.

➡ **Weight of a body in a lift**

- If lift is stationary or moving with uniform speed (either upward or down ward), the apparent weight of a body is equal to its true weight.
- If lift is going up with acceleration, the apparent weight of a body is more than the true weight.
- If lift is going down with acceleration, the apparent weight of a body is less than the true weight.
- If the cord of the lift is broken, it falls freely. In this situation the weight of a body in the lift becomes zero. This is the situation of weight-lessness.
- While going down, if the acceleartion of lift is more than acceleration due to gravity, a body in the lift goes in contact of the ceiling of lift.

Earth's Gravitation

➡ Gravitation plays a crucial role in most processes on the earth. Ocean tides are caused by the gravitational attraction of the moon and the sun towards the earth and its oceans.

➡ Gravitation drives weather patterns by making cold air sink and displace less dense warm air, forcing the warm air to rise.

➡ The gravitational pull of the earth on all objects holds the objects to the surface of the earth. Without it, the spin of the earth would send them floating off into space.

➡ Similarly, the inward pull of gravitation holds stars together. When a star's fuel nears depletion, the processes producing the outward pressure weaken and the inward pull of gravitation eventually compresses the star to a very compact size.

Gravitational Field

➡ The gravitational field strength *g* at a point at a distance *r* from mass M is defined as the force on the unit mass placed at that point, that is

$$g = \frac{GM}{r^2}$$

➡ Therefore, for an object placed on the surface of the earth, the gravitational field strength = $GM/r^2 = g_0$. The units are Nkg^{-1}.

Weightlessness

➡ Weightlessness is the state of not experiencing the effects of gravity. Since weight is a force, weightlessness implies the absence of this force.

➡ But this is only true for a point out in space, infinitely distant from any star of planet.

➡ The condition could also apply at a point where two or more gravitational fields cancel each other.

- If we ignore the attraction of the sun, then there will be a point between the earth and the moon where true weightlessness would occur.

DENSITY AND RELATIVE DENSITY

- The mass per unit volume of a substance is called its density.

$$\text{Density} = \frac{\text{Mass}}{\text{Volume}}$$

- The SI unit of density is kilogram per metre cubed (kg/m^3).
- The relative density of a substance is the ratio of the density of the substance to the density of water.
- Relative density has no unit.

Density of Some Common Substances

Sr. No.	Substance	Density in kg/m^3	Sr. No.	Substance	Density in kg/m^3
1.	Alcohol	790	6.	Lead	11,300
2.	Water	1,000	7.	Mercury	13,600
3.	Aluminium	2,700	8.	Gold	19,300
4.	Steel (vories)	7,800	9.	Platinum	21,500
5.	Copper	8,900			

PRESSURE

- Pressure is defined as force acting per unit area.

$$\text{Pressure} = \frac{\text{Force}}{\text{Area}}$$

- The SI unit of pressure is newton per metre squared or pascal.
- There is a inverse relationship between magnitude of pressure and area of contact.
- It is much easier to cut fruit with a sharp knife than with a blunt one. In the case of a sharp knife the blade makes such a small area of contact with the fruit that the pressure below it, is very high and easily cuts the fruit.
- Broad wooden sleepers are placed below the rails to reduce the pressure exerted by the weight of a train.
- The pressure of water increases with depth, therefore bottom of a dam is made much thicken than the top.
- The pressure exerted on an enclosed liquid at one place is transmitted equally throughout the liquid. This is called Pascal's Principle.

LAW OF FLOATATION

- When a body is immersed in a fluid then if—
  1. the weight of body is equal to upthrust, the body floats with whole of its volume inside the liquid.
  2. the weight of body is more than the upthrust, the body will sink.
  3. the weight of body is less than the upthrust, the body will float with some of its part outside the liquid.
- An iron nail sinks in water whereas a ship made of iron and steel floats. This is due to the fact that a ship is hollow and contains air and, therefore, its density is less than that of water.

- The density of sea water is more than that of river water, due to this a ship sinks less in sea water. It is for this reason that a ship rises a little when it enters a sea from a river.
- It is because of the higher density of sea water that it is easier to swim in the sea.
- A solid chunk of iron will sink in the water but float in mercury because the density of iron is more than that of water but less than that of mercury.

SURFACE TENSION

- Surface tension is that property of liquids owing to which they tend to acquire minimum surface area.
- Surface tension is caused by molecular attractions.
- When a paint brush is dipped in water all its hair spread out but when it is taken out it is covered with a thin film of water which contracts due to surface tension and pulls the hair together.
- Liquid drops, such as raindrops, oildrops, drops of molten metals, dewdrops etc. are all spherical because their surface tend to contract in order to have minimum surface area. For a given volume, a sphere has the minimum surface area.
- Soaps and detergents lower the surface tension of water. This increases the wetting power of water or its ability to detach dirt particles from clothes and utensils.
- Cohesive forces are the forces of attraction acting between molecules of same substance. The liquids for which cohesive forces are large do not wet the walls of the vessel, *e.g.*, mercury. Surface tension forces arise due to cohesive forces.
- Adhesive forces are the forces of attraction acting between the molecules of different substances. If adhesive forces are greater than cohesive force then the liquid wets the walls of the vessel, *e.g.*, water wets the walls of a glass-capillary.
- The force of attraction between unlike molecules is called **adhesion** and that between like molecules **cohesion.**
- The melted wax of a candle is drawn up into the wick by capillary action. Oil rises up a lamp wick for the same reason.
- If one end of a sugar cube is dipped into tea, the entire cube is quickly wet on account of capillary action.
- The fine pores of a blotting paper act as tiny capillary tubes. The ink rises into the blotting paper through these pores.

WORK, ENERGY AND POWER

Work

- Generally, 'work' may refer to any kind of physical or mental activity.
- But according to scientific definition, *work is done only when a force produces motion.*
- Thus work is done on a weight that is being lifted, or on a spring that is being stretched or compressed, or a gas that is undergoing compression in a cylinder.
- When the force acting on a moving body is constant in magnitude and direction, the amount of work done is defined as the product of just two factors: the component of the force in the direction of motion, and the distance moved by the point of application of the force.

- If the magnitude of the force is F and the distance through which the body moves is d in the direction of force, the work.

$$W = Fd$$

- The SI unit of work is joule (J) which is also newton-metre. Work is a scaler quantity.

Energy

- *Energy is the capacity to do work.*
- Energy is used in a number of ways. For example, we utilise the chemical energy locked up in sources like coal, oil, and gas when it is released in the form of heat. Light and sound also carry energy.
- One form of energy can be converted into another form. Energy like work is measured in joule (J).
- Energy is classified into two kinds: kinetic and potential.

Kinetic Energy

- Moving objects, such as bullets, cars and cricket balls, all have kinetic energy.
- Kinetic energy is the energy which is possessed by a body by virtue of its motion.
- Kinetic energy (K.E.) = $1/2\ mv^2$ where m is the mass of the body and v is its speed.
- From the formula of kinetic energy; $1/2\ mv^2$, it is clear that
  (*i*) Kinetic energy of the body is directly proportional to the mass. If the mass is doubled, kinetic energy of the body is doubled, likewise if the mass is halved, the kinetic energy is halved.
  (*ii*) Kinetic energy of the body is directly proportional to the square of velocity of the body.

Potential Energy

- Potential energy is the energy stored in a body or a system by virtue of its position in a field of force or by its configuration. A force active on a body or a system can alter its potential energy.
- There are two common examples of potential energy. The first one is the potential energy of a body due to gravity above the surface of the earth. The second example is the potential energy of a spring when it is compressed or elongnated by an external force.
- Gravitational potential energy (PE) = mgh,

  where m is the mass of the body, g the acceleration due to gravity and h the height of the body above the earth's surface.
- When an object falls from a height, it accelerates and gathers up speed, thereby gaining kinetic energy. This is at the expense of its gravitational potential energy. The total energy consisting of kinetic energy and the gravitational potential energy is conserved.

Energy Related to Mass

- According to Einstien's hypothesis, mass can be converted to energy according to relation,

$$E = mc^2$$

where *'m'* is mass, *'c'* is speed of light.

Value of *'c'* = 3×10^8 m/s.

Conservation of Energy

- According to law of conservation of energy, energy can nither be created, nor be destroyed, it can only be converted from one form to other *i.e.* total energy in a closed system is constant.

Transformation of Energy

- A body placed at a height has potential energy. When it is released, the energy gets converted into kinetic energy by virtue of the motion acquired by the body. And when the body hits the ground, there is a generation of heat, and some kinetic energy is converted into heat energy.
- Similarly, when coal is burnt, the chemical energy of coal is converted into the heat energy. The heat energy converts the water into steam to drive the turbines.
- In all these transformations, energy is never destroyed. The total amount of energy remains the same. It may change from one form to the other.

Power

- The rate at which work is done is called the power.

$$\text{Power} = \frac{\text{work done}}{\text{time taken}}$$

- Power is measured in joules per second (J/s), or watts [W].
- If an engine does 1 joule of useful work every second, it has a power output of 1W.

HEAT

- Heat is one of the most important forms of energy.
- It is the transfer of energy from one part of a substance to another, or from one body to another by virtue of a difference in temperature.
- So, heat is energy in transit; it always flows from a substance at a higher temperature to the substance at a lower temperature.
- According to Kinetic Molecular Theory heat that a body posses is directly related to Kinetic Energy, greater the kinetic energy, hotter is body.
- The French scientist Jacques Charles discovered that heat could be transformed into motion.
- Sir James Prescott Joule, a 19th century physicist later proved that a given amount of mechanical energy always produced the same amount of heat.
- Generally the temperatures are expressed in 'kelvin'.

$$\boxed{K = {}^\circ C + 273}$$

Transmission of Heat

- There are three ways of heat transmission *conduction, convection,* and *radiation*.

Conduction

- Conduction is a process of net energy transfer through a substance without movement of the substance itself.
- All substances conduct heat, some much more effectively than others.
- As a rule, solids conduct heat better than liquids, and liquids better than gases.
- Some solids, particularly metals, are fine conductors. Silver, copper, and aluminium are the best of all.
- On the other hand, many solids, such as wood, paper, and cork, are poor conductors because they have so many air spaces.
- Very poor conductors, such as glass, are called *insulators.* Air is a good insulator.
- A woollen blanket or sweater provides warmth because of the air that is entrapped in its meshes. Air is

also trapped among the long hairs of furs. That is why fur gives excellent protection against cold.

- Houses, for example, are often insulated by a double wall arrangement: an air space is left between the plastering and the outside wall. This sort of insulation is made more effective by placing some loose material, such as mineral wool, in the air space in order to stop any circulation of the air within the double wall.
- The windows of passenger trains often consist of double panes of glass with a thin layer of air between them to protect the pass-engers from extreme cold or extreme heat.
- When we touch an iron object lying in the sun, it appears much hotter than a wooden object in similar circumstances because iron is a good conductor of heat and conducts heat rapidly to the hand while wood, being a poor conductor conducts heat from the touched surface only.
- A carpet on a stone floor feels warm while the floor feels cold though both are at the same temperature. Stone being a good con-ductor takes heat away from your bare feet, thus making your feet feel cold on the floor.
- If a thick layer of ice is formed in and outside the freezer of a refriger-ator, the cooling action is slowed down as ice is a poor conductor. Therefore, defrosting is done to maintain the cooling efficiency of the refrigerator.

Convection

- Convection takes place in liquids and gases. When a portion of a liquid or gas gains heat, its molecules increase their movement and tend to move farther apart.
- Because of this expansion, the warm gas weights less and thus rises.
- The Gulf Stream and Japan Current, who carry warm ocean water from the tropics to the north, are also examples of convection.
- In a refrigerator, convection is used to circulate cold air around the food.
- Convection causes the onshore and offshore winds which sometimes blow on the coast during the summer.

Conductors, Insulators & Semi-Conductors

Good Conductors	Good Insulators	Semi-Conductors
Silver	Oils	Silicon
Copper	Porcelain	Selenium
Gold	Dry leather	Germanium
Aluminium	Silk	
Iron	Sealing wax	
Any other metal	Sulphur	
Acids	Resin	
Water	Rubber	
Human body	Shellac	
	Amber	
	Paraffin wax	
	Glass	
	Dry air	

Radiation

- Radiation does not require any medium; thus radiation can take place in vacuum as well as in air. Heat energy from the sun is transmitted to earth by radiation.
- The higher the temperature of a body, the greater the amount of radiation that it will emit. Radiation emitted by a body is directly proportional to the size of its surface.
- Dark bodies absorb more heat than light coloured and reflect less. Hence dark garments are best for cold weather and light garments for warm weather.
- A *black body* is an ideal energy radiator, which at any specified temperature emits in each part of electromagnetic spectrum. A black body also absorbs all the energy which falls upon it.

WAVES

- A wave is a disturbance which propagates energy from one place to the other without the transport of matter.
- Waves are broadly of two types :
  1. Mechanical Wave
  2. Non-mechanical Wave

Mechanical Waves

- The waves which require material medium (solid, liquid or gas) for their propagation are called mechnical wave or elastic wave.
- The wave motion is classified into two catogories namely transverse and longitudinal wave motion, depending upon the direction of oscillation of the particle during the propagation of progressive mechanical waves in a medium.
- Mechanical Waves are of two types:

Transverse Wave Motion

(*i*) If during the propagation of a mechanical wave in a medium, the particles of the medium vibrate about their mean positions in a direction perpendicular to the direction of propagation of wave, the wave motion is called the transverse wave motion.

(*ii*) All electromagnetic waves are transverse in character.

(*iii*) A transverse wave travels in the form of Crests and Troughs. A crest is a portion of the medium, which is highly raised above the normal positions of rest of the particles of the medium while a trough is a portion of the medium, which is highly depressed below the normal positions of rest of the particles of the medium.

Longitudinal Wave Motion

(*i*) If during the propagation of a mechanical wave in a medium, the particles of the medium oscillate parallel to the direction of propagation of the wave, the wave motion is called the longitudinal wave motion.

(*ii*) For example, when one end of a long spring is tied to a hook in a wall and the other end is moved forward and backward, then every turn of the spring oscillates parallel to the length of the spring and longitudinal waves propagate through the spring.

(*iii*) The states of compression and rarefaction continue to move forward along the length of spring. The distance travelled by the disturbance in the time, the particle of the medium completes one vibration is called wavelength. In case of a longitudinal wave it is found that it is equal to the distance between two successive compressions or rarefactions.

(*iv*) The velocity of longitudinal waves is also given by

$$v = n\lambda$$

Non-Mechanical Waves or Electromagnetic Waves

- The waves which do not require medium for their propagation *i.e.*, which can propagate even through the vacuum are called non mechanical wave.
- Light, heat are the examples of non-mechanical wave. In fact all the electromagnetic waves are non-mechanical.
- All the electromagnetic wave consists of photon.
- The wavelength range of electro-magnetic wave is 10^{-14}m to 10^{4} m
- **Properties of electromagnetic waves**
  - They are neutral (uncharged).
  - They propagate as transverse wave.
  - They propagate with the velocity of light.
  - They contain every and momentum.
  - Their concept was introduced by Maxwell.

Electromagnetic Radiation

- Energy transmitted through space or through a material medium in the form of electromagnetic waves is called electromagnetic radiation.
- Infrared radiation goes through dry air, but not through water vapour. If passed through a simple of person's breath, trasnsmission is altered if a person has consumed alcohol. It enables a precise and quick means to determine a person's blood alcohol count. Police use breath analyzers to detect and catch people driving under the influence of alcohol.
- Photographic film sensitive to infrared rays shows different temperature as different colours. Anything having a higher or lower temperature than the surroundings can be detected by infrared photography.
- Devices called thermographic scanners can produce an on-the-spot T.V. like picture of the infrared emission of various bodies. A person having fever can be spotted in a crowd using such thermographic pictures. Currently, people suffering from H1N1 (swine) flue are being detected at airports by the use of this technique.

Radio and Television Transmission

- Radio waves sent out by radio stations are reflected by the ionosphere (a part of the atmosphere which extends from 60 to 500 km above the earth) and can be received anywhere on the earth.
- Due to slight absorption in the ionosphere, the radio signals received at far-off places are rather weak. At night, the radio reception improves because the layers of the ionosphere are not as exposed to sunlight and are more settled.
- High-frequency waves carrying television signals penetrate the ionosphere and are not received like radio signals. TV transmission was therefore accomplished on a "line-of-sight" basis. The curvature of the earth and mountainous terrains limited the range of TV reception.

- However, geostationary satellites are being used these days for television (and telephone) links between places anywhere on the earth.

SOUND

- Sound travels in the form of waves. It is produced in material medium by a vibrating source.
- Sound waves travel in all directions from source, eventually die out as they occupy more volume as they spread.
- Sound waves are longitudinal waves and are caused by vibrations.
- Sound can only travel through a medium. It cannot travel through a vacuum.
- Sound waves can travel through solids, liquids and gases. Most of the sound waves reaching the ear do so by travelling through air, but it is also possible to hear sounds when swimming underwater.

Speed of Sound

Medium	Speed (m/s)
Air	331
Water	1450
Aluminium	6420
Copper	3560
Granite	6000
Hydrogen	1284
Helium	965
Steel	5941

- Sound travels more rapidly through liquids than through gases, and fastest of all through solids.
- The pitch and loudness of sounds have no effect on their speed.
- In dry air at 0°C, the speed of sound is about 331 metres per second or 750 miles per hour. The presence of water vapour in the air slightly increases this speed. Thus, the speed of sound increases with humidity.
- Sound travels faster through warm air than through cold air. Obvi-ously, the speed of sound is higher on a hot day than on a cold day.
- The speed of sound is much less than the speed of light (3 × 108 m/s).
- Thunder is heard much after the flash of lighting is seen because of the wide difference in the speeds of light and sound. The flash is seen almost instantaneously whereas thunder takes time to reach the earth.
- In a cricket match, spectators hear the sound of ball on a little after they see the batsman actually striking the ball.
- The sound of a jet plane does not appear to come from the plane at all, but from a point far behind it, simply because the plane travels so fast that it moves a long distance in the time it takes the sound to reach our ears.

Types of Sound Waves

Infrasonic

- The longitudinal waves of frequency less than 20 Hertz are infrasonic waves. During an earthquake infrasonic waves pass through the earth's crust. The heart vibrates at infrasonic frequencies.

Ultrasonics

- The longitudinal waves of frequency greater than 20,000 Hz (20 kHz) are ultrasonic. The vibrations of certain crystals (quartz, zinc oxide, barium silicate, etc.) under the influence of an applied alternating voltage produce ultrasonics of frequencies up to well above 10kHz.

- The human ear cannot hear ultrasonics, but dogs, birds, bats and dolphins can hear them. Dogs respond to dog whistles pitched at 25,000 Hz, inaudible to human whistle blowers, and bats emit squeaks at 100,000 Hz and guide themselves in the dark by listening for their echoes from nearby obstructions.
- Ultrasonics are used in cleaning silverwave to catching burglars and drawing electronic portraits (sonograms) of unborn babies. Ultrasonic devices work by either delivering focussed energy or detecting and measuring vibrations from an ultrasonic receiver.

Characteristics of Sound

Loudness

- It depends upon amplitude of vibration of sound making object and distance from the object to ear. Intensity of sound can be measured is "decibel".
- One decibel represents increase in intensity of about 26% which is the smallest change sound can detect.

Increasing Loudness

- Sometimes, it is desirable to increase the loudness of a sound. This can be achieved by setting a greater mass of air into vibration.
- All stringed instruments, such as the violin, sitar, guitar, etc. have sound boxes attached to increase the loudness. When a string of a sitar is plucked, very little air is set in motion due to the small surface area of the string. But the vibration of the string sets the sound box into forced vibrations. When the box vibrates, it moves a large amount of air and increases loudness.
- A loudspeaker has vibrating cone with a large surface area. Thus a large mass of air in contact with the cone is set into vibration producing loud sound.

Pitch and Frequency

- Pitch (shrillness of sound) depends upon its frequency. Pitch is property of sound that we perceive as higher lower tones. It is measured in cycles per second (cps). Higher the frequency, higher will be pitch and vice-versa.
- Audible range of frequency for human is (20-20,000 Hz). 'Beats' are produced by sounds of some Amplitude but slightly different frequency (100 and 104Hz).

Reflection of Sound-Echo

- Waves have the property of being reflected when they meet an obstacle. When a sound wave is reflected by a distant obstacle, such as a wall or a cliff, an echo is heard.
- For an echo to be heard separately from the original sound, it must arrive 0.1 s after the original sound is made.
- This can happen if the minimum distance of the reflecting surface from the source of sound is 17 m.
- If the distance is less than 17 m, the echo cannot be distinguished as a separate sound and gives the impression of the original sound being prolonged. This prolonging of sound by reflection is called reverberation.
- Reverberation is also caused when a series of echoes are heard due to more than one reflecting surface.
- An echo can be used for measuring the speed of sound.

- Exploration of underwater gas and oil is done by detecting the echoes of shock waves produced by explosions on the water surface.
- Echoes of ultrasonic waves are used for measuring the depth of sea-beds or locating submerged objects. An apparatus called Sonar (Sound Navigation and Ranging) is used for this purpose.
- Ultrasonics is also used for detecting flaws in the interiors of solids, destroying micro-organisms, and mapping underground structures for oil and mineral deposits.
- Bats emit ultrasonic waves of frequencies up to 80,000 Hz and use the reflection of these waves (echoes) to determine the presence and the distance of objects on their way and from them respectively.
- Ultrasonics is applied widely in medical diagnosis and treatment. In sounding out the abdomen, as an example, the sound waves pass through the different tissues at speeds that depends on the elasticity and density of the tissue.

Refraction of Sound

- When successive layers of air have different temperatures, the ability of sound to travel faster in warm air than in cold air causes bending of sound. This bending of sound is called refraction.
- On a warm day, the air near the ground is warmer than the air above and so the speed of sound waves near the ground is higher. This causes bending of the sound away from the ground.
- On a cold day or at night, the reverse happens and the sound waves bend towards the earth. Thus on a cold day sounds can be heard over longer distances.

Resonance

- Any vibrating object has a natural frequency, which depends on factors such as the elasticity and shape of the object.
- Whenever an object or a system is set in oscillation at its natural frequency, as a result of impulses received from some other system vibrating with the same frequency, resonance is said to have occurred.
- Resonance can occur in different kinds of systems: acoustical, mechanical, electrical and optical. Resonance results in increased amplitude of vibration.
- The amplitude of a child's swing can be increased by giving it small pushes in rhythm with the frequency of the swing. This is an example of resonance.
- Sometimes the amplitudes that result from resonance can be disastrous. While crossing a suspension bridge soldiers are ordered to break step as otherwise the resonant vibrations caused by their marching can severely damage the bridge.

Doppler Effect

- Doppler effect is an apparent change in the frequency of waves, due to the relative motion of the source of the waves and the observer.
- The classic example of the Doppler effect is the rising pitch of a train whistle as the train approaches an observer and the drop in pitch as it moves away from the observer.
- Not only sound waves, but also light waves, radio waves, and even ocean waves exhibit the Doppler effect.

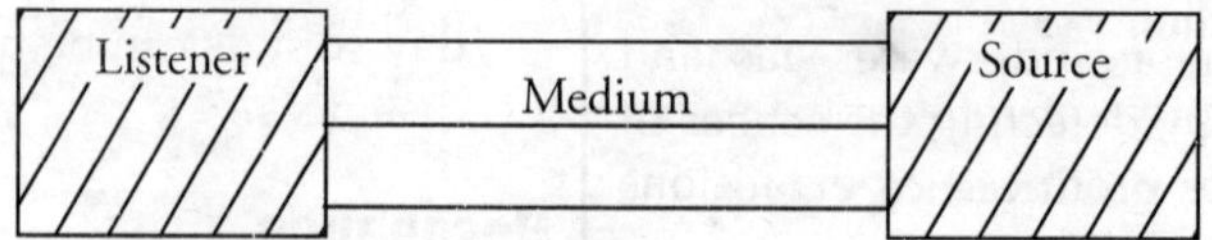

Application of Doppler Effect

- The change in frequency caused by a moving object due to Doppler effect is used to measure their velocities in diverse areas such as military, medical science, astrophysics, etc.
- It is also used by police to check over-speeding of vehicles.
- A sound wave or electromagnetic wave of known frequency is sent towards a moving object. Some part of the wave is reflected from the object and its frequency is detected by the monitoring station. This change in frequency is called Doppler shift.
- It is used at airports to guide aircraft, and in the military to detect enemy aircraft. Astrophysicists use it to measure the velocities of stars.
- Doctors use it to study heart beats and blood flow in different part of the body. Here they use ultrasonic waves, and in common practice, it is called sonography. Ultrasonic waves enter the body of the person, some of them are reflected back, and give information about motion of blood and pulsation of heart valves, as well as pulsation of the heart of the foetus. In the case of heart, the picture generated is called echocardiogram.

LIGHT

- Light is a form of energy which causes the sensation of vision. It travels always in a straight line and at a terrific speed of 300,000 km per second.
- The light of the sun takes about 8-5 minutes to reach the earth.
- Light also produces chemical and heating effects. Its chemical effect is represented by photography and its heating effect is represented by sunlight.

Properties of Light

- The following are the important properties of light:
  - (*i*) Light is a form of energy. In fact, it is a radiant energy *i.e.* energy in motion.
  - (*ii*) Light ray travels in straight lines. This property is known as rectilinear propagation of light.
  - (*iii*) It travels with a speed of 3×10^8 m/s in air or vacuum.
  - (*iv*) Light waves are electromagnetic waves.
  - (*v*) It does not require a material medium for its propagation.
  - (*vi*) It exhibits the phenomena of reflection, refraction, dispersion, polarisation, diffraction etc.

Reflection of Light

- When a ray of light reaches a surface between two types of materials, such as air and glass, several things can happen.
- Some of the light may reflect from the surface, while some may pass through the surface.
- In addition, some of the light may be absorbed by molecules on the surface or within the second material Plane mirror.

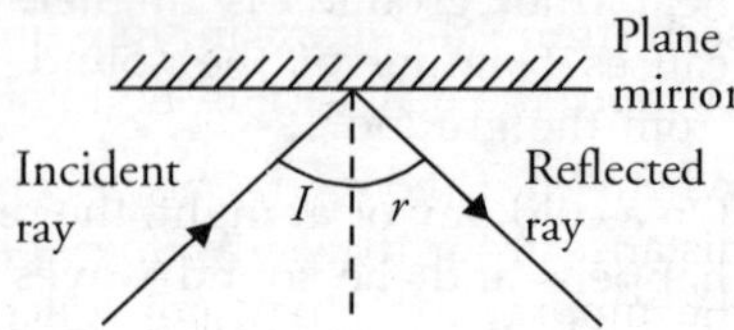

Laws of Reflection

There are two laws of reflection:

1. The angle of incidence equals the angle of reflection (r); the ray leaves the surface at the same angle as it arrives.
2. The incident ray, the reflected ray and the normal all lie in the same plane.

Shadows and Eclipses

- Shadows are formed because light travels in straight lines. If a large or extended source is used, the shadow is larger and has a central dark region, the umbra surrounded by a ring of partial shadow, the penumbra. One can see by the rays that some light reaches the penumbra but none reaches the umbra.

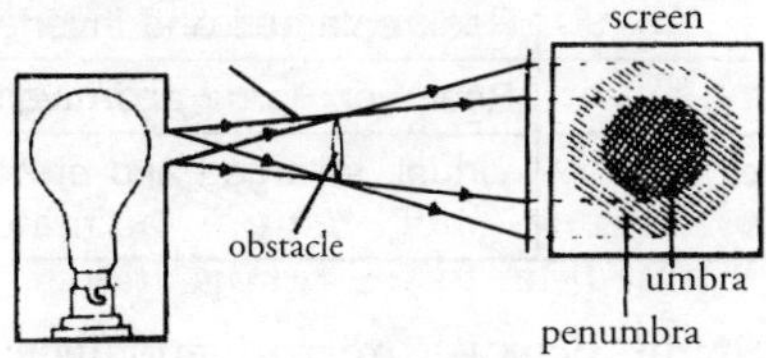

- The formation of eclipses is based on the principle of shadows.
- In case of lunar eclipses, when the moon is situated in the umbra portion of the shadows, the eclipse observed will be total: otherwise it will be partial.
- In the case of solar eclipse the source is bigger than the opaque body (moon), hence there will be both the umbral and penumbral cones behind the moon. When seen from any part in the penumbral portion, the eclipse observed will be partial and when seen from the part in the umbral portion, the eclipse will be total.
- When the moon is at a greater distance from the earth, the apex of the umbral cone may not touch the earth's surface and in that case total eclipse will not be seen from any part of the earth. When seen from the region just below the apex, the sun appears as an annular ring.

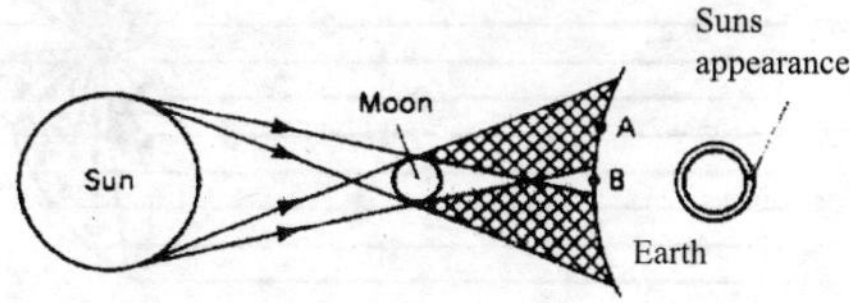

- During a total solar eclipse, although it is day, the sky is dark, stars are visible. The temperature falls and birds stop singing.

Image Formation

- **Image Formation in Plane Mirror:** The image in a plane mirror is:
  - as far behind the mirror as the object is in front and the line joining them is perpendicular to the mirror,
  - the same size as the object,
  - virtual (that is, imaginary),
  - laterally inverted but the right way up.
- A mirror at least half the height of a person is required if the full-length image of the person is to be reflected.

Applications of Plane Mirror

- In Kaleidoscope two strips of plane mirrors placed at 60° with coloured glass peice that produce different pattens on being shapes.
- It is used in periscope, where mirrors facing each other are stationed at 45°. They are used in submarines to see above water.

Image Formation in Spherical Mirrors

- There are two types of curved (or spherical) mirrors; *concave* and *convex*.

Concave Mirrors

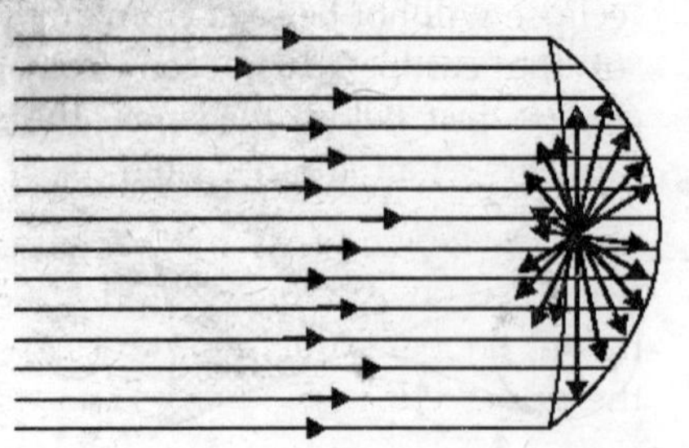

- Not all the rays parallel to the axis of the concave spherical mirror meet exactly at the principal focus. This failure of the rays to converge at a single point is called ***spherical aberration.***
- This effect can be remedied by making the curve of the mirror a paraboloid.
- This mirror is commonly used in searchlights, automobile headlights, and various other devices. Large mirrors used in telescopes are usually paraboloids.

Image Formed in a Concave Mirror

Sr. No.	Position of the Object	Postition of the Image	Nature and Size
1.	At infinity	At the focus F	Real, very small and inverted
2.	Beyond the centre of curvature C	Between F and C	Real, diminished in size and inverted
3.	At C	At C	Real, same size as object and inverted
4.	Between F and C	Beyond C	Real, enlarged and inverted
5.	At F	At infinity	Real, very large and inverted
6.	Between pole of the mirror P and focus F	Behind the mirror	Virtual, enlarged and erect

Convex Mirrors

- Some spherical mirrors use the convex side of a spherical surface. In this case, parallel rays diverge from the surface when they are reflected. However, they all seem to come from a single point behind the mirror (F). This is called a virtual (apparent) focus, because the rays do not actually converge at this point but only appear to do so.
- Convex mirrors can produce only virtual images, which are erect and smaller than the object.
- Small convex mirror are used as rear view mirror in vehicles so that a driver can have a wide field view of the traffic behind. A plane mirror would not give an equally wide view. The drivers of buses can get a clear view of passengers getting in with the help of a convex mirror.
- Also used in supermarkets to deter shoplifters.
- Street lamps are also provided with convex reflectors, as these diverge the light over a large and extended surface.

Image Formed in a Convex Mirror

Position of the Object	Postition of the Image	Size of the Image	Nature of the Image
At infinity	At the focus F. behind the mirror	Highly diminished, point-sized	Virtual and erect
Between infinity and the	Between P and F, behind the mirror	Diminished	Virtual and erect

Refraction

- A swimming pool looks less deep than it really is, and a stick appears to bend when it is placed one end under water.
- These effects and many others are caused by bending of light rays when light passes from one medium into another of a different optical density. This phenomenon of change of direction is called *refraction*.

Atmospheric Refraction

- In the atmosphere there are shifting layers of air of different density. The light of distant stars reaches us after suffering refraction through these shifting layers and gets the twinkling effect.
- It is due to the refraction produced by the earth's atmosphere that the sun is visible for several minutes after it has set.
- If the sun or moon appears elliptical near the horizon, it is because rays from the lower edge of the sun (or moon) are bent more than those from the upper edge.
- Sun is visible two minutes before and after actual sunrise due to refraction.
- Refraction effects may be used to identify small samples of mineral crystals. This is done by immersing them in a succession of liquids, each with a different refractive index.

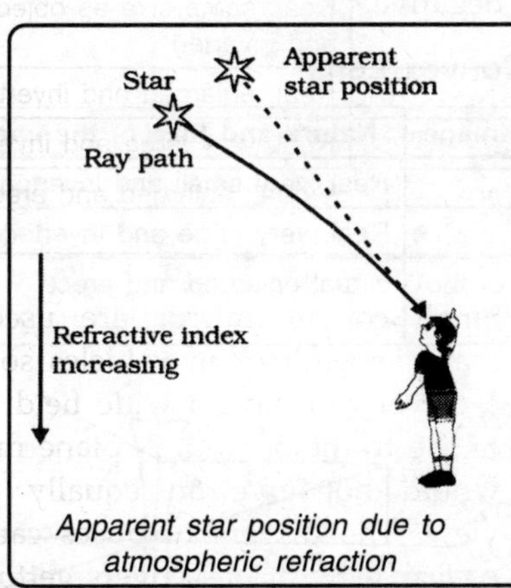

Apparent star position due to atmospheric refraction

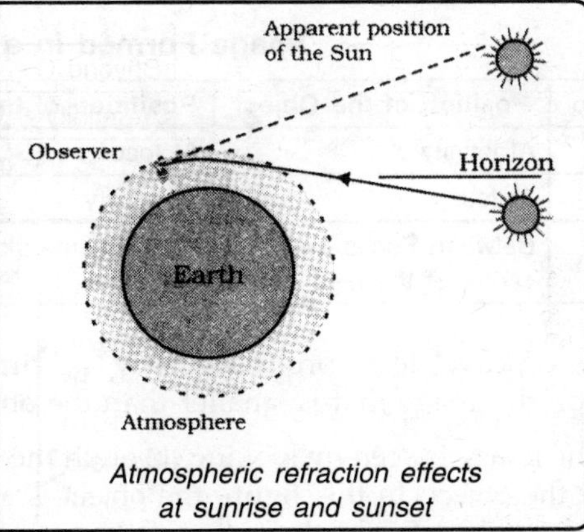

Atmospheric refraction effects at sunrise and sunset

Applications of Total Internal Reflection

- Total internal reflection is the main cause of the brilliance of diamonds. Its critical angle (24.4°) is very small, so that once light gets into diamond, it is very likely to be totally reflected internally. By cutting the diamond suitably, multiple internal reflections can be made to occur.
- Prisms make use of total internal reflection to bend light by 90°, or to invert images without changing their size.
- Mirages seem as a result of the bending of light rays in the atmosphere during abnormal vertical distribution of air density.
- If the air closer to the ground is much warmer than the air above, the rays are bent in such a way that they enter the observer's eyes along a line lower than the direct line of sight. The object is then seen below the horizon, the inferior mirage.
- If the air closer to the ground is much colder than the air above, the rays

are bent in the opposite direction, arriving at the observer's eyes above the line of sight; the object then seems to be elevated or floating in the air, the superior mirage.

- Mirages can be seen most frequently along an overheated highway surface; the inferior mirage of the sky gives the impression of water reflection over a wet pavement, which disappears upon a closer viewing. Mirages are common in deserts.
- Optical fibres too make use of the phenomenon of total internal reflection. When the light is incident on one end of the fibre at a small angle, the light passes inside, undergoes repeated total internal reflections along the fibre and finally comes out.
- Dut to this nature optical fibres have also been used for transmitting and receiving electrical signals which are converted to light by suitable transducers.

Lenses

- A lens is defined as a part of a transparent refracting medium bounded by two surfaces which are generally spherical or cylindrical. One of the surfaces may also be plane.
- The convex (converging) lens are thickest in the middle and thinnest at their periphery. The concave (diverging) lens are thickest at the periphery and thinnest at the middle.
- The focal length of a convex lens is positive and that of a concave lens is negative.

Image Formed in a Convex Lens

Sr.No.	Position of the Object	Positition of the Image	Nature and Size of the image
1.	At infinity	At focus	Real, very small and inverted
2.	At focus	At infinity	Real, very large and inverted
3.	Between Focus and centre of the lens	on the same side of the lens	virtual enlarged and erect

- A concave lens produces only a virtual, upright image that is smaller than the object.
- The image is seen by looking through the lens at the object. In this figure the object is at O, the focus at F and the image at I.

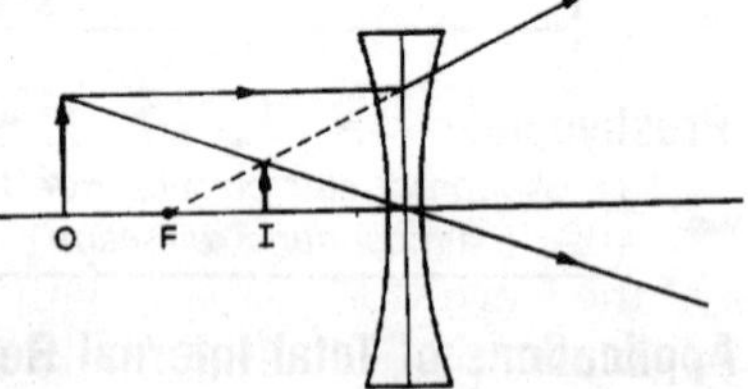

Defects of Vision

Nearsightedness

- When a person sees near objects clearly while distant objects appear blurred it is called nearsightedness or myopia.
- In normal vision, light rays from an object enter the eye and are focused by the lens onto the retina.
- In people with nearsightedness, the distance between the lens and the retina is too long. As a result, light rays from distant objects focus before they strike the retina. Near objects appear clearly because light rays from them focus correctly on the retina.
- Nearsightedness is present at birth and tends to be inherited.

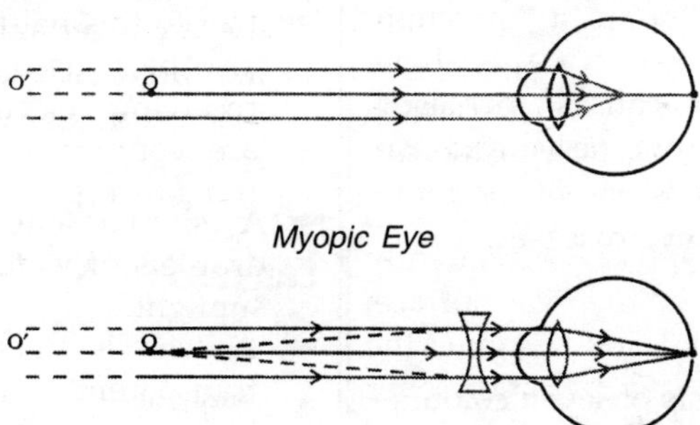

Myopic Eye

Correction for Myopia

Farsightedness

- Farsightedness, also called hypermetropia, is the common name for a defect in vision in which a person sees near objects with blurred vision, while distant objects appear in sharp focus.
- In normal vision, light rays from an object entering the eye are focussed by the lens on the retina.
- In people with farsightedness, the distance between the lens and the retina is too short. As a result, light rays from near objects strike the retina before they are in focus, which causes blurred vision. Distant objects appear clearly because light rays from them focus correctly on the retina.

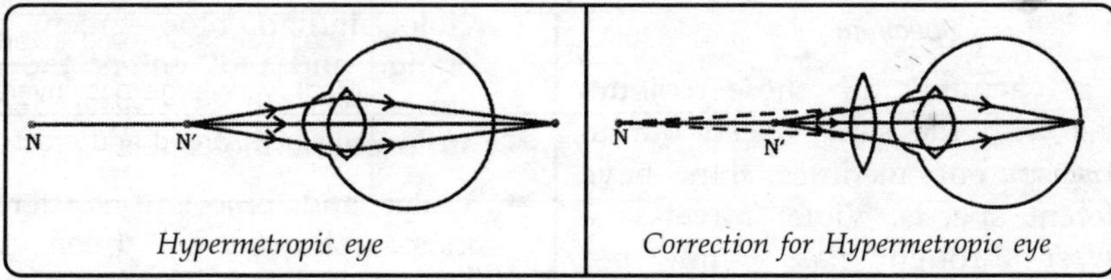

Hypermetropic eye | *Correction for Hypermetropic eye*

Presbyopia

- The power of accommodation of the eye decreases with ageing. Most people find that the near point gradually recedes. As a result, they cannot read comfortably and distinctly without the corrective eyeglasses. This defect is called Presbyopia.
- It arises due to the gradual weakening of the ciliary muscles and diminishing flexibility of the crystalline leans. Sometimes, a person may suffer from both myopia and hypermetropia. Such people often require bi-focal lenses.
- In the most common type of the bi-focal lens is a concave lens, used for distant vision. The lower part of the bi-focal lens is a convex lens, used for reading purposes.

Astigmatism

- This defect is due to the cornea not being spherical. As a result, the rays of light entering the eye in different planes are brought to a focus at varying distances from the retina. So, though the object is a point, the shape of the image may be a line, a circle or any other shape except a point.
- This defect can be corrected by using a cylindrical lens, instead of a spherical lens.

Glaucoma

- A disorder that causes increased pressure on the optic nerve and can lead to blindness, is one of the more serious common eye diseases.

Dispersion

- White light consists of seven colours– violet, indigo, blue, green, yellow, orange, and red. These colours are called the spectrum of the white light. Violet has the minimum wavelength (or maximum frequency) and red the maximum wavelength (or minimum frequency).

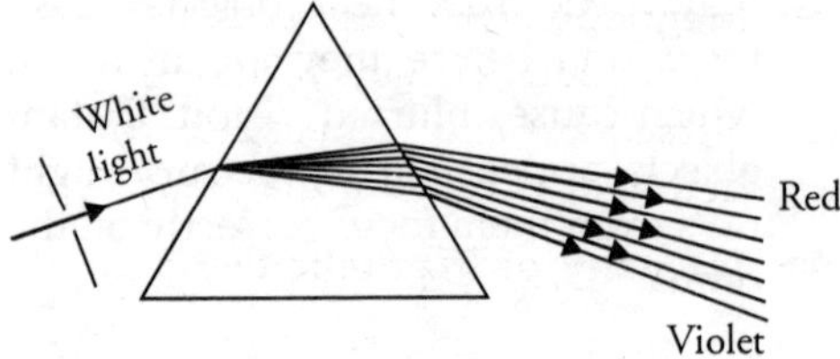

Spectrum

- In a vacuum, all these colours travel with the same speed but in a transparent medium they have different speeds. Violet travels the slowest through glass while red travels the fastest.
- Due to different speeds, the colours are refracted through different angles and, therefore, when a narrow beam of white light passes through a glass prism, it is split up into its constituent colours. This separation of light into colours is called dispersion.

The Rainbow

- The most spectacular illustration of dispersion is the rainbow.
- When the sun shines soon after a shower of rain, a rainbow is seen in the sky opposite the sun. The beautiful colours of the rainbow are due to the dispersion of sunlight by water droplets suspended in the air after rain. The droplets act like prisms. In each droplet there is dispersion as well as total internal reflection.
- A similar effect is produced by droplets of water from a fountain in sunlight.

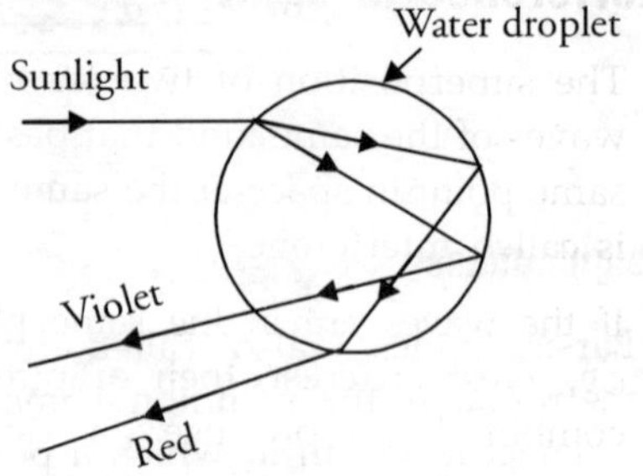

Rainbow

Scattering of Light

- The atmosphere consists of atoms and molecules of air. Thus when sunlight, consisting of seven colours, violet, indigo, blue, green, yellow, orange and red, enters the earth's atmosphere, it is scattered by the atmospheric molecules.
- Violet and blue are scattered the most, followed by green, yellow, orange and red. Thus, the scattered light is predominantly violet and blue. However, our eyes are not very sensitive to violet light and therefore we see a blue sky.
- Red light is scattered the least and therefore, can traverse more atmosphere than any other colour. In the evening, the sun is lower in the sky and its light has to traverse a longer path through the atmosphere to reach an observer. Thus at sunset, blue, green and other colours having been scattered, only red and some orange light reach us and the sun appears a deep orange-red.
- We cannot see stars during the day because of the preponderance of the light scattered by the atmosphere.

- In outerspace, i.e. beyond the atmosphere, there is nothing to scatter the sunlight and therefore the sky appears dark and stars are visible even in the presence of the sun.

Interference of Light

- The superposition of two (or more) waves of the same kind that pass the same point in space at the same time is called interference.
- If the waves are in the same phase, *e.g.*, crest on crest, their amplitudes combine to produce a strong wave. This is called constructive interference.
- If the waves are out of phase, e.g., if crests of one are superposed on the troughs of another, we get destructive interference.
- Beautiful colours seen in soap bubbles and oil films on water are produced due to the interference of white light reflected by these surfaces.

Diffraction of Light

- When a beam of light passes through a narrow slit or an aperture, it spreads out to a certain extent into the region of geometrical shadow. This is an example of diffraction, i.e. of the failure of light to travel in a straight line.

MAGNETISM

- It is the natural force by which a magnet attracts pieces of iron, nickel, cobalt and some alloys containing these metal and these metal is called magnetic.
- **Natural Magnets:** A naturally occurring mineral called magnetite or lode stone.
- **Artificial Magnets:** These are the magnetic elements to which the properties of a magnet have been imparted by artifical means. A steel object is made artificial magnet easily.

Law of Magnetism

- m_1 and m_2 are the pole strength are r is the separation between them. The amount of force exerted by the pole is given by

$$F = \frac{1}{\mu} \cdot \frac{m_1 \cdot m_2}{r^2}$$

- **Magnetic field:** The region around a magnet, in which the force of attraction and repulsion can be detected, is called a magnetic field.
- **Intensity of Magnetic field:**

$$E = \frac{m}{\mu r^2}$$

Properties of Magnet

(*a*) The attractive force are greatest at poles along the axis.

(*b*) Every magnet—natural or aritifical produces a magnetic field around it.

(*c*) It always points along a north-south direction.

(*d*) The pole of a magnet that is directed northward is known as the north pole or +ve pole and the pole that is directed southward is called the south pole or –ve pole.

(*e*) Like poles repel each other and unlike poles attract each other

(*f*) A horse shoe magnet are more powerful than a bar magnet of corresponding size.

- **Dia-magnetic:** The magnetic lines of force of diamagnetic material cannot penetrate certain material as they can penetrate air or vaccum, e.g., bismuth antimony etc.
- **Para-magnetic:** The magnetic lines of force of para magnetic material can penetrate material easily e.g. iron, liquid oxygen etc.
- **Ferromagnetic:** The material by which thunder is easily magnetised called ferro magnetic. *e.g.*, nickel cobalt, iron, etc.
- **Magnetic Moment:** The product of a pole strength and magnetic length is called the moment of the magnet.

  Mathematically,

  $$M = m \times x$$

  It is a vector quantity.

Earth's Magnetism

- The earth is a huge magnet, other magnets will be influenced by it. It is a natural magnet with a North and South magnetic pole, a magnetic axis and a field of force that extends into space. The lines of force of the earth's field are parallel to the surface near the equator.
- **Magnetic Meridian:** If a magnetic needle is hanged freely from its centre of gravity, then the vertical plane passing through the axis of the magnetic needle is known as the magnetic meridian.
- **Angle of Declination:** The acute angle in between magnetic meridian and the geographical meridian is known as the angle of declination at any place.
- **Angle of Dip (θ):** It is the angle at any place which is made in between the horizontal direction and the direction of earth's magnetic field in magnetic meridian.

  Mathematically, $\theta = \tan^{-1}\left[\frac{V}{H}\right]$

  where V = vertical component of earth's magnetic field.

  H = horizontal component of earth's magnetic field.

ELECTRICITY

Electric Charge

- Electric charge is a fundamental property like Length, Mass, and Time. Electric charges are of two types: Positive and Negative.
  - *(i)* A positive ion is an atom from which one or more electrons has been removed, i.e. **positive charge implies the deficiency of electrons.**
  - *(ii)* A negative ion is an atom to which one more electrons has been added, i.e. **negative charge implies excess of electrons.**
- **Units of Charges:** SI system – coulomb

Electric Field

- The region in which a charged particle placed at any point experiences a force, is called electric field. Electric field is measured in terms of electric field intensity $(\vec{E})$. The electric field intensity $\vec{E}$ at any point in an electric field is equal to force experienced by unit positive test charge q_0 placed at that point i.e.

  $$\vec{E} = \frac{\vec{F}}{q_0}$$

Electric Potential

- The electric potential at any point in an electric field is defined as the works done on the system against the electric force in moving an unit positive test charge from infinity (i.e. from beyond the electric field) to that point. If W is the work done in bringing the charge q_0 from infinity to given point, then potential at that point:

$$V = \frac{W}{q_0}$$

Electric Current

- An electric current, is the flow of electrons along a conductor.
- There are two types of currents. Direct current (DC), usually obtained from a battery, flows in one direction only; from the negative terminal of the power sources, through conductors, to the positive terminal.
- Alternating current (AC), on the other hand, flows first in one direction and then in the opposite direction. It always flows from negative to positive terminals, but the polarity (charge) of each terminal alternates from negative to positive.
- Alternating current is used more widely than DC. Its main advantage is that its driving force (voltage) can be readily increased or decreased by transformers. Also, AC machinery is generally simpler to design and build than DC machinery.
- DC, however, is needed in certain electronic devices and for such processes such as charging storage batteries, and electroplating. Also, DC can be produced by batteries, which can be carried about.
- A path along which the current travels is called a *circuit*. A current will only flow if there is a complete circuit to flow around.

Resistance

- A conductor allows an electric current to flow through it, but it does not permit the current to flow with perfect freedom. Collisions between the electrons and the atoms of the conductor interfere with the flow of electrons. This phenomenon is known as resistance.
- Resistance is measured in units called ohms.
- A good conductor is one that has low resistance. A good insulator has a very high resistance.
- At commonly encountered temperatures, silver is the best conductor and copper is the second best.
- Electric wires are usually made of copper, which is less expensive than silver.
- The resistance of a piece of wire depends on its length, and its cross-sectional area, or thickness. The longer the wire is, the greater its resistance. If one wire is twice as long as a wire of identical diameter and materials, the longer wire offers twice as much resistance as the shorter one.
- A thicker wire, however, has less resistance, because a thick wire offers more room for an electric current to pass through than a thin wire does; i.e., a wire whose cross-sectional area is twice that of another wire of equal length and similar material has only half the resistance of the thinner wire.

- Scientists describe this relationship between resistance, length and area by saying that resistance is proportional to length and inversely proportional to cross-sectional area.
- Usually, the higher the temperature of a wire, the greater its resistance.

Domestic Electric Installation

- An electric circuits are arrangement of electric current sources and conducting paths through which a current can continuously flow.

Fuse

- The bulb filament may burn out if too much electric current flows through it. To prevent this from happening, a fuse (circuit breaker) may be placed in the circuit. When too much current flows through the fuse, a wire in the fuse heats up and melts, thereby breaking the circuit and stopping the flow of current. The wire in the fuse is designed to melt before the filament would melt.
- A fuse is a short piece of wire made of a tin-lead alloy, which has a low melting point. When current in a circuit exceeds the specified value due to short circuiting, overloading, voltage fluctuation, etc., the fuse melts and breaks, thereby protecting expensive electrical appliances and also preventing fire accidents. Fuses are always connected in the live wire.
- Nowadays, fuses have been replaced with miniature circuit breakers (MCBs). A circuit breaker is an automatically operated electrical switch designed to protect an electrical circuit from damage caused by overload or short circuit.
- The tin-lead alloy is also used as soldering material in electronic circuits.

Earth

- The earth wire is used for earthing the metal casings of electrical appliances and is a safeguard against shocks.

Flexible Cables

- All electrical appliances are provided with three-core flexible cables. The insulations on the three wires are coloured red or brown (for live connection), black or light blue (for neutral connection), and green or yellow (for earth connection).

Plugs, Sockets and Switches

- A three-pin plug has one pin which is longer and thicker than the other two identical pins. It is for earthing and is connected to the green (or yellow) wire of the appliance. The other two are connected to the red (or brown) and the black (or blue) wires. The earth pin is longer so that an appliance is earthed before it is connected to the live circuit. It is thicker so that it cannot be inserted in the live hole of the socket even by mistake.
- In a socket, the top bigger hole is for the earth, the lower right hole is for the live connection and the left hole is for the neutral connection.
- All switches in a house are put in the live wires. If they were in the neutral wire, the sockets would remain live even when the switches were in the off position. In such a situation one would get a shock from the element of a heater or a stove even when it was cold.

SOME IMPORTANT INVENTORS AND DISCOVERERS

Invention / Discovery	Inventor / Discoverer
• Aeroplane (1903)	Orville and Wilbur Wright (USA)
• Alcohol thermometer (1709)	Fahrenheit (Germany)
• Artificial radioactivity (1934)	Madam J. Irene Curie
• Atom bomb (1941)	Otto Hahn (Germany)
• Atomic structure (1913)	Bohr and Rutherford
• Bakelite (1907)	Lwo H. Backeland (Belgium)
• Ball point pen (1888)	John J. Lord (USA)
• Barometer (1644)	E. Torricelli (Italy)
• Battery (electric) (1800)	A. Volta (Italy)
• Bicycle (1839)	K. Macmillan (UK)
• Bicycle tyre (Pneumatic) (1888)	J.B. Dunlop (UK)
• Bifocal lens (1780)	Benjamin Franklin (USA)
• Car (steam engine) (1769)	Nicolas Cujnot (France)
• Car (petrol engine) (1888)	Karl Benz (Germany)
• Cement (portland) (1824)	Joseph Aspdin (UK)
• Cinema (1895)	Nocolas and Jean Lumiere (France)
• Clock (pendulum) (1657)	Christian Huygens (Netherlands)
• Clock (mechanical) (1725)	I-Hsing and Liang Ling-Tsan (China)
• Cosmic rays (1910)	R.A. Milkan
• Deuterium (heavy hydrogen) (1932)	H.C. Urey
• Diesel engine (1895)	Rudolf Diesel (Germany)
• Dynamite (1852)	Alfred Nobel (Sweden)
• Dynamo (1832)	Hypolite Pixii(France)
• Electric lamp (1879)	Thomas Alva Edison (USA)
• Electric motor {AC) (1888)	Nikola Tesla (Belgium)
• Electric motor (DC) (1873)	Zenobe Gramme (Belgium)
• Electro-magnet (1824)	William Sturgeon (England)
• Electron (1897)	J.J. Thompson (USA)
• Engine (railway) (1814)	Stephenson
• Film (talking) (1926)	J. Engl, J. Mussolle and H. Vogt (Germany)
• Fountain pen (1884)	Lewis E. Waterman (USA)
• Galvanometer (1834)	Andre Marie Ampere (France)
• Glider (1853)	George Cayley (Britain)
• Gramophone (1878)	Thomas Alva Edison (USA)
• Helicopter (1924)	Etienne Oehmichen (France)
• Hovercraft (1955)	C.S. Cockerell (Britain)
• Hydrogen (1766)	Cavendish
• Induction of electric current (1841)	Michael Faraday (England)
• Internal combustion engine (1876)	N. Otto
• Laser (1960)	Charles H. Townes (USA)
• Laws of Gravitation (1687)	Issac Newton (USA)
• Lift (mechanical) (1852)	E. G. Otis (USA)
• Laws of Natural Selection	Charles Darwin (USA)
• Laws of electrical resistance (1826)	Ohm (Germany)

• Locomotive (1804)	Richard Trevithick (UK)
• Loom (power) (1785)	Edmund Cartwright (Uk)
• Loudspeaker (1924)	Rice-Kellogg (USA)
• Match, safety (1855)	J.E. Lundstorm (Sweden)
• Microphone (1876)	Alexander Graham Bell (USA)
• Microprocessor (1971)	Robert Noyce & Gordon Moore (USA)
• Microscope (1590)	Zacharis Janssen (Netherlands)
• Motor cycle (1885)	G. Daimler (Germany)
• Malaria parasite (1897)	Ronald Ross (USA)
• Mercury thermometer (1720)	Fahreinheit (Germany)
• Neon	W. Ramsay (Germany)
• Nylon (1937)	Wallace H. Corothers
• Periodic law	Mehdeleev (Russia)
• Photography (coloured) (1897)	Gabriel Lippman (USA)
• Photography (roll films) (1888)	George Eastman (USA)
• Printing press (circa 1455)	Johan Zu Guttenberg (Germany)
• Printing for the blind (1829)	Louis Braille (France)
• Quantum theory (1901)	Max Planck (Germany)
• Radar (1922)	Allbert H. Taylor and Leo. C. Young (USA)
• Radioactivity of uranium (1896)	Henry Bacquerel (France)
• Record (long playing) (1948)	Petter Goldmark (USA)
• Refrigerator (1851)	James Harrison (Scotland)
• Relativity theory	Albert Einstein (USA)
• Radio transmitter (1914)	Alexander's Sons
• Safety pin (1849)	William Hunt (USA)
• Safety lamp (1816)	Humphrey Devy (USA)
• Sewing machine (1846)	Elias Howe (USA)
• Spinning frame (1769)	Richard Arkrcright (England)
• Steam engine (1639)	Thomas Savery (England)
• Steam engine (1765) (condenser)	James Watt (England)
• Steel production (1885)	Henry Bessemer (England)
• Submarine (1776)	David Bushnell (USA)
• Telegraph (1837)	Sir William Cook (England)
• Telegraph code (1837)	Samel F.B. Morse. (USA)
• Telephone (1876)	Alexander Graham Bell (USA)
• Telescope (1608)	Hans Lippershey (Netherlands)
• Television (1926)	John Logie Baird (Scotland)
• Thermometer (1593)	Galileo Galilei (Italy)
• Transformer (1842)	William Stanley (USA)
• Transistor (1848)	John Bardeen, William Shockley and Walter Brattain (USA)
• Typewriter (1848)	Mitterhofer (Austria)
• Watch (self winding) (1791)	Abraham-Louis Breguet (France)
• Wireless telegraph (1896)	Marconi (Italy)
• X-rays (1895)	Wilhelm von Roentgen (Germany)
• Zip fastener (1891)	Whitcomb L. Judson (USA)

CHEMISTRY

Chemistry is a branch of Science in which we study the properties, composition and structure of materials (all, without any exception) in the world around us.

MATTER AND ITS NATURE

- Any thing that occupies space and has mass or weight is called matter. Matter can exist in any one of the three physical states; solid, liquid, or gas.
- Matter undergoes changes which may be either chemical changes or physical changes.
- When water is transformed into steam it still retains all the chemical properties of water; that is, only its physical state is changed. Upon cooling, it returns to its original liquid state.

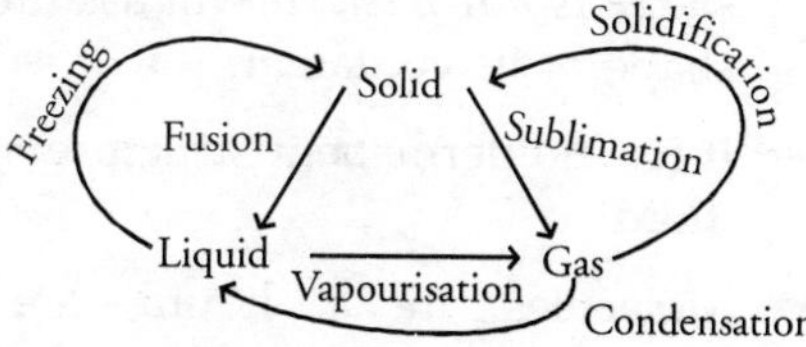

- However, when a piece of wood is burned, the original substance disappears, and new substances are formed. This is a chemical change, the kind of change with which chemistry is primarily concerned.

Classification

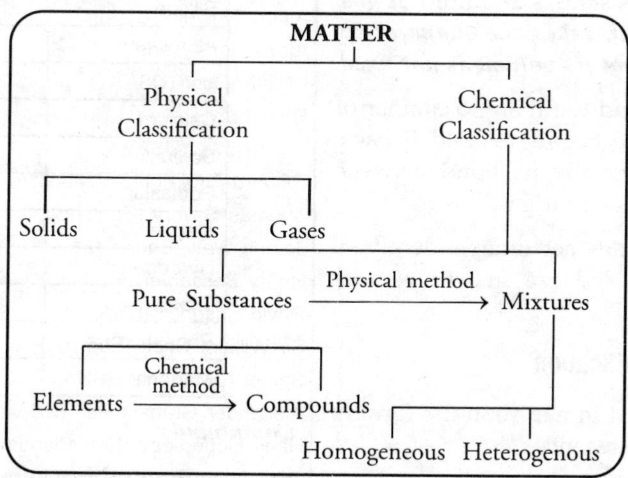

Physical Classification

- The physical classification separates matter into three categories—solids, liquids, and gases—known as the three states of matter.
- Plasma, is considered a fourth state of matter.

Solids

- In a solid the molecules are closely packed together and vibrate about fixed positions. Thus a solid is a rigid substance that has a ***definite volume and a definite shape***.
- Solids maintain their volumes independent of the size or shape of the container in which they are placed.

- Solids are nearly incompressible. They diffuse very slowly in comparison to liquids or gases.
- Solid may be crystalline and amorphous.

Liquids

- A liquid has a ***fixed volume, but its shape is not fixed.*** It will assume the shape of its container.
- It has no permanent structure; it is a 'fluid'.
- Molecules in a liquid are not located in fixed positions, but are free to wander about. However, the molecules exert an attractive force on each other, so that they remain close together.
- Glass is a super cooled liquid.

Gases

- The gaseous state is also fluid. ***A gas, like a liquid, takes the shape of its container, but its volume is not fixed.***
- It will expand to fill any container or until a force begins to hold it back. There is virtually no bond between the molecules of a gas.
- The molecules act independently of each other and are free to wander about.

Chemical Classification

- Matters exist in nature in the form of chemical substances.
- A variety of matter, all samples of which have same composition and properties is called pure substances. Pure substances are divided into **elements** and **compounds.**

Elements

- An element is the simplest form of a pure substance. All subs-tances are ultimately made up of elements. An element may be defined as the *simplest form of matter which cannot be decomposed by ordinary chemical reaction.*
- The earth's crust is made up of a small number of elements. Only eight of the naturally occuring elements make up 99% mass of the earth's crust, oceans and atmosphere.
- If the entire universe is considered, then 90% of matter is hydrogen.
- Helium is the second most abundant element amounting to 9% and the remaining elements make up only 1% of the universe with oxygen, neon, carbon and nitrogen next in order of decreasing abundance.

Elements in Earth's Crust

Elements	Percentage
Oxygen	46.6%
Silicon	27.7%
Aluminium	8.1%
Iron	5.0%
Calcium	3.6%
Sodium	2.8%
Potassium	2.6%
Magnesium	2.1%
Hydrogen	0.14%
Titanium	0.44%
Phosphorous	0.2%
Manganese	0.1%

Compounds

- A compound is a substance made up of elements.
- The gases oxygen and hydrogen combine to form water, a liquid compound.
- The solid potassium and the gases nitrogen and oxygen are found combined in saltpetre (potassium nitrate), a solid compound.

- Chemical compound always contains the same elements in definite (fixed) proportion by weight.

Mixture

- A material obtained by mixing two or more substances (elements or compounds) in any proportions is known as *mixture.*
- In a mixture, the components do not lose their identity. For example, air is a mixture of several gases, syrup is a mixture of sugar and water, gun powder is a mixture of carbon, sulphur and nitrogen.
- The components of a mixture can be easily separated by ordinary methods.
- Mixtures are of two types: *homogeneous mixtures* and *heterogeneous mixtures.*

Homogeneous Mixtures

- Homogeneous mixtures have the same composition throughout the sample. For example salt solution (sodium chloride dissolved in water), sugar solution (sugar dissolved in water), carbonated water (carbon dioxide dissolved in water), etc.

Heterogeneous Mixtures

- Heterogeneous mixtures consist of two or more parts (called phases) which have different compositions. There are visible boundaries of separation between the various constituents, when examined closely under the microscope or even, in certain cases, by the naked eye. For example, undissolved sugar (solid phase) in sugar solution (liquid phase), smoke (mixture of air and carbon particles), mixtures of iron and sulphur, mixture of sand, water and milk etc.

STRUCTURE OF THE ATOM

- Each atom consists of a central core with negatively charged electrons revolving around the core.
- The core consists of positively charged protons and uncharged neutrons.
- The core is called the nucleus of an atom. An atom as such is electrically neutral.
- The atomic weight of an element is a number representing the sum of the constituent protons and neutrons.

Electrons

- J.J. Thomson discovered the charged particles called electrons. They are present in all atoms around the nucleus in fixed energy levels.
- When cathode fall on materials having high atomic mass, new type of penetrating rays of very small wavelengths are emitted which are called X-rays.
- The first precise measurement of charge on the electron was made by Robert A. Mulliken in 1909 by oil-drop experiment.
- The charge on the electron was found to be –1.602 × 10–19 coulomb.

Protons

- The protons were observed by Goldstein in 1896 in a discharge tube with perforated cathode.
- It was observed that a stream of positive charged particles passed through the holes in the cathode in a direction away from the anode.
- A beam of positively charged particles is also known as positive rays.
- This positively charged particle was named proton by Rutherford in 1911.

➡ The positive rays or anode rays travel in straight lines and cast a shadow of the object placed in their path.

Neutrons

➡ Rutherford (1920) suggested that in an atom, there must be present at least a third type of fundamental particles which should be electrically neutral and possess mass nearly equal to that of proton. He proposed the name for such fundamental particle as neutron.

➡ In 1932, Chadwick bombarded beryllium with a stream of a—particles. He observed that the penetrating radiations were produced which were not affected by electric and magnetic fields. These radiations consisted of neutral particles, which were called neutrons.

Atomic Number and Mass Number

Atomic Number

➡ The number of positive charge carried by the nucleus of an atom is termed as atomic number or charge number (Mosley, 1913) and is represented by symbol Z.

➡ Since the charge on the nucleus is equal to the number of the protons (p) in it which, in turn, is equal to the number of electrons (e) in the atom, the atomic number is defined as the number of protons or the number of electrons in a neutral atom.

Mass Number

➡ The total number of the protons and neutrons present in the nucleus of an atom is known as the mass number of the atom.

Atomic Mass Number (A) = total number of proton + total number of neutron.

Dalton's Atomic Theory

The basic postulates of Dalton's atomic theory are as under:

1. All matters is made up of very tiny particles which cannot be further divided. These tiny particles are called atoms.
2. Atoms can neither be created nor destroyed during chemical reactions.
3. Atoms of a particular element are identical in all respects *i.e.,* same size, mass and other properties.
4. Atoms of different elements are different.
5. Atoms combine to form molecules.

Rutherford's Model of Atom

Rutherford (1911) proposed the following atomic model :

1. An atom consists of a tiny nucleus which contains practically the whole mass of the atom. The atom is largely empty.
2. The nucleus is positively charged, and is surrounded by negatively charged electrons. The atom as a whole is electrically neutral.
3. The electrons are not stationary, but are revolving around the nucleus in orbits.

PERIODIC TABLE OF ELEMENTS

➡ In the early 19th century the German chemist **Johann Dobereiner** arranged element with similar properties in groups of three, called ***triads***. He was also the first to investigate the numerical relations between the atomic weights of elements.

➡ In 1864, an English chemist **John Newland** arranged the elements in the order of increasing atomic masses in which the properties of every eighth elements was a repetition of the first one. This relation was called the ***Law of Octaves***.

- In 1870, another German chemist, **Lothar Meyer** classified the elements on the basis of their atomic volumes.
- Finally, the Russian chemist **Dmitri Mendeleev** and the German chemist Julius Lothar Meyer independently discovered the periodic law. It states that the properties of elements are periodic functions of their atomic weights.
- Mendeleev published his report in 1869—a year earlier than Meyer.
- Both scientists arranged the elements in order of increasing atomic weights and groups, or families, of related-elements. In this way they obtained a natural classification based on the properties of elements.
- In 1912, **Mosley** proposed that the physical and chemical properties of the atoms of the elements are determined by their atomic number and not their atomic mass. Thus the physical and chemical properties of the elements are periodic function of their atomic numbers. This is known as **Modern Periodic law.**

Extended Form of the Periodic Table

Group / Period	IA	IIA	IIIA	IVA	VA	VIA	VIIA	VIII			IB	IIB	IIIB	IVB	VB	VIB	VIIB	0
1	H 1																	He 2
2	Li 3	Be 4											B 5	C 6	N 7	O 8	F 9	Ne 10
3	Na 11	Mg 12											Al 13	Si 14	P 15	S 16	Cl 17	Ar 18
4	K 19	Ca 20	Sc 21	Ti 22	V 23	Cr 24	Mn 25	Fe 26	Co 27	Ni 28	Cu 29	Zn 30	Ga 31	Ge 32	As 33	Se 34	Br 35	Kr 36
5	Rb 37	Sr 38	Y 39	Zr 40	Nb 41	Mo 42	Tc 43	Ru 44	Rh 45	Pd 46	Ag 47	Cd 48	In 49	Sn 50	Sb 51	Te 52	I 53	Xe 54
6	Cs 55	Ba 56	La* 57	Hf 72	Ta 73	W 74	Re 75	Os 76	Ir 77	Pt 78	Au 79	Hg 80	Tl 81	Pb 82	Bi 83	Po 84	At 85	Rn 86
7	Fr 87	Ra 88	Ac† 89	Rf 104	Db 105	Sg 106	Bh 107	Hs 108	Mt 109									

The Rare Earths

* Lanthanide series	Ce 58	Pr 59	Nd 60	Pm 61	Sm 62	Eu 63	Gd 64	Tb 65	Dy 66	Ho 67	Er 68	Tm 69	Yb 70	Lu 71
†Actinide series	Th 90	Pa 91	U 92	Np 93	Pu 94	Am 95	Cm 96	Bk 97	Cf 98	Es 99	Fm 100	Md 101	No 102	Lr 103

CHEMICAL BONDING

- A chemical bond is defined as a force that acts between two or more atoms to hold them together as a stable molecule.
- The electronic configuration of all noble gas (except Helium) in the valance cell is eight, which corresponds to stable state and maximum stability.
- All the atoms have urge to attain a stable state configuration of eight electron in their valance shell. This principle of attaining maximum of eight electron in the valance shell is called Octet Rule.
- Every object in universe lose energy to attain a stable state.
- Atoms have high potential energy. An atom combine with another atoms to form molecules. It loses

some amount of potential energy to attain a stable state.

Types of Bonding

➡ Atoms attains a stable configuration by losing, gaining or sharing electrons. There are three principal type of chemical bondings.

1. Ionic bonding;
2. Covalent bonding;
3. Metallic bonding.

Ionic Bond

➡ An Ionic bond is formed by the complete transference of one or more electrons from the outer energy shell of one atom to the energy shell of another atom.

➡ The crystals of sodium chloride obtained actually consist of a large number of Na^+ and Cl^- ions. The electrostatic attraction between the oppositely charged Na^+ and Cl^- is called an Ionic bond. In sodium chloride

$$Na^+ :\ddot{\underset{..}{Cl}}: \rightarrow Na^+ + [:\ddot{\underset{..}{Cl}}:]$$

Characteristics

1. Ionic compounds do not exhibit isomerism.
2. Ionic compounds are crystalline solids.
3. Ionic compounds have high mp and bp.
4. Ionic compounds are generally soluble in polar solvents like water and undergo ionic dissociation which makes the solution good conductor of electricity.
5. In molten state, the ionic compounds are good conductors of electricity.

Covalent Bond

➡ G.N. Lewis, an American chemist, was first to suggest that atoms may combine by sharing electrons in their outer shell with one another. The shared electrons contribute towards the stability of both atoms. This type of linkage is called the covalent linkage or the covalent bond. The compounds formed by this mechanism are called covalent compounds.

➡ Formation of covalent bond in terms of decrease of energy : The bond formed by mutual sharing of a pair of electrons between the two atoms of the same or different elements is known as a single covalent bond and is represented by a line (–). The compound so formed is known as a covalent compound. Examples:

$$H\cdot + \cdot H \rightarrow \quad H:H \quad H-H$$

Two hydrogen atoms (1) — Hydrogen molecule (Single covalent bond)

$$:\ddot{\underset{..}{Cl}}: + :\ddot{\underset{..}{Cl}}: \rightarrow :Cl:Cl: \quad Cl-Cl \text{ or } Cl_2$$

Two Chlorine atoms (2,8,7) — Chlorine molecule (Single covalent bond)

➡ Each line (–) represents a pair of electrons, contributed and shared by the two atoms. When two pairs of electrons are shared, it is known as a double bond. Examples:

$$\ddot{\underset{..}{O}}: + \ddot{\underset{..}{O}}: \longrightarrow (:\ddot{O}::\ddot{O}:) \longrightarrow O=O$$

Two oxygen atoms (2, 6) — Oxygen molecule (Double bond)

$$2[\cdot\dot{C}\cdot] + 4[H\cdot] \quad \begin{matrix} H & & H \\ C & :: & C \\ H & & H \end{matrix} \quad \begin{matrix} H & & H \\ | & & | \\ C & = & C \\ | & & | \\ H & & H \end{matrix}$$

Two carbon atoms (2, 4) — Four hydrogen atoms (1) — Ethylene molecule (Double bond)

Metallic Bond

➡ Metals are made up of positive ions packed together. The negatively charged electrons hold the ion together. The number of positive and negative charge is exactly balanced.

CHEMICAL REACTIONS

- A chemical reaction is a process which transforms one or more substances (called *reactants*) into new substances (called *products*) by the breaking of bonds and the making of new bonds. For *e.g.*

  H — H + I — I ⟶ 2H — I

- Chemical reactions are generally accompanied by heat changes.
- A reaction in which heat is evolved is called the **exothermic chemical reaction**.
- A reaction in which heat is absorbed is called **endothermic chemical reaction.**

  Endothermic Reaction

  A + B ⟶ C + D + Heat Absorbed

  Exothermic Reaction

  A + B ⟶ C + D + Heat Evolved

Forms of Energies Involved in Reactions

Forms of energy generally involved in chemical reactions are heat, light and electricity.

Photochemical Reactions

- Some reactions produce light while other reactions take place by the absorption of light. These reactions are called *photochemical reactions.* Some common examples of photochemical reactions are photos-ynthesis by the plant in sunlight.
- ***Photography*** uses photochemical reaction. The photographic film is coated with the compound silver bromide AgBr, which is sensitive to light. When light falls on the film, then the compound is chemically affected. When the film is developed the photographic image, is obtained.

Electrolytic Reaction

- The sodium and chlorine combine to give NaCl with the release of lot of energy. This reaction can be reversed, if energy is supplied to NaCl in form of electricity to molten NaCl or in other words by electrolysing NaCl. The process of electrolysis is carried out in an *electrolytic cell.*
- The electricity from a battery is passed through molten NaCl by two electrodes.
- The electrode is connected to the positive terminal of the battery is called *anode.*
- The electrode connected to the negative terminal of the battery, is called *cathode.*

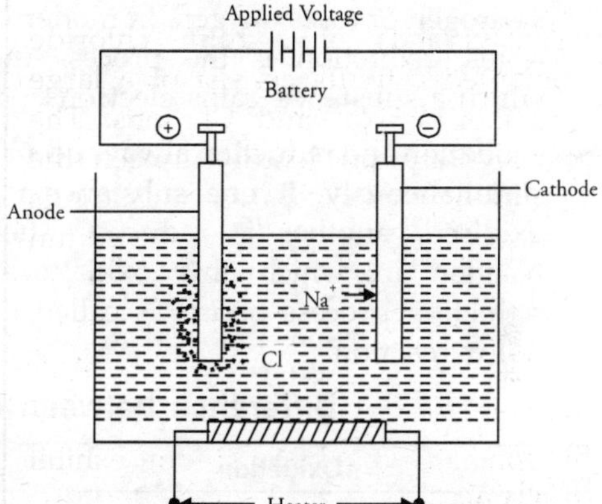

Faraday's Law of Electrolysis

- Michael Faraday (1833) discovered certain relationships between the quantity of current passed through a solution of an electrolyte and the amount of substances liberated (or deposited) at the electrodes during electrolysis.
- He gave the results in the form of two laws of electrolysis.
- ***First Law of Electrolysis***: "The amount of any substance deposited (or dissolved) at an electrode during electrolysis is directly proportional to the quantity of electricity passed."

➥ *Second Law of Electrolysis*: The amount of different substances deposited (or dissolved) at electrodes by the passage of the same quantity of electricity are proportional to their chemical equivalents (E), *i.e.*,

$$W \propto E$$

OXIDATION AND REDUCTION

➥ Oxidation is a process in which a substance adds on oxygen or loses hydrogen.

➥ The current definition of oxidation is the process in which a substance loses electrons.

➥ Reduction, on the other hand, is a process in which a substance adds on hydrogen or loses oxygen. In modern terms, reduction is the process in which a substance gains electrons.

➥ Oxidation and reduction always occur simultaneously. If one substance is oxidised, another is reduced. The reaction in which this oxidation-reduction process occurs is called a redox reaction.

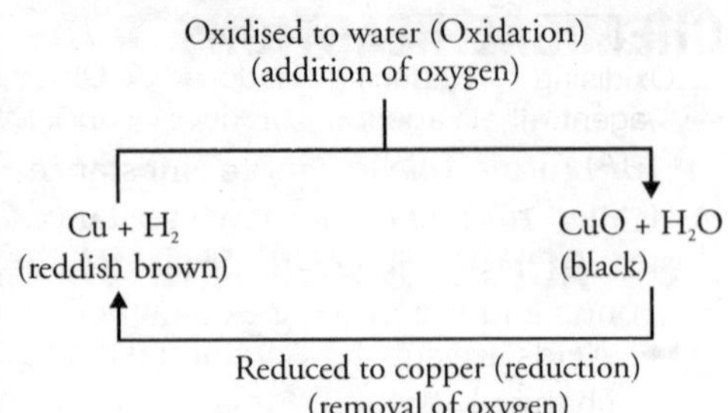

➥ Oxidising agents are substances which bring about the oxidation of other substances, e.g., potassium permanganate, potassium dichromate, nitric acid, hydrogen peroxide, etc.

➥ Reducing agents are substances which bring about the reduction of other substances, e.g., hydrogen sulphide, hydrogen, carbon, sulphur dioxide, etc.

➥ There are a number of oxidation-reduction reactions that are of industrial use. The production of metals from their ores invariably involves these two processes. Organic compounds are also synthesised by various oxidation—reduction techniques.

Difference between Oxidation & Reduction

	Oxidation		Reducation
1.	Addition of oxygen or electro-negative element is known as oxidation.	1.	Removal of oxygen or electro-negative element is known as reduction.
2.	Removal of hydrogen & electro-positive element is known as oxidation.	2.	Addition of hydrogen & electro-positive element is known as reduction.
3.	Increase in valency or oxidation number is known as oxidation.	3.	Decrease in valency & oxidation number is known as reduction.
4.	Loss of electron is known as oxidation $Na \rightarrow Na^+ + e$	4.	Gain of electron is known as reduction $X + e \rightarrow X^-$

Redox Reactions

➥ It is evident that if one substance loses the electrons, another substance at the same time must gain electrons because the electrons cannot be the products of any chemical change.

➥ In any chemical process, oxidation can occur only if reduction is also taking place side by side and *vice versa*. This is the reason that reactions involving oxidation and reduction are called redox reactions.

➥ During redox reaction, there is transference of electrons from the *reducing agent* to the oxidising agent.

C^- → A^+ + B^-

Oxidising agent (A) | Reducing agent (B) | Reduced product | Oxidized product

ACIDS, BASES AND SALTS

➡ Acids are substances that tasted sour, changed the colour of the litmus paper from blue to red, reacted with certain metals to give off hydrogen gas, and formed carbon dioxide with carbonates. Above all, acids are able to neutralize bases.

Types of Acids

(i) *Hydro Acids :* They contain other non-metallic element rather than hydrogen and do not have oxygen.

(ii) *Oxy Acids :* They contain another element besides oxygen and hydrogen.

(iii) *Strong Acids :* These dissociate completely even in concentrated solutions. *e.g.*— HCl, HNO_3, etc.

(iv) *Weak Acids :* These dissociate partially in water,

e.g.— K_2SO_4, Al_2 (SO_4), $24H_2O$

Uses of Acids

➡ **Sulphuric acid** is used in greater quantities than any other chemical. It enters into the manufacture of explosives, dyestuffs, and drugs. It is used in oil and sugar refining and in the preparation of fertilizers. H_2SO_4 is also used in lead storage battery in motor vehicles or in inverter.

➡ **Hydrochloric acid** serves in the manufacture of glue, gelatin, and dextrose, and in cleaning metals. Doctors prescribe very dilute hydrochloric acid for certain cases of indigestion.

➡ **Nitric acid** is used in large quantities in the manufacture of fertilizers and of explosives and also in the preparation of dyes and plastics.

➡ **Acetic acid** is a good solvent for certain organic substance. It plays an important part in the preparation of cellulose acetate, which is used as a plastic and in the manufacture of acetic fibre.

➡ **Hydrofluoric acid** is used in making refrigerants and certain plastics. It has the useful property of being able to etch glass.

Bases

➡ Bases are considered substances that tasted bitter, felt slippery, changed the colour of litmus paper from red to blue. Above all, bases are able to neutralize acids.

(i) *Strong Base:* These dissociate completely even in concentrated solution. *e.g.*–NaOH, KOH etc.

(ii) *Weak Base:* These dissociate partially in water.

e.g.—NH_4OH, $Mg(OH)_2$ etc.

Uses of Bases

➡ **Sodium hydroxide** is mainly used in the rayon, soap, paper, and petroleum industries.

➡ **Hydrated lime** (calcium hydroxide) serves to raise the pH of soils and to make insecticides and many other chemicals.

➡ **Ammonium hydroxide** is another important base. It is used as a raw material for making many important compounds, including the fertilizers.

Salts

➡ Salt is a compound formed when one or more of the hydrogen atoms of an acid are replaced by one or more cations of the base. *e.g.* Sodium Chloride (NaCl).

Uses of Salts

- Common salt, **sodium chloride**, is undoubtedly the most valuable to map of all the salts. It is used to prepare various compounds of the metal sodium. It is also the principal source of the gas chlorine, which is used for bleaching, for purifying water and in many plastics. Salt is also an important preservative of meat, fish, hides, skins and various other products.
- The salt called **sodium bicarbonate** ($NaHCO_3$) is an essential ingredient in baking powders.
- Epson salts (magnesium sulphate, $MgSO_4$ $7H_2O$) and **colomel** (mercurous chloride, Hg_2Cl_2) have medicinal uses.
- **Gypsum** (calcium sulphate, $CaSO_2$, $2H_2O$) yields Plaster of Paris and is also used in the manufacture of gypsum wallboard.
- Hypo, (or sodium thiosulphate, $Na_2S_2O_3$. $5H_2O$) plays an important part in photography as a fixing agent.
- A list of some salts of potassium, alone, provides a good idea of the wide-ranging uses of salts.
- **Potassium carbonate** (K_2CO_3) is used in making glass, dyes, and some soaps.
- **Potassium bromide** (KBr) is used in photography.
- **Potassium nitrate** (KNO_3) is used in the production of gunpowder.
- **Potassium chloride** (KCl) and **potassium sulfate** (K_2SO_4) are used in making fertilizers.
- Pure **monopotassium tartrate** ($K_2H_4C_4O_6$), called cream of tartar, is used in the manufacture of baking powder.

OCCURRENCE OF METALS

- The earth's crust is the major source of metals. Seawater also contains some soluble salts such as sodium chloride, magnesium chloride, etc.
- The elements or compounds, which occur naturally in the earth's crust, are known as minerals.
- At some places, minerals contain a very high percentage of a particular metal and the metal can be profitably extracted from it. These minerals are called ores.

Properties of Metals

Physical Properties

- All metals are solid except mercury which is a liquid.
- Most of the metals are *hard* and have *high melting and boiling points*.
- Metals are *malleable* i.e. they can be beaten into sheets. Gold and silver are the best malleable metals and these can be hammered into foils.
- Most of the metals are *ductile* i.e., they can be drawn into thin wires.
- All metals are good conductors of heat, silver is the best and lead (Pb) is the poorest conductor of heat among metals.
- Metals also show *high electrical conductivity*. The best conductors of electricity are silver, copper, gold, aluminum and tungsten.

Metallurgy

- The process of extracting a metal in the free state from its ore is known as Metallurgy.
- **Minerals:** The compound of a metal found in nature is called a mineral. A mineral may be a single compound or a complex mixture.

- **Ores:** Those minerals from which metal can be economically and easily extracted are called ores. All ores are mineral but all minerals are not ores.
- **Gangue (or matrix):** The ore is generally associated with earthy impurities like sand, rocks and limestone known as gangue or matrix.
- **Flux:** A substance added to ore to remove impurities is called flux. There are two typs of flux:

  Acidic flux is added to remove basic impurity

  $$\underset{\text{acidic flux}}{SiO_2} + \underset{\text{basic impurity}}{FeO} \longrightarrow \underset{\text{Ferrous silicate}}{FeSiO_3}$$

  Basic flux is added to remove acidic impurity.

  $$\underset{\text{basic flux}}{CaCO_3} + \underset{\text{acidic impurity}}{SiO_2} \longrightarrow \underset{\text{Calcium silicate}}{CaSiO + CO_2}$$

- **Slag:** Combination of gangue with flux in ores forms a fusible material which is called slag.

  $$\text{Gangue} + \text{flux} \longrightarrow \text{slag}$$

  $$SiO_2 + CaO \longrightarrow CaSiO_3$$

- **Concentration:** The process of removal of gangue from the ore is known as concentration of ore. Concentration of ore can be carried out in the following ways depending upon the nature of the ore.
  1. Gravity separation
  2. Magnetic concentration
  3. Froth floatation process
  4. Chemical methods
- **Calcination:** Calcination is a process in which ore is heated, generally in the absence of air, to expel water from hydrated oxide or carbon dioxide from a carbonate at temperature below their melting point example:

  $$Al_2O_3 \cdot 2H_2O \xrightarrow{\Delta} Al_2O_3 + 2H_2O$$

  $$CaCO_3 \xrightarrow{\Delta} CaO + CO_2$$

- **Roasting** : Roasting is a process in which ore is heated usually in the presence of air, at temperatures below its melting points.

  $$ZnS + 2O_2 \longrightarrow ZnSO_2;$$

  $$CuS + 2O_2 \longrightarrow CuSO_4$$

- **Smelting:** The reduction of oxide ore with carbon at high temperature is known as smelting.

  $$F_2O_3 + 3C \longrightarrow 2Fe + 3CO;$$

  $$PbO + C \longrightarrow Pb + CO$$

  A series is obtained by arranging the metals in decreasing order of reactivity which is known as Acitivity series.

- **Corrosion:** The process of slow conversion of metals into their undesirable compounds (usually oxides) by reaction with moisture and other gases present in the atmosphere is called corrosion.

  Rusting or Iron, Green coating on the surface of copper, tarnishing of silver etc. are examples of corrosion.

  The formula of rust is $Fe_2O_3 \cdot xH_2O$.

  Reacitvity of the metal, Presence of impurities, Air and moisture, Strains in metal, Presence of electrolytes etc. are factor which affect the corrosion.

THE NON-METALS

- Elements in the periodic table are divided broadly into metals and non-metals.
- There are only 22 non-metallic elements out of which 11 are gases, (*e.g.* oxygen, nitrogen and chlorine) one liquid (bromine) and remaining 10 are solids (*e.g.* carbon, sulphur, phosphorous and iodine). These non-metallic elements are placed on the right-hand side of the periodic table.

- Non-metals have usually low densities, are brittle and do not give sheets (non-malleable) or wires (non-ductile).
- They don't possess lustre and cannot be polished. They have lower melting and boiling point.
- Non-metals are generally bad conductors of heat and electricity. Unlike metals, non-metals have no free electrons. Only graphite, an allotropic form of carbon is an exception and is a good conductor of electricity.
- Unlike metals, non-metals are electronegative that is, they have a tendency to accept electrons and form negative ions.
- They give acidic or neutral oxides on combination with oxygen.
- These oxides are formed by sharing of electrons i.e., covalent oxides are formed. They have high electronegativity.

Hydrogen

- Hydrogen is the first chemical element in the periodic system.
- Hydrogen is most abundant element in the Universe. It is about 92% in Universe followed by Helium 7%, rest of the element present in Universe is about 1%.
- Hydrogen is the third most important element on earth.
- Its three isotopes are Protium (^1_1H), Deuterium or Heavy Hydrogen (^2_1H), and Tritium (^3_1H).
- Heavy water (D_2O) is used in nuclear reactor for slowing down fast moving neutrons (i.e. it acts as a moderator).
- Hydrogen is colourless, tasteless and odourless gas.
- It is the lightest known element. Therefore hydrogen gas is filled in balloon which is used for advertisement.
- It is slightly soluble in water because its molecules are non-polar.
- Hydrogen molecules combined with metals (Sodium, Potassium, Calcium etc.) upon heating to form corresponding hydrate. These hydrates are ionic in nature (*e.g.* NaH, CaH_2 etc.)

Uses of Hydrogen

1. It is used for the manufacturing of ammonia, methyl alcohol, HCl etc.
2. Hydrogen is the lightest gas therefore it is used for filling in different type of balloons, but as the gas is inflammable it is replaced by inert gas helium.
3. Hydrogen is used for hydrogenation or hardening of oils. Oils are polyunsaturated in nature (contains large number of double bonds). Hydrogenation eliminates the double bond.

   $$\text{Vegetable oil} + H_2 \xrightarrow[473\,k]{\text{Ni}} \underset{\text{(Solid)}}{\text{Fat}}$$

   The vegetable ghee such as Dalda, Rath, etc. are prepared by this process.
4. The oxy-hydrogen flame and atomic hydrogen flame contains hydrogen gas which are used for cutting and welding steel and other hard metals.
5. Several fuel gases (*e.g.* coal gas, water gas, oil gas) contains hydrogen as important constituents.

Oxygen

- Oxygen is a colourless, odourless gas.
- Chemically very active, among its most abundant binary compounds are water and silica.

- In air, Oxygen (21%) is second most element after Nitrogen (78.1%).
- It is the abundant element of earth crust, and is mainly present as silicates, carbonates and oxides of metals.
- A most useful element, both combustion and respiration involve oxygen.
- It has many uses. Oxyacetylene burners produce very high temperature flames for cutting and welding metals.
- When steel is being made, oxygen is used to remove the impurities from the molten iron.
- Pure oxygen stored in cylinders, is used to support breathing—to help patients in hospitals, and for high altitude or underwater work.
- Space rockets have to carry liquid oxygen in order to burn their fuels in space.
- In manufacturing liquid rocket fuels, liquid oxygen is used to burn either liquid hydrogen or kerosene.
- The **oxygen cycle** is an important natural process. Respiration and commercial activities transform oxygen to carbon dioxide and other gases.
- Photosynthesis by green plants uses carbon dioxide to release oxygen.

Sulphur

- Sulphur occurs in nature both in the combined and free state.
- In combined state it is a constituent of many important metallic minerals like Cinnabar (HgS), Zinc blende (ZnS), Copper pyrites ($CuFeS_2$) etc.
- Underground sulphur is mined by a special technique called **Frasch process.**
- Sulphur occurs in several allotropic forms. Sulphur burns with a blue flame to give sulphur dioxide. It is used for vulcanizing rubber, in the manufacture of dyes, explosives e.g., gunpowder and various chemicals for killing moulds and pests, and in medicine.
- Hydrogen sulphide is prepared by reacting boiling sulphur with hydrogen gas. Small quantities of hydrogen sulphide are present in air. Blackening of oil paints, tranishing of silverware and blackening of white paint is due to the presence of this gas which forms sulphides of silver in case of silver and sulphides of lead in case of all kinds of paints.
- Hydrogen sulphide is used in laboratory for qualitative inorganic analysis i.e., for the identification of metallic ions. It is also used as a reducing agent.

Nitrogen

- Nitrogen is a gas under normal conditions. Its molecular formula is N_2.
- Molecular nitrogen is the principal constituent of the atmosphere (78% by volume of dry air), in which its concentration is a result of the balance between the fixation of atmospheric nitrogen by bacterial, electrical (lightning), and chemical (industrial) action, and its liberation through the decomposition of organic materials by bacterial or combustion.
- It is a constituent of all proteins (both plant and animal) as well as of many other organic materials. Its chief mineral source is sodium nitrate.

- Because of the importance of nitrogen compounds in agriculture and the chemical industry, much of the industrial interest in elementary nitrogen has been in processes for converting element nitrogen into nitrogen compounds.
- Nitrogen is also used for filling bulbs of incandescent lamps and, in general, wherever a relatively inert atmosphere is required.
- In its liquid form (215°C below zero) nitrogen is used for preserving frozen food.
- Bull semen is frozen in liquid nitrogen at artificial insemination centres for cattle.

Phosphorus

- For every form of life, phosphates play an essential role in energy-transfer during metabolism, photosynthesis, nerve function, and muscle action.
- The nucleic acids which is hereditary materials contain phosphates. Some coenzymes and animal skeletons contains a calcium phosphate.
- Phosphorus is an important ingredient in fertilizer manufacture.
- Other important uses are as builders for detergents, nutrient supplements for animal feeds, water softeners, additives for food and pharmaceuticals, coating agents for metal surface treatment, additives in metallurgy, plasticizers, insecticides and additives for petroleum products.
- Red phosphorus is used in safety matches.
- Phosphorus is solid at room temperature.
- The **white phosphorus** is highly reactive, soft waxy substance which ignites spontaneously in air at 35°C. It is therefore kept under water to prevent ignition. The white phosphorus on heating at about 250°C, in presence of sunlight is converted into **red phosphorus.**
- Phosphate (P_2O_5) is used in water softening, fireproofing fabrics (ammonium phosphate), pharmaceutical (toothpaste) etc.

Silicon

- Silicon is the second most abundant element on earth after oxygen.
- Silicon does not only occur as an element naturally but also in the forms of silicon dioxide and silicates.
- Silicon dioxide, also known as **silica**, occurs as **quartz** which is a crystalline solid, and in an impure form as sand and sandstone.
- Silicates occur naturally in igneous rocks and clay. **Mica** is a transparent mineral made up of silicate sheets.
- Silicon is a hard shiny grey solid with a high melting point. Its structure is similar to that of diamond.
- Silicon is a semiconductor.
- Silicon is used in making microprocessors or silicon chips. A microprocessor is made up of many thousands of transistors arranged on a single chip of silicon.
- Glass is made by heating silicon dioxide in the form of sand with sodium carbonate and calcium carbonate to a temperature of about 1500°C.

CARBON AND ITS COMPOUNDS

- Carbon is widely distributed in nature in the form of coal, petroleum and metal carbonates of electropositive metals.
- All living systems contain carbon compounds. Carbon is also present as CO_2 in the atmosphere.
- The isotope ^{14}C has a half-life of 5770 years and is used in **radiocarbon dating** to determine the age of archaeological specimens of organic origin.

Allotropy of Carbon

- The occurrence of an element in a variety of forms having different physical properties (*e.g.*, crystal shape) but similar chemical properties is known as *allotropy*. The various forms are called the allotropic forms, or simply as allotropes.
- The two well-known allotropes of carbon were **diamond** and **graphite**.
- A third form of carbon known as **Fullerenes** were discovered by H.W. Kroto, R.F. Curl and R.E. Smalley.

Diamond

- Due to its hardness, it is used for cutting glass, making bores for rock drilling and for making abrasives.
- Diamond is used in jewellery as a precious stone. When it is cut at certain angles and polished, brilliant light is refracted from its surfaces, which makes it a precious gem.
- It is used for grinding and polishing hard materials. Diamond is also used for making dies for drawing thin wires from metals.

Graphite

- Graphite is used in making electrodes. It is used as a lubricant for heavy machines.
- It is used in the manufacture of crucibles which can withstand high temperatures.

Coal

- Coal is used as a fuel for gas. It is used also in the manufacturing of fuel gases like coal gas, water gas, producer gas etc.

Charcoal

- Charcoal is prepared by strong heating of wood in a limited supply of air.
- ***Wood Charcoal*** is highly porous used as an adsorbent for gases and in making gas masks.

IMPORTANT FACTS

- ***Coal gas*** is a mixture of H_2, CH_4, CO and other gases like N_2, C_2H_4, CO_2 etc. It is obtained by the destructive distillation of coal at about 1000°C.
- ***Natural Gas*** is a mixture of gaseous hydrocarbons viz. methane (85%), ethane, propane, butane etc. Liquefied petroleum gas (LPG) is also a mixture of gaseous hydrocarbons mainly butane and propane.
- ***Gobar Gas*** contains CH_4, CO_2 and H_2 and is produced by the fermentation of gobar in absence of air.
- ***Oil Gas*** is a mixture of H_2, CH_4, C_2H_4, CO and other gases like CO_2. It is obtained by the thermal cracking of Kerosene oil. It is used in laboratories.

- *Animal Charcoal* or bone black is prepared by destructive distillation of bones. The carbon content in it is 10% and is mainly used for decolourising sugar syrup in the manufacture of sugar and other organic substance.
- *Sugar Charcoal* is the purest form of amorphous carbon and is obtained by the action of concentrated H_2SO_4 on cane sugar.

Carbon Compounds

Carbon Monoxide

- Carbon monoxide is commercially produced by the passage of steam over hot coke. This reaction also produces hydrogen and the mixture of CO and H_2 known as **water gas** or **synthesis gas.**
- Carbon monoxide is a colourless, odourless and an extremely poisonous gas.
- It binds tightly to the iron atom of the haemoglobin in red blood cells and thereby inhibits their ability to bind with oxygen and carry it to the brain and other body tissues.

Carbon Dioxide

- Carbon dioxide is formed in the combustion of carbon and other fossil fuels in an excess of oxygen.
- Carbon dioxide is a colourless gas.
- It is heavier than air. Unlike carbon monoxide, CO_2 is not poisonous but does not support life in humans or animals. It can cause suffocation and eventually death on account of lack of oxygen.
- Carbon dioxide is slightly soluble in water. Soda water and other aerated soft drinks are solutions of CO_2 in water under pressure.
- The Main Application of CO_2 is as a Refrigerant. Solid carbon dioxide can sublime to the gaseous state without passing through the liquid stage and hence is called **DRY ICE.** It is used as a coolant for preserving perishable food items such as meat.

Hydrocarbons

- Hydrocarbons are organic compounds containing carbon and hydrogen only. Example : methane, ethane, propane, butane, benzene.
- Hydrocarbons occur abundantly in nature, largely in petroleum, natural gas and coal.
- They can be considered as the parent organic compounds from which other organic compounds are derived.
- The major use of hydrocarbons is as fuels and as petro-chemicals.
- Hydrocarbons are of two types:
  - *(i)* ***Saturated Hydrocarbons:*** A hydrocarbon in which the carbon atoms are attached by single covalent bonds only is called a *saturated hydrocarbons.* The hydrocarbons methane, ethane, propane and butane form a series of carbon compounds belonging to a family of alkanes.
  - *(ii)* ***Unsaturated Hydrocarbons:*** A hydrocarbon in which the two carbon atoms are attached by a double bond or a triple bond is called an *unsaturated hydrocarbon.* Unsaturated hydro-carbons are of two types:
    - (*a*) those containing double bonds—*alkenes,* and
    - (*b*) those containing triple bonds—*alkynes.*

BIOLOGY

Biology is the Study of life and living organism. The term biology was coined by Jean Baptiste Lamarck and G. Treviranus independently in 1802.

CELL : THE BASIC UNIT OF LIFE

- All organisms are composed of cells. The cell is the structural basis of life. Organisms may be made up of one or more cells.
- If the organisms are made up of a single cell, they are called *unicellular organisms*, e.g. amoeba, chalamydomonas, bacteria, and many fungi; while the organisms made up of a few cells (e.g. some algae and fungi) to several million cells are called *multicellular organisms*.
- Robert Hooke in 1665, was the first to identify cells.
- In the early 19th century, Matthias Schleiden, Theodor Schwan, and others recognized the universal occurence and importance of cells and formulated a comprehensive cell theory in 1838-39 which states that:
  - (*i*) The cell is the smallest unit of living matter capable of assimilation, respiration, growth and reproduction; and
  - (*ii*) The cell can live independently and reproduce its own kind (in other words, all cells come from pre-existing cells).
- Max Schutze (1861) proposed that living matter of an organism is protoplasm and the cell is simply an accumulation of protoplasm limited by an outer membrane and containing a nucleus.

Types of Cells

The living organisms have two types of cells.

- **Prokaryotic Cells:** These are the cells without definite nucleus, i.e. nucleus is not bound by a nuclear membrane. It is called nucleoid *e.g.* bacteria, Blue-Green Algae. (Cyanobac-teria) PPLO, etc.
- **Eukaryotic Cells** : These have a definitely organised nucleus with a definite nuclear membrane which surrounds the genetic material and it has membrane bound cell organelle such as mitochondria, lysosomes, chloroplasts etc., *e.g.* animal cells, plant cells, fungi, algae, etc.

Structure of the Cell

Plasma Membrane

- Most cellular organelles such as mitochondria, chloroplasts, lysosomes, peroxisomes, Golgi apparatus, nucleus and endoplasmic reticulum are all enclosed by the unit membrane.
- The cell surface membrane or plasma membrane is the outer covering of each cell. It is present in cells of plants, animals and microorganisms.
- Plasma membrane is a living, thin, delicate, elastic, selectively permeable membrane. It is about 7 nm (70Å) thick.
- Plasma membrane permits the entry and exit of some materials in the cells. It also prevents movement of some other materials. Therefore, the plasma membrane is called a selectively permeable membrane.

Cell Wall

- In plant cells, there occurs a rigid cell wall which lies outside the plasma membrane. Cell wall is non-living and freely permeable and is secreted by the cell itself for the protection of its plasma membrane and cytoplasm.
- It determines the shape of a plant cell and prevents desiccation of cells.
- It is made up of a fibrous polysaccaride (carbohydrate) called cellulose. The plant cell wall, thus, consists of tiny cellulose fibres called microfibrils, glued together by a mixture of polysaccharides.
- Each microfibril is made up of thousands of cellulose molecules bound together by pectins and hemicellulose.

Functions of Cell Wall: Cell wall of plants has the following functions:

- It permits the plant cell to become turgid. As water enters the vacuole by osmosis, the plant cell expands. The cell wall has to be strong enough to resist this expansion and so enable the cell to become turgid.
- It provides mechanical strength to support the cell. The cellulose microfibrils are very strong. The strength may be increased by the addition of lignin in tissues such as xylem. In cells such as collenchyma, extra cellulose is added to the cell wall to increase mechanical support.
- It is freely permeable to water and substances in solution.
- It has narrow pores, called pits, through which fine stands of cytoplasm, called plasmodesmata, are able to pass. These intercellular connec-tions allow exchange of materials between the living cell contents.
- The cell walls of adjacent cells are glued together by the middle lamella. Middle lamella is a jelly-like substance made up of calcium and magnesium pectate.

Nucleus

- The nucleus is a major, centrally located spherical cellular component. It is bounded by two nuclear membrane, both forming a nuclear envelope.
- Nuclear envelope encloses a space between two nuclear membranes and is connected to a system of membranes called the ER.
- The nuclear envelope separates the nucleus from the cytoplasm.
- The nuclear envelope contains many pores (the nuclear pores) and encloses the liquid ground substance, the nucleoplasm. Nucleopores allow transfer of materials between the nucleoplasm and the cytoplasm. Within nucleoplasm are embedded two types of nuclear structures–the nucleolus and chromatin material.
- The nucleolus may be one or more in number and is not bounded by any membrane. It is rich in protein and RNA (ribonucleic acid) molecules and is the site of ribosome formation.
- Nucleolus is known as factory of ribosomes. Ribosomes are helpful in protein synthesis in the cytoplasm.

Functions

- The nucleus controls all metabolic activities of the cell. If the nucleus is removed from a cell, the protoplasm ultimately dries up and dies.
- It regulates the cell cycle.
- It is concerned with the transmission of hereditary traits from the parent to offspring.

Cytoplasm

- The part of the cell which occurs between the plasma membrane and nuclear envelope is called the cytoplasm.
- The inner granular mass of the cytoplasm is often called endoplasm, while the outer, clearer (glassy) layer is called cell cortex or ectoplasm.
- Cytoplasm consists of an aqueous ground substance, the cytosol, containing a variety of cell organelles and other inclusion such as insoluble waste and storage products (starch, glycogen, lipid, etc.)

Ribosomes

- Ribosomes are dense, spherical and grannular particles which occur freely in the matrix (cytosol) or remain attached to the endoplasmic reticulum (RER).
- Chemically, the major constituents of ribsomes are the ribonucleic acid (RNA) and proteins. Lipids are not present in ribosomes.
- Ribosomes are not bounded by a membrane. They are present both in prokaryotic and eukaryotic cells (except mammalian RBC).
- Ribosomes play an important part in the synthesis of proteins.

Golgi Apparatus (Golgi Body or Golgi Complex)

- Golgi apparatus consists of a set of membrane-bounded, fluid-filled vesicles, vacuoles and flattened cisternae (closed sacs).
- Cisternae are usually stacked together (placed one above the other) in parallel rows. It exists as an extensive network near the nucleus in the animal cells.
- Cisternae are formed at one end of the stack, called *cis* face of Golgi. They are budded off as vesicles at the other face of Golgi apparatus, called *trans* face of Golgi.
- Golgi apparatus is absent in bacteria, blue-green algae, mature sperms and red blood cells of mammals and other animals.

***Functions*:**

- The main function of the Golgi apparatus is secretory. Golgi apparatus acts as a way-station or assembly area for the storage, processing and packaging of various cellular secretions. It packages materials synthesized in the cell and dispatches them either to intracellular targets such as plasma membrane and lyysosomes or extracellular targets (*e.g.*, zymogens).
- It produces vacuoles or secretory vesicles which contain cellular secretions, e.g., enzymes, proteins, cellulose, melanin pigment, lacto-protein of milk, etc.
- Golgi apparatus is also involved in the synthesis of cell wall, plasma membrane and lysosomes.

Lysosomes

- Lysomes are simple tiny spherical sac-like structures evenly distributed in the cytoplasm.
- Each lysosome is a small vesicle surrounded by a single membrane and contains powerful enzymes. These enzymes are capable of digesting or breaking down all organic materials.
- Lysosomal enzymes are made by RER.

***Functions*:**

- Lysosomes serve as intracellular digestive system, hence, called digestive bags. They destroy any foreign material which enter the cell such as bacteria and virus. In this way they protect the cells from bacterial infection.

- Lysosomes also remove the worn out and poorly working cellular organelles by digesting them to make way for their new replace-ments. In this way, they remove the cell debris and are also known as demolition squads, scavengers and cellular house-keepers. Thus, lysosomes form a kind of garbage disposal system of the cell.
- During breakdown of cell structure, when the cell gets damaged, lysosome may burst and the enzymes eat up their own cells. Therefore, lysosomes are also known as suicide bags of a cell.

Mitochondria

- The mitochondria (singular : mitochondrion) are tiny bodies of varying shpaes (cylindrical, rod-shaped, spherical) and size (0.2 mm to 2 mm), distributed in the cytoplasm.
- Each mitochondrion is bounded by a double membrane envelope. Outer membrane is porous. The inner membrane is thrown into folds and, therefore, have an area several times the surface of area of the outer membrane.
- The interior cavity of the mitochondria is filled with a proteinaceous (gel-like) matrix which contains a few small-sized ribosomes, a circular DNA molecule and phosphate granules.
- Mitochondria are absent in bacteria and the red blood cells of mammals.

***Functions*:**

- Mitochondria are sites of cellular respiration. They use molecular oxygen from air to oxidise the carbohydrates and fats (lipids) present in the cell to carbon dioxide and water vapour.
- Oxidation releases energy, a portion of which is used to form ATP (adenosine triphosphate).
- Since the mitochondria synthesize, energy-rich compounds (ATP), they are known as 'power house' of the cell. The energy stored in ATP is used by the cell.

Plastids

- Plastids occur in most plant cells and are absent in animal cells. Like the mitochondria, the plastids also have their own genome (i.e., DNA) and ribosomes.
- They are self-replicating organelles like the mitochondria, *i.e.*, they have the power to divide.
- Plastids are of following three types:
  1. **Chromoplasts:** Coloured plastids except green colour).
  2. **Chloroplasts:** Green-coloured plastids.
  3. **Leucoplasts:** The colourless plastids.

Chloroplasts

- Chloroplasts are present in green algae and higher plants.
- They have the green pigment called chlorophyll and they are involved in the photosynthesis of food. So chloroplasts are the "kitchens of the cells".
- Each chloroplast is bounded by two unit membranes like the mitochondria. It shows two distinct regions:
  1. **Grana** are stacks of membrane-bounded, flattened discoid sacs containing the molecules of

chlorophyll. They are the main functional units of chloroplasts.

2. **Stroma** is the homogeneous matrix in which grana are embedded. Stroma contains a variety of photosynthetic enzymes, starch grains, DNA and ribosomes.

- Granum is the site of light reaction during photosynthesis, while stroma is the site of dark reaction during photosynthesis.

Functions: Plastids perform the following functions:

- Chloroplasts trap solar energy and utilise it to manufacture food for the plant.
- Chromoplasts impart various colours to flowers to attract insects for pollination.
- Leucoplasts store food in the form of carbohydrates (starch), fats and protein.

Vacuoles

- Vacuoles are fluid-filled or solid-filled and membrane-bounded spaces. They are a kind of storage sacs.
- In animal cells, the vacuoles if present are small and temporary. They store water, glycogen and proteins.
- The vacuolar membrane is typically a single unit membrane and is often associated with the maintenance of water balance (e.g., they serve as osmoregulatory organelles in protozoans) or ingestion of nutrient material (food vacuole).
- Thus, food vacuole of a single celled organism such as amoeba or Paramecium contains the food item that the animals has consumed.
- In plant cells, the vacuoles are large, distinct and permanent.
- In mature plant cells the vacuole occupies almost the entire (*i.e.*, 90%) volume of the cell. Because of central position of vacuole, the nucleus and other cell organelles in plant cells are pushed near the boundary wall.
- The vacuole is bounded by a membrane, called tonoplast. The vacuole is filled with cell sap which is a watery solution rich in sugars, amino acids, proteins, minerals and metabolic wastes (such as anthocyanins, alkaloids).

Functions:

- Vacuoles help to maintain the osmotic pressure in a cell (osmoregulation). They store toxic metabolic by-products or end products of plant cells.
- They provide turgidity and rigidity to the plant cells.

Peroxisomes

- Peroxisomes are small (0.3 to 1.5 mm in diameter) and spherical organelles containing powerful oxidative enzymes. They are bounded by a single membrane.
- Peroxisomes are mostly found in kidney and liver cells.
- Inner contents of peroxisomes are finely granular, but sometimes a crystalline core is visible by electron microscope in the centre of peroxisomes. This crystalline core is a crystallized protein, called catalase enzyme.

Functions:

- Peroxisomes are specialised for carrying out some oxidative reactions, such as detoxification or removal of toxic substances from the cell.

Centrosome

- Centrosome is found only in animal cells. It is not bounded by any membrane but consists of two granule-like centrioles.
- Centrioles are hollow and cylinderical structure which are made up of microtubles.
- In plant cells, the polar caps perform the function of centrioles.

Functions:

- Centrosome helps in cell division in animal cells. During cell division centrioles migrate to the poles of animal cells and are involved in the formation of the spindle.
- In plant cells, cell division involves polar caps for the spindle formation.

ORGANISATION OF THE LIVING BODY

Plant Tissues

- A group of similar cells specialized for a particular function is called a tissue.
- Tissues in plants are classified into two major groups— meristematic tissues and permanent tissues.

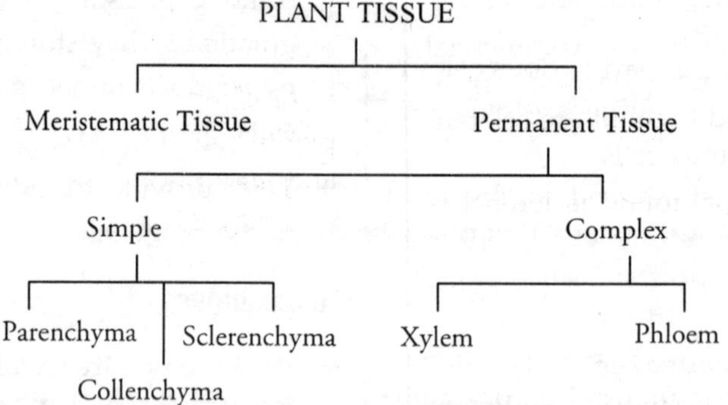

Meristematic Tissues

- These tissues consist of cells that are capable of active and repeated division. The cells are closely packed and so there are no intercellular spaces.
- The cell walls are thin, and the cytoplasm dense and without vacuoles. The cells are spherical or polygonal in shape with large nuclei.
- Meristematic tissue is found mostly at the tips of roots and stems where there is active growth.

Permanent Tissues

These consist of cells that have lost their capacity for division. Though derived from meristematic tissues, they assume different permanent shapes; and, depending upon their structure, permanent tissues are classified into simple or complex tissues.

(a) Simple Permanent Tissues : These are composed of similar cells. There are three distinct types of simple permanent tissues: parenchyma, collenchyma and sclerenchyma.

- *Parenchyma* is a living tissue consisting mostly of round or oval thin-walled cells with intercellular spaces, and constitutes the bulk of the plant body. The main functions of this tissue are manufacture and storage of food, depending upon the plastids that are present.

- ***Collenchyma*** consists of fairly elongated living cells that thicken particularly along the corners. The cell walls are made of mixture of cellulose and pectin. These cells are found mostly in herbaceous plants, providing mechanical support.
- ***Sclerenchyma*** consists of long, narrow, fibre like cells, pointed at both ends and with thick lignified walls that gradually lose protoplasm and so are dead when fully formed. Sclerenchymatous cells are usually found in patches and provide mechanical strength.
  - ❑ The fibres of commercial importance derived from jute and coconut are sclerenchymatous cells.
  - ❑ Oval or round sclerenchymatous cells found in fruits like the pear are called stone cells or *sclereids.*

(*b*) Complex Permanent Tissues: A complex tissue is made up of different types of cells, but working together as a unit. Xylem and phloem are the two complex tissues, both are concerned with the transportation of materials besides the epidermal tissue.

- ***Xylem:*** Commonly called wood, it conducts water and raw materials from the roots to the leaves and consists of two major cell types, tracheids and vessels, both of which are dead.
- ***Phloem:*** This tissue transports manufactured food from the leaves to all other parts of the plant and consists chiefly of sieve tubes and companion cells, both of which are *living.*

Morphology of the Plant

➥ There are three kinds of organs in plants—roots, stems, and leaves.

➥ The reproductive structures-cones and flowers—of higher plants are sometimes referred to as separate organs. Actually they are specialized stems.

➥ Roots, stems, and leaves are called vegetative organs.

Root Systems

➥ The first root to develop in a plant is the primary root. It arises from the embryo contained in the seed. When the seed germinates, the tiny rootlet emerges and penetrates the soil.

➥ Generally, the root systems of seed plants fall into two classes—*fibrous* and *tap root.*

➥ In the fibrous system, there are many branches that are about equal in diameter. A system of this kind may be very extensive.

➥ In a tap root system, the primary root that develops from the embryo grows faster than the branches that arise from it. It becomes a main root that grows down through the soil, with much smaller roots branching from it.

➥ Roots anchor the plant body firmly in the soil. They absorb water and mineral nutrients from the soil, conduct these materials upward into stems, and transport food downward from stems.

➥ Many roots store food produced during the growing season, such as carrots and beets. In these, food is accumulated in the roots during the first year, flowers and seeds are produced in the second.

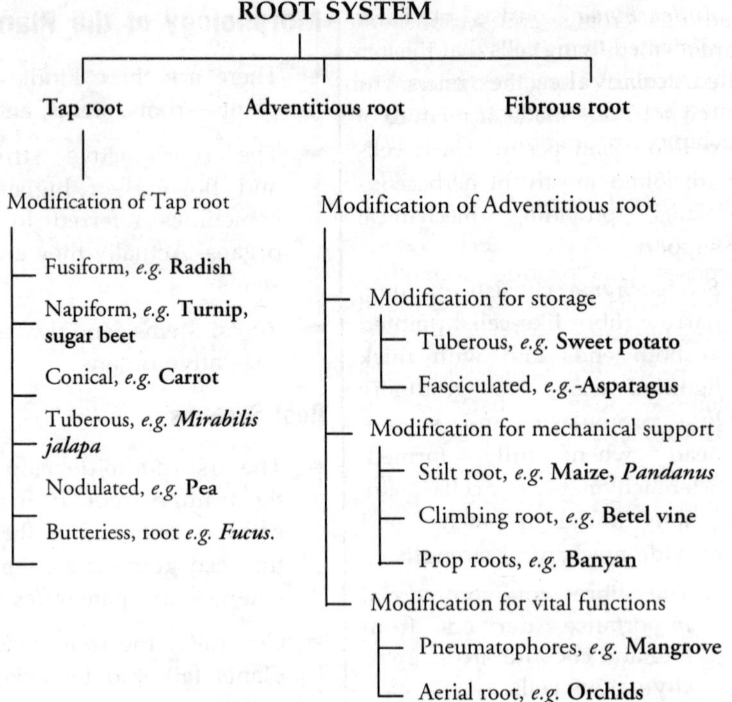

- Certain roots arise neither from primary nor secondary roots but from stems or leaves. They are called *adventitious roots*.
- A new plant can develop from the bulb of the tulip plant because adventitious roots grow from it. This is called *vegetative propagation*.
- The stems of certain plants, such as the banyan tree, bear aerial roots. These grow downward until they penetrate the ground. They are called *prop roots*.
- Mangrove trees, which grow along ocean shores in tropical regions, also put forth prop roots. They reach the water and penetrate the sandy bed.
- The aerial roots of orchids play an important part in the life of the plant. They serve to anchor to the tree or other supports on which the orchid grows.
- They also absorb water from the moisture in the air or from the rain. The *stilt roots* supporting structure in maize and sugarcane.

Stems

- The first stem develops from the plumule of embryo. A miniature stem emerges as the seed germinates.
- Generally; it makes its way upward through the soil and into the air. As long as its growing point remains alive, it becomes longer. In time, branches develop.
- Stems that grow above the ground in this way are called aerial stems.
- Most essential characteristics of stem is that it bears nodes and internodes and buds is present at the nodes.
- In certain plants, such as potatoes, we find fleshy, thickened undergroud stems known as *tubers*. They develop buds-"eyes" of potatoes.
- A *bulb* is very short underground stem that bears a cluster of thick, overlapping leaves. These leaves store food. Onions, tulips, lilies, and other familiar plants develop bulbs, each of which can give rise to a new plant.

- Gladiolus, crocus, and various other plants form underground stems called ***corms.*** These resemble bulbs somewhat. However, the stems are much more prominent and the leaves are generally smaller and thinner than those of bulbs.
- Like roots, stems serve several purposes. They produce and support leaves, which are the food-making centres of plants.
- They provide passage ways along which various substances are transported within the plant.
- Stems also serve as a storage place for foods. And in certain cases, parts of stems propagate plants.

Leaves

- The stem and leaves constitute the shoot system of the plant. Leaves are perhaps the most important vegetative organ of the plants.
- Generally a leaf consists of a *leaf stalk*, or *petiole*, and the *leaf proper*, called *a blade*.
- In many trees, each leaf consists of a single blade and petiole.
- In other trees the leaf blade is divided into several *leaflets* each attached to the same petioles. The latter is called *complex*, and the former, *simple* leaf.
- The leaves of most plants have a similar microscopic structure. There is a surface layer of cells, the epidermis, covered on the outside with a waxy coating or cuticle. The hairs found on some leaves are outgrowths of epidermal cells.
- The epidermis has various openings, or pores, known as stomata (singular, "stoma").
- Gases such as carbon dioxide, oxygen, and water vapour pass in or out through these pores. Each stoma is surrounded by a pair of cells called guard cells.

Flower

- Clove is obtained from flower bud. Flower is the reproductive part of plant.
- In flower Calyx, Corolla, Androecium and Gynoecium are found. Out of these androecium is male sex organ and the gynoecium is female sex organ.
- **Androecium:** Unit of androecium is stamen. There is one or more stamens in the androecium. Pollen grains are found in anther.
- **Gynoecium :** Unit of gynoecium is carpel. There are three parts of carpel—***1.*** Ovary, **2.** Style and ***3.*** Stigma.
- Flower having both stomen and carpel is called bisexual flower.
- **Pollination:** After maturation of Anther, the process of transfer of pollen grains to stigma is called pollination. Pollination is of two types—1. Self-pollination 2. Cross pollination.
- **Fertilization:** Pollen tube reaches the egg cell after entering ino the ovule through a pore called micropyle. After that a male nucleus fuse with egg-cell. This is called fertilization. Fertilized egg is called zygote.

  In angiosperm, the fertilization is triple fusion where as in other category of plants it is double fusion.
- **Syngamy:** Fusion of gametes resulting in the formation of diploid zygote is called syngamy.
- **Parthenocarpy:** In some plants fruits are developed from ovary without fertilization. This type of fruit is called parthenocarpy. Normally these types of fruits are seedless. Example: Banana, Papaya, Orange, Grapes, Pine-apple etc.

- In the majority of flowering plants, out of four magaspores, the ratio of functional and degenerate megaspores is 1 : 3.
- Parthenogenesis, Apogamy and saprophytic budding are an irregular mode of reproduction resulting in the development of embryo without fertilization.
- Bulbil take part in vegetative reproduction.
- The inflorescence of wheat is spike.
- Photoperiodism affects the flowering of plant.
- Pollination in maize takes place by air.

Formation of Fruits

- Fruit is a matured or ripened ovary developed after fertilization.
- Formation of fruit takes place from ovary.

  Fruits are divided into three types:
  1. Simple fruits: like Banana, Guava etc.
  2. Aggregate fruits: Strawberry, Custard apple etc.
  3. Composite fruits: Jackfruit, Mulberry etc.
- In the development of some fruits, Calyx, Corolla and Thalamus takes part. These types of fruits are calld False fruits.

  Example: Apple, Jackfruit, Pear etc.
- Water of coconut is liquid nucellus.
- The medicinal plant used in the preparation of skin care is aloevera.
- In the seed of neem major pesticidal properties are present.
- The alkaloid naturally found in Coffee, Cocoa and Cola nut is Caffeine.
- Hot peppers are hot due to presence of capsaicin.
- A clone is a group of genetically identical individuals obtained through micropropogation.
- Origin place of maize is America.
- Seedless fruit are of no use in coconut and pomegranate.
- Papaya is the source of papain.
- Vivipary germination is found in mangroove plant.

Some Fruits and Their Edible Parts

Fruit	Edible Part
Apple	Fleshy thalamus
Pear	Fleshy thalamus
Mango	Mesocarp
Guava	Entire fruit
Grapes	Pericarp & Placenta
Papaya	Mesocarp
Coconut	Endosperm
Tomato	Pericarp and Placenta
Banana	Mesocarp & Endocarp
Wheat	Starchy endosperm
Cashewnut	Peduncle & Cotyledons
Litchi	Fleshy Aril
Gram	Cotyledons & Embroyo
Groundnut	Cotyledons
Mulberry	Entire fruit
Jackfruit	Bract, Perianth & Seed
Pine apple	Bract & Perianth
Orange	Juicy hair

Animal Tissues

Animal tissues are divided into four major classes on the basis of their functions.

Epithelial Tissues

- It consists of closely-packed cells that form a continuous layer covering the surface of organs or lining the cavities of the body.
- Since the cells are closely packed, there is very little space between them; the absence of intercellular space is characteristic of epithelial tissues.

- The cells in this tissue remain attached to the basement membrane that separates it from the other tissues that lie beneath.
- Though, the primary function of the epithelium is protection, it may be sensory or may be concerned with absorption, secretion, or reproduction.

Connective Tissues

- The connective tissues include a variety of tissues that are specialized to connect and bind the various parts of the body together and to provide support.
- The presence of a matrix composed of intercellular material secreted by the cells is a characteristic feature of connective tissues.
- There are five distinct types of connective tissues: areolar tissue, adipose tissue, cartilage, bone and blood.

(a) *Areolar Tissue*:

- This consists of irregular cells scattered in a soft matrix traversed by elastic yellow fibres and bundles of tough white fibres.
- The sub-cutaneous connective tissue below the skin is a good example of areolar tissue. It binds the skin with the underlying parts.

(b) *Adipose Tissue*:

- This is a connective tissue modified for storing up fat. The matrix is less conspicuous. The cells are generally large, and are round or oval in shape, with prominent central vacuoles that push the cytoplasm and the nuclei to the periphery of the cells.
- The vacuoles in the cells contain fat. Adipose tissue is found between the internal organs and below the skin. The yellow bone marrow is also an example of adipose tissue.

(c) *Cartilage*:

- This is a supporting tissue. The intercellular material or matrix is slightly hardened by the deposition of inorganic salts, chiefly those of calcium.
- The rounded cells lie mostly in groups within special spaces called lacunae.
- The matrix may be traversed by elastic fibres, or white fibres, or by both, and accordingly it comes to have different textures.
- The bridge of the nose and the external ears are supported by cartilage.

(d) *Bone*:

- This is another, perhaps more familiar, supporting tissue, which is characterized by its hard matrix impregnated with large quantities of inorganic salts of calcium and phosphorus.
- Long bones have large central cavities containing the yellow marrow that stores fat. At the ends of these bones are several small spaces containing the red marrow where red blood cells are produced.
- The hard and solid part of the bone is the bone tissue.

(e) *Blood*:

- This is a connective tissue with a liquid matrix adapted for the transportation of nutritive materials, respiratory gases, excretory materials and other substances from one part of the body to another.
- This tissue not only connects the different parts but also establishes a continuity within the body. It consists of 55% plasma and 45% blood cells.

- The plasma is a straw-coloured, watery part containing about 90% water, the remainder being solids, like salts and proteins, in solution.
- *Fibrinogen*, a soluble protein of plasma, precipitates into fibrin threads when the blood clots.
- The blood cells are of three kinds—***red blood cells, white blood cells***, and ***blood platelets***.

➡ The red blood cells (erythrocytes) form the vast majority. The blood contains about 5 million of them per cubic millimetre. Each red cell is a circular, bioconcave disc without a nucleus. It contains haemoglobin, the respiratory pigment that chiefly carries oxygen from the lungs to the other parts of the body.

➡ The nucleated white blood cells (leucocytes), numbering about 9000 per cubic millimetre, are shapeless and contain no pigment. They are the ***'police force'*** of the body and protect it from disease-producing organisms.

➡ The blood platelets (thrombocytes), the smallest of the blood cells, are responsible for the clotting of the blood when blood vessels are damaged.

Muscular Tissues

➡ Muscles constitute nearly half the weight of the body, and are composed of elongated cells adapted for contraction and relaxation and thereby cause movement.

➡ Since muscle cells are drawn out into long structures they are also known as muscle fibres.

➡ These are of three kinds: *Non-Striated Muscle, Striated Muscle,* and *Cardiac Muscles.*

➡ **Non-striated Muscle:**

- This consists of spindle-shaped cells, each with a centrally-located long nucleus. The cells are arranged to form a sheet of muscular tissue, commonly found in the wall of the digestive tract, urinary bladder and other internal organs.
- Since one is not aware of their contraction, they are also called *involuntary muscles.*

➡ **Striated Muscle:**

- These muscles are attached to the skeleton they are also called skeletal muscles.
- Each cell in this muscle is a long cylindrical structure with longitudinal (*i.e.* lengthwise) and cross striations and has a number of nuclei placed along the periphery.
- The cells are bundled up and enclosed by connective tissue sheaths. These sheaths continue as the tendon that connects muscles with the bones.
- Since their contraction is under conscious control, they are also called *voluntary muscles.*

➡ **Cardiac Muscle:**

- These are found only in the heart and are capable of rhythmical contractions.
- The cells, arranged end to end, branch and unite in such a way as to form a continuous network. Each cell has a single centrally located nucleus and a striated appearance.

Nervous Tissues

➡ This is composed of highly specialized cells called *neurons* that are capable of receiving stimuli, conducting impulses from one part of the body to another, and discharging these impulses.

➡ Each neuron has a cell body with a central nucleus and two sets of fibres called *dendrites* which carry the message towards the cell body, and a single long fibre called *axon* which carries the message away from the cell body. Axons may be naked or insulated by a fatty substance.

NUTRITION

- Food is any substance used by a living body to aid growth, maintain and repair body tissues, regulate body processes, and supply energy.
- Nutrition is the process by which food is taken in and used by body.
- Nutrition may also be defined as the science concerned with the study of food and its relation to health.

Types of Food Stuffs

- A living organism consists largely of compounds of carbon plus water. About 60% of most animals and over 90% of most plants is water.
- The carbon compounds of organisms are called *organic compounds* (carbohydrates, lipids, proteins and vitamins). An organism also contains small amounts of inorganic matter like mineral salts.

Carbohydrates

- These are compounds containing carbon, hydrogen and oxygen.
- Some common sources of carbohydrates are rice, wheat, maize, potato, banana, sugar etc.
- Carbohydrates are divided into three main groups:
  1. **Monosaccharides** are simple sugars consisting of three or more carbon atoms. Examples - Ribose, deoxyribose, (pentoses); glucose, fructose and galactose (hexoses.)
  2. **Disaccharides** are formed by the union of two monosaccharides. Examples – Maltose (malt sugar) = glucose + glucose, lactose (milk sugar) = glucose + galactose, sucrose (cane sugar) = glucose + fructose.
  3. **Polysaccharides** are made up large number (300 to over 1000) of monosaccharides units. Example – starch and cellulose are common in plants; glycogen and chitin are common in animals.

Functions of Carbohydrate

- Carbohydrate works as fuel. During the process of respiration, glucose break into CO_2 and H_2O with the release of energy. One gram of glucose gives 4.2 kilo calories energy.
- Glucose is the source of immediate energy production in the cell.
- Nucleic acids are polymers of nucleosides and nucleotides and contain pentose sugar.
- Lactose of milk is formed from glucose and glactose.
- Glucose is used for the formation of fat and amino acid.
- Carbon skeleton of monosaccharides is used in the formation of fatty acid, chitin, cellulose etc.

Fats

- Though these are also compounds of carbon, hydrogen and oxygen, the amount of oxygen present is much less than that in the carbohydrates molecule.
- A molecule of fat consists of fatty acids and glycerol.
- Fats contain twice as much energy as carbohydrates, and so are best suited for storing energy. This explains

why the body converts excess carbohydrates into fats.

- Apart from being an important source of energy, fat also provide important structural components.
- Vegetable oils, fatty meat, nuts, butter and milk are natural sources of fat. Plants are the ultimate source of some of the essential fatty acids.

Functions of Fat

- It provides energy to the body.
- It remains under the skin and prevents the loss of heat from the body.
- It make the food material testy.
- It protects different parts of the body from Injury.
- Due to the lack of fat skin gets dried, weight of the body decreases and the development of the body checked.
- Due to the excessiveness of fat the body gets fatty, heart disease takes place and blood pressure increases.
- Rancidity is defined as oxidation of fat and oils that change the taste and smell of food.

Proteins

- In addition to the carbon, hydrogen and oxygen, proteins contain nitrogen with or without phosphorus and sulphur.
- Proteins are extremely complex compounds formed from simple units called amino acids. About twenty different amino acids are found in living organisms.
- Though proteins can yield the same amount of energy as carbohydrates, they provide mostly the building materials for the synthesis of protoplasm.
- After water, proteins are the main constituents of protoplasm.
- Enzymes which control, the life processes in a cell are proteins.
- Proteins can be used for respiration when carbohydrates and lipids are not available.
- The natural sources of protein are fish, meat, egg, milk butter and pulses like beans and peas.

Functions of Protein

- It takes part in the formation of cells, protoplasm and tissues.
- These are important for physical growth. Physical growth hampers by its deficiency. Lack of proteins causes *Kwashiorkor* and *Marasmus* diseases is children.
- In case of necessity these provide energy to tbe body.
- Control the development of genetic characters.
- Helpful in conduction also.

Minerals

- Although needed in very small quantities, mineral salts of various kinds are essential for the proper functioning of the body.
- They yield no energy but are important constituents of certain tissues, besides playing a major role in the regulation of metabolic activities.
- Calcium is the principal component of the skeleton.
- Blood contains about 0.9 per cent salt, most of which is sodium chloride. Certain mineral salts play an important role in the regulation of the osmotic pressure, both within the cells and in the body fluids that surround them.
- The minerals are important for muscular contraction; for transmission of nerve impulses; for the

formation of bones and teeth; for the formation of respiratory pigments; and for the formation of hormones. In fact, they are extremely essential for life.

➥ Meat, eggs, milk, cheese and vegetables are important sources of minerals, and usually, the body gets adequate amounts of them from a normal diet.

Mineral Salts and their Importance

	Minerals	Importance	Source	Requirement
1.	Iron	Essential for the formaiton of haemoglobin	Meat, eggs, green-vegetable	18 mg
2.	Calcium	Principal component of skeleton, and teeth; essential for contraction of heart muscle, and blood coagulation	Milk, eggs, green-vegetables.	1200 mg
3.	Phosphorous	Essential for the formation of bone and teeth; also for muscular contraction; for nucleic acids and phospholipids synthesis; to maintain blood pH.	Milk, eggs	1200 mg
4.	Sodium	Important constituent of body fluids (blood and lymph); transmission of nerve impulses.	Common salt, milk	3500 mg
5.	Potassium	Intracellular osmotic pressure; transmission of nerve impulses	Meat, vegetables.	1000 mg
6.	Iodine	Essential for the formation of thyroxine.	Sea foods, common salt.	0.15 mg
7.	Magnesium	Activates certain enzymes.	Green-vegetables, meat.	400 mg
8.	Sulphur	Constituent of hair, nails and corneous layers of skin	Meat, fish, eggs.	—
9.	Chlorine	Essential for maintaining osmotic pressure of body fluids.	Common salt, milk	3500 mg
10.	Fluorine	Helps in enamel formation of teeth.	Drinking water, milk	—

Vitamins

➥ Though these are needed in very small quantities, they are essential to life, as they form a part of various enzymes and act as catalysts.

➥ Vitamins are simple organic compounds.

➥ In general, the animal body cannot manufacture vitamins, and therefore they must be present in the diet. Plants are our ultimate source of vitamins.

➥ Vitamins are divided into two main groups: Fat-soluble vitamins A, D, E & K. Water-soluble vitamin B complex and C.

Water

➥ We may live for days without food, but not without water. It is an essential constituent of protoplasm and the body fluids.

➥ Water is indispensable for digestion, for metabolic processes, for removal of metabolic wastes, for the distribution and regulation of body heat, and for keeping the body cool.

- The water requirements of the body are met by drinking water and other liquid foods. Even solid foods contain a good amount of water.

DIGESTIVE SYSTEM

- The human digestive system consists of (1) the digestive tract, or the series of structures and organs through which food passes during its processing and (2) other organs that contribute juices necessary for the digestive process.
- The digestive tract begins at the mouth and ends at the anus.

The Mouth

- Ingestion and mastication, or chewing, takes place in the mouth with the help of teeth.
- The tongue helps to work the food into a ball or bolus so that it can be swallowed.
- When food is swallowed the soft palate closes the opening to the nasal cavity and the epiglottis closes the opening to the trachea. The bolus is pushed along the oesophagus to the stomach by *peristalsis*.

The Stomach

- The stomach is a muscular bag in which a meal is temporarily stored. Its contents are passed on gradually to the small intestine.
- *Peristalsis* (type of movement) helps to mix the food with gastric juice, and so turn it into a watery paste called *chyme.*

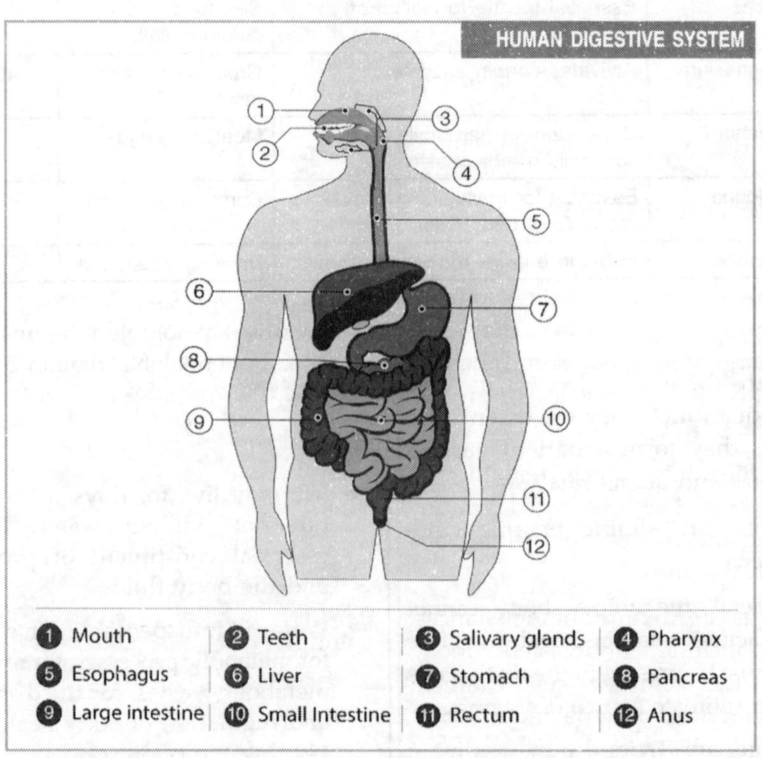

- The mucous helps to protect the stomach wall from its own secretions of hydrochloric acid and pepsin.
- Some absorption of small molecules such as glucose, salt, alcohol takes place in the stomach.

The Small Intestine

- The first, slightly wider part of the small intestine is called the *duodenum.* The duodenum is about 25 cm long. The middle part of intestine is called *jejunum* which is about 8 feet long. The *ileum,* is the longest part of the gut. The ileum is about 12 feet long.
- The later stages of digestion takes place in the small intestine. The walls of the ileum produce intestinal juice, and the digestive processes of the duodenum continue for a time in the ileum.
- Bile and pancreatic juice is also emptied into the duodenum. Nearly all the absorption of digested materials takes place through the wall of the ileum through the villi.

Large Intestine or Colon

- Large intestine is about 5 feet long. The contents of the intestine contain a high proportion of water. The walls of the large intestine absorb much of this water, so it is not lost from the body.
- The semi-solids which remain are called faeces. They are stored in large intestine and passed out at intervals through the anus.
- Faeces is a mixture of substances which include undigested food, mainly the cellulose cell wall of plants and dead bacteria and mucous and dead cells from the gut walls.
- The cells lining the gut have a limited life. They are constantly dying or wearing away and being renewed. Surplus bile and other secretions colour the faeces. The walls of the colon absorb vitamin K which is synthesised by some intestinal bacteria.

Function of Liver

- The liver is found only in vertebrates. Liver is about 1.5 kg. It is the largest gland of body. The liver stores carbohydrate as glycogen, lipids, mineral salts, vitamins A, D, and B_{12}.
- The liver helps to keep the blood sugar (glucose) level constant, which in turn helps to keep the osmotic pressure of the blood constant.
- The liver synthesize a variety of products. These include most of the *plasma proteins* and *bile.* Bile is stored in the gall bladder and passed into the duodenum to help in digestion. Bile contains salts which help in emulsification of fats and absorption of food.
- The liver converts toxins into harmless substances. Many of the toxic by-products of the body's own metabolism are made harmless in the liver. Example : the conversion of nitrogenous waste products to urea.

Absorption

- About 90 per cent of digested food and 10 per cent of water and minerals are absorbed by the small intestine.
- In order to enhance the absorption capacity of the small intestine its epithilial lining is thrown into a number of folds called *villi.*
- The membrane of each villus is further folded into a number of smaller *microvilli.*

- The villi have a rich supply of blood capillaries.
- Simple sugars and amino acids are absorbed, through the intestinal wall into the blood capillaries. These are then carried by the portal vein to the liver before release into general circulation.
- The glycerides and fatty acids are transported usually, via the lymph vessels (lacteals) and thoracic duct to the blood.
- Absorption in stomach occurs only to a limited extent. The large intestine absorbs much of the residual water from undigested food.

RESPIRATION SYSTEM

- All living organisms respire. In fact, respiration is one of the basic characteristics of living organisms so that if an object does not respire, it is considered non-living.
- All living organisms and their component tissues and organs (in case of multicellular organisms) are involved in diverse activities all the time. For all these activities, energy is required which is made available through the process of respiration.
- The energy is made available in the form of ATP *(Adenosine triphosphate)*, referred to as the *energy currency of the cell*, which is synthesised during the breakdown (oxidation) of the food substances consumed by the organisms.
- Not only this, respiration is also the source of *cabon-skeletons* (small organic molecules) that are required for the synthesis, of other complex biomolecules that make up the body of the organism.

Aerobic and Anaerobic Respiration

- Respiration which uses oxygen is called *aerobic respiration*.
- Which respiration takes place in absence of oxygen it is called *anaerobic respiration*.
- Very little energy is released during anaerobic respiration because glucose is not completely broken down into carbon dioxide and water, it is changed into alcohol or lactic acid.
- **Fermentation.** The ***fermentation*** (from the Latin meaning 'to boil') is the partial break down of glucose under anaerobic condition to yield ethanol and CO_2. This is carried out by microorganisms (yeast).

Human Respiratory System

- In human beings lungs are the respiratory organs (pulmonary respiration). Lungs communicate with the atmospheric air through nostrils, pharynx (throat), larynx (voice-box), trachea (windpipe), bronchi and bronchioles.
- These bronchioles terminate into millions of tiny sacs like structures called alveoli.
- The thin walls of alveoli are lined with a network of blood capillaries.
- Alveoli have a far larger surface area than the total skin surface and consequently provide for greater respiratory exchanges.
- Lungs are located in the thorax cavity. Diaphragm and the intercostal muscles, help in contraction and expansion of the lungs during breathing.
- Respiratory gases are exchanged between the alveolar air and the blood in alveolar capillaries.

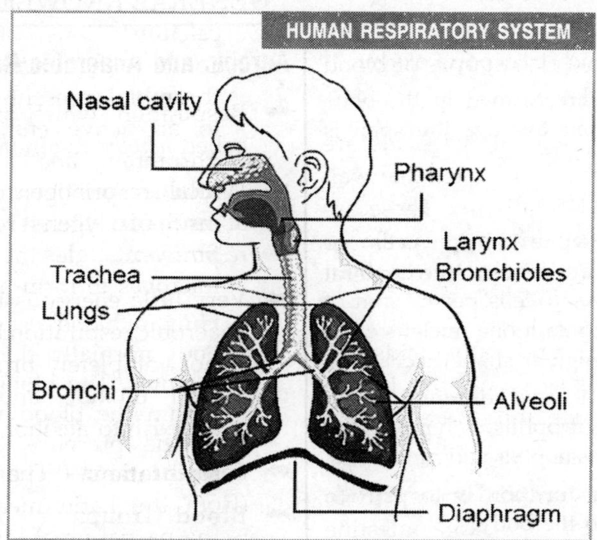

- Most of the oxygen entering the blood combines with haemoglobin to form oxyhaemoglobin and is thus transported by RBC.
- The high pO_2 and low pCO_2 in the alveoli haemoglobin takes up large volumes of oxygen in the lungs.

CIRCULATORY SYSTEM

Human Blood

- Blood is the circulatory fluid of the circulatory system. It is a specialized connective tissue which performs the following vital functions:
  - (*a*) In respiration, transport of oxygen from the lungs to the tissues and of carbondioxide from the tissues to the lungs.
  - (*b*) In nutrition, transport of absorbed food substances to the cells;
  - (*c*) In excretion, transport of metabolic wastes to the kidneys, skin and intestine for their removal;
  - (*d*) In regulation of metabolism, transport of hormones from their site of production to that of their action;
  - (*e*) In other regulatory mechanisms, maintenance of body temperature, osmo-regulation, and acid-base balance;
  - (*f*) In clotting of blood.

Blood and its Composition

- Blood is a red sticky fluid, slightly alkaline in nature. It is composed of a fluid portion, the *plasma* (50-55% of the volume) and three types of corpuscles (45-50% of the blood volume) namely *erythrocytes* (red blood corpuscles, RBC), *leucocytes* (white blood corpuscles or WBC) and *blood platelets*. The corpuscles are embedded in the plasma.
- **Plasma:** Plasma is light yellow fluid with 90-92% water, 6-9% proteins and 1% of dissolved substances. Plasma acts in blood clotting and in defence of the body against diseases.
- **RBC**
  - RBC or red blood cells or erythrocytes number about 5 million per cu mm of blood in man. RBC cells are *devoid of nuclei*.

- RBC mainly consist of *haemoglobin*, a pigment which transports oxygen.
- These cells are formed in the bone marrow. Their average life span is 110 to 120 days.

➥ WBC

- WBC or white blood cells or leucocytes, are larger, fewer-about 5 to 9 thousand cells per cu mm of blood and contain one nucleus each. They are irregular shaped cells.
- They are of five different types namely—neutrophils, lympocytes, basophils, eosinophils and monocytes.
- Their major function is to provide immunity to the body.
- The WBCs have a life span of less than 2 weeks and they are produced in the red bone marrow.
- An overproduction of WBCs results into a disease called leukemia.

➥ Platelets

- Platelets or thrombocytes are small spherical bodies numbering about 300,000 per cu mm of blood.
- They play an important role in the formation of a solid plug called clot at the site of injury to a blood vessel, so as to prevent further loss of blood. Blood platelets are enucleated.
- They live for only a few hours.

➥ Blood Clotting

- In case of injury the blood loss occurs. To prevent this loss, animals have evolved an elaborate mechanism which results in the clotting or coagulation of blood. During this process a series of chemical reactions take place resulting in the formation of a clot that plugs a broken vessel.
- When injury occurs, the damaged tissues and blood platelets release a substance called thromboplastin. On exposure to air the platelets disintegrate. In the presence of calcium ions thrombo-plastin converts the inactive enzyme prothrombin (present in the plasma) to an active enzyme, thrombin. Thrombin finally converts the soluble fibrinogen of plasma into insoluble fibres of fibrin. The fibrin entangles the blood cells and microbes to form a clot.
- Human blood escaping from the body normally clots within 3 to 4 minutes. The blood does not clot within the blood vessels because of the presence of an enzyme, antihrombin (heparin).

➥ Blood Groups

- The four types of blood are called blood groups, and are known by the letters A, B, AB and O.
- Before the blood transfusion can take place it is necessary to make sure that the donor's and recipient's blood will mix together without agglutination.
- Blood groups which mix without agglutination are said to be compatible.

➥ Blood compatibility depends upon chemicals called agglutinogen or antigens on the surface of the red cells, and chemicals called agglutinin or antibodies in the plasma.

➥ There are two types of antigens: A and B; and two types of antibodies: anti-A and anti-B.

- ***Blood group A*** has A antigen on its red cells and anti-B antibody in its plasma.
- ***Blood group B*** has B antigen on its red cells and anti-A antibody in its plasma.
- ***Blood group AB*** has A and B antigens on its red cells and no antibodies in its plasma.
- ***Blood group O*** has no antigens on its red cells but has both anti-A and anti-B antibodies in its plasma.

EXCRETION SYSTEM

- Excretion is the process by which an organism gets rid of the waste products of its metabolism.
- Most waste products become toxic, if allowed to accumulate in an organism, and may fatal from organism. Therefore every living thing has some means of getting rid of its waste products.
- These mechanisms may also be used to get rid of other unwanted substances such as superfluous water, and salts, so as to aid in osmoregulation.

Waste Products

- Urine is composed of water (95%), urea (2%) uric acid (0.05%). Amount of urine secreted per day is 1.5 to 2 litres.
- Protein metabolism results in nitrogenous wastes such as ammonia, urea and uric acid.
- While the carbon dioxide is eliminated by the respiratory system, the nitrogenous materials are taken care of by the specialized excretory organs.

Human Excretory System

- The human excretory or urinary system is typical of that of all mammals. It consists of two *kidneys* where urine is produced by filtration, secretion, and reabsorption; the *ureter tubes* that transport the urine; the *bladder* where the urine is stored; and the *Urethra* through which the urine is voided.
- In humans, kidneys are paired bean-shaped organs about five inches long.
- The functional units of kidney are called nephrons, which are about a 1,000,000 in each kidney.
- Each nephron has Bowman's capsule at one end (a double-walled cup) and the rest part of the nephron is differentiated into a coiled proximal convoluted tubule, a 'U' shaped tin Henle's loops, and a distal convoluted tubule.

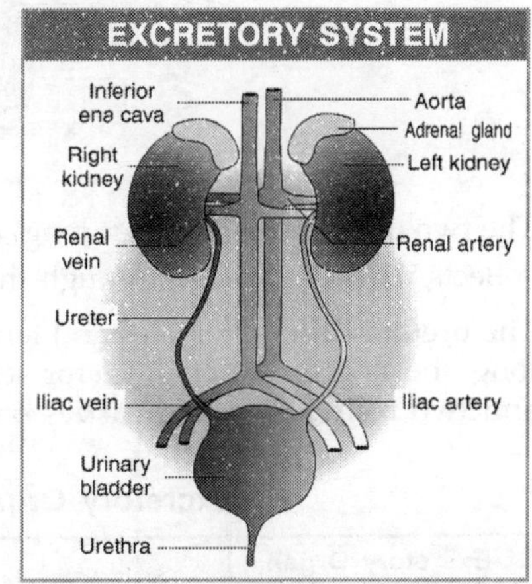

- Urine formation begins in Bowman's capsule which encloses a dense cluster of microscopic blood vessels, the glomerulus.
- Under the driving force of blood pressure, plasma filters from the blood.
- Proteins and about 80 per cent of the water are held back in this process.
- The filtrate passes through the inner wall of the capsule and moves into the tubule.
- The proximal tubule passes from Bow-man's capsule in the renal cortex into the medula and makes a U-turn (Henle's loop).
- The distal convoluted tubule then re-enters the cortex and joins with several other distal tubules to form a collecting tubule, which carries the urine to the renal pelvis and the ureters.
- The ureters move the urine to the bladder in peristaltic waves.

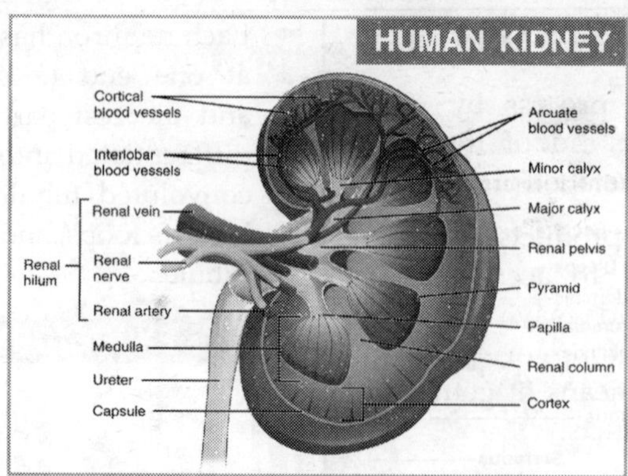

- The two ureters (10-12 inches long) enter the hollow muscular bladder where urine collects until it is voided through the urethra in urination (or micturition).
- The urethra differs in males and females. In human males it is about eight inches long and is also the channel for semen in ejaculation. In women it is only one and two inches long and carries only urine.

Excretory Organs of Human Body

	Excretory Organ	Substances Excreted
1.	Kidneys	Excretion of nitrogenous wastes, Excess of acids or bases, Osmoregulation and homeostasis, Regulation of mineral salts.
2.	Liver	Formation of urea by ornithine cycle, Formation of bile pigments.
3.	Sweat glands of skin	Excretion of mineral salts, small amounts of urea, waxes, sterols and a number of hydrocarbons (sebum), Osmoregulation.
4.	Oil glands of skin	Excretion of carbon dioxide.
5.	Lungs	Excretion of water by evaporation.
6.	Intestine	Excretion of undigested food with bile pigments, salts like calcium phosphate.

THE SKELETAL AND MUSCULAR SYSTEM

- A *skeleton* is a part of an animal which provides support for the rest of the body. Nearly every species of multi-cellular animal has a skeleton. Most are made of hard material *e.g.* bone, cartilage, chitin.
- They are either *exoskeletons* on the outside of the body (*Example:* insect skeletons) or *endoskeletons* inside the body (*Example:* vertebrate skeletons). Some animals have a hydrostatic skeleton which consists of fluid under pressure *e.g.* earthworm.
- ***Bone*** is a very hard material, found only in vertebrates. It is made up of living cells, calcium phosphate (a mineral salt), and collagen (a protein).
- ***Cartilage*** is a second skeletal tissue of vertebrates. It is more plastic and resilient than bone, but not so hard. These properties make it a suitable covering for surfaces where bones meet (articular surfaces) at movable joints.

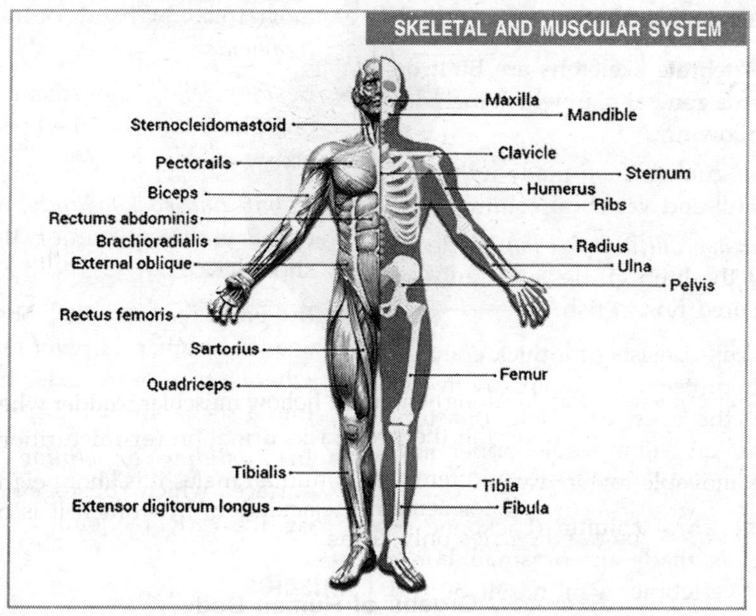

Functions of Skeleton

- The skeleton helps to give body its shape, and provides a frame from which organs are suspended.
- The skeleton surrounds and protects soft parts of the body, *e.g.* in vertebrates, the skull protects the brain.
- In most animals the skeleton provides a system of levers which can be moved, and attachments for the muscles which move them.

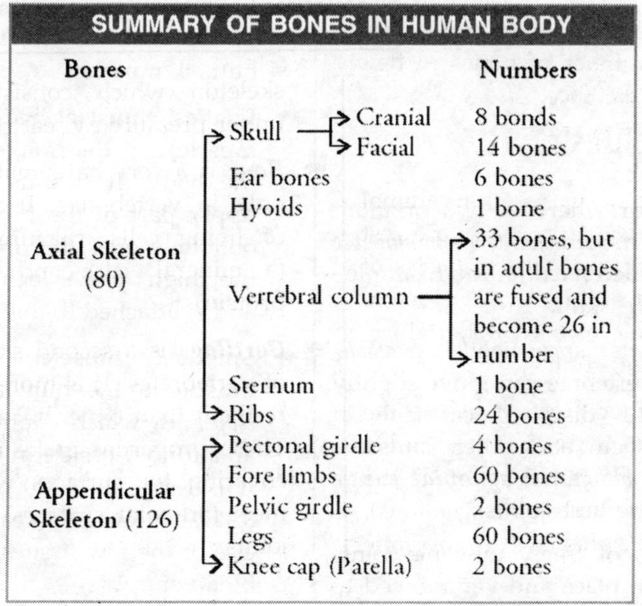

SUMMARY OF BONES IN HUMAN BODY

Bones			Numbers
Axial Skeleton (80)	Skull	Cranial	8 bonds
		Facial	14 bones
	Ear bones		6 bones
	Hyoids		1 bone
	Vertebral column		33 bones, but in adult bones are fused and become 26 in number
	Sternum		1 bone
	Ribs		24 bones
Appendicular Skeleton (126)	Pectoral girdle		4 bones
	Fore limbs		60 bones
	Pelvic girdle		2 bones
	Legs		60 bones
	Knee cap (Patella)		2 bones

The Vertebrate Skeleton

- All vertebrate skeletons are built on the same general plan which includes the following:
  - (*i*) *An axial skeleton*, made up of the skull and vertebral column
  - (*ii*) *An appendicular skeleton*, made up of the limb girdles and limbs or paired fins in fish.
- The skull consists of a thick cranium which protects the brain cavities to house the eyes, ears, and olfactory organs; an immovable upper jaw; and a movable lower jaw.
- The vertebral column (backbone or spine) is made up of small bones called vertebrae. A rat has 46-50 and humans have 33 *vertebrae.*
- The vertebrae form a hollow tube (the neural canal) which contains and protects the spinal cord.
- The *limb girdles* comprise the *pectoral girdle* (shoulder gridle), to which the fore-limbs are attached, and the *pelvic girdle* (hip gridle) to which the hind-limbs are attached.
- Total bones in human endoskeleton are 206 (number of bones in newly born baby is 306).

Joints

- Joints occur wherever two or more bones touch. Some *joints are immovable* and are called ***fixed joints,*** Example– those in the skull.
- Some *joints are slightly movable,* example vertebrae can move slightly against the discs of cartilage in between them and other *joints are freely movable* called **synovial** joints, example the limb joints.
- The bones of freely movable joints are held in place and yet allowed to move freely by bands of fibres called ***ligaments.***
- In *hinge joints,* movement occurs in one plane only *e.g.* the knee and the elbow joints.
- In ***ball-and-socket joints,*** movement occurs in three planes *e.g.* the hip, the shoulder.
- In ***pivot joints*** one bone twists against another. A pivot joint occurs where a peg on the axis vertebra fits into a socket in the atlas vertebra.
- In a ***sliding or gliding joint*** the surfaces which rub together are flat *e.g.* the vertebrae joint.

Muscles

- Muscles, the tissues attached to bones, are composed of fibres. They are capable of contracting and relaxing to effect body movement.
- There are about 630 important muscles in human body, which normally account for 40 per cent of the weight.
- **Largest muscle:** The bulkiest muscle in the body is *gluteus maximus* or buttock muscles.
- **Longest muscle:** Sartorius (tailor's muscle) is the longest muscle in the body. It has its origin in the upper part of the hip bone, crosses obliquely over the upper portion of the thigh, passes behind the femur and is attached to the tibia in the leg.
- **Smallest muscle:** The smallest muscle in the human body is the *stapedius,* which controls the stapes, an auditory ossicle in the middle ear. It is less than 1/20 of an inch and 0.127 cm long. The ear also contains one of the few tissues, which has no blood supply.

NERVOUS SYSTEM

- The nervous system, is an organized group of cells specialized for the conduction of a stimulus impulse from a sensory receptor through a nerve cell network to the site at which the response occurs.
- The nervous system enables a multi-cellular animals to respond to changes in their external and internal environment.
- Nerve tissue is composed primarily of cells called neurons.
- Animals have a nervous system for controlling and coordinating the activities of the body. But plants have neither a nervous system nor muscles.

Nervous System of Humans

- A nerve consists of several bundles of nerve fibres commonly called fasciculi.
- A fascicle contains connective tissue (endoneurium). surrounded by connective tissue sheath (perineurium).
- Each nerve is surrounded by a dense layer of connective tissue called epineurium.
- Each nerve has its own supply of small blood vessels.
- The functional unit of nervous system is nerve cell or neuron, which have a special structure but vary greatly in size and shape.

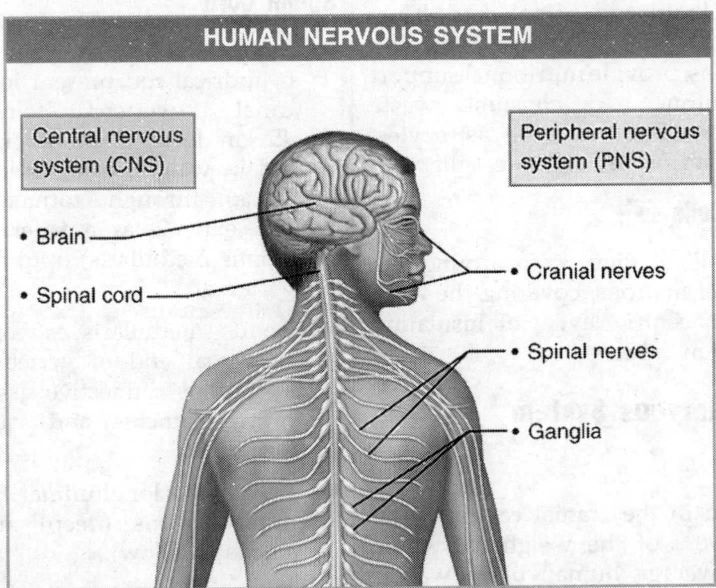

- Each neuron has a cell body (encloses cytoplasm and a nucleus, usually a single axon a variable number of dendrites.
- 3 types of neurons:
  1. **Multipolar neuron:** One long axon with many dendrites, most common type e.g., pyramidal cells is cerebral cortex.
  2. **Bipolar neuron:** Neuron has two processes, an axon at one end and a dendrite at the other end. e.g., bipolar neurons in the retina of eye.

3. **Paurounipolar or Unipolor neuron:** The cell body on a side branch of the main axon e.g. cells of dorsal root ganglion.
   - **Neuroendocrine System:** A network of endocrine glands whose hormone production is controlled by commands form the CNS.
   - **Nuclei:** Mass of neurons clustered inside the CNS.
   - **Ganglia:** Mass of neurons clustered inside the PNS.
   - **Tracts:** Bundles of nerve fibres within the CNS.
   - **Nerves:** Bundles of nerve fibres within the PNS.

Neuroglia or Glial Cells or Glia

- Packing and supporting cells found in the brain and spinal cord. They perform many house keeping functions, provide nutritional support to neurons and consume waste products. They may be astrocytes, oligodendrocytes and microglia.

Schwann Cells

- In the PNS, they wrap around the axons of neurons, covering the axon with concentric layers of insulating plasma membrane.

Central Nervous System

Brain

- Situated in the cranial cavity of the skull, 98% of the weight of whole CNS, average human brain weight from 1200-1400 gm, possess about 100 billion neurons, protected by meninges.
- In lower vertebrates (e.g., amphibians) there are two meninges, durameter and piaarachnoid membrane.
- The brain is made of three major parts: the forebrain, midbrain, and hindbrain.
- The forebrain consists of the cerebrum, thalamus, and hypothalamus.
- The midbrain consists of the tectum and tegmentum.
- The hindbrain is made of the cerebellum, pons, and medulla.
- The mid-brain pons and medulla together are referred as the brainstem.

The Hindbrain

- The hindbrain is also known as Reptilian Brain.
- It is the oldest part of the human brain. It manages our primal instincts and most basic functions like the instincts of survival, dominance, mating, and the basic functions of respiration and heartbeat.

Spinal Cord

- Long, soft, whitish, slightly lattened, cylindrical rod present in the neural canal of vertebral column, about 45 cm long, 2 cm thick, about 35 gm in weight, exists from the skull (atlas) through formen magnum and extends as a taper to a point (conus medullaris) upto first lumbar vertebra.
- Conus medullaris is connected to coccygeal end of vertebral column by fibrous connective tissue derived from piameter and called filum terminale.
- It has two longitudinal fissures i.e., dorsal sulcus (deep) and ventral sulcus (shallow).
- The diameter is not uniform, has two swellings i.e., upper cervical and lower lumbar swelling.
- **Neurocoel or central canal:** Narrow longitudinal canal of spinal cord, connected anteriorly with fourth ventricle of medulla oblongata but is closed posteriorly. It is lined by a single layered cuboidal epithelium called ependyma.

- Central canal is tilled with cerebrospinal fluid. Dorsal septum is a thin sheet of connective tissue which extends from dorsal fissure to inward.
- Spinal cord conducts sensory and motor impulses to and from the brain i.e., acts as link between brain and the peripheral nerves and also controls reflex actions of the body.

Autonomous Nervous System

- Auto functioning or self governed, maintains homeostasis, controlling the smooth muscles, cardiac muscles and certain glands by both feedback loops and antagonistic control.
- Formed of two systems.
  (*a*) Sympathetic nervous system
  (*b*) Parasympathetic nervous system.
- **Functions of Sympathetic Nervous System:**
  1. It narrows the blood vessels in the skin.
  2. By its action hair gets erected.
  3. It reduces the secretion of salivary glands.
  4. It increases the hearth beat.
  5. It increases the secretion of sweat glands.
  6. It stretches the pupil of eye ball.
  7. It relax the muscles of urinary bladder.
  8. It reduces the speed of contraction & relaxation of intestine.
  9. The rate of respiration increase.
  10. It increases the blood pressure.
  11. It increases the sugar level in the blood.
  12. It increases the number of Red Blood Corpuscles in the blood.
  13. It helps in clotting of blood.
  14. Collective impact of this affects fear, pain and anger.
- **Functions of Parasympathetic Nervous System:** The functions of this system is normally the opposite of Sympathetic Nervous system. For example:
  1. It widens the lumen of blood vessels except the coronary blood vessels.
  2. It increases the secretion of saliva and other digestive juices.
  3. The contraction of pupil is caused by this.
  4. It creates contraction in the other muscles of the urinary bladder.
  5. It creates contraction and motion in intestinal walls.
  6. The effect of this nervous system collectively creates the occasion of rest and joy.

REPRODUCTION SYSTEM

- Reproduction is the production of a new generation of individuals of the same species. It is one of the fundamental characteristics of living organisms.
- It involves transmission of genetic material from one generation to the next, ensuring that the species survive over long periods of time, even though individual members of the species die.
- There are two basic types of reproduction, asexual and sexual.
- Asexual Reproduction is reproduction by a single organism without production of gametes. It usually results in the production of genetically identical offspring, the only genetic variation arising as a result of random mutation among the individuals.
- Sexual Reproduction is the fusion of two gametes to form a zygote, which develops into a new organism.

- It leads to genetic variation, which is advantageous to the species because it provides the raw material for natural selection and, therefore, evolution. Eventually, new species may form, the process known as speciation.
- Increased variation can be achieved by the mixing of genes from two different individuals, the process known as genetic recombination.

Reproduction in Human Beings

- The female reproductive system consists of *two ovaries,* and a duct system of *two fallopian tubes,* and *uterus and a vagina.* ***Ovaries produce ova and secrete oestrogens and progesterone.***
- The fallopian tubes conduct the ovum towards the uterus; the uterus lodges the growing foetus and opens to the exterior through the vagina.
- *Gametogenesis* is the formation of gametes for sexual reproduction. Gametogenesis is carried out in the *gonads.* The gametogenesis in male gonad is called *spermatogenesis.* It is the production of sperms in the testes. The gametogenesis in female gonad is called *oogenesis.* It is the formation of ova in the ovary.
- ***Spermogenesis*** or transformation of spermatogonia (male germ cells present in seminiferous tubules) into spermatozoa occurs in seminiferous tubules in four stages:
  - **(*i*) Proliferation phase :** In this stage the spermatogonial cells have diploid number *of* chromosomes (46 in man) which undergo several mitotic divisions to increase their number,
  - **(*ii*) Growth phase:** The spermatogonia cells increase in the dimensions and are called primary, spermatocytes in this stage,
  - **(*iii*) Maturation phase:** Primary spermatocytes undergoes first meiotic division to produce two smaller secondary spermatocytes and these two further divide to give four spermatids and;
  - **(*iv*) Transformation phase:** The spermatid in this final stage acquires a tail and anterior acrosomal cap (head cap) and is transformed into spermatozoan.
- ***Oogenesis*** is the transformation of oogonia (female germ cells) into ova. It takes place in the Graafian follicle of ovaries and is completed in the three stages:
  - (*i*) *Proliferation phase:* The oogonia cells which have a diploid number of chromosomes undergo several mitotic divisions in the foetus upto six months;
  - (*ii*) *Growth phase:* The oogonium increases in size and is transformed into a primary oocyte; and
  - (*iii*) *Maturation phase:* The primary oocyte undergoes meiosis in two steps. The first reduction division leads to the formation of two unequal daughter cells—the larger constitute the secondary oocyte, whereas the smaller, consisting mainly of the nucleus, forms the first polar body, that subsequently degenerates.
- An ovum and a second polar body result from the second meiotic division or second maturation division prior to fertilization.
- Like the first, the second polar body also disintegrates after some time. Thus, a single mature cell is produced from one primary oocyte.

Fertilization and Embryo Development

- During sexual union, the sperms are discharged into the vagina. Each discharge of semen contains millions of sperms. However, only one of them fuses with the ovum to fertilize it.

➥ The sperms deposited in the vagina swim up to the uterus and further up through the fallopian tubes where if a sperm meets an ovum, it fuses with it resulting into the formation of a zygote.

➥ The zygote moves down the oviduct, reaches the uterus and gets embedded in the endometrium on the 24th day of the menstrual cycle.

➥ The zygote divides repeatedly to form an *embryo.*

➥ The process, delivery of foetus (childbirth) is called *parturition.*

➥ The mammary gland of female during pregnancy undergo differentiation to produce milk towards the end of pregnancy. This is called *lactation.*

➥ The milk produced during the initial few days of lactation is called *colostrum.* It contains several antibodies which develop resistance to new born babies.

SCIENCE & TECHNOLOGY

ATOMIC ENERGY

➥ India's Atomic Energy Commission (AEC) was established in August 1948 within the Department of Scientific Research, which was set up in June 1948.

➥ The Department of Atomic Energy (DAE) came into existence in August 1954 through a Presidential Order. Thereafter, a Government Resolution in 1958 transferred the DAE within the AEC.

➥ The Secretary to the Government of India in the DAE is the ex-officio Chairman of the AEC. The other Members of the AEC are appointed on the recommendation of the Chairman of the AEC

➥ The Indian nuclear programme was conceived based on, unique sequential three-stages and associated technologies essentially to aim at optimum utilization of the indigenous nuclear resource profile of modest Uranium and abundant Thorium resources. This sequential three-stage program is based on a closed fuel cycle, where the spent fuel of one stage is reprocessed to produce fuel for the next stage.

➥ The commercial nuclear power program of the first stage (comprising of PHWRs and imported LWRs) is being implemented by Nuclear Power Corporation of India Limited (NPCIL), and the second stage (comprising of Fast Breeder Reactors) by Bharatiya Nabhikiya Vidyut Nigam Limited (BHAVINI), both companies owned fully by the union government in accordance with the provisions of the act.

➥ **STAGE 1: Pressurized Heavy Water Reactor using**

- Natural UO2 as fuel matrix.
- Heavy water as moderator and coolant.

➥ **STAGE 2: Fast Breeder Reactor:** India's second stage of nuclear power generation envisages the use of Pu-239 obtained from the first stage reactor operation, as the fuel core in fast breeder reactors (FBR).

➥ **STAGE 3: Breeder Reactor:** The third phase of India's Nuclear Power Generation programme is breeder reactors using U-233 fuel. India's vast thorium deposits permit design and operation of U-233 fuelled breeder reactors.

Indian Nuclear Power Plants in Operation

Unit	Type	Gross Power (MWe)	Date of Operation
Tarapur Atomic Power Station (TAPS), Maharashtra	BWR	160	October 28, 1969
Tarapur Atomic Power Station (TAPS), Maharashtra	BWR	160	October 28, 1969
Tarapur Atomic Power Station (TAPS), Maharashtra	PHWR	540	August 18, 2006
Tarapur Atomic Power Station (TAPS), Maharashtra	PHWR	540	September 12, 2005
Rajasthan Atomic Power Station (RAPS), Rajasthan	PHWR	0	December 16, 1973
Rajasthan Atomic Power Station (RAPS), Rajasthan	PHWR	200	April 1, 1981
Rajasthan Atomic Power Station (RAPS), Rajasthan	PHWR	220	June 1, 2000
Rajasthan Atomic Power Station (RAPS), Rajasthan	PHWR	220	December 23, 2000
Rajasthan Atomic Power Station (RAPS), Rajasthan	PHWR	220	February 4, 2010
Rajasthan Atomic Power Station (RAPS), Rajasthan	PHWR	220	March 31, 2010
Rajasthan Atomic Power Station (RAPS), Rajasthan	PHWR	700	March 17, 2025
Madras Atomic Power Station (MAPS), Tamil Nadu	PHWR	220	January 27, 1984
Madras Atomic Power Station (MAPS), Tamil Nadu	PHWR	220	March 21, 1986
Kaiga Generating Station (KGS), Karnataka	PHWR	220	November 16, 2000
Kaiga Generating Station (KGS), Karnataka	PHWR	220	March 16, 2000
Kaiga Generating Station (KGS), Karnataka	PHWR	220	May 6, 2007
Kaiga Generating Station (KGS), Karnataka	PHWR	220	January 20, 2011
Kudankulam Nuclear Power Station (KKNPS), Tamil Nadu	VVER -1000 (PWR)	1000	December 31, 2014
Kudankulam Nuclear Power Station (KKNPS), Tamil Nadu	VVER -1000 (PWR)	1000	March 31, 2017
Narora Atomic Power Station (NAPS), Uttar Pradesh	PHWR	220	January 1, 1991
Narora Atomic Power Station (NAPS), Uttar Pradesh	PHWR	220	July 1, 1992
Kakrapar Atomic Power Station (KAPS), Gujarat	PHWR	220	May 6, 1993
Kakrapar Atomic Power Station (KAPS), Gujarat	PHWR	220	September 1, 1995
Kakrapar Atomic Power Station (KAPS), Gujarat	PHWR	700	June 30, 2023
Kakrapar Atomic Power Station (KAPS), Gujarat	PHWR	700	March 31, 2024

Research Reactors

- The research reactor programme of DAE provided research and development support to the nuclear power programme, produces radioisotopes for use in health care, agriculture, industry and research, and provides manpower training.
- The research reactors set up by DAE so far, have been Apsara (1mW, Fuel: Enriched Uranium-Aluminium alloy), CIRUS (40MW, Fuel: Natural uranium), Zerlina (zero energy, Natural Uranium), Purnima I-III (Fuel: Plutonium/Uranium-233), Dhruva (100 MW, Fuel: Natural

Uranium) at Trombay (Maharashtra), and Kamini (30kW, Fuel : Uranium-233-A1 alloy) and Fast Breeder Test Reactor (40MW, Fuel : Uranium-Plutonium carbide) at Kalpakkam (Tamil Nadu).

- Of the research reactors, Zerlina was decommissioned in 1984, and Purnima series made way for Kamini.
- Dhruva, CIRUS and Apsara are used for producing radioisotopes besides their use in research and development relating to nuclear technologies and materials, applied and basic research, and training.
- KAMINI is used mainly for radiography of various materials, and FBTR is the test bed for the development of fuel, blanket and structural materials for fast breeder reactor programme.

Nuclear Explosion

- Smiling Buddha was the assigned code name of India's first successful nuclear bomb test on 18 May, 1974.
- The bomb was detonated on the army base, Pokhran Test Range (PTR), in Rajasthan by the Indian Army under the supervision of several key army officials.
- ***Pokhran-I*** was also the first confirmed nuclear weapons test by a nation outside the five permanent members of the United Nations Security Council.
- Officially, the Indian Ministry of External Affairs (MEA) claimed this test was a "peaceful nuclear explosion", but it was actually an accelerated nuclear program.
- ***Pokhran-II*** was the series of five nuclear bomb test explosions conducted by India at the Indian Army's Pokhran Test Range in May 1998. It was the second Indian nuclear test.
- Pokhran-II consisted of five detonations, of which the first was a fusion bomb and the remaining four were fission bombs.
- These nuclear tests resulted in a variety of sanctions against India by a number of major states, including Japan and the United States.

SPACE PROGRAMME

- Despite being a developing economy with its attendant problems, India has effectively developed space technology and has applied it successfully for its rapid development and today is offering a variety of space services globally.
- During the formative decade of 1960s, space research was conducted by India mainly with the help of sounding rockets.
- The Indian Space Research Organisation (ISRO) was formed in 1969.
- Space research activities were provided additional fillip with the formation of the Space Commission and the Department of Space by the government of India in 1972. And, ISRO was brought under the Department of Space in the same year.

Satellite Launch Vehicle (SLV)

- The Satellite Launch Vehicle (SLV or SLV-3) was a 4-stage solid-propellant light launcher. It was intended to reach a height of 500 kilometres and carry a payload of 40 kilograms.
- Its first launch took place in 1979 with two more in each subsequent year, and the final launch in 1983. Only two of its four test flights were successful.

Augmented Satellite Launch Vehicle (ASLV)

- The Augmented Satellite Launch Vehicle (ASLV) was a five-stage solid propellant rocket with the capability of placing a 150-kilogram satellite into Low Earth Orbit.
- This project was started during the early 1980s to develop technologies needed for a payload to be placed into a geostationary orbit. Its design was based on Satellite Launch Vehicle.
- The first launch test was held in 1987, and after that three others followed in 1988, 1992 and 1994, out of which only two were successful, before it was decommissioned.

Polar Satellite Launch Vehicle (PSLV)

- The Polar Satellite Launch Vehicle (PSLV) is an expendable launch system developed by ISRO to allow India to launch its Indian Remote Sensing (IRS) satellites into Sun synchronous orbits.
- PSLV can also launch small satellites into geostationary transfer orbit (GTO).
- The reliability and versatility of the PSLV is proven by the fact that it has launched, as of June 2022, 345 satellites/spacecraft into a variety of orbits.
- The maximum number of satellites launched by the PSLV in a single launch is 104, in the PSLV-C37 launch on 15 February 2017.

Geosynchronous Satellite Launch Vehicle (GSLV)

- The Geosynchronous Satellite Launch Vehicle (GSLV) is an expendable launch system developed to enable India to launch its INSAT-type satellites into geostationary orbit and to make India less dependent on foreign rockets.
- At present, it is ISRO's second-heaviest launch vehicle and is capable of putting a total payload of up to 5 tons to low Earth orbit. The vehicle is built by India, originally with a cryogenic engine purchased from Russia, while the ISRO developed its own cryogenic engine.
- The first version of the GSLV (GSLV Mk.I), using the Russian cryogenic stage, became operational in 2004, after an unsuccessful first launch in 2001 and a second, successful development launch in 2003.
- The first attempt to launch the GSLV Mk.II with an Indian built cryogenic engine, GSLV-F06 carrying GSAT-5P, failed on 25 December 2010.
- On 5 January 2014, GSLV-D5 launched GSAT-14 into its intended orbit. This marked the first successful flight using the indigenous cryogenic engine, making India the sixth country in the world to have this technology.
- Again on 27 August 2015, GSLV-D6 launched GSAT-6 into a transfer orbit. ISRO used the indigenously developed Cryogenic Upper Stage (CUS) for third time in this GSLV flight.
- On 8 September 2016, GSLV-F05 launched INSAT-3DR, a weather satellite weighing 2,211 kg into a geostationary transfer orbit (GTO). GSLV is designed to inject 2–5 tonnes (2.2–5.5 tons) -class of satellites into GTO. The launch took place from the Second Launch Pad at Satish Dhawan Space Centre SHAR (SDSC SHAR), Sriharikota.

Geosynchronous Satellite Launch Vehicle Mark-III (GSLV-Mk III)

- GSLV-Mk III is a launch vehicle, capable to launch four-tonne satellites into geosynchronous transfer orbit (GTO). GSLV-Mk III is a three-stage vehicle with a 110-tonne core liquid propellant stage flanked by two 200-tonne solid propellant strap-on booster motors (S-200).
- The upper stage is cryogenic with a propellant loading of 25 tonnes. The vehicle has a lift-off mass of about 640 tonnes and is 43.43 metres tall.
- According to ISRO, the payload fairing has a diameter of 5 metres and a payload volume of 100 cubic metres. It allows India to become less dependent on foreign rockets for heavy lifting.
- A GSLV Mk III-D1 carrying the communication satellite GSAT-19 lifted off from the second launch pad at Satish Dhawan Space Centre in Sriharikota on 5 June, 2017, and placed the communication satellite into a geosynchronous transfer orbit sixteen minutes after takeoff. GSAT-19 satellite has a mass of 3,136 kg (6,914 lb), and is configured around ISRO's standard I-3K bus.
- On 14 July GSLV-Mk III was supposed to launch Chandrayaan-2 but due to some technical issues regarding the helium tank it was postpone to 22 July 2019. On 22 July 2019 the GSLV-Mk III launched India's second moon mission 'Chandrayaan-II' successfully into Earth orbit.

Satellite Programmes

- India's first satellite, the Aryabhata, was launched by the Soviet Union on 19 April 1975 from Kapustin Yar using a Cosmos-3M launch vehicle.
- This was followed by the Rohini series of experimental satellites, which were built and launched indigenously.
- At present, ISRO operates a large number of earth observation satellites.

The INSAT Series

- INSAT (Indian National Satellite System) is a series of multipurpose geostationary satellites launched by ISRO to satisfy the telecomm-unications, broadcasting, meteorology and search-and-rescue need of India.
- Commissioned in 1983, INSAT is the largest domestic communication system in the Asia-Pacific Region.

The IRS Series

- Indian Remote Sensing satellites (IRS) are a series of earth observation satellites, built, launched and maintained by ISRO. The IRS series provides remote sensing services to the country.
- The Indian Remote Sensing Satellite system is the largest collection of remote sensing satellites for civilian use in operation today in the world.
- All the satellites are placed in polar Sun-synchronous orbit and provide data in a variety of spatial, spectral and temporal resolutions to enable several programmes to be undertaken rlevant to national development.

Radar Imaging Satellites

- ISRO currently operates three Radar Imaging Satellites (RISAT). RISAT-1 was launched from Sriharikota Spaceport on 26 April, 2012 on board a PSLV. RISAT-1 carries a C band synthetic aperture Radar (SAR) payload, operating in a multi-polarisation and multi-resolution mode and can provide images with coarse, fine and high spatial resolutions.

- India also operates RISAT-2, which was launched in 2009 and acquired from Israel at a cost $ 110 million.
- RISAT-2B was launched from Sriharikota Spaceport on 22 May, 2019 on board a PSLV.

Other Satellites

- ISRO has also launched a set of experimental geostationary satellites known as the GSAT series. Kalpana-1, ISRO's first dedicated meteorological satellite, was launched by the Polar Satellite Launch Vehicle on 12 September 2002. The satellite was originally known as MetSat-1. In February 2003 it was renamed to Kalpana-1 by the Indian Prime Minister Atal Bihari Vajpayee in memory of Kalpana Chawla—a NASA astronaut of Indian origin who perished in the Space Shuttle Columbia disaster.
- ISRO has also launched the Indo-French satellite SARAL on 25 February, 2013. SARAL (or "Satellite with ARgos and AltiKa") is a cooperative altimetry technology mission. It is being used for monitoring the oceans surface and sea-levels.
- In June 2014, ISRO launched French Earth Observation Satellite SPOT-7 (mass 714 kg) along with Singapore's first nano satellite VELOX-I, Canada's satellite CAN-X5, Germany's satellite AISAT, via the PSLV-C23 launch vehicle. It was ISRO's 4th commercial launch.
- On December 05, 2024 ISRO launched Proba-3, an Earth Observation Satellite, via PSLV-C59 launch vehicle.

South Asia Satellite

- The South Asia Satellite (GSAT-9) is a geosynchronous communications satellite by the Indian Space Research Organisation (ISRO) for the South Asian Association for Regional Co-operation (SAARC) region. The satellite was launched on 5th May, 2017.
- During the 18th SAARC summit held in Nepal in 2014, Indian Prime Minister Narendra Modi mooted the idea of a satellite serving the needs of SAARC member nations, part of his Neighbourhood first policy.

IRNSS Satellite Navigation System

- IRNSS is an independent regional navigation satellite system being developed by India. It is designed to provide accurate position information service to users in India as well as the region extending up to 1500 km from its boundary, which is its primary service area. IRNSS will provide two types of services, namely, Standard Positioning Service (SPS) and Restricted Service (RS) and is expected to provide a position accuracy of better than 20 m in the primary service area.
- It is an autonomous regional satellite navigation system being developed by Indian SPace Research Organisation, which is under total control of Indian government.
- ISRO on 1 July 2013, launched from Sriharikota the First Indian Navigation Satellite the IRNSS-1A. The IRNSS-1A was launched aboard PSLV-C22.

Astrosat

- The Astrosat is India's first multi wavelength space observatory and full-fledged astronomy satellite. Its observation study includes active galactic nuclei, hot white dwarfs, pulsations of pulsars, binary star systems, supermassive black holes located at the entre of the galaxies etc.

Extraterrestrial Exploration

Lunar : Chandrayaan-1

- The Chandrayaan-1 was India's first mission to the Moon. The unmanned lunar exploration mission included a lunar orbiter and an impactor called the Moon Impact Probe.
- ISRO launched the spacecraft using a modified version of the PSLV on 2 October 2008 from Satish Dhawan Space Centre, Sriharikota. The vehicle was inserted into lunar orbit on 8 November, 2008.
- It carried high-resolution remote sensing equipment for visible, near infrared, and soft and hard X-ray frequencies. during its 312 days operational period (2 years planned), it surveyed the lunar surface to produce a complete map of its chemical characteristics and 3-dimensional topography. The polar regions were of special interest, as they possibly had ice deposits.
- The spacecraft carried 11 instruments: 5 Indian and 6 from foreign institutes and space agencies (including NASA, ESA, Bulgarian Academy of Sciences, Brown University and other European and North American institutes/ companies), which were carried free of cost.
- Chandrayaan-1 became the first lunar mission to discover existence of water on the Moon.

Mars Orbiter Mission (Mangalyaan)

- The Mars Orbiter Mission (MOM), informally known as Mangalyaan, was launched into Earth orbit on 5 November, 2013 by the Indian Space Research Organisation (ISRO) and has entered Mars orbit on 24 September 2014. India thus became the first country to enter Mars orbit on its first attempt. It was completed at a record low cost of $74 million.
- **Chandrayaan-2:** Chandryaan was India's second mission to the Moon, which included an orbiter and lander-rover module. Chandrayaan-2 was launched on India's Geosynchronous Satellite Launch Vehicle Mark III (GSLV-MkIII) on 22 July, 2019. But the mission failed on 7 September, 2019 during soft-landing, South Pole's on Moon's surface when it was just 2 km above the surface. The science goals of the mission were to further improve the understanding of the origin and evolution of the Moon.
- **Chandrayaan-3:** The Chandrayaan-3 spacecraft's Vikram lander on August 23, 2023 touched near the South Pole (The presence of frozen water on the moon is one of the main reasons) of the moon and becomes first country in the world for any space programme to land on the South Pole and the fourth to land on the moon. India now has joined the US, Russia and China as the fourth country to successfully land on the lunar or moon surface.
- **Aditya-L1:** On 2nd September, 2023, the first Solar Mission, named as Aditya-L1 was launched by ISRO after success of Chandrayaan mission. It will study the energy sources from the sun. The Sun Space Mission Aditya-L1 shall use the Polar Satellite Launch Vehicle (PSLV) with seven payloads (Instruments on Board). The spacecraft shall be based in a halo orbit around Lagrange point-1 (L1) of the Sun-Earth system, which is about 1.5 million kilometres from the Earth, while a satellite placed in the halo orbit will have the major advantage of continuously viewing the Sun wihout any eclipses.

- **Small Satellite Launch Vehicle:** The SSLV or Small Satellite Launch Vechicle is in development for commercial launching small satellites with a payload of 500 kg to Low Earth Orbit. SSLV is a four staged vehicle with three solid propellant based stages and a Velocity Trimming Module. On August 08, 2024 ISRO launched EOS-08, via the SSLV-D3.
- **Unified Launch Vehicle:** The ULV or Unified Launch Vehicle is a launch vehicle in development by the Indian Space Research Organisation (ISRO). The project's core objective is to design a modular architecture that will enable the replacement of the PSLV, GSLV Mk II and GSLV Mk III with a single family of launchers. The SCE-200 engine can even be clustered for heavy launch configuration. The ULV will be able to launch 6000 kg to 10,000 kg of payload into GTO.

Space Technology Incubation Centre

- ISRO has opened Space Technology Incubation Centres (S-TIC) at premier technical universities in India which will incubate startups to build applicaitons and products in tandem with the industry and would be used for future space missions. The S-TIC will bring the idustry, academia and ISRO under one umbrella to contribute towards research and development (R&D) initiatives relevant to the Indian Space Programme.

DEFENCE

Tanks and Missiles

- Vijayanta is India's first indigenous tank.
- T-55 and T-72 are Soviet-built battle tanks.
- Arjun Most sophisticated battle tank designed by the DRDO and developed at Avadi. The 58.5 tonne tank with its state-of-the-art technology, superior fire power, mobility and weapon system is rated among the top three MBTs in the world.
- Agni II is an inter-continental ballistic missile with a strike range of 2000+ km and a payload capacity of 1,000 kg of conventional or nuclear weapons.
- Prithvi, the 8.5 metre short range surface-to-surface missile, has a range of 150 km to 250 km. It is designed for quick mano euvrability and wartime efficiency.
- Trishul is a surface-to-air missile with radar guided weapons, used against aircrafts and helicopters.
- Nag is an anti-tank missile with a range of 4 km, launched from a tracked carrier or a helicopter.
- Pinaka is a mobile weapon, system, having 12 solid propellant rockets configured for launch from a Tatra 8-wheel truck. It has a range of 40 km.
- Akash is a multi-target medium range surface-to-air missile (guided).
- The Shaurya missile is a short-range surface-to-surface ballistic missile developed for use by the Indian Army. Capable of hypersonic speeds, it has a range of 600 km and is capable of carrying a payload of one-tonne conventional or nuclear warhead.
- Nirbhay is Long Range Sub-Sonic Cruise Missile under development and testing.
- Prahaar is a solid-fuelled Surface-to-surface guided short-range tactical ballistic missile that would be equipped with omni-directional warheads and could be used for hitting both tactical and strategic targets.

BRAHMOS

- BrahMos Supersonic anti-ship cruise missile, (said to be the only such missile in the world), is jointly developed by India and Russia.
- BrahMos has a target range of about 290 km with 200-300 kg of payload of conventional warhead mass depending on the version, an ability to engage shore-based radio-contrast targets, and can fire from multiple platforms like ship, land, submarine and air.
- Launched from a ship, it can fly up to a height of 14 km at Mach 2 speed (twice the speed of sound), has a preset trajectory, with a sensor on the head detecting the target and changing the missile's course to strike up to 20 km from targeted range.
- BrahMos, a combined term from Brahmaputra and Moscow, is the only supersonic cruise missile in the world. All other cruise missiles including those in the US, are subsonic or fly below the speed of sound.

LAKSHYA

- The pilotless target aircraft, Lakshya was successfully inducted into the IAF with a squadron having conducted sorties in 2001.
- Lakshya is to be used for ground-air, air-air and ship-air missile target practice.

NISHANT

- Nishant is India's indigenous remote piloted, vehicle (RPV).
- Earlier called the Falcon, Nishant is intended for battlefield surveillance and reconnai-ssance roles.
- It incorporates advanced design features comparable or superior to those developed elsewhere in the world.
- Capable of carrying a 45-kg pay-load, it could cruise at about 150 kmph and fly for more than five hours.
- It could be controlled from the ground for distances up to 160 km. But is also programmed for autonomous flight.
- Made entirely of fibre reinforced glass, it is difficult to detect on radar.
- Its radio links to the ground are difficult to jam since they use the spread spectrum technique.

HELINA

- Helina, (Helicopter-launched Nag) with a range of 7-8 km, launched from twin-tube stub wing-mounted launchers on board the armed HAL Dhruv and HAL Light Combat Helicopter produced by state-owned Hindustan Aeronautics Ltd (HAL).
- It will be structurally different from the Nag.
- On July 13, 2015, three round trials of Helina were conducted at Chandhan firing range in Jaisalmer, Rajasthan.
- The missile was test fired from HAL Rudra and two missiles succeeded in hitting the targets at a range of 7 km, while one reportedly missed the target.

- Astra is a 'Beyond Visual Range Air-to-Air Missile' (BVRAAM) being developed for the Indian Air Force.
- Agni V is an inter-continental ballistic missile with a strike range of 5000-6000 km.
- **Naval Fleets:** The Indian Navy consists of sophisticated missiles-capable warships, guided missile destroyers, aircraft carriers, frigates and advanced submarines.

Warships

- INS Savitri is the first warship fabricated at the Hindustan Shipyard Limited, which joined the Navy in 1990.
- INS Delhi is the largest and most sophisticated, indigenously fabricated warship; it joined the fleet in 1997.
- INS Ghariyal is indigenously built, and was commissioned in 1997.

- INS Mysore is the second of the most powerful class of warships, built indigenously and commissioned in 1999.
- INS Brahmaputra has 16 Russian made Uran surface-to-surface missiles and its helicopters carry two long-range Sea Eagle air-to-surface missiles. It was commissioned in 2000.
- INS Tillanchang is the second indigenous warship in the Trinkat class fast attack craft series commissioned in 2001 at Visakhapatnam.
- INS Kulish is a frontline warship commissioned in 2001 at Garden Reach, the third of Kova-class guided missile corvettes and carries 16 'Uran' tactical surface-to-surface missiles.
- INS Talwar was built by Russia for the Indian Navy. It was commissioned in St. Petersburg in 2003. It boasts of weapons and sensors with a far greater range than what the Indian Navy has at present. Its main attack weapon is the vertical-launch club-N missile system.
- INS Satpura is the second indigenously built stealth warship, second of the P-17 frigate series. It has advanced surface-to-surface and surface-to-air missiles and hi-tech radar and communication equipment on board. It was launched in June 2004 at the Mazagaon Docks, Mumbai.
- INS Tabar, commissioned in 2004. It has the Russian Kashtan close in weapon system.
- INS Kesari, the fourth indigenously built landing ship tank (large) was commissioned at the Visakhapatnam naval base of the Indian Navy in April 2008.
- INS Airavat, the fifth indigenously built landing ship tank (large) was commissioned to the Indian Navy in May 2009.

Submarines

- INS Shalki, the first indigenously built submarine, commissioned in 1994.
- INS Shankul, the second indigenously built submarine comm-issioned in 1994.
- INS Sindhughosh, the Indian variant of the Kilo class diesel-electric submarine. Designated 877 EKM, Sindhughosh submarines were designed as part of Project 877, and built under a contract between Rosvooruzhenie (Russia) and the Ministry of Defence (India).
- INS Arihant, India's first nuclear submarine (earlier known as ATV Advanced Technology Vessel) was launched in July 2009 at Visakhapatnam.
- INS Chakra, under a 10-year lease from Russia since 2012. Negotiations are underway to lease an additional Akula-class attack submarine.

Missile Boats

- INS Vibhuti, the first indigenously built missile boat launched at Mazagaon Dock, Mumbai in 1991.
- INS Vipul, the second missile boat built at Mazagaon Dock, Mumbai, after INS Vibhuti. It consists of surface-to-surface and surface-to-air missiles. It was commissioned in 1992.
- INS Nashak is the country's third missile boat launched in 1993.
- INS Prahar is the indigenously built fastest missile boat in the world, inducted into the Navy in 1997. It parks a powerful punch in the form of ship-to-surface KT 138 missile.

- INS Prabhat is the indigenously built Nashak-Class boat whose weapon package includes surface-to-surface missiles with associated surveillance system. It was launched in 2000.

Aircraft Carrier

- INS Vikrant is the only aircraft carrier with the Indian Navy after the decommissioning of INS Virat. It is the first aircraft carrier to be built in India.

Frigates

- INS Talwar;
- INS Shivalik;
- INS Beas;
- INS Satpura;
- INS Sahyadri;
- INS Brahmaputra;
- INS Betwa;
- INS Ganga;
- INS Gomti.

MULTIPLE CHOICE QUESTIONS

1. Distance covered by object is .... to time.

A. equal proportional
B. directly proportional
C. inversely proportional
D. double proportional

2. Match List-I with List-II:

List-I (Vitamin)	List-II (Alternative Name)
(a) Vitamin A	1. Ascorbic acid
(b) Vitamin B_{12}	2. Retinol
(c) Vitamin C	3. Cobalamin
(d) Vitamin D	4. Ergocalciferol

Codes:

	(a)	(b)	(c)	(d)
A.	2	1	3	4
B.	1	2	3	4
C.	3	2	4	1
D.	2	3	1	4

3. In what form is the energy derived from the food that we eat is stored in our body?

A. Maltose
B. Glucose
C. Glycogen
D. Starch

4. Which one of the following statements about lysosomes is not correct?

A. They are waste disposal system of the cell
B. They breakdown all inorganic materials
C. These are also referred to as 'suicidal bags'
D. Lysosomes stop entry of foreign materials

5. In which one among the following the vegetative propagation takes place through Eye Buds?

A. Potato B. Ginger
C. Onion D. Sugarcane

6. Which one among the following diseases is caused due to deficiency of Vitamin D in humans?

A. Befiberi B. Scurvy
C. Rickets D. Pneumonia

7. Which one among the following combinations most appropriately represent the components of balanced diet?

A. Carbohydrate, vitamins, proteins, fat, minerals, fibres and water

B. Carbohydrate, vitamins, proteins, fat and minerals
C. Carbohydrate, vitamins, proteins, minerals and water
D. Vitamins, proteins, fat, minerals, fibres and water

8. In which part or organ of human body cartilage is not found?
A. Nose
B. Trachea
C. Bronchiole
D. Knee joint

9. Which one among the following processes is not part of chemical weathering?
A. Solution
B. Hydration
C. Reduction
D. Thawing

10. Which one among the following fertilizers is a source of nitrogen?
A. Superphosphate
B. potassium sulphate
C. Bone meal
D. urea

11. J.G. Mendel is known for his work in the field of:
A. Biotechnology
B. Genetics
C. Parasitology
D. Medical engineering

12. Sound travels fastest in:
A. Air B. Water
C. Vacuum D. Iron

13. The maximum displacement of the particle in a wave motion is called:
A. Phase
B. Frequency
C. Amplitude
D. Time period

14. Each magnet has _____ poles:
A. 2 B. 3
C. 4 D. 5

15. pH factor is used to measure:
A. Colour of a liquid
B. Acidity of a liquid
C. Density of a liquid
D. Turbidity of a liquid

16. The common salt contains:
A. Sodium and sulphate
B. Sodium and nitrate
C. Sodium and chloride
D. Calcium and sulphate

17. Brass contains the metals of:
A. Copper and zinc
B. Copper and iron
C. Copper and tin
D. Sodium and iron

18. Goitre is caused by the malfunctioning of:
A. Liver B. Brain
C. Spleen D. Thyroid

19. The blood pressure of a normal man is:
A. 1,00,150 mm Hg
B. 50,100 mm Hg
C. 80,120 mm Hg
D. 200,300 mm Hg

20. Deficiency of Vitamin B causes:
A. Rickets B. Scurvy
C. Beri-Beri D. Night blindness

21. The largest organ in the human body is:
A. Kidney B. Liver
C. Heart D. Pancreas

22. Largest number of satellites belong to the planets
A. Mercury B. Jupiter
C. Saturn D. Neptune

23. Time taken by light to travel from sun to earth is:
A. About 8 minutes
B. About 17 seconds
C. About 129 years
D. About 6 months

24. The planet nearest to the sun is:

A. Mars B. Venus
C. Mercury D. Earth

25. Comets are heavenly bodies, known for their:

A. Brilliant shine
B. Tails
C. Position near polar star
D. Frequency of appearance

26. The first satellite to go into space was:

A. Explorer
B. Luna
C. Sputnik
D. Challenger

27. The first women to go in space was:

A. Yuri Gagrin
B. Nadio Comonseshki
C. Rita Phillips
D. Valentina Tareshkova

28. The first man reached moon in:

A. 1961 B. 1965
C. 1969 D. 1971

29. India joined the space club in:

A. 1975 B. 1978
C. 1979 D. 1982

30. India's range of geostationary satellite is:

A. IRS B. INSAT
C. Rohini D. Bhaskara

31. Green colour of the leaves is due to:

A. Mitochondria
B. ATP
C. Chlorophyll
D. Vacuole

32. Glucose belongs to the category of:

A. Carbohydrates
B. Proteins
C. Vitamins
D. Fats

33. Number of pairs of chromosomes in man is:

A. 6 B. 17
C. 20 D. 23

34. Which among the following belongs to mammals category?

A. Sparrow B. Peacock
C. Bat D. Pigeon

35. Photosynthesis, is the process by which?

A. Plants take fresh air
B. Plants produce food
C. Plants suck water
D. Plants transport food

36. Reflex actions of body are controlled by:

A. Brain
B. Heart
C. Pituitary gland
D. Spinal cord

37. The heartbeat of a normal adult is:

A. 18 B. 72
C. 80 D. 120

38. Oranges are good source of:

A. Vitamin A
B. Vitamin B
C. Vitamin C
D. Vitamin D

39. Gland to be called master gland is:

A. Thyroid
B. Pancreatic
C. Lymph
D. Pituitary

40. The lens in our eyes is:

A. Concave
B. Convex
C. Double convex
D. Double concave

41. Antipyretics are medicines used for:

A. Controlling fever
B. Controlling heart beat
C. Controlling blood pressure
D. Controlling viral infection

42. Which disease is caused by the bite of insects:
A. Cholera B. Smallpox
C. Measles D. Malaria

43. Penicillin is produced from a:
A. Bacteria B. Virus
C. Fungi D. Algae

44. Which class of animals can live in water as well as land:
A. Mammals
B. Amphibians
C. Anthropoids
D. Reptiles

45. Organic chemistry is the study of compounds of:
A. Oxygen B. Nitrogen
C. Carbon D. Sulphur

46. Dry ice is:
A. Ordinary ice at –30°C
B. Compressed CO_2
C. Compressed CI_2
D. Water under pressure

47. Permanent hardness of water is due to:
A. Chlorides and sulphates of calcium and magnesium
B. Bicarbonates of calcium and Magnesium
C. Carbonates of calcium and sodium
D. Nitrates of calcium, magnesium and sodium

48. Amalgam is an alloy, containing:
A. Magnesium
B. Iron
C. Calcium
D. Mercury

49. Metal that floats on water is:
A. Iron B. Sodium
C. Calcium D. Potassium

50. PVC is made from:
A. Ethene
B. Propene
C. Vinyl-chloride
D. Butane

ANSWERS

1	2	3	4	5	6	7	8	9	10
B	D	C	B	A	C	A	C	D	D
11	**12**	**13**	**14**	**15**	**16**	**17**	**18**	**19**	**20**
B	D	C	A	B	C	A	D	C	C
21	**22**	**23**	**24**	**25**	**26**	**27**	**28**	**29**	**30**
B	B	A	C	B	C	D	C	A	B
31	**32**	**33**	**34**	**35**	**36**	**37**	**38**	**39**	**40**
C	A	D	C	B	D	B	C	D	C
41	**42**	**43**	**44**	**45**	**46**	**47**	**48**	**49**	**50**
A	D	C	B	C	B	A	D	D	C

6 Computer

INTRODUCTION

- A computer is an electronic device that accepts an input, processes it and gives the output or the result.
- Input is the raw data given to the computer.
- Process is the mathematical or logical calculation done on the raw data.
- Output is the result or the information received after the data is processed.
- Input devices help to feed data or instructions into the computer.
- Keyboard is an input device which operates like a typewriter. It has many additional keys. Thus, it can do many things that a typewriter cannot.
- Mouse is another input device. It is also known as a pointing device. Computer mice are of two types: mouse with roller ball and optical mouse.
- Output devices give the result or the information. The most commonly used output devices are computer monitor and printer.
- Once information has been sent to a computer by one of the input devices, it is processed by CPU. CPU stands for Central Processing Unit.
- Memory Unit is the storage area of a computer. The computer has a large storage capacity. This capacity is measured in terms of bytes.
- Primary memory is also called the internal memory. It is the main area where the data is stored in the computer.
- Secondary memory is also called the external memory. Here the data is stored on a long-term basis.
- Computers are used in many areas like education, science, business, music, entertainment, multimedia, etc.
- A computer can only work based on the instructions given to it. It does not have decision-making capacity and does not have an intelligence of its own.

Types of Computer

According to size and capacity these are following types of Computer:

- **Micro Computer:** These computers are used by individual, thus also called PC or Personal Computer. These days PCs are largely used for domestic and official purposes etc.

- **Mini Computer:** This type of computer is comparatively larger than that of micro computer. This is 5 to 50 times more powerful than that of a Micro Computer.
- **Main Frame Computer:** These are large sized computers. By Time Sharing and Multi Tasking techniques many people rather more than 100 people can work at a time on different terminals of this computer.
- **Super Computer:** These are very powerful computers and have more storage capacity. These are the most expensive and the fastest computers, able to process most complex jobs with a very high speed.
- **Quantum Computer:** The development of this type is in final stage. Probably Quantum Computers will be more advanced than that of human brain. In Quantum Computers Q-Bit will be used in lieu of Binary Bits.

Hardware and Software

- Hardware in a computer is any physical device, something that one is able to touch. For example, computer monitors and a computer's mouse are all hardware.
- Hardware is usually enclosed in a case or chassis.
- Software, on the other hand, is a collection of instructions and codes installed into the computer, that cannot be touched. For example, an internet browser and the Internet itself constitute software.
- Software can be divided into two groups—system software for operating systems, and application software like word processing, and computer games.

Operating System

- An operating system is the most important software that runs on a computer.
- It manages the computer's memory, processes, and all of its software and hardware.
- The operating system of a computer is important, because it allows to communicate with the computer without knowing how to speak the computer's 'language'.

Computer Program

- A computer is nothing but a machine that has the ability to perform mathematical operations very rapidly and very accurately, but it can do nothing without the aid of a program written by a human being.
- A computer program is a sequence or a set of instructions that a computer can interpret and execute.
- The program is written in code, and must be translated into a 'machine language' that the computer understands.
- This translation is performed by compilers, interpreters, and assemblers.
- The program tells the computer how to accept some type of input, manipulate that input, and give the output that is needed.
- Without a program, a computer is quite useless to us.

Some High Level Languages

- **FORTRAN:** This language was developed for solving the mathematical formulae very quickly and conveniently.

- **COBOL:** This language was developed for the commerical purposes. For the processing of this language a group of sentences is selected called paragraph and all paragraphs composed are called a section, while all sections composed are called a division.
- **BASIC:** In basic a definite part of the prescribed instruction is only inserted in the computer.
- **ALGOL:** This was basically fabricated and designed for the complex algebraic calculations.
- **PASCAL:** It is an amplified and modified form of ALGOL.
- **COMAL:** This computer language is used for the students of secondary level.
- **LOGO:** This language is used for children and kids for drawing Graphic line diagrams.
- **PROLOG:** This language is developed in 1973 in France and this language is used for Artificial Intelligence which is capable and equivalent to the logical program.
- **FORTH:** This language was invented by Charles Mure which is frequently used in all types of the works in the computer.

Computer Virus

- VIRUS, an acronym for Vital Input Resource Under Siege, a term widely used in computer security, is a self-propagating programme that destroys hard drives, crash personal computers and overwhelm critical networks that run business.
- A computer virus is so called because the 'infection' can spread from one disk to another, even across machines.
- It is a piece of software that can replicate itself from one computer to another, without the user being aware of it.
- Some viruses are relatively harmless, but others can damage or destroy data.
- They are written by anonymous programmers, often maliciously, and are spread along telephone lines or on pen drives.
- Antivirus software can be used to detect and destroy well-known viruses, but new viruses continually appear and these may bypass existing antivirus programmes.

INTERNET BASICS

Introduction

- The word Internet is a contraction of international and network. It is often called Net also.
- Internet is a worldwide system of linked computer networks.
- It links computers with different operating systems and storage techniques.
- It is as significant as the invention of the printing press, the telephone or the television.
- It has brought immense change to the world.
- Since the industrial revolution of the 18th century, it is the most significant business development. The Internet has thus come to mean all activity and interaction which takes place on the network such as e-mail and the world wide web (www) etc.
- It has been designed to operate even if one network was destroyed.

➥ Information Superhighway is an all encompassing title for on-line information access which is Internet itself.

NETWORKING

When a group of computers are linked together so that they can share information and resources, it is called computer networking. The computers are connected by cables, and each network has a hub where all the cables on the network come together. Networking makes it possible to share files or peripherals, such as a printer. For example, when the computers in an office are networked, files and printers can be shared by everyone. To set up a network you will need a gateway or router for the different computers to be connected. The Internet is an excellent example of networking.

Background

➥ The concept of the Internet was born as part of the quest to find a solution to one of the major strategic military dilemmas of the nuclear age: how to ensure that communication could continue during and after a nuclear war.

➥ In the early 1960s, the RAND Corporation (a prominent think tank) made public the concept of a communication network with its vulnerability factored into the design. The idea was that if a network in its entirety is innately unreliable, then each contributing part of the whole must be able to function independently in the tasks of sending, receiving, and storing information.

➥ In this way, each packet of information would travel the network like a giant game of hot potato, the packet always staying airborne so that the dismantling of any host computer (or server) would never impact the travelling packet's ability to reach its destination.

Internet Service Providers

➥ The Internet is the backbone of the on-line world. To get directly connected to the Internet, one can subscribe to a service called an Internet Service Provider (ISP). There are different types of ISPs and most are commercial enterprises.

Useful Parts of the Internet

➥ **Browser:** It is a programme which allows users to surf through the Internet and use of e-mail. Best known are: Netscape Communicator, and Microsoft Internet Explorer.

➥ **E-mail:** E-mail is an essential tool for most businesses because it is the most efficient way of sending messages very quickly and cheaply. Documents or graphics can be attached to an e-mail message, saving courier or postal service charges.

➥ **World Wide Web:** Another essential to the Web offers access to a world of information that can help organizations reduce their costs and develop individual relationships with their customers. The Web is also a vital business research tool.

➥ **Newsgroups:** Newsgroups can be very useful for conducting customer research or for keeping up to date with industry news. Newsgroup users post messages for others to read and respond to. Most e-mail programmes also read newsgroups.

➥ **Mailing Lists:** Mailing lists covering thousands of specialist topics are available by e-mail. Many Web sites offer their users regular updates of information by e-mail.

➥ **Chat-Rooms:** Internet chat rooms allow people to congregate and 'chat'. Text typed on one keyboard can be seen on other users' screens. While public chat rooms have little business value, private ones can usefully be set up for meetings.

➡ **FTP (File Transfer Protocol):** FTP allows files to be transferred to and from servers on the Internet, whatever type of computer one uses. Modern Web browsers incorporate FTP ability. Much information and even software is freely available from FTP servers.

DIFFERENCE BETWEEN WWW AND INTERNET

The www, or the World Wide Web, is a huge collection of documents stored in computers around the world. These millions of documents are known as web pages. A collection of documents run by one person or organization is called website. A computer with one or more websites is known as a host or server. The www differs from the Internet in that the Internet refers to all the interconnected national networks, while the 'world wide web' is just one of these networks. However, the www is so vast and widespread that it is often confused with being the same as the Internet.

Computer Terminology

➡ **Bit:** The bit is a unit of measurement of the electronic data. One bit is either 0 or 1 but not both. On composing 8 bits, 1 byte is formed.

➡ **Byte:** Total eight bits compose a byte. Thus 8 bits = 1 byte.

➡ **Boot:** The starting work done by the operating system in any computer to bring the computer in full working condition is called boot.

➡ **Compiler:** The program which converts high level languages into the languages of machine is called compiler.

➡ **Cursor Key:** The buton found to be on Key-Board on which there is a symbol of an arrow is called cursor-key. It is used to move cursor on the screen.

➡ **CD-ROM:** A CD like of music CD in which data can be stored substantially called CD-ROM. In a CD with comparison to floppy extremely more datas can be stored but one problem in it is that one time recorded data can not be deleted or modified.

➡ **Chip:** It is a thin slice on which by a special mechanism a circuit is designed which is normally made from Silicon.

➡ **Database:** The collection of datas in which from phone book to inventory management of any company are inlisted and enclosed are called Database.

➡ **Floppy Disc:** It is like a tape recorder casette in which datas are stored but it is very small and convenient to carry. Today the floppy disc which are used has its size up to of 3.5 inch.

➡ **Giga Byte:** 1024 Mega Byte (MB) is called 1 Giga Byte (GB).

Thus 1 Mega Byte = 1024 × 1024 Bytes.

Today fabricated Hard Discs are of the order of Giga Bytes.

➡ **Hard Disc:** It is datas storage device which is kept inside the cabinet and through it a great amount of datas are collected and stored. Also Hard Discs are of different shapes and sizes thus user select it appropriately.

➡ **Memory System:** The place where computer data and program are temporarily kept is called Memory system. Usually memory is implied from RAM.

➡ **Modem:** The device which converts digital signals into analogue signals and vice-versa is called Modem.

➥ **Mother Board:** Inside the cabinet of the computer there is a board on which CPU, Memory etc circuits are connected is called Mother Board and on it some other cards may also be attached.

➥ **Network:** The net of the various computers in which computers are interconnected by the cable or any medium is called Network. The main advantages of the Network is user file can be utilised or shared by the another.

➥ **Pixel:** The smallest part of any image is called pixel. A pixel of a monitor is represented by a very small dot (.). Such various dots compose an image. At a particular place if there be a large number of pixels then the quality of the image would be fine.

➥ **Pointer:** The component in the form of indicator which is attached to the mouse and controlled through it, appears on the computer screen is called pointer. The direction in which mouse pad is moved, pointer also moves in that direction.

➥ **RAM:** It is Random Access Memory (a place) where datas to be processed are kept temporarily and it is unstable memory.

➥ **ROM:** It is Read Only Memory and it is stable or Non-volatile memory which doesn't ended after power off.

➥ **Scanner:** It is a device through which graphic image is transformed to digital image and the scanners are of usually two types one desktop and another hand operating.

➥ **System Unit:** The box like cabinet part of desktop pc is called system unit and inside it mother board and another chips are attached.

➥ **Touch Screen:** The computer in which by touching monitor, instructions are given on the behalf of Key-Board.

➥ **Virus:** A software which is fabricated or automatically to damage the data is called computer virus. Normally virus tends to damage the files by entering through the operating system.

ABBREVIATIONS RELATED TO COMPUTERS

➥ ALGOL	:	Algorithmic Language
➥ ALU	:	Arithmetic Logic Unit
➥ ARPA	:	Advanced Research Project Agency
➥ ASCII	:	American Standard Code for Information Interchange
➥ ABC	:	Atanasoff-Berry Computer
➥ AGP	:	Accelerated Graphics Port
➥ AI	:	Artificial Intelligence
➥ AMD	:	Advanced Micro Devices
➥ ANSI	:	American National Standards Institute
➥ ASIC	:	Application Specific Integration Circuit
➥ BASIC	:	Beginer's All Purpose Symbolic Instruction Code
➥ BCD	:	Binary Coded Decimal Code

- ➡ BIOS : Basic Input-Output System
- ➡ BEMA : Business Equipment Manufacturers Association
- ➡ BCR : Bar Code Reader
- ➡ BPI : Bytes Per Inch
- ➡ BPS : Bits Per Second
- ➡ CAD : Computer Aided Design
- ➡ CAM : Computer Aided Manufacturing
- ➡ CD : Compact Disk
- ➡ C-DAC : Centre for Development of Advanced Computing
- ➡ CDMA : Code Division Multiple Access
- ➡ C-DOT : Centre for Development of Telematics
- ➡ CD-ROM : Compact Disk–Read Only Memory
- ➡ COBOL : Common Business Oriented Language
- ➡ COMAL : Common Algorithmic Language
- ➡ CPU : Central Processing Unit
- ➡ CAL : Computer Aided Learning
- ➡ CD-R : Compact Disk-Recordable
- ➡ CD-R/W : Compact Disk-Read/Write
- ➡ CLASS : Computer Literacy And Studies in School
- ➡ CMOS : Complementry Metal Oxide Semiconductor
- ➡ CPI : Character Per Inch
- ➡ CRS : Computerised Reservation System
- ➡ CU : Control Unit
- ➡ DOS : Disk Operating System
- ➡ DTP : Desk Top Publishing
- ➡ DTS : Digital Theatre System
- ➡ D/A : Digital-to-Analog
- ➡ DBMS : Data Base Management System
- ➡ DDS : Digital Data Storage
- ➡ DPI : Dots Per Inch
- ➡ DRDO : Defence Research and Development Organisation
- ➡ DSDD : Double Sided Double Density
- ➡ DTR : Data Terminal Ready
- ➡ DVD : Digital Video/Versatile Disk
- ➡ EBCDIC : Extended Binary Coded Decimal Interchange Code
- ➡ E-Business : Electronic Business

- E-Commerce : Electronic Commerce
- E-mail : Electronic Mail
- EDP : Electronic Data Processing
- EEPROM : Electrically Erasable Programmable Read Only Memory
- ENIAC : Electronic Numerical Integrator and Calculator
- EPROM : Erasable Programmable Read Only Memory
- ERNET : Education and Research Network
- FORTRAN : Formula Translation
- FAX : Far Away Xerox
- FAT : File Allocation Table
- FD : Floppy Disk
- FDM : Frequency Division Multiplexing
- FET : Field Effect Transistor
- FLOP : Floating Point Operation
- FSK : Frequency Shift Keying
- FTP : File Transfer Protocol
- GIAS : Gateway Internet Access Service
- GB : Giga Bytes
- GIGO : Garbage In-Garbage-Out
- GIS : Geographical Information System
- GPL : General Public License
- GPS : Global Positioning System
- GUI : Graphical User Interface
- HLL : High Level Language
- HTML : Hyper Text Markup Language
- HTTP : Hyper Text Transfer Protocol
- HP : Hewlett Packard
- IBM : International Business Machines
- I/O : Input-Output
- IRC : Internet Relay Chat
- ISDN : Integrated Services Digital Network
- ISO : International Standards Organisation
- ISP : Internet Service Provider
- IT : Information Technology
- JPEG : Joint Photographic Expert Group
- JRE : Java Runtime Engine

- ➥ JSP : Java Server Pages
- ➥ KB : Kilo Bytes
- ➥ Kb : Kilo bits
- ➥ KIPS : Knowledge Information Processing System
- ➥ LAN : Local Area Network
- ➥ LCD : Liquid Crystal Display
- ➥ LDU : Liquid Display Unit
- ➥ LLL : Low Level Language
- ➥ LASER : Light Amplification for Stimulated Emission of Radiation
- ➥ LD : Laser Diode
- ➥ LED : Light Emitting Diode
- ➥ LISP : List Processing
- ➥ LSD : Least Significant Digit
- ➥ LSI : Large Scale Integration
- ➥ MAN : Metropolitan Area Network
- ➥ MICR : Magnetic Ink Character Recognition
- ➥ MIPS : Millions Instructions Per Second
- ➥ MOPS : Millions of Operations Per Second
- ➥ MODEM : Modulator-Demodulator
- ➥ MB : Mega Bytes
- ➥ MHz : Mega Hertz
- ➥ MIDI : Musical Instrument Digital Interface
- ➥ MOS : Metal Oxide Semiconductor
- ➥ MPEG : Moving Pictures Expert Group
- ➥ MP-3 : MPEG-1 Audio Layer 3
- ➥ MS : Microsoft
- ➥ MSI : Medium Scale Integration
- ➥ MTBF : Mean Time Between Failure
- ➥ NICNET : National Information Centre Network
- ➥ NIU : Network Interface Unit
- ➥ NTSC : National Television Standards Committee
- ➥ OCR : Optical Character Recognition
- ➥ OMR : Optical Mark Reader
- ➥ OOP : Object Oriented Programming
- ➥ OS : Operating System
- ➥ OSS : Open Source Software

- PROM : Programmable Read Only Memory
- PSPDN : Pocket Switched Public Data Network
- PSTN : Public Switched Telephone Network
- PAL : Phase Alternation Line
- PC : Personal Computer
- PCB : Printed Circuit Board
- PCI : Peripheral Component Interconnect
- PDA : Personal Digital Assistant
- PDF : Portable Document Format
- PL/1 : Programming Language/1
- PM : Phase Modulation
- POST : Power On Self Test
- PPM : Pages Per Minute
- PROLOG : Programming in Logic
- RABMN : Remote Area Business Message Network
- RAM : Random Access Memory
- ROM : Read Only Memory
- RGB : Red, Green, Blue
- RPG : Report Program Generator
- RS-232 : Recommended Standard 2-3-2
- SCSI : Small Computer System Interface
- SEQUEL : Structured English Query Language
- SIMM : Single In-Line Memory Module
- SNOBOL : String Oriented Symbolic Language
- SSI : Small Scale Integration
- SVGA : Super Video Graphics Array
- TCP : Transmission Control Protocol
- TB : Tera Byte
- TDM : Time Division Multiplexing
- UPS : Uninterruptable Power Supply
- ULSI : Ultra Large Scale Integration
- UNIVAC : Universal Automatic Computer
- UPC : Universal Product Code
- URL : Uniform Resource Locater
- USB : Universal Serial Bus
- UVEPROM : Ultra Violet Erasable Programmable Read Only Memory

- ➡ VDU : Video Display Unit
- ➡ VLSI : Very Large Scale Integration
- ➡ VAN : Value Aided Network
- ➡ VCR : Video Cassette Recorder
- ➡ VGA : Video Graphics Array
- ➡ VIRUS : Vital Resources Under Seize
- ➡ VSAT : Very Small Aperture Terminal
- ➡ VSNL : Videsh Sanchar Nigam Limited
- ➡ WAN : Wide Area Network
- ➡ WAP : Wireless Application Protocol
- ➡ WWW : World Wide Web
- ➡ WMAX : World Wide Interoperability for Microwave Access
- ➡ WLL : Wireless Local Loop
- ➡ WMP : Windows Media Player
- ➡ WORM : Write Once-Read Many
- ➡ XML : Extensible Markup Language
- ➡ XMS : Extended Memory Specification
- ➡ 2G : Second Generation Wireless Networking
- ➡ 3G : Third Generation Wireless Networking Technology
- ➡ 4G : Fourth Generation Wireless Networking Technology
- ➡ 5G : Fifth Generation Wireless Networking Technology

MULTIPLE CHOICE QUESTIONS

1. Machine language is different

A. for some computer
B. for each kind of computer c.p.u.
C. Both (A) and (B)
D. None of the above

2. A programmer if write instructions in machine language can specify an....... bit with the numerical 1.

A. on B. off
C. into D. None of these

3. Every operation that the computer is capable of performing is indicated by a specific

A. code B. language
C. binary code D. None of these

4. The assembly programmer must use the proper code for

A. each operation
B. each high level language
C. all arithmetic operations
D. all languages

5. Machine language is also called

A. language
B. machine
C. binary representation
D. None of the above

6. An 'on' bit indicates the presence of an
A. electric current
B. off
C. address
D. None of these

7. Programming language can be divided into.....categories.
A. four broad B. three
C. five D. six

8. The operating system contains
A. same programs repetitively
B. several types of programs
C. a few programs
D. None of the above

9. Utility programs performs
A. specialized and useful functions
B. all functions
C. a few functions
D. None of the above

10. The supervisor program is the major component of the
A. system B. operating system
C. all system D. language

11. When the computer is first turn on, the supervisor program is the.......... to be used.
A. last program
B. first program
C. middle program
D. None of the above

12. A job is a unit of work to be processed by the
A. CPU B. ALU
C. TD D. memory

13. A computer can only execute instructions that are in
A. secondary memory
B. machine language
C. pascal
D. None of the above

14. English-like programs such as those written in Pascal must use for their execution, a
A. language program
B. language translation program
C. Both (A) and (B)
D. None of the above

15. Language translation program translates the English-like program into
A. other language
B. other program
C. machine language
D. None of the above

16. There are..........types of language translation programs.
A. four B. two
C. three D. five

17. A utility program can translate data from a format to:
A. another format
B. any machine language
C. Both (A) and (B)
D. None of the above

18. The supervisor schedules the order of input and
A. other operations
B. a few operations
C. output operations
D. None of the above

19. When the computers were first developed, machine language was the only way they could be
A. used
B. programmed
C. Both (A) and (B)
D. None of these

20. Assembly language is also referred as
A. low-level language
B. high-level language
C. Both (A) and (B)
D. None of the above

21. The word size of a microprocessor refers to:
A. The amount of information that can be stored in a byte
B. The amount of information that can be stored in a cycle

C. The number of machine operations performed in a second
D. The maximum length of an English word that can be input to a computer

22. Bar codes store information using:
A. Punch holes
B. Thick and thin lines
C. Magnetized spots
D. Bits

23. Below are examples of real security and privacy risks EXCEPT:
A. hackers B. identity theft
C. spam D. viruses

24. Which is an electronic device that can store temporarily a single bit of data?
A. Accumulator
B. Buffer
C. Memory
D. Latch

25. The first generation computers were characterised by:
A. Micro processor chips
B. Thermionic valves
C. Transistors
D. Integrated circuits

26. The ability to recover and read deleted or damaged files from a criminal computer is an example of a law enforcement specialty known as:
A. robotics
B. computer forensics
C. simulation
D. animation

27. A modern digital computer has:
A. Extremely high speed
B. Large memory
C. Almost unlimited army
D. All of these

28. What is the full form of COBOL?
A. Common Business Objective Language
B. Command Byte Oriented Language
C. Common Business Oriented Language
D. Character Business Oriented Language

29. Find the invalid combination.
A. Dot Matrix Printer - Impact Printer
B. Laser Printer - Non Impact Printer
C. Daisy Wheel Printer - Non Impact Printer
D. Inkjet Printer - Non Impact Printer

30. In which generation of computers transistors were used?
A. First generation computers
B. Second generation computers
C. Third generation computers
D. Fourth generation computers

31. Which computer system is mainly used in Weather forecasting and Disaster control?
A. Super computer
B. Mainframe computer
C. Micro computer
D. Personal computer

32. A factor which would strongly influence a business person to adopt a computer is its:
A. Accuracy
B. Reliability
C. Speed
D. All of these

33. The output quality of a printer is determined by:
A. Dot per sq. inch
B. Dot per inch
C. Dots printed per unit time
D. All of above

34. The first microprocessor built by the Intel Corporation was called:
A. 8008 B. 8080
C. 4004 D. 8800

35. When was the first minicomputer built?
A. 1965 B. 1962
C. 1971 D. 1966

36. The first digital computer built with IC chips was known as:
A. IBM 7090
B. Apple-1
C. IBM System/360
D. VAX-780

37. What is the name of the British gentleman who was the first to put forward in 1952 the idea for the integrated circuit?
A. Jack S. Kilby
B. G.W. Dummer
C. William Shockley
D. John Bardeen

38. The magnetic tape consists of a plastic type with a surface coating of magnetic material. When was it invented?
A. 1968 B. 1964
C. 1956 D. 1946

39. A German mathematician who invented a calculator, for addition, subtraction, multiplication and division, His name was:
A. Napier B. Pascal
C. Leibniz D. Hollerith

40. Who invented analytical machine?
A. Charles Babbage
B. Hollerith
C. Pascal
D. Napier

41. Modern computers are very reliable but they are not:
A. Fast B. Powerful
C. Infallible D. Cheap

42. A complete microcomputer system consists of:
A. Microprocessor
B. Memory
C. Peripheral equipment
D. All of the above

43. Modem is a/an:
A. input device
B. output device
C. both (A) and (B)
D. storage device

44. Computer peripherals do not include:
A. UPS
B. Speaker
C. Microphone
D. Microwave

45. This device helps us to change our voice into electronic signals, is called:
A. Speakers
B. Mouse
C. Microphone
D. Motherboard

ANSWERS

1	2	3	4	5	6	7	8	9	10
B	A	C	A	C	A	A	B	A	B
11	12	13	14	15	16	17	18	19	20
B	A	B	B	C	C	A	C	B	A
21	22	23	24	25	26	27	28	29	30
B	B	C	D	B	D	D	C	C	B
31	32	33	34	35	36	37	38	39	40
A	D	B	C	A	C	B	C	C	A
41	42	43	44	45					
C	D	C	D	C					

World : Miscellaneous

NATIONS AT A GLANCE

Country	Area (sq km)	Capital	Currency	Languages
Afghanistan	652,090	Kabul	Afghani	Pashto, Dari, Uzbeck, etc.
Albania	28,748	Tirana	Lek	Albanian, Greek
Algeria	2,381,741	Algiers	Algerian Dinar	Arabic (official), French, Berber dialects
Andorra	465	Andorra la Vella	Euro	Catalan (official), French Spanish
Angola	1,246,700	Luanda	Kwanza	Bantu, Portuguese (official)
Antigua and Barbuda	442	St. John's	East Caribbean Dollar	English
Argentina	2,766,890	Buenos Aires	Argentinian Peso	Spanish, Italian, Amerindian
Armenia	29,800	Yerevan	Dram	Armenian, Azeri
Australia	7,686,850	Canberra	Australian Dollar	English, Italin, Greek
Austria	83,855	Vienna	Euro	German, Croatian, Turkish
Azerbaijan	86,600	Baku	New Manat	Azeri, Russian Armenian, Lezgins
Bahamas	13,939	Nassau	Bahamian Dollar	English, Creole
Bahrain	687.75	Manama	Bahraini Dinar	Arabic (official), English
Bangladesh	143,998	Dhaka	Taka	Bengali (official), English
Barbados	430	Bridgetown	Barbados Dollar	English, Creole
Belarus	207,600	Minsk	Belarusian Ruble	Belarusian, Russian
Belgium	30,528	Brussels	Euro	Flemish (Dutch), French, German
Belize	22,963	Belmopan	Belize Dollar	English (official), Spanish, Maya, Creole
Benin	112,622	Porto-Novo	Franc CFA	French, African languages

Country	Area (sq km)	Capital	Currency	Languages
Bhutan	38,394	Thimphu	Ngultrum, Indian rupee	Dzongkha (official), Nepali, Assamese
Bolivia	1,098,581	La Paz	Boliviano	Spanish, Quechua, Aymara
Bosnia and Herzegovina	51,129	Sarajevo (Bosnia)	Marka	Bosnian, Surbian, Croatian
Botswana	581,370	Gaborone	Pula	English, Setswana, Shona
Brazil	8,511,965	Brasilia	Real	Portuguese
Brunei Darussalam	5,765	Bandar Seri Begawan	Brunei Dollar	Malay (official), Chinese, English
Bulgaria	110,994	Sofia	Lev	Bulgarian, Turkish
Burkina Faso	274,200	Ouagadougou	Franc CFA	French, Tribal languages
Burundi	27,835	Bujumbura	Burundi Franc	Kirundi and French (official)
Cambodia	181,035	Phnom Penh	Riel	Khmer, Vietnamese
Cameroon	475,442	Yaounde	Franc CFA	French and English (both official)
Canada	9,976,140	Ottawa	Canadian Dollar	English, French
Cape Verde	4,033	Praia	Cape Verdean Escudo	Portuguese, Creole
Central African Republic	622,436	Bangui	Franc CFA	French (official), Sango, Bandu, Baya, local language
Chad	1,284,000	N'djamena	Franc CFA	French and Arabic (official)
Chile	756,945	Santiago	Chilean Peso	Spanish
China	9,596,960	Beijing	Yuan, Hongkong Dollar	Mandarin, Wu, Cantonese Hsiang
Colombia	1,141,748	Bogota	Colombian Peso	Spanish
Comoros	1,862	Moroni	Comoros Franc	Comorian, French, Arabic
Cango Republic	341,821	Brazzaville	Franc CFA	French, Kongo, others
Congo, Demo. Republic	2,345,410	Kinshasa	Franc (CDF)	French, Lingala, Semahili, Kongo
Costa Rica	51,100	San Jose	Costa Rican Colon	Spanish
Cote D'Ivoire	322,463	Yamoussoukro	Franc CFA	French, African languages
Croatia	56,538	Zagreb	Euro	Croatian, Serbian
Cuba	110,860	Havana	Cuban Peso	Spanish
Cyprus	9,251	Nicosia	Euro	Greek, Turkish (official), English
Czech Republic	78,864	Prague	Koruna	Czech, Moravean Slovakian
Denmark	43,075	Copenhagen	Danish Krone	Danish
Djibouti	23,200	Djibouti	Djibouti Franc	Arabic, French, Afar, Somali
Dominica	749	Roseau	East Caribbean Dollar	English and Creole

Country	Area (sq km)	Capital	Currency	Languages
Dominican Republic	48,442	Santo Domingo	Dominican Peso	Spanish, Creole
Ecuador	272,045	Quito	US Dollar	Spanish (90%), Quechua
East Timor	14,874	Dili	US Dollar	Portuguese, Tetun
Egypt	1,000,250	Cairo	Egyptian Pound	Arabic
El Salvador	21,041	San Salvador	Colon	Spanish
Equatorial Guinea	28,051	Malabo	Franc CFA	Spanish (official), French, Fang
Eritrea	117,400	Asmara	Nakfa	Tigre, Tigrinya
Estonia	45,200	Tallinin	Euro	Estonian (official), Russian
Ethiopia	1,133,380	Addis Ababa	Birr	Amharic (official), Tigriniya
Fiji	18,333	Suva	Fijian Dollar	Fijian, Hindustani, English (official)
Finland	335,145	Helsinki	Euro	Finnish, Swedish
France	543,965	Paris	Euro	French, Arabic
Gabon	267,667	Libreville	Franc CFA	French (official) and Fang
Gambia	11,295	Banjul	Dalasi	Native tongues, English (official)
Georgia	69,700	Tbilisi	Lari	Georgian (official), Russian, Armenian
Germany	357,022	Berlin	Euro	German, Turkish
Ghana	238,537	Accra	Cedi	English (official), Native tongues
Greece	131,957	Athens	Euro	Greek
Grenada	378	St George's	East Caribbean Dollar	English, Creole
Guatemala	108,889	Guatemala City	Quetzal	Spanish, Mayan languages
Guinea	245,857	Conakry	Guinean Franc	French (official), native tongues
Guinea Bissau	36,125	Bissau	Franc CFA	Portuguese Creolo, African language
Guyana	214,969	Georgetown	Guyana Dollar	English (Official), Amerindian dialects
Haiti	27,750	Port-au-Prince	Gourde	French, Creole
Honduras	112,088	Tegucigalpa	Lempira	Spanish, Amerindian languages
Hungary	93,030	Budapest	Forint	Hungarian
Iceland	102,820	Reykjavik	Icelandic Krona	Icelandic
India	3,287,263	New Delhi	Rupee	Hindi, English (official) and Regional languages
Indonesia	1,919,443	Jakarta	Rupiah	Bahasa Indonesia (official), Dutch, English

Country	Area (sq km)	Capital	Currency	Languages
Iran	1,648,000	Teheran	Rial	Farsi (Persian), Kurdish
Iraq	438,317	Baghdad	Iraqi Dinar	Arabic (official), Kurdish
Ireland	70,282	Dublin	Euro	Irish, English
Israel	20,772	Jerusalem	Shekel	Hebrew, Arabic
Italy	301,278	Rome	Euro	Italian
Jamaica	10,991	Kingston	Jamaican Dollar	English, Creole
Japan	377,812	Tokyo	Yen	Japanese
Jordan	89,206	Amman	Jordanian Dinar	Arabic (official), English
Kazakhstan	2,717,300	Akmola	Tenge	Kazakh (Qazaq) official language, Russian
Kenya	582,646	Nairobi	Kenyan Shilling	English, Swahili (national)
Korea, North	120,538	Pyongyang	Won	Korean
Korea, South	99,263	Seoul	Won	Korean
Kuwait	17,820	Kuwait	Kuwaiti Dinar	Arabic and English
Kyrgyzstan	1,98,500	Bishkek	Kyrgyz Som	Kirghiz (Turkic origin): Russian (official)
Laos	236,800	Vientiane	Kip	Lao (official); French
Latvia	64,600	Riga	Lats	Latvian, Russian
Lebanon	10,400	Beirut	Lebanese Pound	Arabic (official), French, English
Lesotho	30,355	Maseru	Loti	English, Sesotho (official), Zulu & Xhosa
Liberia	111,369	Monrovia	Liberian Dollar	English (official)
Libya	1,759,998	Tripoli	Libyan Dinar	Arabic, Berber
Liechtenstein	157	Vaduz	Swiss Franc	German
Lithuania	65,200	Vilnius	Litas	Lithuanian, Russian, Polish
Luxembourg	2,586	Luxembourg	Euro	Latzeburgish, French, German
Macedonia	25,713	Skopje	Denar	Macedonian, Albanian, Turlush
Madagascar	587,050	Antananarivo	Malagasy Franc	Malagasy, French
Malawi	118,484	Lilongwe	Kwacha	English (official), Chichewa (Nat.)
Malaysia	332,965	Kualalumpur	Ringgit	Malay (official), Chinese, Tamil, English
Maldives	298	Male	Rufiyaa	Divehi
Mali	1,240,140	Bamako	Franc CFA	French (official), African languages

Country	Area (sq km)	Capital	Currency	Languages
Malta	316	Valletta	Euro	Maltese and English
Marshall Island	181	Dalap-Uliga-Djarrit	US Currency	Marshallese (official), English
Mauritania	1,030,700	Nouakchott	Ouguiya	Arabic (official) and French
Mauritius	2,040	Port Louis	Mauritian Rupee	English (official), French, Creole, Hindi, Urdu, Hakka
Mexico	1,972,545	Mexico City	Mexican Peso	Spanish, American languages
Micronesia	701	Palikir	US Dollar	English (official), Chuukee
Moldova	33,700	Chisinau	Maldovian leu	Romanian, Russian
Monaco	2	Monaco-Ville	Euro	French, Monegasque, Italian
Mongolia	1,565,000	Ulan Bator	Tugrik	Mongolian, Kazakh
Morocco	446,550	Rabat	Dirham	Arabic, French, Berber
Mozambique	799,380	Maputo	Metical	Portuguese (official), Makua
Myanmar	676,577	Nay Pyi Taw	Kyat	Burmese; minority languages
Namibia	824,268	Windhoek	Namibian Dollar	Afrikaans, German, English (official)
Nauru	21.3	Yaren	Australian Dollar	Nauruan, English
Nepal	147,181	Kathmandu	Napalese Rupee	Nepali, Maithili, English, Bhojpuri
Netherlands	41,526	Amsterdam	Euro	Dutch, Frisian
New Zealand	270,534	Wellington	New Zealand Dollar	English, Maori
Nicaragua	130,671	Managua	Cordoba	Spanish
Niger	1,267,044	Niamey	Franc CFA	French (official), Hausa
Nigeria	923,773	Abuja	Naira	English (official), Hausa
Norway	323,878	Oslo	Norwegian Krone	Norwegian
Oman	309,500	Muscat	Oman Rial	Arabic (official); Baluchi also English
Pakistan	803,936	Islamabad	Pakistan Rupee	Urdu (National), English (official), Punjabi, Sindhi
Panama	77,082	Panama City	Balboa	Spanish (offi.), English
Papua New Guinea	462,840	Port Moresby	Kina	English
Paraguay	406,752	Asuncion	Guarani	Spanish (offi.), Guarani
Peru	1,244,284	Lima	Sol	Spanish, Quechua, Aymara
Philippines	300,000	Manila	Peso	Filipino, English, Cebuano, Ilocano, Tagalog

Country	Area (sq km)	Capital	Currency	Languages
Poland	312,685	Warsaw	Zloty	Polish, German
Portugal	88,940	Lisbon	Euro	Portuguese
Qatar	11,437	Doha	Qatari Riyal	Arabic; English is also widely spoken
Romania	237,500	Bucharest	Leu	Romanian (offi.), Hungarian
Russia	17,075,200	Moscow	Ruble	Russian, Tatar, Ukrainian
Rwanda	26,338	Kigali	Rwanda Franc	Kinyarwanda and French
St. Kitts & Nevis or (St. Kitts 169–Nevis 93)	262	Besseterre	East Caribbean Dollar	English, Creole
St. Lucia	617	Castries	East Caribbean Dollar	English and Creole
St. Vincent & the Grenadines	388	Kingstown	East Caribbean	English and Creole
Samoa	2,831	Apia	Tala	Samoan and English
San Marino	62	San Marino	Euro	Italian
Sao Tome and Principe	958	Sao Tome	Dobra	Portuguese
Saudi Arabia	2,200,000	Riyadh	Riyal	Arabic, Creole
Senegal	196,722	Dakar	Franc CFA	French (off.); Wolof, Fulani
Serbia	77,453	Belgrade	Serbean Dinar	Serbian, Hungarian
Seychelles	455	Victoria	Seychelles Rupee	English & French (official), Creole
Sierra Leone	71,740	Freetown	Leone	English (official), Mende, Temne, Krio
Singapore	639	Singapore	Singapore Dollar	Malay, Chinese (Mandarin), Tamil, English
Slovakia	49,035	Bratislava	Euro	Slovak (official), Hungarian
Slovenia	20,251	Ljubljana	Euro	Slovenian, Serbo-Crotian
Solomon Islands	28,370	Honiara	Solomon Islands Dollar	English, Pidigan, 80 other languages and dialects
South Africa	1,219,090	Pretoria	Rand	Africans, English, 9 other official languages
Somalia	637,657	Mogadishu	Somali Shilling	Somali (official), Arabic, English, Italian
South Sudan	644,329	Juba	Sudanese Pond (Sudeni)	Arabic, Dinka, local language
Spain	504,782	Madrid	Euro	Spanish, Basque, Catalan
Sri Lanka	65,610	Colombo	Sri Lanka Rupee	Sinhala, Tamil, English
Sudan	1,861,484	Khartoum	Sudanese Pound	Arabic, English, Tribal dialects

Country	Area (sq km)	Capital	Currency	Languages
Surinam	163,820	Paramaribo	Surinam Guilder	Dutch, Surinamese, English, Hindi
Swaziland	17,400	Mbabane	Emalangeni, S. African Rand	English, Swazi (official)
Sweden	449,964	Stockholm	Krona	Swedish
Switzerland	41,293	Berne	Swiss Franc	German, French, Italian
Syria	185,180	Damascus	Syrian Pound	Arabic, Kurdish, Armerian
Taiwan	36,182	Taipei	New Taiwan Dollar	Chinese (Mandarin)
Tajikistan	143,100	Dushanbe	Somoni	Tajik, Uzbek, Russian
Tanzania	945,037	Dodoma	Tanzanian Shilling	Swahili, English, local languages
Thailand	513,115	Bangkok	Baht	Thai (Siamese), Chinese
Togo	56,785	Lome	Franc CFA	Ewe, Mina (south), Kabye, Cotocoli (north), French (off.)
Tonga	748	Nuku'alofa	Pa'anga	Tongan, English
Trinidad and Tobago	5,124	Port-of-Spain	Trinidad and Tobago Dollar	English (official), Hindi
Tunisia	164,150	Tunis	Tunisian Dinar	Arabic, French
Turkiye	779,452	Ankara	Turkish Lira	Turkish, Kurdish
Turkmenistan	488,100	Ashgabat	Manat	Turkmen, Russian, Uzbek
Tuvalu	24	Vaiaku	Australian Dollar	Tuvaluan, English
Uganda	241,038	Kampala	Ugandan Shilling	English (official), Swahili, Luganada
Ukraine	603,700	Kyiv (Kiev)	Hryvnia	Ukrainian, Russian
UAE	77,700	Abu Dhabi	Dirham	Arabic, English
UK	243,609	London	Pound Sterling	English Welsh, Scots Gaelic
USA	9,629,091	Washington DC	US Dollar	Predominantly English, sizable Spanish
Uruguay	176,215	Montevideo	Peso	Spanish
Uzbekistan	447,400	Tashkent	Som	Uzbek, Russian, Tazik
Vanuatu	12,190	Port Vila	Vatu	English, Bislama, French
Vatican City	0.5	—	Euro	Italian
Venezuela	912.050	Caracas	Bolivar	Spanish, Indian dialects
Vietnam	329,566	Hanoi	Dong	Vietnamese (official), Khmer, Chinese, Thai
Yemen	527,970	Sana'a	Rial	Arabic
Zambia	752,618	Lusaka	Kwacha	English and local dialects
Zimbabwe	390,759	Harare	Zimbabwean Dollar	English (official), Ndebele, Shona

Countries and their Parliament

Country	Parliament	Country	Parliament
Afghanistan	Shora	**Israel**	Knesset
Albania	People's Assembly	**Japan**	Diet
Algeria	National People's Assembly	**Kenya**	National Assembly
Australia	Parliament	**Korea (North)**	Supreme People's Assembly
Austria	National Assembly	**Korea (South)**	National Assembly
Bangladesh	Jatia Parliament	**Malaysia**	Parliament (Dewan Rakyat and Dewan Negara)
Bhutan	Tasongadu	**Mongolia**	Great People's Khural
Botswana	National Assembly	**Nepal**	National Panchayat
Brazil	National Congress	**Netherlands**	Staten General
Britain	Parliament (House of Commons and House of Lords)	**New Zealand**	Parliament (House of Representatives)
Canada	Parliament	**Norway**	Storting
China, Mainland	National People's Congress	**Pakistan**	National Assembly
China, National	Yuan (National Assembly)	**Russia**	Duma
Colombia	Congress	**South Africa**	Parliament
Denmark	Folketing	**Spain**	Cortes
Egypt	People's Assembly	**Sweden**	Riksdag
France	Parliament	**Switzerland**	Federal Assembly
Germany	Bundestag (Lower House) and Bundesrat (Upper House)	**Syria**	People's Council
India	Sansad (Lok Sabha and Rajya Sabha)	**Turkiye**	Grand National Assembly
Indonesia	People's Consultative Assembly	**USA**	Congress (House of Representatives and Senate)
Iran	Majlis	**Vietnam**	National Assembly
Iraq	National Assembly	**Zambia**	National Assembly
Ireland	Oireachtas		

Official Books of Various Countries

Name of the Book	Country
Blue Book	Any official report of the British Government
Green Book	Official Publication of Italy and Iran
Grey Book	Official reports of the Japanese and Belgian Governments
Orange Book	Official publication of the Netherlands
White Book	Official publication of Germany, China and Portugal
Yellow Book	Official book of the French
White Paper	Short pamphlet giving authoritative account of facts issued by the Indian Government stating its views on a particular issue for the knowledge of general public

Political Parties of Some Countries

Country	Political Parties
Australia	Liberal Party, Labour Party
Bangladesh	Bangladesh National Party, Awami League, Jatiya Party
China	Communist Party of China
France	Socialist Party, National Front, Union for French Democracy
India	• Bhartiya Janta Party (BJP), • Indian National Congress (INC), • Nationalist Congress Party (NCP), • Communist Party of India (CPI), • Communist Party of India (Marxist) (CPM), • Bahujan Samaj Party (BSP)
Iraq	Bath Party
Israel	Labour Party, Likud Party, Hamas Party, Shas Party
Nepal	Nepali Communist Party, Nepali Congress Party
Pakistan	Muslim League, Pakistan Peoples Party
Russia	Communist Party, Liberal Democratic Party, Russian Choice
South Africa	African National Congress, National Party, Inkatha Freedom Party
Sri Lanka	United National Party, Freedom Party
UK	Conservative Party, Labour Party, Liberal Democratic Party
USA	Republican Party, Democratic Party

Important News Papers

Newspaper	Country	Newspaper	Country
The Morning Herald	Australia	People's Daily	China
The Age	Australia	Mainichi Daily News	Japan
Globe and Mail	Canada	The New Zealand Herald	New Zealand
The Gazette	Canada	The Press	New Zealand
International Herald Tribune	France	The Times	UK
Die Welt	Germany	The Scotsman	UK
The Sun	Britain	The Guardian	UK
New York Times	USA	The Herald	UK
Washington Post	USA	The Courier	UK

Signs and Symbols

Blind folded Woman Holding a Balance Scale	Justice
Black arm-band	Sign of mourning or protest
Dove	Peace
Flag upside down	Distress
Flag flown at half mast	National mourning
Green Light	Traffic signal for 'go'
Lotus	Culture and Civilization
Maharaja	Air India
Olive Branch	Peace
Red Cross	Hospital (or medical aid)
Red Flag	Revolution
Red Light	Danger; Traffic signal for 'stop'
Red Triangle	Family Planning
Two bones crossing each other diagonally with a skull in the upper quadrant	Danger
Two hands protecting a lamp	Life Insurance Corporation
V (letter)	Victory
White Flag	Truce
Wheel	Progress

Intelligence Agencies of Some Prominent Countries

Country	Intelligence Agency
India	Research & Analysis Wing (RAW), Intelligence Bureau (I.B.), Central Bureau of Investigation (C.B.I.)
Pakistan	Inter Service Intelligence (I.S.I.)
U.S.A.	Central Intelligence Agency, Federal Bureau of Investigation
Britain	Military Intelligence (M.I.)-5 and 6, Special Branch, Ultra, Joint Intelligence Organisation
Israel	Mosad
Egypt	Mukhabarat
Japan	Nicho
Russia	K.G.B. (Komitel Gosudarstvennoy Bezopasnosty) (Committee for State Security)
Canada	Security Intelligence Service
S. Africa	Bureau of State Security
Iran	Sabak
Iraq	Al-Mukhabarat
Australia	Australian Security and Intelligence Organisation
France	S.D.E.C.E.
Spain	C.E.S.I.D.

First in the World (Male & Female)

✦ First President of USA	George Washington
✦ First Prime Minister of Great Britain	Robert Walpole
✦ First Secretary General of United Nations	Trygve Lie
✦ First country to make education compulsory	Prussia/Germany
✦ First country to win the World Cup Football	Uruguay (1930)
✦ First men to climb Mt. Everest	Sherpa Tenzing Norgay & Sir Edmund Hillary (29th May, 1953)
✦ First man to reach North Pole	Robert Edwin Peary (USA)
✦ First man to reach South Pole	Roald Amundsen (Norway)
✦ First religion of the World	Sanatan Dharma
✦ First country to Print books	China
✦ First country to issue paper currency	China
✦ First country to start Civil Services Competition	China
✦ First country to make a constitution	United States of America
✦ Pakistan's first Governor General	Mohammad Ali Jinnah
✦ First summit of NAM was organised in	Belgrade (former Yugoslavia)
✦ First European to visit China	Maffeo Polo
✦ First University of the world	Takshashila/Taxila University
✦ First man to set foot on the Moon	Neil Armstrong (U.S.A.)
✦ First man to go into space	Major Yuri Alekseyevich Gagarin (former USSR)
✦ First Space Shuttle launched	Columbia (April 12, 1981)
✦ First Space Ship landed on Mars	Viking-I (July 20, 1976)
✦ First Woman Prime Minister of England	Margaret Thacher
✦ First Woman Prime Minister of any muslim country	Benazir Bhutto (Pakistan)
✦ First man to fly an aeroplane	Wright Brothers (Wilbur & Orville Right)
✦ First person to sail around the world	Ferdinand Magellan
✦ First country to send human to Moon	United States of America
✦ First country to launch satellite into space	Russia (former USSR)
✦ First country to host the modern Olympic games	Greece
✦ First President of the Republic of China	Dr. Sun Yat-sen
✦ First city to be attacked with Atom Bomb	Hiroshima (Japan)
✦ First Radio Telescope Satellite was launched into space	Japan
✦ First Russian (Soviet) Prime Minister to visit India	V.I. Bulganin
✦ First Woman Prime Minister of a country	Sirimavo Bhandarnaike (Sri Lanka)
✦ First Woman cosmonaut in space	Valentina Tereshkova (former USSR)
✦ First Woman to climb Mt. Everest	Junko Tabei (Japan)
✦ First deaf and dumb to cross the Srait of Gibralter	Taranath Shenoy (India)
✦ First Woman President of UN General Assembly	Smt. Vijyalakshmi Pandit (1953)
✦ First European Invader of Indian soil	Alexander, The Great

✦ First Woman to reach the North Pole	Ann Bancroft
✦ First Woman to reach Antarctica	Caroline Mikkelsen's
✦ First Woman to be a working member of an Antarctic Expedition	Jackie Ronne
✦ First man to draw the map of earth	Anaximander (610-542 BC)
✦ First man to compile Encyclopaedia	Aspheosis (Athens)
✦ The oldest man to climb Mt. Everest	Yuichiro Miura (Japan), 2013
✦ First Woman President of a country	Marma Estela I.M. Cortas de Peron (Argentina)
✦ First Space Tourist (Male)	Denis Tito (USA)
✦ First Space Tourist (Female)	Mrs. Anousheh Ansari (Irani American)
✦ First Asian to win Wimbledon Trophy	Arthur Ashe (USA)
✦ First man to win Nobel Prize for Literature	Sully Prudhomme (France)
✦ First man to win Nobel Prize for Peace	Jean H. Dunant (Switzerland) & Frederic Passy (France)
✦ First man to win Nobel Prize for Physics	W.C. Rontgen (Germany)
✦ First man to win Nobel Prize for Chemistry	J.H. Van't Hoff (Howlland)
✦ First manto win Nobel Prize for Medicine	Emil Adolf Von Behrig (Germany)
✦ First man to win Nobel Prize for Economics	Ragnar Frisch (Norway) & Jan Tinbergen (Howlland)

National Emblems of Some Countries

Country	Emblem	Country	Emblem
U.K.	Rose	France	Lily
U.S.A.	Bald Eagle	Iran	Lion and Sun
Italy	Coat of arms	Spain	Eagle
Australia	Golden Wattle	Canada	Maple Leaf, Lily
India	Lion Capital	New Zealand	Silver fern
Bangladesh	Water Lily	Germany	The Federal Eagle
Netherlands	Coat of arms	Norway	Coat of arms

Superlatives (World)

The Largest, Biggest, Smallest, Longest, Highest etc.

✦ Tallest Building	Burj Khalifa, Dubai (UAE)
✦ Largest City (in population)	Tokyo (Japan)
✦ Biggest City (in area)	Jiuquam Gansu, China (Area: 1,67,996 sq.km.)
✦ Largest Continent	Asia
✦ Smallest Continent	Australia
✦ Largest Country (in area)	Russia
✦ Tallest Animal (on land)	Giraffe
✦ Largest Bird	Ostrich

✦ Smallest Bird	Bee Humming Bird
✦ Largest Coral Formation	The Great Barrier Reef (Australia)
✦ Longest Day	June 21 (in Northern Hemisphere)
✦ Shortest Day	Dec. 22 (in Northern Hemisphere)
✦ Largest Delta	Sundarbans, India (8000 sq. miles)
✦ Largest Desert (world)	Sahara, Africa (84,00,000 sq. km)
✦ Longest Epic	The Mahabharata
✦ Largest Island	Greenland
✦ Deepest Lake	Baikal (Siberia, Russia); depth 5314 feet (1637m)
✦ Highest Lake	Titicaca (Bolivia) 12,645 ft. above sea level
✦ Largest Lake (Fresh water)	Lake Superior, U.S.A.
✦ Largest Lake (Salt water)	Caspian Sea (3,71,000 sq.km.)
✦ Biggest Library	Library of the Congress (Washington)
✦ Highest Mountain Peak (world)	Everest (Nepal) 29,035 ft. (8,850 m)
✦ Highest Mountain Range	Himalayas
✦ Longest Mountain Range	Andes (S. America) about 7000 km in length
✦ Deepest and Biggest Ocean	The Pacific
✦ Largest Peninsula	Arabia (32,50,000 sq.km.)
✦ Largest Planet	Jupiter
✦ Brightest and Hottest Planet	Venus
✦ Farthest Planet (from the sun)	Neptune
✦ Nearest Planet (to the sun)	Mercury
✦ Smallest Planet	Mercury
✦ Largest Platform (Railway)	Grand Central Terminal, New York (USA)
✦ Longest Railway Line	Trans-Siberian Railway (5,772 miles long)
✦ Longest River	Nile (6690 km), Amazon (6570 km)
✦ Brightest Star	Sirius A (also called Dog Star)
✦ World's tallest Statue	'Statue of Unity' (182 m) Gujarat
✦ Tallest Statue (bronze)	Bronze Statue of Lord Buddha, Tokyo (Japan)
✦ Longest Rail Tunnel	Gotthard Tunnel (Switzerland), 57 km
✦ Longest Tunnel (Road)	Laerdal, Norway
✦ Highest Volcano	Ojos del Salado, Andes, Argentine-Chile (6885 m)
✦ Largest Volcano	Mauna Loa (Hawaii)
✦ Longest Wall	Great Wall of China (1500 miles)
✦ Highest Waterfall	Salto Angel Falls (Venezuela)
✦ Longest Strait	Straight of Malacca
✦ Largest Gulf	Gulf of Mexico, Shoreline 2100 miles
✦ Largest River Basin	Amazon Basin (27,20,000 sq.miles)
✦ World's Rainiest spot	Mawsynram, India (11,873 mm)
✦ Lightest Gas	Hydrogen

✦ Lightest Metal	Lithium
✦ Highest Melting Point	Tungsten, 3422 °C
✦ Hardest substance (synthetic)	Wurtzite boron nitride
✦ Hardest substance (comes from meteorites)	Lonsdaleite
✦ Hardest Natural Substance (found on earth)	Diamond
✦ Longest Animal	Blue whale (recorded L: 106 ft, W: 195 tons)
✦ Longest Life-span of an Animal	190 to 200 years, (Giant tortoise)
✦ Largest Land Animal	African Bush Elephant
✦ Fastest Animal	Cheetah (Leopard) 70 m.p.h
✦ Longest Jump Animal	Kangaroo
✦ Longest Poisonous Snake	King Cobra
✦ Biggest Flower	Raffesia Arnoldi (Java)
✦ Largest Church	Basilica of St. Peter, Vatican City (Rome) Italy
✦ Largest Temple	Angkor Wat (Combodia)
✦ Largest River in Volume	Amazon, Brazil
✦ Longest Corridor	Ramanathaswamy Temple's Corridor, Rameshwaram (5000 feet)
✦ Largest Animal of the Cat Family	Lion
✦ Most Intelligent Animal	Chimpanzee
✦ Bird, that never makes its nest	Cuckoo
✦ Wingless Bird	Kiwi
✦ Reptile which changes its colours	Chameleon
✦ Largest Mammal	Blue Whale
✦ Largest Democracy	India
✦ Largest Neck Animal	Giraffe

Geographical Epithets

Epithet	Country/Place	Epithet	Country/Place
China's Sorrow (Yellow River)	Hwang Ho (China)	Land of Cakes (or Oat cakes)	Scotland
City of Arabian Nights	Baghdad (Iraq)	Land of Golden Fleece	Australia
City of Dreaming Spires	Oxford (England)	Land of Kangaroos	Australia
City of Golden Gate	San Francisco (USA)	Land of Lilies	Canada
City of Magnificent Distances	Washington DC (USA)	Land of Morning Calm	Korea
City of Palaces	Kolkata, Mysore (India)	Land of the flying Fish	Barbados
City of Popes	Rome (Italy)	Land of the Golden Pagoda	Myanmar
City of Seven Hills	Rome (Italy)	Land of the Humming Bird	Trinidad
City of Skyscrapers	New York (USA)	Gateway of India	Mumbai (India)

Epithet	Country/Place	Epithet	Country/Place
Bengal's Sorrow	Damodar River (India)	Gift of the Nile	Egypt
Blue Mountains	Nilgiri Hills	Gate of Tears	Bab-el-mandab, Israel
Britain of the South	New Zealand	Golden City	Aberdeen (Scotland)
Cockpit of Europe	Belgium	Grant White Way	Broadway (New York)
Dark Continent	Africa	Hermit Kingdom	Korea
Dairy of northern Europe	Denmark	Herring Pond	Atlantic Ocean
Emerald Island	Ireland	Island of Cloves	Madagascar
Empire City	New York	Island Continent	Australia
Eternal City	Lhasa (Tibet)	Island (Isle) of Pearls	Bahrain
Garden of England	Kent (England)	Key of the Mediterranean	Gibraltar
Garden of India	Bengaluru (India)	Land of Snow	Canada

Important Days (India and World)

JANUARY	
✦ Louis Braille Day	4th January
✦ National Youth Day (Birthday of Swami Vivekanand)	12th January
✦ Army Day (India)	15th January
✦ Rashtriya Balika Diwas	24th January
✦ Tourism Day (India)	25th January
✦ Republic Day (India)	26th January
✦ International Day of Commemoration in Memory of the Victims of the Holocaust	27th January
✦ Martyrs' Day (India)	30th January
✦ Leprosy Prevention Day	30th January
✦ Sarvodaya Day (India)	30th January
FEBRUARY	
✦ World Braille Day	2nd Monday in Feb.
✦ World Radio Day	13th February
✦ Valentine Day	14th February
✦ World Day of Social Justice	20th February
✦ International Mother Language Day	21st February
✦ Central Excise Tax Day	24th February
✦ National Science Day	28th February
MARCH	
✦ National Safety Day (Security of Industrial Institutions)	4th March
✦ International Women's Day, UN Day for Women's Rights & International Peace	8th March
✦ Commonwealth Day	2nd Monday in March
✦ World Kidney Day	10th March

✦ Central Industrial Security Force (CISF) Foundation Day	11th March
✦ World Consumer Rights Day	15th March
✦ Ordnance Factories Day	18th March
✦ International Day of Happiness	20th March
✦ World Forestry Day, International Day for the Elimination of Racial Discrimination	21st March
✦ World Water Day	22nd March
✦ World Meteorological Day	23rd March
✦ Ram Manohar Lohia's Birthday (Anniversary)	23rd March
✦ Bhagat Singh, Sukhdev and Rajguru's Martyrdam Day	23rd March
✦ World TB (Tuberculosis) Day	24th March
✦ Sacrifice Day of Ganesh Shankar Vidyarthi	25th March
✦ National Day of Bangladesh	26th March
✦ World Theatre Day	27th March
APRIL	
✦ World Autism Awareness Day	2nd April
✦ International Day for Mine Awareness and Assistance in Mine Action	4th April
✦ National Maritime Day	5th April
✦ World Health Day	7th April
✦ Special Protection Group (SPG) Foundation Day	8th April
✦ World Homeopathy Day (Birthday of Samuel Hanimen)	10th April
✦ World Aeronautics and Cosmology Day	14th April
✦ Ambedkar's Birth Anniversary	14th April
✦ World Haemophillia Day	17th April
✦ World Heritage Day/International Day for Monuments and Sites	18th April
✦ Indian Civil Service Day	21st April
✦ International Mother Earth Day	22nd April
✦ World Books and Copyright Day	23rd April
✦ Panchayat Divas (India)	24th April
MAY	
✦ International Labour Day (Worker's Day or May Day)	1st May
✦ World Asthma Day	1st Tuesday of May
✦ World Press Freedom Day	3rd May
✦ World Laughter Day	1st Sunday of May
✦ World Red Cross Day	8th May
✦ International Thalassemia Day	8th May
✦ World Migratory Birds Day	2nd Saturday of May
✦ Mother's Day	2nd Sunday of May
✦ National Technological Day	11th May
✦ International Nurses Day	12th May
✦ International Day of Families	15th May

✦ World Telecommunication/Information Society Day	17th May
✦ Anti-Terrorism Day, World Day for Cultural Diversity for Dialogue & Development	21st May
✦ International Day for Biological Diversity	22nd May
✦ Death Anniversary of Jawahar Lal Nehru	27th May
✦ International Day of UN Peacekeepers	29th May
✦ World No-Tobacco/No-smoking Day	31st May
JUNE	
✦ International Day of Innocent Children Victims of Agression	4th June
✦ World Environment Day	5th June
✦ World Oceans Day	8th June
✦ Father's Day (in many countries)	3rd Sunday of June
✦ World Elder Abuse Awareness Day	15th June
✦ World Day to Combat Desertification & Drought	17th June
✦ World Refugee Day	20th June
✦ International Day of Yoga	21st June
✦ UN Public Service Day	23rd June
✦ International Day (UN) against Drug Abuse and Illicit Trafficking, International Day in Support of Victims of Torture	26th June
JULY	
✦ Doctor's Day (Birthday of Dr. Bidhan Chandra Roy)	1st July
✦ State Bank of India Foundation Day	1st July
✦ International Day of Cooperatives	1st Saturday of July
✦ World Population Day	11th July
✦ International Nelson Mandela Day	18th July
✦ Kargil Victory Day (India)	26th July
✦ CRPF Foundation Day	27th Day
AUGUST	
✦ International Day of Friendship	1st Sunday of Augt.
✦ Hiroshima Day	6th August
✦ Quit India Day (India), Nagasaki Day, International Day of the World's Indigenous People	9th August
✦ International Youth Day	12th August
✦ Independence Day (India)	15th August
✦ World Humanitarian Day	19th August
✦ National Sports Day (Birthday of Dhyanchand)	29th August
✦ International Day against Nuclear Tests	29th August
SEPTEMBER	
✦ Teacher's Day (Birthday of S. Radhakrishnan)	5th September
✦ International Literacy Day	8th September
✦ UN Day for South-South Cooperation	12th September

✦ World Fraternity and Apology Day	14th September
✦ Hindi Divas (Day)	14th September
✦ International Day of Democracy	15th September
✦ Engineer's Day (Birthday of M. Vishweshwaraiya)	15th September
✦ World Ozone Day/International Day for the Preservation of the Ozone Layer	16th September
✦ Railway Police Force (RPF) Foundation Day	20th September
✦ International Day of Peace, Alzheimer's Day	21st September
✦ World Tourism Day	27th September
✦ World Heart Day	29th September
✦ World Deaf Day	Last Sunday of Sept.
OCTOBER	
✦ International Day for Older Persons	1st October
✦ Mahatma Gandhi's Birthday (International Day of Non-Violence)	2nd October
✦ Birthday of Lal Bahadur Shastri	2nd October
✦ World Habitat Day	1st Mon. of October
✦ World Animal Welfare Day	4th October
✦ World Teacher's Day	5th October
✦ World Wild Animal Day	6th October
✦ Indian Air Force Day	8th October
✦ World Post Day	9th October
✦ International Day of the Girl Child	11th October
✦ Birthday of Loknayak Jay Prakash Narayan	11th October
✦ UN International Day for Natural Disaster Reduction	2nd Wed. of October
✦ World Standards Day	14th October
✦ World Food Day	16th October
✦ World Allergy Awareness Day	16th October
✦ International Day for the Eradication of Poverty	17th October
✦ World Iodine Shortage Day	21st October
✦ UN Day, World Development Information Day	24th October
✦ World Thrift Day/World Savings Day	31st October
✦ Death Anniversary of Indira Gandhi	31st October
NOVEMBER	
✦ International Day for Preventing the Exploitation of the Environment in War & Armed Conflict	6th November
✦ National Education Day (Birth of Maulana Azad)	11th November
✦ Children's Day (Birth anniversary of Jawaharlal Nehru)	14th November
✦ World Diabetes Day	14th November
✦ International Day for Tolerance	16th November
✦ National Press Day	16th November
✦ World Students Day	17th November

✦ World Day of Rememberance for Road Traffic Victims	3rd Sun. of Nov.
✦ National Journalism Day	17th November
✦ World Adult Day	18th November
✦ Universal Children's Day, Africa Industrialization Day	20th November
✦ World Television Day	21st November
✦ International Day for the Elimination of Violence Against Women, World Non-veg Prevention Day	25th November
✦ World Environment Protection Day	26th November
✦ National Law Day	26th November
✦ International Day of Solidarity with the Palestinian People	29th November
DECEMBER	
✦ World AIDS Day	1st December
✦ International Day for the Abolition of Slavery	2nd December
✦ World Diabled Day/Internatonal Day of Persons with Disabilities	3rd December
✦ Chemical Disaster Prevention Day	4th December
✦ Navy Day (India)	4th December
✦ International Volunteers Day	5th December
✦ International Civil Aviation Day	7th December
✦ Armed Forces Flag Day	7th December
✦ International Anti-Corruption Day	9th December
✦ International Human Rights Day	10th December
✦ World Children's Fund Day	11th December
✦ International Mountain Day	11th December
✦ National Energy Conservation Day	14th December
✦ International Migrants Day	18th December
✦ Liberation Day of Goa	19th December
✦ International Human Solidarity Day	20th December

World Organisation and their Headquarters

✦ United Nations High Commission for Refugees (UNHCR)	Geneva
✦ International Atomic Energy Agency (IAEA)	Vienna (Austria)
✦ United Nations Industrial Development Organisation (UNIDO)	Vienna (Austria)
✦ UNCTAD (United Nations Conference on Trade and Development)	Geneva
✦ WWF (World Wildlife Fund)	Gland (Switzerland)
✦ International Olympic Committee (IOC)	Lausanne, Switzerland
✦ CHOGM (Commonwealth Heads of Governments Meet)	London
✦ OPEC (Organisation of Petroleum Exporting Countries)	Vienna
✦ OECD (Organisation for Economic Co-operation and Development)	Paris
✦ CENTO (Central Treaty Organisation)	Ankara (Turkiye)
✦ Commonwealth	London
✦ BRICS	Shanghai (China)

✦ European Union (EU)	City of Brussels (Belgium)
✦ GATT (General Agreement on Tariffs & Trade)	Geneva
✦ Amnesty International	London (England)
✦ Asian Development Bank (ADB)	Mandaluyong (Philippines)
✦ ASEAN (Association of South-East Asian Nations)	Jakarta (Indonesia)
✦ NATO (North Atlantic Treaty Organisaiton)	Brussels (Belgium)
✦ African Union (AU)	Addis-Ababa (Ethiopia)
✦ International Committee of the Red Cross (ICRC)	Geneva (Switzerland)
✦ SAARC (South Asian Association for Regional Corporation)	Kathmandu (Nepal)
✦ United Nations Environment Programme (UNEP)	Nairobi (Kenya)
✦ INTERPOLE (International Police)	Lyons (France)
✦ World Trade Organisation (WTO) (w.e.f. Jan. 1, 1995)	Geneva (Switzerland)
✦ League of Arab States	Cairo (Egypt)
✦ COMECON	Minsk (Belarus)
✦ World Council of Churches (WCC)	Geneva
✦ European Energy Commission (EEC)	Luxembourg
✦ Economic Commission of Africa (ECA)	Addis-Ababa
✦ Economic Commission of West Asia (ECWA)	Beirut, Lebanon
✦ World Health Organisation (WHO)	Geneva
✦ World Intellectual Property Organisation (WIPO)	Geneva
✦ World Meteorological Organisaiton (WMO)	Geneva
✦ Voluntary Service Overseas (VSO)	London
✦ Woman Aid International	London
✦ European Free Trade Association (EFTA)	Geneva
✦ Organisation of Arab Petroleum Exporting Countries	Kuwait
✦ International Bank for Reconstruction and Development (IBRD)	Washington
✦ Organisation of Economic Cooperation and Development (OECD)	Paris
✦ Organisation of the Islamic Conference (OIC)	Mecca
✦ European Council	Brussels
✦ European Space Research Organization (ESRO)	Paris
✦ BENELUX Economic Union	Brussels
✦ Economic and Social Commission for Asia and the Pacific (ESCAP)	Bangkok (Thailand)
✦ Economic Commission for Europe (ECE)	Geneva
✦ Economic Commission for Latin America and the Carribbean (ECLAC)	Santiago (Chile)
✦ Economic and Social Commission for Western Asia (ESCWA)	Beirut, Lebanon
✦ ANZUS Council	Canberra (Australia)
✦ United Nations Centre for Human Settlements (UNCHS)	New York
✦ United Nations International Children's Emergency Fund (UNICEF)	New York
✦ United Nations Fund for Population Activities (UNFPA)	New York
✦ United Nations Development Programme (UNDP)	New York

✦ United Nations Institute for Training and Research (UNITAR)	Geneva
✦ World Food Programme (WFP)	Rome (Italy)
✦ Food and Agriculture Organisation (FAO)	Rome (Italy)
✦ International Civil Aviation Organisation (ICAO)	Montreal (Canada)
✦ International Fund for Agricultural Development (IFAD)	Rome
✦ International Labour Organisaiton (ILO)	Geneva
✦ International Monetary Fund (IMF)	Washington
✦ International Telecommunication Union (ITU)	Geneva
✦ United Nations Educational, Scientific and Cultural Organisaiton (UNESCO)	Paris
✦ Universal Postal Union (UPU)	Bern (Switzerland)

Seas of the World

Name	Area (km^2)	Average Depth (m)	Name	Area (km^2)	Average Depth (m)
South China Sea	2,319,000	1652	Sea of Japan	1,007,800	1350
Caribbean	2,718,200	2647	Andaman Sea	797,700	870
Mediterranean	2,965,800	1429	North Sea	575,200	94
Bering	2,291,900	1547	Black Sea	507,900	2243
Gulf of Mexico	1,592,800	1486	Red Sea	438,000	491
Sea of Okhotsk	1,589,700	838	Baltic	422,200	55
East China Sea	1,249,200	188	Gulf of St. Lawrence	236,600	148
Hudson Bay	1,232,300	128	Gulf of California	62,000	180

News Agencies of Some Countries

Country	Agencies
India	Press Trust of India (PTI), United News of India (UNI), Samachar Bharti, Univarta
China	Xinhua, China News Service
Japan	Kyodo, Jiji Press
Indonesia	Antara
Iran	Islamic Republic News Agency (IRNA), ISNA, ILNA etc.
U.S.A.	Associated Press (AP), United Press International (UP)
U.K.	Reuters, Press Association
Russia	Telegraph Agency of the Sovereign States (TASS), Interfax
Malaysia	Malaysian National News Agency (BERNAMA)
Italy	Agenzia Nazionale Stampa Associata (ANSA)
Israel	Jewish Telegraphic Agency
France	Agence France Presse (A.F.P.)
Germany	Deutsche Presse Agentur (D.P.A.)
Palestine	WAFA, Ma'an News Agency
Australia	Australian Associated Press (A.A.P.)
Russia	Novosti
Pakistan	Associated Press of Pakistan (APP)
Egypt	Middle East News Agency (MENA)

Changed Names of Cities, States and Countries

Old Name	New Name
Abyssinia	Ethiopia
Angora	Ankara
Allahabad	Prayagraj
Banaras	Varanasi
Bangalore	Bengaluru
Bikramgarh-Bhatinda	Bathinda
Bombay	Mumbai
Baroda	Vadodara
Batavia	Jakarta/Djakarta
Basutoland	Lesotho
Bechuanaland	Botswana
British Guiana	Guyana
Burma	Myanmar
Ceylon	Sri Lanka
Christiana	Oslo
Cochin	Kochi
Constantinople	Istambul
Calcutta	Kolkata
Calicut	Kozhikode
Cape Canaveral	Cape Kennedy
Cawnpore	Kanpur
Central Provinces	Madhya Pradesh
Dacca	Dhaka
Dahomey	Benin
Dutch East Indies	Indonesia
Dutch Guiana	Surinam
Ellice Islands	Tuvalu
Formosa	Taiwan
Gauhati	Guwahati
Gold Coast	Ghana
Gurgaon	Gurugram
Holland	Netherlands
Ivory Coast	Cote d'Ivoire
Jubbulpore	Jabalpur
Jullundur	Jalandhar
Leopoldville	Kinshasa
Madras	Chennai
Madagascar	Malagasy

Old Name	New Name
Machukuo	Manchuria
Malaya	Malaysia
Mysore	Mysuru
Mesopotamia	Iraq
New Hebrides	Vanuatu
Northern Rhodesia	Zambia
Nippon/Nihon	Japan
Nyasaland	Malawi
Ooty/Ootacamund	Udhagamandalam
Orissa	Odisha
Panjim	Panaji
Petrograd	Leningrad
Palghat	Palakkad
Peking	Beijing
Poona	Pune
Persia	Iran
Pondicherry	Puducherry
Pretoria	Tshwane
Quilon	Kollam
Rhodesia	Zimbabwe
Rangoon	Yangon
Salisbury	Harare
Siam	Thailand
Saigon	Ho Chi Minh City
South West Africa	Namibia
Sandwich Islands	Hawaiian Islands
Stalingrad	Volgograd
Simla	Shimla
Spanish	Equatorial
Tanjore	Thanjavur
Trichur	Thrissur
Turkey	Turkiye
Tanganyika and Zanzibar	Tanzania
Trivandrum	Thriuvananthapuram
United Provinces	Uttar Pradesh
Uttaranchal	Uttarakhand
Upper Volta	Burkina Faso
Vizagapattam	Visakhapatnam
Zaire	Republic of Congo

WORLD ORGANISATIONS

United Nations

The United Nations is an association of 193* sovereign States which have voluntarily agreed to work for world peace and security.

- **Origin:** The name "United Nations" was devised by President Franklin D. Roosevelt.

  The United Nations Charter was drawn up by the representatives of 51 countries at the United Nations Conference on International Organization, which met at San Francisco on June 26, 1945. The Charter was signed on June 26, 1945. Poland, not represented at the Conference, signed it later and became one of the original 51 Member States.

  The United Nations officially came into existence on October 24, 1945, when the Charter had been ratified by China, France, the former USSR, the United Kingdom and the United States, and by a majority of other signatories.

- **Aims and Objectives:** ***Primary:*** The purposes of the UN can be divided into three groups, viz. *security, welfare* and *human rights.* The member-nations undertook to carry out four main duties (to settle disputes peacefully, to refrain from threatening or using force, to assist in carrying out the Charter, and not to assist an aggressor). The UN affirms faith in the human rights of all without distinction of race, language, sex or religion.

- **New Objectives:** *Disarm, decolonise, develop* are the three new objectives set forth by the United Nations.

**Latest entrant to the UN is South Sudan.*

- **Headquarters:** In August, 1946, an interim headquarters was set up at Lake Success in New York. In December 1946, the United Nations secured a permanent site, gifted by John D Rockefeller, on Manhattan Island, New York. The offices of the United Nations were shifted to the new building in Manhattan in 1951. The first meeting of the General Assembly was held there in October 1952.

- **Official Languages:** The recognised official languages of the UN are: English, French, Chinese, Russian, Arabic and Spanish. The working languages are English and French only.

- **Flag:** The flag is light blue in colour and emblazoned in white; in its centre is the UN's symbol—a polar map of the world embraced by twin olive branches open at the top.

- **Finance:** The UN is financed by the contributions from member States. All member States contribute to the expenses of the budget and to the Working Capital Fund on a scale determined by the General Assembly each year on the recommendation of its committee on contributions.

- **Membership:** Membership is open to all peace-loving States which adhere to the principles of the United Nations Charter. New members are admitted by the General Assembly only on the recommendations of the Security Council.

- **Major Organs:** The UN has six major organs: *(1)* General Assembly, *(2)* Security Council, *(3)* Economic and Social Council, *(4)* Trusteeship Council, *(5)* International Court of Justice, and *(6)* Secretariat.

1. **General Assembly:** The General Assembly occupies the central position in the structure of the UN. It consists of representatives of all the member nations. Each nation can send five representatives, but each has only one vote. It meets regularly once a year. Special and emergency session can also be summoned at the behest of the Security Council or otherwise. The Assembly discusses ways and means of preserving peace, disarmament, peaceful uses of atomic energy, economic development and social progress, the well-being of the people in non-self-governing colonies, human rights, etc. The President of the General Assembly is elected for a year. The Assembly passes the entire budget of the United Nations.
2. **Security Council:** It is the executive body of the UN. It is mainly responsible for maintaining international peace. It has 15 members, 5 of which (USA, UK, Russia, France and China) are permanent members. There are ten non-permanent members elected by a two-thirds majority of the General Assembly for a two-year term and are not eligible for immediate re-election. Its presidency is held for one month in rotation by member States in the English alphabetical order of their names.
3. **Economic and Social Council:** The Economic and Social Council consists of 54 members elected by the 2/3 majority of the General Assembly. The council meets usually twice a year.
4. **Trusteeship Council:** The Trusteeship Council prepares people for self-government or independence. Membership consists of permanent members of the Security Council plus those nations which administer trust territories, and the needed additional members to maintain an equal balance between administering and non-administering nations. The latter are elected by the General Assembly. The Trusteeship Council supervises the administration of various territories governed by nations designated by the UN as trustees.
5. **International Court of Justice:** The Court has 15 judges; no two of whom may be nationals of the same State. The Judges are elected by the General Assembly and the Security Council sitting independently. Their term of office is nine years, but they are eligible for re-election. The Court elects its own President and Vice-Presidents for a term of three years. The full Court of Judges usually sits but a quorum of nine Judges is sufficient to constitute the Court.
6. **Secretariat:** The Secretariat is under the Secretary General who is the chief administrative officer of the UN. He is assisted by an international staff appointed by him. The Secretary General makes an annual report to the General Assembly and such other reports as may be necessary from time to time.

Specialised Agencies

These specialised agencies are separate autonomous organisations which have their own membership, legislative and executive bodies. But they work with the UN, and ECOSOC coordinates their activities.

➥ **The International Labour Organisation (ILO):** One of the oldest of the specialised agencies, (established in 1919) brings together representatives of governments, labour and management, to improve working conditions, trade union rights, safety and social security of the labour through international conventions. *Headquarters:* Geneva (Switzerland).

➥ **The Food and Agriculture Organisation (FAO):** FAO helps the nations of the world increase the output of farmlands, forests and fisheries and raise nutrition levels. FAO was established in 1945. *Headquarters:* Rome (Italy).

➥ **The United Nations Educational, Scientific and Cultural Organisation (UNESCO):** Established in 1946, it seeks to promote peace through International collaboration on education for all. UNESCO projects range from literacy campaigns and training of teachers, scientists, technicians and engineers, to fostering mutual appreciation of different cultures and providing technical assistance in developing mass communications. *Headquarters:* Paris (France).

➥ **The World Health Organisation (WHO):** It is an agency for international cooperation and helps nations launch campaigns to stamp out diseases like malaria and tuberculosis, coordinates efforts to prevent the spread of epidemics, trains health workers at all levels and promotes international medical research. The agency came into being in 1948. *Headquarters:* Geneva (Switzerland).

➥ **The International Bank for Reconstruction and Development (IBRD) or World Bank** makes loans for economic development and helps with the flow of investment from one country to another. The Bank was established on December 27, 1945. *Headquarters:* Washington (USA).

➥ **The International Finance Corporation (IFC):** Established in 1956 as an affiliate of the World Bank, it promotes economic development through investments in private enterprise, without government guarantee, in less developed areas. *Headquarters:* Washington (USA).

➥ **The International Development Association (IDA):** Established in 1960 as another affiliate of the World Bank, it extends credits on easier terms than are normally available for import and development projects in under-developed countries. *Headquarters:* Washington (USA).

➥ **The International Monetary Fund (IMF):** Founded in 1945, it enables countries to work together on international monetary problems, on currency convertibility and stabilisation questions. *Headquarters:* Washington (USA).

➥ **The International Civil Aviation Organisation (ICAO):** Established in 1947, it adopts international standards with guarantee that no matter where an aircraft is operated, safety and an adequate degree of uniformity are maintained. It helps to simplify customs, immigration and public procedures at international airports. *Headquarters:* Montreal (Canada).

➥ **The Universal Postal Union (UPU):** The establishment of the Union has made it possible to standardise the basic charges applied to postal items. Thus the rates of postage for international mail paid by users all over the world are uniformly fixed to a great extent. *Headquarters*: Berne (Switzerland).

➡ **The International Telecommunication Union (ITU):** The International Telegraph Union, founded in Paris in 1865, and the International Radio-telegraph Union, founded in Berlin in 1906, were merged by the Madrid Convention of 1932 to form the ITU. It promotes the improvement and extension of all forms of international telecommunication, such as telephone calls, cables, radio and television broadcasts and telecasts and space communication. It also allocates frequencies for radio and television stations throughout the world. *Headquarters:* Geneva (Switzerland).

➡ **The World Meteorological Organisation (WMO):** It develops weather-forecasting services through international collaboration and makes possible the rapid interchange of weather information. *Headquarters:* Geneva (Switzerland).

➡ **The International Maritime Organisation (IMO):** Established in 1958, it works to enhance safety at sea. It also helps increase shipping facilities for the expansion of trade without discrimination and seeks to end unfair restrictive practices by shipping concerns. *Headquarters:* London (England).

➡ **World Intellectual Property Organisation (WIPO):** WIPO was established in 1970. The purposes of the agency are to promote the protection of intellectual property throughout the world, and to ensure administrative co-operation among States in the enforcement of various international agreements. *Headquarters:* Geneva (Switzerland).

➡ **International Fund for Agricultural Development (IFAD):** Established in 1977, the International Fund for Agricultural Development is the first international institution established

YEARS OBSERVED BY UN

✦ **1967:** International Tourism Year; ✦ **1968:** Human Rights Year; ✦ **1970:** International Education Year; ✦ **1972:** International Book Year; ✦ **1973:** Copernicus Year; ✦ **1974:** World Population Year; ✦ **1975:** International Women's Year; ✦ **1979:** International Year of the Child; ✦ **1981:** International Year of Disabled; ✦ **1983:** World Communication Year; ✦ **1985:** International Youth Year; ✦ **1986:** International Year of Peace; ✦ **1987:** International Year of Shelter for the Homeless; ✦ **1990:** International Literacy Year; ✦ **1992:** International Space Year; ✦ **1993:** International Year for World's Indigenous People; ✦ **1994:** International Year of Family; ✦ **1995:** International Year of Tolerance; ✦ **1996:** Inter-national Year for the Eradication of Poverty; ✦ **1998:** International Year of Oceans; ✦ **1999:** International Year of Older Persons; ✦ **2000:** International Year of Culture of Peace; ✦ **2001:** International Year of Volunteer; ✦ **2002:** International Year of Ecotourism; ✦ **2003:** International Year of Clean Water; ✦ **2004:** International Year of Rice; ✦ **2005:** International Year of Sports and Physical Education; ✦ **2006:** International Year of Deserts and Desertification; ✦ **2008:** International Year of Potato; ✦ **2009:** International year of Astronomy; ✦ **2010:** Inter-national Year of Bio Diversity; ✦ **2011:** International Year of Forest; ✦ **2012:** International Year of Co-operatives; ✦ **2013:** International Water Cooperation Year; ✦ **2014:** International Year of Family Farming; ✦ **2015:** International Year of Soil; ✦ **2016:** International Year of Pulses; ✦ **2017:** International Year of Sustainable Tourism for Development; ✦ **2019:** International Year of Indigenous Languages; ✦ **2020:** International Year of Plant; ✦ **2021:** International Year of Peace and Trust. ✦ **2022:** International Year of Artisanal Fisheries and Aquaculture. ✦ **2023:** International Year of Millets. ✦ **2024:** International Year of Camelids. ✦ **2025:** International Year of Glaciers Preservation; International Year of Quantum Science and Technology; International Year of Cooperatives; International Year of Peace and Trust.

exclusively to provide additi-onal resources for agricultural and rural development and to channel them to the poorest rural populations.

It is the first UN agency to introduce weighted voting—it means member-state's voting right being directly linked to the amount of money it contributes. In other words, those who pay more will have greater say in decision-making process in the agency.

Other Organs of the UN

Some important organs are: United Nations Conference on Trade and Development (UNCTAD), United Nations International Children's Emergency Fund---now United Nations Children's Fund (UNICEF), United Nations Industrial Devel-opment Organisation (UNIDO), United Nations University (UNU), United Nations Emergency Force (UNEF), Economic and Social Commission for the Asia and the Pacific (ESCAP).

Other Important Related Bodies

- **International Atomic Energy Agency (IAEA):** It has no formal status of a specialised agency of the UN. It was established in 1957 with an objective of accelerating and enlarging the role of atomic energy to peace, prosperity and health. *Headquarters:* Vienna (Austria).
- **World Trade Organisation (WTO):** The WTO came into being on January 1, 1995 when the formally transformed itself into this organisation as a major entity overseeing international trade. The WTO was set up as a result of a world trade treaty known as the 'Final Act' (of the Uruguay Round of trade negotiations). The Final Act which was signed at a ministerial conference at Marrakesh in Morocco in April 1994, contains 28 agreements on world trading relations. The 166 member WTO aims at the liberalisation of world trade. It administers trade agreements through various councils and committees. It is a watchdog of international trade, regularly examining the trade systems of individual members. Its code of conduct includes the principle of non-discrimination between trading partners and equal treatment for imports and domestic goods in internal markets. The WTO is open to all nations who merely undertake to comply with the rules of the membership. These are, that the member-countries should practise free trade, establish a fixed level of import tariff and finally accept the verdict of the WTO in any dispute with another member-country. *Headquarters:* Geneva.

Other Important Organisations/ ALLIANCES

- **The Arab League:** It was set up by a covenant signed in 1945. 22 Arab States are its members.
- **The Asian Development Bank:** It started functioning in 1966. The Bank is the Asian counterpart of the inter-American Development Bank and the African Development Bank with headquarters at Manila. One of the objectives of the Bank is to promote intra-regional trade.
- **Association of South-East Asian Nations (ASEAN):** It was established in 1967 at Bangkok, Thailand, to accelerate economic progress and maintain the economic stability of South-East Asia. The present members of the ASEAN are Indonesia, Malaysia, the Philippines, Singapore, Thailand, Brunei, Myanmar, Laos, Cambodia and Vietnam. The supreme body of the ASEAN is the Ministerial Conference of the Foreign Ministers of member States. Its day-to-day operations are looked after

by a Standing Committee formed by the Conference. *Headquarters:* Jakarta (Indonesia).

- **Commonwealth of Nations:** It is a free association of 56 countries which were once under the British rule and have since become independent. Main member countries are: UK, Canada, Australia, New Zealand, India, Sri Lanka, Pakistan and Bangladesh. *Headquarters:* London, UK. The main principle of Commonwealth is able to influence international society for the benefit of mankind. The Commonwealth Heads of Governments Meet (CHOGM) has now acquired international significance.
- **European Union (E.U.):** It is the new name of European Economic Community (EEC) or European Common Market (ECM). Now a union of 27 European Nations. Members are: France, Germany, the Netherlands, Belgium, Italy, Luxembourg, Ireland, Denmark, Greece, Spain, Portugal, Austria, Finland, Sweden, Cyprus, Czech Republic, Estonia, Hungary, Latvia, Lithuania, Malta, Poland, Slovakia, Slovania, Romania, Croatia and Bulgaria.
- **INTERPOL:** It is the popular name of the International Criminal Police Organisation (ICPO). With headquarters at Paris, it has over 194 affiliated countries which have joined hands through it to fight against international crime.
- **Non-Aligned Movement (NAM):** It is an organisation of 120 countries mostly developing ones. The principles of non-alignment were defined in the Bandung (Indonesia) Declaration of 1955 and were reiterated in Brioni (Yugoslavia) Declaration of 1956 by Jawaharlal Nehru, J.B. Tito and Gamel Abdil Nasser. The first Non-Aligned Conference was held at Belgrade in 1961. The basic thrust of the movement is in favour of peace, disarmament, development, independence and eradication of poverty and illiteracy.
- **North Atlantic Treaty Organisation (NATO):** The treaty was signed at Washington on April 4, 1949, by the Foreign Ministers of Belgium, Canada, Denmark, France, Iceland, Italy, Luxembourg, the Netherlands, Norway, Portugal, UK and USA. Greece and Turkiye became members of the organisation in 1952 and German Federal Republic in 1955. Spain joined in 1982 as the 16th member and Poland, Hungry and Chezch Republic were the last entrant in 1999. Romania, Bulgaria, Slovakia, Lithuania, Slovenia, Latvia and Estonia become member in 2004. Finland and Sweden became its 31st and 32nd members in 2023 and 2024. Its headquarters is at Brussels (Belgium).
- **Nuclear Non-Proliferation Treaty (NPT):** The treaty became effective in March 1970 to: *(a)* bind nuclear powers against sharing or passing on their nuclear weapons or secrets to any non-nuclear-powers, *(b)* make non-nuclear countries agree to renouncing their option to accept from nuclear powers or to produce their own nuclear weapons, and *(c)* institute an international control and inspection system. India refused to sign the treaty. On May 11, 1995, a global conference decided to extend the 25-year-old treaty indefinitely and thus perpetuating an international system in which only 5 nations namely the USA, Russia, Britain, France and China can legitimately possess nuclear weapons. The three nations that have not signed the treaty are India, Israel and Pakistan.
- **Organisation of the Petroleum Exporting Countries (OPEC)** constituted in 1973. Its members

are: Algeria, Gabon, Indonesia, Iraq, Kuwait, Libya, Nigeria, Qatar, Saudi Arabia, United Arab Emirates, Equador, Iran and Venezuela. OPEC countries supply 85 per cent of the world oil products. *Headquarters:* Vienna, Austria.

➡ **International Red Cross:** Two International organisations are known respectively as *International Committee of the Red Cross* and the *League of Red Cross Societies,* both with headquarters in Geneva, Switzerland. The first of these is a wholly international agency unconnected with any national society, and attempts to maintain the basic Red Cross principles of the Geneva Convention; the second agency is a federation of autonomous national Red Cross societies designed to further co-operation among them.

➡ **South Asian Association for Regional Cooperation (SAARC):** Launched in December 1985, SAARC is a eight-member body---India, Maldives, Pakistan, Bangladesh, Sri Lanka, Bhutan, Nepal and Afghanistan. With its headquarters at Kathmandu, it aims at mutual cooperation in matters of common interest.

➡ **AFTA (ASEAN Free Trade Area):** It became operative on 1st January, 1993. Its members are ASEAN countries namely Brunei, Indonesia, Malaysia, the Philippines, Singapore, Thailand, Vietnam, Laos, Myanmar and Cambodia.

➡ **NAFTA (North America Free Trade Agreement):** With USA, Canada and Mexico as its members, it became operative on 1st January, 1994. It aims to eliminate tarrifs over a period of 15 years. Time frame to achieve specific goals relating to agriculture, automobiles, textiles, communications, etc. are clearly specified.

➡ **SAPTA (South Asian Preferential Trade Arrangement):** With Bangladesh, Bhutan, India, Maldives, Nepal, Pakistan, Sri Lanka and Afganistan, it aims at assuming a strong trading bloc.

➡ **Amnesty International:** A global human rights organisation, it was established in May 1961. It is a voluntary body with over 11,00,000 members in more than 150 countries of the world. It was awarded Nobel Peace Prize in 1977. *Headquarters:* London.

➡ **BIMSTEC:** The Bay of Bengal Initiative for Multi-Sectoral Technical and Economic Cooperation (BIMSTEC) is a regional organization comprising seven Member States lying in the littoral and adjacent areas of the Bay of Bengal constituting a contiguous regional unity. This sub-regional organization came into being on 6 June, 1997 through the Bangkok Declaration. It constitutes seven Member States: Five deriving from South Asia, including Bangladesh, Bhutan, India, Nepal, Sri Lanka and two from Southeast Asia, including Myanmar and Thailand. Initially, the economic bloc was formed with four Member States with the acronym 'BIST-EC' (Bangladesh, India, Sri Lanka and Thailand Economic Cooperation). Following the inclusion of Myanmar on 22 December 1997 during a special Ministerial Meeting in Bangkok, the Group was renamed 'BIMSTEC' (Bangladesh, India, Myanmar, Sri Lanka and Thailand Economic Cooperation). With the admission of Nepal and Bhutan at the 6th Ministerial Meeting (February 2004, Thailand), the name of the grouping was changed to 'Bay of Bengal Initiative for Multi-Sectoral Technical and Economic Cooperation' (BIMSTEC).

MULTIPLE CHOICE QUESTIONS

1. Which of the following countries does not shares border with Israel?

1. Egypt 2. Jordan
3. Syria 4. Iran
5. Yaman 6. Lebanon

Choose correct answer following codes given:

A. Only 1 and 6
B. Only 2 and 4
C. Only 3 and 4
D. Only 4 and 5

2. Which one of the following countries is not a member of the Quadrilateral Security Dialogue, also known as 'QUAD'?

A. India B. China
C. Australia D. Japan

3. Consider the following statements about United Nations Environment Assembly:

1. The United Nations Environment Assembly was created in 1992 at the Earth Summit in Rio de Janeiro.
2. The United Nations Environment Assembly is the world's highest-level decision-making body on the environment.
3. The Assembly meets annually to set priorities for global environmental policies and develop international environmental law.

Which of the above statements is/are incorrect?

A. Only 1
B. Only 2
C. Only 1 and 3
D. Only 2 and 3

4. Which of the following port is not correctly matched with their country?

A. Rotterdam – Netherlands
B. Igarka – China
C. Montecidio — Uruguary
D. Jakarta – Indonesia

5. Which of the following is/are correctly matched?

1. 2 December – World Computer Literacy Day
2. 4 December – Indian Air Force Day
3. 5 December – World Soil Day
4. 9 December – International Human Rights Day

Select the correct answer from the code given below:

A. Only 2 and 3
B. Only 1 and 4
C. Only 1 and 3
D. Only 2 and 4

6. Houthi rebels/tribals hail from:

A. Syria
B. Lebanon
C. Yemen
D. Palestine

7. Consider the following statements about the 'Asia-Pacific Economic Cooperation' (APEC):

1. It is an international non-governmental organization for public-private sector collaboration.
2. It is headquartered in Singapore.
3. The heads of government of all APEC members except China attend an annual APEC Economic Leaders' Meeting.

Which of the above statements is/ are correct?

A. Only 1
B. 1 and 3
C. 1, 2 and 3
D. Only 2

8. Consider the following:

1. Asian Infrastructure Investment Bank.
2. Missile Technology Control Regime.
3. Shanghai Cooperation Organization.

India is a member of which of the above?

A. Only one
B. Only two
C. All three
D. None

9. Which of the following is not yet a member of the Group of Twenty or G20?

A. Argentina
B. Mexico
C. Turkey
D. Malaysia

10. The term 'Two state Solution' is sometimes mentioned in the new in the context of the affairs of:

A. China B. Israel
C. Iraq D. Yemen

11. World Social Protection Report is published by:

A. World Bank
B. World Health Organization
C. International Labour Organization
D. World Economics Forum

12. Which of the following is not the member of the G20?

A. Indonesia
B. Singapore
C. Mexico
D. Turkey

13. An inverted pyramid of biomass can be found in which eco-system?

A. Grassland B. Marine
C. Forest D. Tundra

14. Where is the World Organization for Animal Health (WOAH) headquartered?

A. Paris B. Rome
C. Colombo D. Tokyo

15. On which day is 'International Tiger Day' is celebrated every year?

A. 29 July B. 28 July
C. 27 July D. 26 July

16. Which of the following is not a member of South Asian Preferential Trade Agreement (SAPTA)?

A. China
B. Maldives
C. Bangladesh
D. Nepal

17. What is the capital of Azerbaijan?

A. Baku B. Nassau
C. Manama D. Belmopan

18. 'Awami League' is a political party of which country?

A. Bangladesh
B. Iraq
C. Israel
D. Nepal

19. 'The Sun' is a famous Newspaper of which country?

A. Canada
B. Australia
C. Britain
D. New Zealand

20. 'People's Daily' is a famous Newspaper of which country?

A. Japan B. China
C. USA D. Canada

21. 'Mosad' is a Intelligence Agency of which country?

A. Japan B. Russia
C. Israel D. Egypt

22. What is the National Emblem of Spain?
A. Eagle
B. Lily
C. Rose
D. Lion and Sun

23. Minsk is the capital of which country?
A. Belgium B. Belarus
C. Finland D. Gambia

24. What is the capital of Namibia?
A. Palikir
B. Bamako
C. Windhoek
D. Amman

25. Freetown is the capital of which country?
A. Serbia
B. Seychelles
C. Samoa
D. Sierra Leone

26. "Rand" is the currency of which country?
A. South Africa
B. Spain
C. Sudan
D. Surinam

27. What is currency of Armenia?
A. Kwanza B. Dram
C. Kyat D. Sol

28. Which country is called 'Islands of Cloves'?
A. Madagascar
B. New Zealand
C. Belgium
D. Canada

29. 'World Water Day' is celebrated on:
A. 22nd January
B. 22nd March
C. 22nd June
D. 22nd July

30. 'Gold Coast' is old name of which country?
A. Ghana B. Harare
C. Zimbabwe D. Guyana

ANSWERS

1	2	3	4	5	6	7	8	9	10
D	B	C	B	C	C	D	C	D	B
11	**12**	**13**	**14**	**15**	**16**	**17**	**18**	**19**	**20**
C	B	B	A	A	A	A	A	C	B
21	**22**	**23**	**24**	**25**	**26**	**27**	**28**	**29**	**30**
C	A	B	C	D	A	B	A	B	A

India : Miscellaneous

NATIONAL INSIGNIA

NATIONAL INSIGNIA

National Flag

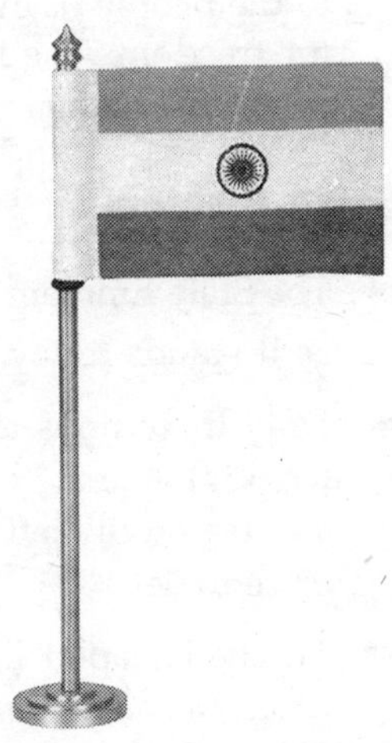

- The National Flag is a horizontal tricolour with three equal horizontal strips—deep saffron strip at the top, the white strip in the middle and the dark-green strip at the bottom.
- The ratio of the width to the length of the flag is 2 : 3.
- In the centre of the white band is a wheel (with 24 spokes) in navy blue.
- It is an exact replica of the wheel on the capital of the Ashoka Pillar at Sarnath.
- The National Flag was adopted by the Constituent Assembly of India on July 22, 1947 and presented to the nation on behalf of the women of India at the midnight session of the Assembly on August 14, 1947.
- According to Dr. S. Radhakrishnan, the saffron colour represents the spirit of renunciation, the white band stands for truth and purity and the green colour signifies growth.
- The wheel (chakra) signifies progress---that is the sign of life.

National Anthem

- Rabindranath Tagore's song *Jana-gana-mana* was adopted as the National Anthem of India on January 24, 1950.

Jana-gana-mana-adhinayaka, jaya he
Bharata-bhagya-vidhata.
Punjab-Sindh-Gujarat-Maratha-
Dravida-Utkala-Banga
Vindhya-Himachala-Yamuna-Ganga
Uchhala-jaladhi-taranga.
Tava shubha name jage,
Tava shubha asisa mage,
Gahe tava jaya-gatha
Jana-gana-mangala-dayaka, jaya he
Bharata-bhagya-vidhata,
Jaya he, jaya he, jaya he,
Jaya jaya jaya, jaya he!

- The complete song consists of five stanzas.
- The first stanza, which has been adopted as national anthem and is usually sung on ceremonial occasions reads as follows:
- The above is the full version of the National Anthem as adopted and its playing time is about 52 seconds. A short version consisting of the first and last lines of this stanza (playing time approximately 20 seconds) is also played on certain occasions.

National Song

- The National Song is Bankim Chandra Chatterjee's *Vande Mataram* which occurs in his novel *Anand Math*. The song had been a source of inspiration to the people of India in their struggle for freedom. The following is the text of its first stanza:

> Vande Mataram!
> Sujalam, suphalam, Malayaja-shitalam,
> Shasyashyamalam, Mataram!
> Subhrajyotsna, pulakitayaminim,
> Phullakusumita-drumadala-shobhinim,
> Suhasinim, sumadhura-bhashinim,
> Sukhadam, varadam, Mataram!

State Emblem

- The State Emblem of India is an adaptation from Sarnath Lion Capital of Ashoka as it stands today.
- Only three lions are visible, the fourth being hidden from the view. The wheel (chakra) appears in relief in the centre of the abacus with a bull on the right and a horse on the left and the outlines of other wheels on the extreme right and the extreme left.
- The bell-shaped lotus has been omitted. The words, "Satyameva Jayate", taken from *Mundaka Upanishad* meaning "truth alone triumphs" are inscribed in Devanagari script below the emblem. The lion capital was adopted as the State Emblem by the Government of India on January 26, 1950.

National Calendar

- The unified Indian National Calendar to be used for official purpose, was introduced from March 22, 1957. The new calendar is based on the Saka era and has a normal year of 365 days. The dates of this calendar permanently correspond with the dates of Gregorian calendar—Chaitra 1 falling on March 22 in a normal year and on March 21 in a leap year.

Months of the National Calendar

1.	Chaitra	2.	Vaisakha
3.	Jyeshtha	4.	Asadha
5.	Sravana	6.	Bhadra
7.	Asvina	8.	Kartika
9.	Agrahayana	10.	Pausa
11.	Magha	12.	Phalguna.

Chaitra is the first month and Phalguna is the last month of the year.

- **NATIONAL BIRD AND ANIMAL:** They are peacock and tiger respectively.

First in India

First Governor of Bengal	Lord Clive (1757-60)
First Governor General of India	Lord William Bentinck
First Indian Author to get Anderson Award	Ruskin Bond
First American President to Visit India	Dwight Eisenhower
First Indian to Reach the South Pole	Col. IK Bajaj
First Indian Cosmonaut to go into space	Sqn. Ldr. Rakesh Sharma
First Indian Commander-in-Chief of Free India	Gen. K.M. Cariappa
First Indian Judge of International Court of Justice	Dr. Nagendra Singh
First President of Indian National Congress	W.C. Banerjee
First Indian to pass ICS	Satyendranath Tagore
First Field Marshall	Gen. S.F.J. Manekshaw
First President of India to Die in Office	Dr. Zakir Hussain
First Indian P.M. to resign from office	Morarji Desai
First Indian to get Jnanpith Award	G. Shankar Kurup
First Speaker to Lok Sabha	GV Mavlankar
First President of Indian Republic	Dr. Rajendra Prasad
First Prime Minister of Independent India	Pt. Jawaharlal Nehru
First Post Office opened in India	Calcutta (Kolkata) (1727)
First Indian to reach Antarctica	Lt. Ram Charan (1960)
First Deputy Prime Minister of India	Sardar Vallabh Bhai Patel
First Prime Minister to loose an election	Indira Gandhi
First Man to climb Mt. Everest twice	Nawang Gombu
First Indian recipient of 'Oscar Award'	Bhanu Athaiya
First To Win World Billiards Trophy	Wilson Jones
First British PM to visit India	Harold Mc Million
First Test-tube baby of India	Indira (Baby Harsha)
First Indian to swim across the English Channel	Mihir Sen
First Foreign recipient of Bharat Ratna	Khan Abdul Gaffar Khan
First India's University	Nalanda University
First Chief Justice of India	Justice Hiralal J. Kania
India's first Election Commissioner	Sukumar Sen
First Asian Games organised	Delhi in 1951
First Indian Missile	Prithvi
First e-business Newspaper of India	Financial Express
First person to get Paramvir Chakra	Major Somnath Sharma
First Indian scientist to get a Nobel Prize	C.V. Raman (Physics)
India's first Open University	Andhra Pradesh Open University
First Education Minister of Independent India	Maulana Abul Kalam Azad

First Indian Pilot	J.R.D. Tata (1929)
First Indian to Win Magsaysay Award	Acharya Vinoba Bhave (1958)
First Indian Nobel Laureate	Rabindra Nath Tagore
First Indian to get Bharat Ratna Award	C. Rajagopalachari
First Nuclear Submarine of India	I.N.S. Chakra
First Muslim President of Indian Republic	Dr. Zakir Hussain

First Indian Women

First Indian Woman to go into Space	Kalpana Chawla
First Woman President of Indian National Congress	Annie Besant
First Indian Woman President of INC	Sarojini Naidu (1925)
India's first Woman Ruler on Delhi's Throne	Razia Sultan
First Indian Woman to win the Booker Prize	Arundhati Roy
First Indian Woman to get Bharat Ratna	Smt. Indira Gandhi
First Woman Musician to Get 'Bharat Ratna'	MS Subbulakshmi
India's First Woman President	Smt. Pratibha Patil
India's First Woman Prime Minister	Indira Gandhi
India's First Woman IPS officer	Kiran Bedi
India's First Women Governor	Sarojini Naidu
First Indian Woman to Get the Noble Prize	Mother Teresa
First Woman to get Jnanpith Award	Ashapurna Devi
First Indian Woman Airline Pilot	Durga Banerjee
First Indian Woman Railway Driver	Ms. Surekha Yadav
First Indian Actress to be awarded Padama Shree	Nargis Dutt
First Indian Woman to head a Nationalised Bank	Ranjana Kumar (Indian Bank)
First Indian Woman High Court Judge	Mrs. Anna Chandy
Recipient of Dada Saheb Phalke Award	Devika Rani
First Woman Chairman to NABARD	Ranjana Kumar
First Indian Woman to become Miss Universe	Sushmita Sen
First Indian Woman to become Miss World	Reita Faria
First Indian Woman to climb Mt. Everest Twice	Santosh Yadav
First Indian Woman to win a WTA title	Sania Mirza
First Woman Judge of Supreme Court	Fatima Bibi
First Indian Woman Ambassador at the United Nations	Vijayalaxami Pandit
First Indian Woman to win a Gold in Asian Games	Kamaljeet Sandhu
First Indian Woman to fly an aircraft	Sarla Thakral
First Woman to get Ashok Chakra	Nirja Bhanot
First Woman Chief Minister of a state	Sucheta Kriplani (U.P.)
First Indian Woman to across English Channel	Arati Saha (Gupta)

Famous Musical Instrument and their Exponent

Sarangi	Ustad Bendu Khan, Pt. Ramnarayanji, Aruna Kale, Santosh Mishra, Indralal, Ashiq Ali Khan etc.
Nadaswaram	Sheikh Chinna Maulana, Rajaratna Pillai, Niru Sami Pillai, N. Krishnan etc.
Simphoni	Zubin Mehta
Guitar	Vishwa Mohan Bhatt, Jatin Mazumdar, Brij Bhushan Kabra, Sri Krishna Nalin, Keshav Jalegaonkar etc.
Mandolin	U. Srinivas, Khagen Dey, Snehashish Mozumder, etc.
Vichitra Veena	Ahmed Raza Khan, Abdul Aziz Khan etc.
Piano	V. Balsara
Ghatam	T.H. Vinayakaram
Harmonium	Jnan Prakash Ghosh, Shri Purushottam Walawalkar, Appa Jalgaonkar etc.
Jal Tarang	Himanshu Biswas, Jagdish Mohan, Ghasiram Nirmal, Ram Swaroop Prabhakar etc.
Surbahar	Imrat Khan, Anapurna Devi etc.
Israj	Alauddin Khan
Mohan Veena	Pt. Vishwa Mohan Bhatt
Sitar	Pt. Ravi Shankar, Nikhil Banerjee, Ustad Vilayat Khan, Shujaat Khan, Jaya Biswas, Debu Chaudhuri, Nishaat Khan, Bande Hasan, Sahid Parvez, Uma Shankar Mishra, Buddhaditya Mukherjee, Anushka Shankar etc.
Tabla	Ustad Shafat Ahmed Khan, Swapan Chaudhary, Zakir Hussain, Latif Khan, Allah Rakha, Gudai Maharaj, Kishan Maharaj, Faiyaz Khan, Sukhbinder Singh etc.
Flute	Pannalal Ghosh, Hari Prasad Chaurasia, Raghunath Seth, B. Kunjumani, Rajendra Prasanna, Rajendra Kulkarni, Prakash Saxena etc.
Sarod	Ustad Amjad Ali Khan, Ustad Ali Akbar Khan, Ustad Alauddin Khan, Hafiz Ali Khan, Zarin Daruwala, Mukesh Sharma, Vasant Rai, Biswajit Roy Chaudhury, Sharan Rani etc.
Shehnai	Ustad Bishmillah Khan, Daya Shankar, Jagannath, Hari Singh, Shailesh Bhagwat, Ali Ahmad Hussain Khan etc.
Violin	Dr. Smt. N. Rajan, Vishnu Gobind (VG) Jog, L. Subramaniam, Sangitha Rajan, Kunakudi Vaidyanathan, Sisirkana Dhar Choudhury, Lalgudi Jayaraman, R.P. Shastri, Suryadev Pawar, Govind Swami Pillai, T.N. Krishnan etc.
Veena	S. Balachandran, Badruddin Dagar, Kalyan Krishna Bhagavatar, B. Doraiswami Iyengar, Gopal Krishna, Asad Ali Khan etc.
Santoor	Pt. Shiv Kumar Sharma, Tarun Bhattacharya, Bhajan Sopori, etc.
Pakhawaj	Ustad Rehman Khan, Gopal Das, Chhatrapati Singh, Ramakant Pathak, Arun Saiwal etc.
Rudra Veena	Ustad Sadiq Ali Khan, Zia Moinuddin Dagar, Asad Ali Khan, etc.
Mridang	Thakur Bhikam Singh, Palghat Raju, T.K. Murthy, U.K. Sivaram, K.R. Mani etc.

Important Classical Dances and Artists

Dances	Artists
Kathakali	Vallthol Narayana Menon, Uday Shankar, K. Krishnan Nair, Shanta Rao, Mrinalini Sarabhai, Anand Sivaraman, Krishnankutty etc.
Kathak	Birju Maharaj, Lacchu Maharaj, Sukhdev Maharaj, Sitara Devi, Gopi Krishna, Shovana Narayan, Malvika Sarkar, Chandralekha, Bindadin Maharaj, Acchan Maharaj, Narayan Prasad.
Manipuri	Guru Amli Singh, Atamb Singh, Nalkumar Singh, Jhaveri Sisters (Darshana, Nayana, Suwarna, Ranjana Jhaveri), Savita Mehta, Kalawati Devi, Charu Mathur, Sonarik Singh, Gopal Singh, Bimbavati Devi etc.
Mohiniattam	K. Kalyankutty Amma, Bharati Shivaji, Ragini Devi, Sri Devi, Shanta Rao, Tara Nidigadi, Geeta Gayak etc.
Bharatnatyam	Yamini Krishnamurthy, Sonal Man Singh, Rukmini Devi Arundale, T. Balasaraswati, Padma Subrahmanyam. S.K. Saroj, Rama Gopal, Leela Samson, Mrinalini Vikram Sarabhai, Vijaynathimala Bali, Malvika Sarkar, Priyadarshini Govind, Hema Malini, etc.
Kuchipudi	Yamini Krishnamurthy, Vedantam Lakshminarayan Shashtri, Radha Reddy, Raja Reddy, Swapnasundari, Vempati Chinna Satyam etc.
Odissi	Sanjukta Panigrahi, Sonal Man Singh, Kiran Segal, Madhavi Mudgal, Kali Charan Patnaik, Indrani Rahman, Sharon Lowen, Myrta Barvie (Argentine) Renowed Teachers : Monan Mahapatra, Kelucharan Mahapatra, Pankaj Charan Das, Harekrishna Behra etc.

Hill Stations of India

Name	State/UT	Height above Sea Level (ft)
Almora (Kumaon hills)	Uttarakhand	5500
Cherrapunji (Shillong)	Meghalaya	4455
Coonoor (Nilgiri hills)	Tamil Nadu	6740
Dalhousie	Himachal Pradesh	7867
Darjeeling	West Bengal	7168
Gulmarg	Jammu & Kashmir	8850
Kasauli (Shimla)	Himachal Pradesh	7200
Kodaikanal	Tamil Nadu	7200
Mahabaleshwar	Maharashtra	4500
Mt. Abu	Rajasthan	4500
Mussoorie	Uttarakhand	7500
Nainital	Uttarakhand	6400
Ootacamund	Tamil Nadu	7500
Pachmarhi	Madhya Pradesh	3500
Shillong (Khasi hills)	Meghalaya	5000
Shimla	Himachal Pradesh	7000
Srinagar	Jammu and Kashmir	5250

Important Monuments : INDIA

Name	Location	Features
	ANCIENT SITES	
Lothal	Gujarat	Archaeological excavations revealed existence of Indus Valley Civilization
Nalanda	Near Patna (Bihar)	Ruins of ancient Buddhist University founded by Kumaragupta in AD 427
Sarnath	Varanasi (UP)	Famous for stupas where Buddha preached his first sermon
Ajanta Caves	Sambhaji Nagar (Maharashtra)	Buddhist monasteries with unique architecture, sculpture and Paintings
Elephanta Caves	Island near Mumbai	Consisting of 7 caves famous for the 'Trimurti' and other sculptures
Ellora Caves	Sambhaji Nagar (Maharashtra)	Ancient cave temples especially famous for 'Temple of Kailash'
Jallianwala Bagh	Amritsar (Punjab)	Famous for indiscriminate firing by Gen. Dyer on April 13, 1919, on people attending a public meeting demanding independence
	MEMORIALS AND MONUMENTS	
Akbar's Tomb	Sikandra, Near Agra (Uttar Pradesh)	Famous for its carvings and architecture of Hindu and Mughal art
Anand Bhawan	Prayagraj (UP)	Ancestral house of the Nehru family which Mrs. Indira Gandhi gifted for conversion into a national memorial
Bibi-ka-Maqbara	Aurangabad (Maharahstra)	Mausoleum built by Aurangzeb (AD 1660) in memory of his wife Rabia Durrani
Gandhi Sadan	New Delhi	Birla House where Mahatma Gandhi was assassinated in 1948.
Jamia Milia	Delhi	Muslim Univerity founded by Dr. Zakir Hussain
Kranti Maidan	Mumbai	Historical venue where Gandhiji gave 'Quit India' call in 1942.
Rajghat	New Delhi	Samadhi of Mahatma Gandhi on the banks of the Yamuna.
Shakti Sthal	New Delhi	Situated on the banks of Yamuna where Mrs Indira Gandhi was cremated.
Shantivana	New Delhi	Near Rajghat where Pandit Jawaharlal Nehru was cremated.
Teenmurti House	New Delhi	Residence of the first Prime Minister of India, Pandit Jawaharlal Nehru, now converted into a national memorial.
Rashtriya Smriti Sthal (Sadaiv Atal)	New Delhi	Samadhi of Atal Behari Vajpayee on the Bank of Yamuna.
Ahmed Shah's Tomb	Ahmedabad, Gujarat	Domed structure, famous for paving of multi-coloured marble.
Sher Shah Suri's Tomb	Sasaram, Bihar	Domed structure
Vijay Ghat	New Delhi	Samadhi of Lal Bahadur Shastri on the banks of Yamuna

Name	Location	Features
IMPORTANT TEMPLES AND MOSQUES		
Khajuraho Temples	Khajuraho, MP	Famous sculptures depicting art of love; built some time in AD 950-1050
Mahabalipuram Temples	Mahabalipuram, Tamil Nadu	Also called 'Seven Pagodas'
Mahakali Temple	Ujjain	Shiva Mandir
Meenakshi Temple	Madurai, Tamil Nadu	Dedicated to the Goddess Meenakshi
Moti Masjid	Agra, UP	Built by Mughal Emperor Shahjahan
Sun Temple or Konark Temple	Konark, Odisha	The mythological conception of the Sun God riding a twenty-four wheeled chariot drawn by seven horses, carved in stone.
Omkar Temple	Omkarji, MP	Shiva Temple on an island in the Narmada river, also called 'Black Pagoda'
Ahmed Shah's Mosque	Ahmedabad	Built in AD 1414, its pillars have Hindu emblems
Bodh Gaya Temple	Bodh Gaya, Bihar	60-m high temple built by Ashoka, site where Buddha attained Enlightenment
Bhubaneshwar Temple	Bhubaneshwar, Odisha	Stone temples
Dilwara Temples	Mt Abu, Rajasthan	Lavishly decorated with carvings, Jain temples
Golden Temple	Amritsar, Punjab	Sacred shrine of the Sikhs
Jagannath Temple	Puri, Odisha	Dedicated to Lord Jagannath, an incarnation of Vishnu
Jama Masjid	Delhi	Biggest mosque in India built by Mughal Emperor Shahjahan
OTHER STRUCTURES—GATES / TOWERS / PILLARS		
Buland Darwaja	Fatehpur Sikri, Agra, Uttar Pradesh	38m high gate built by Akbar, is India's highest gate
Gateway of India	Mumbai, Maharashtra	Built in 1911 to commemorate the visit of King George V of the UK
Qutab Minar	New Delhi	72.5 m high stone tower; tallest minerat in India built by Qutabuddin Aibak as a Victory Tower
Gol Gumbaz	Bijapur, Karnataka	India's largest dome built on the tomb of Sultan Mohammed Adil Shah covering an area of 1630 m^2
Sanchi Stupa	Sanchi, Bhopal	One of the earliest stupas, 17m high and 36.5 m in diameter, made of bricks and sandstone
Sarnath Stupa	Varanasi, Uttar Pradesh	22m hgh and 28m in diameter, stone structure built on the spot where Lord Buddha delivered his first sermon
FORTS, GARDENS		
Red Fort	New Delhi	Built by Shahjahan, made of red stone
Rashtrapati Bhawan	New Delhi	India's biggest residential building

Name	Location	Features
Moghul Gardens	New Delhi	Garden of Rashtrapati Bhawan
Shalimar Gardens	Srinagar, J&K	Pleasure resort in Kashmir
Vrindaban Gardens	Mysore, Karnataka	Unique gardens adjacent to the Krishna-rajasagar Dam
Ramanathaswamy Corridor	Rameshwaram, Tamil Nadu	India's longest corridor — 1220 m long
Gomateswara Statue	Sravanabelagola, Karnataka	India's tallest stone statue of the Jain sage Gomateswara
Agra Fort	Agra, UP	Originally built by Akbar and additions made by Shahjahan containing famous buildings (Royal Palace Shish Mahal, Moti Masjid, Diwan-i-Aam, Diwan-i-Khas)
Gwalior Fort	Gwalior, MP	One of the biggest forts containing famous buildings like Man Mandir, Palace of Man Singh, etc.
Hawa Mahal	Jaipur, Rajasthan	Multi-storeyed pink coloured building
Hindola Mahal	Mandu, MP	The walls sloping at an angle of over 77° create an illusion that the entire building sways.
Jantar Mantar	New Delhi	Ancient observatory

Superlatives (India)

The Largest, Biggest, Smallest, Longest, Highest etc.

The Highest Dam	Tehri Dam, on Bhagirathi river (Uttarakhand)
The Largest Desert	Thar (Rajasthan)
The Largest Cave Temple	Kailash Temple (Ellora, Maharashtra)
The Largest Mosque	Jama Masjid (Delhi)
The Highest Peak	Godwin Austen/K-2 (8611 m)
The Longest Tunnel (Road)	Shyama Prasad Mukherji (Chennai-Nashri (Patnitop)) Tunnel, NH-44 (J&K)
The Largest Delta	Sundarbans (W. Bengal)
The State with Maximum Forest Area	Madhya Pradesh
The Longest Corridor	Corridor of Ramnathaswami Temple (Tamil Nadu)
The Highest Waterfall	Kunchikal (Karnataka)
The Longest Road	NH-44 (3,745 km)
The Highest Gateway	Buland Darwaza, Fatehpur Sikri (UP)
The Longest River	The Ganga
The Largest Museum	Indian Museum (Kolkata)
The Largest Dome	Gol Gumbuz, Bijapur (Karnataka)
The Tallest Statue	Statue of Unity (Gujarat)
The Largest Public-Sector Bank	State Bank of India
The Biggest Cantilever Bridge	Rabindra Setu or Howrah Bridge (Kolkata)
The Longest Canal	Indira Gandhi Canal or Rajasthan Canal (Rajasthan)
The Longest Railway Platform	Hubballi (Hubli) (Karnataka), 1507 m long

The Longest Railway Tunnel	T-50 Tunnel (Khari-Sumber Section) (J&K) 12.77 km
The Most Populous City	Mumbai (Maharashtra)
The Largest Sea Bridge	Bandra-Worli / Rajiv Gandhi Sea Link (Mumbai)
The Longest Passenger Train	Vivek Express
The Longest Passenger Train Route	Dibrugarh to Kanyakumari
The Oldest Church	St. Thomas Syro-Malabar Catholic Church (Kerala)
The Longest National Highway	NH-44 (Srinagar to Kanyakumari)
The State with Longest Coast Line	Gujarat
The Highest Lake	Tso Lhamo/Cholamu Lake (Sikkim)
The Largest Saline Water Lake	Chilka Lake (Odisha)
The Largest Fresh Water Lake	Lake Wular (Kashmir)
The Longest River of Southern India	Godawari
The Longest Dam	Hirakud Dam (Odisha)
The Highest Gallantry Award	Param Vir Chakra
The Longest River Bridge	Bhupen Hazarika (Dhola Sadiya) Bridge : 9150 m
The Largest Animal Fair	Sonepur (Bihar)
The Largest Auditorium	Sri Shanmukhanand Hall (Mumbai)
The Highest Road	Leh-Manali Highway Khardung La (Leh-Manali)
The Deepest River Valley	Bhagirathi and Alaknanda
The Largest River without delta	Narmada and Tapti
The Biggest River Island	Majuli Brahmaputra river (Assam)
The Largest Planetarium	MP Birla Planetarium (Kolkata)
The Highest Airport	Leh Airport (Ladakh)
The Highest Award	Bharat Ratna
The Largest Gurudwara	Harmandir Saheb (Golden Temple) Amritsar
The Biggest Church	St. Cathedral at Old Goa
The Tallest TV Tower	Rameshwaram TV Tower, Tamil Nadu (323 m)
The Longest Sea Beach	Marina Beach (Chennai)

DEFENCE

- The President of India is the Supreme Commander of the country's armed forces though the operational and administrative control rests with the Ministry of Defence and headquarters of respective service.
- Defence comes directly under the purview of the Central Government. Defence Minister is responsible to Parliament for all matters concerning defence. It also shows that armed forces in India are under the control of legislature.
- There are three services. Army, Navy and Air Force and each is headed by a chief. The post of Chief of Defence Staff (CDS) was created in 2019. Various Commissioned ranks in the three services are as follows.

Commissioned Ranks in Defence Services

Army	Navy	Air Force
General	Admiral	Air Chief Marshal
Lieutenant General	Vice Admiral	Air Marshal
Major General	Rear Admiral	Air Vice Marshal
Brigadier	Commodore	Air Commodore
Colonel.	Captain	Group Captain
Lieutenant Colonel	Commander	Wing Commander
Major	Lieutenant Commander	Squadron Leader
Captain	Lieutenant	Flying Lieutenant
Lieutenant	Sub-Lieutenant	Flying Officer

PARTS OF DEFENCE

Army

- The army is organised into one training command and 6 operational commands, viz.. Southern, Eastern, Western, Central, Northern and Southern-western command. Training command is located in Shimla.
- Army consists of a number of arms and services like Armoured Corps, Regiment of Artillery, Corps of Air Defence Artillery, Army Aviation Corps, Corps of Engineers, Corps of Signals, Mechanised infantry, Infantry, Army Service Corps, Army Medical Corps, Military Nursing Services, Army Ordnance Corps, Corps of Electrical and mechanical engineers, Remount and Veterinary Corps, Military Farms Service, Army Education Corps, Intelligence Corps, Corps of Military Police, Army Postal Service, Judge Advocate General Department, Army Physical Training Corps, Pioneer Corps, Territorial Army and Defence Security Corps.

Training Centres for Army

- Military College of Telecommunication Engineering, Mhow
- College of Military Engineering, Kirkee
- Armoured Corps Centre and School, Ahmednagar
- The College of Combat, Mhow.
- Institute of Defence Management, Secundrabad
- The School Artillery, Deorali
- The Infantry Schools, Mhow and Belgaum
- The Army Ordnance School, Jabalpur
- The Army Services Corps School, Barielly
- The Army and Air Transport School, Agra
- The Corps of military police centre and school, Bengaluru
- The Electrical and Mechanical Engineering School, Vadodara
- Military College of Electronics and Mechanical Engineering, Secundrabad
- Remount Veterinary Corps Centre and School, Meerut
- Intelligence Training School and Depot, Pune

Navy

- The Navy which is responsible for defence and security of the country's maritime interests and assets, divided into three commands-Western, Eastem and Southern with their headquarters being at Mumbai, Visakhapatnam and Kochi respectively.

- Western and Eastern commands have operational fleet comprising warships, submarines, frigates and other vessels.
- Southern Command is responsible for training activities of the Indian Navy.

Training Centres for Navy

- INS Vendurutty, Kochi
- INS Garuda, Kochi
- INS Shivaji, Lonavala
- INS Valsura, Jamnagar
- INS Circars, Visakhapatnam
- INS Hamala, Mumbai
- INS Kistna (Training Ship)
- INS Angrca, Mumbai
- Naval Academy, Kochi
- Sailor's Training Establishment, Dabolin

Air Force

The airforce, protecting the frontiers and sky of the country, has five operational commands and two functional commands. The operational commands are on geographical basis, viz., Western, South-western, Central, Eastem and Southern Air commands. The functional commands are Maintenance and Training commands.

Training Centres for Air Force

- Flying School, Bidar
- Air Force Flying School, Jodhpur
- College of Air Warfare, Secundrabad
- Air Force Administrative College, Coimbatore
- Navigation and Signals School, Hyderabad
- Air Force Technical College, Jalahalli
- IAF Paratroopers Training School, Agra
- Air Force Academy, Hyderabad
- Fighter Training Wing and Helicopters Training School, Hakimpet

Territorial Army

- It is a voluntary part-time civilian force which plays a useful role in the defence of the country.
- The territorial army was raised in 1949.
- Employees of government departments and public sector units can join the Territorial Army.
- Their units have played important role during disturbances by assisting the Army.
- Eco Task Forces, raised from Territorial Army units have done excellent work of environment upgradation in Rajasthan, UP and J&K.

Coast Guard

- The Indian Coast Guard came into being on Aug. 19, 1978.
- The duties of the youngest armed force of the country are:
  1. Safety and protection of offshore installations and artificial islands;
  2. Protection of fishermen in distress;
  3. Protection of maritime environment;
  4. Assisting customs in anti-smuggling operations and
  5. Safety of life and property at sea.
- The service has Advanced Offshore Patrol Vessels (AOPVs), Offshore Patrol Vessels (OPVs), Fast Patrol Vessels (FPVs), Interceptor Boats (IBs) and Interceptor Crafts (lCs), Darnier Aircrafts and Chetak Helicopters.

➥ In addition, Six Hovercrafts, two Fast Patrol Vessels, two Interceptor Boats, one Advanced Offshore Patrol Vessel, four Pollution Control vessels, four Advance Light Helicopters and three medium range surviellance Aircrafts have also been approved in the Coast Guard Development Plan.

NCC

➥ The National Cadet Corps was set up in 1948.

➥ The air wing of the NCC was started in 1950 and naval wing in 1952.

➥ The initial aims of the NCC were:

1. To develop character, comradeship, ideals of service and capacity for leadership in the youth of the country;
2. To stimulate interest in the defence of the country by providing training to youth and
3. To build up a reserve to enable the armed forces to expand rapidly in a national emergency.

➥ The functioning of the NCC is a dual responsibility of the centre and the states. The NCC does not act as the feeder for cadets into the defence forces. However, it does encourage and assist cadets to do so. The NCC trains cadets to take appropriate place in the society, in all walks of life and in service of the nation.

Combined Training Institutes for Defence Services

➥ National Defence Academy, Khadakvasala

➥ Indian Military Academy, Dehradun

➥ National Defence College, New Delhi

➥ Defence Services Staff College, Wellington

➥ Rashtriya Indian Military College, Dehradun

➥ Armed Forces Medical College, Pune

MULTIPLE CHOICE QUESTIONS

1. National Defence Academy is located in:
   A. Khadakvasala
   B. Dehradun
   C. New Delhi
   D. Pune

2. What is the total number of languages that have been given the status of 'Classical Language' in India?
   A. 6 B. 8
   C. 10 D. 11

3. Antyodaya Diwas is celebrated in honour of whose birth anniversary?
   A. Mahatma Gandhi
   B. Jawaharlal Nehru
   C. Pandit Deendayal Upadhyay
   D. Subhas Chandra Bose

4. .... is associated with 'Videshiya' folk dance.
   A. Bihar
   B. Jharkhand
   C. Uttar Pradesh
   D. Madhya Pradesh

5. 'Karagam', a religious folk dance is associated with:
   A. Tamil Nadu
   B. Kerala
   C. Andhra Pradesh
   D. Karnataka

6. Which one of the following is essentially a solo dance?
   A. Kuchipudi
   B. Kathak
   C. Manipuri
   D. Mohiniattam

7. Which one of the following pairs of folk dance forms and states is not correctly matched:
   A. Korku : Maharashtra
   B. Jhumar : Haryana
   C. Thali : Himachal Pradesh
   D. Rakhal : Manipur

8. Zubin Mehta is related with which musical instrument?
   A. Guitar B. Simphoni
   C. Piano D. Sarangi

9. Headquarter of western command of Indian Army is located in:
   A. Ambala
   B. Patiala
   C. Chandigarh
   D. Jaipur

10. Which was the first missile boat of India?
    A. INS Vinash
    B. INS Khukri
    C. INS Shakti
    D. INS Ajay

11. Which was the first frigate naval ship in India?
    A. INS Vinash
    B. INS Khukri
    C. INS Shakti
    D. INS Ajay

12. Which among the following does not belong to the Commissioned Ranks in the Army service?
    A. Brigadier
    B. Colonel
    C. General
    D. Commander

13. Headquarter of Training Command of Indian Army is located in:
    A. Hyderabad B. Shimla
    C. Mathura D. Agra

14. Meenakshi Temple is located in which state?
    A. Tamil Nadu
    B. Kerala
    C. Maharashtra
    D. Himachal Pradesh

15. The first woman to be the speaker of Lok Sabha is:
    A. Vijay Lakshmi Pandit
    B. Sarojini Naidu
    C. Indira Gandhi
    D. Meira Kumar

16. The 'first lady' of the Indian Silver Screen is:
    A. Madhubala
    B. Devika Rani
    C. Durga Khote
    D. Nargis Dutt

17. When is the Army Day?
    A. 15 January
    B. 15 February
    C. 15 March
    D. 15 April

18. The name of India's first aircraft carrier is:
    A. INS Nilgiri
    B. INS Himgiri
    C. INS Khukri
    D. INS Vikrant

19. Imrat Khan is a renowned player of:
    A. Surbahar B. Tabla
    C. Sarod D. Flute

20. Appa Jalgaonkar is a renowned player of:
    A. Harmonium
    B. Ghatam
    C. Piano
    D. Mandolin

21. Mahabalipuram Temples are located at:

A. Madhya Pradesh
B. Odisha
C. Tamil Nadu
D. Karnataka

22. Ms. Vijaya Mehta has earned distinction in which fo the following field?

A. Theatre
B. Film Direction
C. Classical Dance
D. Journalism

23. The Flag on half pale represents:

A. War
B. National Mourn
C. Defeat
D. Victory

24. Who composed the 'Bande Mataram'?

A. Bankim Chandra
B. Aurobindo Ghosh
C. Rabindranath Tagore
D. Mukunda Das

25. 'Bibi-ka-Maqbara' is located at:

A. Sambhaji Nagar
B. Ahmedabad
C. Sasaram
D. Mumbai

ANSWERS

2	3	4	5	6	7	8	9	10
D	C	A	A	D	A	B	C	A

13	14	15	16	17	18	19	20
B	A	D	B	A	D	A	A

24	25
A	A

9 Abbreviations

A

AC	Ashok Chakra; Alternating Current
AD	Anno Domini (In the year of Christ)
ADB	Asian Development Bank
AI	Air India
AIDS	Acquired Immune Deficiency Syndrome
AITUC	All India Trade Union Congress
APEC	Asia-Pacific Economic Cooperation
ASEAN	Association of South-East Asian Nations
ASLV	Augmented Satellite Launch Vehicle
ASOCHAM	Associated Chambers of Commerce and Industry
ATM	Automated Teller Machine

B

BBC	British Broadcasting Corporation
BC	Before Christ
BCCI	Board of Control for Cricket in India.
BHEL	Bharat Heavy Electricals Limited
BRO	Border Roads Organisation
BoP	Balance of Payment
BSF	Border Security Force

C

CAG	Comptroller and Auditor General
CAS	Chief of Army Staff; Chief of Air Staff
CBI	Central Bureau of Investigation
CHOGM	Commonwealth Heads of Government Me

- CIA Central Intelligence Agency (US)
- CID Criminal Investigation Department (Police)
- CITU Centre of Indian Trade Unions
- COFEPOSA Conservation of Foreign Exchange and Prevention of Smuggling Act
- CSIR Council of Scientific and Industrial Research
- CTBT Comprehensive Test Ban Treaty

D

- DC Direct Current; Deputy Commissioner; District Collector
- DDT Di-chloro Di-phenyl Tri-chloroethane
- DMK Dravida Munnetra Kazhagam
- DNA Deoxyribose Nucleic Acid
- DRDO Defence Research and Development Organisation

E

- ECG Electro-cardio-gram
- EEZ Exclusive Economic Zone
- EFTA European Free Trade Association
- EPF Employees Provident Fund
- EPZ Export Processing Zone
- ESCAP Economic and Social Council for Asia and Pacific
- ESMA Essential Service Maintenance Act

F

- FAO Food and Agricultural Organisation (UN)
- FDI Foreign Direct Investment
- FERA Foreign Exchange Regulation Act
- FICCI Federation of Indian Chambers of Commerce and Industry
- FIR First Information Report

G

- GATT General Agreement on Tariffs and Trade
- GAIL Gas Authority of India Limited
- GDP Gross Domestic Product
- GIC General Insurance Corporation
- GMT Greenwich Mean Time
- GNP Gross National Product
- GST Goods and Services Tax

H

- HAL Hindustan Aeronautics Limited
- HMT Hindustan Machine Tools
- HUDCO Housing and Urban Developing Corporation

I

- IA Indian Airlines; Indian Army
- IAEA International Atomic Energy Agency
- IBRD International Bank for Reconstruction and Development (World Bank)
- ICBM Inter Continental Ballistic Missile
- IDBI Industrial Development Bank of India
- ILO International Labour Organisation
- IMF International Monetary Fund
- INSAT Indian National Satellite System
- INTERPOL International Police Organisation
- ISI Indian Standards Institute; Inter-Service Intelligence
- ISRO Indian Space Research Organisation

J

- JAL Japan Airlines
- JCO Junior Commissioned Officer
- JNU Jawaharlal Nehru University
- JP Janata Party; Jayaprakash Narayan
- JPC Joint-Parliamentary Committee
- JRC Joint Research Centre
- JRY Jawahar Rozgar Yojana

K

- KG Kindergarten
- Kg Kilogram
- KKK Ku Klux Klan (Racist group of US)
- Km Kilometre; Kumari
- KW Kilowatt

L

- LASER Light Amplification by Stimulated Emission of Radiation
- LCA Light Combat Aircraft

- LCM Lowest Common Multiple
- LIC Life Insurance Corporation
- LL B Legum Doctor (Bachelor of Laws)
- LPG Liquefied Petroleum Gas
- LTTE Liberation Tigers of Tamil Eelam

M

- MBBS Bachelor of Medicine and Bachelor of Surgery
- MBT Main Battle Tank
- MCC Melbourne Cricket Club (Australia)
- MCI Medical Council of India
- MFN Most-Favoured Nation
- MODVAT Modified Value Added Tax

N

- NABARD National Bank for Agriculture and Rural Development
- NAFTA North American Free Trade Agreement
- NASA National Aeronautics and Space Administration (US)
- NATO North Atlantic Treaty Organisation
- NHRC National Human Rights Commission
- NPTC National Power Transmission Corporation

O

- OAS Organisation of American States
- OECD Organisation of European Cooperation and Development
- OIL Oil India Limited
- ONGC Oil and Natural Gas Corporation
- OPEC Organisation of Petroleum Exporting Countries
- OTCE Over-The-Counter Exchange of India

P

- PCI Press Council of India
- PIN Postal Index Number
- PIO Person of Indian Origin
- PLO Palestinian Liberation Front
- PSLV Polar Satellite Launch Vehicle
- PVC Param Vir Chakra
- PWD Public Works Department

Q

- QTY Quantity
- QALY Quality
- qH Every Hour

R

- RAF Rapid Action Force; Royal Air Force
- RADAR Radio Detection and Ranging
- RBC Red Blood Corpuscles
- RAW Research and Analysis Wing
- RNA Ribo Nucleic Acid
- RPF Railway Protection Force
- RSS Rashtriya Swayamsevak Sangh

S

- SAARC South Asian Association for Regional Corporation
- SAF South Asian Federation
- SAPTA South Asian Preferential Trade Arrangement
- SDR Special Drawing Rights
- SEATO South East Asia Treaty Organisation
- SEBI Securities and Exchange Board of India
- SEZ Special Economic Zone
- START Strategic Arms Reduction Talks
- STD Subscriber Trunk Dialing
- SWAPO South West African People's Organisation

T

- TA Territorial Army; Travelling Allowance
- TADA Terrorists and Disruptive Activities (Prevention) Act
- TB Tuberculosis (tubercle bacillus)
- TIFR Tata Institute of Fundamental Research
- TNT Tri-Nitro Toluene
- TRYSEM Training of Rural Youth for Self Employment
- TTE Travelling Ticket Examiner

U

- UGC University Grants Commission
- UNO United Nations Organisation
- UNCTAD United Nations Conference on Trade and Development
- UNDC United Nations Disarmament Commission
- UNEDA United Nations Economic Development Administration
- UNESCO United Nations Educational, Scientific and Cultural Organisation
- UNHCR United Nations High Commissioner for Refugees
- UNI United News of India
- UNICEF United Nations International Children's Emergency Fund

V

- VAT Value Added Tax
- VDIS Voluntary Disclosure of Income Scheme
- VHP Vishwa Hindu Parishad
- VRS Voluntary Retirement Scheme
- VSAT Very Small Aperture Terminal

W

- WAAF Women's Auxiliary Air Force
- WAC Women's Auxiliary Corps
- WBC Wage Board Commission; World Boxing Council; White Blood Corpuscles
- WHO World Health Organisation
- WTO World Trade Organisation

X

- X'mas Christmas

Y

- YHA Youth Hostels Association
- YMCA Young Men's Christian Association
- YWCA Young Women's Christian Association

Z

- ZETA Zero Energy Thermonuclear Agency
- ZG Zoological Garden
- ZPG Zero Population Growth

MULTIPLE CHOICE QUESTIONS

1. What is the full form of "CAG"?
   A. Comptroller and Auditor General
   B. Chief of Auditor General
   C. Central Accounts General
   D. None of these
2. What is the full form of "BCCI"?
   A. Board of Control for Cricket in India
   B. Board of Commission for Cricket in India
   C. Board of Cabinet for Cricket of India
   D. Board of Communication for Cricket in India
3. What is the full form of "FAO"?
   A. Foreign Agro Organisation
   B. Food and Agricultural Organisation
   C. Federation of Agricultural Organisation
   D. First Agro Organisation
4. What is the full form of "GST"?
   A. Goods and Services Tax
   B. General Services Tax
   C. Gross Savings Tax
   D. None of these
5. What is the full form of "UGC"?
   A. Union Grants Commission
   B. United Grants Commission
   C. University Grants Commission
   D. Univesity Grade Commission
6. What is the full form of "ATM"?
   A. Automated Tallying Machine
   B. Automated Teller Machine
   C. Automated Totalling Machine
   D. Automated Transaction of Money
7. What is the full form of "AIDS"?
   A. Acquired Immune Deficiency Syndrome
   B. Acquired Immunity Deficiency Syndrome
   C. Acquired Immune Decency Syndrome
   D. Acquired Immune Defense Syndrome
8. What is the full form of "BRICS"?
   A. Bangladesh, Romania, Indonesia, Cambodia and South Africa
   B. Botswana, Rwanda, Ivory Coast, Croatia and South Africa
   C. Bangladesh, Romania, India, Cambodia and South Africa
   D. Brazil, Russia, India, China and South Africa
9. What is the full form of "IRBM"?
   A. Intermediate Resource Ballistic Missile
   B. Intermediate Range Ballistic Missile
   C. Intermediate Range of Ballistic Missile
   D. Intermediated Range Ballistic Missile
10. What is the full form of "PSLV"?
   A. Polarised Source Laser Viewing
   B. Polar Survey Landing Vehicle
   C. Polar Satellite Launch Vehicle
   D. Precise Source Locating Vision

ANSWERS

1	2	3	4	5	6	7	8	9	10
A	A	B	A	C	B	A	D	B	C

Books & Authors

INDIAN AUTHORS

Books	Authors
A Suitable Boy	Vikram Seth
Ain-i-Akbari	Abul Fazal
Ajatshatru	Jai Shankar Prasad
Akbarnama	Abul Fazal
Anandmath	Bankim Chandra Chatterjee
Arthashastra	Kautilya
Baburnama	Babur
Bhagwat Gita	Ved Vyas
Broken Wing	Sarojini Naidu
Buddha Charitran	Ashvaghosha
Chidambra	Sumitranandan Pant
Devdas	Sarat Chandra
Geet Govind	Jaye Dev
Gitanjali	Rabindranath Tagore
Godan	Munshi Prem Chand
God of Small Things, The	Arundhati Roy
Guide, The	R.K. Narayan
India Wins Freedom	Maulana Abul Kalam Azad
Indian War of Independence	V.D. Savarkar
Justice of Peace Ke Aansu	Janardan Prasad Singh
Kadambari	Bana Bhatt
Kamasutra	Vatsyayana
Kamayani	Jai Shankar Prasad
Mahabharata	Ved Vyas
Meghdoot	Kalidas

Books	Authors
My Experiments with truth	Mahatama Gandhi
My Music, My Life	Ravi Shankar
My Truth	Indira Gandhi
Padmavati	Malik Mohammad Jyasi
Prithviraj Raso	Chandra Bardai
Raghuvamsa	Kalidas
Rajtarangini	Kalhana
Ramayana	Valmiki
Ram Charita Manas	Tulsidas
Saket	Maithili Sharan Gupt
Shakuntala	Kalidas
Shahnama	Firdausi
Unhappy India	Lala Lajpat Rai
Urvashi	Ramdhari Singh 'Dinkar'
Uttara-Ramcharita	Bhava Bhuti
Venisamphar	Naryana Bhatt
Vinay Patrika	Tulsidas
Virangana	Maithili Sharan Gupt
Vish Vriksha	Bankim Chandra Chatterjee
War of Indian Independence	Veer Savarkar
Yama	Mahadevi Verma
Yashodara	Maithili Saran Gupt

FOREIGN AUTHORS

Books	Authors
A Farewell to Arms	Ernest Hemingway
A Midsummer Night's Dream	Shakespeare
Adventures of Sherlock Holmes	Sir Arthur Conan Doyle
Animal Farm, The	George Orwell
Anna Karenina	Count Leo Tolstoy
Antony and Cleopatra	William Shakespeare
Arabian Nights	Sir Richard Burton
Arms and the Men	George Bernard Shaw
Asian Drama	Gunnar Myrdal
Communist Manifesto	Karl Marx
Crime and Punishment	Fyodor Dostoevsky
Das Kapital	Karl Marx
Divine Comedy	A. Dante

Books	Authors
Gathering Storm	Winston Churchill
Good Earth	Pearl S. Buck
Great Expectations	Charles Dickens
Hemlet	William Shakespeare
Illiad	Homer
Jungle Book	Rudyard Kipling
Julius Ceaser	William Shakespeare
Lajja	Teslima Nasreen
Macbeth	William Shakespeare
Mein Kampf	Adolf Hitler
Merchant of Venice, The	William Shakespeare
Midnight's Children	Salman Rushdie
Mother	Maxim Gorky
Mother India	Kathereine Mayo
Odyssey	Homer
Oliver Twist	Charles Dickens
Origin of Species	Charles Darwin
Othello	William Shakespeare
Paradise Lost	John Milton
Prince, The	Niccolo Machiavelli
Pride and Prejudice	Jane Austin
Principia	Issac Newton
Professor, The	Chariotte Bronte
Pygmaliun	George Bernard Shaw
Robinson Crusoe	Daniel Defoe
Romeo and Juliet	William Shakespeare
Satanic Verses	Salman Rushdie
Sense and Sensibility	Jane Austen
Shame	Salman Rushdie
Sohrab and Rustam	Matthew Arnold
Sons and Lovers	D.H. Lawrence
Tempest, The	William Shakespeare
The Affluent Society	J.K. Galbraith
Three Musketeers	Alexander Dumas
Treasure Island, The	Robert Louis Stevenson
Twelfth Night	William Shakespeare
Ulysees	James Joyce
Unto this Last	John Ruskin
Utopia	Thomas Moore

Books	Authors
Wake-up India	Annie Besant
War and Peace	Leo Tolstoy
Waste Land, The	T.S. Eliot
Wealth of Nations, The	Adam Smith
Wuthering Heights	Emily Bronte

LATEST BOOKS AND AUTHORS

Books	Authors
Cricket My Style	Kapil Dev
Sunny Days	Sunil Gavaskar
Freedom from Fear	Aung San Suu Kyi
My Childhood Days	Taslima Nasreen
The City of Joy	Dominique Lapierre
God of Small Things	Arundhati Roi
Disgrace	J.M. Coetzee
Speed Post	Shobha De
Interpreter of Maladies	Jhumpa Lahiri
The Brief History of Time	Stephen Hawking
Living History	Hillary Rodham Clinton
Business at the Speed of Thought	Bill Gates
The Accidental Prime Minister— The Making and Unmaking of Manmohan Singh	Sanjaya Baru
Ignited Minds	Dr. A.P.J. Abdul Kalam
Wings of Fire	Dr. A.P.J. Abdul Kalam
Prophet Song (Winner of Booker Prize-2023)	Paul Lynch
Long Walk to Freedom	Nelson Mandela
The Writer and the World	V.S. Naipaul
Two Lives	Vikram Seth
The Namesake	Jhumpa Lahiri
India First	K.R. Malkani
Straight From the Heart	Kapil Dev
Relationship	Kuldip Nayar
My Life	Bill Clinton
Jinnah-India, Partition, Independence	Jaswant Singh
My Country : My Life	L.K. Advani
The White Tiger (Winner of Booker Prize 2008)	Arvind Adiga
Orbital (Winner of Booker Prize 2024)	Samantha Harvey

Famous Authors in Different Languages

Languages	Authors
English	William Shakespeare, John Milton, Chaucer, Spenser, Lord Byron, P.B. Shelley, John Keats, Francis Bacon, T.S. Eliot, Cecil Dlay Lewis, Alduous Huxley, W.B. Yeats, Bunyan, Dryden, Dr. Johnson, Alexander pope, Robert Browning, Charles Lamb, Charles Dickens, Thomas Hardy, W.M. Thackeray, George Eliot, Alfred Tennyson, Robert Bridges, George Bernard Shaw, D.H. Lawrence, Oliver Goldsmith, Sheridan, Walter Scott, William Wordsworth, S.T. Coleridge, Henry Fielding, Somerset Maugham.
French	Imile Zola, Gustave Flaubert, Moliere, Proudhon, Jean Paul Sartre, Le Sage, Victor Hugo, Alexander Dumas, Balzac.
German	Goethe, Hoffman, Lessing, Schelling, Schaupenhuer, Heinrich Heine, Guenter Grass.
Russian	Tolstoy, Mikhail Solokhov, Turgenev, Dostoevsky, Maxim Gorky, Techov, Alexander Salzhenitsyn, Boris Pasternak.
Greek	Homer, Aesop, Aristophanes, Euripedes, Herodotus, Hesoid, Theocritus, Xenophon, Aeschylus, Sophocles.
Latin	Dante, Boccacio, Terence, Virgil, Ovid, Horace, Seneca.
Persian	Ghalib, Umar Khyyam, Abul Fazal, Amir Khusro, Faiz, Firdausi, Mohd. Iqbal Saddi.
Spanish	Juan Valera, Lope De Vega, Cervantes.
Norwegian	John Bojer, Ibsen.

Greatest Poets

Language	Poet	Language	Poet
Hindi	Tulsidas	Greek	Homer
Sanskrit	Kalidas	English	Shakespeare
Bengali	Rabindra Nath Tagore	German	Goethe
Urdu	Mirza Galib	Italian	Dante
Persian	Sheikh Saadi	French	Sully Proudhone
Latin	Virgil	Punjabi	Waris Shah

MULTIPLE CHOICE QUESTIONS

1. The book *The Insider* is written by:
A. Madhav Rao Scindia
B. Nana Patekar
C. Shobha De
D. P V Narasimha Rao

2. *India Wins Freedom* was written by:
A. Dadabhai Nauroji
B. Ashfaqulla Khan
C. Sarojini Naidu
D. Maulana Abul Kalam Azad

3. *A Tale of Two Cities* is, in fact, the story of two famous cities. Those cities are:
A. Paris and New York
B. London and New York
C. London and Paris
D. Stockholm and New York

4. *Ben Hur* was penned by:
   A. Lewis Wallace
   B. Lord Byron
   C. William Shakespeare
   D. None of the above

5. *Panchatantra* was written by:
   A. R K Narayan
   B. R K Laxman
   C. Vishnu Sharma
   D. None of the above

6. Arundhati Roy has been awarded the prestigious:
   A. Booker's Prize – 1997
   B. Jnanpeeth Award – 1997
   C. Sahitya Akademi Award – 1998
   D. None of the above

7. Who wrote *Odyssey*?
   A. George Orwell
   B. Homer
   C. Dom Moraes
   D. None of the above

8. Which one of the following was not written by Shakespeare?
   A. *As You Like It*
   B. *Mcbeth*
   C. *Hamlet*
   D. *A Farewell to Arms*

9. Lewis Carol wrote a masterpiece. What is its name?
   A. *Don Quixote*
   B. *Alice in Wonderland*
   C. *Adventures of Robinson Crusoe*
   D. *Great Expectations*

10. The *Tamil Ramayana* is the work of:
   A. Tulsidas B. Jayangondar
   C. Kambar D. Veda Vyas

11. In *Shrimad Bhagwat Geeta,* Lord Krishna teaches his disciple Arjuna to:
   A. rise to the occasion and fight with his near and dear ones
   B. withdraw from the battlefield
   C. do his duty and not to expect anything in return
   D. attack the enemy in a planned and meticulous approach

12. Who wrote *Origin of Species*?
   A. Charles Darwin
   B. Alexander Flaming
   C. G.B. Shaw
   D. D.H. Lawrence

13. The poet and the well-known friend of Prithvi Raj Chauhan, who wrote *Prithvi Raj Raso,* was:
   A. Harisena
   B. Vishnu Datt
   C. Chand Bardai
   D. None of the above

14. The first book was printed in India in the year 1561. Its name was:
   A. *The spiritual Compendium of the Christian Life*
   B. *Aain-e-Akbari*
   C. *Babur Nama*
   D. *Ram Charit Manas*

15. The famous book *Runs and Ruins* was written by:
   A. Sir Donald Bradman
   B. Sunil Gavaskar
   C. Kapil Dev
   D. Richard Hadlee

16. Adam Smith wrote the following famous book:
   A. *The Wreck*
   B. *Dr Zhivago*
   C. *The Wealth of Nations*
   D. *Tarzan of the Apes*

17. H.G. Wells is known as a
   A. poet
   B. science-fiction writer
   C. thriller-fiction writer
   D. essay writer and critic

18. Tukaram wrote his devotional songs in this language:
   A. Urdu B. Gujarati
   C. Hindi D. Marathi

19. Our ancient scholars and writers used this language for their social, religious and political books and works

A. Tamil
B. Sanskrit
C. Urdu
D. Hindi (Devanagari)

20. *Gora* is the hero of a book written by Rabindra Nath Tagore. What is the name of the book?

A. *Geetanjali* B. *Patanjali*
C. *Gora* D. *Twelfth Night*

21. Who is the author of the book *The Celestine Vision*?

A. Paul Hockins
B. Salman Rushdie
C. Joseph Conrad
D. James Redfield

22. *Godaan* was written by Munshi Prem Chand and it depicts:

A. the methodology for taking adequate care of the cows
B. exploitation of simple rural folk by the rich landlords of rural India
C. the mutiny of 1857 in which, Indians refused to bite the Kartoos made with cow beef
D. None of the above

23. Manu wrote a book during ancient times in which, he divided the Aryan society into four distinct classes. What was the name of the book?

A. *Arthashastra*
B. *Manusmriti*
C. *Moti Mahal*
D. *My Truth*

24. R. Venkataraman wrote *My Presidential Years*. What was the main theme of the book?

A. It described the aristocratic procedures being followed in the Rashtrapati Bhawan during his tenure as President
B. It described the power equations and ploys in the centre and in the states during his term
C. It described how he felt caged while he was President due to a load of procedures and formalities
D. It explained the machinations of the political party which was in power during his tenure as President

25. The total number of Puranas written during the Vedic age is:

A. 22 B. 9
C. 18 D. 25

ANSWERS

1	2	3	4	5	6	7	8	9	10
D	D	C	A	C	A	B	D	B	C
11	**12**	**13**	**14**	**15**	**16**	**17**	**18**	**19**	**20**
C	A	C	A	B	C	B	D	B	C
21	**22**	**23**	**24**	**25**					
D	B	B	C	C					

11

Awards and Honours

INTERNATIONAL AWARDS

Nobel Prize

- Nobel Prizes are awarded each year under the will of Alfred Bernhard Nobel (1833-96), Swedish chemist and engineer.
- The interest of the fund is divided annually among the persons who have made the most outstanding contribution in various fields. In all, there are six prizes.
- The prizes are awarded to persons who have made outstanding contributions in the fields of Physics, Chemistry, and Physiology or Medicine, Literature and World Peace. The sixth prize, that is The Nobel Prize for Economic Sciences was established in 1967 by Risk Bank, the Swedish Bank, in celebration of its 300th anniversary and was awarded for the first time in 1969. Other awards were started in 1901.
- **Indians Honoured with Nobel Prize:** So far, five Indians have been honoured with these prizes. Their names are
  - *(i)* Rabindra Nath Tagore for Literature, for his book 'Gitanjali', in 1913,
  - *(ii)* Dr. C.V. Raman for Physics in 1930, for his discovery of 'Raman Effect',
  - *(iii)* Mother Teresa for Peace in 1979,
  - *(iv)* Prof. Amartya Sen in 1998 for Economics and
  - *(v)* Kailash Satyarthi for Peace in 2014.
- In addition, four non-resident Indians have also been awarded the Nobel Prize. They are:
  - *(i)* Hargobind Khurana for Medicine in 1968,
  - *(ii)* Subramanian Chandrasekhar for Physics in 1983,
  - *(iii)* Venkatraman Ramkrishnan for Chemistry in 2009,
  - *(iv)* Abhijit Vinayak Banerjee for Economics in 2019.

2025 Nobel Prizes

The winners of 2025 Nobel Prizes has been declared in October 2025. The Winners are:

- **Physics:** John Clarke, Michel H. Devoret and John M. Martinis (All USA) for the discovery of macroscopic quantum mechanical tunnelling and energy quantisation in an electric circuit.

- **Chemistry:** Susumu Kitagawa (Japan), Richard Robson (Australia) and Omar M. Yaghi (USA) for the development of metal-organic frameworks.
- **Medicine or Physiology:** Mary E. Brunkow; Frederick J. Ramsdell and Shimon Sakaguchi (All USA) for their discoveries concerning peripheral immune tolerance.
- **Economics:** Joel Mokyr (USA), Philippe Aghion (UK) and Peter Howitt (USA) for having explained innovation-driven economic growth.
- **Literature:** László Krasznahorkai (Hungary) for his compelling and visionary oeuvre that, in the midst of apocalyptic terror, reaffirms the power of art.
- **Peace:** Maria Corina, Machado, for her tireless work promoting democratic rights for the people of Venezuela and for her struggle to achive a just and peaceful transition from dictatorship to democracy.

Ramon Magsaysay Award 2025

The Ramon Magsaysay Award, named after a Philippines President, who died in an air crash in 1957, is given annually to Asian nationals or institutions who have made worthy contributions to public service, community leadership, journalism, literature and the creative arts and international understanding. It carries a gold medal, a certificate and US$ 50,000. It is awarded on August 31, every year. The Ramon Magsaysay Award is Asia's highest honor and is widely regarded as the region's equivalent of the Nobel Prize. It celebrates the memory and leadership example of the third Philippline president after whom the award is named, and is given every year to individuals or organizations in Asia who manifest the same selfless service and transformative influence that ruled the life of the late and beloved Filipino leader.

Magsaysay Awards 2025: The 2025 awardees are:

- **Foundation to Educate Girls Globally (India):** The first Indian organization to win, it is recognized for its innovative approach to tackling cultural stereotypes and empowering millions of girls in rural India through education.
- **Shaahina Ali (Maldives):** Honored for her significant work in the environmental sector in the Maldives.
- **Flaviano Antonio L. Villanueva (Philippines):** Awarded for his dedication to uplifting and supporting the poor and marginalized communities in the Phillippines.

Man Booker Prize 2025

Flesh by David Szalay was named the winner of the Booker Prize 2025 at a ceremony in London on 10 November, 2025. Szalay receives £50,000 and a trophy, which was presented to him by last year's winner, Samantha Harvey. Written in spare prose and spanning decades – from a Hungarian housing estate to the mansions of London's rich elite – Flesh is a propulsive novel centred on an emotionally detached man who is unravelled by a series of events beyond his grasp. The novel is the sixth work of fiction by David Szalay, who was previously shortlisted for the Booker in 2016.

Mahatma Gandhi Peace Prize

- This award, which carries an amount of ₹ 1 crore and a citation, was instituted by the Government of India in 1994, during the 125th birth anniversary celebrations of Mahatma Gandhi.

- The first person to receive this award in 1995, was Dr. Julius K. Nyerere, former President of Tanzania.
- The winner of 2021 is Gita Press, Gorakhpur.

Jawaharlal Nehru Award for International Understanding

- The Government of India instituted the Jawaharlal Nehru Award for International Understanding in 1965 as a tribute to the memory of the late Prime Minister for his lifelong dedication to the cause of world peace and international understanding. The award, which is given away annually to an eminent person for outstanding contribution towards the promotion of international understanding, goodwill and friendship among the people of the world, carries an amount of Rs. 25 lakh (convertible into foreign currency) and a citation. The award is administered by the Indian Council for Cultural Relations and is made by a seven-member independent jury which includes the Vice-President and the Chief Justice of India. The first person to receive this award in 1965, was U. Thant former Secretary General of the UN.

Bafta Awards - 2026

- The 79th British Academy Film and Theatre Awards, popularly known as the BAFTA Awards, were conferred in different categories at a star-studded awards ceremony on February 22, 2026 at the Royal Festival Hall in London, England. Winners of BAFTA 2026 are: • ***Best Film:*** One Battle After Another; • ***Best Director:*** Paul Thomas Anderson *(One Battle After Another)*; • ***Best Leading Actress:*** Jessie Buckley *(Hamnet)*; • ***Best Leading Actor:*** Robert Aramayo *(I Swear)*; • ***Best Supporting Actor:*** Sean Penn *(One Battle After Another)*; • ***Best Supporting Actress:*** Wunmi Mosaku *(Sinners)*; • Best Original Screenplay: Sinners *(Ryan Coogler)*; • ***Best Adapted Screenplay:*** One Battle After Another (Paul Thomas Anderson); • ***Best Animated Film:*** *Zootropolis 2*; • ***Best Documentary:*** *Mr. Nobody Against Putin*; • ***Best Cinematography:*** *One Battle After Another*; • ***Best Costume Design:*** Frankenstein; • ***Best Editing:*** *One Battle After Another*; • ***Best Original Score:*** *Sinners*; • ***Best Special Visual Effects:*** *Avatar : Fire and Ash*; • ***Best British Short Animation:*** *Two Black Boys in Paradise*; • ***EE Rising Star Award:*** Robert Aramayo.

Indira Gandhi Prize for Peace, Disarmament and Development 2025

- The award was instituted in the memory of Mrs. Indira Gandhi, to foster creative cooperation among nations of the world, ushering in of a new international economic order and the enrichment of the human spirit. The winner of 2025 is Mozambican rights activist and humanitarian Graca Machel.

Oscar Awards

This prestigious award of film world is given annually by 'National Academy of Motion Picture Arts & Sciences' of America.

98th Oscar Awards, 2026

- The 98th Academy Awards, popularly known as Oscar awards, 2026 were conferred in different categories for outstanding films at grand award ceremony on March 16, 2026 in Los Angeles, USA. The winners are: • ***Best Film:*** *One Battle After Another*; • ***Best Actor:*** Michael B Jordan *(Sinners)*; • ***Best Actress:*** Jessie Buckley *(Hamnet)*; • ***Best Supporting Actor:*** Sean Penn *(One Battle After*

Another); • ***Best Supporting Actress:*** Amy Madigan *(Weapons)*; • ***Best Director:*** Paul Thomas Anderson *(One Battle After Another)*; • ***Best Cinematography:*** Autumn Durald Arkapaw *(Sinners)*; • ***Best Original Screenplay:*** Ryan Coogler *(Sinners)*; • ***Best Adapted Screenplay:*** Paul Thomas Anderson *(One Battle After Another)*; • ***Best Original Score:*** Ludwig Goransson *(Sinners)*; • ***Best Sound:*** F1–Gareth John, Al Nelson, Gwendolyn Yates Whittle, Gary A Rizzo and Juan Peralta; • ***Best Visual Effects:*** Joe Letteri, Richard Baneham, Eric Saindon and Daniel Barrett *(Avatar : Fire and Ash)*; • ***Best Original Song:*** Golden KPop Demon Hunters; • ***Best International Feature Film:*** Sentimental Value; • ***Best Documentary Short Film:*** All the Empty Rooms; • ***Best Editing:*** Andy Jurgensen *(One Battle After Another)*; • ***Best Documentary Feature Film:*** *Mr. Nobody Against Putin*; • ***Best Animated Film:*** *KPop Demon Hunters*; • ***Best Animated Short Film:*** *The Girl Who Cried Pearls*; • ***Best Costume Design:*** Kate Hawley *(Frankenstein)*; • ***Best Makeup and Hair Styling:*** Mike Hill, Jordan Samuel and Cliona Furey *(Frankenstein)*; • ***Best Prodution design:*** Tamara Deverell and Shane Vieau *(Frankenstein)*. • ***Best Live Action Short Film:*** *The Singers.*

Grammy Awards 2026

➡ 68th Grammy Awards, one of the most prestigious awards in music world, were conferred in different categories at an award ceremony in Los Angeles on February 01, 2026. **Major Winners:** • ***Song of the Year:*** *Wildflower* (Billie Eilish) • ***Record of the year:*** *Luther* (Kendrick Lamar feat SZA) • ***Album of the year:*** *Bad Bunny* (Debí Tirar Más Fotos) • ***Best new artist:*** Olivia Dean • ***Best pop vocal album:*** *Mayhem* (Lady Gaga) • ***Best pop solo performance:*** *Messy* (Lola Young) • ***Best pop duo/group performance:*** *Defying Gravity* (Cynthia Erivo & Ariana Grande) • ***Best dance/ electronic recording:*** *End Of Summer* (Tame Impala) • ***Best Dance electronic album:*** *Eusexua* (FKA Twigs) • ***Best Rock song:*** *As Alive As You Need Me To Be* (Nine Inch Nails) • ***Best Metal Performance:*** *Birds* (Turnstile) • ***Best Rap Performance:*** *Chains & Whips* (Clipse, Pusha T & malice feat Kendrick Lamar & Pharrell Williams) • ***Best Rap Album:*** *GNX* (Kendrick Lamar) • ***Best Country Solo Performance:*** *Bad As I Used To Be* (Chris Stapleton) • ***Best Country Song:*** *Bitin' List* (Tyler Childers) • ***Best R&B Song:*** *Folded* (Kehlani) • ***Best Comedy Album:*** *Your Friend, Nate Bargatze* (Nate Bargatze) • ***Best Jazz vocal Album:*** *Portrait* (Samara Joy).

NATIONAL AWARDS

Bharat Ratna and other national honours and awards are conferred on Republic Day in recognition of exceptional and distinguished services of high order in any field.

Bharat Ratna

➡ This award is given for exceptional work for the advancement of art, literature and sciences and in recognition of public service of the highest order. The decoration is in the form of a peepal leaf, about 5.8 cm long, 4.7 cm wide and 3.1 mm thick. It is of toned bronze.

➡ On its obverse, is embossed a replica of the sun, 1.6 cm in diameter, below which the words "Bharat Ratna" are embossed in Hindi. On the reverse, are state emblem and the motto, also in Hindi. The emblem, the sun and the rim are of platinum. The inscriptions are in burnished bronze.

➡ The following celebrities have received this award so far.

Name	Year	Name	Year
C. Rajagopalachari	1954	Rajiv Gandhi (Posth.)	1991
S. Radhakrishnan	1954	Subhash Chandra Bose (Withdrawn)	1992
Dr. C. V. Raman	1954	Maulana Abul Kalam Azad (Posth.)	1992
Jawaharlal Nehru	1955	J.R.D. Tata	1992
Dr. Bhagwan Das	1955	Satyajit Ray	1992
M. Visweswaraiya	1955	No Award	1993-96
No Award	1956-57	A.P.J. Abdul Kalam	1997
Govind Ballabh Pant	1958	Gulzari Lal Nanda	1997
Dr. D. K. Karve	1958	Aruna Asaf Ali (Posth.)	1997
No Award	1959-60	M. S. Subba Lakshmi	1998
Dr. B.C. Roy	1961	C. Subramaniam	1998
P.D. Tandon	1961	Jaya Prakash Narayan (Posth.)	1999
Dr. Rajendra Prasad	1962	Prof. Amartya Sen	1999
Dr. Zakir Hussain	1963	Pandit Ravi Shankar	1999
Dr. P.V. Kane	1963	Gopinath Bordoloi	1999
No Award	1964-65	No Award	2000
Lal Bahadur Shastri (Posth.)	1966	Ms. Lata Mangeshkar	2001
No Award	1967-70	Bismillah Khan	2001
Mrs. Indira Gandhi	1971	No Award	2002 to 2008
No Award	1972-74	Pt. Bhimsen Joshi	2009
V. V. Giri	1975	Sachin Tendulkar	2014
K. Kamraj (Posth.)	1976	C.N.R. Rao	2014
No Award	1977-79	Madan Mohan Malaviya (Posth.)	2015
Mother Teresa	1980	Atal Bihari Vajpayee	2015
No Award	1981-82	Nanaji Deshmukh (Posth.)	2019
Acharya Vinoba Bhave (Posth.)	1983	Bhupen Hazarika (Posth.)	2019
No Award	1984-86	Pranab Mukherjee	2019
Khan Abdul Ghaffar Khan	1987	No Award	2020 to 2023
M.G. Ramchandran (Posth.)	1988	Karpoori Thakur (Posth.)	2024
No Award	1989	L.K. Advani	2024
Dr. B.R. Ambedkar (Posth.)	1990	Charan Singh (Posth.)	2024
Nelson Mandela	1990	P.V. Narasimha Rao (Posth.)	2024
Morarji Desai	1991	M.S. Swaminathan (Posth.)	2024
Vallabh Bhai Patel (Posth.)	1991		

Note:

1. No Republic Day civilian awards were announced on the eve of Republic Day in 1993, 1994 and 1995 because the government decided to wait for the Court's verdict on the constitutionality of these awards.
2. During the Janata Party regime (1977-79), the institution of Republic Day Awards was abolished. It was, however, revived by the Congress Government in 1980.

GALLANTRY AWARDS

- **Param Vir Chakra:** The highest decoration for valour is the Param Vir Chakra which is awarded for the most conspicuous bravery or some daring or pre-eminent act of valour or self-sacrifice in the presence of the enemy, whether on land, at sea or in the air. The decoration is made of bronze and is circular in shape. It has, on the obverse, four replicas of "India's Vajra" embossed round the state emblem in the centre. On the reverse, the words "Param Vir Chakra" are embossed both in Hindi and English with two lotus flowers in the middle. The decoration is worn on the left breast with a plain purple coloured ribbon about 3.2 cm in width.
- **Maha Vir Chakra:** The Maha Vir Chakra is the second highest decoration and is awarded for acts of conspicuous gallantry in the presence of enemy, whether on land, at sea or in the air. It is made of standard silver and is circular in shape. Embossed on the obverse, is a five point heraldic star with domed centrepiece bearing the gilded state emblem in the centre. The words "Maha Vir Chakra" are embossed both in Hindi and English on the reverse with two lotus flowers in the middle. The decoration is worn on the left breast with a half-white and half-orange ribbon about 3.2 cm in width, the orange being near the left shoulder.
- **Vir Chakra:** The Vir Chakra is third in the order of awards given. Its ribbon is golden with one dark-blue strip down the centre.
- **Ashok Chakra:** This is awarded for the most conspicuous bravery or some daring or pre-eminent act of valour or self-sacrifice during peace time.
- **Vishisht Sewa Medal:** It is awarded to the personnel of all the three defence forces, in recognition of distinguished service of most exceptional and high order.
- **Jeevan Raksha Awards:** The medals are awarded for meritorious acts or a series of acts of a human nature displayed in saving a person from drowning, fire and rescue operations in mines etc. Sarvottam Jeevan Raksha Padak is awarded for conspicuous courage under circumstances of very great danger to the life of the rescuer. Uttam Jeevan Raksha Padak is awarded for courage and promptitude in saving life under circumstances of great danger to the life of the rescuer. Jeevan Raksha Padak is awarded for courage and promptitude in saving life under circumstances of grave bodily injury to the rescuer.
- **Two New Medals:** Two new medals have been introduced since 1988. These are the Uttam Seva Medals and Yudh Seva Medals.

Literary Awards

- **Bharatiya Jnanpith Award:** The *Bhartiya Jnanpith Award* has been sponsored by Bharatiya Jnanpith, a cultural-literary society, founded in 1944 by the noted industrialist, Shanti Prasad Jain, with the twin object of rediscovering the neglected treasures of Indian philosophy and of encouraging creative writing in various modern Indian languages. The award carries with it a cash prize of ₹ 21 lakh, a citation and a replica of the Vagdevi, the symbol of outstanding literary achievement.

Renowned Tamil poet, lyricist and writer R. Vairamuthu has been given Jnanpith Award for 2025.

- **Saraswati Samman 2024:** Given to an outstanding literary work of an Indian language recognised by our Constitution. The value of the prize is ₹ 15 lakh. The award for the year 2024 has been given to renowned Sanskrit Scholar Mahamahopadhyaya Sadhu Bhadreshdas for his book *'Swaminarayana Siddhanta Sudha'* in Sanskrit.
- **Vyas Samman 2024:** This is awarded by KK Birla Foundation for outstanding Hindi Literary work by an Indian citizen that was published in the past decade. This carries a cash prize of ₹ 4.0 lakh. The award for 2024 has been given to Noted Hindi writer Suryabala for her novel *"Kaun Des Ko Vasi : Venu Ki Diary"*.

National Sport Awards-2024

- **Major Dhyan Chand Khel Ratna Award:** Gukesh D. (Chess), Harmanpreet Singh (Hockey), Praveen Kumar (Para-Athletics), Manu Bhaker (Shooting).
- **Arjuna Awards:** Jyothi Yarraji (Athletics), Annu Rani (Athletics), Nitu (Boxing), Saweety (Boxing), Vantika Agrawal (Chess), Salima Tete (Hockey), Abhishek (Hockey), Sanjay (Hockey), Jarmanpreet Singh (Hockey), Sukhjeet Singh (Hockey), Rakesh Kumar (Para-Archery), Preeti Pal (Para-Athletics), Jeevanji Deepthi (Para-Athletics), Ajeet Singh (Para-Athletics), Sachin Sarjerao Khilari (Para-Athletics), Dharambir (Para-Athletics), Pranav Soorma (Para-Athletics), H Hokato Sema (Para-Athletics), Simran (Para-Athletics), Navdeep (Para-Athletics), Nitesh Kumar (Para-Badminton), Thulasimathi Murugesan (Para-Badminton), Nithya Sre Sumathy Sivan (Para-Badminton), Manisha Ramadass (Para-Badminton), Kapil Parmar (Para-Judo), Mona Agarwal (Para-Shooting), Rubina Francis (Para-Shooting), Swapnil Suresh Kusale (Shooting), Sarabjot Singh (Shooting), Abhay Singh (Squash), Sajan Prakash (Swimming), Aman (Wrestling).
- **Arjuna Awards (Lifetime):** Sucha Singh (Athletics), Murlikant Rajaram Petker (Para-Swimming)
- **Dronacharya Awards (Regular Category):** Subhash Rana (Para-Shooting), Deepali Deshpande (Shooting), Sandeep Sangwan (Hockey).

  Dronacharya Awards (Lifetime Category): S Muralidharan (Badminton), Armando Agnelo Colaco (Football).

OTHER AWARDS

- **Dada Saheb Phalke Award:** The prestigious Dada Saheb Phalke Award is given to the persons for outstanding contribution to the growth and development of Indian cinema. The award comprises a Swarna Kamal, a cash component of ₹ 15 lakhs and a shawl.

  Dada Saheb Phalke Award 2023: Renowned Malayalam actor Mohanlal has been honoured with the Dada Saheb Phalke Award (2023) for his contribution to Cinema.
- **G.D. Birla Award for Humanism:** The G. D. Birla award for humanism carries a cash prize of ₹ 3 lakh and the other two awards carry a cash prize of ₹ 1 lakh each.
- **Lal Bahadur Shastri National Award 2024:** The 25th Lal Bahadur Shastri National Award for Excellence-2024 was presented by Shri Jagdeep

Dhankhar, Hon'ble Vice President of India to Smt. Rajshree Birla, Chairperson, Aditya Birla Centre for Community Initiatives and Rural Development, on 1st October 2024.

71st National Film Awards 2023 (Declared in 2025)

The winners of the 71st National Film Awards are announced at the National Media Center in New Delhi on August 01, 2025 with the Hindi film 12th Fail emerging as the Best Feature Film. **The winners. are:** • ***Best Feature Film:*** 12th Fail • ***Best Actor (Leading Role):*** Shah Rukh Khan (Jawan) and Vikrant Massey (12th Fail) • ***Best Actress (Leading Role):*** Rani Mukerji (Mrs Chatterjee vs Norway) • ***Best Actor (Supporing Role):*** Vijayaraghavan (Pookalam), Muthupettai Somu Bhaskar (Parking) • ***Best Actress (Supporting Role):*** Urvashi (Ullozhukku), Janki Bodiwala (Vash) • ***Best Action Director:*** Nandu-Prudhvi (HanuMan) • ***Best Choreography:*** Vaibhavi Merchant (Rocky Aur Rani Kii Prem Kahaani) • ***Best Lyrics:*** Kasarla Shyam (Ooru Palleturu – Balagam) • ***Best Music:*** GV Prakash Kumar (Vaathi), Harshavardhan Rameshwar (Animal) • ***Best Editing:*** Midhun Murali (Pookkaalam) • ***Best Sound Design:*** Sachin Sudhakaran, Hariharan (Animal) • ***Best Screenplay:*** Sai Rajesh (Baby), Ramkumar Balakrishnan (Parking) • ***Best Female Playback Singer:*** Shilpa Rao (Chaliya – Jawan) • ***Best Debut Film:*** Aatmapamphlet.

Miss Universe India-2025

Rajasthan's Manika Vishwakarma was crowned Miss Universe India 2025 in Jaipur as she took over the title from last year's winner Rhea Singha. Tanya Sharma from Uttar Pradesh was the first runner-up, Mehak Dhingra from Haryana was the second runner-up, and Amishi Kaushik was the third runner-up. Manika Vishwakarma won the Miss Universe Rajasthan title before stepping onto the national stage.

Jamnalal Bajaj Awards-2025

Each of the award comprises a cash prize of ₹ 20 lakh, a trophy and citation. It is given for outstanding role in different walks of life. The winners of 2025 awards are: • Hasmukh Babubhai Patel (Constructive Work) • P.M. Murugesan (Application of Science & Technology for Rural Development) • Triveni Acharya (Development and Welfare of Women and Children) • Sekacheva Lyudmila Leonidovna (Promoting Gandhian Values Outside India by Individuals other than Indian Citizens). The Jamnalal Bajaj Awards 2025 event was held on 10th November, 2025 in Mumbai.

MULTIPLE CHOICE QUESTIONS

1. In which of the following years 'Nobel Prizes' were instituted?

A. 1910 B. 1905
C. 1901 D. 1911

2. The writer who refused the Nobel Prize for Literature was:

A. Winston Churchill
B. Prem Chand
C. Jean Paul Sartre
D. None of the above

3. Which country awards the Noble Prize?

A. USA B. India
C. Russia D. Sweden

4. In which of the following years Arjuna Awards were instituted
A. 1951 B. 1971
C. 1961 D. 1965

5. National Awards for Popularising Science was instituted in the year
A. 1981 B. 1985
C. 1987 D. 1988

6. The Government of which state has instituted the 'Tansen Samman'?
A. Madhya Pradesh
B. Uttar Pradesh
C. Gujarat
D. Maharashtra

7. Gujarmal Modi Award is given in the field of
A. Dance B. Science
C. Cinema D. Literature

8. Who returned the award of 'Sir' given by the British government in protest against the "Jallianwala Bagh Massacre" on April 13, 1919?
A. Prem Chand
B. Thomas Roe
C. Rabindra Nath Tagore
D. Dada Bhai Naoroji

9. Nobel Prize is not awarded in the following disciplines
A. Chemistry and Physics
B. Literature and Peace
C. Economics and Medicine
D. Geography and Space Research

10. In which year Nehru Award for International Understanding instituted?
A. 1965 B. 1969
C. 1974 D. 1964

11. Which of the following Indians was awarded Legion D award, the highest civilian awards of France?
A. Jawahar Lal Nehru
B. Satyajit Ray
C. Mother Teresa
D. Shahrukh Khan

12. 'Pulitzer' prizes are awarded to Americans for excellence in
A. Films B. Journalism
C. Medicine D. Social Work

13. C.V. Raman received Nobel Prize in the year
A. 1934 B. 1931
C. 1932 D. 1930

14. Saraswati Samman is awarded by
A. Government of India
B. Sahitya Academy
C. K.K. Birla Foundation
D. Lalit Kala Akademi

15. On which day every year National Awards for Teachers are announced?
A. August 15
B. September 5
C. November 19
D. November 14

16. The National Award given to the distinguished sportsmen/women in India is known as
A. Dronacharya Award
B. Param Vir Chakra
C. Arjun Award
D. Nehru Award

17. The prestigious Ramon Magsaysay Award was instituted in the memory of Mr Ramon Magsaysay who was
A. the Secretary – General of UN
B. the Commander of NATO in Europe
C. the President of the Philippines
D. the President of Cambodia

18. The Kalinga Prize is awarded by UNESCO but it was founded by an Indian. His name is
A. Biju Patnaik
B. Sharad Pawar
C. C.V. Raman
D. Piloo Modi

19. Who was the first Indian to receive the World Food Prize?
A. Dr. M.S. Swaminathan
B. Dr. Amrita Patel
C. Dr. Verghese Kurien
D. None of these

20. Jesse Owens Global award is given in the field of:
A. Literature
B. Sports
C. Science
D. Journalism

21. B.C. Roy Award is given in the field of:
A. Music
B. Journalism
C. Medicine
D. Environment

22. Grammy Awards are given in the field of
A. painting B. architecture
C. music D. rock dance

23. The highest civilian award of India is
A. Padma Vibhushan
B. Padma Shri
C. Bharat Ratna
D. Param Vir Chakra

24. The highest military award of India is
A. Shaurya Chakra
B. Param Vishisht Sewa Medal
C. Param Vir Chakra
D. Kirti Chakra

25. 'Victory Medal' is awarded in:
A. UK B. USA
C. Russia D. France

26. Abel Prize is associated with:
A. Film
B. Mathematics
C. Music
D. Creative Writing

27. First Miss World Competition was established by 'Miss World Incorporation' in the year:
A. 1941 B. 1950
C. 1951 D. 1957

28. The size of an Olympic medal is .... mm and thickness is .... mm.
A. 50, 2.5 B. 60, 3.0
C. 60.5, 3.5 D. 55.2, 2.5

29. "Dhanwantari Award" is given in the field of:
A. swimming
B. Bharata Natyam
C. cinema
D. medicine

30. In which year was Pulitzer Prize established?
A. 1912 B. 1916
C. 1917 D. 1922

31. Which is the second Highest Civilian award in India?
A. Padma Vibushan
B. Padma Shri
C. Bharat Ratna
D. Ashok Chakra

32. Who is the first Asian winner of Nobel prize?
A. C.V. Raman
B. Rabindranath Tagore
C. Mother Teresa
D. Hargobind Khurana

33. The second highest gallantry award in India is:
A. Padma Bhushan
B. Vir Chakra
C. Mahavir Chakra
D. Ashok Chakra

34. 'Mubarak-Al-Kabir' medal is the highest honour of
A. Kuwait
B. Iran
C. Afghanistan
D. Iraq

35. Bharatendu Harish Chandra awards are given annually for:
A. best local self administration
B. showing kindness and generosity of unusual kind
C. promoting original writing in Hindi
D. None of the above

36. Tulsi Samman is given in the field of ....
A. Folk Arts
B. Cinema
C. Creative Writing
D. Sports

37. Liberty Medal is the highest honour of which government?
A. India B. UK
C. USA D. Australia

38. Nobel Prizes are not given for which of the following fields?
A. Physics
B. Chemistry
C. Peace
D. Music

39. Oscar award is related to:
A. Books
B. Politics
C. European Community
D. Films

40. Who is not eligible for Bharat Ratna?
A. A government official
B. A sportsperson
C. A film actress
D. A Prime Minister

ANSWERS

1	2	3	4	5	6	7	8	9	10
C	C	D	C	C	A	B	C	D	D
11	**12**	**13**	**14**	**15**	**16**	**17**	**18**	**19**	**20**
B	B	D	C	B	C	C	A	C	B
21	**22**	**23**	**24**	**25**	**26**	**27**	**28**	**29**	**30**
C	C	C	C	B	B	C	B	D	C
31	**32**	**33**	**34**	**35**	**36**	**37**	**38**	**39**	**40**
A	B	C	A	C	A	C	D	D	A

Sports

TERMINOLOGY

- **Badminton:** Ace, Alley, Backhand, Block, Carry, Checking the Smash, Court, Cross-court, Double hit, Drop shot, Fault, Forehand, Frame, Game point, Kill, Lob, Love, Net, Racket, Rally, Serve, Short Serve, Shuttle (also called bird), Side-out, Underhand.
- **Billiards and Snooker:** Angle, Around the table, Balk, Ball, Break, Bridge, Cannon, Cue, Cue ball, Coup, Follow, Hazard, Inning, Miss, Nurse, Pocket, Pot, Pyramid, Red ball, Rests, Run, Set-up, Short, Swing, Table
- **Boxing:** Apron, Attack, Back-pedal, Backhand punch, Blocking, Bolo, Bout, Butt, Chop, Combination, Cut, Dive, Elbowing, First blood, Floor, Full count, Gloves, Heeling, Holding, Hook, Jab, Mouthpiece, Punch, Ring, Scoring, Second, Spar, Warning.
- **Cricket:** All-rounder, Ashes, Backfoot, Bails, Ball, Bat, Batting, Batsman, Beamer, Bouncer, Boundary, Bowler, Bowling crease, Byes, Caught and bowled, Call, Catch, Caught behind, Century, Cheeky single, Chinaman, Checker, Clean bowled, Cover, Cover-point, Cross bat, Cut, Cutters, Dead ball, Extras, Fast medium, Follow-on, Front foot, Full toss, Glance, Googly, Guard, Gully, Half Volley, Hat trick, Hit-wicket, Hook, In-swinger, Late cut, Leg break, Leg side, Maiden, Mid off, Mid on, Mid wicket, Night watchman, Point, Off-drive, Opener, Over, Overthrow, Over the wicket, Pitch, Pull, Round the wicket, Square cut, Square-leg, Sweep, Toss, Umpire, Wicket keeper, Yorker.
- **Golf:** Ace, Address, Air shot, Apron, Away, Ball mark, Birdie, Bogey, Bye, Chip, Club, Cup, Drive, Eagle, Fluff, Halved, Handicap, Hazard, Hole, Honour, Hook, Jigger, Lie, Par, Pin, Pitch, Putt, Run, Slice, Stance, Swing, Tee, Wedge
- **Hockey:** Backpass, Bully, Carrying the ball, Centre forward, Charging, Corner, D, Defender, Dribbling, Flick, Forward, Foul, Free hit, Fullbacks, Goal, Halves, Hit, Hooking, Intercepting, Long corner, Obstruction, Off-side Penalty Corner or Short Penalty stroke, Push, Reverse Stick, Scoop, Sixteen yard hit, Stick, Striking circle, Tackling, Through pass, Trapping, Twenty-five-yard line, Undercutting

➥ **Shooting:** Air gun, Barrel, Bore diameter, Bull, Calibre, Canting, Drag, Firearm, Grip, Long rifle, Muzzle velocity, Rifle, Sighters, Snap, Stock.

➥ **Soccer:** Bicycle kick, Body swerve, Box or the penalty area, Carrying, Chesting, Clearing, Corner kick, Corner flags, Cross, Cross over, D, Direct free kick, Dive, Double Foul, Dribble, Drop ball, Extra-time, Finishing, Flank, Foul, Goal kick, Goal posts, Goals, Half-volley, Hat trick, Heading, Indirect free kick, Interception, Kickoff, Linesman, Linkman, Lob, Marking, Nutmeg, Obstruction, Off-side, Pass, Penalty spot, Reverse pass, Scissor kick, Shadow marking, Sidelines, Striker, Sweeper, Tackle, Throw-in, Tripping, Winger, Yellow card

➥ **Swimming:** Backstroke, Butterfly, Breast stroke, Castle, Crawl, False start, Freestyle, Kicking, Leg, Medley relay, Pool, Touch

➥ **Tennis:** Ace, Advantage, Back-court, Backhand, Ball boy or ball girl, Break, Bye, Centre line, Chip, Chop, Court, Dead, Deuce, Double fault, Down-the-line, Drop shot, Drop volley, Error, Face or a racket, Fault, Fore court, Frame, Game, Game point, Ground stroke, Let, Line ball, Lob, Love, Match point, Net, Net ball, Overhead smash, Passing shot, Rally, Retire, Return, Serve, Service, Set, Set point, Short ball, Smash, Stroke, Toss, Underhand, Vol'ey.

FAMOUS CUP AND TROPHIES : WORLD

American Cup	Yacht racing
Ashes	Cricket (England Vs Australia)
Canada Cup	Golf (World Championship)
Colombo Cup	Soccer
Champions trophy	Hockey (Men) (top six teams in the world)
Corbillon Cup	Table Tennis (Women) — World Cup
Davis Cup	Lawn Tennis (Men)
Derby	Horse Racing (England)
Indira Gandhi Gold Cup	Hockey (Women) (India)
Jules Rimet Cup	Soccer — World Cup (Men)
King's cup	Air races (England)
Merdeka	Soccer (Men) (Malaysia)
Prince of Wales Cup	Golf (England)
Rothman's Cup	Cricket
Ryder Cup	Golf (England)
Swaythling Cup	World Table Tennis (Men)
Thomas Cup	World Badminton (Men)
Tunku Abdul Rahman Cup	Badminton
Uber Cup	World Badminton (Women)
Walker Cup	Golf (England)
Wightman Cup	Lawn Tennis (Women)
Wimbledon	Lawn Tennis (England)

FAMOUS CUP AND TROPHIES : INDIA

Aga Khan Cup	Hockey (Mumbai)
All-India Maharaja Ranjit Singh Gold Cup	Hockey
All India Guru Nanak Championship	Hockey (Women)
Barna Bellack Cup	Table Tennis (Men)
Beighton Cup	Hockey (Men)
Mumbai Gold Cup	Hockey
Burdwan Trophy	Weightlifting
C K Naidu Trophy	Cricket
DCM Trophy	Football
Dhyan Chand Trophy	Hockey
Dr B C Roy Trophy	National Junior Football
Duleep Trophy	Cricket
Durand Cup	Football
Ezra Cup	Polo
IFA Shield	Football
Irani Cup	Cricket
Deodhar Trophy	Cricket
Jayalakshmi Cup	National Women Table Tennis
Kuppuswamy Naidu Trophy	Hockey
Lady Ratan Tata Trophy	Hockey
Maulana Azad Trophy	Inter University Games
Murugappa Gold Cup	Hockey
National League	Football
Nehru Trophy	Hockey
Obaidullah Gold Cup	Hockey
Radha Mohan Cup	Polo
Rajkumari Challenge Cup	Junior Girls Table Tennis
Ramanujam Trophy	Junior Boys Table Tennis
Ramnivas Ruia Challenge Gold Trophy	Bridge
Rangaswami Cup	National Men's Hockey
Ranji Trophy	National Men's Cricket
Rohinton Baria Trophy	Inter-University Cricket
Rovers Cup	Football
Santosh Trophy	National Men's Football
Subroto Cup	Inter-School Football
Vizzy Trophy	Cricket
Wellington Trophy	Rowing

Places Associated with Sports

Place	Sports	Place	Sports
Aintree	Horse-racing (England)	Henley	Boat race (England)
Blackheath	Rugby football (England)	Hurlingham	Polo (England)
Brooklyn	Baseball (USA)	Leeds	
Cheapuk Ground	Cricket (Chennai)	Lords	Cricket (England)
Donchester	Horse-racing (England)	Oval	
Eden Gardens	Cricket (Kolkata)	Madison Square Garden	Boxing (England)
Epsom	Derby horse-racing (England)	Wimbledon	Tennis (England)
Forest Hills	Tennis (USA)	Yankee Stadium	Boxing (USA)

Stadium in Various Cities of India

- **Delhi:** Ambedkar Stadium, Arun Jaitley Stadium, Jawaharlal Nehru Stadium, Indira Gandhi Indoor Stadium, Shivaji Stadium, National Stadium.
- **Mumbai:** Brabourne Stadium, Wankhede Stadium.
- **Kolkata:** Eden Gardens, Salt Lake Stadium, Ranjit Stadium, Subhas Sarovar.
- **Chennai:** Nehru Stadium, Chidambaram Stadium, Chepauk.
- **Cuttack:** Barabati Stadium.
- **Kanpur:** Green Park.
- **Jamshedpur:** Keenan Stadium.
- **Nagpur:** Vidarbha CA Ground
- **Jaipur:** Swai Mansingh Stadium
- **Gwalior:** Roop Singh Stadium
- **Pune:** Nehru Stadium
- **Vadodara:** Moti Bagh Stadium
- **Patna:** Moin-ul-Haq Stadium
- **Hyderabad:** Lal Bahadur Stadium
- **Patiala:** Yaduvindra Stadium.
- **Bengaluru:** Chinnaswami Stadium.
- **Siliguri:** Kanchenjunga Stadium.
- **Faridabad:** Mayur Stadium.
- **Vishakhapatnam:** Indira Priyadarshini Stadium
- **Ahmedabad:** Narendra Modi Stadium.

OLYMPIC GAMES

- The Greeks used to hold competitive games in the ancient period to keep their men fit.
- The first games were held in 776 BC at Olympus Mount in honour of God Zaus.
- The Olympic games continued to be held, after intervals of 4 years till 394 AD when the decline in Greek civilization led to their end.
- In the modern times a French baron named Pierre de Coubertin revived the modern games.
- The first modern Olympics were held in Athens (Greece) in 1896.
- Since then, they are being held every four years except for breaks during world wars.
- The Olympic flag is white in colour with five coloured rings, each ring symbolic of a continent. Summer as well as Winter Olympics are held in the same year.

Olympic Games (Venues and Dates)

Year	Venue	Year	Venue
1896	Athens (Greece)	1972	Munich (Germany)
1900	Paris (France)	1976	Montreal (Canada)
1904	St. Louis (USA)	1980	Moscow (USSR)
1908	London (Britain)	1984	Los Angles (USA)
1912	Stockholm (Sweden)	1988	Seoul (South Korea)
1920	Antwerp (Belgium)	1992	Barcelona (Spain)
1924	Paris (France)	1996	Atlanta (America)
1928	Amsterdem (Netherlands)	2000	Sydney (Australia)
1932	Los Angles (USA)	2004	Greece (Athens)
1936	Berlin (Germany)	2008	Beijing (China)
1948	London (Britain)	2012	London (Britain)
1952	Helsinki (Finland)	2016	Rio-de-Generio (Brazil)
1956	Melbourne (Australia)	2020	Tokyo (Japan) [held in 2021]
1960	Rome (Italy)	2024	Paris (France)
1964	Tokyo (Japan)	2028	Los Angeles, USA (to be held)
1968	Mexico City (Mexico)		

Paris Olympics-2024

The 33rd Summer Olympic Games, the biggest multi-sport event of the world, was organized with great splendor and success in Paris, the French capital city from July 26 to August 11, 2024. About 7000 athletes from 205 nations and one refugee team took part in the opening ceremony labeled as 'Parade of nations' on July 26 organized on the River Seine passing through the historic monuments of the French capital. The United States of America (USA) emerged as the most successful country in the Paris Olympics 2024 in terms of number of medals. The USA topped the medal table with total 126 medals in its kitty including 40 gold and 44 silver medals. Another sport powerhouse of the world China also won 40 gold medals but finished second on the medal table with total 91 medals. China could win 27 silver medals. Japan secured total 45 medals including 20 gold and 12 silver medals. Host France secured total 64 medals including 16 gold and 26 silver medals and rest the bronze medals. The Paris Olympic Games came to a conclusion on August 11, 2024 with a grand and spectacular closing ceremony. International Olympic Committee President Thomas Bach praised the Games in Paris in his speech at the closing ceremony. IOC President Thomas Back presided over the Olympic flag handover ceremony, with the flag being passed from the Mayor of Paris, Anne Hidalgo, to the Mayor of Los Angeles Karen Bass as the next Olympic Games in 2028 will be organized in Los Angeles, the USA.

MEDALS TALLY

Rank	Country	G	S	B	Total
1	USA	40	44	42	126
2	China	40	27	24	91
3	Japan	20	12	13	45
4	Australia	18	19	16	53
5	France	16	26	22	64
6	Netherlands	15	7	12	34
7	Great Britain	14	22	29	65
8	South Korea	13	9	10	32
9	Italy	12	13	15	40
10	Germany	12	13	8	33
11	New Zealand	10	7	3	20
12	Canada	9	7	11	27
13	Uzbekistan	8	2	3	13
14	Hungary	6	7	6	19
15	Spain	5	4	9	18
16	Sweden	4	4	3	11
17	Kenya	4	2	5	11
18	Norway	4	1	3	8
19	Ireland	4	0	3	7
20	Brazil	3	7	10	20
21	Iran	3	6	3	12
22	Ukraine	3	5	4	12
23	Romania	3	4	2	9
24	Georgia	3	3	1	7
25	Belgium	3	1	6	10
26	Bulgaria	3	1	3	7
27	Serbia	3	1	1	5
28	Czech Republic	3	0	2	5
29	Denmark	2	2	5	9
30	Azerbaijan	2	2	3	7
30	Croatia	2	2	3	7
32	Cuba	2	1	6	9
33	Bahrain	2	1	1	4
34	Slovenia	2	1	0	3
35	Chinese Taipei	2	0	5	7
36	Austria	2	0	3	5
37	Hong Kong	2	0	2	4
37	Philippines	2	0	2	4
39	Algeria	2	0	1	3
39	Indonesia	2	0	1	3
41	Israel	1	5	1	7
42	Poland	1	4	5	10
43	Kazakhstan	1	3	3	7
44	Jamaica	1	3	2	6
44	South Africa	1	3	2	6
44	Thailand	1	3	2	6

Rank	Country	G	S	B	Total
—	Indi. Neutral Athletes	1	3	1	5
47	Ethiopia	1	3	0	4
48	Switzerland	1	2	5	8
49	Ecuador	1	2	2	5
50	Portugal	1	2	1	4
51	Greece	1	1	6	8
52	Argentina	1	1	1	3
52	Egypt	1	1	1	3
52	Tunisia	1	1	1	3
55	Botswana	1	1	0	2
55	Chile	1	1	0	2
55	Saint Lucia	1	1	0	2
55	Uganda	1	1	0	2
59	Dominican Republic	1	0	2	3
60	Guatemala	1	0	1	2
60	Morocco	1	0	1	2
62	Dominica	1	0	0	1
62	Pakistan	1	0	0	1
64	Turkiye	0	3	5	8
65	Mexico	0	3	2	5
66	Armenia	0	3	1	4
66	Colombia	0	3	1	4
68	North Korea	0	2	4	6
68	Kyrgyzstan	0	2	4	6
70	Lithuania	0	2	2	4
71	India	0	1	5	6
72	Moldova	0	1	3	4
73	Kosovo	0	1	1	2
74	Cyprus	0	1	0	1
74	Fiji	0	1	0	1
74	Jordan	0	1	0	1
74	Mongolia	0	1	0	1
74	Panama	0	1	0	1
79	Tajikistan	0	0	3	3
80	Albania	0	0	2	2
80	Grenada	0	0	2	2
80	Malaysia	0	0	2	2
80	Puerto Rico	0	0	2	2
84	Cape Verde	0	0	1	1
84	Ivory Coast	0	0	1	1
84	Peru	0	0	1	1
84	Qatar	0	0	1	1
84	Refugee Olympic Team	0	0	1	1
84	Singapore	0	0	1	1
84	Slovakia	0	0	1	1
84	Zambia	0	0	1	1

India in Paris Olympics-2024

India won 6 medals in the Paris Olympics 2024 and secured 71st position on the medal table. India won one silver and 5 bronze medals this time. Manu Bhaker won the first medal for Inida at the Paris 2024 Olympics. She bagged a bronze and became the first Indian woman to win a Olympic shooting medal. She then created history by becoming the first Indian to win two medals at a single edition of the Olympics after she clinched a mixed team 10 m air pistol bronze with Sarabjot Singh. Swapnil Kusale added a third medal in shooting to make it India's biggest haul in sport in a single edition of the Olympics. Swapnil won a bronze medal. The Indian men's hockey team matched their Tokyo 2020 success with the bronze in Paris while Neeraj Chopra became the most successful individual Olympian after he claimed a silver medal in the javelin throw. Later, Aman Sehrawat became India's youngest Olympic medallist when he won bronze in wrestling.

INDIA'S MEDAL WINNERS IN PARIS OLYMPICS-2024

Silver Medal

- **Neeraj Chopra** (Men's Javelin Throw)

Bronze Medal

- **Manu Bhaker** (Women's 10 m air pistol event)
- **Manu Bhaker and Sarabjot Singh** (10 m air pistol mixed team event)
- **Swapnil Kusale** (Men's 50 m rifle 3 positions)
- **Indian Hockey Team** (Men's Hockey)
- **Aman Sehrawat** (Men's 57 kg freestyle event)

Paris Paralympics-2024

After successful and splendid hosting of the Summer Olympic Games in Paris, France successfully organized the Paris Paralympic Games 2024 from August 28 to September 8, 2024 in Paris. More than 4,000 athletes with physical, visual and intellectual impairments from across the globe took part in the splendid opening ceremony of the 17th edition of the Summer Paralympic Games 2024 on August 28, 2024 in Paris. China reasserted itself as a major sport powerhouse by securing the top postion on the medal tally of the Paris Paralimpic Games 2024 with total 220 medals in its kitty including 94 gold and 76 silver medals. Great Britain finished distant second with total 124 medals including 49 gold medals on the medal tally. Host France secured 8th position on the medal tally by securing total 75 medals including 19 gold medals. Indian para athletes gave a splendid performance in the Paris Paralympics 2024 as India's paraathletes delivered their best-ever performance at the Paris games, earning an incredible 29 medals—7 gold, 9 silver, and 13 bronze— securing an 18th-place finish in the overall medal tally. This achievement represents a watershed moment for Indian para-sports, showcasing the potential of Indian athletes on the global stage. This achievement surpasses the 19-medal haul from tokyo 2020, which included five golds. The record haul also meant that India crossed the 50-medal mark in their Paralympic history.

19th Asian Games-2022

➡ 19th Asian Games, also referred to as the Asiad, was successfully organized in Hangzhou, China from September 23 to October 8, 2023. Chinese President Xi Jinping officially opened the 19th Asian Games on September

23, 2023 at Hangzhou Olympic Sports Centre Stadium in the Eastern city of Hangzhou in a spectacular opening ceremony. Approximately 12,000 athletes from 45 participating nations took part in the 40 sports events in 61 disciplines with total 483 golds at stake in the 19th Asian Games. Host China emerged the overall champion of the 19th Asian Games in Hangzhou by securing the top spot on the medal tally with total 383 medals including 201 gold and 111 silver medals in its kitty. Japan secured the second spot on the medal tally with 188 medals including 52 gold medals.

- India's campaign at the 19th Asian Games in Hangzhou ended with 28 gold, 38 silver and 41 bronze to a total of 107 medals.
- This is the best-ever performance of the Indian contingent at the continental event. It was the first time in Asian Games history that India's medals taly crossed the three-figure mark.

22nd Commonwealth Games 2022

- The 2022 Commonwealth Games, officially known as the XXII Commonwealth Games and commonly known as Birmingham 2022, was an international multi-sport event for members of the Commonwealth of Nations took place in Birmingham, England from 28 July to 8 August 2022.
- The Games was the largest ever held, with 72 Commonwealth Games Associations took part in the event. With 67 Gold, the Australia reclaimed the top position and most medals overall (178).
- England finished second and Canada finished third position. India finished 4th position with 61 medals (22 Gold, 16 silver and 23 Bronze).
- It was the first major international multi-sports event to be an integrated event, meaning that the para and non-para games held at, the same time. In addition, it was the first games to host more women's gold medals than men's.
- **India in Commonwealth Games 2022:** Olympic medalist PV Sindhu and the men's hockey team captain Manpreet Singh led as the flag bearer of the Indian contingent in the Commonwealth Games 2022 opening ceremony in Alexander Stadium in Birmingham. India was represented by 215 athletes who took part in 141 events across 19 sporting disciplines. The Indian contingent comprised 111 male and 104 female athletes. India secured fourth position on the medal tally by clinching total 61 medals including 22 gold and 16 silver medals. India's campaign in Birmingham ended with gold medals for PV Sindhu, Lakshya Sen and Satwiksairaj-Chirag Shetty in badminton and Sharath Kamal in table tennis. Sathiyan G won bronze in TT while the men's hockey team won silver in the final on August 8.

World Cup Football 2022

- The 2022 FIFA World Cup was an international football tournament contested by the men's national teams of FIFA's member associations and 22nd edition of the FIFA World Cup. It took place in Qatar from 20 November to 18 December 2022, making it the first World Cup held in the Arab world and Muslim world, and the second held entirely in Asia after the 2002 tournament in South Korea and Japan. Argentina won the FIFA World Cup 2022, defeating

France 4-2 on penalties following a 3-3 stalemate in a thrilling final at Doha's Lusial Stadium. After 36 years, Argentina won its third World Cup.

ICC Men's T-20 World Cup-2026

➡ The 2026 ICC Men's T20 World Cup was the tenth edition of the ICC Men's T20 World Cup, co-hosted by Board of Control for Cricket in India and Sri Lanka Cricket from 7 February to 8 March 2026. A total of twenty teams competed in 55 matches across five venues in India and three in Sri Lanka. India were the defending champions, having won the 2024 edition. They defended their title by defeating New Zealand by 96 runs in the final, Narendra Modi Stadium, Ahmedabad, becoming the first team to win two consecutive T20 World Cups, the first country to win the title at home and the first team to win the tournament three times.

ICC Men's World Cup Cricket-2023

➡ The ICC Men's ODI World Cup 2023, the 13th edition of the international cricket event, was successfully organized from October 5 to November 19, 2023 at different venues in India. Total 10 countries took part in this mega event, comprising total 48 matches in this world cup including the final. After league matches, New Zealand, South Africa, Australia and host India secured their places in the semi-final of the event. In the first semi-final, India emerged victorious against New Zealand by 70 runs in Wankhede Stadium, Mumbai while Australia defeated South Africa by 3 wickets in the second semi-final in Eden Gardens, Kolkata. India came into the final with 10 wins on the trot. Australia emerged champion of the ICC Man's ODI World Cup 2023, beating host India by 6 wickets on November 19, 2023 at the Narendra Modi Stadium, Ahmedabad. Australia won the toss in the final and asked Team India to bat first. India batting collapsed miserably in the final and set just 241 runs target before Australia which chased down the target at its 4 wickets cost with 7 overs to spare. It was Australia's record-extending 6th ICC Men's ODI World Cup 2023.

SOME SIGNIFICANT RESULTS

Tennis

➡ **Wimbledon Open (July, 2025)**–*Men's Singles:* Jannik Sinner (Italy); *Women's Singles:* Iga Swiatek (Poland)

➡ **Australian Open (Jan., 2026)**–*Men's Singles:* Carlos Alcarez (Spain); *Women's Singles:* Elena Rybakina (Kazakhastan)

➡ **French Open (June, 2025)**–*Men's Singles:* Carlos Alcarez (Spain); *Women's Singles:* Coco Gauff (USA)

➡ **U.S. Open (Sept., 2025)**–*Men's Singles:* Carlos Alcaraz (Spain); *Women's Singles:* Aryna Sabalenka (Belarus).

➡ **Madrid Open (May, 2025, Shanghai)**–*Men's Singles:* Casper Ruud (Norway); *Women's Singles:* Aryna Sabalenka (Belarus)

➡ **Italian Open (May, 2025)**–*Men's Singles:* Carlos Alcaraz (Spain); *Women's Singles:* Jasmine Paolini (Italy)

Cricket

➡ **ICC Men's T-20 World Cup (March 2026, Ahmedabad)**–India defeated New Zealand

➡ **ICC Champions Trophy (March 2025, Dubai)**–India defeated New Zealand

- **ICC Men's Asia Cup (Sep., 2025, Dubai)**–India defeated Pakistan
- **Women's Premier League-WPL (Feb. 2026, Vadodara)**–Royal Challengers Bengaluru (RCB) defeated Delhi Capitals.
- **Vijay Hazare Trophy 2025-26 (Jan. 2026, Bengaluru)**–Vidarbha defeated Saurashtra.
- **ICC Women's World Cup (Nov. 2025, Mumbai)**–India beat South Africa.

Football

- **SAFF U17 Women's Championship (August 2025, Thimphu)**–India beat Nepal.
- **Santosh Trophy, 2025-26 (Feb. 2026, Assam)**–Services beat Kerala.
- **Durand Cup (August, 2025, Kolkata)**–North East United beat Diamond Harbour.
- **Indian Super League (ISL), 2024-25**–Mohun Bagan beat Bengaluru FC.
- **SAFF U17 Football Championship (Sep. 2025, Colombo)**–India beat Bangladesh.
- **SAFF U19 Football Championship (May 2025, Arunachal Pradesh)**–India defeated Bangladesh.

Hockey

- **Asia Cup (Men's) (Sept. 2025, Rajgir)**–India beat South Korea.
- **FIH Hockey Men's Junior World Cup (Dec. 2025, Chennai)**–Germany defeated Spain.
- **Sultan Azlan Shah Cup Hockey Tournaments (Nov. 2025, Ipoh)**–Belgium defeated India.

Badminton

- **India Open (Jan. 2025, New Delhi)**–*Men's:* Viktor Axelsen (Denmark) *Women's:* An Se-Young (South Korea).
- **BWF Japan Open (July 2025, Tokyo)**–*Men's:* Shi Yuqi (China) *Women's:* An Se-Young (South Korea).
- **All England Badminton Championship (March 2025, Birmingham, England)**–*Men's:* Shi Yuqi (China), *Women's:* An Se-young (South Korea).
- **Indonesia Open (June 2025, Jakarta)**– *Men's:* Anders Antonsen (Denmark), *Women's:* AN Se Young (South Korea).

Chess

- **FIDE World Chess Championship (Dec. 2024, Singapore)**–D. Gukesh (India).
- **45th Chess Olympiad (Sept. 2024, Budapest)**–India wins maiden gold medals in both open and women's event.
- **Norway Open (May 2025, Stavanger)**–Magnus Carlsen (Norway).
- **FIDE Women's World Cup (July 2025, Batumi)**–Divya Deshmukh (India).
- **FIDE World Cup (Nov. 2025, Goa)**–Javokhir Sindarov (Uzbekistan).

Golf

- **Hero Indian Open Championship (March 2025, Gurugram)**–Eugenio Chacarra (Spain).
- **US Open (June, 2025, Oakmont, Pennsylvania)**–J.J. Spaun (USA).

Billiards/Snooker

- **Asian Snooker Championship (Feb. 2025, Doha)**–Mens: Pankaj Advani (India).
- **World Billiards Championship (April 2025, Ireland)**–Sourav Kothari (India).

MULTIPLE CHOICE QUESTIONS

1. The first winning stroke in Lawn Tennis gives the player:

A. 2 points B. 1 point
C. 10 points D. 15 points

2. Which of the following game is played for stipulated period of 70 minutes?

A. Hockey B. Football
C. Rugby D. Basketball

3. Neeraj Chopra is associated with which game.

A. Polo B. Javelin Throw
C. Tennis D. Cricket

4. Arjuna Award has been instituted for outstanding contribution in the field of:

A. Social Service
B. Games and Sports
C. Literature
D. Art and Music

5. Murugappa Gold Cup is associated with:

A. Football B. Polo
C. Hockey D. Bridge

6. Jimmy Connors and Geoff Boycott are related with following games respectively:

A. Tennis, Football
B. Tennis, Cricket
C. Chess, Cricket
D. Football, Hockey

7. Which of the following is the first Indian player to achieve 'Bharat Ratna'?

A. Marry Kom
B. Dhanraj Pillay
C. Sachin Tendulkar
D. Sunil Gavaskar

8. Which Indian player won gold medal in Tokyo Olympic–2020?

A. S. Mirabai Chanu
B. Neeraj Chopra
C. P.V. Sindhu
D. Manika Batra

9. The term 'Steeple Chase' is associated with which of the following games

A. Polo
B. Tennis
C. Horse Racing
D. Cricket

10. With which game is the term 'butterfly stroke' associated?

A. Swimming
B. Cricket
C. Gliding
D. Skiing

11. The first Olympic games were revived by ..... in 1896 at Athens

A. Lord Welsley
B. Queen Elizabeth-I
C. Baron Piere de Cubertin
D. None of the above

12. The national game of the USA is:

A. swimming
B. baseball
C. athletics
D. None of the above

13. Jules Rimmet Cup is associated with:

A. hockey B. archery
C. football D. table tennis

14. The approximate weight of a cricket ball is:

A. 5.25 Oz
B. 6.30 Oz
C. 7.20 Oz
D. 8.25 Oz

15. The number of players on each side in a basketball match is:

A. 10 B. 6
C. 5 D. 8

16. The first woman in the history of US open Championship to have played 100 matches, is:

A. Martina Navaratilova
B. Chris Evert
C. Steffi Graf
D. Helena Sukova

17. Swaythling Cup is associated with:

A. World Table Tennis Tournament (men)
B. World Table Tennis Tournament (university)
C. World Table Tennis tournament (women)
D. World Hockey Tournament (university)

18. Which one of the following is not a cricket - playing nation?

A. West Indies
B. Zimbabwe
C. Kenya
D. Columbia

19. The first recipient of Major Dhyanchand Khel Ratna Award (1991-92) was:

A. Geet Sethi
B. N Kunjurani Devi
C. V Anand
D. P.K. Garg

20. The first Olympic Games were held at Olympia (Greece) in the year:

A. 300 BC B. 776 BC
C. 500 BC D. 394 AD

21. Which of the following is the National Game of Spain?

A. Bull fighting
B. Baseball
C. Rugby
D. Golf

22. 'Ashes' is the name of a series between .... and .... and it relates to ....

A. Pakistan, Australia, Hockey
B. India, England, Cricket
C. England, Australia, Cricket
D. New Zealand, Australia, Cricket

23. The term "Butterfly Stroke" is associated with:

A. Kabaddi
B. Wrestling
C. Polo
D. Swimming

24. Which is the national sport of Canada?

A. Field Hockey
B. Cricket
C. Lacrosse/Ice Hockey
D. Volleyball

25. 'Gambit' is a term normally associated with:

A. Bridge
B. Chess
C. Billiards
D. Polo

26. 'Bunker' and 'Chukker' are the two terms associated with

A. Polo
B. Rowing
C. Bungey Jumping
D. Ice Hockey

27. A Lawn Tennis court measures:

A. 78 feet by 28 feet
B. 79 feet by 29 feet
C. 76 feet by 26 feet
D. 70 feet by 24 feet

28. Who scored the fastest timing (in case of an under-13 swimmer) for crossing the English Channel?

A. Arati Saha
B. Uday Shenoy
C. Rihen Mehta
D. Rupali Ramdas Ropal

29. Which one of the following has been entrusted with the responsibility of training coaches in various disciplines of sports?

A. Tata Football Academy
B. Ministry of Human Resource Development
C. Netaji Subhash Institute of Sports
D. Lakshmibai National College of Physical Education

30. Name the first oldest person to climb the Mount Everest:

A. Santosh Yadav
B. Sundare Sherpa
C. Ramon Balanco Saurez
D. Ang Rita Sherpa

31. Archery is the National Sport of which country?

A. Afghanistan
B. India
C. Japan
D. Bhutan

32. Who was the first deaf & dumb swimmer in the world to swim 30 km Gibralter strait?

A. Des Renford
B. Mihir Sen
C. Arti Pradhan
D. Taranath Shenoy

33. The height of the net in the centre of the tennis court is:

A. 3 feet, 5 inches
B. 3 feet, 2 inches
C. 2 feet, 8 inches
D. 2 feet, 6 inches

34. 'Canon' is a sports term associated with the following game.

A. Billiards B. Volleyball
C. Shot-Put D. Table Tennis

35. The Himalayan Mountaineering Institute is located in:

A. Leh B. Darjeeling
C. Kohima D. Dispur

36. The diameter of a golf hole is:

A. 4.36 inches
B. 4.50 inches
C. 5.63 inches
D. 4.75 inches

37. The total distance of a Marathon Race is .... miles and .... yards.

A. 29, 388 B. 26, 380
C. 26, 385 D. 25, 372

38. The first woman, who won six gold medals in a single Olympics tournament, was:

A. Evelyn Ashford
B. Florence Griffth Joyner
C. Kristin Otto
D. Susi Susanti

39. In which year on account of a decree issued by Roman Emperor the Olympic Games were ceased to be played?

A. 350 AD B. 394 AD
C. 300 BC D. 384 AD

40. Putney (UK) is a place most frequently associated with:

A. swimming
B. horse racing
C. boat rowing
D. polo

41. .... has Cricket as its national sports.

A. Jamaica
B. India
C. Sri Lanka
D. United States

42. The term 'Finesse' is normally associated with this game.

A. Chess B. Bridge
C. Snooker D. Rowing

43. The following trophy is not associated with cricket.

A. Ranji Trophy
B. Rohintan Baria Trophy
C. Singer-Akai-Nidahas Trophy
D. Asia Cup

44. Tonya Harding is a controversial athlete and has been associated with the following game.

A. Rowing
B. Table Tennis
C. Figure Skating
D. Boxing

45. When and where the first Asian Games were held?

A. 1955, Seoul
B. 1951, New Delhi
C. 1954, Manila
D. 1970, Bangkok

46. Olympic Games were first started by which country and in which year?

A. France (1924)
B. Greece (1896)
C. Greece (1890)
D. France (1894)

47. What is the measurement of a Golf Hole?

A. 3½ inch in diameter
B. 4½ inch in diameter
C. 7½ centimeter in diameter
D. 10 inch in diameter

48. Bandy is national sport of which country?

A. Latvia B. Peru
C. Russia D. Lithuania

49. K Sasikaran is well known as a:

A. table tennis player
B. swimmer
C. chess player
D. football player

50. If we are using the following words in a game. Which game are we playing?

Break, Cannons, Cue, In off, Jigger, Scratch

A. Polo B. Bridge
C. Billiards D. Baseball

ANSWERS

1	2	3	4	5	6	7	8	9	10
D	A	B	B	C	B	C	B	C	A
11	**12**	**13**	**14**	**15**	**16**	**17**	**18**	**19**	**20**
C	B	C	A	C	B	A	D	C	B
21	**22**	**23**	**24**	**25**	**26**	**27**	**28**	**29**	**30**
A	C	D	C	B	A	A	D	C	C
31	**32**	**33**	**34**	**35**	**36**	**37**	**38**	**39**	**40**
D	D	B	A	B	B	C	C	B	C
41	**42**	**43**	**44**	**45**	**46**	**47**	**48**	**49**	**50**
A	B	D	C	B	C	B	C	C	B